W9-CNC-781

▼

THIS IS
PR

THE REALITIES
OF
PUBLIC RELATIONS

FIFTH EDITION

▼

THIS IS
PR

THE REALITIES
OF
PUBLIC RELATIONS

Doug Newsom
Texas Christian University

Alan Scott
University of Texas at Austin

Judy VanSlyke Turk
University of South Carolina

WADSWORTH PUBLISHING COMPANY
Belmont, California   A Division of Wadsworth, Inc.

Executive Editor:	Kris Clerkin
Development Editor:	John Bergez
Editorial Assistants:	Patty Birkle, SoEun Park
Production:	Cecile Joyner, The Cooper Company
Permissions Editor:	Jeanne Bosschart
Designer:	Janet Bollow
Print Buyer:	Karen Hunt
Copy Editor:	Steven Gray
Cover:	Vargas/Williams/Design
Compositor:	Thompson Type, San Diego
Printer:	Arcata Graphics/Fairfield

Cover photographs:

Background:	Copyright 1992 Craig Aurness/Westlight
Memorial steps:	TIB/West/C. L. Chryslin © 1992
Recycling:	TIB/West/A. T. Willett © 1992
Audio-visual meeting:	TIB/West/Lou Jones © 1992

© 1993 by Wadsworth, Inc. All rights reserved. No part of this book may be reproduced, stored in a retrieval system, or transcribed, in any form or by any means, without the prior written permission of the publisher, Wadsworth Publishing Company, Belmont, California 94002.

1 2 3 4 5 6 7 8 9 10—97 96 95 94 93

**LIBRARY OF CONGRESS
CATALOGING-IN-PUBLICATION DATA**

Newsom, Doug.
   This is PR: the realities of public relations / Doug Newsom, Alan Scott, Judy VanSlyke Turk. — 5th ed.
      p.   cm.
   Includes bibliographical references and index.
   ISBN 0–534–17262–8
   1.   Public relations.   I.   Scott, Alan, [date].
II.   Turk, Judy VanSlyke.   III.   Title.
HM263.N49   1992   92–10718
659.2—dc20

▼

**TO OUR COLLEAGUES
AND
OUR STUDENTS,
WHO HAVE MADE US BETTER TEACHERS
AND
PR PRACTITIONERS**

▼

ABOUT THE AUTHORS

▼ DOUG NEWSOM, Professor of Journalism at Texas Christian University and coordinator of the Media Studies graduate program, is chair of the College of Fellows, the organization of senior accredited practitioners and educators in the Public Relations Society of America. She is also the senior co-author of three leading textbooks: *Public Relations Writing*, 3rd ed., with Bob Carrell; *This Is PR*, 5th ed., with Alan Scott and Judy VanSlyke Turk; and *Media Writing*, 2nd ed., with the late James Wollert. She has been president of the Association for Education in Journalism and Mass Communication, Southwest Education Council for Journalism and Mass Communication, Texas Public Relations Association, the North Texas Chapter of the Public Relations Society of America, and Chair of TCU's Faculty Senate. Dr. Newsom's four earned degrees are from the University of Texas at Austin. In 1982 she was named Educator of the Year by the Public Relations Society of America. In 1988, while a Fulbright lecturer in India, she gave public relations workshops and seminars throughout the country.

▼ ALAN SCOTT is Professor Emeritus, College of Communication, at the University of Texas at Austin and a fellow in the Public Relations Society of America College of Fellows. He is a founder of the Texas Public Relations Association and

was for 15 years its Executive Director. Readers of *Public Relations News* named him among the 40 outstanding public relations leaders in the world. He was named Educator of the Year in 1972 by the Public Relations Society of America and is considered the first college instructor to teach public relations full time.

▼ JUDY VANSLYKE TURK, Dean and Professor at the College of Journalism and Mass Communications at the University of South Carolina, was the Public Relations Society of America's 1992 Educator of the Year. She also is a member of the College of Fellows of the Public Relations Society of America, in recognition of her accomplishments and leadership in the field of public relations and in public relations education. She is editor of *Learning to Teach: What You Need to Know to Develop a Successful Career As a Public Relations Educator*, a publication of the Educators' Section of PRSA, which she chaired in 1992. She also has chaired the Educational Affairs Committee of PRSA (1992) and the Public Relations Division of the Association for Education in Journalism and Mass Communication (1988). She is a member and past chair of the Educator Advisory Committee to the Institute for Public Relations Research and Education.

▼

BRIEF CONTENTS

▼

DETAILED CONTENTS

▼

PREFACE

Changes in the practice of public relations require writers on the subject to update their texts frequently, even though public relations principles are rooted in "the eternal verities."

One source of changes in the practice is innovation in the larger social, economic and political environment, where developments have been rapid and dramatic. Consequently, this edition stresses the global perspective, recognizing that technology has made the world our neighborhood. The expanded awareness found in public relations today, however, does not translate into more generalized messages. Although you might imagine that practitioners now emphasize the macro level and rely primarily on mass media, they actually tend to work at the micro level and use specialized media.

Messages go to people who are members of "publics"—groups connected by some common bond of interest. But we must remember that people think individually before they act collectively.

The need to know more about the environment for public relations practice and about the publics who create that environment has pushed research to the forefront of public relations activity. Behind this push is an increased demand by top management for accountability: proof of results. When management pays to have something happen, it wants followup proof that something did or an explanation for why something didn't.

This results orientation sometimes encourages illegal or unethical behavior, despite greater public consciousness by organizations of the long-term value of being recognized as ethical and responsible. But in general, firms seem to be moving toward what PR pioneer Edward L. Bernays called the underpinning of public relations practice: the Jeffersonian concept of winning and deserving public support.

Unfortunately, among nonpractitioners PR is still not very well understood. Many people don't know what practitioners do. Some reasons for this lack of understanding have to do with the roles public relations practitioners take in relation to an organization, while others involve the rapid growth of the field and the diversity of its practice.

▼ ORGANIZATION AND PERSPECTIVE

Since this book is designed to give you a survey of the field, it stresses the essentials. One goal is to give you a good idea of what it's like to work in various areas of public relations practice. As in all previous editions, the fifth edition of *This Is PR* uses gender-neutral language and employs representative examples to illustrate key points.

The first part of the book introduces you to the practice of public relations in various settings, examines where public relations practices began and suggests where the field may be going.

The second part of the book explores the backbone of public relations practice: research applications, research techniques, publics and public opinion. In Part Three, modes of persuasion and communication theories are discussed in relation to the goal of influencing publics.

After learning these fundamentals, you will move into a critical area of public relations practice: law and ethics. This book can't make lawyers out of you, but it can give you the groundrules for keeping out of trouble. Although the ethics chapter focuses on general ethical concerns, it provides a frame of reference for the discussions of public relations practice that follow.

Part Four discusses public relations strategy as a problem-solving device for an organization. Various channels of communication are investigated, to show you how to reach your publics effectively through the tactics you employ. The way all of this fits together is demonstrated in the final chapters on campaigns, cases and crises.

▼ CONTRIBUTORS AND CRITICS

Colleagues and students from all over the world have made helpful suggestions for revising this book. Some of our reviewers have been with us through several editions, and we're grateful for their candor and constructive criticism.

We would especially like to thank those who combed the fourth edition to suggest changes: Susan Caudill, University of Tennessee at Knoxville; James A. Danowski, University of Illinois at Chicago; John Detweiler, University of Florida; Wallace E. Knight, Marshall University; John V. Pavlik, Columbia University; Susan C. Pendleton, Mansfield University; Tommy V. Smith, Texas Tech University; William Thompson, University of Louisville; and Sharon Yoder, California State University at Chico. We also appreciate the recommendations made by those who read drafts of this edition: Lynn Masel-Walters, Texas A&M University; and Ruth Ann Weaver-Larisey, University of Georgia.

Finally, thanks go to Kris Clerkin, our editor and friend, and to Steven Gray for his careful copy editing.

▼

THIS IS
PR
—
THE REALITIES
OF
PUBLIC RELATIONS

▼

PUBLIC RELATIONS:
ROLE, ORIGINS
AND FUTURE

This unit identifies the origins of PR activities, discusses the scope and nature of public relations work and examines the organizations and people who use and benefit from public relations. Finally, it offers some insight into what the future may hold for you as a PR practitioner.

▼

CHAPTER 1

THE REALITIES
OF
PUBLIC RELATIONS

In my opinion, the best prevention and the most effective form of communication is behavior itself!

Stephen A. Greyser, professor of business administration,
Harvard Business School

PR Fundamentals

Maintain the integrity and credibility of yourself and your client.

Practice or adopt policies that are in the public as well as private interest.

Don't do or say or write anything you wouldn't want to see on the front page of the *New York Times.*

Kerryn King, late senior consultant, Hill & Knowlton, New York

The woman sitting in front of the computer had just completed a newsletter design for a client. While that was printing, she began to proof another client's ad for a national magazine, and the logo in that ad reminded her that she needed to call a graphics artist who was supposed to show her several different logo designs for a client whose company had changed its name.

For that client, too, she needed to review the next day's shooting schedule with the photographer. The company now needed all new brochures, media kits, and presentation folders, as well as such items as business cards and stationery. Even the sign on the building needed to be replaced with the new design. All of the organization's materials, from corporate biographies to product descriptions, had to be changed. That would involve so much rewriting that she decided to enlist the aid of a publicity writer she worked with occasionally, so her staff writer wouldn't be overloaded.

For the client undergoing reorganization, she had also agreed to do a communications audit—interviews and surveys with employees, customers and suppliers to help the restructured entity clarify its image. She had explained to the new management that mergers and restructuring tend to obscure an organization's image. Although such confusion eventually dissipates without any special planning, valuable opportunities can be lost if the organization's various publics are not actively helped to understand the changes. The woman needed to get in touch with the research organization she used to handle telephone interviews. She would have to structure the questionnaire, pretest it and then train the callers in how to use it in conducting interviews.

After completing the audit, she would be responsible for making a formal presentation of her findings and recommendations to the company's board of directors. She made a note to be sure to get the new display element for her laptop computer as soon as possible, so she would have plenty of time to practice using it while she spoke.

As the woman continued working, the fax machine began printing a message. She glanced at the cover sheet and saw that it was from an agency in Singapore she frequently worked with. A client of the agency was coming to the United States on business and would need some assistance. The fax identified the dates and places involved and spelled out the help the agency thought the client would need from her. The printout ended with a request for a return message confirming general arrangements. The woman liked working with the Singapore group because they reacted enthusiastically to her ideas and encouraged her to contribute to their broad overall plans. She laughed to herself remembering a sketch one of them had faxed to her with an accompanying note saying, "color it American." In return, she counted on their cultural help with her Pacific Rim business.

Similarly, she counted on help with the European marketplace from a former college roommate who was a German national and had returned home to work with a big public relations firm before going into business for herself. She also had a contact in Mexico City, which she had developed through several international public relations professional meetings, and she was just beginning to work with a new colleague in Canada. Although her own firm was small, her activities on behalf of clients often spanned the globe. When she came to work in the morning, she often found that the fax

▼ **PR involves responsibility and responsiveness in policy and information to the best interests of the organization and its publics.**

had been busy overnight, transmitting inquiries or requesting information from professional associates around the world.

This woman is a practitioner of public relations—a field that has emerged in recent years as a global phenomenon. The consistency of the practice, despite differences in the social, economic and political climates in various parts of the world, can be traced to the growing body of knowledge about and the general acceptance of what public relations is. The creator of the profession's international code of ethics, Lucien Matrat, offers these thoughts:

> Public relations, in the sense that we use the term, forms part of the strategy of management. Its function is twofold: to respond to the expectations of those whose behaviour, judgements and opinions can influence the operation and development of an enterprise, and in turn to motivate them. . . .
>
> Establishing public relations policies means, first and foremost, harmonizing the interests of an enterprise with the interests of those on whom its growth depends.
>
> The next step is putting these policies into practice. *This means developing a communications policy which can establish and maintain a relationship of mutual confidence with a firm's multiple publics.*[1] [Emphasis ours.]

▼ WHAT IS PUBLIC RELATIONS?

The public relations practitioner serves as an intermediary between the organization that he or she represents and all of that organization's publics. Consequently, the PR practitioner has responsibilities both to the institution and to its various publics. He or she distributes information that enables the institution's publics to understand its policies.

Public relations involves research into all audiences: receiving information from them, advising management of their attitudes and responses, helping to set policies that demonstrate responsible attention to them and constantly evaluating the effectiveness of all PR programs. This inclusive role embraces all activities connected with ascertaining and influencing the opinions of a group of people (see Example 1.1). But just as important, public relations involves responsibility and responsiveness in policy and information to the best interests of the organization and its publics.

The complexity of PR's role prompted the Public Relations Society of America (PRSA) to define fourteen activities generally associated with public relations: (1) publicity, (2) communication, (3) public affairs, (4) issues management, (5) government relations, (6) financial public relations, (7) community relations, (8) industry relations, (9) minority relations, (10) advertising, (11) press agentry, (12) promotion, (13) media relations, (14) propaganda. PRSA's definitions of these activities are listed in the Glossary.

Another organization produced a consensus definition of PR much earlier than PRSA did. The First World Assembly of Public Relations Associations, held in Mexico City in August 1978, defined the practice of public relations as "the art and social science of analyzing trends, predicting their consequences, counseling organizational leaders, and implementing planned programs of action which will serve both the organization and the public interest."

As a practical matter, good public relations involves confronting a problem openly and honestly and then solving it. In the long run, the best PR is disclosure of an active social conscience.

▼ TEN BASIC PRINCIPLES OF PUBLIC RELATIONS

We can describe the function and role of public relations practice by stating ten basic principles:

1. Public relations deals with reality, not false fronts. Conscientiously planned programs that put the public interest in the forefront are the basis of sound public relations policy. (*Translation*: PR deals with facts, not fiction.)

2. Public relations is a service-oriented profession in which public interest, not personal reward, should be the primary consideration. (PR is a public, not personal, service.)

3. Since the public relations practitioner must go to the public to seek support for programs and policies, public interest is the central criterion by which he or she should select these programs and policies. (PR practitioners must have the guts to say no to a client or to refuse a deceptive program.)

4. Because the public relations practitioner reaches many publics through mass media, which are the public channels of communication, the integrity of these channels must be preserved. (PR practitioners should never lie to the news media, either outright or by implication.)

5. Because PR practitioners are in the middle between an organization and its publics, they must be effective communicators—conveying information back and forth until understanding is reached. (The PR practitioner probably was the original ombudsman/woman.)

6. To expedite two-way communication and to be responsible communicators, public relations practitioners must use scientific public opinion research extensively. (PR cannot afford to be a guessing game.)

7. To understand what their publics are saying and to reach them effectively, public relations practitioners must employ the social sciences—psychology, sociology, social psychology, public opinion, communications study and semantics. (Intuition is not enough.)

EXAMPLE 1.1 ━━━━━━━━━━━━━━

Public Relations: A Graphic Definition

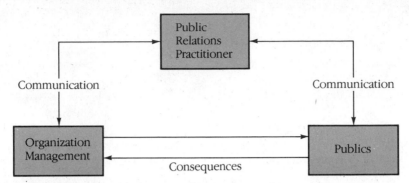

SOURCE: Drawing reproduced courtesy of James E. Grunig from a July 1979 newsletter to the Public Relations Division of the Association for Education in Journalism and Mass Communication.

The PR problems an individual practitioner will address depend on his or her organization's definition of public relations and on its PR activities. The diagram above defines PR in terms of relationships. PR activities differ among corporate, government, association, education and nonprofit public relations.

The diagram shows that a relationship exists between an organization and its publics whenever one has a consequence for the other. Thus, if an organization's acts have an impact on a group, that group comprises a public for the organization. Conversely, if a group can affect an organization, it is a public for that organization. When consequences ensue—when one does something that affects the other—the organization and the publics must communicate with one another. Management delegates this function to the public relations practitioner. This person communicates with management for two reasons: to be able to explain management decisions to the public, and to explain public opinion to management. He or she also communicates with the public for two reasons: to be able to explain public opinion to management, and to explain management decisions to the public.

Although this is what PR practice should be, it doesn't always work that way. PR practice exists today in various arrested stages of development.

8. Because a lot of people do PR research, the PR person must adapt the work of other, related disciplines, including learning theory and other psychology theories, sociology, political science, economics and history. (The PR field requires multidisciplinary applications.)

9. Public relations practitioners are obligated to explain problems to the public before these problems become crises. (PR practitioners should alert and advise, so people won't be taken by surprise.)

10. A public relations practitioner should be measured by only one standard: ethical performance. (A PR practitioner is only as good as the reputation he or she deserves.)

> ▼ **Public relations may include press agentry, promotion, public affairs, publicity and advertising, and may coexist with marketing and merchandising.**

▼ PR AND RELATED ACTIVITIES

Public relations may include all of the following activities, but it is never confined to any one of them: press agentry, promotion, public affairs, publicity, and advertising. PR activities also coexist with marketing and with merchandising, which are not synonymous terms. Since many people confuse public relations with one or more of these activities, let's distinguish among them explicitly.

Press Agentry

Because PR's origins are associated with press agentry, many people think that press agentry and public relations are the same. But press agentry involves planning activities or staging events—sometimes just stunts—that will *attract attention* to a person, institution, idea or product. There is certainly nothing wrong with attracting crowds and giving people something to see or talk about, provided that no deception is involved. Today's press agents are polished pros who steer clear of fraud and puffery, unless it is done strictly in fun and is clearly recognizable as such.

Although a press agent's principal aim is to attract attention, rather than to educate or promote understanding, some press agents manage to do both. For example, one summer the Dallas Symphony Orchestra put on a series of free outdoor concerts with a program of light classical music to stimulate interest in its season ticket sales drive.

The events attracted a warm response from music lovers and probably helped people see the symphony as a "fun-giving" rather than as solemn and formal. Press agentry can thus be an effective element in a larger public relations effort.

Promotion

A hazy line separates yesterday's press agentry from today's promotion. Although promotion incorporates special events that could be called press agentry, it goes beyond that into *opinion making*. Promotion attempts to garner support and endorsement for a person, product, institution or idea. Promotional campaigns depend for their effectiveness on the efficient use of various PR tools; and in many cases more is not better (see Chapter 6 on publics and public opinion). Examples of promotion are the various fund-raising drives conducted by churches, charities, health groups and conservation interests. Among the most successful promoters in the country are the American Red Cross, American Cancer Society and United Way. Promotion, fund raising and all the attendant drum beating constitute one variety of PR activities that may be incorporated into an overall public relations program. What makes promotion activities worthwhile is the merit of the cause. The legitimacy of the cause is also important from a purely pragmatic viewpoint: It won't receive media coverage if it isn't legitimate news and if it can't maintain public support.

Public Affairs

Many public relations people use the term *public affairs* to describe their work, but this is misleading. Public affairs is actually a highly specialized kind of public relations that involves *community relations* and *governmental relations*—that is, dealing with officials within the community and working with legislative groups and various pressure groups such as consumers. It is a critical part of a public relations program, but it is not the whole program. For example, eighteen months before the Dallas/Fort Worth Airport was to open, two

PR firms were hired—one to handle public affairs, and the other to handle media relations. There were good reasons for having two firms. Public affairs were complex, not only because the airport was paid for by cities in two different counties, but also because the airport was located astride two counties and within the municipal boundaries of four suburban cities. The media relations were complex, too, since they involved arranging special events, advertising and publicity connected with the opening; producing informational materials about the airport; and conducting media relations that were international in scope.

In agencies of the federal government, including the military, the term *public affairs* is commonly used to designate a broader responsibility than *public information*, which consists merely of publicity—handing out information. Thus a public information officer is a publicist, whereas a public affairs person in government often has policy-making responsibilities. Because a rather short-sighted law precludes government use of people identified as public relations personnel (see Example 1.2), military public affairs officers often have responsibility for all facets of internal and external public relations.

The unfortunate effects of this law could be countered at the very highest level of government, since the President of the United States appoints the country's most visible PR person, the presidential press secretary. It might make sense to rename the job "public relations counselor" and then employ an accredited public relations practitioner in that post. That person could name a publicity chief for news announcements. A public affairs department could then be set up to work with Congress, and a public affairs officer in the State Department could be appointed to handle relationships with other nations.

Publicity

A college student's first awareness of public relations activity is often through some personal experience with publicity. A note comes from home,

---

EXAMPLE 1.2

Why the U.S. Government Uses the Term "Public Affairs"

An October 22, 1913, Act of Congress often is interpreted as precluding governmental use of public relations talent. The prohibitive words were attached to the last paragraph of an Interstate Commerce Commission statute: "Appropriated funds may not be used to pay a publicity expert unless specifically appropriated for that purpose." The amendment to the bill was introduced by Representative Frederick H. Gillett and thus is referred to in public relations literature as the Gillett Amendment. Most public relations activity of that period was publicity, and the intent of the amendment was to identify and control publicity. Legislators were concerned that the government would become involved in propaganda directed at U.S. citizens. Most responsible PR practitioners would like to see this amendment repealed, since government currently carries out PR functions anyway, but masks them. As a result, taxpayers cannot get any information about how much money is spent for PR.

"Congratulations on making the dean's list. Love, Aunt Susie." A clipping is attached. How did that get into the hometown newspaper? Mother? No. The university's news bureau sent the paper a story with the student's name in it.

Because publicity is used to call attention to the special events or the activities surrounding a promotion, there is confusion about this term. *Public relations* is often used as a synonym for *publicity*, but the two activities are not the same. Publicity is strictly a communications function, whereas PR involves a management function as well. Essentially, publicity means *placing information in a news medium*, either in a mass medium such as television or newspapers or in a specialized medium such as corporate, association, trade or industry magazines, newsletters or even brochures (such as quarterly corporate reports).

Publicists are writers. Use of the term *public relations* by institutions to describe publicity jobs is unfortunate. Publicists perform a vital function—disseminating information—but they generally do not help set policy. Only PR counselors, usually at the executive level, are in a position to effect substantive management changes.

Publicity isn't always good news. In a crisis, for example, it's often important for the organization to tell its story before the news media develop it on their own. In these situations, the publicist is an inside reporter for internal and external media.

Publicity is *not* public relations. It is a tool used by public relations practitioners. Some writers do choose careers as information writers, but they are *publicists*, not public relations practitioners.

Advertising

Public relations differs from both advertising and propaganda. Matrat explains why:

> The strategy of advertising is to create desire, to motivate demand for a product.
>
> The strategy of propaganda is to generate conditioned reflexes which will replace reasoned actions. *Public relations is the strategy of confidence, which alone gives credibility to a message.*[2] [Emphasis ours.]

Designing ads, preparing their written messages and buying time or space for their exposure are the tasks of advertising. Although advertising should complement a total PR program, it is a separate function. A public relations person who has no expertise in advertising should arrange to hire an agency to work under his or her supervision.

Advertising is needed for special events and for successful promotion. Although it is a major part of marketing, it has its own needs for research and testing. Advertising in the form of paid-for time or space is a PR tool often used to complement publicity, promotions and press agentry. (For the kinds of advertising most public relations practitioners tend to be closely involved in, see Chapter 11.)

Marketing

As in advertising, research and testing play a vital role in marketing, but the kind of testing used in advertising may be only a part of market research. Marketing specialists want to know two things: Is there a need or desire for a product or service? If so, among which audiences and in what form is it most likely to be well received? Marketing is directed toward consumers, although it also interacts with other publics such as the sales force, dealers, retailers and the advertising department. Market research is invaluable to the PR practitioner because it provides information about consumers—an important PR public.

All marketing activities have public relations implications, and occasionally they have a direct impact. For example, a marketing campaign launched to promote a new type of double-edged razor blade turned into a public relations problem when samples of the product (enclosed in an envelope with promotional literature) were inserted into newspapers, provoking complaints that, for instance, a dog cut its mouth and children got to the blades before their parents. On another occasion some recipients of a strongly lemon-scented dishwashing powder that had been sent to households as a sample mixed it with water and drank it, mistaking it for instant lemonade mix. Most often, however, marketing is an asset to public relations.

In the 1980s the term *marketing/public relations* became popular as a way to describe public relations activities involved in marketing, but it caused further muddling of the component terms. In reality, the activities involved are not PR, but they do include promotion (usually sales promotion), press agentry (special events, special appearances) and publicity.

The 1985 definition of *marketing* adopted by the American Marketing Association (AMA) shows the relationship: "Marketing is the process of planning and executing the conception (product), pricing, promotion and distribution (place) of ideas, goods and services to create exchanges that satisfy individual and organizational objectives."[3] The AMA includes in that definition the activities (ideas and services) of nonprofit organizations as well as products sold for profit.

Merchandising

In contrast to marketing, merchandising is concerned with the *packaging* of a product, an idea or perhaps even a president.[4] Its research asks what subtle emotions play a part in acceptance of the product, what shape of package is easiest to handle, what color is likely to attract more attention or what kind of display will make people react. The answers are important to salespeople and dealers and provide a valuable supplement to the marketing and advertising research in a campaign. Merchandising experts are strong in graphics, color, tactile responses and emotional reactions to physical imagery. Their work is a frequent and vital part of the public relations milieu. However, it is not in itself public relations.

▼ THE PR PRACTITIONER: PERSONAL TRAITS AND EDUCATION

It takes a multitalented person to perform well the many activities encompassed by public relations. According to former PRSA president Pat Jackson, publisher of *pr reporter*, the PR practitioner today needs to be a researcher, counselor, strategic planner, educator, communicator and cheerleader.[5] In this section, we look at the personal traits and educational background needed by a person choosing a career in public relations.

▼ **PR practitioners must be creative, well-adjusted and capable of mastering diverse skills.**

Personal Traits

PR practitioners have to master diverse skills. They must be creative in solving problems and well-adjusted enough to withstand the considerable stress involved in working between the institution and its various (and numerous) publics. Solving the problems encountered in public relations often requires teamwork and a tolerance for different views. As a public relations person, you must gather different views and help hammer them into a solution. At the same time, you must express confidence and hope that a solution can be found. In a crisis, people in an organization tend to look to the public relations person for answers. Confidence and hope come only from viewing and presenting problems with complete honesty and learning to live with some that seem (for the moment at least) insoluble, while diligently pursuing solutions. This leaves no room for the view of public relations as providing a cover-up for problems or difficulties.

Bernays lists eleven personal characteristics needed by the PR practitioner: (1) character and integrity, (2) a sense of judgment and logic, (3) the ability to think creatively and imaginatively, (4) truthfulness and discretion, (5) objectivity, (6) a deep interest in the solution of problems, (7) a broad cultural background, (8) intellectual curiosity, (9) effective powers of analysis and synthesis, (10) intuition, (11) training in the social sciences and in the mechanics of public relations.[6]

Most of these characteristics relate to the individual's effectiveness as a problem sensor and problem solver—a critical role for the PR person.

Education

As interest in public relations continues to grow, both in the United States and abroad, concern about what is being taught and who is teaching it increases. Senior practitioner and author Sam Black, who wrote the International Public Relations Association's 1990s Gold Paper on public relations education, urges that there be more coordination of educational standards.[7] He cites the conflict between proponents of skills-based study, to prepare technically competent people, and supporters of programs that prepare students for the upper-level skills of management counseling. Most educators agree that proficiency in both areas is necessary and that a liberal arts background is an essential starting point. Black suggests that most study beyond the level of basic skills should occur at the post-graduate level, but he is concerned about the lack of faculty.[8] He recommends that public relations curricula be built around the International Public Relations Association's "Wheel of Education" (see Example 1.3). "Unfortunately," Black observes, "there are times when public relations becomes a small spoke in the wheel of education for a related discipline."[9]

Because many practitioners come into public relations from other fields, and because public relations practice is constantly growing and changing, a practitioner's education can be divided into two parts: preliminary (pre-practice) education at either the undergraduate or the graduate level, and continuing education, which PRSA now requires of its members to maintain their accreditation.

Preliminary Education The exact contours of an ideal pre-entry education for the field of public relations are still a subject of debate among educators and practitioners, despite a great deal of research. The formal education of PR practitioners in U.S. colleges and universities has been developed through the cooperative efforts of professionals in PR education and in PR practice. The first nationally accepted standard for public relations education was developed in 1975[10] and was updated in 1981.[11] Because colleges and universities outside of the United States also began offering public relations courses, another model was developed to include all schools.[12,13]

In 1987, another study commission presented a report that called for mastery of specific skills, preparation in a second field and adoption of an approved curriculum for universities where a PRSSA (Public Relations Student Society of America) chapter had a charter.[14] Four years before this commission's report appeared, another commission developed a model for earning a professional master's degree in public relations,[15] and made recommendations for the doctoral program. The three areas of conflicting opinion about where and how public relations education should occur were described by E. W. Brody as follows: (1) maintaining PR education at the undergraduate level versus transferring this function to the graduate level; (2) awarding a master's degree in PR after the traditional undergraduate education in PR versus awarding a master's degree in business administration after the same undergraduate education; (3) a stronger component of PR studies in the undergraduate education versus a traditional liberal arts program.[16]

Specific preferences about career preparation may vary, but experts agree that public relations practice demands expertise in the following:

▼ *Planning:* Ranges from counseling top management in problems other than PR to dealing with the details of the PR department's own organization and functioning; includes developing policy, procedures and actions and communicating these to other departments.

▼ *Managing:* Goes beyond managing the PR department itself to interpreting top management's directives to the entire organization, participating in association activities, coordinating all outside agencies and activities, accumulating information about the organization and preparing and allocating the corporate PR budget.

EXAMPLE 1.3

The Wheel of Education for Public Relations

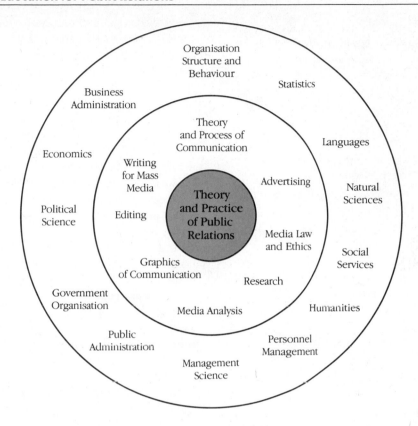

The educational curriculum for a student who wishes to enter the profession can be pictured as a series of three concentric circles. The smallest circle encloses subjects that specifically address public relations practice. The middle circle contains subjects in the general field of communication. The largest circle represents subjects taken in a general liberal arts and humanities course of study. All of the subjects named are essential elements in the background of a successful PR practitioner.

SOURCE: Reprinted from "Public Relations Education—Recommendations and Standards" (September 1990), p. 2, with permission of the International Public Relations Association.

▼ *Advising:* Relates to researching the opinions, attitudes and expectations necessary to provide authoritative counsel, as well as educational and informational materials, to stockholders, lobbyists and others.

▼ *Analyzing:* Consists of examining trends and their consequences and preventing conflict and

misunderstandings by promoting mutual respect and social responsibility.

▼ *Industry Relations:* Involves helping to attract and retain good employees and working with personnel to improve employer-employee relations; initiating communication systems with employees and suppliers; helping improve labor relations by participating in meetings and conferences with labor representatives; and working closely with labor negotiators in labor contracts and discussions.

▼ *Economic Relations:* Entails maintaining relations with competitors, dealers and distributors; encompasses advertising and promotion, which often requires working closely with marketing and merchandising departments and harmonizing public and private interests.

▼ *Social Relations:* Includes being concerned with human relations—preservation of personal dignity, employee protection (security), and social welfare—incorporating recreational, medical and civic activities.

▼ *Political Activities:* Calls for being involved with the community's administrative, educational and religious groups, as well as with legislative bodies and international contacts; also implies an interest in the international affairs of the world community.

▼ *Communication:* Requires knowing how to communicate through mass media and specialized media via advertising and publicity and how to set up a system for a two-way flow of reliable information.

▼ *Educational Activities:* Covers working with all publics (educational institutions, employees, consumer groups and company representatives such as salespeople and dealers) arranging appearances and writing speeches for corporate executives, and developing in-house educational activities such as employee training programs.

Continuing Education   Offered and pursued sporadically at best, continuing education in PR consists largely of seminars given by educators and practitioners. In some of these seminars, continuing education credits can be earned while the practitioner prepares for an accreditation exam. Other seminars are developed by employers for their own employees. Growth in the field, especially in areas of specialization, forces many PR practitioners to perform demanding jobs using outdated skills.

To remedy this situation, the International Association of Business Communicators and PRSA have identified skills that are appropriate for different career levels. The Public Relations Foundation of Texas has published a handbook for career guidance, written by counselor Jim Haynes. At Texas Public Relations Association meetings, workshops and presentation sessions are ranked by skill level. However, there is no systematic plan of progress from one level to another.

Corporate and organizational management often faults continuing education programs for failing to teach public relations practitioners the business of the organization in which they work. This suggests that, as a means of learning a specialized area of public relations practice, workshops in communication may not be priorities for PR practitioners. Certainly a PR person benefits from learning the business of his or her organization—whatever it might be—in depth. For both the organizational staff person and the agency person, knowing the world of business is critical. This means understanding government and corporate regulations, as well as finances.

▼ THE JOB OF THE PR PRACTITIONER

The daily work of a PR practitioner depends on his or her job level. Frank Wylie, former PRSA president and now both a consultant and an educator at California State University at Long Beach, has stated that upper-level public relations people divide their time in the following way: 10 percent on techniques, 40 percent on administration and 50 percent on analysis and judgment. In contrast, the average entry-level PR employee generally spends 50 percent of his or her job time on techniques, 5 percent on judgment and 45 percent on running like hell![17]

Wylie notes that "every beginner is a 'go-fer,' and it's important that you not only go for something, but that you bring back something usable."[18] The retrieval emphasis implies reportorial skills, including knowledge of research techniques.

Other skills Wylie stresses are thinking (first and foremost), writing of all types, speaking, being persuasive, understanding and appreciating media, knowing graphics and photography, respecting deadlines and developing an ability to deal with and solve multiple PR problems at one time.[19]

Three Basic Roles

The way a PR person applies his or her special skills depends on the role he or she plays in an organization. The three main roles are as a *staff member*, as an *agency employee* and as an *independent PR practitioner* who might from time to time function as a *PR counselor*. We will consider each of these roles separately.

Staff Members Staff public relations practitioners are employees of commercial or nonprofit organizations or of divisions of government such as local, state or federal agencies. They perform highly specialized tasks in their organization, but they get a paycheck just as other employees do, and they share the same corporate or institutional identity. Specific needs of the organization usually determine a staff member's job description.

Staff positions with small organizations often include responsibility for external relations. In the case of a small nonprofit organization, the PR person typically works either with volunteers who provide professional expertise of various kinds or with outside suppliers whose services may be bought on a limited basis or donated.

Staff positions with larger organizations can involve responsibility for all other communications functions that report to public relations, and in some instances for human relations (personnel) as well. Large organizations are likely to buy services such as research, audio-visuals (everything from employee training videos to video news releases and commercials) and perhaps even the annual report from outside suppliers.

Commercial and Nonprofit Organizations Public relations people in institutions—whether commercial or nonprofit—may have skilled jobs in a PR department, may be middle managers of some aspect of PR activity or may function as professional staff. Increased use of computer technology is likely to decrease the number of practitioners working at the lower-level jobs and increase the number working at the middle manager and professional levels; the rather small number of positions at the senior level of policy making is unlikely to be affected.[20]

Public relations jobs are now considered a route to top management, but handling the different publics of a modern corporation is demanding, and some PR people find the demands overwhelming. For instance, investor relations is an area that many executives would like to put under the PR umbrella. However, they often find that their PR people are simply not trained to handle it, and as a result they must go outside the organization for assistance. Thus, one of the highest-paid PR people of the 1980s was Herbert Schmertz, a lawyer by training, who managed Mobil's public, government and investor relations.

Government Job descriptions for PR positions in government vary dramatically. Some people who are called public information officers are really publicists, while others with precisely the same title may have all the responsibilities of a corporate vice president for PR.

Usually, though, the person with the more comprehensive job is called a public affairs officer. The anachronistic 1913 law prohibiting public relations work in government from being acknowledged as such accounts for this. Many people hired for PR work by government (the world's largest employer of public relations talent, despite the law) are really only communications technicians. Such people perform jobs involving PR skills (publicity, news releases, brochures, promotions and so on), but they are not planners or counselors. Until the law is changed, there cannot be a civil service job description and test for top public relations practitioners at the policy-making level.

Agency Employees   Each agency or firm has its own internal structure, but generally the president of the firm shares in handling accounts, as do the salespeople, who may also be account executives. A firm may employ a bookkeeper, a secretary, a publicity writer, an advertising or graphics specialist and an artist. In some instances the writer may prepare both publicity and advertising copy, and the artist may be responsible for illustrations and layout.

Large firms have copy editors, media specialists, several artists and a production facility. Most firms, even the largest ones, arrange contracts with printers, typesetters and photographers. More recently, desktop publishing has come to the aid of writers and artists by making their jobs more efficient and easier to coordinate. Computer software programs that include type and graphics make almost instant page makeup possible in-house. These systems usually make the writer the production person as well. The writer actually develops the final format of the publication. The artist provides original designs and artwork.

Beginning in the late 1970s and early 1980s, several large public relations firms were acquired by advertising agencies. In one transaction, J. Walter Thompson acquired Hill & Knowlton for $28 million. In another important merger, Dudley-Anderson-Yutzy, a PR firm, became a part of Ogilvy and Mather, an advertising firm, which was renamed the Ogilvy Group. Then in 1989 the Ogilvy Group and J. Walter Thompson merged, through a hostile takeover. The British-owned WPP Group PLC is run by Martin Sorrell. WPP has grown even faster than its chief competitor (also British) Saatchi & Saatchi PLC. In addition to owning the world's largest PR firm, Hill-Knowlton, WPP owns the largest custom market research company, Research International, and the largest direct-marketing company, Ogilvy Direct.[21]

Mergers have also created giant communications operations with advertising and public relations capabilities. For instance, Young and Rubicam bought Burson-Marsteller and Marsteller, Inc., for about $20 million; and Benton and Bowles acquired Manning, Selvage and Lee for $2 million. The first big merger (1978) was of Carl Byoir & Associates (one of the oldest PR firms) with Foote, Cone & Belding.

The intertwining functions these mergers produced has been recognized by some colleges and universities, which now combine the academic programs of advertising and PR.

Apparently the trend toward amalgamation is continuing. Many advertising agencies have moved into related fields: public relations, specialized advertising to and for selected groups (doctors, for example), merchandising (including package design), direct marketing and/or sales promotion. Some agencies have bought successful companies to put under a corporate umbrella. Others have created their own divisions. Some have integrated the various units into a superteam. Others operate the units separately and independently but find it advantageous to be able to present themselves as a "full-service" agency. PR counselor Philip Lesly fears that the trend may limit PR to a communications role, subservient to marketing and stripped of its counseling role. Although some agencies use PR mostly for product/service support, others allow PR free rein to pursue its full range of functions.

Independent Practitioners/Counselors
The *independent* public relations practitioner is usually hired to accomplish a specific task—one that is ordinarily (but not always) predetermined. Payment may take the form of a flat fee, a fee plus expenses or a base fee plus hourly charges and

expenses. The less experienced the independent practitioner, the more often he or she will have to work for a flat fee. Although some experienced independents prefer to bill for actual costs, they price a job based on the hours required to complete it multiplied by an hourly rate. They then increase these costs by a certain percentage to cover overhead and profit.

Independent public relations practitioners sometimes function as PR counselors. Indeed, some independent practitioners work almost exclusively as counselors.

A PR counselor is called in at in advisory level and works for a consultant's fee, which he or she sets, with hours and expenses added. The counselor studies and researches a situation, interviews the people involved, outlines recommendations and makes a formal presentation of these. The program is then implemented by other PR workers at the organization or at an agency. (See Chapter 10 for details of billings.) Counselors may work independently, or they may be associated with a firm as senior members. Some independent PR practitioners do various PR jobs, but most are strictly counselors.

Some counselors are sensitive about their role because people tend to view them as strong behind-the-scenes influence peddlers. Another misconception is that counselors are simply unemployed would-be senior staffers. Public confusion is understandable, however, because counselors are *advisers* who possess special areas of expertise, most of it gained in agency or corporate work. Their value resides in their experience; in the people they know and are able to call upon; and in their skill as researchers, analyzers, communicators and persuaders.

Some counselors develop reputations for helping institutions prepare for and handle crisis communication. Others are known for their ability to help institutions establish and maintain good government relations (at all levels, but primarily the federal level). Still others are called on for their ability to help with internal problems, typically ones involving employee relations. Counselors, as

senior practitioners, often develop staffs that include younger people who have particular strengths or specializations.

Specific Areas of PR Specialization

The breadth of PR services gives individuals a wide career choice. Many practitioners are experienced in more than one area.

Nonprofit Organizations   The growing number of nonprofit organizations offers a practitioner several advantages and opportunities, although the compensation is often lower here than in other areas. The structure of these organizations (small production staff answerable to a volunteer board of directors) means that the nonprofit PR person generally has a great deal of freedom in designing a program. An attractive program that does not require a large bankroll probably will be accepted.

This kind of PR work usually entails a considerable amount of promotional activity and sometimes fund raising and foundation grant seeking. A particular plus, however, is the reception given to publicity materials by news media representatives, who usually make every effort to use information from nonprofit institutions as long as the preparation is professional. Even advertising gets a break with special rates (sometimes called "church rates"). The only drawback besides red ink is frequent dependence on volunteer support in many areas. Responsibility for training volunteers usually falls on the PR people, and they must recognize that volunteers' interest in and enthusiasm for the organization can be stimulated and sustained only by a viable program.

The number and variety of nonprofit organizations are expanding rapidly, increasing the need for public relations practitioners in this area. Categories include museums, hospitals, social service and health-care groups plus professional organizations of all types.

Educational Institutions   Educational institutions are usually nonprofit organizations as well, but they may be either public or private. The private institutions generally conform to the nonprofit organizational pattern. Although they have significant dealings with government, their work is quite unlike that of public institutions, which, being a part of government, are more open to the scrutiny of taxpayers and the whims of politicians. The type of PR practiced in state educational institutions is often suited to a person who enjoys dealing with the government.

PR people in all educational institutions are likely to be involved in development, which includes fund raising. The functions of PR and of development are separate, but the two groups must work closely together. In fact, the two functions are often lumped together under the umbrella term *institutional advancement* (a term used by CASE, the Council for Advancement and Support of Education).

The title "vice president for development" or "director of university relations" is commonly assigned to the individual who supervises both the PR and the fund-raising functions. Sports information may be included under public relations or kept separate from it in an athletic department; in the latter case, the person responsible for it reports to the athletic director who in turn reports to the president. This arrangement can cause problems, however, because university sports are often involved in controversies that affect university relations.

Fundraising or Donor Relations   Although many public relations people will tell you that they "don't do fundraising," just as many others say that they "don't do advertising," those who do it well are in great demand.

Fundraising is sometimes called donor relations. First and foremost, the fundraiser must identify sources of potential support through research. Then he or she must inform those sources of the value of the organization, so they will consider making a gift to it. In the case of individual donors, this usually means cultivating a relationship be-

tween that person and the organization over a period of time. If the source is a foundation, the informational task means writing a grant proposal that explains the value of the organization seeking the funds and identifies it closely with the mission of the foundation.

The third aspect of donor relations—the actual solicitation—takes many forms. It may involve an elaborate presentation book prepared just for that individual, or it may employ a videotape that can be used repeatedly in combination with personally directed appeals. It generally involves a series of letters requesting funds, and in broader appeals it may include brochures and telephone solicitations. Face-to-face meetings also are used for the personal appeal, and these can be one-on-one or one to a group of potential donors. In the case of large gifts, a strong tie is usually built between the institution (some element or some person in it) and the donor.

The next step is to provide some appropriate recognition for the donor that reflects the size of the gift and the nature of the appeal. (Nothing is more upsetting to a donor than getting an expensive "reward," since this signals that a good portion of the money raised is being spent on thank-yous instead of on the primary mission of the organization.)

Finally, the donor's relationship to the organization must be sustained in a way that is mutually satisfying. The fundraiser wants the donor to give again, especially if the organization has annual fundraising events (as do public television stations). Even if the gift was substantial and there is no reason to expect another, the fundraiser still wants the donor to have an ongoing relationship with the organization and to feel good about having given. Donors often attract other donors, but only when they feel good about their experience.

Research: Trend Analysis, Issues Management and Public Opinion Evaluation   Some PR practitioners specialize in research that focuses on capturing information to help organizations plan better by anticipating currents of change. Some engage in analyzing trends to enable their organization to detect, adapt to and even take advantage of emerging changes. Issues management is centrally concerned with watching the horizons for change through many types of research. By determining in advance what developments are likely to become important to one or more of its publics, an organization can plan to meet the challenge, rather than being taken by surprise. Much of the research underlying trend analysis and issue anticipation consists of monitoring public opinion and evaluating the consequences of attitude changes to the organization and its publics.

By the mid-1970s, as many as one in five Fortune 500 companies had on the payroll a "futurist" whose role was to serve management as an early warning system.[22] The 1970s were a decade of uncertainty. Most Americans worried about economic problems and shortages of natural resources, especially energy. Many people also lacked confidence in American institutions. These concerns continued into the 1980s, giving impetus to planning based on predictions of internal company development and external social, political and economic conditions.

The 1990s will emphasize detection of emerging issues and surveillance of social and economic trends as important PR functions. These developments cast PR people more in their role as social scientists. Information and intelligent analysis can help restore public confidence in our economy and government. The challenge facing PR practitioners is to provide leadership in developing creative, pragmatic communications programs that provide the public with complete, candid, factual and understandable information. Further, PR workers must pioneer new skills to use in maintaining good relations with their publics.

International PR for Organizations and Firms
The globalization of news media, the unification of the world's economy and the emergence of multinational companies have helped expand this area of public relations. *International PR* is not limited to businesses, however, because many nonprofit organizations and associations are international in scope. PR firms often have offices abroad to represent both their own domestic clients and foreign clients. Corporate PR people abroad function just as their counterparts do at home, working with community leaders, government officials and media. They provide a crucial link between the branch organization and the home office.

International PR requires extra sensitivity to public opinion because practitioners deal with people whose language, experience and frame of reference differ from their own. Areas of special concern are language (and knowledge of its nuances); customs affecting attitudes toward media, products/services and symbols that stem from customs; and laws. The last area is particularly significant, because incompatibilities between one country's laws and another's may make harmonious relationships impossible.

Financial PR or Investor Relations Sometimes referred to as *investor relations*, financial PR includes such activities as preparing material for security analysts to study, developing an annual report that is acceptable to auditors and intelligible to stockholders and knowing when and to whom to issue a news release that could affect corporate stock values. It is a rather hazardous occupation because a wrong move can have such grave re percussions. On the other hand, it is exciting, remunerative and challenging.

Industry Public relations for industry also requires a good feel for political PR-public affairs, because so much of industry is regulated by government. A person working for a company that handles government contracts must develop a high tolerance for bureaucratic delay. One PR staffer for a defense contractor has said that the average time required to get an "original" release—one with all new material—cleared for dissemination to the news media is twenty-three days. Since much of the emphasis in industrial public relations is on internal PR, and in particular on labor relations, a strong background in the social sciences and business helps.

PR practitioners in the utilities industry must work with both government and consumers. They must also know financial PR, because most utilities are publicly held. Finally, industry's PR practitioners may be involved in product promotion, which requires an understanding and appreciation of marketing and advertising activities.

General Business or Retail PR   Sometimes called *retail PR*, business PR is somewhat broader than the term *retail* implies. It involves working with government regulatory bodies, employees, the community, competitors and, generally, the full complement of publics both inside and outside the company. Consumers represent an increasingly significant external public because they talk to politicians and can arouse public opinion against a business. Product promotion—of a service or of goods—is another common aspect of general business. For that reason, the business setting is a likely place to find the *marketing/public relations* title.

Government   The four areas in this category all have the same focus, but their internal workings vary.

Federal, State or Local Government Employment Although the federal government is prohibited from labeling PR activities as such, it (like state and local governments) uses PR talent under a variety of titles: public information officer, public affairs officer, or departmental assistant.

Nongovernmental Organizations' Government Relations   The term *public affairs* is also used by institutions to designate the working area of staff members who deal with government. Most institutions, whether commercial or nonprofit, have specialists who handle their relations with relevant departments of government on federal, state and local levels. In this context public affairs work consists of dealing with problems that come under the jurisdiction of elected or appointed public officials.

Political Public Relations   Political PR involves working with candidates for office—and often continuing to work with them after their election—to handle problems, strategies and activities such as speech writing or publicity. Many PR practitioners will not support a cause or person they cannot endorse. Others see PR advice as being like legal counsel and offer their services to anyone who is willing to pay for them.

For government, public affairs and politics, a strong background in government and history is useful. Political PR, like other things of public relations activity, can be high-pressure, especially since the Freedom of Information Act has made government secrets more generally available. In addition, recent restrictions on campaign financing mean that PR people must be even more judicious in collecting, reporting and spending money. State and federal laws must be obeyed to the letter.

Lobbying   Many lobbyists are not public relations specialists at all (many are former government officials). But many public relations practitioners get involved in lobbying activities through their jobs with corporations or utilities. Some PR practitioners become professional lobbyists, at which point they generally represent a particular industry (such as oil and gas) or special interest (such as senior citizens or health-care organizations). Lobbyists work closely with the staffs of federal and/or state representatives and senators, who depend on them to explain the intricacies and implications of proposed legislation. Lobbyists draw on information furnished by their sponsors to persuade lawmakers to adopt a particular point of view.

Health Care   Hospitals, health-care agencies (such as nursing home corporations), pharmaceutical companies, medical clinics, health-science centers and nonprofit health agencies (for example, those combating heart disease, cancer, and birth defects) all employ public relations personnel. The demand in this field is for PR practitioners who either know or have the educational background to learn about medical science, to translate that information accurately for the organization's publics. A heavy marketing component also exists in this area, which means that the PR person needs to have good advertising as well as public relations skills.

Sports   Before sports became big business, the term *public relations* was sometimes used to describe a job that actually combined press agentry and publicity. Today, however, business enterprises in professional sports are of such size and scope that the PR title is legitimate. Professional teams have intricate relations with investors, their own players, competing teams and players, stadium owners, transportation and housing facilities (at home and on the road), community supporters, media (with regard both to publicity and to contractual obligations, as in live coverage) and other important publics. Most pro sports organizations employ full-time staff PR people, and they contract for special PR activities as well. Sports are also increasingly important to colleges and universities. Sports information officers in these institutions handle relations with media and fans.

Leisure Time   The leisure-time market, which has been expanding since World War II, includes all recreation-related industries. It covers real-estate promotion for resort locations, public park development, resorts and hotels, travel agencies, airlines and other mass transportation systems, sports, hobbies and crafts, and some educational, entertainment and cultural activities. The focus of PR activity in this market is promotions, and the only real hazard is the somewhat erratic economy. Creative and inventive public relations generalists can function here quite comfortably.

▼ THE FUNCTION OF PUBLIC RELATIONS IN BUSINESS AND SOCIETY

Traditionally, three different functions have been ascribed to public relations. According to one point of view, public relations serves *to control publics*, by directing what people think or do in order to satisfy the needs or desires of an institution. According to a second point of view, PR's function is *to respond to publics*—reacting to developments, problems or the initiatives of others. According to a third point of view, the function of public relations is *to achieve mutually beneficial relationships among all the publics that an institution has*, by fostering harmonious interchanges among an institution's various publics (including such groups as employees, consumers, suppliers and producers).[23]

Stephen A. Greyser, a Harvard University business professor and consumer researcher, calls this third view of the function of PR, where the consumer is seen as a partner of business, the *transactional model*. Greyser has developed two other models: the *manipulative model*, which looks upon the consumer as victim; and the *service model*, which sees the consumer as king. According to Greyser, the consumer still sees some distance between the current marketplace and the ideal service model.[24]

The three traditional views of PR are each discernible in the history of public relations (see Chapter 2). Greyser's manipulative model describes public relations during the era of communicating and initiating. His service model describes practices that predominated during the era of reacting and responding. Greyser's transactional model describes public relations during the era of planning and presenting.

The current era of professionalism has seen practitioners beginning to control PR's development, use and practice. This current conception of the uniqueness of public relations is well expressed in the following words of Philip Lesly:

> Public relations people have the role of being always in the middle—pivoted between their clients/employers and their publics . . . This role "in the middle" does not apply to any other group that deals with the climate of attitudes. Experts in other fields—journalists, sociologists, psychologists, politicians, etc.—are oriented in the direction of their specialties.[25]

EXAMPLE 1.4

Grunig's Four Models of PR Practice

1. *Press Agentry/Publicity Model.* This model exemplifies the first historical stage of public relations, in which the aim is to "publicize the organization, its products, and its services in any way possible." Promotion of sport and theatrical events is typical. Product promotion in support of marketing objectives is also prevalent. These activities involve only one-way communication dedicated to "help the organization control the publics that affect it." The complete truth is not always told.

2. *Public Information Model.* This historically second stage of public relations seeks to "disseminate information to the public as truthfully and accurately as possible." It is used primarily by government agencies, nonprofits and associations. Practitioners in these organizations serve as "journalists in residence"; they try to represent both organizational and public interests.

3. *Two-Way Asymmetric Model.* This model is tilted in favor of the organization. It uses public relations to "persuade the public to agree with the organization's point-of-view." Feedback is used for manipulative purposes, i.e., "to determine what public attitudes are toward the organization and how they might be changed." Business firms in highly competitive markets use this model.

4. *Two-Way Symmetric Model.* Here the organization attempts to reach a "state-of-affairs" with its publics that is acceptable to all. The purpose of public relations is "to develop mutual understanding between the management of the organization and publics the organization affects." Instead of thinking of the organization as the source of communication and the publics as the receiver, both are conceived as groups engaged in a transaction. Highly regulated business firms such as a telephone company are likely to subscribe to this model.

SOURCE: Reprinted with permission of *pr reporter*, Exeter, N.H.

James E. Grunig, who has developed four models of PR practice, defines public relations as "the management of communication between an organization and its publics."[26] Although many PR practitioners might argue that PR involves managing more than communication, few would fail to recognize the four models presented in Example 1.4.

Another way of talking about the different approaches to PR is from the standpoint of practitioner self-description. PR educator Lalit Acharya suggests that environment might explain the self-perceptions of a practitioner.[27] Self-described roles, largely the conceptual work of Glen M. Broom and George D. Smith,[28] include *expert prescriber*, an authoritarian and prescriptive model; *communications technician*, a supportive, skills-oriented model; *communication facilitator*, a liaison model; *problem-solving process facilitator*, a confrontational model; and *acceptant legitimizer*, a yes-person model. Acharya examined these descriptions in terms of "perceived environmental uncertainty" for the practitioner and concluded that a public relations practitioner (as an individual) may play a number of these roles, depending on the environment in which he or she functions in any given case.

Actually these self-described roles may be telescoped into only two: manager (who supervises technical staff and participates in planning and policy making as counsel to management) and technician (who performs the skills jobs that PR demands). A test of the conceptual research in which surveys were mailed to 136 PR practitioners in Washington state suggests that this is the case.[29] If the roles really are more diverse, as the earlier descriptive work suggests, the particular roles chosen may depend on the degree of encouragement or discouragement for individual initiative present in the public relations practitioner's own environment.

Acharya's work primarily describes practitioner behavior in terms of the external environment of public opinion, but internal environments (such as open or closed communication systems) also can affect practitioner behavior. In fact, some research indicates that PR practitioners who work in participative environments (where employees make job-related suggestions and generally take a more active role in determining their work environment) see themselves as less constrained than those who work in authoritarian environments (where employee input is strongly discouraged).[30] It may be that the self-described "technician" doesn't have the option of being a manager, because of authoritarian top management and a closed communication environment. Michael Ryan, who has investigated participative versus authoritative environments, observes:

> Practitioners who work in authoritative environments might attempt to change those environments by educating management about the advantages—indeed, the necessity—of involving public relations persons in decision-making at the highest levels and of removing constraints on their freedom to act professionally.[31]

While Ryan recognizes that the task of transforming an organization from authoritative to participative might not be included in a PR person's job description, he notes that accomplishing such a change might be among the most significant contributions a practitioner could make. In any case, Ryan suggests that "public relations persons would do well to seek out participative environments and to avoid authoritative environments."[32]

The Values of Public Relations

The lack of consistency in PR practices is due to PR's rapid growth and the absence of any mechanism of control over both practice and practitioners. Public relations may still be observed *in practice* in each of the eras Greyser and Grunig identify. The development of professionalism should give some consistency to PR practice and strengthen the values of public relations, which include the following:

▼ Public relations represents and articulates the desires and interests of various publics to society's sometimes unresponsive institutions. While interpreting and speaking for publics, it also speaks to them for the institutions.

▼ **The three traditional interpretations of the function of public relations—controlling publics, responding to publics and achieving mutually beneficial relationships among all publics—correspond to the manipulative, service and transactional models of PR.**

▼ Public relations helps establish smoother relationships between institutions and society by encouraging mutual adjustments to benefit society.

▼ Public relations offers ways to work out differences cooperatively so that coercion or arbitrary action does not become necessary.

▼ Public relations provides information for the communication system to help it keep people informed about various aspects of their lives.

▼ Public relations personnel can and frequently do help stimulate an institution's social conscience.

▼ Public relations functions in all aspects of life, since its principles reflect the basic human impulses of seeking acceptance, cooperation or affection from others. Public relations practice just formalizes that activity.[33]

▼ Public relations can help management formulate better objectives, advocate them and teach them.

Doing these things is part of the social responsibility of all institutions—public or private, profit making or nonprofit.

PR as Counsel for Social Responsibility

Management must be responsible and responsive to its publics; otherwise, it will have to combat a hostile environment. Unfortunately, the pattern of action has often been just the opposite, according to social scientist Hazel Henderson, who identified the following "normal" pattern of business response to social issues: (1) Ignore the problem. (2) If publicity calls widespread attention to the problem, admit its existence but present business as a victim of circumstances it cannot alter. (3) When the public takes the problem to lawmakers, lobby, testify in legislative hearings and advertise to get opinion leaders to believe that the proposed solutions constitute government interference in the private economy. (4) After new regulations are final, announce that business can live with the new law.[34]

Not only does such behavior justify public pressure for government intervention as the only way to achieve needed changes—just what business does not want—but it also undermines a company's credibility. First, the behavior is reactive, as the late William A. Durbin, former chairman of Hill & Knowlton, pointed out. Second, it is defensive, suggesting that there is a fundamental conflict between public welfare and industry. Third, the posture business takes in explaining how it is a victim of circumstances evidences a preference for quantification (as in talking about "nonproductive dollars") when the public is focused on something qualitative like "clean air." Fourth, the pattern of response concentrates on the means and ignores the end—an end that business might actually support, like clean air.[35]

All large institutions are challenged these days, not only businesses: governments, schools and colleges, professional sports, churches, health groups, fund-raising groups, even the news media. With the prevalence of such crises in public confidence, the role of the PR practitioner becomes critical.

Probably the biggest obstacles to "ideal" public relations, as media scholars David Clark and William Blankenburg observe, are economics and human nature:

The plain fact is that managers are hired to make money for owners, and that a conscience can cost money. In the long run, it is money well spent, but many stockholders and managers fix their vision on the short run. Then, too, an abrupt change in corporate policy amounts to a public confession of past misbehavior—or so it seems to many executives. The natural temptation is to play up the good, and to let it go at that.[36]

As a result, in the 1970s a whole "new math" entered the corporate structure. Executives committed to being responsive and responsible attempted to explain social costs to chief financial officers, security analysts and stockholders. The *Wall Street Journal* called it "the Arithmetic of Quality":

The social critics of business are making headway. Increasingly, corporations are being held to account not just for their profitability but also for what they do about an endless agenda of social problems. For business executives, it's a whole new ball game. Now they're struggling to come up with a new way to keep score.[37]

In the 1980s and into the 1990s, with a downturn in the economy, the job became more difficult.

Many examples of the problems of accountability can be found. How can a profit-and-loss statement be made to reveal on the credit ledger the good a company does when its personnel advise minority businesspeople struggling to succeed in a ghetto? How can the installation of pollution-control devices at a factory be calculated as a positive accomplishment, rather than as a drag on productivity? How can the expense of hiring school dropouts and putting them through company-financed training programs be manifested as a credit rather than as a debit? Conversely, how can the "bad" a company does (by polluting, using discriminatory hiring practices and the like) be measured and reflected as a negative factor in the company's performance?

Despite these problems, social responsibility is widely recognized today as an essential cost of doing business in the United States. A good indication of how seriously major companies now regard "social accounting" is the big jump onto the "green" bandwagon that occurred in the early 1990s. According to the *Wall Street Journal* many companies have appointed environmental policy officers.[38] But some of these companies were merely being duplicitous—promoting some environmental efforts while continuing to pollute in another area.[39] Perhaps the reason for this is that some who espoused the environmental cause and wanted to devote more than "window dressing" to it found that the social accounting was quite costly, because it entailed top-to-bottom organizational reform. Still, a company does better to anticipate environmental accountability than to ignore it and eventually face a fine from the Environmental Protection Agency, as Disney Industries did in 1990. The pressure comes from consumers; and PR firms with environmental specialists, such as GSD&M in Austin, Texas, find that explaining their clients' environmental activities (as opposed to telling people what they make, sell or do) consumes inordinate amounts of time.[40]

All of this has meant that public relations has had to expand its role as (1) *a problem finder and problem solver or preventer* and (2) *an interpreter—a communications link*. Let's consider these two requirements individually.

PR as Problem Finder, Solver and Preventer

PR people have to be problem finders and solvers and, preferably, problem preventers. Such work involves identifying issues and understanding what images are projected.

In 1965, PR practitioner Philip Lesly outlined the six major problems he saw for business in the second half of this century.[41] These problems—which may also apply to large nonprofit institutions—are, Lesly said, "the most intangible, immeasurable, and unpredictable of all elements affecting a business":

1. The main problem in production is no longer how to increase the efficiency of factories and plants, but how to deal with the attitudes of people whose jobs will be changed or eliminated by the introduction of more efficient methods.

2. The principal problem of growth through innovation is not how to organize and administer development programs, but how to deal with the reactions of intended customers and dealers to the product.

3. The personnel problem is not how to project a firm's manpower needs and standards, but how to persuade the best people to work for the company—and then to stay and do their best work.

4. The financing problem is not how to plan for the company's funding, but how to deal with the attitudes of investors.

5. The problem in advertising is not how to analyze in minute detail the media, timing and costs, but how to reach the minds and hearts of the audience.

6. The problem of business acceptance is no longer how to demonstrate that an institution is operating in the public interest, but how to get people to understand that its cornucopia works better when it has a minimum of restraints.

Each problem Lesly isolated suggests a need for awareness of and sensitivity to what is going on in the public mind. To probe the public consciousness, PR people have turned to pollsters and futurists.

Years ago, no one foresaw the role that the public relations practitioner or consultant is now playing in relation to current social crises. No longer primarily a communicator, today's PR practitioner is a sort of moderator who tries to prevent crises from getting out of hand. Some of the tools used, such as personnel contact and the media—mass and specialized—remain the same. However, the

▼ **Social responsibility, historically ignored by most institutions, increasingly is recognized as an essential "cost" of doing business.**

measure of performance is not how effectively the client's message gets across but whether a flareup that might injure a client's business can be avoided. One major obligation is to help clients conduct their business in a way that responds to the new demands made by concerned scientists, environmentalists, consumerists, minority leaders, employees and underprivileged segments of the community.

The most valuable type of public relations activity involves planning to prevent problems or at least to solve them while they are still small.

PR as Interpreter and Communications Link

Perhaps, as suggested by Daniel H. Gray, a management consultant noted for his work on the social role of business, social accounting doesn't exist.[42] Indeed, the system needed may well be more concerned with communications than with accounting.

Communications audits—internal, external or both—have become common for institutions trying to track problem areas. Philip Lesly has observed that institutions must function in a human climate, and thoughtful managers recognize that they don't have the expertise to deal with this element unaided. As human patterns become more complicated, they demand greater expertise and experience. Consequently, says Lesly, "Communications sense and skills, which have been vital and have always been scarce, are becoming more vital and scarcer still."[43]

This is where the PR practitioner comes in, of course. He or she must act as an interpreter or communications link between an organization and its publics. Lesly adds,

> Public relations is a bridge to change. It is a means to adjust to new attitudes that have been caused by change. It is a means of stimulating attitudes in or-

der to create change. It helps an organization see the whole of our society together, rather than from one intensified viewpoint. It provides judgment, creativity and skills in accommodating groups to each other, based on wide and diverse experience.[44]

David Finn, cofounder of the PR firm of Ruder & Finn, says:

> Twenty years ago public relations had its eye on the social sciences, with the full expectation that new discoveries would soon be made which would elevate the art of mass communications into a respectable and responsible profession. Ten years ago some of us thought computer technology was going to do the trick and the phrase "opinion management" emerged as a possible successor to the long-abandoned "engineering of consent." As things turned out, it is not the technique of public relations which has changed so much as the subject matter with which we are concerned.[45]

Emphasizing PR's role as a communications link, Finn focused on four developments that he held to be true of the job: (1) resolving conflicts may require modifying many opinions, including those held by the public relations consultant and the client; (2) patterns of communications in the future may revolve increasingly around smaller groups; (3) the random benefits of public relations activities not directly tied to corporate interests will increase; (4) new methods of research now being developed will be especially relevant to situations where opinions change rapidly.[46]

Public relations, one writer notes, does not "create the corporate image or reputation"; rather, "it interprets and advocates the policies, statements, and activities which qualify the corporation for its reputation."[47] In other words, PR cannot fabricate a corporate image; it must start with reality and seek to match the image to the truth.

Perceptions of Public Relations

Both the functions and the values of public relations are poorly understood by management. Consequently, PR practitioners must comprehend and be prepared to respond to popular perceptions of their field, in order to correct mistaken ideas and avoid false expectations.

Often, the first challenge that faces PR people is to get management to accept the expertise it already pays for. Management is therefore the first public that must be sold on the value of public relations. Evidence suggests that corporate executives go to the public relations staffs they already employ only for advice on communications problems, not for insights into public perceptions that may be causing those problems.

For public relations to be an effective instrument in any situation, management must have a clear conception of the breadth of its role—such as in counseling, research and planning—beyond communication, and the PR practitioner must be prepared to assume any aspect of that role. In an article for *Harvard Business Review,* Robert S. Mason, PR consultant and head of his own agency, cautions management not to hire a new public relations director until the parameters of the job are clearly understood by all (see Example 1.5). If management only wants a communications technician, it should not hire a highly skilled public relations person who is qualified to participate in policy decisions. But, Mason warns, since almost every policy decision has some public relations implications, management would do well to seek the more expensive, better-equipped public relations practitioner. As Mason notes, most PR directors have an independent orientation that adds a significant dimension to the decision-making process. When the role is clearly defined, evaluation of PR performance is easier. Mason adds, "Meaningful evaluation of PR's performance can only occur in an environment where PR itself is managed consciously as a rational function."[48]

One problem with PR evaluation, according to a professional newsletter, is the lack of agreement about how the function is to be measured. It might be helpful to measure the PR function by determining how it contributes to an organization's financial health. At least seven contributions of PR to an organization's financial well-being are identifiable and measurable.[49]

▼ **PR people have to be interpreters, functioning as a communications link between an institution and all of its publics.**

___

▼ *Publicity and promotion* help pave the way for new ideas and products.

▼ *Internal motivation* can increase team effort and build morale.

▼ *Eliminating surprises* through interpretation of publics to the institution and vice versa may avoid disruptive controversies.

▼ *New opportunities* are identified by PR's outreach to all publics, as a result of which new markets, new products, new methods and new ideas may be discovered.

▼ *Protection of present position* can be handled by PR only when an institution is under siege, because then the public's perception of the institution's true values must be nurtured.

▼ *Overcoming executive isolation* enables management to know what is really going on.

▼ *Change agentry* helps persuade an institution's publics to overcome a natural resistance to necessary change.

For some time now, the role of public relations has been in flux. It has changed from being responsible for "making the cash register ring" to handling the "myriad social problems that beset the corporation," says Harold Burson, chairman of Burson-Marsteller.[50] There are three reasons for the change, Burson believes. The first is affluence: Energies once directed toward making a living are now diverted toward effecting social change. The second is technology, which has made bigness possible but has reduced the impact of the individual. The third is the transnational or multinational character of the large, modern corporation, which knows no boundaries.[51]

▼ Many people wrongly assume that public relations means image-making in the sense of creating a false front or cover-up.

Many people wrongly assume that public relations is preoccupied with image-making in the sense of creating a false front or cover-up. Unfortunately, this misperception of public relations is reinforced by periodic reports of just such behavior on the part of individuals identified as public relations specialists. For example, the term "spin doctor," which suggests media manipulation through "doctored" (that is, deceptive) accounts or interpretations of events, gained currency in the 1990s.[52] In fact, a *New York Times* story about a media relations course being taught in business schools was headlined, "Media Manipulation 101."[53] At least most media relations instructors are teaching better answers than the following response received by a reporter investigating the troubled Los Angeles–based Security Pacific Bank: "[A] bank spokeswoman says that regulators aren't at the bank; she added that if they were, she wouldn't be permitted to say so."[54]

Students probably won't have to wait until they get a public relations job to discover the unfavorable perception of public relations some people have. In fact, in many departments of journalism and mass communications where public relations is taught, negative attitudes toward public relations as an area of study appear to be common.[55]

It doesn't help, either, when someone like Eugene Kennedy—Loyola University psychology professor and former priest—is quoted in the *New York Times* as saying, "You call in public relations operatives when the truth won't do. . . . That's why

EXAMPLE 1.5

Ad for PR Talent?

Misperceptions about the field of public relations are often reflected in ads like this one.

800 — General Help Wanted

PR GRAD

I have great entry level position for you. Plan special events, coordinate special interest groups, office management, clerical responsibilities, phone work. Must be good typist & people person. Full, low salary, great experience. Call 467-2296.

P.R.—the very letters evoke subtle maneuvers and manipulation of opinion—has become, in business and in politics, the substitute for genuine moral and ethical sense."[56] It's not uncommon for PR to be used as a pejorative term, and educating misinformed people about what PR really is and does poses a significant challenge.

▼ OPPORTUNITIES AND CHALLENGES IN PUBLIC RELATIONS

If research findings of early 1990 hold true for you as a public relations practitioner, you'll change jobs with some frequency (every 3 to 5 years); devote a good bit of your time to such traditional tasks as media relations, special events and publicity; work in the corporate sector; and be paid on the basis of your gender (women in public relations earn less for the same work than men).

A survey conducted by *pr reporter* showed that 33.3 percent of respondents had been with their current employer for three years or less, and 54.8 percent had been in their current position for

THE LITTLE WOMAN

Reprinted with special permission of King Features Syndicate, Inc.

© King Features Syndicate, Inc., 1975. World rights reserved

"So you're in public relations. Is that where you get me to like something I wouldn't like at all if you didn't do what you do to make me like it?"

three years or less. The newsletter's survey found that 75.9 percent had been in their current position for five years or less. The highest turnover was in travel/tourism, followed by financial service organizations, state government, nonprofit social service organizations and advertising agencies. Organizations where relatively many practitioners had been employed for ten years or more included the federal government, utilities, transportation, banks and consumer products companies.[57]

When the Public Relations Society of America surveyed its members in 1990, it found that 41 percent of respondents were working in the corporate sector—manufacturing, utilities, finance, media/communications, scientific/technical and travel/resorts/hotels/entertainment. The next highest

concentration was 27 percent in government/health care/nonprofits (including religious/charitable organizations, associations/foundations and education).

PRSA respondents were allowed to list up to six specialties or tasks they performed. The three most common ones listed were media relations (81 percent), special events (70 percent) and publicity (69 percent). Other frequently cited tasks and specialties were corporate communications (61 percent), community relations (58 percent), generalist activities (47 percent), public affairs (46 percent), employee relations (41 percent), issues management (40 percent), and advertising (40 percent).[58] This

▼ **More women are now entering the PR field, but at lower pay than men at the same level receive and with less access to the top.**

▼ **Four observations about PR: (1) the better the education, the better the job; (2) two currently controversial areas of PR practice are education and licensing; (3) PR jobs are highly stressful; (4) PR people must function effectively in a "global village."**

---

study for Career Press shows that, for entry-level people, the first job in public relations may be in a related field or in one of the specialties.[59]

Whatever the PR job, some observations about career opportunities and challenges can be made uniformly. First, salaries are largely affected by gender, experience, education, age, job title and duties, as well as by the type, size and location of the organization. Generally speaking, though, the better educated the person is, the higher his or her average salary will be. This is true regardless of the person's college major, although age and gender are major factors.

The median salary for people with one to four years' experience was $44,250 ($53,637 for men and $35,933 for women). PR practitioners with five to nine years' experience were making $44,158 if they were men and $36,520 if women. Those with ten to fourteen years' of experience were making $52,721 if men, and $43,668 if women. With fifteen to nineteen years' experience, men were making $60,781 to women's $50,104; and with twenty or more years' experience, men were making $68,963 to women's $55,898. Practitioners who were men over 35 years old made 35 percent more than did women of the same age; those 35 and under made 24 percent more.[60]

Although more women are entering the field, their pay and authority remain less than men's. Most women feel that their path to management is blocked, and women who are minorities feel that racism and sexism combine to keep them from the top. Many women have attempted to circumvent the problem by opening their own public relations firms.

A second general observation is that, since anyone can be designated as a public relations practitioner, two currently controversial areas in public relations are educational preparation and licensing for the practice.

A third point is that PR jobs are all stressful. In fact, PR practice has been listed as one of the top ten fields for stress. Psychologist Thomas Backer has identified eight reasons for this: (1) *negative leverage,* the result of the high visibility of mistakes PR professionals make, multiplies the stress impact; (2) *multiple bosses* (and publics), exist within the institution's structure (and there is the stress of a responsibility to all of the different publics as well); (3) *time pressures* are constant because almost all major tasks are on tight schedules; (4) *lack of understanding* of the PR role results in such disparaging labeling as "flacks"; (5) *intangible results* remain a problem, despite better gauges for measuring PR's effectiveness; (6) *lack of respect* for public relations work occurs because everyone thinks he or she can do it; (7) *values conflicts* often occur when the PR practitioner's personal values differ from those of his or her client or institution; (8) *multiple emergencies* are common in PR practice because crises tend to spark others.[61]

A fourth observation is that not all PR people appreciate that the information age has created a "global village." Several studies indicate that cross-cultural awareness penetrates the PR function only when the situation is forced by the activities of the institutions involved (multinational companies, high-tech companies, governments and nonprofit organizations with international ties). Clearly, educators and public relations practitioners in the field should be taking the initiative in creating such awareness among their publics.

▼ SUMMARY

The practice of public relations is now global, but some basic principles apply to it regardless of where it is practiced. PR is a public service that deals with reality. Practitioners must say no to deception, and they must not lie to news media. PR practitioners are the link between an organization and its publics, which means that they have to work from a strong research basis; intuition is not enough. PR often uses research from other related disciplines in developing counsel or advice. Because a PR person only has credibility to offer, he or she is only as good as his or her deserved reputation.

The term *public relations* often is used by people who really mean publicity. But PR isn't publicity or advertising or propaganda. Public relations constitutes the responsibility and responsiveness of an organization to its publics.

Press agentry consists of gaining attention through events, whereas promotion involves garnering support for an organization, person or product. Public affairs is government relations, from inside or outside; and publicity means using a mass or specialized medium to gain attention. Advertising is purchased time or space, marketing is selling, and merchandising is packaging. (Ideas and people can be "packaged" and "sold" just as products or services can.) A public relations person may be involved in any or all of these activities while practicing public relations.

The demands of PR work require a person with a particular temperament—someone who enjoys being a problem sensor and a problem solver. Experts generally agree on the educational preparation a public relations practitioner needs for entry-level work; but while continuing education for public relations practitioners is recognized as a necessity, it is less structured and not very well defined. Often what the PR practitioner most needs to learn is the field he or she is working in, rather than any aspect of communications. The failure of trained PR practitioners to learn the business in which they are working is frequently cited by management as the reason for hiring someone who does (such as an engineer or accountant) and teaching that person public relations.

Many specialized areas of public relations change periodically, and the demand for them changes with the business, social, political and economic environment. (Information on PR careers appears in the *Instructor's Guide* to this text.)

The practice of public relations is traditionally viewed as falling into one of three forms: the PR staff person working in-house for an organization; the PR firm or agency person working with and representing clients; or the independent PR practitioner, who often is a counselor. These three types of practitioners are often seen as personally taking on either the role of technician (that is, someone who performs the mechanics of the job as suggested by the client or management), or the role of manager (that is, an active participant in planning and decision making).

One determinant of which role a practitioner ultimately plays may be the environment in which the person tries to practice. This may also be a factor in the maturity or type of public relations being practiced. Four models of PR practice have been developed: press agentry/publicity; public information; two-way asymmetric (often found in marketing communications); and two-way symmetric (generally recognized as the most desirable and effective model).

The value of public relations lies in its power to serve as a two-way link and negotiator between an organization and its publics, to build understanding and resolve conflicts. In this role, public relations can strengthen management's sense of social responsibility. But although offering counsel in the area of social responsibility is one of the jobs of public relations, such counsel is not always well received. In any case, the most valuable service PR people provide to an organization is as problem finders, solvers and preventers and as interpreters of communications between the organization and its publics.

The common public perception of PR is unflattering, and fallout from popular misunderstandings can be experienced even by college students on their own campuses. Overcoming these misunderstandings in order to educate people about what public relations practice can and should be is one of the biggest challenges facing practitioners.

▼ NOTES

[1]Lucien Matrat, "The Strategy of Confidence," *International Public Relations Review*, 13(2), (1990), pp. 8–12. The quoted language is on p. 8.

[2]Ibid., p. 8.

[3]*pr reporter*, 28(36) (September 9, 1985), p. 1.

[4]Joe McGinniss, *The Selling of the President, 1968* (New York: Trident Press, 1968).

[5]Pat Jackson, "The Practice of Public Relations, 1982," *pr reporter,* 25(1) (January 4, 1982), p. 3.

[6]Edward L. Bernays, *pr reporter*, 25(50) (December 20, 1982), pp. 1–2.

[7]Sam Black, *Public Relations Education—Recommendations and Standards.* International Public Relations Association, Gold Paper no. 7 (September 1990), p. 5.

[8]Ibid., p. 6.

[9]Ibid., p. 8.

[10]Carroll Bateman and Scott Cutlip, "A Design for Public Relations Education," *Report of the Commission on Public Relations Education* (New York: Foundation for Public Relations Research and Education, 1975).

[11]Kenneth Owler Smith, "Report of the 1981 Commission on Public Relations Education," *Public Relations Review,* 8(2) (Summer 1982), pp. 61–70.

[12]IPRA Education and Research Committee with the IPRA International Commission on Public Relations Education, "A Model for Public Relations Education for Professional Practice." International Public Relations Association, Gold Paper no. 4 (January 1982).

[13]Robert Kendall, James L. Terhune and Michael B. Hesse, eds., *Where to Study Public Relations—A Student's Guide to Academic Programs in the U.S. and Canada, 1982* (New York: PRSA/PRSSA; San Francisco: IABC).

[14]William P. Ehling and Betsy Ann Plank, "The Design for Undergraduate Public Relations Education," Report of the 1987 Commission on Public Relations Education (New York: Public Relations Society of America).

[15]Michael Hesse and Paul Alvarez, Report of the 1983 Commission on Graduate Education in Public Relations (New York: Public Relations Society of America). Also published in summary in *Public Relations Journal* (March 1984), pp. 22–24.

[16]E. W. Brody, "What Ought to Be Taught Students of Public Relations?" *Public Relations Quarterly,* 30(1) (Spring 1985), p. 8.

[17]Frank Wylie, "The New Professionals." Speech to the First National Student Conference, Public Relations Student Society of America, Dayton, Ohio (October 24, 1976); published by Chrysler Corporation, p. 5.

[18]Ibid., p. 6.

[19]Ibid., pp. 6–11.

[20]Daniel Goleman, "The Electronic Rorschach," *Psychology Today* (February 1983), p. 43.

[21]Randall Rothenberg, "Brits Buy Up the Ad Business," *New York Times Magazine* (July 2, 1989), p. 14.

[22]Liz Roman Gallese, "More Companies Use 'Futurists' to Discern What Is Lying Ahead," *Wall Street Journal* (March 31, 1975), pp. 1, 10.

[23]Task Force on Stature and Role of Public Relations, "Report and Recommendations," Public Relations Society of America (November 1980).

[24]Stephen A. Greyser, "Changing Roles for Public Relations," *Public Relations Journal,* 37(1) (January 1981), p. 23.

[25]Philip Lesly, *Managing the Human Climate,* 54 (January–February 1979), p. 2.

[26]James E. Grunig, "What Kind of Public Relations Do You Practice? New Theory of Public Relations Presents Four Models," *pr reporter,* 27, *purview* (April 9, 1984), p. 1.

[27]Lalit Acharya, "Public Relations Environments," *Journalism Quarterly,* 62(3) (Autumn 1985), pp. 577–84.

[28]Glen M. Broom and George D. Smith, "Testing the Practitioner's Impact on Clients," *Public Relations Review* (1979), pp. 47–59.

[29]Joey Reagan, Ronald Anderson, Janine Sumner and Scott Hill, "A Factor Analysis of Broom and Smith's Public Relations Roles Scale," *Journalism Quarterly,* 67(1) (Spring 1990), pp. 177–83.

[30]Michael Ryan, "Participative vs. Authoritative Environments," *Journalism Quarterly,* 64(4) (Winter 1987), pp. 853–57.

[31]Ibid., p. 855.

[32]Ibid., p. 856.

[33]From Task Force on Stature and Role of Public Relations, "Report and Recommendations," p. 9.

[34]Henderson is quoted by William A. Durbin, "Managing Issues Is Public Relations Responsibility," in "tips and tactics," biweekly supplement of *pr reporter,* 16(9) (May 15, 1978), pp. 1, 2.

[35]Durbin, "Managing Issues," pp. 1, 2.

[36]David G. Clark and William B. Blankenburg, *You & Media* (San Francisco: Canfield Press, 1973), p. 175.

[37]Frederick Andrews, "Puzzled Businessmen Ponder New Methods of Measuring Success," *Wall Street Journal* (September 9, 1971), p. 1. Reprinted with permission of the *Wall Street Journal,* © Dow Jones & Company, Inc., 1971.

[38]Joann S. Lublin, "'Green' Executives Find Their Mission Isn't a Natural Part of Corporate Culture," *Wall Street Journal* (March 5, 1991), pp. B1, B6.

[39]Ginny Carroll, "Green for Sale," *National Wildlife,* 29(2): (February–March 1991), pp. 24–28.

[40]Lublin, p. B6. Charles T. Salmon in his preface to *Information Campaigns: Balancing Values in Social Change,* p. 9, says that there is a fundamental tension between social marketing and the social values influencing such activity.

[41]Philip Lesly, "Effective Management and the Human Factor," *Journal of Marketing,* 29 (April 1965), pp. 1–4. Reprinted by permission of the American Marketing Association.

[42]Andrews, "Puzzled Businessmen Ponder New Methods," p. 1.

[43]Philip Lesly, "Challenges of the Communications Explosion," *The Freeman* (October 1973), pp. 607–8.

[44]Ibid.

[45]David Finn, "Modifying Opinions in the New Human Climate," Ruder & Finn Papers no. 1, reprinted from *Public Relations Quarterly,* 17 (Fall 1972), pp. 12–15, 26.

[46]Ibid.

[47]John Cook, "Consolidating the Communications Function," *Public Relations Journal,* 29(8) (August 1973), pp. 6–8, 27–28.

[48]Robert S. Mason, "What's a PR Director for Anyway?" *Public Relations,* no. 21490, pp. 95–101; article reprinted from *Harvard Business Review,* no. 74510 (September–October 1974).

[49]"Eight Ways Public Relations Contributes to the Bottom Line," *pr reporter,* 26(1) (January 3, 1983), pp. 1–2. Used by permission.

[50]Harold Burson, "The 'Bottom Line' in Public Relations," *Burson-Marsteller Report,* 46 (November 1980), pp. 1–4; adapted from Burson's acceptance address when he was named Public Relations Professional of the Year.

[51]One company's chart of PR corporate duties is in the instructor's supplement to the text.

[52]David Shaw, "'Spin Doctors' Provide New Twist," *Los Angeles Times* (August 26, 1989), sec. 1, p. 24.

[53]Claudia H. Deutsch, "Media Manipulation 101," *New York Times* (January 21, 1990), sec. 3, part 2, p. 29.

[54]Herb Greenberg, "Banking Blues," *San Francisco Chronicle* (January 14, 1991), p. C1.

[55]Peter Habermann, Lillian Lodge Kopenhaver and David L. Martinson, "Sequence Faculty Divided on PR Value, Status and News Orientation," *Journalism Quarterly,* 65(2) (Summer 1988), pp. 490–96.

[56]James Cox, "Bishops' account ignites P.R. schism," *USA Today* (April 24, 1990), p. 28.

[57]"Do High Turnover, Job Mobility Damage Professionalism? Survey Finds 33% of Practitioners with Current Employer 3 Years or Less, 76% in Current Position 5 Years or Less," *pr reporter,* 33(3) (January 15, 1990), pp. 1, 2.

[58]David Y. Jacobson and Nicholas J. Tortorello, "PRJ's Fifth Annual Salary Survey," *Public Relations Journal,* 46(6) (June 1990), pp. 18–25.

[59]Ronald W. Fry, ed., *Public Relations Career Directory,* 4th ed. (Hawthorne, N.J.: Career Press, 1990). See also Carolyn A. Stroman and Michael Andrew Williams, eds., *Minorities and Communication* (Washington, D.C.: Howard University Center for Communication Research, 1991), p. 80.

[60]Jacobson and Tortorello, "PRJ's Fifth Annual Salary Survey," pp. 18–25.

[61]"Public Relations One of Top 10 Fields for Stress," *pr reporter* (January 24, 1983), p. 1.

Selected readings, activities and assignments appropriate to this chapter can be found in the *Instructor's Guide.*

CHAPTER 2

▼

PR'S ORIGINS
AND
EVOLUTION

Public relations has always played a part in free societies and the democratic process, and it still does. I think we need to appreciate that heritage.

Harold Burson, chairman of Burson-Marsteller

Today's public relations worker has inherited a legacy of criticism.

From *The Mass Media and Modern Society*, by Theodore Peterson, Jay W. Jensen and William L. Rivers

The public relations field, in all its variety, inventiveness, flamboyance and solemn pretentiousness, can perhaps best be approached, at the outset, by an examination of a representative sampling of its hardiest practitioners.

Irwin Ross, *The Image Merchants*

Opinions differ about where, when and by whom the words "public" and "relations" were first combined into "public relations." Some authorities say Thomas Jefferson used the term in 1807; others say that the term was coined by lawyer Dorman Eaton in an address to the Yale graduating class of 1882.[1] Regardless, "public relations" was not used in its modern sense until 1897, when it appeared in the Association of American Railroads' *Yearbook of Railway Literature*.[2] The real success of the term can be credited to Edward L. Bernays, whom Irwin Ross calls "the first and doubtless the leading ideologue of public relations."[3]

Bernays was the first to call himself a "public relations counsel," which he did in 1921. Two years later he wrote the first book on the subject, *Crystallizing Public Opinion*,[4] and taught the first college course on PR at New York University. Thus it was around the turn of the twentieth century that PR came into being as a term, as a profession and as an academic discipline.

Like his uncle, Sigmund Freud, Bernays devoted his career to the study of the human mind. His specialty was mass psychology—how the opinions of large numbers of people can be influenced effectively and honorably. When he arrived on the scene, public opinion was considered the province of philosophy. Sociology was in its infancy, and Walter

Lippmann had just begun to define what Bernays calls "the American tribal consciousness." Bernays's approach to psychology is exemplified in the advice he gave the Procter and Gamble Company several decades ago when it presented him with a problem: a boycott of its products by black people. Bernays advised Procter and Gamble to eliminate its racist advertising campaign, to hire blacks in white-collar jobs and to invite black people to open-house gatherings at the plant.

The Bernays style was often subtle. For example, he helped the Beech-Nut Packing Company sell bacon, not by promoting bacon itself, but by promoting what all America could respond to—a nutritious breakfast. In 1918 Bernays even changed the course of history, by convincing Tomas Masaryk, the founder of modern Czechoslovakia, to delay announcement of that country's independence by a day in order to get better press coverage.

Bernays, who celebrated his 100th birthday in 1991, adamantly believes that his profession is more than mere press agentry. He was not, however, above staging events. In 1924 he helped President Coolidge counteract his aloof image by staging a White House breakfast, to which Al Jolson and several other movie stars were invited. In 1929 he publicized the fiftieth anniversary of the electric light bulb by having Thomas Edison reenact its discovery in the presence of President Hoover.

On the other hand, Bernays turned down an appeal through an intermediary for PR assistance from Adolf Hitler in 1933, just before Hitler came to power. A correspondent for the Hearst newspapers told Bernays, however, that—during an interview with Joseph Goebbels, Hitler's minister of propaganda, some years later—he saw Bernays' 1923 book, *Propaganda*, on the Nazi's desk.[5]

▼ SEEKING THE PR "SOURCE SPRING"

For all his influence on the field of public relations, Bernays is not its "founder." In fact, some authorities say Bernays learned public relations while serving on George Creel's Committee on Public

▼ **Although public relations developed its form and substance in the United States, varieties of PR practice are now firmly established around the world.**

Information, which was dedicated to gaining popular support for the United States' war effort during World War I.

Public relations probably has no single "founder," but public relations practitioners in the United States often look to Ivy Lee as the first practitioner of what became modern-day public relations practice.

Without a doubt, public relations developed faster in the United States than in other countries.[6] Historian Alan R. Raucher attributes this to the nation's social, political, cultural and economic climate, as well as to the power of its media to render all large public institutions vulnerable to public opinion.[7] Public relations practice also has become an important export service, as other nations have developed their own versions of the practice.

Public relations as a concept has no central, identifying founder, national origin or founding date because it focuses on efforts to influence—not only opinions but behavior. This very element has created the greatest criticism of public relations. Historians who view public relations as a significant positive influence regard it as a broker for public support of ideas, institutions and people. Others, however, contend that this entails the sacrifice of individual freedom, which is usurped by majority decision. Of course, the same tradeoff is central to the nature of democracy itself; but this does not dispose of the problem that public opinion is subject to misuse (see Chapter 6).

PR Functions Throughout History

Since the effort *to persuade* underlies all public relations activity, the general endeavor of public relations is as old as civilization itself. For society to exist, people must achieve some minimum level of

EXAMPLE 2.1 ■■■■■■

PR's Early Best Sellers

St. Paul wrote his *Epistles* to encourage membership growth and to boost the morale of the early Christian churches, which were spread about the Roman Empire. His PR campaign was a great success, and his slogans and words of encouragement are still quoted.

Dante Alighieri wrote his *Divine Comedy* in Italian rather than in Latin to reach a wider local audience. In the book, Dante, a political activist, eloquently put forth his moral, political and intellectual views.

William Shakespeare's historical plays contained poetry and ideas for the intellectuals and jokes and violence for the rest of the audience. But they also appealed to those in power by glorifying and reinterpreting the War of the Roses to justify the Tudor regime.

John Milton spent much of his career writing pamphlets for the Puritans. He also wrote for the Cromwell government. His greatest work, *Paradise Lost*, is a beautiful and influential statement of Puritan religious views.

---

agreement, and this agreement is usually reached through interpersonal and group communication. But reaching agreement often requires more than the simple act of passing on of information; it demands a strong element of persuasion. Today persuasion is still the driving force of public relations, and many of the tactics that modern PR people use to persuade have been used by the leaders of society for thousands of years.

Monuments and other art forms of the ancient world reflect early efforts at persuasion. Pyramids, statues, temples, tombs, paintings and early forms of writing announce the divinity of rulers, whose power derived from the religious convictions of the public. Ancient art and literature also celebrated the heroic deeds of leaders and rulers, who were considered gods or godlike. Speeches by the powerful or power-seeking used institutionalized rhet-

oric (artificial or inflated language) as a principal device for persuasion.

Looking at some of the early techniques and tools used in persuasion can help put today's PR activities in perspective. Certainly such an overview will reveal that, in the process of its development, PR has amalgamated various persuasive techniques that have proved their utility and effectiveness through the centuries (see Example 2.1).

As Theodore Lustig, Sun Chemical Corporation's communications manager, points out:

> The ancients had to make do with what they had. Two media, sculpture and coins, were particularly effective, and their use for political ends was refined between the fourth century B.C. and the establishment of the Byzantine Empire in the sixth century A.D., the beginning of the Dark Ages.[8]

Lustig cites as an example Philip II of Macedonia. By 338 B.C., Philip had subjugated all the city-states in the Hellenic peninsula under his dominion. Gold and ivory statues of Philip adorned temples along with those of the gods. Philip was thus a good role model for his son, Alexander the Great. In the thirteen years of Alexander's reign and conquests (336–323 B.C.), he managed to erect idealized images of himself across Africa, Asia Minor and India. According to Lustig, these image-making lessons were not lost on the first Roman emperor, Augustus.

All Roman emperors, from Augustus on, made use of the ultimate promotion campaign: they proclaimed themselves gods and required the people to worship them.[9] Augustus also had Virgil's *Aeneid* published, for propaganda purposes. This epic poem glorified the origin of the Roman people and, by implication, the house of Caesar.

PR Uses and Strategies Throughout History

Throughout history, PR has been used to promote wars, to lobby for political causes, to support political parties, to promote religion, to sell products, to raise money and to publicize events and people.

Indeed, most of the uses modern society has found for public relations are not new, and modern PR practitioners have learned a lot by studying the strategies employed by earlier experts.

In 1095 Pope Urban II promoted war against the Muslim caliphate to the east. He sent word through his information network—cardinals, archbishops, bishops and parish priests—that to fight in this holy war was to serve God and to earn forgiveness of sins. It also gave Christians a once-in-a-lifetime chance to visit the holy shrines. The response was overwhelming, even though the Crusades were not an unqualified success.

In 1215 Stephen Langton, Archbishop of Canterbury, used promotion tactics to lobby for a political cause. He mobilized an influential group of barons to stand up for their rights against King John, and these men ultimately forced the king to agree to the terms of the Magna Carta—a document that has been used as a political banner ever since by people combatting political oppression and control. In the fifteenth century, Niccolo Machiavelli, an Italian statesman and political philosopher, used his talents as a publicist to support a political party in power. His *The Prince* and *Discourses* are essentially treatises on how to govern people firmly and effectively. Machiavelli's political psychology seems quite modern. His work for Cesare Borgia relied heavily on opinion control and propaganda—techniques associated today with "issues management."

PR-related activities have been used to promote religion throughout the ages. In 1622 Pope Gregory XV established the *Congregatio de propaganda fide*, the Congregation for Propagating the Faith, to handle missionary activity. From that institution we have retained the word *propaganda*. In 1351 John Wycliffe called for reform of the Catholic Church and, in particular, for an English translation of the Bible to give the word of God more directly to more people. Wycliffe took his campaign to the people themselves, addressing them on the streets and in public places. Although it was forbidden, he and his followers also distributed books, tracts and broadsides.

▼ **The use of PR to promote political, commercial and religious goals goes far back into history.**

PR Tactics Throughout History

Various functions and uses of public relations have certainly existed throughout civilized history. The same cannot be said, however, for many of the *tactics* of twentieth-century PR, since these often depend on relatively recent inventions. For example, much of modern PR relies on electronic communication—telegraph, telephone, facsimile, telex, even satellites—and on electronic mass media—movies, radio and television. PR also has been radically affected by the rise of the computer.

Of course, not all tactics of modern PR are of recent origin. PR still uses *rhetoric*, which is as old as human speech; *symbols*, which have been around as long as the human imagination; and *slogans*, which date back to people's first consciousness of themselves as groups.

Before the Industrial Revolution, the most significant period in the development of PR tactics was a 100-year period starting about 1450. During that time the Renaissance reached its height, the Reformation began and the European rediscovery of the New World occurred. These events gave people a new view of themselves, of one another and of their environment.

The period also marked the beginning of the age of mass media: around 1450 Johann Gutenberg invented printing from movable type, and the press was born. Few other inventions have had such a profound effect on human culture. Spinoffs of this discovery have been used by PR practitioners ever since, in books, advertising posters, handbills, publicity releases, party publications, newspapers and so on. Of course, these media existed before Gutenberg and his press, but never before could they be produced so efficiently to reach and persuade so many people at once.

EXAMPLE 2.2

Capsule History of PR in the United States

In the United States the development of PR has gone through five distinct stages:

1. **Preliminary period**—an era of development of the channels of communication and exercise of PR tactics (publicity, promotion and press agentry)

2. **Communicating/initiating**—a time primarily of publicists, press agents, promoters, and propagandists

3. **Reacting/responding**—a period of writers hired to be spokespeople for special interests

4. **Planning/preventing**—a maturing of PR as it began to be incorporated into the management function

5. **Professionalism**—an effort by PR to control its development, use and practice on an international level

These stages of evolution are marked by particular periods in U.S. history, which fall into the following divisions:

1600–1799
Initial Colonization—American Revolution

1800–1899
Civil War
Western Expansion
Industrial Revolution

1900–1939
Progressive Era/Muckrakers
World War I
Roaring Twenties
Depression

1940–1979
World War II
Cold War of the 1950s
Consumer Movement

1980–Present
Global Communication

▼ THE BEGINNINGS OF PR IN THE UNITED STATES, 1600–1799

As Example 2.2 indicates, the United States has witnessed five periods or stages in the development of public relations.

During the early colonization of America, PR was used to sell a vital product, real estate. The Virginia Company in 1620 issued a broadside in England offering 50 acres of free land to anyone who brought a new settler to America before 1625. In 1643 PR was used in the colonies to raise money. Harvard College solicited funds by issuing a public relations brochure entitled *New England's First Fruits*.[10] Another college was the first to use a pub-

licity release in the New World to publicize an event. King's College (now Columbia University) sent an announcement of its 1758 commencement to various newspapers, where the item was printed as news.[11] Even sports sponsorship is not new. The first recorded intercollegiate competition was an 1852 rowing match between Harvard and Yale, sponsored by the Boston, Concord and Montreal railroads.

By the time of the American Revolution substantial advances had been made in public relations uses and tactics. Although public relations as such did not exist in 1776, many of PR's functions, uses and tactics were already well developed by that time. The patriots who promoted the American

Revolution overlooked no opportunity to use PR in their efforts to persuade—that is, to boost the war effort and to rally support for their new political plans. To this end they employed a wide variety of PR tools—newsletters, newspapers, heroes, slogans, symbols, rhetoric, organizations, press agentry and publicity—as well as rallies, parades, exhibitions, celebrations, poetry, songs, cartoons, fireworks, effigies and even crude lantern slides.

American patriots made the most of heroes (George Washington, Ethan Allen), legends (Yankee Doodle, the Spirit of '76), slogans ("Give me liberty or give me death!"), symbols (the Liberty Tree) and rhetoric (the speeches of John Adams and the writings of Thomas Jefferson, including the Declaration of Independence). They founded public-spirited organizations (the Sons of Liberty, the Committee of Correspondence). They grabbed every opportunity to interpret events in a light most favorable to their cause: a brawl on March 5, 1770, in which five unruly Bostonians were shot was billed by the revolutionary press as the "Boston Massacre" and denounced as an atrocity to inflame passions against the British.

When there was no event to exploit, the patriots didn't hesitate to create one. On December 16, 1773, a group of them put on war paint and feathers, boarded a British ship and tossed its cargo of tea leaves overboard. The Boston Tea Party, whose main function was to attract attention, has been called an early example of American press agentry. Historian Richard Bissell states, "Of all the crazy hooligan stunts pulled off by the colonies against England, the Boston Tea Party was the wildest."[12]

One of the best of the patriotic publicists was Samuel Adams, a man who had failed at every business venture he had tried previously. His specialty was what Bernays later labeled "crystallizing public opinion." Adams was one of the first to cry out against taxation without representation. He publicized the Boston Massacre, staged the Boston Tea Party and signed the Declaration of Independence. One historian offers the following assessment of Adams: "He was indignant, impassioned, incensed and outraged. He was the first American to get up

▼ **The American revolutionaries employed a wide variety of PR tools in pursuit of their political objectives.**

in a public assembly and declare for absolute independence. As an agitator he makes Vladimir Ilich [Lenin] and Trotsky look like pikers."[13]

Adams understood that the press could be the emerging nation's most powerful weapon. When the American Revolution began, there were thirty-seven newspapers in the colonies, and they served as a focal point for political appeals.[14] Many of these papers were owned and run by patriotic writers and editors such as Benjamin Franklin of the *Pennsylvania Gazette*[15] and Isaiah Thomas of the *Massachusetts Spy*—a man who often found it necessary to relocate his operations. A woman active in the cause was Hannah Bunce Watson, who took over publication of the *Connecticut Courant* at the death of her husband and contributed extensively to the revolutionists' propaganda war.[16]

The printing press was used for other forms of propaganda, too, such as books of political philosophy by Jean Jacques Rousseau and inflammatory pamphlets by Thomas Paine. The works of both men were distributed widely to promote the spirit of rebellion.

Following independence, another massive effort at persuasion was necessary to push for reform of the short-lived Articles of Confederation. The men who drafted the Constitution conducted an intense PR campaign to sell the document to their colleagues and to the American people. Their propaganda took the form of eighty-five letters written to the newspapers. These letters, by Alexander Hamilton, James Madison and John Jay, became known as the *Federalist Papers*, and they did much to shape the political opinions of citizens of the young nation. The Bill of Rights, a propaganda piece supported by that spectacular campaigner Patrick Henry, guaranteed citizens numerous rights against the federal government, including freedom of the

▼ **Special-interest groups—for example, the suffragists (people in favor of women's right to vote) and the abolitionists (those who opposed slavery)—adopted PR strategies to promote their causes.**

press. The resulting climate of free interchange encouraged the evolution of public relations into a full-fledged practice. If the Bill of Rights had not been adopted, public relations would never have become what it is today.

▼ COMMUNICATING/INITIATING: THE ERA OF PRESS AGENTRY AND PUBLICITY, 1800–1899

Although PR tactics were initially used in the United States for political purposes, as the nation developed and the nineteenth century progressed, all aspects of life fell under the influence of two PR tools: press agentry and publicity.

Government and Activists

In the 1830s, political sophistication got a boost from the PR innovations of Amos Kendall, the first man to function (although without the title) as a presidential press secretary—to Andrew Jackson. Kendall, an ex-newspaper reporter, held the official position of fourth auditor of the treasury,[17] but in fact he wrote speeches and pamphlets, prepared strategy, conducted polls, counseled the president on his public image, coordinated the efforts of the executive branch with other branches of government and with the public and constantly publicized Jackson in a favorable light.

PR techniques were also important in the heyday of the political machine. By the late 1850s, the Tammany Hall organization of New York was using interviews to gather information about the public mood. This marked the beginning of poll taking by special interest groups for strategic planning and publicity.[18]

Although public relations had always been employed in political campaigns in an effort to persuade, the 1888 Harrison–Cleveland presidential race showed a growing sophistication in its use. First, far greater use was made of the press—newspapers, pamphlets, fliers and the first official campaign press bureau—during that election year. The political campaign grew even more sophisticated during the 1896 race between Bryan and McKinley.[19] Both parties established campaign headquarters and flooded the nation with propaganda. Campaign trains and public opinion polls were also used extensively.[20]

Politicians were not the only ones to sell their ideas through PR. Agitators of many persuasions discovered that publicity could help change the nation's thinking. By relying mainly on appeals to public sentiment, groups such as the antivivisectionists, the American Peace Party and the Women's Christian Temperance Union met with varying success. Leaders of the women's suffrage movement publicized their cause at the 1876 Centennial celebration in Philadelphia; on July 4 Elizabeth Cady Stanton, Susan B. Anthony and Matilda Joslyn Gage staged a demonstration to dramatize that their rights as citizens had not yet been won.[21]

The most compelling protest movement of the nineteenth century was the abolitionist or antislavery movement, which consisted of many allied organizations. These organizations found that their cause was helped not only by news releases and press agentry stunts but also by getting public figures and newspaper editors to endorse their efforts and ideas. Forming an editorial alliance with a mass medium extended the reach of their message and gave it prestige and credibility.

Harriet Beecher Stowe used the partisan press to publicize the antislavery cause. Her best known work, *Uncle Tom's Cabin, or Life Among the Lowly*, was first published in serial form in an abolitionist journal. When the novel appeared as a book in 1852, 300,000 copies were sold above the Mason–Dixon Line.

The fund drive, a very successful PR practice first used to raise money for military purposes, came into existence during the Civil War. During that war, the Treasury Department put Jay Cooke, a banker, in charge of selling war bonds to the public. Not only did the bonds finance the army, but the mass sales effort also roused public opinion in support of the Union cause.[22] Similar fundraising programs were later used to finance war efforts during World Wars I and II.

National Development

PR was also an important factor in the United States' westward development. The western frontier was sold like real estate by the forerunners of modern PR practitioners, who made the most of legends and heroes. As early as 1784, for example, John Filson promoted land deals by making a legendary figure out of Daniel Boone, an unschooled, wandering hunter and trapper.[23] Almost a century later, George Armstrong Custer was likewise made into a hero—partly to justify U.S. policy toward the American Indian, partly to promote the settling of the West and partly to sell newspapers and dime novels.

In the 1840s, various publicists actively encouraged interest in the West. Reverend Jason Lee and some Methodist missionaries promoted the Willamette Valley near Salem, Oregon, an area where Nathanial Wyeth had tried to establish colonies twice before. The missionaries were there to Christianize the Flathead Indians, and it wasn't until Lee's publicity that white settlers began to come. Lee wrote letters to religious publications and went on a speaking tour throughout the East in 1838. The lower San Joaquin Valley was promoted by John Marsh, and Sacramento by John Sutter. Each man wrote articles for newspapers and magazines touting his preferred region for its healthfulness, and playing up themes of patriotism and manifest destiny.

Perhaps the most effective publicist of westward expansion was *New York Tribune* publisher Horace Greeley, whose editorial "Go West, Young Man, and

▼ **PR strategies were widely used by developers to encourage white settlers to move to the West.**

Grow Up with the Country" changed the lives of many people and the demographics of the entire nation.

But if the West was sold by PR techniques, it also was exploited by some of those same techniques. Press agent Matthew St. Clair Clarke brought Davy Crockett, the frontier hero, to the public's attention in the 1830s and used Crockett's glory to win political support away from Andrew Jackson. Two generations later, the adventures of Western personalities like Buffalo Bill, Wyatt Earp, Calamity Jane and Wild Bill Hickock were blown out of all proportion (to the benefit of their promoters in the eastern press) to give people a glamorous picture of the American frontier. Even outlaws like Jesse James became adept at using the press for glory—and to mislead the authorities.

Culture

The role of PR in the growth of America's entertainment industry was substantial. In fact, PR's immediate predecessor, press agentry, grew up with the entertainment business in the nineteenth century, a flamboyant era of road shows and circuses. P. T. Barnum was one of many circus showmen who employed press agentry (see Example 2.3).

Publicity stunts were even used occasionally to attract attention to books and their authors. For example, in 1809 the *New York Evening Post* ran a story about the mysterious disappearance of one Diedrich Knickerbocker from his residence in the Columbian Hotel. In followup stories, readers learned that Knickerbocker had left a manuscript, which the hotel's owner offered to sell to cover the cost of the unpaid bill. Later, the publishing house

EXAMPLE 2.3 ■■■■

Phineas Taylor Barnum (1810—1891)

The most famous and successful of nineteenth-century press agents was P. T. Barnum, who created, promoted and exploited the careers of many celebrities, including the midget General Tom Thumb, singer Jenny Lind and Chang and Eng, the original Siamese twins. Early in his career, in 1835, Barnum exhibited a black slave named Joice Heth, claiming that she had nursed George Washington 100 years before. Newspapers fell for the story, intrigued by its historical angle. Then, when public interest in Joice Heth began to die down, Barnum kept the story alive by writing letters to the editor under assumed names, debating her authenticity. Barnum didn't care what the papers said, as long as he got space. When Heth died, an autopsy revealed her age to be about 80. With the fraud exposed, Barnum claimed that he also had been duped.* Was this true? Why not? After all, "There's a sucker born every minute."

The great circus showman was himself often the center of public attention, for which he credited his own press agent, Richard F. "Tody" Hamilton.** However, the term *press agent* was first formally used by another circus. In 1868 the roster of John Robinson's Circus carried the name W. W. Duran with the title Press Agent.†

*Edward L. Bernays, *Public Relations* (Norman: University of Oklahoma Press, 1952), pp. 38–39.
**Dexter W. Fellows and Andrew A. Freeman, *This Way to the Big Show* (New York: Viking Press, 1936), p. 193.
†Will Irwin, "The Press Agent: His Rise and Decline," *Colliers*, December 2, 1911, pp. 24–25. (William Henry Irwin)

of Inskeep and Bradford announced in the same newspaper that they were publishing the manuscript, entitled *Knickerbocker's History of New York*. The whole story was a hoax, a publicity campaign conducted by the book's real author, Washington Irving.[24]

In the field of education, the value of PR was recognized even before the Revolution. In the nineteenth century, the trend continued. In 1899, Yale University established a PR and alumni office, showing that even the most established institutions were ready to enlist the budding profession to help them create favorable public opinion.[25] In 1900 Harvard University hired the Publicity Bureau—the nation's first PR firm, formed in Boston in 1900—but refused to pay the bureau's fees after about 1902. Nevertheless, the bureau continued to service the client for the prestige that it received.

Business and Industry

The development of industry during the 1800s brought about the most significant changes in the history of PR. The technological advances of the Industrial Revolution changed and modernized the tactics and techniques of PR. Steam power and inventions like the linotype made newspapers a truly democratic, nationwide mass medium.

Although the early industrialists used advertising to sell their wares and services to a growing market, they were not very interested in other functions of public relations. The prevailing attitude of the "robber barons" of the latter half of the century was summed up by William Henry Vanderbilt, head of the New York Central Railroad: "The public be damned."[26] J. P. Morgan, another railroad tycoon, echoed this sentiment when he said, "I don't owe the public anything." During the years between the Civil War and the turn of the century, industrial profit and power controlled and reshaped American life. Industrial magnates were answerable to no one and were immune to pressure from government, labor or public opinion.

An example of the corporate attitude at this time was the behavior of steel tycoon Andrew Carnegie in 1892, during the Homestead strike. When labor problems in his steel plant erupted into violence, Carnegie retired to his lodge in Scotland, 35 miles from the nearest railroad or telegraph. Carnegie wanted to be known as a cultured philanthropist, and he let the London press know that he remained aloof from the labor struggle only to protect his company from his own generosity. But professionally, he had not amassed a fortune of $400 million by worrying about the working or living conditions of his poorly paid employees, and he was content to have his right-hand man, Henry Clay Frick, crush their strike and their union with the help of the state militia.[27]

In time, industry had to reckon with the monster it had created—a labor force unwilling to be further exploited by the likes of Carnegie, Morgan and oil magnate J. D. Rockefeller. As the twentieth century progressed, labor disputes came to be fought more and more with public relations, less and less with violence.

Nonetheless, even in the 1800s, a few large corporations recognized that in the long run they would have to woo the public's favor. In 1858 the Borden Company, a producer of dairy products, set a PR precedent by issuing a financial report to its stockholders.[28] In 1883 an even more important precedent was set by Theodore N. Vail, general manager of the American Bell Telephone Company. Vail wrote to the managers of local exchanges, urging them to reexamine the services they were offering and the prices they were charging.[29] His letter is significant because it shows concern for the consumer and an interest in improving relations between the telephone company and the general public.

In 1877, Jay Gould opened a "literary bureau" for the Union Pacific Railroad, for the purpose of attracting immigrants to the West.[30] In 1888, the Mutual Life Insurance Company hired an outside consultant, Charles J. Smith, to write press releases and articles to boost the company's image.[31] In 1889 the Westinghouse Corporation established, under the directorship of ex-newspaperman E. H. Heinrichs, what was essentially the first in-house publicity department.[32]

This was also the period when department stores first appeared in the United States. The originator of the concept, John Wanamaker, was also the best in the business at public relations. When the Philadelphia store opened in 1876, Wanamaker

▼ Educational institutions formalized their public relations activities by opening their own PR offices or using one of the new agencies.

used publicity to generate interest in the new idea of a store that covered a full two acres. He gave visitors copies of a self-printed 16-page "souvenir booklet" that explained the store's departments, hiring policies and dedication to customer service. Salespeople were instructed in how to capture quotes from visitors that could later be incorporated in news releases.[33] Wanamaker also founded the *Farm Journal*, which he published for years, and he began publishing *The Ladies Home Journal* to sell ladies' fashions.[34] Macy's, Bloomingdale's, Lord & Taylor and Marshall Field quickly caught on and began publishing their own magazines and souvenir books.[35]

Press Agents and Publicists

It has often been said that twentieth-century public relations grew out of nineteenth-century press agentry. In some ways this is true. Certainly, many early PR practitioners got their start as press agents. Although few of these PR pioneers were as flamboyant as the great showman, P. T. Barnum, many were publicity writers whose main target had always been the press. The greatest of the publicity consultants was Ivy Ledbetter Lee (see Example 2.4).

Press Agentry   Press agentry really began in about 1830, with the birth of the penny press. When newspaper prices dropped to a penny each, circulation and readership boomed, but so did the price of newspaper advertising. To reach the huge new audience without paying for the opportunity, promoters and publicity people developed a talent for "making news." The object was simply to break into print, often at the expense of truth or dignity.

Press agents exploited freaks to publicize circuses, invented legends to promote politicians, told outrageous lies to gain attention and generally provided plenty of popular entertainment if not much real news.

The cardinal virtue of press agentry was its promptness. Indeed, it was often so prompt that its practitioners spent practically no time verifying the accuracy or value of its content. But ultimately the effectiveness of a press release depended on its creator's imagination, and imagination remains a necessary talent for effective PR today.

Publicity   Many early publicists were no more careful with the facts than their press agent contemporaries—neither were journalists of that day. Most publicists continually tried to "plant" stories in newspapers, hiding their source. In that respect, Ivy Lee represented a new kind of publicist (see Example 2.4). Perhaps the essential difference can be found in Lee's "Declaration of Principles" (1906), in which he defined the important ideals of public relations, his new profession: "Our plan is, frankly and openly . . . to supply the press and public of the United States prompt and accurate information concerning subjects which it is of value and interest to the public to know about."[36]

Lee's career spans the earlier era of communicating/initiating and the subsequent era of reacting/responding (1900–1939). At the dawn of the twentieth century PR's incubation period had drawn to a close. America was now a powerful, industrialized nation with sophisticated mass media and a well-informed public. The time was right for a mode of practice that would synthesize and coordinate the various talents—publicity, promotion, propaganda and press agentry—that had developed in tandem with the nation's growth.

▼ REACTING/RESPONDING: THE TIME OF REPORTERS-IN-RESIDENCE, 1900–1939

Public relations development grew significantly in the first four decades of the twentieth century, as publicists became spokespersons for organizations. As the age of unchecked industrial growth ended, industry faced new challenges to its established way of doing business. The new century began with a cry of protest from the "muckrakers"—investigative journalists who exposed scandals associated with power capitalism and government corruption. The term *muckraker* is a metaphor taken from John Bunyan's *Pilgrim's Progress*. It was first used in its modern sense by Theodore Roosevelt, who applied it pejoratively to journalists who attacked the New York Police Department in 1897, while he was commissioner. Later as President, with a consumer protection platform and a trust-busting program, Roosevelt came to appreciate the muckrakers.[37]

The Turn of the Century

Perhaps the first of the muckrakers was Joseph Pulitzer, whose editorials supported labor in the Homestead strike of 1892. "The public be informed," his slogan for an earlier campaign in support of labor, parodied the contemptuous attitude of William H. Vanderbilt.[38] But the great age of muckraking journalism began in the twentieth century.[39]

Lincoln Steffens, staff writer for *McClure's* magazine, wrote articles and books exposing corruption in municipal politics. Frank Norris, who covered the Spanish–American War for *McClure's*, took on the railroads and the wheat traders in his novels *The Octopus* (1901) and *The Pit* (1903). Ida Tarbell's *History of the Standard Oil Company* (1904), which began as a series for *McClure's* in 1902 and consisted mainly of interviews with former Rockefeller employees, exposed the company's corruption and its unfair competition with smaller companies. In 1906, Upton Sinclair described

EXAMPLE 2.4

"THE FATHER OF PUBLIC RELATIONS"

After graduating from Princeton, Ivy Lee became a reporter in New York City but soon gave that up to become a political publicist. Then, in 1904, he and George F. Parker formed the nation's third publicity bureau. By 1906 he was the most inspiring success in the young field of PR and found himself representing George F. Baer and his associates (who were allied with the J. P. Morgan financial empire) in a public controversy over an anthracite coal strike. Lee tried a radical approach: Frankly announcing himself as a publicity consultant, he invited the press to ask questions, handed out news releases and presented his client as cooperative and communicative.*

Lee's "Declaration of Principles," issued in 1906 to city editors all over the country, won respect for public relations (and didn't hurt the Baer bunch either). That same year, Lee represented the Pennsylvania Railroad when an accident occurred on the main line. Instead of hushing up the incident, Lee invited the press to come, at company expense, to the scene of the accident, where he made every effort to supply reporters with facts and to help photographers. As a result, the Pennsylvania Railroad and the railroad industry got their first favorable press coverage in years.**

Lee's remarkable, straightforward style came from his frank admiration of industry and capitalism, and he made it his goal to get big business to communicate its story to the public. By the time he was 30, Lee had sired a profession, chiefly by introducing and promoting its first code of ethics.

Lee's career continued to be successful, if not so influenced by high ideals. He began working for the Rockefeller family in 1913, when he presented the "facts" about a coal strike in Colorado that resulted in an incident known as the Ludlow Massacre. Lee later admitted that the "facts" he handed out about the bloody affair were the facts as management saw them, and that he had not checked them for accuracy.†

Lee's many clients included the American Russian Chamber of Commerce and the German Dye Trust, from whom he earned $25,000 a year and a sticky PR problem of his own—how to defend his work for a Nazi organization. He was also heavily criticized for his support of Soviet Russia and his encouragement of U.S.–Soviet ties.

Lee once wrote, "The relationship of a company to the people . . . involves far more than *saying*—it involves *doing*."‡ Nevertheless, it is perhaps an example of Ivy Lee's public relations talent that he is now remembered not so much for what he *did* at the height of his career as for what he *said* when he was still in his twenties.°

*Frank Luther Mott, *American Journalism* (New York: Macmillan, 1950), pp. 179–180.

**Irwin Ross, *The Image Merchants* (Garden City, N.Y.: Doubleday, 1959), p. 31.

†Ibid.

‡Ibid., p. 32.

°For a defense of Lee's often-criticized international activities, see the letter to the editor of *PR Review*, 13(3) (Fall 1987), pp. 12–13, by James W. Lee, II, his son.

---

the unsavory conditions that existed in the meatpacking industry in his novel *The Jungle*. These articles and books resulted in social legislation that remains the law of the land today.

Big business also was under fire from the government. President Theodore Roosevelt considered it the federal government's job to uphold the public interest in the battles that flared among management, labor and consumers. Using the Sherman Antitrust Act of 1890, he challenged big business—including U.S. Steel, Standard Oil and the Pennsylvania Railroad—to respond to popular displeasure.

An era of social consciousness was dawning. Proof that the former attitude was giving way came in 1899 with the founding of the first national consumer group, the National Consumers League (NCL), which was formed from state consumer leagues by Florence Kelley and Dr. John Graham Brooks.[40] The fledgling NCL supported the work of Harvey W. Wiley, a Department of Agriculture chemist who for more than twenty years gathered information to prove the need for a federal food and drug law. The first Pure Food and Drug Act was passed in 1906.

Industry *had* to respond. It could no longer afford simply to ignore the public and the press. Threatening to withhold advertising from uncomplimentary media did not have the desired effect. No longer could the railroads neutralize the press by giving free passes to reporters. No longer would the public buy statements like that of coal industrialist George F. Baer, who in 1902 told labor to put its trust in "the Christian men whom God in His infinite wisdom has given control of the property interests of the country."[41] When the coal industry came under fire again in 1906, the coal owners had learned their lesson; and instead of relying on puffery and rhetoric, they enlisted the talents of the young ex-newspaper reporter, Ivy Lee.

It is no coincidence that most of the first generation of public relations specialists came from the newspaper profession. Newspaper advertising had long been the only way that many companies communicated with their markets. Newspapers also were the medium in which many companies were being attacked. And newspaper coverage had been the main goal of nineteenth-century press agents, whose legacy inspired the first publicity agencies of the twentieth century.

The first publicity firm, the Publicity Bureau, was formed in Boston in 1900.[42] The idea of publicity caught on quickly, and soon several such firms—composed largely of ex-newspaper people—had appeared, including the firm of William Wolf Smith in Washington, D.C., which specialized in publicity aimed at influencing legislators.[43] From a historical standpoint, however, the most important publicity bureau during this period was the one operated by George F. Parker and Ivy Lee. Although that company lasted only four years, it launched the career of Ivy Lee, who is often called the father of public relations.

The public relations profession grew rapidly, and before long publicity became a standard and necessary tool for many businesses, individuals and organizations. Big businesses especially, such as communications, railroads and the automobile industry, found that publicity agencies and in-house publicity bureaus improved their relations with both the public and the government. In 1904 two major state universities—the University of Pennsylvania and the University of Wisconsin—set up publicity bureaus.[44]

By 1917, enough colleges had public relations and development officers for these individuals to form their own organization, the American Association of College News Bureaus. Later it was renamed the American College Publicity Association, and then the American College Public Relations Association; and today it is known as CASE, the Council for the Advancement and Support of Education. CASE's roots in ACPRA make it the oldest public relations organization in the world.[45] (The first association of public relations people was the Bank Marketing Association, formed in 1915 as a section of the Associated Advertising Clubs.)[46]

Publicity also proved valuable for public service organizations. The Young Men's Christian Association (YMCA) employed a full-time publicist to call attention to its fund drive in 1905.[47] The National Tuberculosis Association started a publicity program in 1908, and the American Red Cross followed suit the same year.[48] The Marine Corps established a publicity bureau in 1907 in Chicago.[49] In 1909 the Trinity Episcopal Church in New York City hired Pendleton Dudley as a public relations counsel to help combat criticism of its ownership of slum tenements.[50] Three years later the Seventh Day Adventist Church established a formal publicity bureau to answer complaints about its opposition to Sunday closing laws.[51]

Publicity in support of a product was used by National Cash Register founders John and Frank Patterson, who employed newsletters, brochures and flyers in the world's first direct-mail campaign.

Many useful tactics and techniques were developed during this early period. One PR pioneer who contributed a number of new ideas was Samuel Insull, publicity expert for the Chicago Edison Company.[52] Insull had a demonstration electric cottage constructed in 1902 to show how convenient the new technology was. In 1903 he communicated with the company's customers via bill stuffers and a house publication that was distributed to the community. In 1909 Insull became the first person to make PR-related movies.[53] (This was appropriate, since Thomas Edison himself was one of the first movie tycoons.)

Larger organizations, such as the Ford Motor Company, helped broaden business's interest in the public relations function. In 1908 Ford established a house publication, *Ford Times*, which is still printed today.[54] In 1912 the company began using public opinion surveys for market research.[55] And in 1914 Ford established the first corporate film department.[56]

The first formally designated press bureau in the federal government was founded in 1905 by the U.S. Forest Service.[57] The aggressiveness of its promotions is said to have been one of the elements leading to the 1913 federal ban on hiring public relations people (see Chapter 1).[58] However, Walter Lippmann's concern over the infiltration of German propaganda into American newspapers in the years immediately preceding World War I was another contributing factor, as was the growing resentment by newspaper reporters and editors of publicists.[59] Ivy Lee himself was attacked in muckraker Upton Sinclair's exposé of the newspaper business, *The Brass Check*, written in 1919.[60] Journalists particularly resented PR people's control over access to sources and their "prepackaged" news.[61] Advertisers, too, were unhappy with publicists for getting what they saw as "free advertising" in news columns.

Making the World Safe for Democracy

By the time the United States entered World War I in 1917, the war had been going on for several years, and PR had proved itself an effective weapon of persuasion for Europeans. The British, in particular, directed a "hands across the sea" propaganda campaign at the United States government and people, urging them to join the fight. They publicized the Allies' view of the *Lusitania* incident, for example, characterizing the Germans (whose submarine had sunk the ocean liner) as vicious "Huns." When President Wilson finally gave up his policy of peacemaking and neutrality, the United States entered the war with money, military might and a highly sophisticated public relations effort.

In selling the war as one destined "to make the world safe for democracy," the U.S. government solicited cooperation from many sources. AT&T was convinced that the government needed control of the phone company for the war effort.[62] The press was persuaded to exercise self-censorship and to contribute free advertising space for the war effort.[63] Academics served too. College professors acted as a force of Four-Minute Men, meaning that they were prepared to speak for that length of time on propaganda topics relating to the war. The world, not just the classroom, was their forum.

The government also solicited cooperation directly from the public: Herbert Hoover's Food Administration persuaded American citizens to conserve food during this time of emergency. The greatest example of the government's salesmanship, however, was the Liberty Loan Drive, which financed the war.

The genius behind America's wartime public relations effort was George Creel, a former newspaper reporter whom President Wilson appointed as chairman of the newly formed Committee on Public Information. The success of the Liberty Loan Drive and the effectiveness of U.S. wartime propaganda at home and abroad were both attributable to the Creel Committee. (Creel's propaganda was

▼ **The United States' entry into World War I led to creation of the Creel Committee, to win public support for American participation in the conflict.**

not as heavy-handed as that of the British government. In particular, Creel toned down the assaults on the German character and emphasized loyalty more than fear as the basis for support.)

The committee also created a legacy for the PR profession. Many members of the committee who learned their craft in wartime went on to practice it in peacetime. Included among these were Edward L. Bernays[64] and Carl Byoir.[65] As assistant chairman of the Creel Committee, Byoir publicized the draft and was in charge of distributing the *Red White and Blue Textbooks*, which described the goals of the war. He went on to become one of America's most successful public relations practitioners.

The Advertising Boom and the Roaring Twenties

The early twentieth century was a period of tremendous growth in the advertising industry. In 1916 Stanley B. Resor bought the J. Walter Thompson Company, which had been founded in 1864 and was at the time the largest advertising agency in the world.[66] Resor focused the agency's work on fact finding and scientific research. He was cofounder of the American Association of Advertising Agencies in 1917 and also helped to found the Advertising Research Foundation, the Audit Bureau of Circulations and the National Outdoor Advertising Bureau.[67] Working with him was his wife, Helen Lansdowne Resor, who, as head of the copy department, worked to ensure the ads were effective in their appeals to women.[68]

The 1920s were characterized by prosperity, power and pleasure. In spite of a national mood of isolationism, the United States' economic boom was heard around the world. Much of the boom was the sound of advertising, which continued its rapid expansion during this decade. In 1920, for example, the Illinois Central Railroad began what was to become the oldest continuous national advertising campaign in America.[69]

During this period, advertisers also discovered many new media. In 1921 an NBC radio station in New York broadcast the first paid commercial over the airwaves. Suddenly advertisers had a new medium, in addition to newspaper ads, billboards, streetcar signs and direct mailing. Advertisers in the 1920s also explored film, flashy trademarks and even skywriting. And advertising was itself adopted by health and public service organizations, by churches and by political parties and candidates. By 1929 advertising was a billion-dollar industry. Many sociologists attacked the economic wastefulness of the profession's mass media appeals, but none disputed the effectiveness of its sophisticated psychology.

Public relations in general also grew in scope and in stature during the 1920s. Books and courses were offered on the subject, and social scientists began to take notice. Among them was Walter Lippmann, a former adviser to President Wilson, who expressed concern over the implications of public opinion molding. In *Public Opinion* (1922), he wrote that the public no longer formed its own opinions, particularly about government policy; instead, people's opinions, like their knowledge, were fed to them by the media in the form of slogans and stereotypes.[70] He pointed out, however, that opinion molding is a two-way street. Society contains "innumerable large and small corporations and institutions, voluntary and semi-voluntary associations, national, provincial, urban and neighborhood groupings, which often as not make the decisions that the political body registers."[71]

Social scientists' interest in public opinion was shared by industry. Many companies, including AT&T, had learned from their experiences in World War I that social responsibility was good for public relations and hence good for business.[72] Thus the field of opinion research grew as companies developed tactics for finding out what their stockholders, their markets, and the general community wanted. AT&T's cooperation with the government during the war had earned it the confidence of the government and of the people. When Arthur Page joined the company in 1927 as vice-president and in-house public relations expert, he stressed several opinions that have affected modern PR ever since: that business begins with the public's permission and survives because of its approval; that businesses should have public relations departments with real influence in top management; and that companies should find out what the public wants and make public commitments that will work as "hostages to performance." Page insisted that PR is built by performance, not by publicity[73] (see Example 2.5).

The New Deal

The mood of the 1930s differed drastically from that of the 1920s. Following the stock market crash of 1929, the U.S. economy plunged into a depression from which it did not fully recover for ten years. Public relations during this time faced many challenges, as industry was forced to defend itself against public distrust, a discontented labor force and strict regulation by the Roosevelt administration. The greatest challenge to PR, however, was the job of selling good cheer to a confused and frightened populace. The challenge was felt by government, and successive presidents responded by trying to convince the country that a return of prosperity was just around the corner and that the only thing to fear was fear itself. The challenge was also felt by industry, and in 1938 the National Association of Manufacturers and the U.S. Chamber of Commerce conducted a comprehensive campaign based on the slogan "What helps business helps you."[74]

PR continued to develop as a field of practice during the 1930s. The National Association of Accredited Publicity Directors was founded in 1936. The American Association of Industrial Editors, founded two years later, was an indirect descendant of some earlier groups, including the Association of House Organ Editors, which had been formed in 1915. The American Council on Public Relations was founded in 1939 by Rex Harlow,[75] but

EXAMPLE 2.5

PR at AT&T—A Long History

In 1938 Arthur Wilson Page, first vice-president for public relations of the American Telephone and Telegraphy Company, told an international management congress that "the task which business has, and which it has always had, is of fitting itself to the patterns of public desires." A familiar saying of the PR pioneer was that in a democratic society no business could exist without public permission nor long succeed without public approval. Page also helped to popularize opinion survey techniques. In doing so Page was following through on the philosophy of a predecessor who was very conscious of public opinion: Theodore Vail, AT&T president in the early 1900s, had sent a series of questions about service to Bell telephone exchange managers to inquire about how well Bell was serving its customers. He understood the power of public opinion, noting it was based on information and belief. When public opinion was wrong, it was because of wrong information, and Vail said it was "not only the right, but the obligation of all individuals . . . who come before the public, to see the public have full and correct information." The long history of PR at AT&T makes even more amazing public support of the 1982 consent decree that separated individual Bell companies from each other and from AT&T. Page's philosophy and views of public relations are kept alive today by members of the Arthur Page Society, a professional membership organization founded by Bell public relations practitioners.

SOURCE: E. M. Block, "Arthur Page and the Uses of Knowledge," Inaugural Lecture, Arthur Page Lecture and Awards Program, College of Communication, University of Texas at Austin, April 22, 1982. Reprinted with permission of E. M. Block.

it had no chapters. The National Association of Accredited Publicity Directors, which changed its name in 1944 to the National Association of Public Relations Counsel, had chapters and requirements for professional experience. This group merged with Harlow's ACPR in 1948.

▼ **The economic crash of the 1930s stirred industry's concern for social responsibility as a way to regain public esteem and confidence.**

Another significant development during the 1930s was the institution of the Gallup Poll, which gave a boost to the sophistication and credibility of opinion research.[76]

Many trends in the development of public relations during the 1930s are reflected in the history of General Motors. When Paul Garrett joined GM in 1931 as its one-man PR department, most people distrusted big business. GM's Board of Directors wanted Garrett to help the billion-dollar corporation look small to win public favor, but Garrett did not believe in this approach. Good PR, he felt, had to work from the inside out. Corporate policies in the public interest had to provide the basis for public acceptance.[77] Management had to earn the goodwill of the public by acting, not by selling a false image. Garrett insisted that it was in the company's best interest to "place the broad interest of the customer first in every decision of the operation of the business."[78]

Despite its adoption of Garrett's views, General Motors' problems were far from over. Events worked against GM in 1937 when the Congress of Industrial Organizations (CIO) got involved in a labor dispute that resulted in a forty-four-day sitdown strike.[79] At a time when public sentiment was strongly anti-union, the CIO won a major victory for labor by getting public opinion on its side and forcing the nation's third largest corporation to recognize the union. But although the corporation lost the battle with labor, under Garrett's leadership it continued to wage the war for good public relations. In 1938 Garrett said, "The challenge that faces us is to shake off our lethargy and through public relations make the American plan of industry stick."[80]

In 1939 *Fortune* magazine carried an article on Paul Garrett, describing his activities "carry[ing] out a long-range program of finding out what people like and doing more of it."[81] This was the first time an important magazine reported on a corporation's public relations, and the description itself showed how the function had evolved into one directly concerned with corporate policy.

The Increasing Influence of U.S. Presidents as Opinion-Makers

The management of news by U.S. presidents goes back to George Washington, who leaked his Farewell Address to a favored publisher who he knew would give it a good display. When Thomas Jefferson was in Washington's cabinet, he put a newspaper reporter on the federal payroll to establish a party newspaper that would represent Jefferson's point of view; later, when he became president, he relied heavily on his "party press" and limited other newspapers' access to him.

Abraham Lincoln sought out newspaper editors who he believed might convey his ideas sympathetically to the people and thus help win their support for his policies. The significance he placed on public opinion is apparent in his famous statement, "Public sentiment is everything. With public sentiment, nothing can fail; without it, nothing can succeed. Consequently, he who moulds public sentiment goes deeper than he who enacts statutes or pronounces decisions."

Theodore Roosevelt developed the "trial balloon" device, calling favorite reporters to the White House to get their reaction to his ideas before trying them out on the public. He was sensitive to media coverage and once waited to sign a Thanksgiving Proclamation until the Associated Press photographer arrived.[82]

However, Calvin Coolidge is credited with having arranged the first pure photo opportunity, some twenty years later, on the occasion of his 55th birthday. The taciturn president liked photo sessions because he didn't have to talk during them.[83]

Woodrow Wilson developed the first regular formal press conferences, although he later regretted the idea, for he was a reserved man and never won popularity with the press. He also complained that the press was interested in the personal and the trivial rather than in principles and policies—to which the press responded that presidents just want journalists to print what they tell them, not what the public wants to know.

Franklin Roosevelt's candor and geniality delighted reporters, but even he sometimes regretted holding press conferences; and once, in a pique, he said that he would like to award a Nazi Iron Cross to a news reporter whose stories he felt had earned it. Roosevelt staged a great many photo sessions so that photographers wouldn't take candid pictures that called attention to his paralysis.[84]

Roosevelt, more than any of his predecessors, used public relations tactics to sway public opinion; and the development of mass media technology during the 1930s enhanced his efforts (see Example 2.6). In the decades following his death, he has drawn increasing retrospective criticism for "managing news," as have more recent presidents and their spokespeople. There may be some justification for this criticism, since the executive branch can end most independent reportorial investigations into its affairs by claiming "executive privilege." No one expects to find out too much from the judiciary branch, because of restrictions on what can be discussed, in keeping with the American Bar Association's code of judicial conduct; but in the legislative branch, what one party won't tell, the other will.

▼ PLANNING/PREVENTING: THE GROWTH OF PR AS A MANAGEMENT FUNCTION, 1940–1979

With the advent of the 1940s, the nation's mood changed again. The country was soon at war, and, as in World War I, the most conspicuous public relations efforts either served the war effort directly or were obvious by-products of a wartime economy.

EXAMPLE 2.6

PR Stands for President Roosevelt

Franklin Delano Roosevelt used every possible public relations device to sell the radical reforms of his New Deal to the American people. Advised by PR expert Louis McHenry Howe, FDR projected an image of self-confidence and happiness—just what the American public wanted to believe in. He talked to them on the radio. He smiled for the cameras. He was mentioned in popular songs. He even allowed himself to be one of the main characters in a Rodgers and Hart musical comedy (played by George M. Cohan, America's favorite Yankee Doodle Dandy). Of course, FDR's public image didn't succeed with everybody, and in some households *Roosevelt* is still a dirty word. But in general, the American people liked FDR, and they showed it by putting him in the White House four times.

Louis McHenry Howe also encouraged Eleanor Roosevelt to expand her public activities. She had joined the National Consumers League as an 18-year-old volunteer and was very interested in public issues. With Howe's help, she developed news conferences for women reporters only—"news hens," they came to be called. Nevertheless, they got exclusives from Eleanor, despite being excluded from most other news meetings because of their gender.

SOURCE: L. L. L. Golden, *Only by Public Consent: American Corporations Search for Favorable Opinion* (New York: Hawthorn Books, 1968), pp. 37–39.

World War II

When the United States entered World War II, PR firms quickly seized the opportunity to enlist in the cause. The prestigious PR firm of Hill & Knowlton, for example, firmly established itself by representing war industry groups such as the Aviation Corporation of America, the American Shipbuilding Council and the Aeronautical Chamber of Commerce.[85] Overall, the PR effort during World War II

> ▼ **The PR effort during World War II was much more sophisticated, coordinated and integrated than the one during World War I.**

was much more sophisticated, coordinated and integrated than the one during World War I.

Communications scholar Charles Steinberg believes that World War II caused public relations to develop into a "full-fledged profession."[86] In 1947 Boston University established the first full school of public relations, later "public communications."[87] By 1949, 100 colleges and universities across the nation were offering courses in PR.

Two significant events in government affected the future of public relations. One was the appointment of former newscaster Elmer Davis, as director of the Office of War Information (OWI). Davis's program was even larger than George Creel's had been but it was focused exclusively on the task of disseminating information worldwide. OWI was a forerunner of the U.S. Information Agency (Service), and unlike Creel, Davis was not an advisor to the president. At OWI evidence of government-planted disinformation began to appear.

The second event to affect PR practice was the creation of a War Advertising Council, which handled war-related public service announcements and created slogans like "Loose lips sink ships." The two organizations were tremendously successful in winning support for the United States at home and abroad, in helping sell war bonds and in winning cooperation from the public, from industry and from labor.

The use of films for PR purposes expanded greatly during this period. In 1943, for example, Frank Capra made a documentary film for the U.S. Signal Corps to inspire patriotism and build morale.[88] The government was not alone in using film for PR, however; Hollywood also made countless movies glorifying American fighting forces. The persuasive power of film was not lost on industry officials. In 1948 filmmaker Robert Flaherty made the documentary "Louisiana Story"[89] for Standard Oil.

Individual companies adapted to the war in different ways, often with the help of PR. Because of wartime ink shortages, the American Tobacco Company had to change the color of the Lucky Strike package from green to white. Thanks to PR, the change caused the company only a moment's regret. It launched a new campaign promoting a new slogan: "Lucky Strike Green Has Gone to War." Lucky Strike smokers everywhere were proud of their new white package because it signified that their brand was doing its part for America.

For Standard Oil of New Jersey, the war created a public relations crisis. At hearings of Senator Harry Truman's Committee on National Defense, Assistant Attorney General Thurman Arnold charged Standard Oil with "acting against American intent."[90] The charge involved a deal that Standard Oil had made with a German company many years earlier. In response, the oil company's marketing director, Robert T. Haslan, mounted a public opinion campaign, sending letters to customers and stockholders and hiring Earl Newsom as outside PR counsel. Eventually, Standard Oil beat the charges and came out of it with public support.[91]

In 1945 the same public relations fervor that helped sell the war effort contributed to the postwar industrial recovery. In that year, Henry Ford II, the new president of Ford Motor Company, hired Earl Newsom as a PR consultant. Newsom helped Ford compose a letter to the United Automotive Workers (UAW) during a strike at General Motors, urging the union to be reasonable and fair. He also helped Ford with his speech to the Society of Automotive Engineers in January 1946 and with an important anti-labor address to the Commonwealth Club in San Francisco the following month. With Newsom's help, young Ford became a public figure—a respected and publicized spokesperson for responsible business management.[92]

Earl Newsom was one of the first of a new type of PR practitioner: the public relations counselor. He did not send out news releases or hold press conferences; he simply advised. But his advice was valued and effective. His career also demonstrated the power of PR counselors to affect the policies and behavior of their clients.

The Fabulous Fifties and the Military-Industrial Complex

During the 1950s, America again experienced a booming economy, this time based largely on rising production of consumer goods. The population was growing faster than ever, and more and more people were getting good educations and entering the white-collar work force. Technology progressed on all fronts: television, satellites, atomic energy, the computer. Industry, in spite of "labor pains," continued to grow at home and abroad. Yet the mood of the nation reflected fear—of Communists, Russians, the bomb, McCarthyism, technology, juvenile delinquency and mass conformity, to name a few. In 1955 Sloan Wilson examined society and described the American white-collar worker in his best-selling novel, *The Man in the Gray Flannel Suit*. The hero, Tom Rath, was an in-house PR person for a large broadcasting corporation.

Public relations grew with the economy. That Wilson's typical businessperson was a PR practitioner shows how well established the profession had become. In 1953 the International Chamber of Commerce set up a commission on public relations, and in 1954 the Public Relations Society of America (PRSA) developed its first code of ethics.[93] A year later the International Public Relations Association was founded. Its individual members currently represent more than 60 countries. Many public relations organizations in other countries also have founding dates in the period from 1955 to 1960.

By the end of the 1950s, a number of women had entered the field, including several who ranked among the nation's top PR people: Doris E. Fleischman Bernays, early PR pioneer; Denny Griswold, former editor and publisher of *Public Relations News*; Jane Stewart, president of Group Attitudes Corporation; and Leone Baxter, president

▼ **PR counseling came into prominence in the postwar period.**

of Whitaker and Baxter in San Francisco.[94] In 1957 President Eisenhower appointed Anne Williams Wheaton his associate press secretary, drawing nationwide attention to PR as a potential career for women.[95]

The affluence of the 1950s encouraged businesses to find new uses for their money, and one job of public relations was to help them reinvest it in society—not only in tax-sheltering foundations, but also in health and community interest campaigns, public service drives and educational seminars. By encouraging corporate investment in society, PR gained greater respect and increased its own influence within corporations.

Television, which conquered America in the 1950s, had an enormous effect on the growth of public relations. This powerful medium's capacity for persuasion was evident from the start. Social scientists criticized television's pervasive control over public opinion, but it soon became clear that TV could create harmful as well as helpful PR. For example, Joseph McCarthy's credibility was weakened when his hectoring manner and his five o'clock shadow were exposed to the scrutiny of viewers across the nation. The Revlon Company first enjoyed glorious PR from its sponsorship of the nation's most popular TV program, but when the "$64,000 Question" was exposed as a fraud, Revlon suffered acute embarrassment and a wave of public criticism for its failure to meet its social responsibility.

Honesty in public relations became a serious issue during the 1950s. In the bitter competition between truckers and the railroads to win the nation's long-haul freight business, both groups relied heavily on PR. The Eastern Railroad Presidents' Council hired Carl Byoir and Associates to represent it, and the Pennsylvania Motor Truck Association hired Allied Public Relations Associates. By

▼ PR's development toward professional status in the 1950s raised concerns about the need for control over the ethics of PR practitioners.

1953 the two parties also had hired lawyers, and the case was in court.

The truckers charged that the railroads (and their PR firm) were violating the Sherman Antitrust Act by trying to drive the truckers out of business and by characterizing them as (in the words of federal judge Thomas J. Clary) "law-breakers, road-hoggers, completely indifferent to the safety of others on the highway and moochers on the public through failure to pay their way."[96] Byoir and Associates created many "front" organizations with the single purpose of agitating against the trucking industry.

In response, the agency argued (Byoir himself died before the struggle was resolved) that the anti-trucking coalition did not violate antitrust laws but merely exercised fundamental rights of free speech. A ruling from the U.S. Supreme Court in 1961 upheld Byoir's position and established the PR practitioner's right to represent a client's case in public even if the presentation is dishonest. Thus the legal question was resolved, while the ethical one was raised to a new level of urgency.[97]

Ethical problems like this led to PRSA's first code of ethics, a very brief statement promulgated in 1954. In 1959 PRSA adopted a Declaration of Principles and a more developed code of ethical behavior.[98] To avoid being accused of creating a paper tiger, PRSA established a grievance board in 1962 to conduct hearings whenever a PRSA member suspected another member of violating the code.[99] Two years later, PRSA approved a voluntary accreditation program open to all members of the society. This was the first step in recognizing a level of professional accomplishment in public relations and the first step toward establishing and policing standards of behavior among practitioners.

Transition in the Turbulent Sixties and Seventies

The 1960s and early 1970s were years of great crisis and change in the United States. Public relations talent was called upon to cope with the drama and the trauma. Modern PR practitioners needed a broad knowledge of the social sciences, as well as communication and management skills. In addition, nonmarketing problems received new emphasis, more attention was given to the worldwide consumer movement, corporate–government relationships were scrutinized, PR people gained increasing responsibility within the corporate structure, a more demanding role for PR in multinational companies and cries for help came from all sectors in dealing with dissident youth and minorities. Communications satellites, the awesome power of nuclear weaponry and the emergence of electronic information storage for data processing had made the globe smaller but had not diminished its problems.

One fundamental change in the United States actually began in the 1950s, signaled by the U.S. Supreme Court's landmark school desegregation decision of 1954, *Brown v. Board of Education of Topeka*, and involved a reassessment and legal reform of black and white race relations. During the 1950s in Montgomery, Alabama, Martin Luther King, Jr., began expressing his vision of what U.S. society could achieve if racism were ended. He used many public relations techniques to gain support for his cause, and he was skillful in working with the news media. His "I Have a Dream" speech and other eloquent sermons and addresses, as well as his adoption of nonviolent protest patterned on the approach developed by Mahatma Ghandi, helped launch a civil rights movement that produced many social changes, especially in the 1960s. King's assassination in April 1968 shocked the nation, and made his name a rallying cry for supporters of the continuing movement to achieve racial equality in the United States.

The nation seemed to divide on one point after another: civil rights, disarmament, the space program, the Vietnam war and the peace movement, conservation, farm labor, women's liberation, nuclear energy, the Watergate affair and on and on. In the debate over each of these issues, public relations was important to both sides. For example, PR professionals conducted seminars to train people within the power structure in how to respond directly to activists and how to answer them indirectly through news media and other public channels of communication. But the activists used PR just as effectively, capturing public attention with demonstrations, organizations and powerful rhetoric. Conservatives charged that the Chicago riots of 1968 smacked of press agentry. Radicals retorted that the same could be said of the Gulf of Tonkin incident.

Dow Chemical Company faced a PR crisis when antiwar consumers boycotted its household products, including Saran Wrap, because Dow also manufactured the incendiary chemical napalm, used to great destructive effect in the Vietnam war. Industry was chagrined by such protests, since contributing to the war effort had always been good for PR in the past. When no way could be found to popularize the Vietnam war, the United States signed a peace treaty ending the involvement of American troops—a decision that was announced (prematurely) during the last month of Richard Nixon's re-election campaign in 1972.

The Rise of Consumerism

In the United States, the consumer movement produced much of the criticism of institutions. Because of its increased visibility, many people assumed that the movement was new. It wasn't. The first national consumer group, the National Consumers League, had been founded from ninety state affiliates in 1899. Early issues it supported were minimum wage laws, improved working hours, occupational safety, abolition of sweatshops and child labor and improved working conditions for migrant farm workers. In supporting the 1906 Pure Food and Drug Act, the league formed food committees that set standards for food manufacture, inspected food manufacturing establishments and

▼ **The fractionalization of the nation in the 1960s and 1970s underscored society's need for public relations people who were good social scientists and good counselors.**

certified their safe working conditions by attaching a White Label, a logo similar to today's union label, to products.

Another organization that has been a longtime consumer advocate is the Consumers Union of the United States. It began as part of Consumer's Research, Inc., the first product-testing organization supported by consumers, and was established as a separate entity in 1936. Consumers Union is an independent, nonprofit organization that tests and evaluates such products as appliances, automobiles and packaged food. Since its founding, it has published the results of its tests in a monthly magazine, *Consumer Reports*, along with articles designed to help consumers spend more wisely and to make them aware of current consumer problems. The organization has always pressed for increased consumer protection by calling attention to what it believes are unsafe products. It has also concerned itself with weaknesses in consumer legislation and with the reluctance or failure of government regulatory agencies to act on behalf of consumers.

Sarah Newman, executive director of the National Consumers League from 1962 to 1975, has pointed out the major tactical differences between consumer-oriented organizations of earlier periods and those of the 1970s. For one thing, consumer advocates in the 1970s were more program-oriented. Consumer advocates during earlier periods did not resort to militancy. They also had to do much of the watchdog work themselves, because no regulatory agency was responsible for ensuring the safeness of most consumer products. By the late 1970s, Newman's own group was involved in such issues as equal credit, no-fault insurance and uniform beef grading. The NCL also pushed for creation of an agency for consumer advocacy.

Until the late 1960s, the U.S. economy had been run on the basis of increasing productivity. The supposition was that a ready market existed for all goods that could be conceived, produced, promoted and sold. Whatever it was, someone would buy it. This idea served as a cornerstone in the foundation of the American dream. But then a superabundance of goods resulted in a glutted marketplace and a surfeited public.

These surpluses led to more careful scrutiny of the consumer economy. At first only a few voices were raised, but the protesters found some dynamic allies, such as Ralph Nader. Their voices of dissent were eventually heard by some people sensitive to the sounds of the marketplace—people in public relations and advertising. Advertisers began finding flaws in the old edict of the business world: "If we can make it, you can sell it." As one disgusted advertising man exclaimed during this period: "I keep trying to tell those guys [his clients] that you can't fool the public." Although their clients may have been unaware of the changes that were occurring, many PR agencies certainly felt the mood of the marketplace; and in some of the largest and most prestigious, departments of consumerism or divisions of consumer studies began to appear.

Consumerism has been called "buyer's rights,"[100] "a cause or movement that advances the rights and interests of the consumer"[101] or a movement "seeking to increase the rights and powers of buyers in relation to sellers."[102] Whatever its title and definition, the essence of consumerism is perhaps best expressed by Margot Sherman, a retired senior vice-president of McCann Erickson (a New York agency), who had been in charge of setting up the agency's division of consumerism:

> On this business of consumerism, I suppose as a concept it was probably born in March 1962, when President Kennedy declared, "Every consumer has four basic rights—the right to be informed, the right to safety, the right to choose, and the right to be heard"!

Someone else sensitive to public sentiment—a politician—had given the movement a bill of rights. President Kennedy identified consumers as the only important group in contemporary society that was not effectively organized. He then appointed ten private citizens to serve on a Consumer Advisory Council, and he placed a consumer adviser, Esther Peterson, on his staff. Every U.S. president since Kennedy has followed his lead in having a staff consumer advisor.[103]

The Sentiment Behind Consumerism   The sentiment behind the consumer movement was best defined by Ralph Nader:

> Indeed the quality of life is deteriorating in so many ways that the traditional measurements of the "standard of living" according to personal income, housing, ownership of cars and appliances, etc., have come to sound increasingly phony.[104]

The sentiment was in fact a reaction to a "hostile environment." And the movement's character at a particular point in time, according to Edgar Chasteen, depended on the behavior of the "enemy," as defined by the movement.[105]

The enemy was business. In bewilderment, business looked on as a generation of consumers whose basic needs had been satisfied reacted adversely to old methods of persuasion. Evidently, the techniques that sold products also created expectations that could not be satisfied. A gap materialized between reality and the anticipation of rewards. In addition, consumer dissatisfaction was both the cause and the effect of another wave of investigative (or muckraking) journalism.[106]

To measure the intensity of consumer satisfaction/dissatisfaction, business used five common techniques: (1) statistics such as sales, profits and market share; (2) behavioral measures such as repeat purchases, acceptance of other products in the same line and favorable word-of-mouth publicity; (3) direct observation; (4) dissatisfaction indices such as recorded complaint data; (5) surveys and interviews to unearth reticent respondents. The hazards of using these techniques and the difficulties involved in measuring consumer satisfaction and dissatisfaction are legion.[107]

A thorough look at the activist requires a look at the adversary as well. Ralph Nader has said that the principal concern of the consumer movement has always been the "involuntary subeconomy"—unwritten price-fixing for goods and services, and inflationary agreements with labor and suppliers. These factors force up the costs of consumer goods and services, and the higher costs must be accepted because no other sources of the goods or services exist. Because there are no controls and no choices, the system is "involuntary"; because it underlies the economic structure, it constitutes a "subeconomy." Writing in 1973, Nader noted that the consumer movement has had limited success in improving regulatory action and encouraging private litigation. Its main achievement has been to create an awareness among consumers that they are being cheated and endangered. Nader conceded that the consumer movement has yet to devise an economic and policy-making framework to counterbalance or deplete the power of corporations to impose involuntary expenditures:[108]

> To some extent, consumerism as we know it was born of public frustration during a period of social turmoil, which saw unrest over civil rights issues and a divisive war in Southeast Asia. We entered a strobe-light existence, and with every blink of the flashing light, society had changed a little more before our very eyes! In short, the storm of the 1960s blew away many of the road signs that had helped us find our way comfortably along in the more predictable decades that came before.[109]

The Impact of Consumerism   Most consumer activists of the 1960s and 1970s were members of what has been called the "silent generation." This generation was proportionally smaller because its members were Depression or post-Depression babies.[110] For it, quality of life was understood in terms of a standard of living.[111,112] But not until confronted with the hostile accusations of the "antimaterialistic" younger generation of the 1960s did the silent generation recognize two salient questions: (1) At whose expense does a better living come? (2) What is the real value of all this? Robert

Glessing has perceptively commented that "the unpreparedness of the silent generation was at least part of the cause of the student protest movements."[113]

But after taking a careful and critical look at its own lot, the silent generation began borrowing tactics from the youth revolt. Suddenly meat boycotts were being staged by matrons who were definitely over 40.[114] Although Rachel Carson's *Silent Spring* was published in 1962 and Ralph Nader's consumer statistics tips to Congress began appearing in 1960 (even before his 1965 publication *Unsafe at Any Speed*), the consumer movement did not become formidable until the early 1970s.[115] In 1972 and 1973, however, the Public Relations Society of America appointed a task force to examine the impact of consumerism on business.[116] By this time, class action suits were being filed; pressure was being brought to bear on regulatory agencies to enact stricter criteria and to enforce them; stockholders' meetings were losing their predictability because minor shareholders were appearing and demanding social accountability; employees were more likely to become litigants than loyalists.[117]

By 1967 President Lyndon Johnson had decided that consumer complaints were so politically significant that he appointed Betty Furness consumer advisory counsel.[118] By 1971 there were four national consumer organizations: the Consumer Federation of America, the Nader Organization and the two older associations, the National Consumers League and the Consumers Union.[119]

The consumer movement even reached that bastion of authoritarianism, the military. Complaints about the food in mess halls got a hearing, not a court-martial. Although the volunteer army may have influenced some of these changes, it is important to look at some dates. Permissiveness in dress,[120] one of the first changes, was championed by the secretary of the Navy, Admiral Elmo R. Zumwalt, in 1970, three years before the end of the draft.[121]

Communication Problems and Public

Opinion   The consumer movement clearly demonstrates some lack of communication between business and consumers, a deficiency that the following statement makes clear:

> The consumerism movement not only mirrors the inability of the business sector to discern what factors of inherent consumer motivations promulgate (dis)satisfaction, but also reflects a growing concern for the "quality of life," which seems to be a popular cause, as well as a goal to collectively attain.[122]

In commenting on a 1977 Louis Harris survey, financial columnist Sylvia Porter asked how closely the views of senior business managers, consumer activists and government regulators matched the views of the general public. The answer was "not closely," with senior management "less in touch with public opinion than are any of the other groups." As Porter said:

> Consumer activists would prefer to concentrate on electric utilities, the advertising industry, nuclear power plants and banks.
>   Business executives want reforms in hospitals, the medical profession, garages, home building and the legal profession.
>   Only one common perception is shared by every group surveyed: mistrust of the honesty and accuracy of advertising.[123]

The Harris survey had found that more than a third of all adults were bothered by poor-quality or dangerous products that failed to live up to advertising claims. They were distressed at the failure of companies to show legitimate concern for the consumer. They were bothered by poor after-sales service and repairs and by misleading packaging or labeling. More than half of the respondents thought they were receiving a worse bargain in the marketplace than they had been getting ten years earlier. Moreover, consumers expected things to get worse in three areas: product durability, product repair and the reliability of manufacturer's claims for products. Although the public expressed a desire for more information about subjects of concern to consumers, the poll found little public confidence in the accuracy and reliability of media news.

The Scope of the Problem   The word *corporate*, as used in the consumer movement, should be interpreted in its broadest sense. Under fire, in addition to businesses, were all large institutions—hospitals, fund-raising public health associations, major-league sports teams, public and private educational institutions on all levels and religious groups. The biggest guns of all have been leveled at government administrators. The news media have suffered from adverse public opinion, too, as have newsmakers themselves, due to lawsuits, public attacks and threats of government intervention.

The harsh realities are clearly set forth by mass media scholars David Clark and William Blankenburg:

> The sturdiest obstacles to "ideal" public relations are economics and human nature. The plain fact is that managers are hired to make money for owners, and that a conscience can cost money. In the long run, it is money well spent, but many stockholders and managers fix their vision on the short run. Then, too, an abrupt change in corporate policy amounts to a public confession of past misbehavior—or so it seems to many executives. The natural temptation is to play up the good, and to let it go at that.[124]

Some Conclusions   Consumer groups have "common interest" appeal and extensive networks of relationships, assuring them of a large constituency. Concurrently, business enjoys less product loyalty from customers than it used to, and employee loyalty is almost nonexistent. The link between consumer and employee interests is particularly significant, since it strengthens the collectivity in support of consumer interests.

Consumer activists claim to represent "the people." Government, too, represents "the people." But business appears to represent only its owners—a rather select interest group even in publicly held companies, where the owners are stockholders.

The Impact of the Sixties and Seventies on Public Relations

The urgency of the problems that PR practitioners handled during the crises of the 1960s and 1970s and the expectations of those hiring PR talent gave the role new dimensions. But the new demands also created a crisis of confidence inside and outside public relations. In 1968 the Public Relations Student Society of America formed,[125] and as public relations continued to gain status as an academic discipline, the field for the first time became dominated by people specially trained for the job.

In 1973 the U.S. Supreme Court handed down a decision that fundamentally changed the role of the PR practitioner. In the *Texas Gulf Sulphur* case (discussed further in Chapter 14), the Supreme Court upheld a 1968 decision of the U.S. Circuit Court of Appeals in New York requiring immediate disclosure of any information that may affect the market value of stock in publicly held corporations.[126] This ruling meant that PR had to concentrate more on dealing with public information and less on selecting what information to make public. The Supreme Court also ruled that PR practitioners involved in such cases were "insiders" and therefore were subject to the same trading restrictions as other members of the corporation whose knowledge of special circumstances prohibited them from buying or selling stock.[127] The insider trading scandals of the 1980s severely tested the SEC's ability to enforce insider trading rules.

The Growth of Public Skepticism   Between 1966 and 1977 public confidence in corporate leadership dropped by 31 percentage points. While many executives besieged by negative public opinion bunkered down or toyed with the idea of resigning, one public relations officer decided to take the offensive. Mobil Oil's Herb Schmertz, a lawyer, began running Mobil's issue advertising in 1970. Following the oil shortages of the 1970s and the price acceleration they caused, Schmertz expanded Mobil's aggressive ad program and sought favorable opinion by sponsoring public television's "Masterpiece Theater." Schmertz became a 1970s

personality and had another PR person, William Novak, write his version of the experience.[128] (In 1988, Schmertz resigned from Mobil to start his own PR firm.)

Throughout the 1960s and 1970s there were valid grounds for public skepticism. Although the term *disinformation* didn't gain currency until the 1980s, the U.S. government was giving its citizens a good bit of it all along. One such campaign was engineered by former Assistant Secretary of Defense Paul Nitze. In 1975 intelligence-gathering activities of the CIA revealed that the Soviets' defense industry was *half* as efficient as had previously been supposed. It was therefore costing the Russians twice as much to build their weapons as U.S. analysts had thought. But in October 1975, Secretary of Defense James Schlesinger disclosed that "new intelligence" showed the Soviets were *spending* twice as much, implying that the Soviet military capacity was twice as great as had been estimated theretofore. News of the Soviet spending increase was reported in the mass media and thus was placed on the public agenda. With CIA Director George Bush's help, Nitze put together a study group to reevaluate the CIA data; subsequently, it "leaked" to the *New York Times* its conclusions that the CIA had been "dangerously complacent" in earlier evaluations of Soviet capacity and that the Soviets now had a first-strike capability. The leak was timed for one month before Jimmy Carter took office. So much for his vow to cut the defense budget.[129]

The Seventies in Summary   The Middle East garnered a great deal of attention in the United States in the 1970s. The effects of the oil shortage created by policies of the coalition of oil-producing nations (OPEC—the Organization of Petroleum Exporting Countries) began to be felt as world demand for oil outstripped the supply from non-OPEC sources. In Iran the Ayatollah Khomeini and his fundamentalist Islamic followers overthrew the U.S.-backed shah. Soon thereafter, the American

Embassy in Tehran was seized and its staff held hostage. Other acts of terrorism in the region suggested that the U.S. government was unable to defend its interests in that part of the world.

Problems in the Middle East added to a loss of confidence in the U.S. government at home. Another contributing factor was double-digit inflation, which eroded the economy and caused a serious decline in the standard of living. The nation's first military defeat, in Vietnam, drained people's feelings of nationalism, although the 1976 bicentennial helped revive these to some extent.

During the 1970s, the cultural monopoly of the traditional American family disappeared. More couples lived together outside marriage, and some were of the same sex. Married couples divorced at high rates, and after the 1950s "baby boom," fewer children were born each year, especially to white couples.[130] The ethnic mix in America changed as the black and Hispanic populations, respectively, grew at twice and six times the rate of the white population. The Hispanic community was enlarged by numerous political and economic refugees from Latin America. Southeast Asian refugees, fleeing their homelands in the wake of communist victories there, added another ethnic piece to the American mosaic.

While consumerism and environmentalism both made great strides during the decade, the main social movement of the 1970s was the women's movement. Opponents succeeded in blocking ratification of the Equal Rights Amendment to the Constitution, but the movement helped bring about some fundamental changes in society. Women began to view themselves as complete equals to men and demanded equal treatment in the workplace. Of the 3 million new people in the workforce, 2 million were women; almost half of all married women were employed, one-fourth of them with children under the age of six. Women's wages, though, were only 60 percent of men's. Women in legal careers doubled. Women getting medical degrees accounted for 22 percent of all those who sought such degrees in traditional medicine and 23 percent in veterinary medicine. The percentage of financial officers who were women rose from 18 percent to 30 percent in the decade, and women economists increased from 11 percent to 23 percent. Women in operations system research and analysis more than doubled, and women entered the public relations field in unprecedented numbers.

Presidential Power and Public Opinion in a Climate of Increasing Skepticism   In the 1950s, President Dwight Eisenhower acknowledged the needs of television and radio news media and allowed them to record his press conferences. John Kennedy permitted live TV coverage of his meetings with the press.

Richard Nixon, who blamed TV for his 1960 defeat for the presidency, was determined to master his television technique and did. President Nixon's press secretary was not permitted much candor in his interactions with the media, however, and was not a professional public relations practitioner. In fact, Ronald Ziegler was experienced only in advertising. The only person with media experience, Herb Klein, was relegated to working with newspapers in the "hinterlands," and the only person on Nixon's staff with PR background, William Safire, was strictly a speech writer.

Jimmy Carter hired Jody Powell as his press secretary when he first took office. However, when President Carter felt his work was not being understood correctly by the citizenry, he hired Gerald Rafshoon, the man who had managed his media campaign during his candidacies for governor of Georgia and president of the United States, to coordinate policy statements within the executive branch so that unity and cohesiveness of position were maintained. In response to media descriptions of his role as an "image maker," Rafshoon said he was coordinating, not creating.

President Ronald Reagan's deputy press secretary, Pete Roussel, said he faithfully adhered to what he called the "Press Secretary's Prayer": "Oh, Lord, let me utter words sweet and gentle, for tomorrow, I may have to eat them."[131] Roussel was one of several public-opinion-sensitive specialists on Reagan's staff. Reagan came to be called "the Great Communicator." Recognizing that some people who didn't like what Reagan said nonetheless continued to like him, Colorado Congresswoman Pat Schroeder nicknamed him the "Teflon" president: nothing unpopular that his administration did seemed to stick to him personally. Reagan's administration also employed pollster Richard Beal, whose job was to look at public views on questions likely to arise as issues in the future.

In doing this, Reagan was following a trend that started with John F. Kennedy's use of polling, according to Sidney Blumenthal, author of *The Permanent Campaign*.[132] Blumenthal called Reagan "Communicator in Chief" and made this observation:

> Ronald Reagan is governing America by a new doctrine—the permanent campaign. He is applying in the White House the most sophisticated team of pollsters, media masters and tacticians ever to work there. They have helped him to transcend entrenched institutions like the Congress and the Washington press corps to appeal directly to the people.[133]

In addition to filling the administration's major public relations posts with experienced professionals, Reagan appointed PR pros to many positions not traditionally considered public relations jobs. Of the three top advisers to the president, two were lawyers and one, Michael Deaver, was a public relations professional. Deaver was indicted for influence peddling after he left the White House, and Bernard Kalb of the State Department left in protest when the government got involved in a disinformation campaign.

After press secretary Jim Brady was severely injured in the assassination attempt on Reagan, Larry Speakes became acting press secretary. Speakes sometimes felt that he wasn't sufficiently informed by other administration officials, and some newspeople agreed. However, Speakes said, not knowing is the lesser of the two sins of a press secretary; lying was a "cardinal sin," and unforgivable. Then, after he had left the administration—first to work

for a large public relations firm, and then to direct public relations for a major brokerage firm— Speakes acknowledged he had "made up" quotes he attributed to President Reagan!

There is protection in not knowing because then you can't lie outright. However, if you don't know, you may commit a near-equivalent to lying—misleading. Not knowing everything, Speakes said, left him vulnerable in briefings because he ran the risk of saying something that might embarrass the president. About a fourth of the time he was bound by strict guidelines concerning what he could say to the news media.[134]

The Reagan presidency was one of the most controlled in the history of the office. One indication of this was the number of orchestrated photo opportunities.[135] Additionally, during the Reagan administration, the U.S. Information Agency grew in power and influence. As the U.S. Information Service, it now has offices worldwide and controls an extensive television service called Worldnet, which broadcasts to 100 cities in 79 countries. Concern about Worldnet was expressed in 1987 by Florida Congressman Dan Mica, who observed that it had an "untapped and unlimited potential." The Congressman was concerned "that a particular Administration could use Worldnet as its private propaganda vehicle."[136]

▼ PROFESSIONALISM: AN EFFORT BY PR PRACTITIONERS TO CONTROL PR'S DEVELOPMENT, USE AND PRACTICE ON AN INTERNATIONAL LEVEL, 1980–PRESENT

The confrontations, challenges and turbulence of the 1960s and 1970s led to polarization in the 1980s. This polarization crossed every imaginable social and political boundary. The resulting struggles increased global as well as national tensions between fundamentalists and secularists. At the same time, the centrist position narrowed dramatically.

Historical Developments in the 1980s and 1990s

The interconnectedness and shared experience of our global society was demonstrated in international reactions to everything from natural events such as the return of Halley's comet (1985–1986) to calamities like the Chernobyl nuclear power plant accident in the Ukraine (April 25, 1986) to the world stock market disaster of Black Monday (October 19, 1987), which was precipitated by a drop of 508 points in the Dow Jones industrial average. Individual investors fled the marketplace and complained bitterly about the havoc wreaked by speculators. In 1989 in the United States the "Big Board" initiated a major public information campaign aimed at the 47 million Americans who owned stocks or shares in mutual funds. By 1991 there was some evidence that individual investors had returned to the stock market.

Discoveries of a super nova and of a superconducting substance, as well as breakthroughs in genetic coding research, revitalized confidence in our ability to understand and shape the world. But the proliferation of the deadly disease AIDS (Acquired Immune Deficiency Syndrome) was humbling and defied explanation and control. Both in the United States and abroad, advertising and public relations programs were undertaken to educate the public about AIDS and to impede its progress into a pandemic.

Faith in U.S. institutions was severely shaken in 1986 by a series of events. The first of these was the January 28 explosion of the Challenger space shuttle, which temporarily ended manned space explorations by the United States. NASA's return in 1989 was with the launches of Magellan and Galileo space probes, and with the brilliant success of Voyager 2's flyby of Neptune at the conclusion of its 12-year journey. Then there followed the exciting pictures of Venus. Despite these successes, NASA was feeling the national budget crunch which threatened its future.

Falling oil prices in 1986 caused such economic chaos in the Sunbelt states that more banks failed that year than ever before in the nation's history. The drop in oil prices hurt not only the banks themselves and U.S. oil-producing states, but also Latin American countries that had used their petroleum assets as collateral for loans from U.S. banks that they suddenly had no means of repaying.

Worldwide television audiences witnessed the exposure of an unelected subgovernment in the United States during the Iran-Contra hearings, which investigated unauthorized sales of arms to Iran, supposedly in exchange for American hostages held in Lebanon, with profits from the sales going to the Nicaraguan Contras. President Ronald Reagan claimed to have been unaware of these activities, and Marine Lieutenant Colonel Oliver North of the National Security Council enjoyed a brief career as a national hero before being indicted and sentenced in 1989. (His convictions were overturned later by an appeals court decision that the evidence proving his guilt had not been sufficiently insulated from testimony North had given to Congress under a grant of immunity from prosecution. North pronounced himself "totally exonerated" by this ruling.) Before the dust from this debacle had settled, a new (but lesser) scandal involving Pentagon defense contracts further eroded public confidence in government.

Television audiences also watched the downfall of TV evangelists Jim and Tammy Bakker and Jimmy Swaggart and the collapse of the Bakkers' organization, an event that indirectly led to Jerry Falwell's resignation as head of Moral Majority, the leading fundamentalist organization in the United States.

In the face of falling U.S. prestige, Soviet Prime Minister Mikhail Gorbachev introduced a new climate of *glasnost* (openness) in the USSR. He sent young, effective communicators to represent his nation in preliminary peace talks and agreed to many U.S. positioning statements, much to the dismay of U.S. diplomats. In 1987, he came to the United States and showed that he, too, knew how to handle a media event. But by 1991 Gorbachev was in serious trouble at home, trying to keep the USSR glued together as one state after another voted for independence. By year's end the Soviet Union was defunct, and Gorbachev was head of a Russian "think tank."

The United States hosted another important world leader in 1987, Pope John Paul II, who found his followers in a restive mood as he refused to modify his conservative views on the issues of marriage for priests and nuns, abortion, birth control and homosexuality. The world of public relations got directly involved in that issue because the United States Catholic Conference (USCC) asked Hill & Knowlton to represent it in a public anti-abortion campaign. Robert L. Dilenschneider, then president and CEO of Hill & Knowlton, agreed to take the account, but he didn't anticipate that USCC would announce that fact before he had a chance to tell employees about it. Many of his staffers were quite upset, and some even quit. Dilenschneider later conceded that the internal handling of the affair was not ideal, but he defended his decision to accept the account as a first amendment issue—a rather problematic line of argument because it implies that, much like lawyers, PR practitioners have a societal duty to provide their services to anyone who wants (and can pay for) professional help in framing and disseminating ideas, regardless of how repugnant those ideas may be. Taken to an extreme, this reasoning would find an obligation to provide PR services to hate groups, on the theory that the first amendment guarantees them not merely the right to free speech, but the right to effective speech. In the fall of 1991, Dilenschneider resigned, citing loss of control to the parent company, WPP Group PLC.

Hill & Knowlton also had the account of the Citizens for a Free Kuwait, which it obtained shortly after U.S. troops started their campaign to recapture that country on January 16, 1991. The Desert Storm war, perhaps because of its brevity, success and multinational force, restored a strong feeling of patriotism to citizens of the United States. However, the war's aftermath, especially the Kurdish refugee situation, reminded the international community of the lingering horrors of war. The war also left a substantial number of Kuwaiti oil fields on fire (the last of these fires was put out some six months later) and an oil-drenched, ecologically damaged Persian Gulf. Cynicism replaced patriotism in some quarters after the war, as people became more aware that the "reality" of the coverage they had been exposed to more nearly resembled managed news. The backlash among media personnel against PR control of war information was strong.

The stock market collapse of Black Monday in 1987 represented a frightening but graphic example of imagery and public opinion. The lingering weakness of the market was attributable in part to global discomfort at the U.S. debt, which had reached the trillions of dollars, and at the deadlock between the Reagan administration and Congress over how to deal with it. The friction in philosophies between the executive and legislative branches was apparent in the Iran–Contra hearings, the budget negotiations, and most dramatically in the Senate's refusal to confirm strict constructionist Robert Bork to the Supreme Court. Opposition to his nomination revived the activism of civil rights and the feminist constituencies. Four years later, the nomination of Clarence Thomas to replace Thurgood Marshall on the Supreme Court opened a rift within the black community when law professor Anita Hill's allegations of sexual harassment by Thomas created a national furor over the nature and prevalence of this previously ignored type of crime. Although many people found Hill's testimony at the resulting hearing both plausible and compelling, the U.S. Senate's ninety-eight men and two women narrowly voted to confirm Thomas's appointment to the court.

The most dramatic historical development of the late 1980s was the downfall of communist regimes in Eastern Europe. In the spring of 1989, with neighboring borders relaxed, East Germans began leaving the state in droves. Then in November, the East German government resigned en masse, and on November 10 the Berlin Wall began to come down. Pieces of the wall sold as souvenirs in U.S. department stores at prices from $15 to $25.

By 1990, the U.S. Information Agency had opened the first "American University Bookstore" in East Berlin. The two Germanies were united in October of 1990. Another notable development in November of 1989 was Hungary's withdrawal from the Warsaw Pact; and later in the same month Hungarians voted in their first free election in forty-two years. In Czechoslovakia, voters elected prominent dissident playwright Vaclav Havel president in 1989. The Solidarity trade-union leader Lech Walesa was chosen premier of Poland in August 1989. By 1990, the Voice of America had opened its first Polish office, in Warsaw. Meanwhile, in Bulgaria, seeing the tide of change in 1989, Communist party leader Todor Zhivkov resigned.

The most dramatic climax may have been in Rumania. In December 1989, after his communist government had collapsed, Nicolae Ceausescu was captured, tried in secret and, along with his wife, executed by a firing squad on Christmas Day. Mass graves of suspected government opponents were exhumed, and U.S. families began to adopt orphaned and abandoned Rumanian children. This turned out to be a problem by 1991 when it became clear that many private adoption homes in Rumania were placing children who had been relinquished (either abandoned or sold) by poor families. The U.S. State Department responded by refusing to grant adopting parents visas for the children.

In the Western Hemisphere, Fidel Castro began issuing visas that permitted some people to leave Cuba legally for the first time.

With restraints loosening in much of the communist world, the Western world was shocked to watch on television as Chinese students participating in a pro-democracy movement were attacked by armed troops and tanks near Beijing's Tiananmen Square. Especially apprehensive were the Chinese citizens of Hong Kong, since that island city is due to revert to China in 1997. Many of the students who weren't captured in the subsequent crackdown escaped with the help of an underground movement operating out of Hong Kong.

Two unique elements in the tragic event point out the globlization of today's world. First, the students in revolt were receiving fax messages from Chinese students and sympathizers abroad, and second, the authorities later used television footage to identify the students and track them down. Some received severe prison sentences. This led some U.S. citizens to push for revoking China's "most favored nation" trading status, but President Bush opposed this measure and committed the administration to a policy of keeping the market open.

The mostly nonviolent revolutions of Eastern Europe were followed in 1991 by the disintegration of the Soviet Union into its constituent republics (loosely allied as the Confederation of Independent States). A far more destructive secessionist movement occurred simultaneously in Yugoslavia, where forty-five years of cooperative existence between neighboring states gave way to older enmities and a bitter civil war.

The world's turbulence and turmoil opened markets and new opportunities for public relations practitioners who could cope with the demands of global communications. The new Russian commonwealth presented a particularly challenging opportunity. In response to the new united European market (scheduled for 1992), the United States, on President Bush's initiative, opened expanded trade with Canada and Mexico, as a part of a "united continent" concept.

If any single element characterized the domestic scene in the United States at the beginning of the 1990s, it was increased concern with the environment. Movements to protect tropical rainforests, to end ozone depletion and to limit emissions of chemical pollutants responsible for acid rain burgeoned. Many efforts by government and industry were largely hype disguising an underlying hypocrisy, but public opinion was generally pro-environmentalist.

PR Developments in the 1980s and 1990s

During the 1980s, public relations became greatly enhanced by developments in computer technology. PR newswire services responded to the new technology by using satellite transmissions. In addition to the greater dispersion of information, computer technology brought the microcomputer to the public relations office and, with it, an array of microcomputer techniques. One such technique was desktop publishing, which improved the look of in-house publications and made possible sophisticated graphics for reports, speeches and ads. Improvements in computers also added to the explosion of the PR research industry.

In a move to stress professionalism, PRSA developed and published a "body of knowledge," and it is cooperating with IPRA to produce a comparable international body of knowledge. PRSA also informed all of its accredited members that accreditation must be maintained through continuing education. Senior practitioners were recognized by PRSA through creation of a College of Fellows.

Buyouts of U.S. companies by foreign nations put a new and complicated burden of responsibilities on PR practitioners in the United States. The buyout of Standard Oil by BP (British Petroleum) "constitute[s] a textbook example of the complications that arise in such a transaction."[137] In 1986, when BP was still only a partial owner, Sohio (Standard Oil of Ohio) dropped its name because management felt that its activities were too international to justify using the name of a single state. During the February 1986 name change, the company was restructured and twenty subsidiary companies were sold, requiring an extensive investor and media relations campaign.

Another full-blown information campaign was developed for the May 1987 merger, but it had to be put aside after the British government announced in July 1987 that it was privatizing its one-third share ownership of BP. During that time, under both U.S. and British securities regulations, BP America was forbidden to engage in internal or external communications activity until the share issue was no longer in the registration process—and this process lasted from the end of July until December.

To make matters worse, the British government's BP share offering occurred on Black Monday. To prevent company shares from being bought from a stockbroker at less than the government's asking price, the government promised to support a floor price to reduce risks to brokers who had agreed in advance to buy the full issue.

Finally, in January 1988, BP America began to tell its story with a three-page ad that ran during the first week of the year in most major U.S. dailies. The ad pointed out that BP America "is the 12th largest company in America . . . but you probably never heard of it." The ads were part of a comprehensive campaign that included an intensive media relations emphasis for the business and financial press.[138]

Another trend in public relations was the continued stream of women into the field, as documented and examined in "The Velvet Ghetto."[139] While male PR practitioners moved into CEO slots, women did not. Most women in public relations held lower-status positions and earned considerably less than men in similar positions. Most women at the top reached it by heading their own agencies, although there were exceptions such as Jean Way Schoonover, vice-chairman of Ogilvy Public Relations Group. Alma Triner was vice-president of corporate communication for Arthur D. Little, Inc., until she and several others went into business handling the promotion of entrepreneurial ventures.

Two women were PRSA presidents in the 1980s, following in the footsteps of Betsy Ann Plank, former assistant vice-president for corporate communications at Illinois Bell, who served as PRSA president in the 1970s and now works as an independent consultant; Judith Bogart, former executive vice-president for the southwest office of Diversified Communications, Inc., and now a consultant; and Barbara Hunter, president of Hunter MacKinzie Cooper, Inc.

In 1987, President Reagan appointed Ann Dore McLaughlin to head the Labor Department. She had held high public affairs positions in the Treasury Department and in the Environmental Protection Agency. She had left the number two position in the Interior Department earlier in the year because of a conflict with Secretary of the Interior Donald Hodel.

In 1989 the Episcopal Church (Anglican Communion) elected as its first woman bishop a former public relations practitioner, Barbara Harris. The African-American activist broke a 2,000-year-old barrier for women in Anglican communion.

Media coverage of public relations in the 1980s was extensive and generally hostile—largely because of the perceived manipulation of public attitudes by sophisticated PR campaigns—but the 1990s started out more PR-positive, except for reaction to the government's handling of the Gulf war. Editorialists still refer to "putting public relations spins" on news and using "PR gimmicks," but respect is growing. And in the early 1990s, even with the U.S. economy down and the whole world's economy not doing much better, employment of public relations people around the world was up, and more universities around the world had begun adding public relations courses to their programs.

▼ SUMMARY

While public relations practice as we identify it today has only existed since the beginning of the twentieth century, it has grown from ancient sources. People throughout history have needed to influence public opinion—to persuade others to think or do something—so the strategies of advocacy know no nationality. But the particular social, economic, political and cultural status of news media in the United States gave public relations tactics and strategies a fertile environment in which to flourish.

Historians who view public relations as a significant, positive influence regard it as a broker for public support of ideas, institutions and people. But some critics say that this is accomplished at the sacrifice of individual autonomy.

The beginnings of PR in the United States can be traced to early promotions of the new country designed to attract immigrants and (later) to promote local universities. The American Revolution used many identifiable public relations tactics in an organized campaign to win public support for the establishment of a new nation.

The development of public relations in the United States has five distinct stages—each related to the types of public relations practiced during that epoch. Over time, the stages show a maturing of the practice. The first stage is simply the preliminary one of developing the necessary infrastructure for public relations to be practiced on a large scale; this encompasses the period from the earliest colonization to the early republic, or roughly 1600 to 1799. The second stage, 1800–1899, is characterized by *communicating and initiating* and was a time of press agentry (typified by P. T. Barnum) and publicity. In the early 1900s, there were many publicists, but one took the business of getting recognition to a higher level by setting practical standards for people acting as the spokesperson for clients: Ivy Ledbetter Lee, the father of public relations in the United States.

The third stage, of which Lee was a part, consisted primarily of reacting and responding to criticism when the unfettered economic interests of industry began to run into adverse public opinion, creating a need for reporters-in-residence to act as spokespersons and to obtain favorable press exposure. This period, from 1900 to 1939, was marked by the influential writings of muckrakers, who delighted in exposés of business and government scandals. Just as the American Revolution's war effort had needed a campaign to win public opinion, so did World War I; and recognizing this, President Wilson appointed the Creel Committee to help rally support. One of the members of that committee, Edward L. Bernays, went on to become the leading public relations figure in the United States. Bernays wrote the first textbook on public relations and taught the first university class in this new subject, both in 1923.

The economic depression of 1930 to 1939 crushed the nation's spirit so thoroughly that it took the powerful influence of President Roosevelt, who had outstanding public relations skills and a knack for using the news media, to bring the nation out of the doldrums and help it persevere in World War II. Roosevelt also appointed a committee to drum up support for the war effort, but this one was not an advisory group. The Office of War Information (OWI) was the forerunner of the U.S. Information Agency. A War Advertising Council also was established, and it, together with OWI, united public relations and advertising in a way that provided a model for the later merging of advertising agencies and public relations firms into full-service agencies. Indeed, the wartime era marked the beginning of the fourth stage in PR development, which extends from 1940 to 1979 and is marked by the growth of PR as a management function.

The postwar period witnessed a long period of economic growth that eventually triggered a backlash in the form of a powerful consumer movement rooted in much earlier movements. A hint of the turbulent times to come emerged in the 1950s "Cold War" period—a time of suspicion and intolerance—and the pent-up conflicts exploded in the 1960s. The 1960s and 1970s were marked by the confrontations over civil rights issues, consumer discontent and quality-of-life issues, as well as by a growing public distrust of all institutions. For PR professionals it was a watershed era when media skills and media relations suddenly were not enough. Social scientists of the sort Bernays had long been saying public relations people ought to be were desperately needed by top management. More organizations began to include public relations as a part of the management function.

The fifth stage runs from 1980 to the present and is typified by a new sense of professionalism in the practice of public relations. Domestically, 1980 marked the start of a conservative retrenchment— the Reagan Revolution—after two decades of social ferment and activism. But internationally, technology had made the world a neighborhood, and by the 1980s PR professionals were needed who could interact with their counterparts in other countries and other cultures. The dramatic growth in freedom throughout the world as the 1990s began created even more of a need of public relations skills, and the development of consumer markets where governments previously had been the sole suppliers put a heavy demand on PR talent.

During this period, the high visibility of public relations—not only because of its stature but also because of the pervasiveness of the news media— brought the practice increasing criticism. And as more people went into public relations (often without the necessary qualifications), public relations practitioners began to focus on the importance of insisting on necessary levels of preparation and performance, including the need to promote standards for professional conduct.

▼ NOTES

[1] According to a report by Professor Eric Goldman of Princeton University, referred to by Edward L. Bernays in the International Public Relations Association (IPRA) *Review*, September 1977, p. 4 of reprint. However, according to Sanat Lahiri of Calcutta, president, IPRA, in *pr reporter*, December 17, 1979, the phrase "public relations" was used much earlier by Thomas Jefferson, and this reference appears in the first edition of *Effective Public Relations* by Scott Cutlip and Allen Center (Prentice-Hall, 1952), p. 40.

[2] Ibid.

[3] Irwin Ross, *The Image Merchants* (Garden City, N.Y.: Doubleday, 1959), p. 51.

[4]Edward L. Bernays, *Public Relations* (Norman: University of Oklahoma Press, 1952), p. 84.

[5]Based on Irwin Ross, *The Image Merchants* (Garden City, N.Y.: Doubleday, 1959), pp. 51–64.

[6]J. A. R. Pimlott, *Public Relations and American Democracy* (Princeton, N.J.: Princeton University Press, 1951), pp. 235–41.

[7]Alan R. Raucher, "Public Relations in Business: A Business of Public Relations," *Public Relations Review*, 16(3) (Fall 1990), p. 19.

[8]Theodore Lustig, "Great Caesar's Ghost," *Public Relations Journal* (March 1986), pp. 17–20.

[9]Theodore H. White, *Caesar at the Rubicon* (New York: Atheneum, 1968), p. 9.

[10]Marcus Lee Hansen, *The Atlantic Migration, 1607–1860* (New York: Harper & Row, 1961), p. 30. Also see E. I. McCormac, *White Servitude in Maryland, 1634–1820* (Baltimore: Johns Hopkins University, 1904), pp. 11–14.

[11]Cutlip and Center, *Effective Public Relations*, 4th ed. (Englewood Cliffs, N.J.: Prentice-Hall), p. 49.

[12]Richard Bissell, *New Light on 1776 and All That* (Boston: Little, Brown, 1975), p. 26.

[13]Ibid., p. 32.

[14]Frank Luther Mott, *American Journalism* (New York: Macmillan, 1950), pp. 26–28.

[15]Ibid., p. 33.

[16]Susan Henry, "Work, Widowhood and War: Hannah Bunce Watson, Connecticut Printer," Connecticut Historical Society Bulletin 48 (Winter 1983), pp. 24–39.

[17]Frank Luther Mott, *American Journalism* (New York: Macmillan, 1950), pp. 179–80.

[18]Jerome Mushkat, *Tammany: The Evolution of a Political Machine* (Syracuse, N.Y.: Syracuse University Press, 1971), pp. 373–74. "Public opinions" are noted, not "polls" specifically, in this reference. Also see Gustavas Myers, *The History of Tammany Hall* (New York: Gustavas Myers, 1901).

[19]Stanley L. Jones, *The Presidential Election of 1896* (Madison: University of Wisconsin Press, 1964), pp. 276–96.

[20]Ibid., p. 295.

[21]Deborah J. Warner, "The Women's Pavilion," in *1876: A Centennial Exhibition*, ed. Robert C. Post (Washington, D.C.: Smithsonian Institution, 1976).

[22]Vernon L. Parrington, *Main Currents in American Thought* (New York: Harcourt Brace, 1938) pp. 31–43, especially p. 40.

[23]Cutlip and Center, *Effective Public Relations*, 4th ed., p. 49. Also see John Walton, *John Filson of Kentucky* (Lexington: University of Kentucky Press, 1956).

[24]Bernays, *Public Relations*, pp. 36–39.

[25]Cutlip and Center, *Effective Public Relations*, 4th ed., p. 83.

[26]The rest of the remark, made in 1882 in his private railroad car while being interviewed by reporters was "I don't take any stock in this silly nonsense about working for anybody's good but our own because we're not. When we make a move we do it because it is in our interest to do so." Roger Butterfield, *American Past* (New York: Simon & Shuster, 1947), p. 476.

[27]Richard Bissell, *The Monongahela* (New York: Rinehart, 1952), pp. 184–91.

[28]John Brooks, "From Dance Cards to the Ivy League Look," *The New Yorker* (May 18, 1957), p. 74.

[29]Vail also sought third-party credibility by subsidizing the writing of favorable editorials and by giving newspaper editors free long-distance service. For more on this aspect of Vail, see Marvin N. Olasky, *The Development of Corporate Public Relations 1850–1930*, Journalism Monographs 102, April 1987 (Columbia, S.C.: Association for Education in Journalism and Mass Communication, 1987).

[30]William Faith, "The American Public Relations Experience: 400 Years from Roanoke to Reagan," (New York: Institute for Public Relations Research and Education, forthcoming).

[31]Scott M. Cutlip and Allen H. Center, *Effective Public Relations*, 5th ed. (Englewood Cliffs, N.J.: Prentice-Hall, 1978), p. 73.

[32]Forrest McDonald, *Insull* (Chicago: University of Chicago Press, 1962), pp. 44–45.

[33]Ronald A. Fullerton, "Art of Public Relations: U.S. Department Stores, 1876–1923," *Public Relations Review*, 16(3) (Fall, 1990), p. 69.

[34]Ibid., p. 71.

[35]Ibid., p. 72.

[36]Sherman Morse, "An Awakening on Wall Street," *American Magazine* 62 (September 1906), p. 460.

[37]Faith, "The American Public Relations Experience."

[38]W. A. Swanberg, *Pulitzer* (New York: Scribner's, 1967), pp. 73–122.

[39]Cornelius C. Regier, *The Era of Muckrakers* (Chapel Hill: University of North Carolina Press, 1932).

[40]Douglas Ann Johnson Newsom, "Creating Concepts of Reality: Media Reflections of the Consumer Movement" (Austin: University of Texas unpublished dissertation, 1978).

[41]Ross, *Image Merchants*, pp. 29–30.

[42]Cutlip and Center, *Effective Public Relations*, 4th ed., p. 72. Also see Scott M. Cutlip, "The Nation's First Public Relations Firm," *Journalism Quarterly* 43 (Summer 1966), pp. 269–80.

[43]William Kittle, "The Making of Public Opinion," *Arena* 41 (1909), pp. 433–50.

[44]Cutlip and Center, *Effective Public Relations*, 4th ed., p. 83.

[45]Personal letter from Paul Ridings, PR practitioner and son of J. Willard Ridings, founder of the Department of Journalism at Texas Christian University and ACPRA president 1941–1942. When Paul joined in 1940, they were the association's first father-son team. Paul Ridings, Jr., is also a public relations professional.

[46]Cutlip and Center, *Effective Public Relations*, 4th ed., p. 91.

[47]Scott M. Cutlip, *Fund Raising in the United States: Its Role in America's Philanthropy* (New Brunswick, N.J.: Rutgers University Press, 1965).

[48]Ibid.

[49]Ibid.

[50]Ibid. (letter from Pendleton Dudley to Major Earl F. Storer).

[51]Howard Weeks, "The Development of Public Relations as an Organized Activity in a Protestant Denomination" (Washington, D.C.: American University, unpublished master's thesis, 1963).

[52]McDonald, *Insull*, p. 3.

[53]David L. Lewis, "Pioneering the Film Business," *Public Relations Journal* (June 6, 1971), pp. 14–18.

[54]Cutlip and Center, *Effective Public Relations*, 4th ed., p. 82.

[55]Ibid.

[56]Lewis, "Pioneering the Film Business," pp. 14–18.

[57]Stephen Ponder, "Progressive Drive to Shape Public Opinion, 1898–1913," *Public Relations Review*, 16(3) (Fall 1990), p. 95.

[58]Ibid.

[59]Alan R. Raucher, "Public Relations in Business: A Business of Public Relations," *Public Relations Review*, 16(3) (Fall 1990), p. 21.

[60]Ibid.

[61]Ibid.

[62]L. L. L. Golden, *Only by Public Consent: American Corporations Search for Favorable Opinion* (New York: Hawthorn Books, 1968), pp. 37–39.

[63]George Creel, *How We Advertised America: The First Telling of the Amazing Story of the Committees on Public Information That Carried the Gospel of Americanism to Every Corner of the Globe* (New York: Harper & Row, 1920), especially pp. 18–19.

[64]Bernays volunteered to help on the Foreign Press Bureau and had to have his loyalty investigated by military intelligence, since he was Austrian-born.

[65]*Who Was Who in America*, vol. 3 (Chicago: Marquis—Who's Who, Inc., 1960), p. 129.

[66]Peggy J. Kreshel, "The 'Culture' of J. Walter Thompson, 1915–1925," *Public Relations Review*, 16(3) (Fall 1990), p. 81.

[67]Ibid., p. 86.

[68]Ibid., pp. 87, 88.

[69]Cutlip and Center, *Effective Public Relations*, 4th ed., p. 90.

[70]Bernays, *Public Relations*, p. 84.

[71]Walter Lippmann in *The Essential Lippmann*, ed. Clinton Rossiter and James Lare (New York: Vintage Books, 1963), p. 96.

[72]Golden, *Only by Public Consent*, pp. 37–39.

[73]Cutlip and Center, *Effective Public Relations*, 4th ed., p. 91. Also see George Griswold, Jr., "How AT&T Public Relations Policies Developed," *Public Relations Quarterly*, 12 (Fall 1967), pp. 7–16.

[74]Golden, *Only by Public Consent*, p. 386.

[75]Cutlip and Center, *Effective Public Relations*, 4th ed., pp. 674, 675.

[76]Philip Meyer, *Precision Journalism* (Bloomington: Indiana University Press, 1973), pp. 144–45; also see George H. Gallup and Saul Forbes Rae, *The Pulse of Democracy* (New York: Simon & Schuster, 1940), pp. 41–56.

[77]Bernays, *Public Relations*, p. 112.

[78]Ross, *Image Merchants*, p. 25.

[79]Golden, *Only by Public Consent*, p. 386.

[80]Ross, *Image Merchants*, p. 27.

[81]Bernays, *Public Relations*, p. 112.

[82]George Juergens, *News From the White House: The Presidential Press Relationship in the Progressive Era* (Chicago: University of Chicago Press, 1981), p. 29.

[83]Rodger Streitmatter, "The Rise and Triumph of the White House Photo Opportunity," *Journalism Quarterly*, 65(4) (Winter 1988), pp. 981–86.

[84]Ibid.

[85]Ross, *Image Merchants*, p. 102.

[86]Charles S. Steinberg, *The Creation of Consent* (New York: Hastings House, 1975), p. 27.

[87]Bernays, *Public Relations*, p. 145.

[88]Richard Meran Barsam, *The Nonfiction Film* (New York: E. P. Dutton, 1973), p. 129.

[89]Ibid., pp. 151–56.

[90]Golden, *Only by Public Consent*, pp. 163–72.

[91]Ross, *Image Merchants*, p. 93.

[92]Ibid., pp. 87–88.

[93]Cutlip and Center, *Effective Public Relations*, 4th ed., p. 673. Also see comments in Golden, *Only by Public Consent*, pp. 347–50, and the Public Relations Society of America.

[94]Richard W. Darrow et al., *Public Relations Handbook* (Chicago: Dartnell Corporation, 1967), pp. 55–56.

[95]*Facts on File*, vol. 17, "National Affairs" (New York: Facts on File, 1957), p. 116.

[96]"The Railroad–Truckers Brawl," *Fortune* (June 1953), pp. 137–39, 198–204.

[97]PRSA *Register*. Also see Golden, *Only by Public Consent*, pp. 347–50.

[98]Ibid. (PRSA).

[99]Ibid.

[100]Stephen A. Greyser and Steven L. Diamond, "Business Is Adapting to Consumerism," *Harvard Business Review* (September–October 1974), p. 38.

[101]Public Relations Society of America, "Frustration Shock," slide presentation script, 1974, p. 2. [Hereafter cited as PRSA, 1974.]

[102]Greyser and Diamond, "Business Is Adapting," p. 38.

[103]PRSA, 1974, p. 7.

[104]Ralph Nader, "A Citizen's Guide to the American Economy," ed. Robert R. Evans, *Social Movements* (Chicago: Rand McNally College Publishing, 1973), p. 217.

[105]Edgar Chasteen, "Public Accommodations," ed. Robert R. Evans, *Social Movements* (Chicago: Rand McNally College Publishing, 1973), p. 379.

[106]PRSA, 1974, pp. 3–4.

[107]D. J. Aulik and L. J. Saleson, "Client Satisfaction: Conceptualization, Measurement, and Model Development—A Perspective," paper presented at School of Business, University of Wisconsin at Madison, May 12, 1975.

[108]Nader, "A Citizen's Guide," p. 220.

[109]PRSA, 1974, p. 3.

[110]According to the 1970 U.S. Census, this age group comprised 11 percent of the population.

[111]Louise Cook, "Consumer Voices Being Heard," *Fort Worth Evening Star Telegram* (May 18, 1976), p. 7A.

[112]Anthony M. Orum, ed., *The Seeds of Politics: Youth and Politics in America* (Englewood Cliffs, N.J.: Prentice-Hall, 1972), p. 3.

[113]Robert Glessing, *The Underground Press in America* (Bloomington: Indiana University Press, 1970), p. 51.

[114]1966 *Facts on File*, p. 526.

[115]Bo Burlingham, "Popular Politics," *Economic Working Papers* (Summer 1974), pp. 5–14. See also Cook, "Consumer Voices," op. cit.; Richard Flacks, "The Liberated Generation," in Orum, ed., *The Seeds of Politics*, pp. 267–68; Orum, *The Seeds of Politics*, p. 3.

[116]PRSA, 1974, p. 1.

[117]Ibid., p. 3.

[118]1967 *Facts on File*, p. 85.

[119]1971 *Facts on File*, p. 801.

[120]1970 *Facts on File*, p. 834.

[121]1973 *Facts on File*, p. 84.

[122]Aulik and Saleson, "Client Satisfaction," p. 2.

[123]Sylvia Porter, "'Fair Deal' Wanted, Anybody Listening?" *Dallas Morning News*, May 18, 1977, p. 5C.

[124]David G. Clark and William B. Blankenburg, *You and Media* (San Francisco: Canfield Press, 1973), p. 175.

[125]1970 *Facts on File*, p. 830.

[126]*Facts on File*, vol. 29, "U.S. Developments" (New York: Facts on File, 1969), pp. 266–67; see also vol. 28, p. 625.

[127]Ibid.

[128]Alexander Cockburn and Andrew Cockburn, "Flacks: They Clarify, They Edify, They Stupify—They're PR Specialists and They Get Paid to Change Your Mind," *Playboy* (January 1987), pp. 195–96.

[129]Ibid., p. 196.

[130]Andrew Hacker, "Survey of the 70s," *Britannica Book of the Year, 1980*, pp. 129–37.

[131]Dave Montgomery, "A Texan Meets the Press (and Says a Little Prayer)," *Fort Worth Star Telegram* (April 10, 1983), p. 29A.

[132]Sidney Blumenthal, "Brave New World: Marketing the President," *Dallas Morning News* (September 20, 1981), p. G1.

[133]Ibid.

[134]Maureen Santini, "Presidential Spokesman Speaks on Life under Fire," *Fort Worth Star Telegram* (February 22, 1983), pp. 1, 2.

[135]Streitmatter, "Rise and Triumph of White House Photo Opportunity," p. 985.

[136]Howard Greene, "USIA's TV Network Could Be 'Most Powerful' Propaganda Instrument in History of World," *TV Guide*, 1987, news release, pp. 27–29.

[137]PR Strategies Staff, "Foreign Buy-outs of U.S. Companies Set up New PR Challenge," *PR Strategies, USA*, Vol. 1, No. 1, Feb. 1–15, 1988, Washington, DC, p. 4.

[138]Ibid.

[139]Carolyn Cline, Hank Smith, Nancy Johnson, Elizabeth Lance Toth, Judy VanSlyke Turk, and Lynne Masel Walters, "The Velvet Ghetto" (San Francisco: IABC Foundation, summary report, 1986).

Selected readings, activities and assignments appropriate to this chapter can be found in the *Instructor's Guide*.

CHAPTER 3

▼

PR'S FUTURE

Public relations, in my view, is engaged in the "moving of ideas." Ideas aren't "things"; they're abstracts. Creating ideas isn't a process wherein the most cost-effective system works.

John F. Budd, Jr., chairman and CEO of the Omega Group

Gone are the days of women succeeding by learning to play men's games. Instead the time has come for men on the move to learn to play women's games.

Tom Peters, management consultant

We will need to understand the overall, to broaden our view of the world we live in and of the institutions that employ us. To provide strategic advice, we must understand and identify with the business we're in—not only the public relations part, but the business itself, the business of our client and of our employer.

Harold Burson, chairman of Burson-Marsteller

The "future" encompasses the infinite stretch of time from the present moment forward. To narrow the subject somewhat, this chapter focuses on the role and status of public relations in the field and in the classroom between now and the year 2000. Such a limitation makes the task less awesome, but it may or may not improve predictability. As Prime Minister Brian Mulroney of Canada has said, "The pace of change in international politics is straining mankind's capabilities of assimilation and assessment."[1] And that's only half of it; adjusting to those changes in the social, economic and political environment where public relations operates is intellectually and emotionally taxing.

▼ THE GLOBAL ENVIRONMENT FOR PRACTICING PR

The Canadian prime minister has noted that, already in the early 1990s, some of the characteristics of the world in the year 2000 are apparent: increasing population; increasing prosperity, but with greater disparity between have and have-not nations; the prospect, at least, that middle-income countries can flourish; increasing investment abroad by all nations; growing capabilities of nations to produce and export high-tech products; changing technology, with the knowledge industry dominating the development and use of information technology; and an increasing need for new production strategies aimed at specific markets. All of this points to a highly competitive global environment for business where, Mulroney says, "human resources will be a vital factor."[2] He foresees an increasing demand for people whose education includes an emphasis on science, engineering and language training. Job skills retraining will become a standard feature in the workplace. Two major issues that will have to be addressed are healthcare and the environment. "The environment," Mulroney says, "will have become a truly global issue, and progress will depend on all countries' embracing a new environmental ethic based on the concept of sustainable development."[3]

These predictions come, in part, from an appreciation of the dizzying changes of the 1980s—a decade in which public relations didn't always fare too well. As Ronald E. Rhody, senior vice-president of the Bank of America, has put it:

> The Eighties was a tough decade—inflicting more pain on public relations organizations throughout the country than any other single period in the profession's history. Collectively, we fought more battles, handled more strain, took more casualties than at anytime I suspect any of us can remember.[4]

But Rhody also feels that the practice of public relations emerged stronger, with greater status, authority and compensation for practitioners who met the tests of the decade. The workload for public relations increased during this time, while business staffs were cut back, meaning that more jobs were being given to independent counselors and to firms and agencies.[5]

Much of this new work is being done by women, whose increasing visibility in the field is viewed with alarm by some PR practitioners and with enthusiasm by others. One enthusiast is Tom Peters, co-author of *In Search of Excellence*. He sees women as likely to make better managers for the future business world because business "must become: less hierarchical, more flexible and more fluid."[6] The increasing economic and social power of women is one major ongoing trend in North America, according to Patricia Aburdene, principal in Megatrends Ltd. in Washington, D.C., and co-author with John Naisbitt of the best-seller, *Mega-*

▼ **Some observers speculate that the feminization of public relations may reduce salaries and status in the field.**

---

trends. She also thinks public relations will take a leadership role in the future.[7]

On the other hand, many public relations practitioners fear that the presence of increasing numbers of women in the field is already causing corporate "layering" that lowers the status of the PR function on the corporate ladder; and others believe that, in a global society where women have lower status than men, delegating the PR function to women will denigrate the profession. Few critics are brave enough to voice these concerns loudly, but their murmurings can be heard.

According to Caroline Cline, one of the co-authors of "The Velvet Ghetto," research suggests that "the major problem facing public relations' move into top management today may be not only the large percentage of women in the field, but the dominance of the profession by the intuitive."[8] An intuitive worker "seeks the furthest reaches of the possible and the imaginative, and is comparatively uninterested in the sensory reports of things as they are"; and this conflicts with the methodology of a sensate worker, who "prefers an established way of doing things, relying upon skills already learned, working steadily, and focusing on now." The sensate type of worker accounts for 70 to 75 percent of the American population, Cline says.[9]

For whatever reason—psychological predisposition or gender—women in public relations constitute an unpopular majority and face discrimination in wages and jobs. Of course, this situation might well change if Peters's view of what qualities are needed in management prevails.

Also subject to widespread discrimination are public relations practitioners of color, although their value has increased as businesses have begun to recognize the value of the ethnic market. Just as women have set up their own organizations to improve their prospects for success in the field, so have public relations practitioners of color; they also have their own professional organizations, although a few are members of the predominately white professional organizations as well. The discrimination that forces minorities to set up their own firms and organize their own professional associations may change if Aburdene is correct in seeing cultural diversity in the workplace as a megatrend of the 1990s. Due to a shortage of experienced practitioners in the U.S. labor market, she says, managers in the future will be hiring new workers from among women, minorities and immigrants.[10] Although Aburdene is talking about the workplace in general, her analysis could certainly apply to public relations. In the future, the more astute public relations firms and staffs will rely on cultural diversity among their own practitioners to maintain their sensitivity to issues and audiences on a broad scale. They will not hire a practitioner from a specific ethnic group just to reach that constituency. Aburdene says that managers will need to possess "superb cross-cultural skills" just to superintend the diversified workforce in the United States successfully.[11]

Managing employees in public relations, as well as in other fields, will be more complicated because, as tomorrow's practitioners focus on becoming more professional in what they do, their ties to any specific organization or institution will be reduced. Public relations employees whose positions were eliminated in the mergers and consolidations of the 1980s found that what they needed was not demonstrated loyalty to an employer but "portable professionalism."

The growing trend on the part of public relations people to see themselves as PR people first and only secondarily as employees of a particular organization has some advantages for the field as a whole. Ronald Rhody says that, whereas employees see themselves as a unitary part of their organization, a professional should have a different perspective. While employed by a particular organization, the PR person must demonstrate something short of blind loyalty, because a professional "sees himself or herself as hired to bring expert professional skills or talents to bear on the problems and opportunities at hand."[12]

In some ways, PR practitioners may be reflecting a national trend in the United States—an increase in individualism at the expense of communalism or a sense of belonging. This extends beyond the workplace to encompass various other social, economic and political institutions. But while the increasing commitment to self-interest is readily apparent in the United States, it is not a part of all cultures. In fact, many cultures pride themselves on their sense of community and on their readiness to put the common good above personal benefit.

Understanding different perspectives is especially important to public relations practitioners who work globally and are responsible for employee communications. "Many communicators are not equipped intellectually, educationally and culturally to cope with globalization," says Taki Andriadis, president of Intercultural Public Affairs in Wilmington, Delaware.[13]

Inability to cope with the international scene may be costing U.S. public relations organizations their former preeminence in the world. Although public relations isn't unique to the United States, it did develop most rapidly here, and for many years public relations expertise has been a major service export. But the recent change has been dramatic. According to Jean Farinelli of Creamer Dickson Basford in New York, "A decade ago, the world's five top PR firms were American owned. Today, only one is."[14]

Furthermore, Farinelli says:

[A] study of 400 U.S. and U.K. CEOs found the British are more active users of PR than are Americans. Over half formally integrate PR into corporate planning systems, compared with a third of American companies. PR managers in 50 percent of the British companies report directly to the board compared to a third (generous estimate) in U.S. companies.[15]

She goes on to say that "superb work is coming out of Europe," and she observes that the PR industry in Europe and Japan is now 15 to 20 percent of the size of the U.S. PR industry, whereas only ten years ago it was considerably smaller.[16]

This trend suggests that the practice of public relations may be losing its association with the United States, and that it may eventually be defined in terms quite different from those we now use, as the emphasis shifts toward strategies and away from tactics.

▼ DEFINITION, ROLE AND STATUS OF THE PR PROCESS

Harold Burson points out that the public relations process really has only two components: strategy and execution.[17] As he sees it, PR's greatest contribution is in the area of strategy:

> Our true value, our unique and vital contribution to our clients and employers is the knowledgeable advice we bring to the decision-making process. . . . [T]here's growing importance in the strategic component, in providing input that produces the most effective decision—first about what to do, then about what to say and how.[18]

The execution of the strategy, Burson notes, usually involves communication, which will be important (and increasingly challenging) as the channels of communication—the available media—proliferate.

Recognition of the emphasis on strategy prompts John Budd to suggest renaming the public relations function *ideology*. He believes that the term *public relations* has fallen into "misuse, overuse and abuse." But beyond that, he thinks that circumstances in the future will challenge the accumulated wisdom of what we now know as the field of public relations. Budd says:

> It [the future] will require, as a prerequisite, people skilled in the advancement of ideas, in building broad non-political coalitions and support. It will need people comfortable in dealing with abstracts and converting them to realities. In short, it requires people with minds of originality, endowed with the intellectual resources needed to deal with subjective views, attitudes and behavioral patterns. In short, an ideologist.[19]

An ideologist, Budd explains, "deals with systems of ideas, explaining them and gaining understanding." Calling public relations an ideology doesn't bother him, because he sees both the function and the role of the practice as remaining the same, regardless of the name:

> It may not be the perfect title—but . . . I think it comes closest to what we're about. It is unencumbered by all the baggage of distortions surrounding public relations. To me, it is counterproductive to continually defend public relations as a management value that CEOs rarely accept.[20]

Budd even has drawn up a projected management structure to show where the newly named function would be located (see Example 3.1). Still, changing the practice's name may have little effect on public attitudes toward it; and indeed the term *ideologist* is not without its own share of undesirable connotations, including suggestions of rigidity, intolerance, dogmatism and even extremism. Perhaps the best method of changing suspicious attitudes remains the oldest and hardest way: by earning people's respect and trust through behavior and performance.

Like any developing profession, public relations continues to change; and while it changes, it eludes any firm definition. The formal definition of PR in the *Encyclopaedia Britannica* is as follows:

> [P]olicies and activities designed to convey information about, and improve the public's attitude toward, an individual, corporation, government agency, or other organization. Major responsibilities of public relations departments or agencies include issuing news releases; arranging press conferences; answering correspondence from the public; planning participation in community affairs; preparing films, pamphlets, employee magazines, reports to stockholders, and form letters; planning advertising programs; planning and publicizing exhibitions and tours; and undertaking research surveys to measure public opinion.[21]

Budd is certainly correct in his comment about the misuse, overuse and abuse of the term *public*

EXAMPLE 3.1

John Budd's Projected Management Structure in the Year 2000

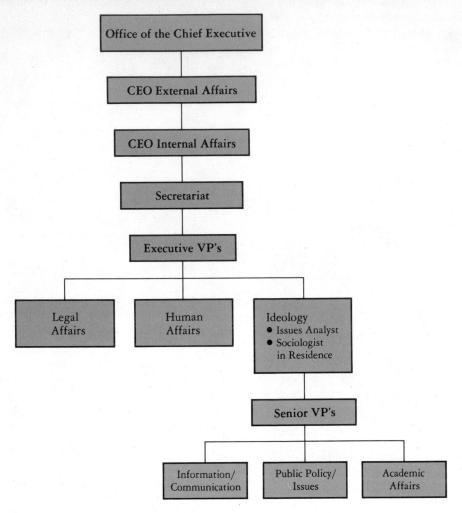

John Budd's Office of the Chief Executive has two co-directors: internal affairs and external affairs, which means that all issues would be given short- and long-term consideration simultaneously. His Secretariat post is a cabinet-like structure held by three executive vice-presidents: of ideology, of legal affairs and of human affairs. The ideology vice-president (formerly called public relations person) is an issues analyst and resident sociologist; under that position are the senior vice-presidents for information/communication, public policy and issues and academic affairs.

SOURCE: Copyright 1989 by John F. Budd, Jr. Reprinted with permission.

relations. The *Britannica* notes, "Public relations has been subject to much criticism, both from social scientists, who criticize its techniques, and from the general public, which distrusts it."[22] It is easy to see valid historical reasons for the criticism: the hucksterism of Barnum and of press agentry in general, the self-defensive whitewashing of problems during the muckraking era, the attempts to manipulate the public during political crises, and so on. Therefore, we must keep an eye on the past, lest we repeat some of the same mistakes.

The early 1980s created enough uncertainty about the role and techniques of public relations that some PR practitioners began to entertain ideas of radical change. In many cases the change began and ended with the occupational title. A 1987 Conference Board study showed *public affairs* as the new umbrella title for public relations activities.[23] That report defined public affairs as external relations and communications comprising government relations (federal, state and local), public relations (primarily media relations), community relations, international public affairs, investor and stockholder relations, corporate contributions, institutional advertising, employee communications and issues management. Public relations practitioners generally classify most of these areas as functions of public relations, while limiting the purview of public affairs to government relations.

Another interesting aspect of the Conference Board report is that most public affairs officers—that is, those currently holding the title—are *not* from the communications field. They are from disciplines related to the institution for which they work, such as art historians for museums and engineers for utilities. Public affairs officers usually hire communication technicians to handle the various tasks for which they are responsible.

The other most common configuration is the vice-president of communication or of relations, such as "university relations" or "industry relations." All other communication activities, including public relations and marketing, fall under that operational title. The vice-president of communication is the policy-making executive who has the ear of the chief executive officer. As was mentioned earlier, some observers speculate that this communication function has developed as part of an organizational layering process to enable CEOs to distance themselves from the female PR officer.

▼ PR IN THE FIELD

It may be that a new name for public relations can be borrowed from another country, and with the new name will come a slightly different conception of what we now call public relations. Meanwhile, we can look at the practice of public relations in the field today to see what some of the current trends suggest for the future—to determine a focus for the future, and to anticipate some of the problems that will have to be faced.

Trends

A number of trends can be identified in recent PR practice.

Growth of the PR Role   Growth of the public relations function has expanded its role so that more types of public relations activities are now included as responsibilities of an organization's public relations practitioner. These include issues management, public affairs, community relations, shareholder/stakeholder relations, corporate contributions/fundraising (nonprofit), all types of organizational advertising (except products and services) and employee communication. The increased workload has not translated into bigger public relations departments, but it has meant that many organizations that never previously had a public relations person now do.

In the larger organizations, where the public relations function is well established, economic conditions have caused staff reductions. Typically, the workload from these reductions has been farmed out to public relations specialists rather than to

▼ **The fact that more people inside and outside the organization are involved in accomplishing PR duties increases the need for coordination and management of the PR function.**

---

larger firms. Many PR firms struggling to meet the demands of the expanded PR function have extended themselves to offer a full range of services to clients, and many firms associated with advertising agencies have taken on entire public relations campaigns. The tendency is for firms/agencies to handle campaigns but not routine public relations projects. The routine work—such as producing employee publications, newsletters and annual reports—has gone to specialists. Because of the complexity of global communications in some organizations, specialty media firms are often used to disseminate almost all of their news releases and to monitor their use.

Increased Organizational Demands for Accountability   Both within the organization and outside it, most public relations practitioners are experiencing pressure for greater accountability, in association with management's increased tendency to set PR goals and to demand evidence of their accomplishment. The evidence deemed acceptable is mainly physical, such as increased market share, successful media placement, funds raised or employee involvement in events. Few organizations use research about opinions and attitudes to measure changes in awareness, understanding and acceptance of the organization and what it is doing. In an occupation whose primary role is to serve as counselor and strategist, at least one major area of effort and achievement remains concealed because employers fail to perform the necessary opinion research.

Increased Struggles over Turf   The demand for results and the spread of public relations activities has created new turf battles, since many individuals whose competence lies in other areas feel qualified to handle PR. Encroachment from marketing appears on the consumer relations side, from finance on the investor relations side, from personnel on the employee relations side, from political scientists on the public affairs side and from lawyers in the counseling/strategy area. Some public relations practitioners say that even their previously undisputed turf of media relations is now contested by former television news producers. Others complain that crisis management is handled by outsiders trained in emergency or disaster response. Organizations still tend to take people who are specialists in the area where the organizational mission is concentrated and make them public relations directors—often because the PR people do not learn the nuances of the organization's business as well as they should.

Sometimes, turf battles may be solved by having the "encroachers" make formal use of public relations talent. Their increased appreciation of public relations as a result of this experience might discourage them from persisting in their "anyone can do PR" attitude. For example, the two most threatening encroachers—law and marketing/advertising—now use public relations firms.

Lawyers use public relations firms to improve their competitive edge and image.[24] According to a *Wall Street Journal* report, law firms' use of PR counsel tripled during the period from 1985 to 1990, so that by 1990 some 75 percent of all major law firms regularly used PR consultants hired on retainer or on an hourly fee basis.[25] The fees are fairly modest, and the clients are sometimes difficult, but the larger public relations firms handling this new professional business describe it as one of the fastest growing specialties.[26] The law firm of Winston & Strawn in Chicago is believed to have been the first to hire a public relations specialist, Loren A. Wittner, as a salaried partner.[27] Wittner, formerly an executive vice-president at Edelman Public Relations Worldwide, had practiced law before joining Edelman, and currently works with the law firm's outside public relations firm.[28]

Having an in-house public relations person is not new to ad agencies, but having a public relations specialist on staff to help improve the position of the agency itself is new. Increasing competition in an era marked by recession has caused agencies to employ someone to look after their own interests, not just those of their clients.[29]

Growing Governmental Use of PR Increasing use of public relations is being made by all governments, especially as many of the previously centralized Eastern European governments began a democratization process. Developing nations (some of which are democracies) frequently have a critical need for public relations. According to Saudi Arabian professor Abdulrahman H. Al-Enad, a considerable gap may exist between the expectations of citizens and the actual benefits that a government still engaged in building infrastructure can deliver. He sees a pressing need to develop an understanding between the citizens and the government.[30] The role of public relations has been poorly understood often by the United States government, too, although any democracy depends on the consent of its citizens. Harold Burson states it succinctly: "Call it what you will, but there it is: advancing information in the public forum, for the purpose of contributing to public opinion. That is public relations. It's implicit to the democratic process."[31]

Another thing implicit to the democratic process is the opportunity for feedback. But because this remains a problem in the U.S., special interest groups have grown to fill the void. Finding ways to respond to government actions is even harder in developing nations that traditionally have a more hierarchical communication system. If governments and their citizens can find ways to communicate better, the result should be an improved level of political and economic stability. Public relations can help develop such relationships in democratizing and developing nations, but PR practitioners

▼ **Resolving turf battles is difficult and frequently organization-specific, but the public relations person's ability to handle internal organizational politics effectively (often by applying techniques of persuasion) is a key element.**

---

must be well trained in understanding different cultures and in communicating among them.

Increased Diversity of PR Publics The publics addressed by public relations are more diverse than ever before, and the stereotypes that once permitted mass communication in each haven't worked for some years. More people are living with unrelated people in a family unit, and more people are choosing to live alone. There are many single fathers in the United States today—and even more single mothers. The age-bracket populations are becoming more evenly divided, so that youth no longer dominates. In fact, traditional couples with young children constitute only 27 percent of all U.S. households.[32] While economic and political changes abroad have enlarged the middle class there, in the United States many formerly middle-class people (especially single mothers) have joined the ranks of the poor.

Since married couples make up a smaller share of the "families" than previously in the United States, significant differences in family and household income exist. While family income has increased because of the rise in two-wage-earner families, the average "household" income is down.[33] Married women contribute to their families' overall affluence, but fewer women than men are wealthy in their own right.[34] While some authorities cite inheritance laws and income taxes as a reason, the real reason may lie in the lower wages women earn for the same occupation. In any case, only 9 percent of U.S. households are classified as affluent; and of these, only 3.6 percent are "very

▼ **With increasing decentralization of power in organizations and a move toward more individual responsibility, PR practitioners must make sure that the organization's messages get *to* the employees and are understood and accepted by them, and that messages *from* employees to top management get heard and answered.**

---

affluent" (that is, have annual incomes of $100,000 or more).[35] This may be part of the reason why consumer expectations are higher than ever before. Since most people have less money to spend, they want more value for it. The change in consumer demand may also be traced in part to the continuing influence of the consumer movement. Improved product quality used to be the most recommended way to respond to consumer demands, but customer service (which has deteriorated in the United States) is now getting more attention. Organizations still have considerable difficulty discovering how to keep consumers satisfied, however, and as a result many are applying the same survey techniques for service issues that they previously used for products.[36]

Public relations people should have been recommending—even demanding—such surveys all along, since public opinion research has been considered a part of public relations work since the 1950s. Moreover, people say that they are willing to pay for improved service.[37] How much they are willing to pay for environmental safeguards through changes in products, services or their own habits will be crucial to the future course of the environmental movement.

Heightened Need for Good Internal PR   You might expect that organizations' internal relations are smoother than their relations with external publics, but that is not the case. The level of em-
ployee satisfaction has been low in recent years—perhaps due to a management attitude (prevalent in times of recession) that the economy has created a "buyers' market" and that management doesn't have to worry too much about employee relations. The dilution of affirmative action laws in the United States also has contributed to workers' unhappiness on the job. However, several Supreme Court decisions on the subject of discriminatory firing have offset this effect somewhat.

A major factor in low employee morale is the failure of management to communicate with employees. The critical phrase here is "communicate with," as opposed to "talk to." Anecdotal information indicates that top management has no idea what the people lower in the organization think, want or need; and some surveys show that little more than 15 percent of a CEO's time is spent communicating with employees, versus 34 percent spent communicating with other CEOs.[38] Unresponsiveness fosters dissatisfied employees and lower productivity. It also can hurt the organization's reputation, since employees are any organization's PR front line.

Another cause of employee alienation is management changes. As Jeff Roach, senior vice-president for public affairs of Canadian Imperial Bank of Commerce, observed, "Investors and customers don't do business with organizations they don't understand, so employees must know what's happening in order to serve them."[39]

Increased Environmental Concerns   Concern for the "environment" within an organization is critical, but many organizations see a marketing advantage in devoting at least public attention to the global environment, as well. However, the global environment is not an easy subject for organizations to handle, because it pits publics against each other in sometimes dire conflict, creating a no-win situation for the organization. A good example of this can be seen in the dilemma of protecting endangered species (such as the spotted owl in Oregon) on the one hand and preserving jobs and economic health (such as in the timber industry) on the other. Feelings run high on both sides, and the timber industry must combat a damaged public image, similar to the one mining and oil and gas exploration companies had before they began repairing the environmental damage done during the course of their activities.

One example of how a timber firm's operations can adversely affect the industry was recorded in a *Wall Street Journal* article, which called the story of Plum Creek Timber Company—a publicly held limited partnership spun off from Burlington Northern, Inc.—"a case study in the public costs of private decisions."[40] Plum Creek Timber, while running an advertising campaign proclaiming that "For Us, Every Day Is Earth Day" was cutting old-growth forest on land that the U.S. government (under President Abraham Lincoln) had ceded to private railroad companies back in 1864. Some trees in the forest predated the nation by a century or more.[41] According to the *Wall Street Journal*, the company was logging the forest at twice the rate it could regenerate itself and had bulldozed a road into at least one wilderness area.[42] It had also made itself one of the Pacific Northwest's most controversial corporate citizens.[43]

According to the *Journal* piece, the case "demonstrates how a boardroom effort to maximize shareholder values can leave an enduring mark upon the land—and some fear, perhaps contribute to an economically crippling regional timber shortage in future decades."[44] The accelerated logging by Plum Creek Timber began in the 1980s, in response to a Japanese demand for fine-grained old wood. In addition, increasing logging profits was part of a larger Burlington-Northern strategy to boost shareholder values during a time of frequent hostile takeovers.[45] The *Journal* quotes Washington state Republican representative Rod Chandler as saying that, within the industry, Plum Creek Timber had earned the sobriquet, the "Darth Vader of the state." Idaho Governor Cecil Andrus, who personally photographed a clearcut area in 1987, commented that the company "appears to be cashing out their equity at everyone else's expense."[46] The company's CEO, David Leland, stated that the com-

▼ **Because the environment is a serious and complicated issue, public relations people have to help organizations resolve the environmental conflicts that their policies create with their publics, so that the practices ultimately adopted are sustainable in the future.**

pany needed "more professional publicity work" to tell people about its reforestation efforts and its attempts to be a good neighbor to those who lived near its operations.[47]

Plum Creek Timber might have learned something from the experience of Manville, which continues to take heat for deaths and injuries attributed to its asbestos products. That company, previously known as Johns-Manville, was faced with so many lawsuits that it declared bankruptcy and set up the Manville Personal Injury Trust to meet the demands of claimants. Now, however, according to a *Wall Street Journal* article, the company is a "born again environmentalist."[48] CEO Tom Stephens told the World Economic Forum in 1990 that problems like his company's asbestos debacle must be anticipated by organizations, and he added, "Nothing like the asbestos nightmare must ever happen again; we at Manville are compelled to share what we have learned from that experience."[49] Among the things company management learned, Stephens said, were (1) to listen to society very carefully, rather than relying on the law, because the company would be held accountable in the *future* for what it did; (2) to reflect on what is ethical, rather than what is expedient; (3) to control its own destiny rather than waiting for government to step in; (4) to be aware of the power of persistence and of how dedicated employees can help an organization through its problems; (5) to seize the environmental initiative. Our policies, he said, must be real, not rhetoric.[50]

▼ **Future practitioners will need to be concerned about credibility, accountability and responsibility.**

Focus

In the field of public relations, the focus of future challenges will be on credibility, accountability and responsibility.

Credibility　From time to time, pollsters publish the results of surveys that ask people in the United States which occupations they respect. Implicit in the word *respect* is confidence and trust. As a group, politicians don't enjoy it. Neither do business leaders as a group. There's no point in even asking about the public relations field per se as long as the term *public relations* is used pejoratively. "That's just a public relations explanation" means "That's just something said to make the speaker look good, and it is only slightly related to the truth." In that sense, public relations is considered by many to be a tool used by the untrustworthy to deceive the unwitting. Thus, neither public relations nor those who use it are trusted, and the very service that is supposed to help an organization win credibility is itself suspect. Marketing doesn't fare any better, since it is seen as just trying to sell or "pawn off" on the credulous some product, service or idea. The unstated but assumed view is that the product, service or idea is probably worthless.

Why is cynicism so rampant? Why is credibility such a thorny issue? Why did *Time* magazine devote a whole issue to ethics in its May 25, 1987, edition? At that time, the world was being entertained by the real-life soap operas of the Iran–Contra hearings, the Wall Street insider trading scandals and the problems of the TV evangelists. We might ask "Why worry about that for the future?" There are two reasons: first, credibility is difficult to win and easy to lose; second, we live in a global village where credibility is not just a domestic issue.

Credibility is based on the realities of behavior as well as on favorable perceptions of that behavior. Public relations professionals face immense challenges in trying to maintain credibility for institutions that have myriad publics in difficult cultural, economic and political settings.

Will public relations practitioners be up to the task? In the 1960s, when institutions turned to their "public relations" people to solve problems, more often than not they found communication specialists—not social scientists who could tell them what to expect and what to do about the problems. A substantial number of public relations practitioners dropped out of the field during that time. What will happen now that the audience is the world? PR practitioners will have to understand media systems and economic systems throughout the world, but even that is not enough. To be effective, they will also have to understand the business of their own institutions, just as well as specialists in the field do, in order to explain the nuances and anticipate the potential impacts of policies to global publics.

Just as important, the public relations practitioner must ensure that the organization communicates with one voice, so that internal and external messages are unified and credible. This means establishing strong liaisons within every facet of the organization's activities.

Accountability　The second important challenge is accountability, which consists of providing substantive verification for the contributions of public relations and establishing a baseline for all publics against which public relations actions can be measured. This means that the contribution of public relations actions must be quantitatively measurable. When public relations people report to operations officers in terms that these officers understand, they win respect for their PR expertise and gain tangible arguments for their budgets. If public relations is ever replaced by marketing, it might be because marketing people are experts at measuring. They have to measure markets, and they have to measure results, so they become experts at offering quantifiable justifications for what they do.

In the past, public relations people claimed results and offered publicity instead of proof, while claiming that public relations was more than publicity and promotion. The future will belong to PR people who can hold their own in doing research, buying research, and evaluating the resulting data. In many cases public relations people will be engaged in measuring changes in behavior.

Responsibility   One difficulty with responsibility is measurability, but another difficulty relates to the question of who is practicing public relations and with what credentials, how much expertise and how much current experience.

Top management expresses some exasperation in trying to identify acceptable public relations talent. It's not like locating a CPA or an attorney— both of whom come with formal credentials. (This is why Edward L. Bernays has argued in favor of licensing PR practitioners.) Most people don't have any idea what IABC's ABC means or what APR represents, and certainly they have no knowledge at all of the PRSA code of ethics. The professional transgressions that this code forbids are precisely the things most people imagine that public relations people do routinely (see Chapter 8). In the future, some way will have to be found for public relations talent to be recognized by the public, and something other than self-declaration will have to be offered to justify functioning at certain levels of expertise.

PR people are also going to have to demonstrate real knowledge and mastery of the industry or field they represent, whether it be chemicals, banking, agriculture, music or fine arts. A CEO can't send a public relations person who doesn't know the field in depth to serve as a spokesperson to knowledgeable employees, to suppliers or to the trade press. You can't speak for the field without understanding it thoroughly and without knowing all the nuances of the written and spoken words that are used to describe it. A PR person who fails to master the

▼ Responsibility entails making sure that the quality of the practitioner's performance is high and that he or she represents the larger interests of the global community.

field in which he or she works is limited to the role of technician.

Another area of responsibility involves management. Whether it operates in a small office or in a large institution, management must make important decisions regarding budgets, personnel and other routine business activities. Learning on the job can be costly, since most PR people are hired for important jobs because of their track records.

Public relations practitioners of the future will not only have to be good, they will also have to be capable of guiding the best talent they can find— male or female. Finding the best talent also means making a special effort to attract minorities from their own agencies and businesses.

Problems

Every field of endeavor has problems, but the difficulties that public relations faces are especially visible because of the nature of the work: counseling management executives whose decisions may subsequently be criticized as poor "public relations" moves (whether or not the action taken was what the PR person advised); interacting with globally connected media, so that PR mistakes are magnified; issuing printed materials that can later come back to haunt the organization because of factual or judgmental errors. The larger public relations grows internationally, and the more sophisticated its audiences become, the more likely PR is to be a target of criticism. The following are problems that have already been isolated and identified by public relations practitioners.

Status   Status continues to be a problem, despite wider acceptance of the public relations function as valuable to an organization. Denny Griswold noted in a 1990 issue of her newsletter, *PR News*, that not a single PR executive was included in the list of 126 leaders featured in *Fortune*'s sixtieth anniversary issue.[51] This problem of nonrecognition and the difficulty PR practitioners often experience internally in gaining acceptance from management may be attributable to the range of activities involved in PR, which give the field a diffused, unfocused look.

Lack of a clear focus for public relations also contributes to turf battles inside organizations. Marketing textbook author Philip Kotler is quoted as having said, after participating in a 1989 colloquium, that he thought he needed to add a chapter on marketing communication to his book, but that he wouldn't call it public relations because that was a separate function.[52] At that time, however, his text dealt with public relations in connection with sales promotion, and he was treating PR as simply another important marketing tool. If people of Kotler's stature are only now beginning to recognize the true dimensions of public relations function, where does that leave everyone else?

It's also difficult for outsiders to develop a strong sense of public relations standards, since they don't know what to look for. Many organizations still don't know how to hire public relations talent. There is little understanding of PR education and of the various accreditation processes. Although most practitioners try to be professional about their work, PR remains a field of endeavor—not a profession—so it's difficult for practitioners to gain recognition for their adherence to a code of ethics or to high standards of professional behavior.

Many executives view the public relations function as fluff—a frill that may be an enhancement but is not an essential. This attitude has been around since the 1950s, when public relations people were identified as "the last to know and the first to go." At that time many PR practitioners were still seen as hired apologists for an organization. This attitude persists, and some people (mostly men) say that the increased number of women in the field doesn't improve the situation. Naturally, women resent the idea that they diminish the prestige of whatever field they're in, be they brain surgeons or public relations counselors.

Research   Perhaps the most serious uncorrected problem in public relations practice is the failure of PR practitioners to use research. Millions of dollars may be spent on messages that haven't been pretested. Followup research is too often oriented toward exposures to messages, rather than toward the messages' impact. And PR planning frequently operates on the basis of routine rather than on the basis of serious study of publics and policies.

Area-Specific Problems   Other problems are specific to certain areas of public relations practice—namely, employee relations, investor relations, media relations and organizational counsel.

Employee relations involves two major problems: (1) how to maintain a strong PR front line (which employees represent) when many employees are in jobs, not careers, and when those who are in careers are primarily interested in their area of expertise and not in the organization that employs them; (2) how to get volunteer readers/listeners/viewers to review employee communications when employees have many other demands on their time and a great deal of competition for their attention.

Investor relations has at least four major problems: (1) how to make investors understand long-term benefits that may not report out well on quarterly statements; (2) how to involve individual investors who are buying shares indirectly (that is, through accounts or funds); (3) how to encourage employee investments; (4) how to capture and sustain analysts' attention.

Media relations includes at least two areas of concern: (1) how to develop continuity of coverage (that is, how to get media to follow an organization over time so that a deeper understanding of the organization is developed); (2) how to use specialized media more successfully to communicate to priority publics, given that no "mass medium" is truly "mass" in its ability to reach publics.

Organizational counsel (the highest level of PR practice in an organization) encompasses two areas that raise special problems: social responsibility and competition.

Social responsibility itself contains two major areas of concern: (1) how to communicate the good a company is doing, in order to create a climate of goodwill and trust in a generally cynical society; (2) how to coordinate all communications (employee, marketing, product/service publicity and so on) so that areas of conflict don't destroy credibility.

In the area of competition, two problems arise: (1) how to issue challenges without engaging in negative attacks (which tend to make already distrustful audiences even more so); (2) how to communicate advantages without hyperbole.

One fundamental problem in the field of public relations involves the connection between public relations practice and education for PR. Many practitioners feel that too many students are being prepared for public relations careers in the first place, and that many of these are taking courses in mass communication theory rather than learning relevant skills—although many PR practitioners also say that they would just as soon train a liberal arts graduate who had no skills. Since all schools accredited by the Accrediting Council on Education in Journalism and Mass Communication must offer liberal arts degrees, the presumption that a liberal arts problem exists constitutes something of a mystery. Actually, most university degrees require only about 30 hours in the major, whatever it happens to be; so out of 120 total hours, typically consisting of forty courses of 3 hours each, only ten classes (one-fourth of the total) are in the major—any major! Therefore, that particular complaint from the field defies easy explanation. The future of education in public relations, however, raises a number of broader issues.

▼ PR IN THE CLASSROOM

The future of public relations education has to be considered on two levels: that provided for full- or part-time college or university students, and that provided for continuing education. Educators should be taking the lead in both, but they aren't. This lack of leadership may stem in part from the limited supply of public relations educators in academic institutions who are available to teach the burgeoning crowds in PR. In any case, higher education has not shown itself able to focus attention on continuing education.

Instead of coming to the educators' rescue with needed resources, most practitioners have focused on setting up their own training facilities. One reason for this is that many people teaching public relations in colleges and universities were pressed into service without having much experience in the field, and many practitioners had little confidence in what was happening in the classroom. Certainly they weren't looking at PR education as the "cutting edge," where practitioners could go to learn how to do their jobs better. The decision not to invest in continuing education at universities—even at universities where public relations programs existed—remains widespread today, and it does not bode well for the future of the field.

Growing demand for PR courses at academic institutions has increased the need for public relations educators with advanced degrees. In response, many academics with public relations interests began doing quantitative research in the field, but this made them seem even more remote to practitioners in the field who did not do any research and did not even pretend to understand it— even when they were buying it from commercial research organizations. This state of affairs has changed somewhat as more researchers holding doctorate degrees have been hired to work in the research departments of public relations firms. However, during the period when demand for public relations education was exploding, the

▼ **PR educators must help practitioners avail themselves of continuing education opportunities and must prepare students just starting in the field.**

gap between education and practice grew, and the courses and workshops that practitioners set up outside the universities for people they were hiring primarily addressed "nuts and bolts" concerns. So much for continuing education at the university level!

If public relations is going to achieve professional status, it will have to switch to the mode adopted by law and medicine, where faculties teaching the field are expected to be at its forefront. In that mode, the field's intellectual resources lie in higher education, not in the practice.

Such a statement suggests that graduate schools for public relations should be centers for research and knowledge, and some are. But controversy continues, in the academic community and in the practice, over whether public relations should even be taught at the undergraduate level. Nevertheless, most PR jobs go to students who have learned public relations in undergraduate programs. In the future, universities will have to fulfill their responsibilities at both undergraduate and graduate levels and will have to live with the continuing debate over what courses they should offer.

Despite years of effort by curriculum committees and commissions made up of educators and practitioners, experts still disagree over what should be taught and who should teach it. Many academics, stung by criticism that they didn't know the field, have gotten experience on the side; and many practitioners who wanted to teach have gone back to school to learn how to do scholarly research.

Another problem associated with public relations in the classroom is the question of where the public relations sequences should be housed. Most PR courses were originally developed in programs of journalism and mass communications, and the Department of Education's designated accrediting body for public relations is the Accrediting Council for Education in Journalism and Mass Communication (ACEJMC), which accredits journalism-based programs, usually. However, news editorial faculty often have negative attitudes toward public relations courses, the students who take them and their own colleagues who teach them.[53] This creates academic friction and hinders advancement of the field's status, since news editorial faculty still tend to be the heads of journalism and mass communication units.

While some journalism and mass communication units would like to get rid of their public relations sections, speech communication units have generally welcomed them. Few speech communication units qualify for accreditation, however, because they typically house highly vocational programs such as speech and hearing, which require many hours of major coursework and have lower liberal arts degree standards. Many authorities advocate teaching public relations in business units, but the business schools scarcely recognize public relations as a field and certainly not as a management function—although some see it as allied (but probably subordinated) to marketing. Naturally, this low esteem doesn't sit well with public relations educators and practitioners.

Ultimately, the squabbling has unfortunate consequences for public relations education and practice. As one of this book's authors said,

> Public relations educators, like those who actually practice public relations, haven't even been able to agree upon a definition of what it is they do and how they're supposed to do it, much less achieve consensus about the parameters of professionalism that should guide their endeavors. Is it any wonder, then, that public relations education— and, indeed the entire public relations practice— faces a lack of credibility and fails to earn support, encouragement and understanding?[54]

▼ SUMMARY

Future public relations practitioners will function in a global environment where high-technology developments have simultaneously increased the potential scope of communication and narrowed the channels of communication. As a result, audiences must be thought of as specific publics marked by cultural diversity. Some issues that already concern public relations practitioners, such as the environment, will attain global scope, and public opinion on these issues will have to be monitored globally.

Today, the challenges are greater and the demand for public relations services higher than previously, but the 1990s will also be a time for PR to recover from the 1980s' downsizing of staffs and PR-bashing by opinion leaders and news media. Many of the new jobs becoming available in public relations in this decade will be filled by women, who historically have been paid less and had lower status than men. Some practitioners fear that this will have a negative impact on PR's occupational status, but some management experts foresee major changes in the business climate that will call for flexibility and a more fluid, less hierarchical organizational structure (in which women work especially well) to build networks across areas of expertise in order to accomplish tasks.

In any case, management in the workplace is gaining importance and becoming more complex, as cultural diversity creates a need for people who are culturally sensitive. Another recent development is increased employee independence, fostered in some ways by the organizational acquisitions and mergers that have destroyed company allegiances. With this independence comes a greater dedication to the task, rather than to the setting where it is being performed. Some observers consider that a desirable trait for public relations practitioners, because it will encourage them to work within a set of standards for practice and to be aware of the special skills and training they bring to their positions.

Public relations practitioners in the United States no longer hold the world's attention as being preeminent in the field, although the United States is recognized as the place where PR grew most rapidly and matured fastest. Other nations are catching up, and in the future the practice of public relations may not even be defined in the same terms as it is today.

The practice of public relations consists of two major elements: strategy and execution. In the future, the emphasis will be on strategy, which implies a growth in the research function. At least one senior counselor sees the practice getting a new name, *ideology*, since the term *public relations* has fallen on hard times.

The misuse and abuse of the term *public relations* may be tied to PR's recent decline in status in the United States, although the field's own history doesn't help, either. Many trends in public relations suggest that, while the function itself is expanding and its use is growing, the battles for turf within organizations are likely to continue. On a positive note, some of the occupations most prone to encroach on public relations are now themselves hiring public relations firms, and that could help matters by creating useful liaisons.

The demand for public relations is especially noticeable among governments—particularly developing and newly democratizing governments. The U.S. government, too, needs improved communication with its own citizens in an age of special interest groups. This suggests that the public affairs specialty of public relations should grow rapidly.

Another expanding area comprises customer, investor and shareholder relations. Employee relations, always a crucial area, has become even more of a challenge now, since listening with cultural understanding is critical to an organization's success.

The biggest area of global public relations involvement is likely to be the environment. Organizations must anticipate how their policies will affect the global community, instead of avoiding the subject and then having to do damage control after the fact.

The three key facets of PR practice will be credibility, accountability and reliability, as a more sophisticated (and more cynical) world scrutinizes what an organization says and compares this to what the organization does. PR people will have to demonstrate real knowledge and mastery of information about the organization they represent, to maintain the quality of their performance.

Problems in meeting the demands of the future abound, but good public relations practitioners should recognize these as opportunities to tackle such longstanding issues as status, focus, turf wars, education and particular difficulties within the PR specialties.

Academics have to get serious about bringing continuing education back into the university so that PR practitioners will look to the universities the way doctors and lawyers look to their academic communities. Currently, practitioners doubt that professors are on the cutting edge, and professors question what is happening (or not happening) in the field. Some of the debate over what public relations people should be learning will never be settled, because what people need to know changes as the field changes. For this reason both preliminary career preparation and continuing education are pressing needs.

▼ NOTES

[1] Brian Mulroney, "The Future Has Started," *Encyclopaedia Britannica Book of the Year 1990, Events of 1989* (Chicago: Encyclopaedia Britannica, 1990), p. 13.

[2] Ibid.

[3] Ibid.

[4] Ronald E. Rhody, "The Matter of Survival," speech at the Public Relations Society of American Management Seminar, Palm Springs, California, June 26, 1990. Reprint #3124 by Bank of America, Box 37000, San Francisco, Calif. 94137.

[5] Ibid.

[6] Tom Peters, "The Best New Managers Will Listen, Motivate, Support," *Working Woman* (September 1990), p. 142.

[7] Patricia Aburdene, speech to the 1990 National Convention of the Public Relations Society of America, New York, November 1990.

[8] Carolyn G. Cline, Michael H. McBride, Kate Peirce, "A Functional Gender-Aschematic Approach to the Feminization of Public Relations: A Review of the Literature and the Possibilities," paper presented to the Committee on the Status of Women at the annual convention of the Association for Education in Journalism and Mass Communication, Minneapolis, Minn., August 1990.

[9] Ibid.

[10] Patricia Aburdene, "How to Think Like a CEO for the 1990s," *Working Woman* (September 1990), p. 137.

[11] Ibid. Also see Leon E. Winter, "Theater Program Tackles Issues of Diversity," in "*Business and Race,*" *Wall Street Journal* (April 18, 1991), p. B1.

[12] Rhody, "The Matter of Survival."

[13] *Public Relations News*, 46(24) (June 18, 1990), Special Report, Part II.

[14] Jean Farinelli, "You'd Better Learn to 'Speak International,'" in *tips & tactics*, supplement to *pr reporter*, 28(9) (June 25, 1990), p. 1.

[15] Ibid.

[16] Ibid.

[17] Harold Burson, "Beyond 'PR': Redefining the Role of Public Relations," speech for the Institute for Public Relations Research and Education, New York City, October 2, 1990, p. 16.

[18] Ibid.

[19] John F. Budd, Jr., "When Less Is More: Public Relations' Paradox of Growth," speech by the 1989 Vern C. Schranz Distinguished Lecturer, Ball State University, Muncie, Indiana, p. 31.

[20] Ibid.

[21]*Encyclopaedia Britannica, Micropaedia*, 15th ed., vol. 8, "Public Relations," p. 285.

[22]Ibid.

[23]Seymour Lusterman, "The Organization and Staffing of Corporate Public Affairs," research report from the Conference Board, 845 Third Ave, New York, NY 10022.

[24]Ellen Joan Pollock, "Lawyers Are Cautiously Embracing PR Firms," *Wall Street Journal* (March 14, 1990), p. B1, B2.

[25]Ibid.

[26]Ibid.

[27]Amy Dockser Marcus and Stephen Wermiel, "Public-Relations Executive Joins Big Law Firm as Salaried Partner," *Wall Street Journal* (February 27, 1990), p. B8.

[28]Ibid.

[29]Thomas R. King, "Agencies Use PR Firms to Attract Clients," *Wall Street Journal* (March 28, 1990), p. B6.

[30]Abdulrahman H. Al-Enad, "Public Relations' Roles in Developing Countries," *Public Relations Quarterly*, 35 (Spring 1990), pp. 24–26.

[31]Harold Burson, "Beyond 'PR': Redefining the Role of PR."

[32]*American Demographics* staff, "More Single Dads, Childless Couples," *Wall Street Journal* (November 12, 1990), p. B1.

[33]*American Demographics* staff, "Income of Households Outpaces Families'," *Wall Street Journal* (November 12, 1990), p. B1.

[34]*American Demographics* staff, "The Rich Are Different from One Another," *Wall Street Journal* (November 12, 1990), p. B1.

[35]Ibid.

[36]Amanda Bennett, "Making the Grade with the Customer," *Wall Street Journal* (November 12, 1990), pp. B1, B8.

[37]Amanda Bennett, "Many Customers Expect Better Service—and They Say They Are Willing to Pay for It," *Wall Street Journal* (November 12, 1990), p. B1.

[38]"Communicating with Employees by CEOs," *PR News*, 46(11) (March 19, 1990), p. 1.

[39]"Focused View of 90s Realities for Public Relations at CPRS Conference: Management and Internal Issues Plus Managing Technological Change Top List," *pr reporter*, 33(25) (June 18, 1990), p. 1.

[40]Dennis Farney, "Unkindest Cut? Timber Firm Stirs Ire Felling Forests Faster Than They Regenerate," *Wall Street Journal* (June 18, 1990), pp. 1, 6.

[41]Ibid.

[42]Ibid.

[43]Ibid.

[44]Ibid.

[45]Ibid.

[46]Ibid.

[47]Ibid.

[48]Marj Charlier, "Manville Tries to Build New Identity as a Firm Keen on Environment," *Wall Street Journal* (May 31, 1990), p. 1.

[49]"Nothing Like the Asbestos Nightmare Must Ever Happen Again, We at Manville Are Compelled to Share What We Have Learned from That Experience—Mainly About Anticipating Issues," *pr reporter*, 33(26) (June 25, 1990), p. 1.

[50]Ibid.

[51]Denny Griswold, *PR News*, 46(11) (March 19, 1990), p. 1.

[52]Glen M. Broom and Kerry Tucker, "An Essential Double Helix," *Public Relations Journal* (November 1989), pp. 40–41.

[53]Peter Habermann, Lillian Lodge Kopenhaver and David L. Martinson, "Sequence Faculty Divided on PR Value, Status and News Orientation," *Journalism Quarterly*, 65(2), pp. 490–96.

[54]Donald K. Wright and Judy VanSlyke Turk, "Public Relations Education: The Unpleasant Realities: Questions and Challenges for a New Decade," report published by the Institute for Public Relations Research and Education, 1990.

Selected readings, activities and assignments appropriate to this chapter can be found in the *Instructor's Guide*.

▼

RESEARCH FOR PR

If you're a skillful PR practitioner, you do research first for backgrounding and program planning. Then you continue the research process to monitor what you are doing. And finally you measure your work's effectiveness to find out how well it turned out. Research and honest evaluation make the practice of PR more precise. This is what Chapters 4 and 5 are about.

Chapter 6 shows you how to apply research in order to examine publics and determine public opinion.

▼

RESEARCH FOR BACKGROUNDING AND PLANNING

Research is the one important source of ideas for public relations practice.

Edward J. Robinson, management training and development authority

We can't manage what we don't measure.

David R. Drobis, president of Ketchum Public Relations and Ketchum Public Relations Worldwide

You have a new public relations job, or you've volunteered to do public relations work for an organization. Before you can function effectively, you must find out what you are supposed to do, for whom and why. You ask a lot of questions, and you look for materials to read—perhaps at the library. Once on the job, you begin discovering helpful information that you put into your computer or file away where you can find it. You ask questions.

You are doing research. Furthermore, you are using the same general methods that every researcher uses: reading available material, and questioning people. The two categories of research methods are *secondary* (reading or consulting available materials that someone else has already compiled) and *primary* (collecting the raw data yourself). This chapter deals with secondary research; primary research is discussed in Chapter 5.

In public relations, the need for systematic research is critical and continuous. Keeping records as you go along will save you from a lot of frantic scurrying when you have to locate specific information. Maybe you've already learned this lesson to the extent of keeping a list of your information sources' phone numbers handy, and updating it regularly.

You have to do research initially to gather facts. Then you have to monitor your progress to see whether what you have planned is going all right or whether changes need to be made. Finally, you evaluate what was accomplished, in order to determine how you need to plan for the future. There's no simple all-purpose formula to follow, because research in public relations is a never-ending process. Example 4.1 indicates the high value organizations place on up-to-the-minute information.

Public relations research concentrates on finding the answers to these questions: Who is our audience? What is our action/message? What channels of communication reach our audiences? What is the reaction to our efforts? What should we do to keep in touch? With every public relations activity, we should consider: How is this activity going to be understood by everyone whom we try to inform or persuade? What are they going to say or do as a result of our efforts? What is their feeling about us (that is, our client—whether an individual or an institution), and what we are doing and saying? Research is used for exploration, description, explanation and control.

Research in public relations supports audience, media and trend analysis; message testing; and issue monitoring, forecasting and evaluating. It often provides essential data for effectively presenting information. This chapter discusses the importance of keeping records, of finding and using existing reports and information and of using research in planning, monitoring and evaluating PR programs.

▼ THE BASICS: RECORD KEEPING AND RETRIEVING

Getting started with a new public relations job or a new client means doing a lot of basic research and setting up a system for accumulating and accessing information. Some large organizations have information systems officers and librarians. Information systems officers manage the current flow of information generated by the organization. Librarians maintain past records, files and documents. You will find that both are invaluable as you gather the information you need.

EXAMPLE 4.1 ▬▬▬▬

Information Gatherers in Washington, D.C.

There's a high value in being the first to get important facts in the decision-making atmosphere of Washington, D.C., so public relations and accounting firms often hire fact-finders, at salaries as high as $50,000 a year, to sit outside committee meetings until they break up and then grab quick briefings from participants. These information gatherers often make getting to know congressional and committee staff people a part of their job, so they have steady sources of strategic information. In discussing this new "paper chaser" role, the *Wall Street Journal* gave the example of a tax analyst for Hill & Knowlton stationing himself at 7:15 A.M. outside the room where the House Ways and Means Committee was meeting. This committee writes the nation's tax laws, and the H&K researcher needed to be there to talk to people as soon as the meeting adjourned or even as people came and went. The *Journal* noted that, by the time the Ways and Means Committee convened (which was several hours after the H&K researcher took his post outside the room), he had 100 or more people behind him, all doing what he was—trying to get critical bits of information for their employers. Sometimes the researchers are on all-night "stake-outs" as meetings go on until early morning. They are prepared to pass the word to their employers even if it's 3 A.M. The information is often critical to decision making, and a client's strategy may depend on a few key facts. The *Journal* said that two rules govern the behavior of these new-style researchers: be accurate and transmit what you get as soon as possible.

SOURCE: Adapted from *Wall Street Journal* (August 3, 1990), p. B3A.

Keeping Records

The kinds of records you will need to accumulate fall into several categories: information about the organization itself (when it was begun, its mission statement, what it makes or does, its history); information about personnel (biographies of current principals and past leadership); and information about ongoing projects or activities. You will need file copies of all of the organization's communication pieces—magazines, newsletters, annual reports, advertising, films and videotapes. These may be on file in the library, but you will need all of the current information right in your office.

Retrieving Information

Systematic record keeping—fact collecting—may be a drudgery, but it can supply critically needed information (such as a record telling you what you did last year when the same problem cropped up), help you plan (such as by telling you what you need to put on the calendar) and help you flesh out stories or identify a news peg. Maintaining a file on all major activities and a general how-to file facilitates planning and reduces strain on the nerves—provided that you can find what you filed.

Recorded information must be kept in an easily retrievable form. It is not valuable unless you have access to it. For example, suppose that you have been touting the high nutritional value of your company's canned peaches, and a competitor releases a "market study" showing that actually its frozen peaches have more nutritional value because so much of yours is destroyed in canning. A newspaper food editor calls you for a comment on the challenge. If it takes you too long to find the nutritional information you need, the competition may win the headlines that day, and you may have to settle for a less prominent display of your answer several days later.

▼ RESEARCH SOURCES

There are two broad categories of research sources: scholarly and commercial. Academic institutions and faculty do scholarly research, sometimes with funding from the government, from foundations or from professional associations. Commercial research is done by specific organizations—research firms, advertising and public relations firms/agencies and independent companies.

Research results that are funded by an academic institution or by a professional association or society are usually published and made public. The results of most commercial research are proprietary and are not made available to others. Scholars, however, may be given limited access to the results. Normally the results are withheld unless the commercial organization sees some benefit in releasing them.

Finding and Using Existing Reports

Research results of all kinds are available. Databases for general and specialized sources can be accessed either on a subscription basis or through purchased searches conducted by reference librarians. Unless the information is needed immediately, searches can be conducted "off-line," at nonpeak hours, to save money. The most familiar databases are CompuServe, The Source, Dow Jones News Retrieval and Nexis/Lexis (Nexis is used by journalists, and Lexis by lawyers). MARS serves the field of advertising and public relations. PR people often need to use communications databases, as well as specialized ones for their organization or client.

Most useful in communicating with publics is information from communications research that shows profiles of audiences and provides credibility ratings for various communication tactics and tools. The research has usually already been done. You simply need to know where to look for it. You must also know enough about research techniques to interpret the results correctly and then apply them. If, for instance, you are interested in advertising for the youth market, you would be interested in a published study by Professor Stephen Unwin, who concluded that "differences in opinion of the advertisements and the products advertised were predictive of response difference between cultures but not between generations and sexes."[1] Social science research also provides a wealth of information. Although such research often is not directly relevant to a particular public relations problem, the PR practitioner can learn how to extract what can be used most effectively.

Research findings are available from various sources. Useful compilations of research information that describe emerging trends are available in books. *Megatrends* by John Naisbett and Patricia Aburdene and *Inside America* by Paul Chance are examples. Membership in an organization like the Newspaper Advertising Bureau, Inc., also can provide ready access to useful research data. One research study conducted by this organization measured the coincidental recall of TV commercials over the 1965–1986 period. Other studies it has done include an examination of the effectiveness of automotive, employment and real estate classifieds, and a study of circulation trends over a fifty-year period.

Periodicals are yet another source of useful information. The public relations newsletter, *pr reporter*, shares studies that its subscribers and readers grant it permission to use. The results of one such study, a banking-customer behavior survey, were made available to *pr reporter* by Carol Morgan Associates. A note in the newsletter directed readers who wanted additional information to contact the agency that conducted the survey.

The results of national surveys are usually obtainable from a number of sources. Some national surveys have individual applications. Thus, if you use the same questionnaire and methodology as the national survey, you can compare one of your publics with the national one.

Research organizations are also sources of information. Research institutions such as Opinion Research Corporation, which was founded in 1938, offer comprehensive reports compiled from var-

▼ **Reports and summaries of much research are readily available in public and specialized libraries. Other sources include social scientists, government agencies and the media.**

ious clients' projects. These reports are not inexpensive (each costs several hundred dollars), but they are considerably cheaper than any comparable research project you might do yourself.[2]

Good survey research is costly. Small organizations, therefore, depend heavily on careful analysis and application of the results of surveys taken by others and published or made available within the industry. Such surveys are commonly performed by professional associations and then made available to their members. Social problems and issues with significance to government or to social agencies are studied and published by public polling agencies. Recent examples include studies that have focused on projections of the numbers of future AIDS (Acquired Immune Deficiency Syndrome) victims and the cost of their treatment.

Mastery of a unique body of knowledge is one of the marks of a true profession. In 1988, a task force appointed by the Public Relations Society of America developed an outline of subject matter essential to the professional practice of public relations. This *Body of Knowledge*, a comprehensive bibliography with each entry annotated (summarized), is available from PRSA in printed form or on computer disks that you can load into your computer to access and read.

From the U.S. Government Printing Office, you can order a catalog of booklets published from government-funded research. You can also get research information, especially demographic information and economic statistics, from state and local governments. The U.S. Census Bureau is *the* source for demographic information.

Fortunately much of this research is available in electronic data banks. A good bit is even accessible

▼ **Survey research is the primary research tool for learning about and describing publics, including their demographics (social and economic status) and psychographics (personality traits).**

to personal computer users, due to the development of the CD-ROM (for *compact disk—read only memory*) technology. Some even offer sound. If you don't have the capacity to access such information with your own computer, you can pay a research librarian to perform the search for you. If you are fishing in unfamiliar waters, a research librarian can be very helpful with descriptions—the key words you use to tap into data banks—and with the choice of data banks themselves. Once you find information, you need to be sufficiently knowledgeable about the research methodology to apply it to a particular client or organization. As an active practitioner in the field, you must be aware of the available literature and of the sources of that literature.

What to Look for in Research Data   Much of the information that public relations practitioners seek involves public opinion—the reported views of designated groups of people. Since public opinion is composed of the collective individual views expressed about a product, service or organization by segments of a community, it follows that both demographics and psychographics must be used to put public opinion into its proper context. The public relations practitioner needs to be sure that the research data contain sound demographic and psychographic information.

Demographics identifies the size of a population and its capacity to expand or decline. It also provides information about a population's gender, level of education, occupation, and income. **Psychographics** reveals the personality traits of an audience. Its value lies in its ability to show likenesses in audiences of great demographic variation. Thus, psychographics can reveal what an eighty-year-old

engineer and a twenty-five-year-old stockbroker have in common. Perhaps they both prefer classical music to popular music, or they both like to grow roses. Psychographics also tells us about life-styles.

Public relations practitioners are interested in the geo-demographic information contained in the research data, as well. Geo-demographics— also known as "cluster demographics," "indirect psychographics," "zip clustering" and "geo-marketing"—identifies geographic areas that are populated by consumers who share demographic and psychographic characteristics. The demographic and psychographic profile of an area is matched against the penetration of a product or service into that same area. Sound geo-demographic information causes universities to recruit new students in areas where large numbers of their alumni live, and it persuades the U.S. Armed Services to recruit in neighborhoods where they have gotten qualified applicants in the past.[3]

Applying Research Information   You'll find yourself relying heavily on survey data for guidance. But two questions should be asked before you use survey research. First, is it valid? Second, what does it mean to me or my client—that is, does it measure what I want to measure? If the answer to the first question is "no" or "probably not," there is no point in using the information. The answer to the second question can serve as a warning signal to the alert public relations practitioner that a problem is brewing. If the answer is "Some of this research does not really apply to our situation," then you must take care to use only the portion of the research that *is* relevant and to do some primary research of your own to get at your problem directly. For instance, a church or denominational office might react to a Gallup religion survey by checking its own statistics on attendance. If attendance is sliding, the prudent move would be to design a survey to answer questions directly relevant to that church or denomination.

Surveys and polls can be extremely useful as long as they are interpreted correctly. The key to successful interpretation is a realistic and objective viewpoint. To assist people in using poll data, the National Council on Public Polls (NCPP) has issued some standards for releasing poll data. NCPP considers it essential that the following information be specifically incorporated in published or broadcast reports on polls: (1) who sponsored the poll; (2) dates of interviewing; (3) method of obtaining the interviews (in-person, telephone or mail); (4) wording of the questions; (5) population that was surveyed; (6) size of the sample; (7) size and description of the subsample, if results are based on less than the total sample.[4]

The American Association for Public Opinion Research (AAPOR) offers a cautionary note, as well. Taking an activist stance, AAPOR writes letters to those who do "alleged" polls, pointing out that these—such as one billed as a "national" poll even though its sample was 80 percent Californian—are not polls at all. AAPOR president Hope Lunin Klapper cited advocacy organizations as being the most frequent abusers of poll methodology, primarily by the way the questions are asked.[5]

One of the biggest stumbling blocks to overall acceptance of market research is implicit in the question, "who is going to test market the test marketers?" The Advertising Research Foundation undertook to find out just how objectively market research firms operate and how valid their findings are. The foundation asked research firms to allow it to audit their research techniques. Its findings were then made available to foundation member firms, and participating research companies received the "Registered for the ARF Open Audit Plan" seal.[6]

▼ USING RESEARCH FOR PLANNING

Research is critical at every step of public relations work, from planning and goal setting to prioritizing publics to evaluating results for purposes of future planning and action. Research information is particularly useful at the initiation stage of a public relations effort. A public relations practitioner interested in putting together a program to bring an organization's goals and objectives to a public's

▼ Being realistic and objective is critical to the proper interpretation of research.

attention begins by examining all available research information indicating how various publics view the organization (or similar organizations). Any other information about the organization's publics also deserves close study.

When a public relations practitioner reaches the point of planning messages for various publics, audience research becomes critically important. If sufficient information about how a target group is likely to respond to a particular type of message is not at hand, the practitioner must make every effort to locate it elsewhere. This may involve asking special departments, such as sales or product research, for specific usable information. The practitioner must be cooperative toward and considerate of the work schedules and time commitments of those approached for help.

Sometimes information about how a particular audience will respond to a particular type of message simply cannot be located. Original research must then be undertaken (see Chapter 5).

Vast quantities of material are available for public relations planning. PR consultant Steve Lee astounded a British client by presenting a 2-inch thick book of information for public relations planning—all from available research sources.

The main stages of the planning phase of research are issue forecasting, learning about publics, planning media use and considering possible outcomes.

Issue Forecasting

Issue forecasting is the research part of issues management and environmental scanning. In issue forecasting, an organization uses collected information to determine how it and its publics might react to a future event, trend or controversy. Of the more than 150 forecasting techniques available, only 9 are commonly used, according to Raymond Ewing,

▼ **The nine principal techniques used in issue forecasting are trend extrapolation, trend impact analysis, scanning, monitoring, the DELPHI technique, cross-impact analysis, computer simulations, scenario writing and technology assessment.**

---

former issues management director of Allstate Insurance.[7]

1. *Trend extrapolation*, one of the most widely used techniques, is based on the assumption that most trends follow the ups and downs of an S curve (∽). Social and environmental factors also have to be considered, however, and events like wars and strikes can intervene.

2. *Trend impact analysis* involves anticipating the impact of future events. Experts review a computer-generated trend and try to list future events that could affect it. Then they describe how this could occur.

3. *Scanning* consists of having a number of people regularly review various general and specialized publications and write abstracts of these, adding their own personal comments. The abstracts are reviewed by an analysis committee, which reports to a steering committee so that the information can be used in planning.

4. *Monitoring* picks up where trend analysis and scanning stop. Once a significant identifiable element is discovered, monitors track its development. Research institutions, for example, use surveys and content analysis of mass media to follow identified issues.

5. *The DELPHI technique* identifies issues by polling experts. Anonymity prevents the experts from being influenced by authority figures, interpersonal persuasion or majority opinion. A summary of the predictions is then circulated among members of a panel, who refine it to reach a consensus.

6. *Cross-impact analysis* attempts to determine how trends discovered or predicted by all other means might occur, influence each other or affect the timing of events.

7. *Computer simulations* apply mathematical formulas to numerical information in order to arrive at a predictive conclusion.

8. *Scenario writing* is a "what if" form of research developed to project a number of possibilities, including unpleasant ones, to help an organization plan for contingencies. Resulting scenarios may be used to sensitize management to issues or to communicate trends to the public.

9. *Technology assessment* attempts to predict the costs, benefits and negative impact of various technologies, to help in planning for development and adoption.

Learning About Publics

After you have accumulated all the facts you need about a given issue or situation, you must begin exploring the publics involved. Reexamine their profiles to see how each might be affected by the situation. This is a critical area, and it is important not to overlook any public. In this manner you will often discover areas that present conflicts of interest between divergent publics. For example, a college PR administrator frequently encounters conflicts of interest among the college's varied publics—trustees, administrators, alumni, faculty, staff, parents and students. Each public might react quite differently to the same issue or situation.

The two main tasks involved in exploring publics consist of prioritizing them by issues and interpreting their behavior.

Prioritizing Publics by Issues   In each planning situation, you have to decide which are the major publics and which the minor ones of your organization. For example, some nonprofit organizations that depend on fundraising are very sensitive to news media coverage, as are all government agencies. But a privately held company with consumer products is not likely to rank news media very high on its list of publics. On the other hand, on *specific* issues, you may have to revise your general ordering of publics. If that privately held company were charged with polluting a major source of drinking water, news media might suddenly rank very high on its list of publics.

"It's not exactly deciding who you can afford to offend," one practitioner said, "It is more deciding which one has to be appealed to most effectively and figuring out how to do that while offending the others the least." To do this at all, you must be aware of what these publics know and what they think they know. Only research will tell you how many real facts a public has, what myths it holds and what rumors it has embraced. Some research professes to have discovered how a public is *likely* to think and what it might do. This claim is worth examining, but cautiously.

Research also helps you examine the dynamics of your publics—how they act collectively. This is something more and more institutions are investigating with employee surveys.

Surveys are one way to measure a public's dynamics on issues and problems, but some managements use a more direct approach with employees and consumers. Managers—even CEOs—sit down with a few employees at a time at different sites to listen to them air complaints and suggestions. For example, officers, accompanied by some directors, of ONEOK (a diversified energy company) go to different locations to present employee awards and hear about problems. The president, who is also chairman, conducts one-on-one meetings with employees and meets with units to hear what they have to say.

Some companies have adopted a Japanese technique called "quality circles," in which groups of employees meet regularly with managers to review problems. Listening to the people who are doing the work and interacting with consumers and suppliers may be good for morale, even if nothing is done. On the other hand, if employees or consumers don't see some tangible evidence of the upward flow of communication, they may lose

▼ **The two main tasks in exploring publics are to prioritize them by issues and to interpret their behavior.**

interest or use the meetings strictly for personal or political benefit. The dynamics of a public often provide clues to possible approaches for effective communication.

Interpreting the Behavior of Publics James Grunig, public relations professor at the University of Maryland, says likenesses between and among publics may depend entirely on specific situations. Any examination of publics, Grunig says, should consider first a grouping by the nature of that public's communication behavior and then a grouping by the similarity of that public's situational perception and behavior—that is, how people look at certain situations and how they behave in them. For example, an ordinarily outgoing and talkative person may be silent and reserved in particular situations. Thus, Grunig says, we must take into consideration that people *control* their behavior. Grouping publics in the two ways that Grunig recommends may help us predict the attitudes people will assume in certain specific situations, as well as offering us a way to understand what is going on in the situations.

Grunig tells us to expect different communications behaviors from information seekers than from information processors.[8] See persuasion and communication theories p. 222 for chart. An information seeker is interested enough in the problem or situation to want to know more about it. An information processor is aware of the communication and may be touched by the message but does not actively seek the information.

For example, suppose that the professor in your class announces that Friday is the last day to add and drop classes. If you are interested in adding or dropping a class, you will try to find out more information about how to do it on or before Friday. You are therefore an information seeker. However, if you do not need the information, you will process it but not seek additional data. Subsequently, if your roommate says, "My schedule is all messed up; I wonder when the deadline is for changing," you might say, "Well, it's Friday, but that's all I know."

The roommate has demonstrated *problem recognition*—one of the communication states that Grunig explains. Problem recognition increases the probability that a person will communicate and seek information about a situation. Communication is reduced, though, if the person thinks that limitations restrict his or her behavior. Grunig calls this behavior *constraint recognition*. These two concepts combine to produce four types of perceived situations: problem-facing behavior (high problem recognition, low constraint recognition); constrained behavior (high problem recognition, high constraint recognition); routine behavior (low problem recognition, low constraint recognition); and fatalistic behavior (low problem recognition, high constraint recognition).

Now add another variable, the *referent criterion*. A referent criterion is a guide or rule by which a person measures a new situation in terms of an old experience. A person who is confronted with a new situation employs an old criterion to handle it. If the old criterion doesn't work this time, the person develops a new criterion to guide his or her behavior (including communication behavior) in the new setting. Grunig has found that, when a person is motivated to communicate about a situation, he or she is also motivated to develop a solution for the situation—an attitude. Therefore, why a person communicates or does not communicate in a situation can be explained by these three variables: problem recognition, constraint behavior and referent criterion.[9]

A fourth variable that helps determine whether a person will be an information seeker or an information processor is *perceived level of involvement*. A person seeks information if involved in a situation but only processes it if not involved. Grunig's four variables now produce sixteen types of communication behavior (four combinations of problem recognition and constraint recognition, subdivided by the presence or absence of a referent criterion and again by the level of involvement). With all four variables under examination, probabilities can be used to decide whether either information seeking or information processing by a particular public is likely to be worth the investment involved in preparing information (brochures, videotapes, films) for that group.

Consider, for example, a new admissions policy that would affect students transferring from two-year colleges. Many of these students may not even be thinking about going on to a four-year institution, while others might entertain the idea if they thought they had a chance to be admitted. Information about a nonrestrictive policy would have to be communicated to the latter group to show them how to qualify for admission—how to overcome obstacles. They constitute a very cost-effective public, since they are actively interested in finding out what to do and what is going on. However, money is wasted on students who are not very interested in a college education, who think getting admitted is impossible, and who really want to obtain a vocational rather than an academic education.

Planning Media Use

Research indicating what media different publics use is widely available from professional, trade and academic journals. Occasionally, research reports from polls appear in the popular press, as well. As a PR practitioner, you want to know how people use media, which media they use and who the users are. When you want to know about a specific medium you can consult reference publications such as *Standard Rate and Data* and the Audit Bureau of Circulation reports, as well as industry guides like *Editor and Publisher*. In addition, a medium will have its own research prepared to sell time or space or to provide editorial guidance.

Considering Possible Outcomes

Any time you consider a public relations plan, you should closely examine everything that can go right and everything that can go wrong. Even just discussing these possibilities can often prevent a poor plan from progressing beyond the talking stage. Few practitioners are willing to share "wild ideas" that were scrapped in the planning stages, but often people with public relations awareness wonder whether an actually adopted plan had ever been put to the "possibilities test."

One example is the nerve gas story. As the result of a reporter's initiative, people learned of an activity that the government had intended to keep secret. Front-page headlines told the nation—with heavy play in the local communities involved—that the government was using train cars to move nerve gas that it had decided to destroy. No one seems to have asked ahead of time, "What if someone finds out and makes this move public?" Surely, if someone had foreseen this possibility, a more careful program would have been worked out for handling the resulting media exposure.

In another case, a university discovered that it would have to increase dormitory room rents. Except for the administration and the school's business office, however, no one knew of the plan—until housing contracts were sent to students who planned to return the following year. The shock and resentment at the last-minute notification caused many students to cancel their contracts and move off campus, while other students felt lingering bitterness toward the institution. Again, you have to wonder why no one asked, "What will be the reaction when these contracts are received?"

Examining the possibilities of any plan often reveals that unexplored areas exist. You must then decide whether additional research is needed. Is the missing information likely to be critical enough to justify the cost? Usually the answer is yes. This is particularly true when you are developing a campaign.

Moreover, even though existing research in each area—the situation, the publics and the media—

may have been applied, pretesting is essential. Secondary research—materials and information from other sources—is certainly important, but each situation is unique and may merit its own testing before you launch an entire campaign. If you receive in the mail one bar of soap of a brand you have never seen before, the accompanying information will probably reveal that you are in a "test market." Sometimes an ad will appear in one split run of a magazine as a test. Or a person may interview you and show you several different ads to get your reaction to each. All such pretests are worth the investment if they prevent an expensive error, indicate an unanticipated response or suggest a different approach.

▼ USING RESEARCH FOR MONITORING

It is important to arrange for feedback after a plan has been set in operation. Careful planning may have preceded a public relations program, but that does not ensure success.

In developing goals, you must use a procedure that will allow you to determine later on whether you have achieved these goals. To accomplish this, you have to build monitoring into your plans. Monitoring can reveal problem areas before they become crises. Monitoring a PR operation involves a specific check on results, as opposed to general monitoring of the climate of public opinion, which goes on in issue management. Monitoring is also different from the final evaluation, which allows you to determine whether your completed program achieves all your goals.

Monitoring can be as simple as checking a broadcast to make sure that advertising is running in the time slots purchased or reading a magazine to confirm that an ad really got in. On the other hand, it may be as difficult as finding out whether a consumer noticed a new package. The benefits of monitoring are illustrated by the example of a resort area's hurried decision to buy radio time after

▼ **Monitoring involves a specific check on results as a campaign or program unfolds.**

discovering that a magazine story counted on to increase Labor Day crowds would, in fact, hit the newsstands the day after the holiday instead of two weeks before. Monitoring also may result in a hurried call to a broadcast station to stop commercials for a special sale because someone failed to notice the termination date given on the commercial, and now all of the sale merchandise has already been sold.

The importance of keeping up with events was not lost on one politician's campaign manager. He had hired youngsters one Friday morning to set up stake signs in supporters' yards. The following Monday he could find no signs in place. He arrived at the office ready to kill a bunch of kids; but instead he had to answer a call from city officials, who informed him that his signs had been removed because all 500 had been placed in the easement area just behind the curb. That was city property, and political signs could not be displayed there. How had the city officials known about this infraction? The candidate's opponent had been "monitoring," of course. Monitoring media use and supplied information is another important part of your work. You need tangible evidence that the message is getting out. For publicity monitoring, you can use services that will clip and tape in areas where you've released information. You generally get reports with the bill when you buy time or space. However, you need to have someone check to confirm that billboards and posters went up on time.

▼ **USING RESEARCH FOR FINAL EVALUATION**

The public relations function doesn't end with the achievement of particular goals or objectives. But certainly you want to look at each goal to see whether and by how much it was achieved. This is the purpose of the final evaluation. After-the-fact measurements of goals provide an estimate of objective achievement and indicate where problems may persist.

Most major agencies have elaborate evaluation systems in place. Ketchum Public Relations, for instance, has a system specifically designed to determine how well publicity reached a target audience and how effective the messages were.[10] Another agency, Burson-Marsteller, uses an Audience Impact and Diagnostics (AID) program to assess the effects of a specific program on audiences."[11]

You should check the effects of your public relations effort on each public, if possible. If that is too costly, at the very least you should look at its effects on your most important publics. You also need to see how the accomplishment of certain goals has modified or changed your overall objective. Here, measurements could suggest a shift in emphasis.

It is therefore wise to adopt the following procedures:

1. Compile the goal results, and interpret their significance to the specific objective set, to the organization's overall objectives and to its mission.

2. Evaluate the impact of actions taken on your publics to see what their attitudes are now toward the organization (and its products, services, management and so on).

3. Determine how the organization's overall objective and mission have been affected.

4. Measure the program's impact in three areas: (a) *Financial responsibility*—going beyond market share to the publics' perception of how an organization gets and spends its money. (b) *Ethics*—the perception by publics of an organization's standards of behavior, a moral judgment of the consequences of what it says and does. (c) *Social responsibility*—publics' perception of whether an organization is a good citizen; for example, whether it contributes to the social, political and economic health of global society.

Research can yield specific information about publics that may prove useful. For example, one survey produced evidence that two-thirds of the public (68 percent) said that knowing more about a company generally makes them think more favorably about it[12] and almost nine out of ten (87 percent) said that, if given a choice of similar products or services, they would choose the one from the company with the best reputation. Both points held up across socioeconomic lines for all major segments of the public.[13]

Research can also reveal something about the effect or impact of certain specific messages, such as anti-union messages conveyed in films. A study of some anti-union films appears to show that these can have an attitudinal effect on workers, strengthening any existing anti-union sentiment. However, some unions have undercut the impact of such films by showing them to workers before management does and then refuting the claims one by one.[14]

One ongoing research effort assesses information about both the public and the message. In it, the American Heart Association tests the impact of its annual Food Festival on grocery shoppers to see if awareness of heart-healthy foods has increased. The survey for the first Food Festival was measured against a prefestival baseline survey, and the survey for succeeding Food Festivals has been measured against previous ones and against the baseline. The survey, conducted by Home Testing Institute, collects information from shoppers who are surveyed about the types of food consumed in their household and about their attitudes toward food consumption. On the basis of survey answers, each consumer is placed in one of five behavioral groups: (1) children in a household, (2) meat-and-potatoes or traditional foods eaters, (3) sophisti-

▼ **The final evaluation assesses whether all of the goals in a public relations plan were achieved.**

cates who dine out and keep mostly adult-oriented foods like wines and cheeses at home, (4) naturalists who eat health-oriented foods and (5) the diet-conscious who choose low-calorie products. In addition, four attitudinal groups have been assembled, based on homemakers' attitudes toward food consumption: (1) nutritionally fit—less concerned with calories and more interested in food value; (2) conventional taste—concerned with foods that taste good, regardless of value; (3) restrictive dieter—focused on losing weight; (4) busy urbanite—ate away from home and was likely to try different foods and drinks. In 1987, for example, the overall findings were positive from a health standpoint, which also reflected well on the credibility of the American Heart Association. As might be expected, the nutritionally fit were the best informed group of consumers.[15]

The Cyclical Effect

Using research helps the public relations practitioner anticipate problems, evaluate ongoing programs, pretest the effectiveness of certain tools, profile a public and its attitudes, accumulate information about effective uses of media and evaluate completed programs and campaigns.

What results is a cycle of research activity (see Example 4.2) that can be described as follows:

1. Research is begun either as routine record keeping or specifically to gather facts for planning purposes.

2. After the PR objective is determined, facts gathered from research are used to formulate a hypothesis, test the hypothesis and make revisions if it does not seem to work.

EXAMPLE 4.2 ▮

The Continuing Cycle of Research

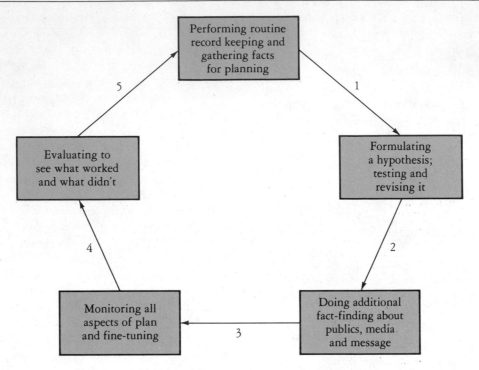

Research begins as routine study to assist in public relations planning, moves on to testing and revising hypotheses, necessitates further fact finding and methodology assessment, shifts to monitoring of the ongoing program, and concludes with a final evaluation of the public relations plan, which provides information to help in planning for the future, thus completing (and restarting) the cycle.

3. Once the PR objective has been developed, additional fact finding may be required to determine what needs to be known about the situations, publics or media to be used. Here we consider how best to present the PR objective to a particular public. We must evaluate the image the public holds and determine whether to keep or modify the present identity. We must also devise methods of reaching the audience and decide what type of message is likely to be most effective—publicity, speech, meeting, display or advertising. In addition, we need to consider the best timing for activities and messages.

4. To be sure the plan is working properly, we monitor.

5. Afterward, an evaluation should be conducted to see what went according to plan, what deviated and why. This evaluation can help clarify a public's profile or suggest greater use of a particular medium, and it may be used as resource information in the development of future plans.

Thus a continuing pattern of research needs to be developed for each public relations situation. The greater the continuity of any research project, the greater its potential effectiveness.

▼ TYPES OF RESEARCH

Research can be either informal or formal. Both are useful and both have limitations. You have to know when informal methods are adequate and when more formal methods are required. Formal research can be divided into two categories: qualitative and quantitative. Qualitative research includes historical and legal research, field studies and the like. It is descriptive and informative but not measurable. Quantitative research can be done in the laboratory or in the field. It is sometimes called a clinical study. Field studies can be observational and thus qualitative, but most field studies in public relations consist of survey research. Quantitative research results in a mathematical analysis because it produces measurable results. There is a place for all types of research. The choice depends upon the purpose of the research and its importance to the client.

How to do your own research is discussed in Chapter 5, which also provides guidelines for evaluating research that you buy from a supplier.

▼ SUMMARY

As a public relations practitioner, you will have to do basic record keeping and fact finding and maintain ready access to all information with a good retrieval system. Most large organizations have information systems officers and librarians to do this work. In smaller organizations, you'll have to set up your own system.

In any case, keeping records will be your job, so you'll have to identify what kinds of records to keep: on the organization's purposes, its history, its products or services, its principals, its publics and the media used to reach them. You will also accumulate examples of all types of communication, such as news releases, annual reports and videotapes.

You'll need to be able to get at that material quickly, too, which is why most record keepers rely on computers with some sort of backup printed system for days when the computers are down (thus the reliance on information systems people and librarians).

Most of the information you'll need is readily available, but you still have to know what to look for and how to apply it to your organization or to the practice of public relations. Some of the relevant information is commercial, and some of it is academic. You can draw from it what you need, if it proves valid.

You'll be using research for planning, monitoring and evaluating. In *planning*, you'll use research to see the range of concerns people have; as a part of environmental scanning; to learn more about publics themselves; to help you prioritize publics on special issues; to interpret the behavior of your publics; to consider possible outcomes of programs; and to review media. In *monitoring*, you'll track the plan as it is implemented. You'll also look at issues as they develop, and examine publics as well as the media that serve them. In *evaluating*, you'll develop some kind of system for seeing how well you succeeded in meeting your goals and objectives and where you fell short. The final evaluation helps you with future planning. Thus, the evaluation brings you back to planning: the research process is ongoing, a continuing cycle.

▼ NOTES

[1]Stephen J. F. Unwin, "How Culture, Age and Sex Affect Advertising Response," *Journalism Quarterly* (Winter 1973), p. 743.

[2]Opinion Research Corporation, Center for Management Research, 850 Boydston St., Chestnut Hill, Mass. 02167.

[3]"Geo-Demographics—Aid in Marketing and Recruiting," *pr reporter's purview* 168 (January 14, 1985), p. 2; see also Ronald L. Vaught, "Demographic Data Banks: A New Management Resource," *Business Horizons*, 27 (November–December 1982), pp. 38–42.

[4]Statement issued in 1978 by the National Council on Public Polls, 1990 M Street, N.W., Washington, D.C. 20036: President Albert H. Cantril, Vice President Burns W. Roper, Secretary-Treasurer Frederick P. Currier and trustees Archibald M. Crossley, Mervin Field, George Gallup, Louis Harris and Richard M. Scammon.

[5]"Gathering Public Opinion Is a Business So Be Wary, Warns AAPOR President; A Survey of New Items to Be Wary Of," *pr reporter* (April 3, 1978), p. 1.

[6]*Advertising and Sales Promotion* (February 1972), p. 38.

[7]Raymond P. Ewing, "The Uses of Futurist Techniques in Issues Management," *Public Relations Quarterly*, 24(4) (Winter 1979), pp. 15–18.

[8]James E. Grunig, "An Assessment of Economic Education Programs for Journalism Students," paper presented to the Public Relations Division, Association for Education in Journalism annual convention, Houston, Texas, August 5, 1979.

[9]Grunig has since stopped using the referent criterion variable because he has found that the other variables yield the same predictions.

[10]"Computer Measuring System for Publicity Compares Exposure in Various Media," *pr reporter* (February 21, 1983), p. 2.

[11]Lloyd Kirban, "Showing What We Do Makes a Difference," *Public Relations Quarterly*, 28 (Fall 1983), pp. 22–27.

[12]Harry O'Neill, "A Good Company Image Can Mean Higher Sales," *ORC Issue Watch*, news release.

[13]Ibid.

[14]Cathy Trost, *Wall Street Journal*, "Labor Letter" (July 17, 1984), p. 2.

[15]American Heart Association, 1986 Food Festival Public Awareness Survey.

Selected readings, activities and assignments appropriate to this chapter can be found in the *Instructor's Guide*.

C H A P T E R   5

▼

RESEARCH PROCESSES, PROCEDURES AND TECHNIQUES

Good research and management's openness to communication, working in tandem, generate a favorable climate for public relations.

Peter Finn, Chairman, Research & Forecasts, Inc., New York

Any superimposing of preconceived ideas which forces patterns upon people's reports loses the richness, the uniqueness, the flavor or the authenticity of what they are trying to say about themselves. What is needed is information which transmits reliability, in people's own terms, what they are feeling.

Hadley Cantril, social psychologist

The kind of research an organization does and the way it uses its research findings tell something about the kind of public relations practice it employs. Research conducted at the University of Maryland attempted to correlate various research techniques (informal research, "mixed" informal and formal research, and scientific research) with the model of public relations practice most generally evidenced by the organization's public relations activities. Organizations where the one-way models of press agentry and of public information predominated typically had no scientific program research. However, the press agentry model was positively correlated with mixed informal and formal research. The two-way models of asymmetric and symmetric public relations practice also were correlated with mixed informal and formal research. However, only the asymmetric model of public relations was positively correlated with all three types—scientific, mixed and informal. The correlation between use of informal research and the asymmetrical model, however, was weak. This suggests that public relations practitioners who employ all three types of research are more likely to be participants in management decision making.[1]

▼ INFORMAL RESEARCH

Informal research is research conducted without generally agreed-to rules and procedures that would enable someone else to replicate the same study. The results of such research can be used only for description and not for prediction (see Example 5.1).

Among the categories of techniques frequently used in informal research are unobtrusive measures, journalistic research, opinion and communication audits and publicity analysis. Intuition and experience also play significant roles, and ethical considerations must be given full weight.

Unobtrusive Measures

Informal research makes extensive use of unobtrusive measures to gather information. Such measures permit researchers to study someone or something without interfering with or interrupting what's going on. Field experiments are often designed to incorporate these techniques. Unobtrusive measures give a researcher a general notion of what has occurred, but no real proof. If, for example, you use several different sources to issue color-coded tickets to an event, you can count how many people used each color of ticket, but you cannot tell where exactly they got them. A classic example of the flawed use of unobtrusive research measures comes from a survey conducted by a museum. Museum administrators assumed that a display's popularity could be judged by the amount of wear on the carpet in front of it. Unfortunately, they failed to take into account the fact that some displays lay along routes that the public often took to get to restrooms and water fountains.[2]

Journalistic Research

When it comes to gathering data, journalists and public relations researchers have a lot in common. For one thing, both rely heavily on unobtrusive measures. Philip Meyer, author of *Precision Journalism*, observed that "the role of the fire-engine researcher may come naturally and readily to journalists. The ground rules are no different from those on which we've always operated: find the facts, tell what they mean, and do it without wasting time."[3] Like other researchers, the journalist is trained to get information from two principal sources: secondary (public records, media files, libraries) and primary (mainly interviews). Practicing sound interviewing techniques is essential. The journalist learns to phrase questions neutrally, to avoid asking "leading" questions or putting words in the mouth of the respondent. A good journalist also learns how to organize questions in a logical sequence, with the easiest ones offered first. The rapport a journalist becomes skillful at developing with interview subjects contributes significantly to eliciting answers from people who are under no obligation to give them. A journalist also learns how to pin down an evasive respondent to get at something only suggested or implied by earlier answers.

The journalist also learns that listening and observing are extremely important to both the reporter and the public relations researcher. A few journalists can recall entire conversations, although most rely on audio and video recorders. These methods, as well as the records journalists use (called archives), and their observations constitute unobtrusive measures.[4]

The tools of reporting are the tools of any other form of primary research. Furthermore, the general researcher, like the journalist, must try to make sense out of all the information he or she has collected. Both must also be sensitive to trends, contradictions and conflicts and must be able to communicate their findings efficiently and effectively—usually under deadline pressure.

EXAMPLE 5.1 ▬▬▬▬

Informal Research: Pluses and Minuses of Various Techniques

Technique	Pluses	Minuses
Unobtrusive measures	1. No "intrusion" that affects publics 2. Physical evidence 3. Can be less costly, more convenient	1. Investigator error 2. Recorder error 3. Fixed data 4. Some physical evidence is not appropriate to psychological or sociological study
Audits	1. Make it possible to locate "problems in the making" 2. Can detect breaks in the communication chain 3. Help develop images that are held by different publics	1. Special sensitivity to "guinea pig" effect—awareness of measure 2. Sensitivity to confidentiality 3. People with less formal schooling may give socially acceptable responses 4. Response to visible cues from interviewer
Publicity analysis	1. Shows evidence of efforts 2. Suggests other opportunities	1. Same as unobtrusive measures 2. Incomplete documentation 3. Difficult to put in context 4. Not a measure of audience impact

Opinion and Communication Audits

Informal research also makes wide use of opinion audits and communication audits. The typical audit procedure for either type of audit is identical (see Example 5.2). Opinion audits may be social, economic or political. Some opinion audits use survey research, but many concentrate on observational data such as economic indicators, trends that note what is happening but do not explain why, and experiential reporting (people recounting individual experiences).

Communication audits are efforts to evaluate various publics' responses to an organization's communication efforts (see Example 5.3). Opinion audits and communication audits can both be done with publics inside or outside an organization.

Either can be used prior to a change (such as at the beginning of a campaign), to establish a benchmark or baseline against which subsequent results can be compared.

Publicity Analysis

Publicity analysis is another often-used tool of informal research. Clippings from print media and transcripts from broadcast publicity can be analyzed to determine the quantity and quality of coverage. Analysis is usually broken down by audience, medium, message and frequency. The prestige of the publication or broadcast source is often taken into consideration as well, to weight the value of the publicity.

EXAMPLE 5.2

Typical Audit Procedure

This audit procedure applies to either opinion audits or communication audits. It uses both formal and informal research techniques.

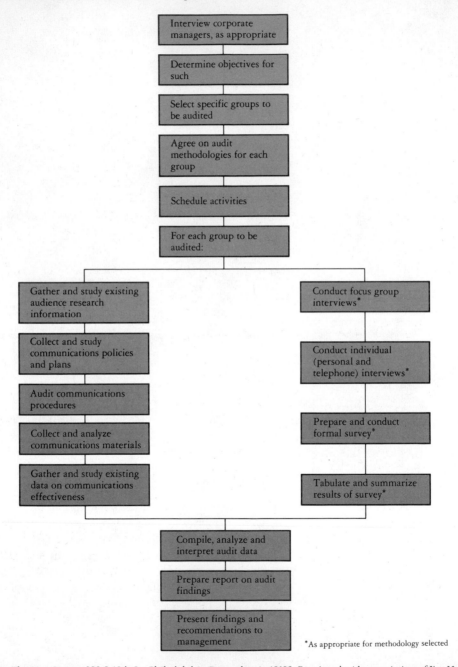

SOURCE: The Hay Group, 229 S 18th St., Philadelphia, Pennsylvania 19103. Reprinted with permission of Jim Haynes.

EXAMPLE 5.3

Communication Audit

A communication audit for an organization involves searching for differences in opinion about the organization among various publics, in order to improve the "fit" so that publics develop the same ideas about what the organization is, does and should be.

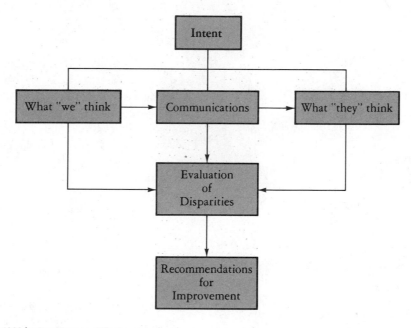

SOURCE: Copyright 1982 by Jim Haynes, APR. Reprinted with permission of Jim Haynes.

The Role of Intuition and Experience

Much informal research is conducted to confirm or deny the validity of a concept that is actually based on intuition or experience: someone simply feels that something is true or that something is happening. Research may not *prove* that the intuition or experience is valid or invalid, however; it usually only *indicates* that it is. But intuition and experience are very important, because they may lead to a larger and more formal study that does yield scientific evidence. While some people assert that formal research only proves what everyone already knows, the results of formal studies sometimes reveal that "common knowledge" is in error—indeed, little more than shared myth.

Responsibility

Following ethical standards in gathering, using and disseminating information is critical when you are conducting any type of research. It can be especially critical in informal research, however, because other researchers are less likely to try to check the results by replication. You must be certain that respondents understand how the study

▼ **Formal research consists of ten steps: state the problem, select a manageable portion to measure, define the measurement, search the literature, develop a hypothesis, design experiments, get the data, analyze them, interpret them and communicate the results.**

---

will be conducted, what its purpose is and how its results will be used. You should protect respondents by guaranteeing them anonymity.

▼ FORMAL RESEARCH

The two types of formal research—qualitative and quantitative—can be conducted either in the laboratory or clinic or in the field (see Example 5.4). While qualitative research describes, quantitative research measures (by counting). Both types follow the same general steps, and in both the researcher is responsible for representing the study honestly, maintaining confidentiality and interpreting data objectively. The responsibility is great because many people are suspicious of research.

Steps in Formal Research

The formal research process usually consists of the following steps:

1. State the problem.

2. Select a manageable (and measurable) portion of the problem.

3. Establish definitions to be used in the measurement.

4. Conduct a search in published literature for studies similar in subject or research approach.

5. Develop a hypothesis.[5]

6. Design experiments.[6] This step includes defining the universe or broad group you want to study and then choosing a sampling method and a sample.

7. Obtain the data.

8. Analyze the data.

9. Interpret the data to make inferences and generalizations.

10. Communicate the results.

A somewhat different formulation of these research steps is given in Example 5.5.

Stating the problem with precision certainly aids in the second step: deciding which part of the problem most requires study or which part lends itself to testing that would cast light into other dark corners. Because they ignore this step, many inexperienced practitioners design unwieldy research projects that attempt to examine too much at once.

A realistic researcher usually designs simple projects that keep the significance of the research in proper perspective. This involves, in each case, isolating a testable portion of the problem and knowing specifically what information is needed. You must take care to spell out what you want to know. Don't set a goal like "Find out how to establish effective communications with employees" when you really want to know whether they would like to have an employee publication. If that is the question, find out what kind of publication they want, how often it should be published and what subjects it should cover.

By establishing definitions, you also set parameters for your research. If you want to find out what people think about the Center for Battered Women, first decide what you mean by "people"—social workers? battered women? everyone in the city or county? only residents of the neighborhood in which it is located? The *purpose* of your study is the determining factor in establishing these definitions.

A literature search simply means seeing if someone has already done some work for you. Has someone conducted research that you can apply or use as a model? To answer this question, you must consult research journals in the social sciences, communications and business. Buried deep in one or more of these may be precisely the information that gives you a unique insight into your research project.

Qualitative Research

Many people are more comfortable with qualitative research than with quantitative, because they are suspicious of statistics and feel that numbers neglect the human side of the story. Undeniably statistics can be used to obscure, distort or exaggerate. Consider, for example, the debates about how many homeless people there are in the United States and how many people may go hungry here (not necessarily the same people). The percentages might be comparatively small, but whatever they are, the human suffering involved is indeed intolerable. Although much formal research could be classified as qualitative, three distinctive techniques are generally employed in qualitative work: historiography (including case studies and diaries), in-depth interviews and focus groups.

Historiography, Case Studies, Diaries   People who write biographies or historical narratives about actual happenings must first collect facts from informed sources—both secondary sources (books, articles, journals and so on) and primary sources (people who were involved in some way). The researchers then organize these facts to provide the necessary background for understanding the problem or issue they are examining. When PR people produce background papers or position papers, they rely on this methodology and reporting technique—called historiography—which reconstructs the past in a systematic and orderly manner. It involves recording, analyzing, coordinating and explaining past events.

Case studies use all available factual data to examine issues, events and organizations systematically. Diaries are used in field studies and consist of detailed reports of personal experiences and actions.

▼ **Qualitative measures include historiography, case studies and diaries; in-depth interviews; and focus groups.**

In-depth Interviews   As is the case with informal audits, most in-depth interviews are conducted with a specifically chosen audience. But in these formal interviews, the questions are pretested and are usually asked of all respondents. The questions are designed to produce open-ended responses that the researcher must interpret. The respondents selected are encouraged to talk freely and fully. This technique is used extensively in motivational research—the study of the emotional or subconscious reasons that lie behind decision making. However, motivational research requires highly trained interviewers and skilled analysis.

Open-ended questions are often used with in-depth interviewing because they give the interviewer an opportunity to follow up equivocal answers with more probing questions. For example, while trying to ferret out employer bias toward hiring members of minority groups, some in-depth interviewers asked general questions at first and then zoomed in with questions like this: "If you had two applicants absolutely equal in terms of educational background and experience, and one was a woman or a member of a minority race, or both, which would you hire?" The employers' answer could then be interpreted directly, based on a particular response.

Some researchers also feel that open-ended questions reduce error in reply since the interviewee can respond in his or her own words, rather than having to fit his or her answer into a category set up by the researcher. Errors are often made in evaluating such questions, however, since interviewers may interpret responses in light of their own opinions. Consequently, most researchers prefer that the answers be coded in the office rather than in the field by the interviewer. This reduces the impact of the interviewer's bias.

EXAMPLE 5.4

Formal Research: Pluses and Minuses of Various Techniques

QUALITATIVE

Technique	Pluses	Minuses
Historiography, case studies, diaries	1. Give insight into situations	1. Difficult to generalize from
	2. Suggest further research to examine the "whys" that it indicates	2. Often lack rigor of scientific method
	3. Provide detail that can put other research into perspective	3. Time-consuming and require boiling down a lot of data that are sometimes selectively presented
In-depth interviews	1. Allow interviewers to follow up on new lines of questioning	1. Difficult to transcribe and code for content analysis
	2. Permit respondent to describe in detail so that more information is available	2. Interviewer sometimes "leads the witness," or otherwise influences response
	3. Permit questions to be broader, more comprehensive	3. Responses often include basically meaningless information
Focus groups	1. Some are quick and less expensive than other research methods	1. Often used as conclusive evidence when they are merely tools to be used with other research
	2. Flexible in design and format	2. Sometimes not handled well by moderator, so that not all participants express opinions
	3. Elicit more in-depth information and often point out "whys" of behavior, as well as showing intensity of attitudes held	3. Sometimes not representative of population

QUALITATIVE

Technique	Pluses	Minuses
Panels	1. Same as focus groups 2. May be chosen to represent a population	1. Same as focus groups 2. Same people used over time "learn" some of the reasons for difficulties and cease to be representative

QUANTITATIVE

Technique	Pluses	Minuses
Content analysis	1. Shows what appeared, how often, where and in what context 2. Allows comparison with other data, especially about publics 3. Useful in tracking trends and in monitoring change	1. Expensive and time-consuming 2. Provides no information about impact of messages and audiences 3. Some information may not be in the media
Survey research	1. Flexible 2. Varied—administered by mail, telephone, computer, personal or group interview 3. Capitalizes on enjoyment of expressing opinion	1. Respondents may not tell the truth, because they don't remember accurately or because they want to appear different from their behavior 2. Inflexibility of instrument doesn't allow for in-depth expression and intensity of true feelings 3. Wrong questions may be asked of wrong people

EXAMPLE 5.5

Research Steps

This diagram for research planning comes from the most used reference in the field, *The Practice of Social Research* by Earl Babbie, 1992 edition, figure 4.1.

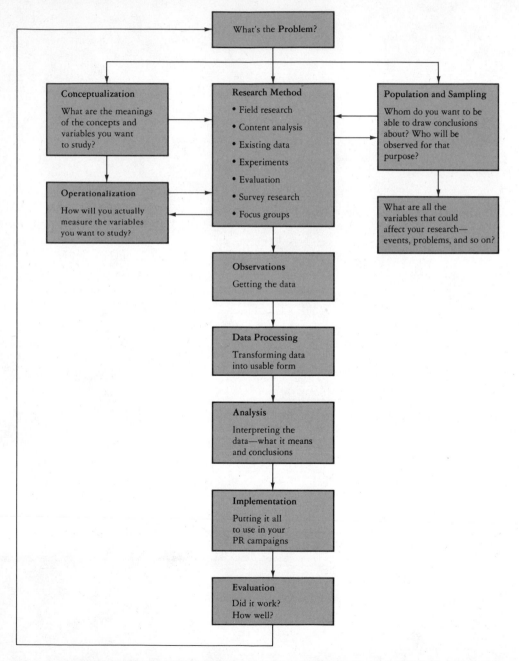

Adapted with permission from Earl Babbie, *The Practice of Social Research*, 6th ed. © 1992 by Wadsworth, Inc.

Focus Groups   In the focus group technique, the interviewees chosen generally represent one specific public, because homogeneous groups usually converse more freely. However, the focus groups may include representatives from each of a number of different publics. In a university setting, such publics might include faculty, staff, administrators, students, alumni and perhaps parents, regents or trustees.

The key to the session's success is the moderator, who must be a skillful interviewer, adept at keeping the conversation moving and tactful when acting as referee or devil's advocate. Research groups often videotape these sessions, too, and they often use a live monitor so that viewers—the researchers or the client—can slip notes to the moderator during breaks in the session and get additional questions on the agenda. The focus interview is often used as a prelude to developing a questionnaire.

Some misuse of this technique appears when reported results are used to make judgments without benefit of more specific research. Focus groups should only be used as a *preliminary or guidance* technique.

Focus groups are not the same as panels, although the two research techniques share some of the same advantages and disadvantages. Panels (groups of people queried on several occasions), are sometimes used for discussions in issue development, but they are not generally considered appropriate for formal research. Focus groups are.

Five steps are followed in focus group research, some of which are identical to the steps involved in overall research methodology.[7]

1. Define the problem to be examined.

2. Choose the part of the problem that will be looked at by the participants.

3. Decide how many focus groups will be needed, and choose the participants. (Because group-selection methods are always likely to create non-representative groups, more than one group will be necessary in almost every situation.)

4. Work out all the details of the session, including notification of the participants, selection of the moderator, physical arrangement of the interview area and compensation of the participants.

5. Prepare all materials that the group will need, including a list of basic questions that will serve as a guide for the moderator.

Quantitative Research

The difference between qualitative research (which is based primarily on description) and quantitative (which is based primarily on measurement) is that quantitative research offers a higher degree of predictability. It is easier to generalize from results of this research in order to make predictions about the larger population from which the research participants were drawn. Quantitative measures include content analysis and survey research, which uses descriptive and inferential statistics.

Content Analysis   Transcripts of panel discussions or interactions, in-depth interviews and focus group interviews are often subjected to content analysis, as are broadcast media transcripts and newspaper and magazine clippings. Content analysis allows for the systematic coding and classifying of written material that relates to the public relations practitioner's organization or client. Content analysis tells what has been published or broadcast and the context in which it was presented. This provides helpful clues to the kinds of information various publics are being exposed to (although not necessarily what they consume and believe).

As a data-gathering technique, content analysis can also be used to assess what is being said about the goals set by the organization and about its specialized areas of interest, such as proposed legislation. The main difficulty with the technique is setting up a model that will give an unbiased analysis.

The classic definition of content analysis was provided by Bernard Berelson, who called it a research technique for the "objective, systematic, and quantitative description of the manifest content of communication."[8] The content analysis research procedure developed by H. D. Lasswell is one of the earliest quantitative measures of communication and follows Berelson's definition. It is *objective* because categories used in the analysis are both precise and normative, with no evaluative terms (good–bad) used. It is *systematic* because selection is by a formal, unbiased system that does not allow for subjective collection of data. It is *quantitative* because the results are usually expressed in some numerical way—in percentages, ratios, frequency distributions, correlation coefficients or the like. It is *manifest* because it is a direct measure, in which no effort is made to figure out the intent of the person using the words; only the fact that the words were used is registered. Some content analysis research designs are more complicated, because they apply symbol or phrase coding to allow for mention of the "context" of the words used.

Content analysis uses variables related to the medium: typography, makeup and layout for print; and camera angles, editing, shot selection, pace and scene locations for broadcast. PR content analysis usually is concerned with the time or space given to an organization and its spokespersons. In broadcasting, the concern is with whether the spokesperson does the talking, the announcer describes the situation or the two work in combination.

Hypotheses can be tested with content analysis and comparisons can be made with normal or real situations by designing a representation of the "normal" or "real world." Sometimes the comparison shows how a group is represented, in contrast to their real role in society. An example would start with a television drama that depicts a two-parent family, both working, with two children. This would be compared to the current reality, which is often a family headed by a single parent who works.

The limits of content analysis are reached in the area of effects; although you can show that something happens, you cannot identify the happening's impact. In addition, the investigation is sometimes limited by a lack of evidence. A final limit to the use of the technique involves the amount of time and tedious effort it demands, although computer software does make the manipulation of data significantly easier.[9]

Some research steps in content analysis are different from those in the basic research process. Once you format the research questions, construct a hypothesis, identify the population and select a sample, you must go on to define a unit of analysis, construct the categories to be analyzed and write descriptions of the categories. After you establish a way to choose material for the various categories uniformly, you must train coders and make sure that they can categorize the items the same way. You can test that ability by applying a coder reliability formula that will check to see whether the definitions are consistently applied. After the collected data are categorized, you analyze them, draw conclusions, and then try to develop some statements indicating a situation or circumstance that supports your hypothesis.

Survey Research   Survey research attempts to measure the practices and preferences of a specified public by tabulating responses to a standardized series of questions. Such research has become an essential basis for assessing a public's actions and opinions. Two types of statistics are used in survey research: descriptive and inferential. Descriptive statistics consists of talking about data in manageable ways. Inferential statistics lets you draw conclusions about a population, based on what you found in the sample.

Basics of Numerical Research

A PR practitioner must master at least the basics of quantitative or numerical research. These include such subjects as sampling, probability and posing research questions.

Sampling   Since a public normally contains a large number of people, it's usually possible to question only a sample of it to determine what the public as a whole thinks. The sample need not be large. Large samples cost too much, and they really do not improve the investigation's accuracy much, once a certain size is reached. With very small sample sizes, predictability increases rather dramatically at first; but once the sample reaches a certain size, error becomes a factor. (Sample error is the degree of discrepancy between the representativeness of the sample and the larger population.) A sample of 1,000 is not likely to be much better than a sample of 500, although a sample of 100 is considerably more reliable than one of 50. That explains why, in a country of more than 211 million, reliable national estimates are made based on samples of only 1,500 to 3,000 people. Researchers do this work within a margin of allowable error. The size of the sample depends on how much error can be tolerated in the results—that is, how close a call you need to make.

Probability   Sampling is based on probability. The researcher is gambling on how probable it is that a sample accurately represents a population. But the gamble is not wild. The people selected for a sample can be chosen *randomly*, and a random sample is usually free of bias or predictability with regard to such things as the income of those chosen. The use of a mechanical method for random selection eliminates any bias that the researcher might have or any peculiar homogeneity that might exist within a group or segment of a group selected for study. (*Bias* is the tendency of an estimate to deviate from the true value, for reasons such as being based on nonrandom sampling.) In a random sample, each element of a population has an equal chance of being selected for study. For exam-

ple, students in a mass communications class were used as subjects for a survey on media use. To select a random sample from the class, the researcher gave every *other* student seated in the classroom a survey to complete. Since seating was a matter of the students' choice, and not simply assigned, every student had an equal chance of being selected for the sample. This is random selection.

But while this group of students constitutes a random sample of the population of students in the room, it does not constitute a sample of people living in that area or of students attending that college or even of students taking classes in mass communications at that college. The population from which the sample was drawn was one particular classroom of students, and that remains the population to which information discovered in the sample survey can legitimately be extrapolated.

In dealing with any large number of events that occur by chance, we can make predictions (or educated guesses) based on the relative frequency of occurrence of certain events among all events that are observed. This involves applying rules of probability. To return to the example of the student survey, because every other student in the classroom was chosen, half of the students (one out of every two) completed the questionnaire. Thus, each student had a 1:2 (or .5) chance of being selected, and this is the probability that any given student would be chosen.

Two types of errors can occur in research that uses probability sampling: sampling errors and nonsampling errors. Sampling errors are the chance difference of an observed phenomenon from the corresponding population constant for which it is a measure. They can occur if a sample is too small for the audience or population being sampled or if the selection is not random enough. *Nonsampling errors* are simply mistakes made by the research team in gathering, recording or calculating data. Nonsampling errors are reduced when fewer data have to be recorded and calculated— another argument for using a small sample size.

As researcher W. Edward Deming observes, a survey's usefulness and reliability "may actually be enhanced by cutting down on the size of sample and using the money so saved to reduce the non-sampling errors,"[10] such as by tracing wrong and missing information. (*Reliability* is the extent to which a test always yields the same results. *Validity* is how well the evidence explains what is occurring—whether the empirical measures are really measuring the desired situation or concept.) These savings, he points out, might free up more time and money for constructing the questionnaire, hiring better interviewers, providing better training and supervision in the field and making more call backs on people not previously at home.

Not all samples are chosen randomly. In fact, there are three major types of nonprobability or nonrandom sampling: accidental, purposive and quota. A reporter who stands outside the campus cafeteria and asks people leaving what they think of the food is getting an *accidental* sample; it is accidental because you never know who will come out. (Suppose you catch all the members of the football team, and they all liked the ground round?) A *purposive* sample is by a reporter who interviews teachers and students in the food and nutrition department about the quality of food in the college cafeteria. (They have been chosen because of their particular expertise or background, and they can be expected to have different ideas about food from their counterparts in, say, engineering.) A *quota* sample is used by a reporter who tries to match the school's population in miniature: the proper proportion of freshmen, transfer students, sophomores, juniors, seniors, staff, faculty. The sample would be improved if the reporter already knew what percentage of these different groups ate regularly in the cafeteria. Each group could then be represented in the sample in the same proportion as its presence in the entire population of students who ate in the cafeteria.

Stratified sampling is similar to quota sampling in that both re-create the population in microcosm and both have population representation. However, the selection process is different. In *stratified sample measurement*, selection is *random* but the overall population has been divided into categories or strata. Selection is therefore a matter of probability. In quota sampling, the interviewer selects participants nonrandomly.

Posing Research Questions   Most quantitative research attempts to answer "what if" or "I wonder if" questions. Research questions are often asked about matters that haven't been looked into often or in depth. Such *exploratory* research looks for indications, not causes. It attempts to get preliminary data so that research questions can be refined for future study and so that hypotheses can be proposed. You might wonder, for example, what conditions (if any) might change the results of your exploratory research, or how other elements of the research questions are related. In doing this, you are attempting to make a prediction (hypothesis) stating your assumption of what is or could be. The reverse of that assumption—what is not or could not be—is called a null hypothesis.

Prediction comes after preliminary or exploratory research and before hypothesis testing. At the exploratory stage, you are saying, "I wonder." At the prediction stage, you are saying, "I think." When you start to test an idea or a hypothesis in quantitative research, your particular research project will dictate whether you should use parametric or nonparametric statistics. You will use parametric statistics for interval and ratio data—data about populations, means and variances. You will use nonparametric statistics for nominal and ordinal data.

Hypothesis testing is always done within some theoretical framework. Most public relations people use one of the communication or persuasion theories. There are five commonly accepted bases for communication theories and two general bases for persuasion theories (see Chapter 7).

The five-step procedure for testing a hypothesis is quite simple:

1. State your hypothesis—what you think is true of the population or universe (generally a PR public) in general. Make sure that the variable you want to measure in your population can be quantified or counted.

2. State the opposite of your hypothesis, the null hypothesis. This is simply a statement of what would be the case if your hypothesis were not true.

3. Determine the probability that you would see the same differences in the population or universe that you see in your sample, if the opposite of what you believe turned out to be true. This is the probability of the null hypothesis being true.

4. If that probability is slight—less than .05—then you reject the null hypothesis, with 95 percent confidence that what you thought was true is true.

5. If that probability is large, you should not reject the null hypothesis, since you still can't be sure whether your original hypothesis is true or not.

Hypothesis testing uses familiar measures: descriptive and inferential statistics. You have been using statistics for a long time. You ask about *means* for test scores, so you know how you ranked in the class. Your interest in statistics began a while ago and was probably developed so that you could respond to parental questions like, "You made a C?" "Yes, but it was a high C, a 78, and the class average was barely 70, 69.5."

▼ AUDIENCE INFORMATION

Most sampling relies on a small unit of the audience that the researcher uses to represent the larger group. The small unit is chosen with the demographics of the larger audience in mind. Some of the research most valuable to people interested in persuasion goes beyond telling who an audience is to telling who the audience thinks it is—or better still, who it wants to be. Information about *who* makes up an audience—age, sex, level of education, geographic location, occupation and such—is

▼ **Public relations research describes populations in terms of who people are (*demographics*) and what people think (*psychographics*).**

called the *demographics*[11] of that audience. But demographics alone isn't enough. A group of individuals, even a large one, may fall into one category in which all demographic data match, and yet they may not think at all alike. A key to how people are likely to respond often lies in their value systems. The study of what goes on inside an audience's head is termed audience *psychographics*[12]

A demographer is a social scientist who keeps an ongoing record of the size and characteristics of human populations and how they change—their births, deaths, longevity, migrations and so on. Demographic statistics are important because of the dollars-and-cents consequences of these changes. Demographic information is important to planners trying to develop educational systems to meet future needs, to utilities managers furnishing equipment and services to changing populations and to many others.

Psychographics is a specialty of psychologists employed by polling and attitudinal research firms to help them figure out what is going on in the minds of people who are members of a particular demographic group. Advertisers have been interested in psychographics for a long time because of the science's relevance to a marketing strategy called "positioning."[13] For example, many commercial products are chemically identical; how they are presented makes all the difference.

The most familiar processes for data gathering by samples are cross-section surveys and survey panels. The most used instrument is the questionnaire, which has many formats. The decision about which one to use depends on which one offers the best solution to the problem at hand.

▼ **The most familiar processes for data gathering by samples are cross-section surveys and survey panels, and the most commonly used instrument is the questionnaire.**

Cross-section Surveys

Three types of samples are widely used in cross-section surveys: probability samples, quota samples, and area samples.

In a *probability sample*, people are chosen at random—ordinarily by using a random number table or a mechanical formula such as every *n*th name on a list, a method called "systematic sampling" or "interval sampling."

In a *quota sample*, a population is analyzed by its known characteristics, such as age, sex, residence, occupation and income level. A sample selection is made by choosing a quota of people with desired characteristics in the same proportion as these characteristics exist in the whole population.

In an *area sample*, geographical areas, such as cities or units of cities, are used; an area sample can be designed by using city directories as sources for housing units. Using a *cluster plan* in an area sample may reduce the time and money spent on travel, although it also somewhat reduces the randomness. (In a cluster plan areas are selected, and sample small block clusters from each area are drawn. A random sample may then be drawn from each cluster.)

Survey Panels

Businesses and institutions often use survey panels, such as consumer panels, in their research. One unusual consumer panel employed by a toy company consists of panelists five years old and under. Once a panel is selected, the members are interviewed several times over a certain period of time. The toy manufacturers get around verbal communication problems by merely watching their consumer panel. Some research firms videotape panel sessions so that the client can see the results without inhibiting panelists by being there. (Using one-way glass in the viewing area doesn't fool many panelists.) Videotaping aids in analyzing the sessions too, because body language as well as words may be evaluated.

Survey panelists are usually selected on a cross-sectional basis and generally by quota, which is effective for controlled experiments. Seldom, if ever, are panelists chosen randomly. One disadvantage with panels is that, over time, they tend to become less representative. For example, newspaper editors have found that citizens on press councils—small panels of readers from the community—tend to become less critical as they learn more about the problems of getting out a daily paper.

Not all survey panels actually meet. Some may participate through teleconferencing. Some may respond only to mailed inquiries of various types, including diaries and questionnaires. Sometimes a panel represents people with vested interests, presumably with the inducement of improved goods or services. But members of some panels are rewarded with gifts.

Questionnaires

The most familiar survey data-gathering device is the questionnaire. A questionnaire is often administered in face-to-face personal interviews, with the interviewer asking the questions and noting the responses on a form. However, it may also be administered over the telephone or by direct mail, or it may be printed either in a mass medium (like a newspaper) or in a specialized one (like an organization's own newsletter).

The telephone survey is more economical than the personal contact survey, but fewer questions can be included, because the interview may be interfering with the interviewee's activities. Asking too many questions shortens responses and upsets respondents' tempers. Moreover, only homes with listed telephones can be reached, and up to 30 percent of the telephones in any area may have unlisted numbers. Thus a telephone survey sample is less likely to represent the entire market accurately. One solution to this problem is to obtain from the telephone company a list of local exchanges (the first three numbers in a seven-digit telephone number) and the number of telephones served by each. A computer can then be programmed to draw four-digit numbers at random to add to the prefix. This method is reliable enough to be used by national research companies.

Computers are being used more widely today to administer questionnaires electronically. They are used for polling, in market research to determine product demand, and even in personnel interviews. Techniques for using computers vary. In some cases, a person may be seated in front of a screen and asked to type simple responses or to punch numbers on a telephone in answer to questions asked by a mechanical voice. Some researchers say that people hang up more often when they are reached by a computer; however, others say that many people prefer to give private information to a computer, because the machine is nonjudgmental.

Often questionnaires are sent by direct mail. When this is done, the researcher can increase the proportion of responses by enclosing a self-addressed, postage-paid envelope. Such questionnaires can be longer than those used in telephone or personal interviews, but a long, formidable-looking questionnaire will draw few responses.

One important element in the rate of return is the respondent's interest in the subject. For general questionnaires sent to a large sample, you can expect a 5 to 20 percent return. But when the rate of returns is this small, the respondents usually do not represent the population well. In contrast, a 30 to 80 percent response to a carefully designed questionnaire is likely if respondents have a vested interest or some special knowledge of the subject. Members of a professional organization, for example, are more inclined to answer a long, detailed questionnaire that asks about their professional interests. Women in Communications, Inc., reported a 75 percent return on a salary questionnaire sent to all its members without a return envelope. Texas

▼ **Developing an effective questionnaire involves carefully studying how it should be administered (by mail, telephone, or some other means) and who the respondents should be.**

Instruments Corporation tried a special gimmick. It got almost a 60 percent response from shareholders to a questionnaire printed on the back of dividend checks.[14]

When people don't have a vested interest, money is the best way to elicit a response. The *Wall Street Journal* quoted an official of a New York market-research firm, Erdos & Morgan, as saying that sending a dollar bill with the questionnaire form usually guarantees at least a 50-percent response.[15] Quarters still work for shorter queries, but Montgomery Ward sends $5 with its ten-page questionnaires. *Newsweek* finds that affluent readers respond better if the publication offers to give a charitable contribution in their name than if it offers them a gift.[16]

In a study collating findings from surveys in the social sciences since 1935, Arnold S. Linsky concluded that researchers may need to change their overall strategy to ensure a high return on mail questionnaires. He found the following devices (listed in descending order of effectiveness) worked best:

1. Send one or more followups, such as postcards or additional letters, as reminders. More intensive followups, such as phone calls or letters sent by special delivery or registered mail, work best.

2. Contact the respondent in some way before the questionnaire is sent. Again, the most effective method of doing this is by phone.

3. Send mail by some type of special handling, such as special delivery, and use a hand-stamped return envelope rather than a postage permit envelope.

4. Send a reward with the mailing. Promises to send something on receipt of the questionnaire are less effective.

5. Make sure that the sponsor of the survey and the name of the person signing the cover letter are both impressive to the audience you are trying to reach.

Linsky's study did not show that guaranteeing the anonymity of respondents constituted a decided asset. Personalizing the questionnaires seems to be somewhat effective but it does confound the anonymity issue, so the situation and the issues might be the deciding points to consider here. The length of the questionnaire was only inconsistently related to the level of returns, so again, a very interested audience (or perhaps a highly rewarded one) may tolerate a longer questionnaire. Appeals for cooperation based on the significance of the study, the personal appreciation the researcher would feel or any other altruistic motivation were ineffective. But evidence is mixed, Linsky reported, on the efficacy of explaining the role and importance of the respondent in the survey.[17]

Alan Andreasen, in *Public Opinion Quarterly*, offered the following advice on conducting questionnaire research:

> Use a cheap method for the first wave, then bear down with a high-return method for the second. This system gives you the advantage of being able to compare first-time respondents with those who had to be nudged and thus estimate the substantive biases, if any, of reluctant respondents.[18]

Increases in postage rates have forced researchers to examine content and systems very carefully to stay within budgets. Some research agencies use Western Union Mailgrams or other electronic mail systems, such as Datapost (a unit of TDX Systems, Inc.), for both speed and drama. The implied urgency of the communication system commands attention. Computer systems offer even more direct access and allow for immediate response. As offices become electronically equipped and more individuals have home computers, research designs for electronically administered surveys can be used.

How to Prepare a Questionnaire The best way to encourage a good response in a survey is to write a good questionnaire. The questionnaire should be clear, simple and interesting (see Example 5.6). You must decide whether the questions should require specific answers or be open-ended and elicit free response. (The latter type is much more difficult to tabulate and almost demands content analysis.)

Some formats dictate the type of questions. In all cases, though, you must try to elicit all pertinent information easily, quickly and in analyzable form. It takes skill to break a general question down into its logical parts. Questions should be definite and separate, not overlapping, and they should invite answers. Be careful of phrasing especially because personal queries often meet with some resentment.

Because the source of a questionnaire may bias the answer, it is sometimes important to hire an outside agency. An interviewer conducting a door-to-door survey for an aluminum foil company received a long list of the many ways one woman used aluminum foil in her kitchen, but when the interviewer talked to the woman's next-door neighbor, who was also her daughter, he was told, "Don't bother going over there. My mother lives there and she doesn't cook a thing. She eats every meal with us." Obviously, the mother just had not wanted to disappoint the interviewer.

It is important to group questions in a logical sequence so that the arrangement encourages response. If a respondent is to fill out a questionnaire unaided, the instructions must explain clearly whether responses are to be checked, underlined or crossed out (see Example 5.7). Many survey results have been skewed because respondents put x's by choices they thought they were deleting. Every question must be accounted for, but there should also be an allowance for "Other," "Does not know," "Does not wish to answer" or "Omitted."

One way to ensure developing a good questionnaire is to pretest it by asking a few people to complete it. Pretesting may tell you which questions are ambiguous or cause resentment. For example, one health-related questionnaire had to be reworked four times when pretests showed that the eight- to twelve-year-olds in the study misinterpreted the questions.[19] Examples 5.8 and 5.9 show an advertisement created by the American Heart Association and a survey questionnaire conducted by National Family Opinion, Inc., to pretest this ad's impact and effectiveness before running it.

Some questionnaires that require a specific response provide no gauge for measuring the *intensity* of the response. However, researchers can use semantic differential scales or summated ratings to get at intensity.

Semantic Differential Scales   A semantic differential questionnaire accounts for intensity by measuring variations in the connotative meanings of objects and words.[20] In this procedure, the respondent rates the object (person or concept) being judged within a framework of two adjectival opposites with seven steps between them. In rating a person, for instance, adjectival opposites might be active–passive or strong–weak. A political pollster may use a semantic differential scale in asking respondents to select qualities, positive or negative, they attribute to persons or issues.

The application of semantic differential scales to marketing was advanced by William Mindak, who views it as a useful tool in rating images of brands, products and companies.[21] As many as nineteen rating scales will reduce to five factors, and a varimax factor analysis can be used for measurement.[22] Weighting of responses is based on the value of the attribute (such as colorful–colorless, measured as positive or negative) to the factor (appearance).

Complex questionnaires and tests have been designed, using the semantic differential technique, to measure changes in attitudes, personality, knowledge and behavior against a background of such variables as education, income, religion, social status, gender, occupation and race. One writer has listed the following measurement dimensions and examples of semantic differential adjectives for each:

▼ *General evaluative dimension:* pleasant–unpleasant, valuable–worthless, important–unimportant, interesting–boring

▼ **Questionnaires can use semantic differential scales or summated ratings to measure the intensity of responses.**

▼ *Ethical dimension:* fair–unfair, truthful–untruthful, accurate–inaccurate, biased–unbiased, responsible–irresponsible

▼ *Stylistic dimension:* exciting–dull, fresh–stale, easy–difficult, neat–messy, colorful–colorless

▼ *Potency dimension:* bold–timid, powerful–weak, loud–soft

▼ *Evaluative dimension:* accurate–inaccurate, good–bad, responsible–irresponsible, wise–foolish, acceptable–unacceptable

▼ *Excitement dimension:* colorful–colorless, interesting–uninteresting, exciting–unexciting, hot–cold

▼ *Activity dimension:* active–passive, agitated–calm, bold–timid[23]

Summated Ratings   Summated ratings are similar to semantic differential scales. Here, however, the responses to a series of statements are selected from among the options, "strongly approve, approve, undecided, disapprove or strongly disapprove." A weight of from 1 to 5 is assigned to each option, so that the high score consistently represents one of the two extremes—for example, 5 for "strongly approve" and 1 for "strongly disapprove." After testing, the weights are totaled and each individual is given a single numerical score. Those who score high and those who score low are selected for further study. Then each question on the questionnaire is evaluated by determining whether the high scorers respond to the particular item with a higher score than do those who are low scorers. Internal consistency in the questions ensure that no correlation of answers appears between these extreme groups. If correlation is found on some questions, these are deleted from the scoring, so that only the items reflecting consistent divergence of opinion are used as a scale.

EXAMPLE 5.6 ▬▬▬▬▬

Tips for Framing Questions

These tips are the suggestions of John R. Wirtz of Dix & Eaton, corporate communication consultants in Cleveland, Ohio.

There are ... some general questions you should always ask yourself when drafting a survey. Some of these questions, and examples of those that may not be obvious to most people include:

1. Are the words understandable?

2. Do they contain abbreviations or unconventional phrases/jargon?

3. Are the questions technically accurate?

4. Are there appropriate time references?

5. Are they too vague?

6. Are they biased? Bias can occur at least four ways:

▼ *Bias from behavioral expectation*

Question: More people have attended pro football games than any other sport. Have you ever seen a pro football game?

1. Yes

2. No

Revision: Have you ever attended a pro football game?

1. Yes

2. No

▼ *Bias from leading information*

Question: If the election were being held today, who would you vote for: Jimmy Carter, the incumbent; Ronald Reagan, the Republican challenger; or John Anderson, the independent?

Revision: If the presidential election were being held today, who would you vote for: Jimmy Carter, Ronald Reagan or John Anderson?

▼ *Bias due to unequal comparison*

Question: Who do you feel is most responsible for the high oil prices?

1. Service station owners

2. People drilling for oil

3. Executives of the oil companies

Revision: Who do you feel is most responsible for the high oil prices?

1. Service station owners who pump it

2. Refiners who process it

3. Businessmen who operate the oil companies

▼ *Bias due to unbalanced categories*

Question: Currently our country spends about $40 billion a year on social services. Do you feel this amount should be:

1. Increased

2. Stay the same

3. Decreased a little

4. Decreased somewhat

5. Decreased a great deal

Revision: Currently our country spends about $40 billion a year on social services. Do you feel this amount should be:

1. Increased significantly

2. Increased a little

3. Stay the same

4. Decreased a little

5. Decreased significantly

7. Are questions offensive? If so, there are at least three ways to overcome offensive questions:

▼ *Using a series*

Question: Have you ever had an abortion?

Revision: As you know, there is a great deal of controversy about abortion in this community. Some folks think it's a serious problem, others do not. Do you consider abortion to be a serious, moderate, slight or no problem at all in your community?

1. Serious
2. Moderate
3. Slight
4. Not at all

During the past few years do you think the number of abortions has increased, stayed the same, or decreased in the community?

1. Increased
2. Stayed about the same
3. Decreased

Please try to recall the time when you were a teenager. Do you recall personally knowing anyone who had an abortion?

1. No
2. Yes

How about yourself? Did you ever consider having an abortion?

1. No
2. Yes

If yes, did you actually have one?

1. No
2. Yes

▼ *Using general categories to overcome offensive questions*

Question: How much money did you earn in 1979? _____ dollars

Revision: Which category below best describes your income during 1979?

1. Less than $7,000
2. $7,000 to $9,999
3. $10,000 to $14,999

4. $15,000 to $24,999
5. $25,000 or more

▼ *Using narrative material to overcome offensive questions*

Question: "Big business is the root of society's problems." Do you:

1. Agree
2. Disagree

Revision: Next, let's talk about your feelings about the relationship between big business and society. Here are various popular opinions, both negative and positive. With each statement, check whether you are in agreement or disagreement.

"Big business is the foundation of our society's problems."

1. Agree
2. Disagree

"Big business is the root of society's problems."

1. Agree
2. Disagree

(Other statements could follow.)

▼ *Do they require too much effort to answer?*

Question: What percent of your time each month is spent on meetings? _____

Revision: How many hours do you spend a month in meetings? _____

How many hours do you spend on the job each month? _____

SOURCE: From "The Communication Audit—Your Road Map to Success." *Journal of Organizational Communication* 10(2) (February 1981), p. 16. Reprinted with permission of John R. Wirtz.

EXAMPLE 5.7

Sample Opinion Survey

The first portion of this survey is designed to elicit responses to nostalgia questions.
The bottom half is attitudinal and value-oriented.

GOOD OLD DAYS

THE "GOOD OLD DAYS", WHILE SUBJECT TO SOME DEGREE OF "SELECTIVE MEMORY", ARE FILLED WITH FOND THOUGHTS OF EVENTFUL TIMES IN OUR LIVES WHEN WE WERE GROWING UP AND/OR ENGAGED IN ACTIVITIES THAT WERE VERY IMPORTANT TO US. MANY TIMES, THE AUTOMOBILE PLAYS A SIGNIFICANT PART IN THOSE MEMORIES.

FIRST

PLEASE TAKE A MENTAL TRIP DOWN "MEMORY LANE" THROUGH SOME OF THE PERIODS AND POSSIBLE MILESTONES IN YOUR LIFE THAT WE'VE SELECTED BELOW, AND TELL US THOSE SITUATIONS IN WHICH A PARTICULAR CAR STANDS OUT IN YOUR MIND.

CHECK (✓) THOSE PERIODS/EVENTS WHICH BRING TO MIND A SPECIFIC CAR YOU OWNED OR PARTICULARLY LIKED AT THAT TIME.

1. WHEN YOU WERE "JUST A KID", AND THINKING ABOUT BEING ABLE TO DRIVE
2. WHEN YOU GOT YOUR DRIVER'S LICENSE AND HAD ACCESS TO A CAR AT LEAST PART OF THE TIME
3. WHEN YOU FIRST ACQUIRED A CAR TO CALL YOUR OWN
4. WHEN YOU WENT OUT ON YOUR FIRST DATE IN A CAR
5. WHEN YOU BOUGHT YOUR FIRST NEW CAR
6. WHEN YOU GRADUATED AND WENT TO WORK FULL TIME (if applicable)

7. WHEN YOU WERE ENGAGED TO BE MARRIED
8. WHEN YOU RETURNED HOME FROM MILITARY SERVICE (if applicable)
9. WHEN YOU STARTED "DOING WELL" IN YOUR JOB OR PROFESSION (if applicable)
10. WHEN YOU REACHED THAT POINT WHEN YOUR LIFE STYLE COULD ACCOMMODATE THE KIND OF CAR YOU REALLY WANTED

ANY OTHERS YOU CAN THINK OF? _____

SECOND

NOW, PLEASE SELECT 4 OF THE MOST SIGNIFICANT PERIODS/EVENTS FROM THE LIST ABOVE IN TERMS OF YOUR MEMORIES OF AUTOMOBILES .... AND TELL US MORE ABOUT THEM.

MOST SIGNIFICANT 4 OR 5 PERIODS/EVENTS (Write in ID Number From the List Above)	OUTSTANDING CAR IN YOUR MIND (Write in Make and Car Line)	DID YOU ... HAVE ACCESS			WAS IT A ...	
		OWN IT	TO USE IT (CHECK ONE)	JUST ADMIRE IT	U.S. CAR	IMPORTED CAR (CHECK ONE)
		□ 1	□ 2	□ 3	□ 1	□ 2
		□	□	□	□	□
		□	□	□	□	□
		□	□	□	□	□

THIRD

THINKING NOW OF THE PRESENT TIME, WHAT CAR (MAKE AND CAR LINE) WOULD BE YOUR "MOST WANTED" CAR, IF PRICE WERE NO OBJECT?

MOST WANTED CURRENT CAR ____ (MAKE) ____ (CAR LINE) ____ DO YOU: OWN IT □ 1 ADMIRE IT □ 2 IS IT: A U.S. CAR □ 1 OR AN IMPORT □ 2

RELATIVE TO YOUR INDIVIDUAL TASTES AND PREFERENCES FOR DIFFERENT KINDS OF CARS THROUGHOUT YOUR LIFETIME, PLEASE TELL US YOUR AGREEMENT OR DISAGREEMENT WITH THE FOLLOWING STATEMENTS.

(5 = STRONGLY AGREE ...... 1 = STRONGLY DISAGREE)

. WHILE MY "NEEDS" MAY HAVE CHANGED THROUGHOUT MY LIFE, I STILL HAVE THE SAME "TASTES": I PREFER "PLAIN VANILLA"...OR A "SPORTY FLAIR"...OR A "TOUCH OF LUXURY", ETC.   5 4 3 2 1

. PEOPLE GROWING UP TODAY HAVE DIFFERENT VALUES FROM THOSE OF YESTERDAY....I THINK WE WILL SEE A DIFFERENT PATTERN OF CAR PREFERENCES (by size...type...U.S. vs. Import, etc.) IN THE FUTURE THAN IN THE PAST.   5 4 3 2 1

. YOUNG PEOPLE'S ATTITUDES GO IN CYCLES. THE RADICALS OF THE 60'S HAVE BECOME QUITE CONSERVATIVE IN THE 80'S. THERE'S NO REASON TO THINK THEY WON'T LIKE THE SAME KINDS OF MATERIAL THINGS SUCH AS THE TYPES OF CARS THAT OLDER PEOPLE LIKE TODAY.   5 4 3 2 1

. YOUNG PEOPLE TEND TO FAVOR SMALL ECONOMY OR SPORTY CARS BUT AS THEY GROW OLDER, THEY USUALLY CHANGE TO SOMETHING BIGGER AND MORE COMFORTABLE.   5 4 3 2 1

. MAYBE WE'LL NEVER GET BACK TO THE ULTRA BIG LUXURY CARS OF THE PAST, BUT THERE ALWAYS WILL BE A DEMAND FOR RELATIVELY LARGE, LUXURY CARS AS WELL AS ECONOMY CARS, SPORTY CARS, ETC.   5 4 3 2 1

. IMPORTS HAVE BEEN GOOD FOR ECONOMY ...AND SPORTS-CARS, BUT FOR FAMILY NEEDS, U.S. CARS TRADITIONALLY HAVE BEEN BETTER.   5 4 3 2 1

. WHEN I BOUGHT MY FIRST CARS, IMPORTS FIT MY BUDGET, AND WHEN I PROGRESSED IN MY "ABILITY TO PAY", I JUST NATURALLY STAYED WITH THE IMPORTS.   5 4 3 2 1

. IMPORTED CARS MAY BE REALLY NICE CARS, BUT I HAVE A STRONG BUY-AMERICAN ATTITUDE.   5 4 3 2 1

. MANY YOUNG PEOPLE DRIVING IMPORTS TODAY WILL SWITCH TO U.S. CARS AS THEIR NEEDS AND TASTES CHANGE WITH AGE.   5 4 3 2 1

. I DON'T THINK MOST PEOPLE ARE LOYAL TO EITHER IMPORTS OR U.S. CARS PER SE, BUT THEY BUY ACCORDING TO THEIR PARTICULAR NEEDS AT THE TIME.   5 4 3 2 1

. ONCE A PERSON OWNS EITHER AN IMPORT OR A U.S. CAR AND HAS GOOD LUCK, HE IS LIKELY TO "STAY LOYAL" TO THE SAME KIND OF CAR NEXT TIME.   5 4 3 2 1

. FOR SOME PURPOSES, U.S. CARS OFFER THE BEST CHOICE, WHILE FOR OTHERS, AN IMPORT IS MUCH BETTER, SO MANY FAMILIES OWN ONE OF EACH.   5 4 3 2 1

SOURCE: Reprinted with permission of the Survey Center, Inc.

EXAMPLE 5.8 ■

Advertisement Published by the American Heart Association

This advertisement was one of seventeen created by the American Heart Association and pretested by National Family Opinion, Inc. (see Example 5.9). Respondents rated the photograph as gripping, the message as strong and the entire ad as eye catching.

This kind of family reunion happens all too often these days. Because too many people don't realize that heart disease, stroke and related disorders will be responsible for almost half of all deaths this year. And that affects a lot of families. Don't wait until it's too late. Don't smoke. Eat a low-fat, low-cholesterol diet. And keep your blood pressure under control. Urge your family members to do the same. And make sure your next family reunion is an especially lively one.

American Heart Association WE'RE FIGHTING FOR YOUR LIFE

This space provided as a public service.

SOURCE: Reproduced with permission. © Magazine Ad Kit, 1987. Copyright American Heart Association.

EXAMPLE 5.9

Survey Questionnaire Conducted by National Family Opinion, Inc., for the American Heart Association

This survey questionnaire was used to pretest seventeen candidate advertisements for the American Heart Association on a sample audience. Responses were used to help identify the most effective and positively received advertisement (see Example 5.8).

1. Have you smoked any cigarettes in the last week?

1 ☐ Yes

2 ☐ No

2. Are you presently trying to reduce fat or cholesterol in your diet?

1 ☐ Yes

2 ☐ No

3. Has your doctor ever told you that you have high blood pressure?

1 ☐ Yes

2 ☐ No

3 ☐ Never been tested for high blood pressure

4. I have personally experienced the difficulties of heart problems because I, someone in my family, or someone close to me has had to deal with them.

1 ☐ Yes

2 ☐ No

5. Have you made a donation to the American Heart Association in the last year?

1 ☐ Yes

2 ☐ No

6. Please indicate your age and sex.

Age: _____ years

Sex: 1 ☐ Male

2 ☐ Female

7. Please tell me how much you agree or disagree with each of the following statements.
(√ *One* box for each statement)

	Completely Agree	Somewhat Agree	Neither Agree Nor Disagree	Somewhat Disagree	Completely Disagree
The ad was eye catching	1 ☐	2 ☐	3 ☐	4 ☐	5 ☐
The ad showed me nothing that would make me change my habits	1 ☐	2 ☐	3 ☐	4 ☐	5 ☐
The ad was clear and easy to understand	1 ☐	2 ☐	3 ☐	4 ☐	5 ☐
The ad was very informative	1 ☐	2 ☐	3 ☐	4 ☐	5 ☐
The ad was alarming	1 ☐	2 ☐	3 ☐	4 ☐	5 ☐
I would be more likely to donate money to the American Heart Association because of this ad	1 ☐	2 ☐	3 ☐	4 ☐	5 ☐
The ad really does not apply to me	1 ☐	2 ☐	3 ☐	4 ☐	5 ☐

8. What would you say is the main idea that the ad is trying to communicate?
(Please be as specific as possible)

_____

_____

9. What, if anything, do you particularly like about this ad?

(Please be as specific as possible)

_____

10. What, if anything, do you particularly dislike about this ad?
(Please be as specific as possible)

_____

_____

SOURCE: Reprinted by permission of National Family Opinion, Inc.

Scale Analysis   In its simplest form, scale analysis involves dichotomous questions—such questions as "Is your grade point average 4.0 (yes or no)?" and "Is it 3.5 (yes or no)?" Such questions often appear on questionnaires about salary and position in relation to years of experience in professional fields. Other questions may be posed along lines of increasing or decreasing agreement or disagreement. These may be presented in the form of a multiple choice.

Respondent-generated Questionnaire: The DELPHI Process   Developed by a Rand Corporation research group, the DELPHI process is a method for polling an audience in order to reach a consensus. Management has used this method to improve relations with employees. The process involves six steps. First, a questionnaire is designed to allow open-ended responses. Second, the sample is chosen on the basis of cost and acceptable level of sampling error. Third, the questionnaire is sent to respondents in the sample as individuals—not handed out by a supervisor or given to the respondents in a general assembly. Fourth, the responses received are all organized into one composite list. Corrections in spelling and grammar are made as a common courtesy, but no value judgments are made, such as discarding an idea because it is too costly or has been tried before. Fifth, each respondent is given a copy of the composite list of responses, together with a rating scale, such as high to low from 5 to 1, and asked to order the responses. Tabulations of this second series of responses—that is, a ranking of items on the list—can be made on a computer. When a number of issues from the list are rated in the highest category, they are grouped according to some relationship of ideas. Once categories of ideas have been developed, the items can be rank-ordered within the categories, according to what the responses were. Sixth, a copy of the ordered list is sent back to each respondent along with his or her individual responses. Of course, this cannot be done if the responses are anonymous; however, if the respondents' anonymity is important, you can provide an automatic copy that they can tear off and keep to compare with the overall results. Employees, for example, can see if their opinions are shared by the majority of their peers. If the results of the polling are to be reported to management for some action, those in the minority may want to present a minority report also. This opportunity to participate in issue description and prioritization has given employees a greater sense of contributing to the organization's overall planning, and it certainly aids in communication.

DELPHI has been used successfully by Charleston County Public Schools in Charleston, South Carolina, to draw out specific proposals concerning school vandalism and student disruptions. Included in the sample with students and teachers were various community groups. The ideas suggested by respondents ranged from improving remedial reading programs to using guard dogs; and as a result of a proposal prepared from the report, the schools were granted more than $1 million to implement the ideas agreed upon.[24]

Do-It-Yourself Versus Supplier Types of Research

In do-it-yourself research, the following points are important:

1. The types of surveys you can best handle yourself are those dealing with (a) the audience—the listeners, viewers or readers of your messages; (b) the market in which you operate—the consumers and users of your products or services; (c) public opinion—what people think about issues, conditions, governments, their lives.

2. Confine your survey to your precinct, city, metropolitan area or county. Difficulties arise when a beginning researcher attempts to cover more extensive territory.

3. Collect information by telephone or face-to-face interviews or observation. Mail surveys have some value, although they are limited in view of the costs involved.

4. Question interviewees directly, but avoid asking them for information about others in the family. Use a standardized questionnaire. Self-administered and leave-behind forms are generally not recommended.

5. Primarily, use closed-ended or structured-type questions, eliciting explicit replies. Although open-ended questions are sometimes necessary, they are more difficult to handle, both during the interview and during tabulation.

6. Make interviews relatively short—from 1 or 2 minutes up to a maximum of 15 minutes. Professionals can successfully handle interviews lasting an hour or more, but such questioning requires wide experience, and the analysis can be ponderous.

7. Gather the information through sampling—a cross-section of relatively few people—rather than through a complete enumeration of the population.

8. An adequate sample can be as small as 100; it is seldom more than 1,000.

The following situations usually call for hiring an outside professional research supplier:

1. Advertising effectiveness can now be measured in new and intriguing ways, but these usually require more technical know-how than the average businessperson or beginning researcher has. Many problems arise in attempting to measure not only advertising effect on sales but exposure to advertising—commercials, print, outdoor and others. It may seem perfectly natural to ask, "What led you to buy that?" or "What type of advertising helps you most?" but such simple approaches usually yield misleading results because respondents are likely to give superficial responses and may not understand really what motivated them.

2. *Motivation research* has become a popular term, but it is widely misused. Properly it refers to research that describes *why* people act as they do. Using it usually requires training in psychology or

at least knowledge of techniques developed by behavioral scientists. You can ask people their reasons for many things, but don't expect to probe their subconscious for basic motives if you are equipped with everyday research tools. In-depth interviewing is one of the techniques of motivation and attitude research. An in-depth interview that probes intensively behind expressed opinions and reactions demands skills not commonly available.

3. Conditional questions are dangerous. Asking a respondent what he or she would do if certain changes were made or if other conditions existed seldom produces realistic results. Perhaps you cannot completely avoid questions like "If the 6 o'clock evening newscast were changed to 7 P.M., would you listen to it more, or less, or about the same?" But, such questions can give you a general indication at best—not a precise estimate.

4. Identifying use of products by volume is difficult. Consumers can readily tell you whether they use a product or not, but it is quite another thing to find out how much they use.

5. Loaded surveys mislead. Some advertising researchers have attempted to "document" what they don't actually have by using "research." Going through the motions of a loaded survey does not produce facts. And even if you proceed in good faith, your eagerness to make a good showing may cause you unconsciously to bias a survey.

6. Trend measurements are not taboo, but for one result to be comparable to a later one, the comparability of each survey in a series must be maintained on several levels—as to method, timing, and manner of being conducted.

7. Panels, requiring that the same people be reinterviewed at intervals or that they do something between intervals, are best left to specialists.

8. Store audits also call for specialists. Although simple in concept, they demand more control than a nonspecialist can exercise.

9. Consumer tests—taste tests, advertising copy tests, package tests and the like—are highly specialized and should be used cautiously, if at all.

10. Ratings—the measurements that tell how many people are listening to a given radio or television station at a given time—are not recommended as part of broadcast do-it-yourself research. There is much more to station research than ratings. Demand for ratings research by radio and television has, indeed, been high, but there are many reasons why they should be left to specialists.

Broadcast Research

Audience Measurement   Some questions and methods are peculiar to broadcast research and some of this research is of value to public relations practitioners. One question often asked is, "How big is my audience?" The three main methods used in broadcast research are diaries, interviews and mechanical audience recorders.

Although it might seem to be a simple task, accurate measurement of audience size is highly technical. One needs only to read the Congressional hearings into ratings to become aware of the intricacies and pitfalls. The National Association of Broadcasters is active in the effort to police ratings through the Broadcast Rating Council, which audits the operations of the major rating services. To be effective and useful, ratings must be comparable from market to market; so they must be tallied by organizations that operate nationally. Ratings are available from such services as American Research Bureau, Hooper, Mediastat, Nielsen, and Pulse. Only if you intend to use audience estimates *internally* and can't afford to retain a professional firm should you try to conduct ratings research yourself. The simplest and least expensive method is usually the telephone coincidental—calling a sample of homes during the time segment you wish to measure.

Evaluating the impact or effect of media on publics can be done in a number of ways, but among the ones most commonly used by broadcasters is the control group study or experiment in which two groups are selected to be matching samples. One is then exposed to the program, while the other is not. The differences are determined

▼ **Broadcast research uses three basic formats: diaries, interviews and mechanical audience recorders.**

through panel studies or surveys, and thus the impact of the program is measured. The survey method is generally used here when a program has been activated in one geographical area and not in another. The panel method may use the already selected advisory group. However, the problem with this test involves matching the two sample populations. Another measurement technique consists of studying similar groups over a long period of time. The measures may involve observable changes over the time span, as well as measurable differences in individual and group reactions. The in-depth interview is a valuable tool for determining reactions to various aspects of a program.[25]

The Diary   When used to measure a program's audience, the diary method requires that some member of a household keep a written log of the household's program listening or viewing. The same information can be obtained by attaching a recorder to the TV or radio to measure the frequency of viewing and channel selection, although the automatic device does not tell when the TV or radio is playing in an empty room.

The Interview   Broadcast researchers use several different types of personal and telephone interviews.

The *personal coincidental* method consists of personal interviews made during a given time period or during a specific program. Respondents are simply asked what program they are listening to or watching at that moment.

The *personal roster recall* consists of showing respondents a list of programs and stations and asking them to indicate which they watched or listened to within the given time span (usually the day before or the week before).

The *unaided personal recall* seeks the same type of information, but respondents are asked to identify what they listened to on the radio or watched on TV during the survey time span without referring to a list. Thus respondents must remember the names of programs and stations through independent recall.

The *telephone coincidental*, a survey method that local stations or area research bureaus can use effectively, is identical to the personal coincidental method, except that it is conducted over the telephone. Along the same lines, the *telephone aided recall* is like the personal roster recall, and the *telephone unaided recall* is essentially the same as the personal unaided recall.

Broadcasting researchers also use *combinations* of these tests: the combined telephone coincidental and telephone recall, the combined telephone coincidental and personal roster recall or the combined telephone coincidental and diary.

Mechanical Audience Recorders The two main types of mechanical audience recorders are people meters and program analyzers. People meters are devices that can be held in the viewer's hand or can rest on top of the TV set. People using these devices can record who is watching as well as what is being watched. The A. C. Nielsen Company has replaced its diary system of 2,400 participants with people meters, and the results have been rather dramatic. The meters indicate that network TV audiences are far smaller than had been suggested by the diary system, and this led to a drop in advertising on TV and an effort by the networks to find a new measuring system.

Another device for obtaining viewer information is the program analyzer. It is now used exclusively by panels, but when cable television becomes more widespread its use may be extended to general audiences. To analyze a program, the viewer or listener presses a button or switch that records his or her reaction to a specific part of the program. There are two buttons—Like and Dislike—and the viewer's reactions are recorded on tape and then matched with the program to see which parts of the show elicited which response. Cable systems equipped with such response buttons have been used to register instant ratings, but only on an experimental basis.

▼ APPLIED RESEARCH: MIXING QUALITATIVE AND QUANTITATIVE MEASURES IN INTERNAL AND EXTERNAL SETTINGS

Research conducted within an organization is often done informally and usually mixes qualitative and quantitative techniques: conferences with employees involved in a particular problem, studies of the organization's records, reviews of employee suggestions and surveys of employee opinions. Some internal research also may take into account external opinion: ideas of opinion leaders that affect the organization's management; incoming mail; reports from field agents or sales personnel; press clippings and monitoring reports on broadcast media; opinion polls, elections and legislative voting patterns or similar reflections of public opinion that may be shared by internal audiences; and the work of advisory committees or panels of people experienced in a particular field. The trouble with internal research is that it is seldom representative and almost always lacks objectivity.

External research is almost always formal. It may involve public opinion—that is, the opinions of large groups of the public (such as a nation) which are usually described demographically—and it always involves monitoring specific target audiences outside the organization that are of particular significance to it. Both qualitative and quantitative methods are used.

Monitoring publics and their environments suggests an old southwestern ranching phrase, "riding the fence." The original phrase refers to checking all the boundaries of a property periodically to make sure that the fences are up and in good repair. In public relations, it means checking the parameters of the institution to see what areas need mending or rebuilding because something either has changed or is likely to change.

When you ride the PR fences you identify issues both inside and outside the organization, analyzing opinion of publics in both places and monitoring the climate of public opinion in both places. You may also be trying to build or rebuild relationships with various publics. And you may be evaluating the effectiveness of your work by measuring conditions before and after to see what the results are.

More and more companies conduct employee surveys to check on the quality of their products, the effectiveness of their advertising and the extent of employee involvement in the local community. These areas go beyond the traditional concerns about employees, although those continue to be of interest, too. In addition to offering insights into what employees are thinking, these surveys provide management with information that can be used to remove sources of employee irritation.[26]

Many nonprofit organizations recognize their members as an internal public and try to find out what these people are interested in. Many national organizations with local chapters have become keenly aware of the grassroots perception of many members that the national office doesn't benefit them directly. Some organizations conduct formal, scientific surveys to keep in touch with their membership and its concerns. Others, like the Public Relations Society of America (through its *Public Relations Journal*), use informal readership surveys. One nonprofit organization, the Dallas Museum of Art,[27] has conducted a number of formal audience surveys and has assembled visitor profiles over the years. It has also employed unobtrusive measures, such as membership attendance at previews.

▼ RESEARCH AND PROBLEM SOLVING

Three types of people don't want to hear about an institution's problems: the ones responsible for them, because the problems make them look bad; the ones whose egos are involved, because the problems are a threat to their expertise; and the

▼ **Monitoring enables management to identify and analyze problems and to develop and test programs to solve those problems.**

helpless, who are usually employees or suppliers, because they can't do anything about the problems and are likely to become victims of any institutional shakeup. When people don't want to hear about a problem, they can either ignore the information that points to it or they can deny that the information is accurate.

In either case, the messenger who draws attention to the problem—for example, a public relations practitioner armed with information obtained through research—is always at considerable risk. People who feel threatened are likely to lash out at the most convenient and visible target. To avoid getting involved in battles that can't be won, you must be a diligent fact-finder and an expert communicator. You must also be sensitive to the natural resistance to certain messages that exists within each public, and you must compensate for the resistance. Finally, you must anticipate that some resistance will be put up in response to any action that you or your organization takes to solve problems. Consequently, in addition to riding the fences, and identifying needed action, you have to be prepared to supervise the action, monitor its likelihood of success and report objectively on the results.

A PR person must above all maintain objectivity in "riding the PR fences." You have to be the one to say, "That looks shaky, and a good strong wind is going to blow it down. It's going to cost plenty to fix it, but it has to be fixed now and fixed right." Or, you might have to say, "There's the hole where the livestock are getting out. We have to repair it now, even if we don't get anything else done." Finding the holes and the potential breakdowns is your job.

How an organization reacts to problems is determined in part by its structure and its corporate culture, which also influence how it communicates about its problems. Organizations maintain either closed or open systems of communication. For example, banks have traditionally maintained closed systems, with little to say publicly when they have faced problems. Deregulation of the industry, however, has forced them to adopt much more open systems. The first banks to find themselves on a list of troubled institutions in danger of closing experienced a rude shock. The industry had operated for years within the secure confines of industry practice. Banks rarely spoke publicly about themselves, justifying their silence on grounds of protecting the confidentiality of their clients. But suddenly they had to communicate with their publics.

Hospitals, too, have traditionally operated as closed systems. But while many closed systems still exist, the marketplace has obviously become more competitive in recent years. Major corporate restructuring, brought about as the result of a takeover or a parent spinoff, has also changed how organizations communicate.

Corporate restructuring is going on at a rate that alarms some observers. Various spokespersons have observed that this restructuring is not particularly good for either business or its customers, although it usually benefits stockholders in the short term. Restructuring almost always disassembles the corporate culture. This is important because communication first occurs internally, within the framework an institution's culture.

External communication—even deliberate external communication, such as marketing—follows from and reflects internal communication. A person who functions objectively within the institution—for example, by communicating honestly with employees—is sometimes perceived as not being a team player and not adhering to the corporate point of view. Objective communication to external audiences may be seen as even more threatening. But objective communicators are valuable assets to an institution. They are alert to problems and potential problems because they have been riding the fences with their eyes and ears open, basing their recommendations and actions on objective research. The idea of doing systematic research isn't always supported by management,

often because the results can be threatening, but there is no substitute for such information in times of need.[28]

Research for Problem Identification

A good way to begin identifying problems is to ask an organization's insiders about them. Employees know an institution better than anyone else. They may only know parts of it really well, but they do interact with people in other sections of it, and they do talk among themselves. Listening to voices of dissent within an institution often provides good clues as to where fences need mending. Unfortunately, this is a little-used technique, perhaps because it strikes management as being subversive. Public relations practitioners, of course, recognize that employees are the front line for public relations because they *are* the institutional image. They have a strong sense of what an institution really is, what its problems consist of, and what its customers think about it. They also represent the institution to its publics. In their neighborhoods and among their friends, they are the authority on the institution. Finding out what employees know or think they know about an institution is a critical monitoring operation.

Employees respond to an external environment, as the public relations practitioners well knows. Anticipating reactions of various publics under certain circumstances is part of the job of the PR person as a social scientist within management. Unfortunately, this role often calls for the PR person to become a devil's advocate, posing hard questions about proposed actions. This can be risky, and it explains why a communications audit is a good research technique for riding the fences. Such an audit combines internal and external research with some quantitative and qualitative evidence.

The right time to do a communications audit is not after you have already detected a problem, but regularly as a part of normal monitoring. A communications audit is especially needed before major changes are anticipated, to give you a benchmark against which to measure internal and external attitudes in the future. The audit begins with an account of what is—a look at policies, procedures, materials and any available data on communication effectiveness. Publics are then studied to identify what is perceived, versus what is; research tools used for this purpose include focus group interviews, individual interviews and perhaps a formal survey. The result provides a comparison of policies and procedures with the image they cast.

Audits can be useful problem predictors. Sometimes you know fences are going to need mending, but you don't know exactly where, when and how much. One predictable problem involves policy changes. Philip Lesly has called public relations practitioners "the bridge for change," and a PR colleague observed, "That's right. It means you get walked on." Anticipating problems and dealing with them while they are small are two major public relations contributions to management. Policy changes (indeed, changes in general) usually mean problems. The role of the public relations practitioner is to help smooth the way for changes by eliminating surprises and building interest and anticipation. The PR person also may have to assume the role of negotiator to help effect a change.

Another type of problem is a *crisis*—anything from an internal breakdown, where someone has embezzled funds or leaked corporate secrets, to a primarily external controversy, where the institution is accused of creating a public hazard. Your institution will inevitably have a crisis of one sort or another. Anticipating it will make it easier to cope with (see Chapter 15).

Research for Problem Analysis

Dissecting a problem sounds simple when you work step-by-step through the procedures. Yet the thing initially identified as the problem rarely turns out to be the problem. It's usually an effect or result of the problem. You have to get to the root of the situation, and the only way to do that is to describe what has happened or is happening in clear declarative sentences. Then you have to do some research—formal or informal—to see if you can get at the cause or causes.

Once you have identified the problem, you should be able to express it in one simple sentence. The next step is to state what you want the outcome to be, again in one simple sentence. Even if the situation is as complex as an attempted takeover, you should express the desirable outcome in a simple statement.

If the desirable outcome cannot be stated, you should set down some possible outcomes as goals, together with the consequences, pro and con, of each. This step involves selecting strategies and the tactics to implement them, as well as research techniques for measuring progress toward your goals. The research can be unobtrusive (like monitoring phone calls or mail) or formal (like a survey). Once your action strategies are set, you must identify the publics and the appeals likely to affect them. Finally, you must choose the media most likely to reach the publics.

Now the easy part begins. You have to orchestrate the organization so that it carries out the strategies and tactics needed to meet the goals, on a timetable and within a reasonable budget.

Constraints of time or resources may force you to modify goals, but usually creative thinking will enable you to overcome these constraints. On the other hand, even when resources are unlimited, you have to set some priorities. This entails deciding what you need to achieve first for a strategy to work. Once you have decided that, you can begin work on a more mechanical timetable that tells you what has to happen first.

For example, if you determine that you have to get neighborhood agreement on the rezoning of some property before the architect's plans for a proposed development are completed, you need to make sure that these meetings are going on while you are working with the architect. You must allow enough lead time to avoid any risk that the finished plans will be "leaked" before the neighbors agree to the zoning change. If this is not done properly, the whole deal could be torpedoed. Once you have made this determination, the mechanics become clear. The staff first has to get in touch with neighborhood group leaders to set up meetings and to prepare information for presentation at those meetings, before work begins on a brochure that will feature the architect's plans and schematics.

In problem situations, your concern is to influence public opinion in a positive way. (Case histories show that successful plans to influence opinion share five problem-solving characteristics: assessment of the needs, goals and capabilities of target publics; systematic campaign planning and production; continuous evaluation; complementary roles of mass media and interpersonal communication; and selection of appropriate media for target audiences. All of these depend on sound research.

In some problem situations, you may be attempting to change behavior, rather than opinions. Four problem-solving characteristics are associated with successful behavior change: education; enforcement (legal measures to force behavior change); engineering (constructing preventives or barriers); and peer support. The communication requirements in behavior change are problem awareness, problem acceptance (belief that it is a real problem) and a feeling that something can be done about it.

Research for Program Development and Implementation

When you develop a program to address a problem, you focus on three major components: the publics involved (prioritized and described in terms of demographics and psychographics); the message statements to each of these publics (slanted for special appeal to each public, but essentially the same, so that the institution speaks with one corporate voice, and phrased as a simple statement); and the media to reach each public (primary and secondary, evaluated for their usefulness in delivering the message in an appropriate, economical and timely manner).

You should plan the program in parts and set achievement goals for each part. Research techniques are built in so you can measure how well the plan is working. Any plan has to be flexible enough to allow for changes as you work through it. The purpose of measuring your achievement as you go along is to fine-tune the plan by eliminating what is not working. This kind of midcourse correction research may also reveal at some point that you must go in an entirely different direction. If this happens you must be prepared to do so.

The danger in measuring results as you go along is that you might draw erroneous conclusions, especially regarding cause and effect. You might, for instance, conclude that, because customers said in a survey that they liked your product, they can be expected to buy it. In the social sciences you deal with people who respond differently under different circumstances. As a result, cause and effect are difficult to determine without extensive replication. In this kind of research, you also run the risk of throwing out information that seems irrelevant but may later turn out to be meaningful. On the other hand, you can become confused and led astray by information that you think is useful but is fundamentally unrelated to the problem.

Deciding which research data are relevant and which are irrelevant is critical to objective thinking. Ego involvement always presents a major problem in any effort to think objectively. The problem is lessened if plans are made by a group rather than by an individual. Information about progress can then be shared with all members of the group. At some point, however, someone has to make critical decisions. It may be the public relations person, or it may be someone else in the management group, acting after receiving an appropriate recommendation from the public relations person.

In any case, the best way to proceed is to make your recommendation as objectively as possible, based on your research findings, anticipating as you do so the positive and negative effects it may have on various publics. These potential effects should not be guessed at. They should be anticipated, based on past responses in similar situations and on what research has shown is likely to happen.

▼ SUMMARY

Research for organizations may be informal, formal or a mix of the two. Formal research includes both quantitative and qualitative methods. Qualitative research techniques include historiography (including case studies and diaries), in-depth interviews and focus groups. Quantitative research—often called "scientific" because it is measurable—generally involves study of media content (using content analysis) and of publics (through survey research). In survey research, questionnaires are used in various formats to measure the degree of intensity of opinions, as well as the opinions themselves.

Broadcast research sometimes goes beyond content analysis to investigate audiences. Some types of broadcast research can be done without special expertise, but other types almost always should be done by a supplier.

In applying research to public relations programming, practitioners use internal and external research and qualitative and quantitative measures. Basing PR programs on research can sometimes be a problem either because it conflicts with the organization's corporate culture or structure or because it is perceived as posing a threat to those in power. Nonetheless, research provides objective information that is essential to sound public relations planning.

▼ NOTES

[1] David M. Dozier, "The Innovation of Research in Public Relations Practice: Review of a Program of Studies," in Larissa A and James E. Grunig, eds., *Public Relations Research Annual*, vol. 2 (Hillsdale, N.J.: Lawrence Erlbaum Associates, 1990), p. 23.

[2] Eugene J. Webb, Donald T. Campbell, Richard D. Schwartz and Lee Sechrest, *Unobtrusive Measures: Nonreactive Research in the Social Sciences* (Chicago: Rand McNally, 1966).

[3] Philip Meyer, *Precision Journalism* (Bloomington: Indiana University Press, 1973), p. 15.

[4] Eugene J. Webb, Donald T. Campbell, Richard D. Schwartz and Lee Sechrest, *Unobtrusive Measures*, p. 3.

[5] In exploratory or descriptive research (which is often done in public relations), you develop, instead of a hypothesis, a simple statement of what you want to find out. You must do this as specifically as possible.

[6] In designing an experiment, you will have to pretest it even if it is exploratory. You will be dealing with respondents' interpretations of your questions, so you need to discover any misconceptions that might skew results.

[7] Roger D. Wimmer and Joseph R. Dominick, *Mass Media Research* (Belmont, Calif.: Wadsworth, 1983). Look especially at "The Methodology of Focus Groups," pp. 153–155. The book also has a moderator's guide. See also Toni H. Lydecker, "Focus Group Dynamics," *Association Management* (March 1986), pp. 73–79; and Amanda Bennett, "Once a Tool of Retail Marketers, Focus Groups Gain Wider Usage," *Wall Street Journal*, (June 3, 1986), sec. 2, p. 34.

[8] Bernard Berelson, "Content Analysis in Communication Research," in Bernard Berelson and Morris Janowitz, eds., *Reader in Public Opinion and Communication*, 2d ed. (Glencoe, Ill.: Free Press, 1953), p. 263.

[9] Noel L. Griese, "Feedback, The Vital Link," *Public Relations Journal*, 33(12) (December 1977), pp. 12–14.

[10] W. Edward Deming, *Sample Design in Business Research* (New York: John Wiley, 1960), p. 61.

[11] Demography is the science of vital statistics. An important factor in this science is the tolerable margin of error. Thus, demography asks, how wrong can you be—5 percent, 10 percent, 20 percent?

[12]Psychographs are charts outlining the relative strength of fundamental personality traits in an individual.

[13]PR clients, like products, can be "positioned," whether they are individuals or institutions. Images are important to positioning, and this means finding an emotional appeal that will segment the market.

[14]Selwyn Feinstein, "Computers Replacing Interviewers for Personnel and Marketing Tasks," *Wall Street Journal* (September 9, 1986), sec. 2, p. 31.

[15]Robert B. May, "Business Bulletin," *Wall Street Journal* (December 30, 1976), p. 1.

[16]"Business Bulletin," *Wall Street Journal* (July 31, 1980), p. 1.

[17]Arnold S. Linsky, "Stimulating Responses to Mailed Questionnaires: A Review," *Public Opinion Quarterly*, 39(1) (Spring 1975), pp. 82–101.

[18]Alan R. Andreasen, "Personalizing Mail Questionnaire Correspondence," *Public Opinion Quarterly* (Summer 1970), pp. 273–277.

[19]Philip Meyer, *Precision Journalism*, pp. 315–16.

[20]Some researchers disagree, saying semantic differential measures *degree* of response but not *intensity*. But others argue that degree itself reflects intensity.

[21]William A. Mindak, "Fitting the Semantic Differential to the Marketing Problem," *Journal of Marketing*, 25 (April 1961), pp. 28–33.

[22]Varimax gives a clearer separation of factors. Most students use computer programs to handle reserve data, but for an explanation of the mathematics see Jae-On Kim and Charles W. Mueller, *Factor Analysis Statistical Methods and Practical Issues* (Beverly Hills, Calif.: Sage, 1978).

[23]Hugh M. Culbertson, "Words vs. Pictures: A Comparison as to Perceived Impact and Connotative Meaning," *Journalism Quarterly* (Summer 1974), pp. 226–37.

[24]John C. Cone, "DELPHI: Polling for Consensus," *Public Relations Journal*, 34(2) (February 1978), pp. 12–13.

[25]Adapted from *A Broadcast Research Primer* (Washington, D.C.: National Association of Broadcasters, 1973), pp. 10–12.

[26]Larry Reibstein, "A Finger on the Pulse: Companies Expand Use of Employee Surveys," *Wall Street Journal* (October 27, 1986), sec. 2, p. 23.

[27]Robert Milbank, Jr., "DMA Visitor Profile." *Dallas Museum of Art Bulletin* (Summer 1986). See also John C. Pollock and Michael Winkleman, "Salary Survey," *Public Relations Journal* (June 1987), pp. 15–17.

[28]Jennie M. Piekos and Edna F. Einsiedel, "Roles and Program Evaluation Techniques Among Canadian Public Relations Practitioners," in Grunig and Grunig, eds., *Public Relations Research Annual*, vol. 2, p. 107. Also see Hugh M. Culbertson and Dennis W. Jeffers, "The Social, Political and Economic Contexts: Keys to Front-End Research, *Public Relations Quarterly* (Fall, 1991), pp. 43, 48.

Selected readings, activities and assignments appropriate to this chapter can be found in the *Instructor's Guide.*

CHAPTER 6

▼

PUBLICS AND PUBLIC
OPINION

The sharp drop in the credibility of most U.S. institutions means that the message must be designed with the background of a specific public in mind, so that it will be fully understood. It means also that the real questions in the minds of these publics must be solicited—and answered.

Carl Hawver, former president, Public Relations Society of America

Nothing is more indivisible in a company than its reputation and the climate in which it does business. These are the concerns of the company's public relations, which must be unified as the *antenna*, the *conscience*, and the *voice* of the whole corporation.

Philip Lesly, author and PR counselor

As I see it, PR is defined in terms of public opinion and behavior. Public opinion is a powerful lever that can motivate an audience to a desired behavior.

Harold Burson, founder of Burson-Marsteller

▼ IDENTIFYING AND DESCRIBING PUBLICS

Every discipline seems to develop its own terminology; and sometimes, the same term is used in different ways by teachers and practitioners in different disciplines. In this book, one exceedingly important term is *audience*, which has a very specific meaning in public relations. And within public relations, the difference between an "audience" and a "public" is likewise essential to understand.

The term *publics* has traditionally meant any group (or possibly, individual) that has some involvement with an organization—its neighbors, customers, employees, competitors and government regulators. You might imagine that "publics" and "audiences" are synonymous. But in important ways they are not.

From a public relations perspective, the term *audience* suggests a group of people who are recipients of something—a message or a performance. An audience is thus inherently passive. But this conflicts with the goal of most public relations programs, which is to stimulate strong audience participation. To help resolve the semantic conflict, a new term evolved to distinguish between passive audiences and active ones. That term is *publics*.

In public relations, the term *publics* ("active audiences") encompasses *any group of people tied together, however loosely, by some common bond of interest or concern*. The best way to understand

▼ *Publics ("active audiences")* encompass any group of people tied together by a common bond of interest.

---

this concept is to think of various publics that you, as an individual, might belong to (see Example 6.1).

First, you belong to a group of consumers that, no doubt, has been well defined by marketing people. You may, for instance, be in the eighteen- to twenty-one-year-old "college" market. This market receives a great deal of attention because—although you may not believe it—it is responsible for a vast outlay of cash. Second, you may have an organizational identity. For instance, if you belong to a social or civic organization—the Rotary, Lions, PTA, League of Women Voters, a fraternity, political action group, professional society or athletic team or club—you are a member of a public. You may also belong to other publics because of your race, religion, ethnic group or national origin. You probably would not want to be thought of as a member of "the general public," and you're not. No one is. *No such public exists.* Instead, you are a member of many definable, describable publics. It is the job of public relations practitioners to identify these.

In traditional public relations literature, publics are divided into two categories: external and internal. *External publics* exist outside an institution. They are not part of the organization, but they do have a relationship with it. Certain external publics, such as government regulatory agencies, have a substantial impact on the organization.

Internal publics share the institutional identity. Thus they include management, employees and supporters (investors, for example). Occasionally the term *internal publics* is used in public relations practice to refer exclusively to employees—that is, workers. This usage is unfortunate, however, because it results in employees' being considered as unrelated to management instead of being thought of as part of the same team. Such thinking has a

ghettoizing effect that creates serious communications problems. In a strong union situation, the separation is real and a team concept is not likely. Still, the adversarial relationship can be healthy as long as communication between the two groups is maintained.

Realistically, the categories internal and external are too broad to be very useful in identifying publics. A more definitive typology has been developed by Jerry A. Hendrix, who identifies the following major publics: media, members/employees, community, government, investor, consumer and special (see Example 6.2). Every organization needs to compile a comprehensive list of its publics.

Any particular public, regardless of its broad category, may become the focal point for a public relations effort. When that occurs, the public singled out for attention is called a "target public" or a "priority public."

The PVI (Public Vulnerability Importance) index has been developed to help organizations identify target or priority publics. The potential *P* of a public plus the vulnerability *V* of the organization to action from that public equals the importance *I* of that public to the organization and to its public relations program (see Example 6.3).

Another PR publics measuring tool, called PR Quotient, has been devised by Richard W. Muller. PR Quotient uses a list of forty questions with weighted responses to evaluate the importance of various publics. (The copyrighted test from *Public Relations Quarterly* (Fall 1990), pp. 11–13, appears in the *Instructor's Guide* to this text.)

Not everyone approves of the connotations of the term "target" in the context of an important public. The dean of communications researchers, Wilbur Schramm, is one authority who disparages it:

For nearly thirty years after World War I, the favorite concept of the mass media audience was what advertisers and propagandists often chose to call the "target audience." . . . A propagandist could shoot the magic bullet of communication into a

EXAMPLE 6.1

One Person's Publics

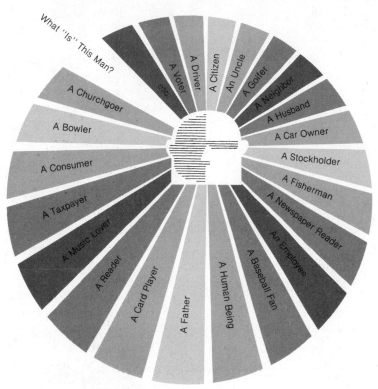

What "Is" This Man?

A Voter, etc. · A Driver · A Citizen · An Uncle · A Golfer · A Neighbor · A Husband · A Car Owner · A Stockholder · A Fisherman · A Newspaper Reader · An Employee · A Baseball Fan · A Human Being · A Father · A Card Player · A Reader · A Music Lover · A Taxpayer · A Consumer · A Bowler · A Churchgoer

SOURCE: Reprinted by permission of Macmillan Publishing Co., Inc., from *Communications: The Transfer of Meaning* by Don Fabun. Copyright © 1968 by Kaiser Aluminum and Chemical Corp., reissued in 1987.

viewer or a listener, who would stand still and wait to be hit!... By the late 1950s the bullet theory was, so to speak, shot full of holes. Mass communication was not like a shooting gallery. There was nothing necessarily irresistible about mass communication or mass propaganda. Many influences entered into the effect of the mass media. The audience was not a passive target; rather, it was extraordinarily active.[1]

Certainly most PR practitioners would agree that a target public is not passive and may exhibit un-

predictable behavior. Still, the idea behind the term is valid—as a silhouette or a statistical profile, and not as a life-size, four-color portrait. Although "priority public" might be more accurate, the term "target public" continues to be used today to signify some definable audience for whom advertising and information are specifically prepared. The "mass audience" is indeed a myth, and the scatter-shot approach is both foolish and uneconomical.

EXAMPLE 6.2

Discovering Publics

Publics for any organization fall into these categories developed by Jerry Hendrix.

MAJOR PUBLICS

Media Publics

Mass media
  Local
    Print publications
      Newspapers
      Magazines
    TV stations
    Radio stations
  National
    Print publications
    Broadcast or cable networks
    Wire services
Specialized media
  Local
    Trade, industry and association publications
    Organizational house and membership
      publications
    Ethnic publications
    Publications of special groups
    Specialized broadcast or cable programs and
      stations
  National
    General business publications
    National trade, industry and association
      publications
    National organizational house and membership
      publications
    National ethnic publications
    Publications of national special groups
    National specialized broadcast or cable programs
      and networks

Member Publics

Organization employees
  Headquarters management
  Headquarters nonmanagement (staff)
  Other headquarters personnel
Organization officers
  Elected officers
  Appointed officers
  Legislative groups
  Boards, committees
Organization members
  Regular members
  Members in special categories—sustaining, emeri-
    tus, student members
  Honorary members or groups
Prospective organization members
State or local chapters
  Organization employees
  Organization officers
  Organization members
  Prospective organization members
Related or other allied organizations

Employee Publics

Management
  Upper-level administrators
  Midlevel administrators
  Lower-level administrators
Nonmanagement (staff)
  Specialists
  Clerical personnel

Secretarial personnel
Uniformed personnel
Equipment operators
Drivers
Security personnel
Other uniformed personnel

Union representatives

Other nonmanagement personnel

Community Publics

Community media
Mass
Specialized

Community leaders
Public officials
Educators
Religious leaders
Professionals
Executives
Bankers
Union leaders
Ethnic leaders
Neighborhood leaders

Community organizations
Civic
Service
Social
Business
Cultural
Religious
Youth
Political
Special interest
Other

Investor Publics

Shareowners and potential shareowners

Security analysts and investment counselors

Financial press
Major wire services: Dow Jones & Co., Reuters Economic Service, AP, UPI
Major business magazines: *Business Week, Fortune,* and the like—mass circulation and specialized
Major newspapers: *New York Times, Wall Street Journal*
Statistical services: Standard and Poor's Corp., Moody's Investor Service, and the like
Private wire services: PR News Wire, Business Wire

Securities and Exchange Commission (SEC), for publicly owned companies

Government Publics

Federal
Legislative branch
Representatives, staff, committee personnel
Senators, staff, committee personnel
Executive branch
President
White House staff, advisers, committees
Cabinet officers, departments, agencies, commissions
State
Legislative branch
Representatives, delegates, staff, committee personnel
Senators, staff, committee personnel
Executive branch
Governor
Governor's staff, advisers, committees
Cabinet officers, departments, agencies, commissions

(Continued)

EXAMPLE 6.2

Discovering Publics (*continued*)

County
    County executive
    Other county officials, commissions, departments

City
    Mayor or city manager
    City council
    Other city officials, commissions, departments

Consumer Publics

Company employees

Customers
    Professionals
    Middle-class
    Working-class
    Minorities
    Other

Activist consumer groups

Consumer publications

Community media, mass and specialized

Community leaders and organizations

Special Publics

Media consumed by this public
    Mass
    Specialized

Leaders of this public
    Public officials
    Professional leaders
    Ethnic leaders
    Neighborhood leaders

Organizations composing this public
    Civil
    Political
    Service
    Business
    Cultural
    Religious
    Youth
    Other

SOURCE: Reprinted with permission from Jerry A. Hendrix, *Public Relations Cases*, 2nd ed., pp. 13–16 (Belmont, Calif.: Wadsworth, 1992). Copyright © 1992 Wadsworth Inc.

Identifying Priority Publics

To see how a public becomes a *priority public*, consider the example of health-care programs. When any national health-care program is proposed, the opinion of the American Medical Association—as a public—is critical; therefore, pro-health-care PR forces must be concerned with AMA members as a target public. Priority publics are generally chosen for economic or political reasons. You don't try to reach everyone—only those whom you have *chosen* to receive a specially designed message.

Sometimes priority publics are determined by large-scale changes in socioeconomic or sociopolitical environments. For example, Otto Lerbinger has identified several relationships that American corporations are reassessing in order to compete in the global marketplace: competitors (more cooperation), suppliers (more long-term relationships), capital (money) suppliers (more long-term and not limited to banks), employees (partnership) and government (cooperative).[2]

As a public relations practitioner, you must carefully study your comprehensive list and identify each public that is especially pertinent to your particular project. You must also designate publics not on your list that might be affected. One way to isolate these peripheral publics (which are not normally a part of your contact list) is to figure out how you would get names, addresses and phone numbers if you needed to contact *each* member of that public directly.

EXAMPLE 6.3

Prioritizing Publics

Prioritizing publics may be done in a number of ways. One informal method is called the PVI index: *P*, the organization's Potential to influence a public, plus *V*, the organization's Vulnerability to that public (which may change over time and in different situations), equals *I*, the Impact of that public on the organization. The higher the *I* value, the greater the impact. Here is a tabular form for "computing" a PVI index.

	P +	*V* =	*I*
Audience or Public	**Potential for Organization to Influence (Scale 1–10)**	**Vulnerability of Organization to Being Affected (Scale 1–10)**	**Importance of Audience to Organization**
———————	———————	———————	———————
———————	———————	———————	———————
———————	———————	———————	———————

The key to identifying and defining priority publics accurately is *research*—finding out who these publics really are and what they think, not what you assume they are or think. An example of what happens when research is ignored is the difficulty an armaments company experienced in a community that the company dominated. Because the company contributed so much to the community's economy, executives couldn't understand reports that their employees were being shunned socially by other members of the community. Eventually this affected the company's ability to recruit top employees locally, regardless of the pay it offered. Finally, an attitude study of the community by an outside research agency revealed that the community did not know what the company's employees did. Because of their high salaries and the access restrictions due to government security, the employees were perceived as being a lot of high-priced Ph.D.s who did nothing but push paper at the expense of the community's tax dollars. An informational campaign conducted within the confines of government security restrictions helped clear up the resentment.

The danger of *assuming* what a major public thinks or knows is quite serious. Alert public relations practitioners consider not only the majority opinion of each public but also the opinions of dissenters. Failure to do so may cause future problems, as the Democratic Party leadership discovered in the early 1970s when faced with demands by women and racial minorities that they be more equitably represented. In 1983 Republican President Ronald Reagan encountered a similar problem when polls reported that women voters saw him as unresponsive to their concerns. Except when votes are being counted, politicians (and organizations) tend to underestimate the significance of publics categorized as "minor."

To develop sensitivity to the attitudes of various priority publics, a PR person must develop empathy for each one, much as an actor studies a role and then becomes the character. The PR person must ask, "If I were this public, with this background, these situations, this set of concepts, how would I react to the set of circumstances being introduced by the institution I represent?" Developing such empathy for a public—trying to imagine how that public will react—not only helps in planning for a specific situation but also helps in media selection.

▼ Target publics can be described in three
ways: nominatively, demographically and
psychographically.

Each institution has its own particular primary publics. A business, for example, has internal primary publics (stockholders, employees, dealers and sales representatives) and external primary publics (customers, government regulatory agencies, suppliers, competitors, the financial community—security analysts and investors in addition to their own stockholders—and the local community). At any time one or more of these primary publics can become a target public.

Describing Priority Publics

Priority publics can be described in any of three ways. The first is merely by giving the public a name, such as "stockholders." The second is by looking at the public's demographics—its statistical characteristics such as age, gender, income, education and so on. The third is by looking at the public's psychographics—its defining emotional and behavioral characteristics. These psychographics often show how one primary public resembles another in interests, attitudes, beliefs or behavior.

Such descriptions are becoming more and more important as the diversity of publics increases. In this regard, AT&T's public relations organization (supposedly the world's largest) has done some target marketing that seems to contradict conventional wisdom. Former Vice President for Public Relations Edwin Block reported, for instance, that supporting the arts is a good business proposition because a large percentage of the people AT&T wants to reach is interested in the arts. People who enjoy symphonic music (a psychographic characteristic) have what Block called "remarkably appealing" demographics of age, educational level and income, and they demonstrate their arts interest by attending cultural events. "If you talk about numbers of people who pay their own good hard money to go to an event, there is a higher percentage of the kind of people we want to reach in the arts."[3]

A more general type of psychographic casting is done by SRI International, which has developed a system called VALS 2 for categorizing publics according to *values, attitudes,* and *lifestyles* (see Example 6.4). VALS 2, an improvement on an earlier program, employs a typology based on psychographics.[4]

In their attempt to predict future behavior from observed or reported behavior, SRI's descriptive categories resemble those resulting from a study by NPD, a market research firm that has categorized people by their eating habits—another expression of values.[5] NPD went beyond traditional market research methods to use, in addition to questionnaires, a research technique borrowed from broadcast research—the diary. The survey spanned two years, and on the basis of the information gathered from it, NPD grouped people into five categories: (1) meat-and-potatoes eaters; (2) families with children (the soda pop and sweet cereal buyers); (3) naturalists (the fresh fruit, granola and yogurt crowd); (4) sophisticates (the brie and chablis bunch); (5) dieters (the consumers of skim milk and sugar substitute). The researchers discovered, however, that the groups behaved consistently but in a manner that casts doubt on the purity of the categories. Naturalists may have eaten sugar less often than others did, but they ate—or at least purchased—chocolate chips more frequently. (The study dealt with frequency, not volume.) There was a logical explanation: the naturalists also liked to cook from scratch, so they probably baked their own cookies (including chocolate chip ones) more often than did people who often bought ready-made cookies.

An NPD competitor, Market Research Corporation of America, has completed a ten-year study of the same subject that it claims is more comprehensive. The bottom line for such studies is to recommend products that people like and will buy. But translating research into action gives most decision makers pause.

Researchers pause, too. It's difficult to predict behaviors from attitudes, but attitudes remain easier to measure than behavior (without invading privacy). Some research indicates that behaviors can best be predicted from attitudes under the following specific circumstances: (1) when multi-item, detailed and highly relative instruments are used; (2) when a common understanding of the attitude questionnaire is shared among respondents and between researcher and respondent; (3) when the behavioral measure is familiar to the respondent; (4) when the attitudinal and behavioral objects are defined so as to achieve common interpretations; (5) when the attitudinal response and behavioral response are defined similarly; (6) when belief intentions (probably that a person will perform a particular act) and normative pressures (group norms tending to induce conformity) are taken into account.[6]

To improve educated guessing before a final decision is made, demographic and psychographic information should be cross-referenced with other statistics. Numerous firms that correlate such data with the outreach potential of various forms of the media.

Simmons Market Research Bureau, Inc., and Mediamark Research, Inc., are two major London-based readership research firms that measure how many people read various magazines and national newspapers and who these readers are demographically. The two seldom agree on specific numbers, as the chart for highest magazine circulation in Example 6.5 indicates. And as you might imagine, publications often challenge their figures. The differences in findings may be due to their different research methodologies. Simmons shows published issues to people and records how many people have read or scanned the issues. MRI shows sample magazine logos on flash cards and counts how many people say they have read that publication in the past seven days (if it is a weekly) or in the past thirty days (if it is a monthly).[7]

Newspaper circulation is measured by the Audit Bureau of Circulation. In addition, most metropolitan daily newspapers have their own research staffs to give them more detailed pictures of who their readers are. In large markets, newspapers hire outside research organizations, but the results are rarely made public. Moreover, the results tend to be applied more by the advertising, marketing and circulation staffs than by the editorial staff. Unfortunately, this means that editorial staffs miss opportunities to take valuable research findings into account on such matters as readability factors and process comprehension. Most newspapers don't have a PR staff, although they may have a promotional staff.

Network television audiences are measured by A. C. Nielsen Company (see Example 6.5). In 1987, the company switched from a diary method of audience response to people meters, as discussed in Chapter 5. The device counts how many people are watching a program and who they are. Obtaining those data requires some button-pushing by the viewers.

The Nielsen change was not popular in the broadcast industry, because the people-meter reports showed a substantial drop in audiences, which forced networks to change the way they sold broadcast time to ad agencies. The Nielsen switch occurred largely in response to pressure from AGB Television Research, Inc., a U.S. subsidiary of London's AGB Research PLO, which operates a people-meter service. Two other Nielsen competitors, Control Data Corporation's Arbitron Ratings Company and R. D. Percy and Company, also use a version of the people-meter measuring device. Nielsen has received such harsh criticism from the U.S. networks that its competitors are hoping to gain market share at its expense.[8]

Research on print and broadcast media publics is used by media to help sell advertising time or space, and by media buyers to determine how to maximize their budgets by reaching their publics most effectively. Specialized firms like Communicate! The Advertising and Public Relations Network

EXAMPLE 6.4

The VALS™ 2 Typology

The VALS 2 typology, developed by the Values and Lifestyles Program at SRI International, is a new psychographic system for segmenting American consumers and predicting consumer behavior.

For over a decade, the Values and Lifestyles Program has been the leader in psychographic consumer segmentation. Its insights have helped countless advertisers, advertising agencies, and media companies improve the effectiveness of their marketing. Now, building on its years of research into consumer attitudes and lifestyles, the VALS Program has created VALS 2, a new typology of American consumers.

VALS 2 is built on a conceptual framework that is called self-orientation, and a new definition of resources.

SELF-ORIENTATION

Consumers pursue and acquire products, services, and experiences that provide satisfaction and give shape, substance, and character to their identities. They are motivated by one of three powerful self-orientations—principle, status, or action. Principle-oriented consumers are guided in their choices by their beliefs or principles, rather than by feelings, events, or desire for approval. Status-oriented consumers are heavily influenced by the actions, approval, and opinions of others. Action-oriented consumers are guided by a desire for social or physical activity, variety, and risk-taking. Each VALS 2 segment has distinctive attitudes, lifestyles, and life goals according to its members' self-orientation.

RESOURCES

Resources, in the VALS 2 system, refers to the full range of psychological, physical, demographic, and material means and capacities consumers have to draw upon. This dimension is a continuum ranging from minimal to abundant. It encompasses education, income, self-confidence, health, eagerness to buy, intelligence, and energy level. Resources generally increase from adolescence through middle-age, while they decrease with extreme age, depression, financial reverses, and physical or psychological impairment.

NETWORK OF DISTINCTIVE INTERCONNECTED SEGMENTS

Using these two dimensions—self-orientation and resources—VALS defined eight segments of consumers who have different attitudes and exhibit distinctive behavior and decision-making patterns. The segments are balanced in size, so that each truly represents a viable target. VALS 2 is a network of interconnected segments. Neighboring types have similar characteristics and can be combined in varying ways to suit particular marketing purposes. The overall system is highly flexible and predictive of consumer behavior.

ACTUALIZERS

Actualizers are successful, sophisticated, active, "take-charge" people with high self-esteem and abundant resources. They are interested in growth and seek to develop, explore, and express themselves in a variety of ways—sometimes guided by principle, and sometimes by a desire to have an effect, to make a change. Image is important to Actualizers, not as evidence of status or power, but as an expression of their taste, independence, and character. Actualizers are among the established and emerging leaders in business and government, yet they continue to seek challenges. They have a wide range of interests, are concerned with social issues, and are open to change. Their lives are characterized by richness and diversity. Their possessions and recreation reflect a cultivated taste for the finer things in life.

THE VALS 2 NETWORK

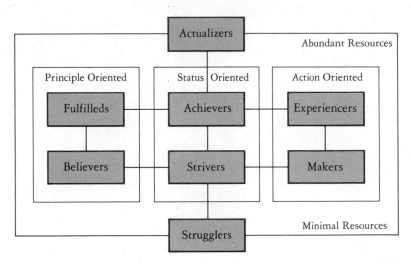

FULFILLEDS AND BELIEVERS: PRINCIPLE-ORIENTED

Principle-oriented consumers seek to make their behavior consistent with their views of how the world is or should be.

Fulfilleds are mature, satisfied, comfortable, reflective people who value order, knowledge, and responsibility. Most are well educated, and in, or recently retired from, professional occupations. They are well-informed about world and national events and are alert to opportunities to broaden their knowledge. Content with their careers, families, and station in life, their leisure activities tend to center around their homes. Fulfilleds have a moderate respect for the status quo, institutions of authority, and social decorum, but are open-minded about new ideas and social change. Fulfilleds tend to base their decisions on strongly held principles and consequently appear calm and self-assured. While their incomes allow them many choices, Fulfilleds are conservative, practical consumers; they look for functionality, value, and durability in the products they buy.

Believers are conservative, conventional people with concrete beliefs based on traditional, established codes· family, church, community, and the nation. Many Believers express moral codes that are deeply rooted and literally interpreted. They follow established routines, organized in large part around their homes, families, and social or religious organizations to which they belong. As consumers, they are conservative and predictable, favoring American products and established brands. Their education, income, and energy are modest but sufficient to meet their needs.

ACHIEVERS AND STRIVERS: STATUS-ORIENTED

Status-oriented consumers have or seek a secure place in a valued social setting. They make choices to enhance their position or to facilitate their move to another, more desirable group. Strivers look to others to indicate what they should be and do, whereas

(Continued)

EXAMPLE 6.4

The VALS™ 2 Typology (*continued*)

Achievers, more resourceful and active, seek recognition and self-definition through achievements at work and in their families.

Achievers are successful career and work-oriented people who like to, and generally do, feel in control of their lives. They value structure, predictability, and stability over risk, intimacy, and self-discovery. They are deeply committed to their work and their families. Work provides them a sense of duty, material rewards, and prestige. Their social lives reflect this focus and are structured around family, church, and business. Achievers live conventional lives, are politically conservative, and respect authority and the status quo. Image is important to them. As consumers, they favor established products and services that demonstrate their success to their peers.

Strivers seek motivation, self-definition, and approval from the world around them. They are striving to find a secure place in life. Unsure of themselves and low on economic, social, and psychological resources, Strivers are deeply concerned about the opinions and approval of others. Money defines success for Strivers, who don't have enough of it, and often feel that life has given them a raw deal. Strivers are easily bored and impulsive. Many of them seek to be stylish. They emulate those who own more impressive possessions, but what they wish to obtain is generally beyond their reach.

EXPERIENCERS AND MAKERS: ACTION-ORIENTED

Action-oriented consumers like to affect their environment in tangible ways. Makers do so primarily at home and at work, Experiencers in the wider world. Both types are intensely involved.

Experiencers are young, vital, enthusiastic, impulsive, and rebellious. They seek variety and excitement, savoring the new, the offbeat, and the risky. Still in the process of formulating life values and patterns of behavior, they quickly become enthusiastic about new possibilities but are equally quick to cool. At this stage in their lives, they are politically uncommitted, uninformed, and highly ambivalent about what they believe. Experiencers combine an abstract disdain for conformity and authority with an outsider's awe of others' wealth, prestige, and power. Their energy finds an outlet in exercise, sports, outdoor recreation, and social activities. Experiencers are avid consumers and spend much of their income on clothing, fast food, music, movies, and video.

Makers are practical people who have constructive skills and value self-sufficiency. They live within a traditional context of family, practical work, and physical recreation and have little interest in what lies outside that context. Makers experience the world by working on it—building a house, raising children, fixing a car, or canning vegetables—and have sufficient skill, income, and energy to carry out their projects successfully. Makers are politically conservative, suspicious of new ideas, respectful of government authority and organized labor, but resentful of government intrusion on individual rights. They are unimpressed by material possessions other than those with a practical or functional purpose (e.g., tools, pickup trucks, or fishing equipment).

STRUGGLERS

Strugglers' lives are constricted. Chronically poor, ill-educated, low-skilled, without strong social bonds, aging, and concerned about their health, they are often despairing and passive. Because they are so limited, they show no evidence of a strong self-orientation, but are focused on meeting the urgent needs of the present moment. Their chief concerns are for security and safety. Strugglers are cautious consumers. They represent a very modest market for most products and services, but are loyal to favorite brands.

SOURCE: Reprinted with permission from the VALS Program, SRI International.

assist in this analysis. It offers the following databases, in addition to various electronic mail and delivery services:

▼ *SRDS:* a list of all major print and broadcast media, mass as well as specialized, arranged by ad rates, circulation, costs and mechanical information

▼ *mediabase:* a list of publication editors and broadcast media contacts, organized by categories

▼ *NEXIS:* a news database that carries PR Newswire, Reuters, NY Times Advertising and Marketing Intelligence, full text of all *Time-Life* publications, and others

▼ *Newsnet:* a collection of industry newsletters

▼ *ADWeek:* directories of advertisers, agencies, media services and other vendors, as well as special reports on the industry from *AdWeek Magazine*

▼ *RAB:* information about cooperative advertising programs, provided by the Radio Advertising Bureau

▼ *PRIZM:* a market research service that provides geo-demographic data according to social and lifestyle classifications

▼ *ACORN:* target marketing information, including VALS, MRI and Scarborough/Simmons

▼ *OTC NEWSALERT:* news about public companies and their regulators, such as the SEC[9]

Companies use specialized services like these because it is less costly to do so than to buy each service separately and try to maintain a usable library of information.

One problem in trying to identify publics relates to their size, location and diversity. The difficulty is compounded by the nature of the organizations that compile the statistics. Depending on its area of interest, each organization may look at the same population and arrive at very different conclusions. For instance, the Census Bureau, the Department of Economic Analysis of the Commerce Department and the National Planning Asso-

▼ **Today's publics are fragmented by technology and population trends, leading to loss of identity, sense of community and creativity.**

ciation (NPA) tried to project what the population of Connecticut would be in the year 2000. Their estimates ranged, respectively, from 3.1 million to 3.6 million to 3.8 million. The Census Bureau looks at population rather than economic figures. The Commerce Department does almost exactly the opposite, and the NPA mixes economics and demographics such as age, race, personal income and industrial activity to project figures by city and county.[10]

Fragmented Publics and Activist Groups

The sheer size of U.S. institutions today has created many problems. Today's consumer faces an endless chain of command in which each person is proficient at buck-passing. As a consequence, both consumers and employees suffer a loss of identity and influence. The fragmentation is exacerbated by differences between what institutions are and what they say they are.

From the PR practitioner's standpoint, dealing with loss of *identity* in an era of increasing sophistication can be difficult. Employees in industry worry about being replaced by robots, and individual achievement is likely to be submerged in group effort. The employee of a large corporation, for example, may wet a finger and try to smear the "signed" signature of a congratulatory letter from management to see whether it is handwritten or just another of the "personalized" computer-written letters everyone gets in the mail. Efforts to personalize, identify and recognize members of a large target public demand originality and heavy financing.

Computer information delivery systems through cable television have further fragmented publics, but they do offer some potential for identifying these publics/users. A study by International

EXAMPLE 6.5

Different Measures of Media Audiences

September 2, 1987

Study in Contrasts

Top five magazines based on total adult readership, in millions

The Simmons List

1	TV Guide	43.2
2	Reader's Digest	37.5
3	People	24.6
4	National Geographic	23.6
5	Time	23.2

The MRI List

1	Reader's Digest	50.9
2	TV Guide	46.8
3	Better Homes and Gardens	35.5
4	People	30.4
5	National Geographic	30.3

NOTE: Excludes Sunday magazines

Sources: Simmons Market Research Bureau Inc; Mediamark Research Inc.

December 28, 1987

How Big an Audience?

Television ratings for adults, age 25–54, for top 10 shows, Nov. 10 to 23

Show	Nielsen Index	People Meters
The Cosby Show	27.4	24.4
Family Ties	27.2	25.5
Cheers	24.1	23.0
Moonlighting	22.7	20.2
Night Court	22.1	20.1
Growing Pains	18.3	17.5
Who's the Boss	17.5	16.1
Family Ties (Special)	17.5	18.8
Murder She Wrote	16.8	14.7
60 Minutes	16.5	18.6

NOTE: One rating point equals 1% of the 97.7 million adults age 25–54

Source: NBC

SOURCE: Reprinted by permission of the *Wall Street Journal*, © 1987 Dow Jones & Company, Inc. All rights reserved worldwide.

Resource Development, "Paperless Consumer Information Services," shows that electronic communication is efficient but that recipients miss the human touch. The most personal form of communication, the letter, has been depersonalized by electronic mail systems. As a result, according to IRD, letters on personal stationery will be even more important, as will greeting cards.

Some personal paper communications, such as newspaper classifieds, will probably be supplanted entirely by electronic ads. Public relations practitioners can, therefore, fill this void in communica-

January 7, 1987

Declining Audience?

Selected cartoon ratings, October and November

Program	1986 Diary Method	1987 People Meters	Pct. Change
Care Bears Family (ABC)			
Household rating	8.5	2.2	− 87%
Children rating	10.4	4.0	− 62%
No. of children viewing (in millions)	8.52	1.88	− 61%
Disney's Adventures of the Gummi Bears (NBC)			
Household rating	4.5	3.2	− 29%
Children rating	10.0	5.8	− 42%
No. of children viewing (in millions)	8.89	2.0	− 41%
Jim Henson's Muppet Babies (CBS)*			
Household rating	4.5	4.7	+ 4%
Children rating	13.4	11.8	− 16%
No. of children viewing (in millions)	4.56	8.86	− 15%
Smurfs (NBC)*			
Household rating	5.6	5.7	+ 2%
Children rating	12.4	9.8	− 21%
No. of children viewing (in millions)	4.22	8.37	− 20%

*9 a.m. to 10 a.m. EST portion

NOTE: A 1986 household rating point equals 1% of the estimated 87.4 million U.S. homes with televisions; a 1987 household rating point equals 1% of the estimated 88.6 million homes with televisions. A 1986 children rating point equals 1% of the estimated 34.4 million children ages two to 11 in U.S. households. Estimates are rounded and are from A.C. Nielsen Co., a unit of Dun & Bradstreet Corp. Changes in ratings also may have been affected by changes in program time periods.

Sources: ABC, NBC

tion with the human touch if they use more personal media, says *pr reporter*:

Depersonalized computer communication will affect many media, adding value to personal ones. Electronic communication will have a high negative impact on catalogs, directories and technical books—most used as references. This information will probably be in data banks. Also, second-class unit messages will be electronically delivered. Very personal media, such as letters on personalized, high-quality stationery, will increase in value due to the human touch.[11]

▼ Issues evaluation and management involve monitoring the socioeconomic and political climates for any event or trend that might
have an impact on public opinion.

PR people must also contend with a population that is losing its *sense of community*. High mobility has weakened family ties, almost dissolved neighborhood alliances, reduced civic involvement and changed loyalties so that, as one editor complained, "No one buys this paper just because it's a hometown newspaper anymore." Mobility has weakened loyalty to employers, too. Other companies can lure executives with promises of greater success and can attract lower-level employees with more money.

In addition, workers suffer from a loss of *creativity*. Because progress in our highly technological society depends to such a great extent on teamwork, individuals often think that their accomplishments are meaningless. No longer does a cobbler make a pair of shoes, see them worn and pride himself on his reputation as a fine craftsman. People on an assembly line feel little personal involvement with the shoes that come off it, and they may be highly critical of the production process itself if they perceive it as producing shoddy merchandise.[12] Some corporations try to combat this discontent by rotating production-line workers from time to time so that they learn new jobs and begin to understand the production process itself; in some instances, however, technological complexity or union restrictions may not allow this.

Fragmentation has resulted in another type of community—constituencies concerned about a particular issue. Activists are often well-organized and build "memberships" as issues arise. Frequently they are first to identify and clarify concerns about situations. For many, their "cause" becomes their reason for being.

▼ ISSUES AND ISSUES EVALUATION/ MANAGEMENT

Issues evaluation and management serve to head off problems that could develop between an organization and its publics. The main task consists of monitoring the socioeconomic and political scene for issues that could have an impact on any of the organization's publics. *Anticipating* issues enables the organization to deal with them before a major problem arises and a crisis ensues. Anticipation and a proactive position (taking the initiative instead of responding or reacting) enable the organization to modify its programs so that they remain in tune with changed circumstances. Monitoring issues helps it foresee when public opinion is likely to build around incidents or trends.

Issues

The handling of issues once they have been identified through monitoring is not a linear action that concludes with achieving a favorable solution. Instead, as consultant John Bitter suggests, it is a cyclical process with five steps: sensing the problem (research), defining the problem (through judgment and priority setting), deriving solutions (through policy and strategy selection), implementing them and evaluating outcomes (see Example 6.6). The process can recur as each portion of a solution is worked through. The feedback causes adjustments in the plans, which in turn causes the next step of the solution to return to step one each time.[13]

Philip Lesly cautions that emphasizing "issues" can lead to a siege mentality. He prefers to call the entire procedure *monitoring*, and he points out that the process lends itself to discovery of both issues and *opportunities*. Lesly also cautions against long-term, fixed planning; the term *issues monitoring* suggests the need to be flexible and responsive to developing situations and trends.

Lesly has developed a comprehensive checklist for issues and opportunities (see Example 6.7).[14] Many organizations have issue-tracking systems,

EXAMPLE 6.6

The Issues Management Process

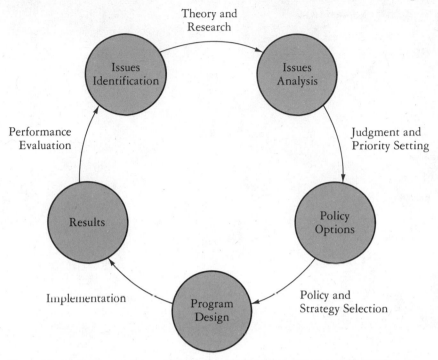

Theory and
Research

Issues
Identification

Issues
Analysis

Performance
Evaluation

Judgment and
Priority Setting

Results

Policy
Options

Implementation

Policy and
Strategy Selection

Program
Design

SOURCE: Reprinted with permission of *International Public Relations Review*, 13(4) (1990), p. 23.

and some use a computer software program that performs a content analysis of daily news from various wire services.

Issues Evaluation and Management

Each person in the monitoring task force must identify and track emerging issues and must evaluate their potential impact on the organization and its publics. Some organizations have developed sophisticated computer models to perform such evaluations.

The evaluation is made by following procedures in Part II of Lesly's chart (see Example 6.7). Then priority publics can be established by following

Part III. Appropriate activities should be subjected to the usual pretests, to make sure that the right message is communicated through the most appropriate medium, as Part IV of the chart suggests. Some of this is contingent on time elements, as Part V indicates, and on budget, as in Part VI. Built in to each of the activities in Part IV should be some method of monitoring for ongoing effectiveness, as well as a system to accommodate final evaluation, as Part VII recommends.

In many instances, the appropriate strategy to use depends on the life-cycle stage of the issue, according to John F. Mahon of the Boston University School of Management.[15] He suggests three strategies: (1) containment, for an emerging issue;

EXAMPLE 6.7

Checklist for Issues and Opportunities

MANAGING THE HUMAN CLIMATE

Guidelines on Public Relations and Public Affairs

I. Structure

  1. Public Issues and Opportunities Task Force

    ▼ Corporate planning

    ▼ Operations

    ▼ Finance

    ▼ Marketing

    ▼ Production

    ▼ Law

    ▼ Government relations

    ▼ Public relations

    ▼ Human resources

    ▼ Outside counsel

II. Preparation for Each Issue or Opportunity

  1. Research what is known about the issue or opportunity

    1.1 Analyze causes

      ▼ Technical factors

      ▼ Supplier fault

      ▼ Company's procedures

      ▼ External problems (blockages, weather, etc.)

      ▼ Snag in employee communication

      ▼ Snag in communication with customers

      ▼ Snag in communication with stockholders

      ▼ Snag in communication with government agencies

      ▼ Snag in communication with legislators

      ▼ Snag in relations with external organizations (environmentalists, minorities, etc.)

    1.2 Study facts, reports, experts within company

    1.3 Review outside sources

      ▼ Government

      ▼ Other industry

      ▼ Associations

      ▼ Libraries

      ▼ Suppliers

      ▼ Publications

    1.4 Analyze the present climate

      ▼ In government

      ▼ Competitors

      ▼ Other industry

      ▼ Critics' groups

      ▼ In media

      ▼ In journals

    1.5 Conduct opinion surveys

      ▼ Among groups affected by issue

      ▼ Activists

      ▼ Employees

      ▼ Stockholders

    1.6 Determine what others are doing on this issue (avoid duplication, coordinate, counteract)

  2. Establish company's position on the issue

    2.1 Write policy as guide for all in company

    2.2 Distribute on need-to-know basis

III. Publics to Be Dealt With

  1. Employees

    1.1 All

    1.2 Select groups

      ▼ Executives

      ▼ Operating staff

      ▼ Subsidiaries' staff

      ▼ Local plant and office level

  2. Government

    2.1 Federal elected officials

    2.2 Federal appointed officials

    2.3 State elected officials

    2.4 State appointed officials

    2.5 Local elected officials

    2.6 Local appointed officials

  3. Financial community

  4. Stockholders

  5. Customers and prospective customers

  6. Unions

  7. Suppliers

  8. Plant and office communities

  9. Academia

  10. Other opinion leaders—churches, civic groups

  11. News media

    11.1 Press

    11.2 TV and radio

  12. Other media

    12.1 Books and reference works

    12.2 Business publications

    12.3 Trade publications

    12.4 Alternative press

IV. Activities

  1. Prepare authoritative document on the issue or opportunity that can be the key source for all concerned with it

    ▼ Distribute to affected government officials and personnel, colleges, journals, public media, other industry members, associations

  2. Designate company representatives on this issue or opportunity, and establish lines of authority for communicating on it

  3. Prepare executives for questioning by media, testifying to committees, conducting meetings

  4. Prepare testimony before Congress, government agencies, etc.

  5. Prepare fact cards on the issue and company sources (with home phone numbers) for distribution to media

  6. Set up emergency plan

    ▼ Line of authority

    ▼ Facilities for the media on the site

  7. Statements ready as responses to charges or questions

  8. Press conference

  9. Press releases

  10. Fact sheets and photos for the media

  11. Videotape

    ▼ Record events

    ▼ Provide proof of developments and deter media distortion

    ▼ Prepare news footage for TV

  12. Literature

(Continued)

EXAMPLE 6.7

Checklist for Issues and Opportunities (*continued*)

13. Employee bulletins or letters

14. Employee publications

15. Advertising

16. Scripts for radio broadcast

17. Customer information—letters and literature

18. Letters to stockholders

19. Bulletin boards

20. Community meetings

21. Speeches

    ▼ Key executives

    ▼ Others at local levels

V. Set Timetable (with built-in flexibility)

VI. Establish Budget

VII. Review and Evaluation

1. Conduct survey as a measure against analysis of problem or opportunity at the start

2. Analyze cost of manpower utilization in terms of alleviation of the problem or progress in fulfilling opportunity

SOURCE: Philip Lesly, "Checklist on Issues and Opportunities," *Managing the Human Climate* 68 (May–June 1981). Reprinted with permission.

---

(2) shaping, for one that has media attention and therefore is on the public agenda; (3) coping, for issues that face legislative, regulatory or interest group action. When an issue is emerging, Mahon recommends dealing directly with the issue or with those who are promoting it, to defuse the situation. The most aggressive stance an organization can take is to shape or define the issue in its own terms. Shaping strategies include total resistance, bargaining, capitulation, termination and cessation of activity. If the issue has reached the coping stage, Mahon says, the organization has no choice but to change its behavior substantially.

Determining an issue's life-cycle stage isn't always easy. Many organizations subscribe to public opinion polling services such as Opinion Research Corporation, whose study of consumer attitudes toward U.S. goods and those made in Japan and Germany appears in Example 6.8, and the *Roper Center Review of Public Opinion and Polling*, which reprinted Gallup studies for various clients on the flag-burning issue (see Example 6.9). Other organizations subscribe to newsletters like *Future Watch* that specialize in monitoring trends.

Handling issues management internally is sometimes difficult, because it is likely to cross many lines of authority and require several levels of technical expertise. A process has to be in place to allow for efficient and effective response. One such process, developed by Dow Chemical, is shown in Example 6.10. In any event, enough publics must be convinced that the issue is a *legitimate concern* to them to motivate them to take or support action in response to it. The hole in the ozone layer is a good example of a longstanding problem that only recently achieved public legitimacy. Polling helps determine this, but the organization most closely associated with the issue must evaluate legitimacy and the implications of action in terms of each of its key publics before setting policy.

One of the hardest parts of handling issues is convincing management that an issue needs to be addressed. Richard Long, manager of Dow Chemical's corporate communications, suggests a four-step process: (1) state the issue or problem in the most specific terms possible, and describe the various effects it can have on the organization; (2) identify adversaries and friends; (3) develop a strategy that includes deciding whether to take the initiative; (4) determine whether to involve coalitions.[16]

According to Richard Claeys and J. Sherman Feher, issue management is at the core of the decision-making process at the Electric Power Research Institute. Issue monitoring and analysis is used to determine the research agenda that justifies EPRI's nonprofit status.[17] Working from different social, economic and political assumptions, EPRI predicts world demand for and supply of natural gas.

A similar method is used by the Gas Research Institute (GRI), one of many organizations that approach issues management from a global perspective. More than ever before, organizations are affected by world events. For example, Jim Morrissey of the American Textile Manufacturers' Institute cited U.S. public opinion polls that tied American politics to world trade issues.[18] This trend seems likely to continue growing because the news media have discovered that the public is interested in international issues and so are giving them greater attention, according to John Merriam, chairman of the Conference on Issues and Media, which created the National Media Index, a computerized database of media coverage.[19]

No organization that has struggled with the South African apartheid issue would argue with Merriam. The South African government's policies on race became a domestic civil rights issue in the United States, and activist organizations began pressuring companies to divest themselves of all holdings in South Africa.

Issue Prediction

Anticipating the impact public opinion will have on issues such as how companies operate in the apartheid society of South Africa is the responsibility of public relations practitioners. They rely on

▼ **Anticipating trouble and heading it off are primary responsibilities of issues management. Some issues managers act as futurists for their organizations.**

issue analysis of the type that Merriam's organization offers, and on opinion polls and annual professional newsletters that predict important global issues and trends, as well as issues and trends of specific importance to PR practitioners. They may also rely on futurists.

A futurist develops a collective consciousness within an organization of the emerging environment. Strategies for dealing with this emerging future then evolve from the collective consciousness. Not only may the futurist be found under many different titles in the organization, he or she also may come from any of a number of educational backgrounds. (The *Futures Research Directory* lists more than 1,100 individuals from 60 countries.) But regardless of title and background, the futurist has to be a superior conceptual thinker.[20]

Futurists are called "issues managers" in some companies, although a more appropriate title might be "issues identifiers, predictors or monitors." The planning they engage in is called a precrisis approach by Archie Boe, who set up one of the first early warning departments when he headed Sears's Allstate Insurance unit. Atlantic Richfield Company also established an issues identification system, because it felt its planning was too numbers-oriented.

Efforts like those of Allstate and Atlantic Richfield to broaden the traditional planning base include the use of computer software services, which are being developed to accumulate files on legislative leaders, prominent spokespeople, voting records, legislation, speeches and other public documents. Computerized storage of information like this makes cross-listing easier and helps PR departments track issues efficiently and retrieve information for reports.

EXAMPLE 6.8

AFFLUENT CONSUMERS GIVE JAPAN, GERMANY HIGHER MARKS THAN U.S. FOR QUALITY PRODUCTS; AMERICANS SEE MUCH CRITICISM OF JAPANESE TRADE PRACTICES AS UNFAIR

A recent survey conducted by Opinion Research Corporation (ORC), of Princeton, New Jersey, reveals that most affluent Americans are favorably impressed by the quality of German and Japanese products; in fact, more Americans rate these countries' products as superior in quality than do so for American goods.

A further reflection of the high regard for Japanese products is that Japan is seen as being unfairly blamed for America's economic problems by much of the American public.

The more upscale segments of the U.S. population have a particularly favorable impression of German and Japanese goods. College-educated consumers, and those with annual incomes of $50,000 or more, are much more likely to believe that the products of Germany and Japan are of superior quality than they are to bestow the same laurels on American manufacturers. About one-third of upper-income consumers designate German and Japanese products as superior in quality; only one-fifth believe U.S. goods to be in the same class. Among college-educated Americans, the results are even less favorable for U.S. manufacturers: German and Japanese products are deemed to be of superior quality by 29% and 37%, respectively. U.S. products are rated this highly by only one college graduate out of ten.

Consumers with the greatest buying power generally shop for quality products, spend the most money, and set the trends for the nation. It's unfortunate that this prime segment is the one most likely to view certain foreign products as being of superior quality to those of their own country. U.S. companies must act quickly and decisively to restore their image at home as a world leader in quality if they hope to regain market share and compete effectively with foreign manufacturers.

Among American consumers overall, the preference for foreign products is less pronounced than among the more affluent segments of the public; nevertheless, Japanese (25%) and German (21%) products do rank ahead of American goods (20%) in terms of ratings for superior quality.

Korean and Taiwanese products continue to suffer from an image of cheapness and shoddy quality. Virtually no one rates the goods of these countries as being of generally superior quality, while more than half rate their quality as not very good or poor.

The praise that Americans lavish on Japanese products may help to explain one aspect of the U.S. public's attitude towards trade with Japan. A majority of Americans (54%) believe there is truth in the statement that the U.S. is blaming Japan for its own economic problems. At the same time, there is a large proportion (42%) who accept the idea that Japanese companies are competing unfairly.

Americans' opinions on this issue are divided along generational lines. The belief that Japanese companies are competing unfairly with their American counterparts is held by 48% of people aged 60 or older, compared to 35% of the under 30 age group. While 40% of senior Americans believe that Japan is being blamed unfairly for the United States' own economic problems, about two-thirds (63%) of young Americans believe Japan is a scapegoat for America's economic woes.

Americans' attitudes, and perhaps even their instincts about Japan appear to be molded by impressions they formed early in life. For some older Americans, Pearl Harbor may have gouged a permanent scar in their perception of Japanese motives and trustworthiness. Younger Americans, on the other hand, grew up associating Japan with top-of-the-line cameras and cars rather than World War II. For older Americans, the attitudes of the young toward Japan may appear to be dangerously naive; for the young, the perceptions of their elders may seem anachronistic and overly suspicious.

(*Continued*)

Country's Products Are of Superior Quality

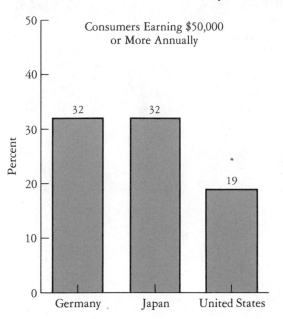

Consumers Earning $50,000 or More Annually

Excludes those having no opinion

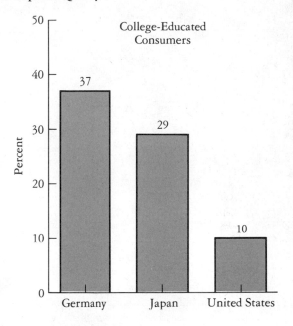

College-Educated Consumers

Excludes those having no opinion

Quality Ratings of United States' and Foreign Products

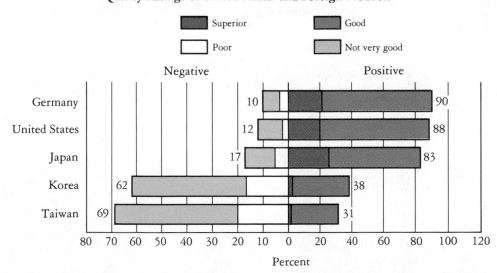

Excludes those having no opinion

Attitudes Toward Trade with Japan

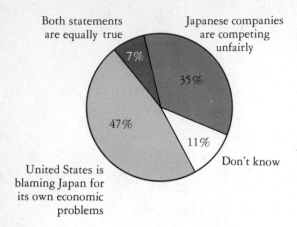

Both statements are equally true — 7%

Japanese companies are competing unfairly — 35%

Don't know — 11%

United States is blaming Japan for its own economic problems — 47%

About the survey: These findings are drawn from a survey of 1,001 adult heads of households conducted by ORC on behalf of Maryland Public Television. Interviewing was conducted January 6–8, 1989. Results from a sample of this size will have an error attributable to sampling of ±3 percentage points at the 95% level of confidence.

The results of this survey were originally reported in Louis Rukeyser's column and on the PBS television special, "Louis Rukeyser's 1989 Money Guide," in late January.

Opinion Research Corporation, which was founded in 1938, is one of the largest firms conducting strategic research and consulting relating to marketing, corporate reputations, service quality and organization effectiveness.

Following are the questions, as asked and in the order asked, and the responses.

I'd like to know how you rate the *overall quality* of products made in various countries. For each country that I mention, please tell me if you think the quality of its products is superior, good, not very good, or poor.

	Superior	Good	Not Very Good	Poor
a. Germany	21%	69	7	3
b. Japan	25%	58	12	5
c. Korea	2%	36	45	17
d. Taiwan	1%	30	49	20
e. The United States	20%	68	10	2

Which of these statements comes closer to your opinion?

1. Japanese companies are competing unfairly with American companies, or   35%

2. The United States is blaming Japan for its own economic problems   47

3. Both statements equally true (volunteered)   7

4. Don't know/no opinion   11

Reprinted with permission of Opinion Research Corporation.

▼ ISSUES AND THE ROLE OF THE PR PRACTITIONER

More than any other executive (except the chief executive), the PR practitioner must know what is going on inside and outside the organization and how the organization's activities and functions interrelate and relate to others'. He or she also is expected to bring awareness and objectivity to the job and to inject unvarnished, usable facts into the decision-making process.

The PR person learns about what is happening outside the organization by being exposed to pressures generated by various groups seeking support. The role of the practitioner here is sensitive and complex.

Sometimes, the PR practitioner must play devil's advocate, raising all the salient arguments against a proposed action and explaining which decisions will have an adverse effect on certain groups. Sometimes actions must be taken that will offend a major public, and management should be warned in advance and offered some way of successfully explaining to the public why the action is necessary.

Years ago, no one foresaw the role public relations now plays in relation to current issues and social crises. No longer primarily a communicator, the PR practitioner must act as an intervenor who tries to prevent a potential problem from getting out of hand. Indeed, the most valuable public relations activity consists of steps designed to prevent problems or at least to solve them while they are small.

Some of the tools the PR practitioner uses, such as personal contact and mass media, remain the same. The proper measure of performance is not how effectively the client's message gets across, however, but whether a flareup that can stop a client's business can be avoided. The public relations practitioner has an obligation to help employers or clients conduct their business in a way that responds to the new demands made by concerned scientists, environmentalists, consumerists, minority leaders, underprivileged segments of the community and employees.

Internal and External Publics

Management's perception of priority publics—both internal and external—is not always accurate, as the following story demonstrates.

The owner of a specialty store with a reputation for expensive, high-quality merchandise was asked by other local retail merchants to join them in a downtown promotional campaign. The owner was skeptical. "We have the carriage trade," she said, "and a great deal of out-of-town, even international business. Frankly, I can't see that it would be worth our time." But then someone who had noticed that the specialty store was highest both in dollar volume and in individual receipts asked the owner where the store's volume of business was centered. Might the customers responsible for all those re-

▼ **As a PR practitioner, you need to know how your messages are likely to affect the various publics you depend on for goodwill.**

ceipts be young professionals, many of whom worked downtown? They were the kind of people who could afford only a couple of high-priced outfits but were willing to make the investment to get the style and quality the specialty store offered. And might these people, since they were climbing the career ladder, tend to buy smaller-priced gifts simply to get the store's label? Intrigued, the owner did some research. She found to her amazement that, although she did have the carriage trade, which made substantial purchases, her daily volume came from downtown career workers. She participated in the downtown promotion and became as excited as any businessperson with a new market discovery.

Knowing who your target publics are implies knowing what to say to them and how to say it (see Exercise 6.11). You need to know how your messages are likely to affect the various publics you depend on for goodwill. A university administrator once forgot this when, during a talk to prospective students and their parents, he thoughtlessly said, "To maintain high standards of teaching, we try to have as few teaching assistants as possible." His remark, dutifully reported in the university's student newspaper, aroused a predictably hostile reaction from graduate students who served as teaching assistants. The president did not set out to offend the TAs, of course; it was just a thoughtless remark, but one he might not have made had he been particularly conscious of the composition of his audience.

Awareness of publics and their responses requires heightened sensitivity, constant alertness and a lot of guessing, unless you have and regularly update a statistical profile of these publics. A trend in public relations away from the artistic to the scientific is noticeable. More and more clients ask

EXAMPLE 6.9

Public Opinion Summary of an Issue by the *Roper Center Review of Public Opinion and Polling*

PUBLIC OPINION ON THE FLAG

On June 21, 1990, the House of Representatives voted 254–177 in favor of a constitutional amendment permitting laws which prohibit the desecration of the US flag. This was 34 votes short of the two-thirds majority required (in each house) under Article V of the Constitution.

What does the US public think about a flag-protection amendment? How strong is public sentiment? How likely is a vote cast in the House June 21 to influence votes cast in the country next November? The data on these two pages summarize what surveys tell us on these questions.

	% Disagree with Court's Decision	% Favor Constitutional Amendment	% Saying Vote on Flag Amendment Is Very Important
All Respondents	58	69	40
By Sex:			
Male	59	67	39
Female	57	70	41
By Education:			
College Graduate	53	56	27
Some College	72	71	34
High School Grad	53	75	46
Less than HS Grad	61	66	50
By Party ID:			
Republican	64	76	41
Democrat	56	63	40
Independent	55	68	37
By Position on Court Decision:			
Agree with decision	—	50	25
Disagree with decision	—	82	51

QUESTIONS: Page 24—The Supreme Court ruled this week that burning the American flag, though highly offensive, is protected under the free speech guarantee of the First Amendment to the Constitution. Do you agree or disagree?; Do you think we should pass a Constitutional Amendment to make flag-burning illegal, or not?; How important is a candidate's position on the flag burning issue when you decide how to vote in an election for Governor, members of Congress, or state legislature? (Gallup/Newsweek, June 13–14, 1990) Page 25—Would you support a new Constitutional Amendment that would make flag-burning illegal? (Gallup/Newsweek, June 23, 1989); Do you think we should pass a Constitutional Amendment to make flag-burning illegal or not? (Gallup/Newsweek, June 13–14, 1990); Should burning or destroying the American flag as a form of political protest be legal or should it be against the law? [If "against the law," ask:] If the only way to make flag destruction illegal was to change the Constitution, would you favor or oppose a Constitutional amendment making it illegal to destroy the flag for political reasons? (CBS News/New York Times, May 22–24, 1990); How important is a candidate's position on the flag-burning issue when you decide how to vote in an election for Governor, member of Congress, or state legislation? (Gallup/Newsweek, June 13–14, 1990).

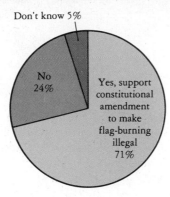

Don't know 5%

No 24%

Yes, support constitutional amendment to make flag-burning illegal 71%

Survey by the Gallup Organization for Newsweek, June 23, 1989

Don't know 5%

No 27%

Yes, should pass a constitutional amendment to make flag-burning illegal 69%

Survey by the Gallup Organization for Newsweek, June 13-14, 1990

"The Congress and the states shall have the power to prohibit the physical desecration of the flag of the United States."

—Proposed amendment

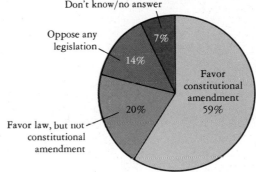

Don't know/no answer 7%

Oppose any legislation 14%

Favor law, but not constitutional amendment 20%

Favor constitutional amendment 59%

Survey by CBS News/New York Times, May 22-24, 1990

How Important?

Those favoring amendment:

Those opposing amendment:

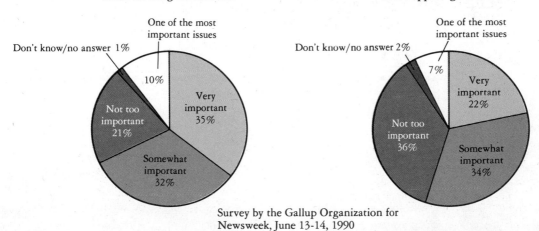

One of the most important issues

Don't know/no answer 1%

10%

Not too important 21%

Very important 35%

Somewhat important 32%

One of the most important issues

Don't know/no answer 2%

7%

Very important 22%

Not too important 36%

Somewhat important 34%

Survey by the Gallup Organization for Newsweek, June 13-14, 1990

EXAMPLE 6.10 ■

Format for Issue Analysis

ISSUE ANALYSIS WORKSHEET

This worksheet is intended as a guide in developing constructive company programs for dealing with emerging and/or current issues. Completion of the worksheet might logically lead to the following steps:

1. An Issue Overview Statement or executive summary which describes the scope, intensity and direction of an issue; no more than two typewritten pages.

2. A Public Affairs Strategy Proposal which spells out a particular course of action for management review and support.

3. A Company Position Paper which defines, in a paragraph or two, the company's response and/or policy on the issue; this should be particularly useful in handling media queries.

ISSUE ANALYSIS

Issue: _____

Management responsibility for the issue:

Who is in *overall* charge? _____

Research: _____

Public Affairs: _____

Government Affairs: _____

Commercial: _____

U.S. Area Management: _____

Manufacturing/Division: _____

Corporate Management: _____

Legal: _____

Who is responsible for handling media calls on this issue?

1. Primary _____

2. Backup _____

Describe the level and intensity of media interest to date. Who are the key reporters and their organizations? Are any "themes" emerging from the news coverage?

What is the potential impact of this issue on the company's operations and/or its reputation?

Describe any state or federal *legislative* implications:

What, if any, are the state or federal *regulatory* implications?

_____

practitioners to back up their advice with scientific evidence. As Wayne Danielson summarizes:

> The point is simply this: Interest in science and in asking the scientific question is part of the spirit of our times. Professional communicators cannot avoid these questions. They encounter them all the time. They frequently ask them themselves. And

they cannot indefinitely avoid giving a scientific as opposed to an artistic answer.

> This is basically what communication research is all about. It is an attempt to give scientific answers to scientific questions about communication.[21]

Being aware of publics and their opinions depends on having ready access to information that

What are the key *legal* implications, e.g., litigation filed or trial dates pending?

What do we know about the public opinion on this issue? Does the evidence suggest that public opinion is (or can be) susceptible to change?

What are the geographic considerations of this issue?

On a scale of 1–10 (10 being the worst), what is our vulnerability to:

____ Bad publicity	____ Congressional testimony	____ Community unrest/fear
____ Significant lawsuits		
____ Customer backlash	____ Plant shut-down	____ Security concerns
____ Employee morale problems	____ Regulatory action	____ Product recall/ban
	____ Drop in stock price	____ Terrorist activity
____ New legislation	____ Network television coverage	

STRATEGIC CONSIDERATIONS

What are the toughest questions we will be asked by key parties in this controversy? What are our answers?

What might (Name of Company) say and/or do to defuse or minimize this issue? How might it be turned into a plus?

Are there opportunities for a coalition approach to the issue? Who are our likely allies, and how can they help us?

Are there opportunities for compromise or joint study of the problem? If this issue has not yet flared, what steps might be taken to begin or accelerate dialogue with our adversaries?

What specific actions must be taken (and by whom) to improve our understanding of this issue?

This format was developed by The Dow Chemical Company and is reprinted here with permission.

helps give an accurate picture of where they stand on issues facing an organization. "The whole world of information has changed. . . . Just about any question you can ask can be answered out of a database," says Andrew Garvin, whose company, FIND/SVP of New York, is in the business of selling answers.[22] Institutions accumulate a wealth of information in their daily operations. Unless some thought is given to how that information might be used, though, it is useless.

Research for sound public relations planning can be built into a record-keeping system, provided that retrieval is also carefully considered. Information about PR audiences is critical, but it only

EXAMPLE 6.11

Internal and External Publics and Media

PR people prioritize publics by knowing the characteristics of members of the various publics, which they discover through advance research.

	Internal	**External**	
		Direct (marketing communications)	*Indirect (institutional communications)*
Publics	Management (top and middle)		
	Staff and employees (union and nonunion employee organizations)	Customers	Potential customers
	Stockholders	Sales representatives	Potential investors (stockholders)
	Directors	Traders and distributors	Financial community
		Suppliers	Special community of institution
		Competitors	Government (local, state, federal)
			Community (environmental)
Media	Personal (person to person/person to group)	Personal (person to person/person to group)	
	Audiovisual (specialized media: films, slides, videotape, closed circuit TV, computer networks)	Audiovisual (films, slides, videotape, mass media, specialized media available to external audiences such as slide presentations, etc.)	
	Publications (specialized media: books, magazines, newspapers, newsletters)	Publications (mass and specialized, including controlled and uncontrolled publicity, as well as institutional and commercial advertising)	
	Direct mail	Direct mail (personalized, institutional and sales promotion)	
	Exhibits (including posters, bulletin board materials and personalized items such as pins and awards)	Exhibits (mass and specialized, including product packaging, graphics and point-of-sale promotions)	
	Critics (individuals and institutions)		

SOURCE: Adapted from Doug Newsom and Bob Carrell, *Public Relations Writing*, 3d ed. (Belmont, Calif.: Wadsworth, 1990), p. 11.

has value if it can be accessed. For example, a team handling reorganization and five-year planning for a professional organization concluded that some basic information about membership was crucial to its decision making and called the organization's national headquarters for the needed facts. They were told that the information had been gathered, but that the organization did not have a software program capable of generating the specifics about members the team needed. The information was therefore of no use to it.

The president of one research company uses a method he calls cross-tabulation of data to develop profiles of his clients' PR publics. He takes a company's own fact-finding operation and extracts from it a general picture of its publics. He combines this with more generally available research in the field, such as published public opinion studies, to get a broad picture. Then he develops a set of questions to use in interviewing small segments of these publics. The quantitative information furnishes the base from which he can go after specific qualitative information—a technique he laughingly calls "coloring by numbers." There may be a broad outline and a number suggesting what color to use, but until colors—the qualitative research—are applied, the picture is not complete.

Internal Publics and Perceptions of the Organization   One important aspect of an organization's internal publics is their perception of the organization: its image in their eyes. A word needs to be said about "images" in connection with public relations. Most PR practitioners would gladly ban use of the word *image* because it's so often misused and misunderstood and because they don't like being depicted as "image makers." Nonetheless, *image* does describe the perception of an organization or individual, and this perception is based largely on what an organization or an individual does and says. Of course, the organization seldom is perceived in exactly the same way by all of its publics at any given time, but we will return to this subject a bit later.

One major contributor to virtually every public's perception of an organization is the organization's

▼ **Collective perceptions about an organization by its publics, based on what it says and does, constitute its image.**

___

employees. To complicate matters, employees are themselves an organizational public that has its own perceptions of the organization. The role of employees is a significant concern in most PR efforts. In looking at the automobile industry, the National Academy of Engineering produced a study funded by the National Science Foundation that noted:

> In the case of productivity, product quality and the role of the work force, we are talking about something close to a cultural revolution, about fundamental changes in the way the business is managed and the ways people at all levels participate in the enterprise.[23]

The lack of homogeneity in any public poses problems for the public relations practitioner trying to evaluate it. This is especially true of employees, since they exist on many different levels: salespeople, clerks and receptionists, technicians, professionals, administrators. Moreover, within each group, some people see themselves as embarked on a career while others see their work only as a job. Beyond that, subgroups exist in all of the main categories—such as professionals, which may include engineers, researchers and lawyers. The way these people work together and the way the administration works with them create a corporate or organizational culture, which strongly affects how employees behave in relationships to each other and to outsiders. This in turn affects how the organization is perceived.

Collective perceptions about an organization by its publics, based on what it says and does, constitute its *image*. "Every organization has an image. The only question is whether it has the image it wants to have—in fact as well as in fantasy," says Harry Levinson, a clinical psychologist. Levinson explains:

[Psychoanalyst Sigmund] Freud points out that individuals in any cohesive organization identify with the ego ideal [ideal stereotype] of their leader. As an organization expands and matures, this ego tends to become the collective aspirations of its people. Diffuse as this may sound, it is real. Industrial psychologists have long known that people, if they have any choice in the matter, will not work for an organization when they disapprove of its image, its self-image, and its ego ideal.[24]

In other words, employee attitudes often accurately reflect an organization's image of itself. Employees who are indifferent to the organization's ideal of itself may stay on the payroll, but they will do nothing beyond the minimum demanded.

For employees to react in any way to an organizational ideal, that ideal must be defined, communicated and understood. Many institutions have never tried to define theirs accurately, and the result is often a fragmented reaction to the institution, its policies and its products. In other instances, the ideal is too vague or is just rhetoric, as when an oil company says it believes understanding and goodwill must be earned through the application of sound and ethical principles in the conduct of every phase of its business, but then embarks on a path of conduct that raises ethical questions that its ideal offers no practical guidance for handling.

The real difficulty is not in stating an ideal, but in living up to it. When an organization fails to act consistently with its projected ideal, employees, customers and the community are disillusioned. But while customers may simply take their dollars elsewhere, employees express their disillusionment in other ways, particularly if economic circumstances do not permit them to quit. If they stay, they often have feelings of depression, apathy, alienation and outright anger. These feelings are compounded if a company advertises that people are its most important asset, but its own employees have a different experience. They will, of course, see their leaders as hypocrites and will react with open or covert hostility.

Negative feelings can also result when employees cannot contribute toward attaining an ideal. For example, a company's pride in the steel panels it makes may be shared by all employees except those in the paint department, who know that the paints they apply will wear off quickly because the company has not invested in the necessary process for baking on the enamels. The resulting cynicism causes high turnover in that department and may undermine morale elsewhere in the company.

Clinical psychologist Levinson compares an organization to a human being:

> If you want to understand a person, you examine him. You may do so systematically, as a physician does, or you may get to know much about him over a long period of time, as a friend does. First, you try to learn who and what he is. Second, you try to learn how he behaves under various circumstances. Third, you want to know what he believes and how he sees the world, how he presents himself to the world and why he does so that way. If there is a wide gap between the image he projects and the person he really is, emotional conflicts are inevitable.[25]

The measures Levinson recommends for determining an organization's image are as follows (see Example 6.12):

▼ *What it does*, as evidenced in its products and services and in the way it regards its employees ("economic units to be purchased and directed" or "capable, mature people").

▼ *What it says*, through communication with employees ("exhortation and persuasion" or "mutual definition of common problems") and with its customers ("someone to be conned by promising more than can be delivered" or "to be duped by clever packaging").

▼ *What people believe it to be.*

Although the best way to find out what various publics think is by scientific research, you can also ask a few informal questions: (1) If the institution has an image, does it live up to it? Or does it say one thing and do another? (2) If the organization has an image, can employees live up to it? Or do

EXAMPLE 6.12

Institutional Image

PROBLEM PROFILE

1. What an institution's employees think it is. ○
What employees want it to be. ⊘

2. What an institution's management thinks it is. △
What management wants it to be. ▽

3. What an institution's external publics think it is. □
What external publics want it to be. ▭

Difficulties occur when the two profiles overlap and the lines are not harmonious. For example, in problem profile 3, the public wants the institution to be ▭ (buses to all major shopping districts on the hour, six days a week, for 50 cents fare), but it is □ (buses to three major shopping districts, 10 A.M. to 6 P.M., five days a week, for 75 cents fare plus area add-on tolls). The result is ▭□, a poor fit.

LEVINSON'S IMAGE THEORY ILLUSTRATED

	Problem Profile	Positive Profile
What an institution does.	○	○
What it says.	□	○
What people believe it to be.	△	○
How these fit.	⧌	◎

Levinson says an institution is a mix of what it does and what people believe it to be. If these fit, the image is consonant.

---

conflicting demands, low pay, or other factors render this impossible? (3) When an image change is necessary, have the employees been helped to make the change through participative management? (4) If the company has no recognizable image, does this result in confusion, limited identification and disparate values?

Internal publics are likely to be particularly sensitive to how an institution is presented to an external public because, as a part of that institution, their ego is involved.

A university that decided to do some preregistration advertising discovered just how touchy such egos can be, when returning students who had heard the radio commercials raised a storm of protest. What the protesters *said* was, "A really excellent institution of higher learning shouldn't have to advertise." However, when the protesters were asked in small group sessions whether it was unseemly to "call attention to the programs and services the university had to offer, just in case people were unaware of them," they agreed that this was acceptable.

The problem, it turned out, involved the type of advertising used. The critics considered broadcasting a bit flamboyant, although they admitted that it was the best way to reach the target audience of eighteen-year-olds. But even here, the medium was not fundamentally at fault in their view; the *style* of commercials was. The protesting students saw the style of the commercials as inconsistent with the image they had of their university. They complained about the lack of "dignity" in the appeals. The problem was rooted in inconsistency of imagery.

The university's solution was to increase student involvement in all its planning for presenting the university to its publics—especially to potential students. The current students needed to feel comfortable with the image being portrayed because they shared that image.

Part of the philosophy behind this solution was that current students, as an internal public, may be the best recruiters a university has. Certainly, they (along with faculty) have the highest credibility among external publics because they are in a position to know how it really functions. Often, however, because of poor internal communications, they don't. The wise public relations practitioner focuses on internal publics to keep them involved and informed, because theirs are the voices likely to be heard and believed by external publics.

Internal publics are popularly considered authorities, whether they really are or not. For example, a plant manufacturing planes for the U.S. government received some unwelcome publicity when one of the multimillion-dollar aircraft failed to function. Since the plane was new, each time one aircraft malfunctioned, all were grounded until the fault could be detected. The community in which the planes were being made was very sensitive to the publicity. One employee, whose job was plant security, told of being asked constantly by people at his church, at his club, at the grocery store and even in his yard, "Come on, tell me, what's *really* wrong with those birds." He honestly didn't know. The reasons, like the plane, were very complex. Besides that, he had no engineering experience and was not involved in the design or construction of the plane. But people sought his judgment and took his words as authoritative because, since he worked there, "he ought to know."

Realizing that each member of an internal public is a potentially significant public relations asset could make most public relations directors' jobs easier. The best way to promote the use of internal publics as PR's front line is to make employees feel involved. PR researcher James Grunig says that a person involved in a situation seeks information, and that a person motivated to communicate about a situation is also motivated to develop a solution for it. For example, a city having difficulty with old gas meters that record higher levels of consump-

tion than actually exist needs to inform those on the front line—the meter readers. They will be in contact with customers, and if they understand the problem and what the company is doing to solve the problem, they are more likely to communicate. If the company goes farther and provides them with information to give customers, the typical communication constraint—that it's someone else's job—is removed. If the company generally keeps its front-line meter readers, receptionists and so on informed, the effectiveness of the PR front line will be much improved.

Internal surveys to find out what employees think of their organization are now as common as external ones. Evidence suggests that labor strife can be reduced by *regular* employee attitude surveys. Such surveys often influence organizational decisions on personnel policies, work practices, communication, productivity, compensation, organizational structure and physical plant improvements (see Example 6.13).

The organizational behavior of employees produces a corporate or organizational culture that contributes significantly to the organization's image. Joseph F. Coates, president of a Washington, D.C., policy research firm that studies the future, views the concept of corporate culture as recognizing that every stable human organization has consistent patterns of behavior reflecting implicit and explicit beliefs and values. Coates says that the cultural characteristics of an organization are usually expressed in positive terms by employees, who often fail to see how outsiders may perceive the same company behavior or policy in negative terms—for example, as "paternalistic," "moralistic" or "intrusive into personal matters," rather than as "offering counseling" or "genuinely concerned."

Coates identifies two widely held beliefs regarding the corporate culture. One is that the corporate culture comes from the top down. The other is that the culture determines or strongly influences a corporation's willingness to embrace change, promote innovation, tolerate dissent, encourage criticism, experiment and allow for other qualities that

EXAMPLE 6.13

Production-line Problem

Should you always take workers' complaints at face value? Think twice before you do! Maybe communications problems are the real cause of the trouble.

St. Louis public relations consultant Alfred Fleishman, in his [1973] book *Troubled Talk*, tells of a client who was having "all kinds of problems" at one of his plants. In this plant, two identical production lines existed side by side.

Employees on the first line complained about their physical working conditions. It was "too cold in the winter, too hot in the summer." There "wasn't enough light. The machines were too close together." Employees complained about high accident rates and other matters. Absenteeism was high.

But researchers noted that employees on the second production line had few complaints, low absenteeism and a low accident rate. So instead of making the physical changes in the factory called for by the first group, the investigators dug deeper. And here's what they found.

In answer to the question "How does your boss criticize you, in public or in private?" more than 75

percent of the first group said the boss always criticized them in public. This compared with about 10 percent in the second group. Other questions revealed similar differences between the two groups. The answers convinced Mr. Fleishman that neither new lights nor new air conditioning and heating systems would solve the problem.

Instead, the supervisor of the first production line was taken off his job and sent back for more training. The supervisor of the second group replaced him. Months later, a follow-up study showed that the first group's complaints had dropped sharply, along with absenteeism and accidents. Nothing physical had changed; only the boss.

SOURCE: Alfred Fleishman and William D. Meyer, *Troubled Talk* (San Francisco: International Society for General Semantics, 1973); printed in "persuasion," 21, edited by Chester Burger, May 27, 1974, supplement of *pr reporter*, Exeter, NH. Used by permission.

---

characterize a competitive firm. Organizations with especially strong corporate cultures *may* enjoy a more cohesive image, but they tend to be less flexible and don't adapt well to change. Furthermore, the influence of the corporate culture is also shaped by its environment (location), its business (for example, TV or manufacturing) and the primary culture of its employees (for example, American or Japanese).

Typically, PR practitioners are not asked to convince employees that they should accept the corporate culture. People usually go to work in a place where they are comfortable. The more common problem public relations must deal with is *changing* a corporate culture when new leadership arrives.

Although he recommends that employees be "brought along" through discussions and requests for their input, Coates concedes that the job is not easy. Philip Lesly is more pessimistic. He says it is akin to "turning over an elephant with a shoe horn."[26] People are more likely to change their jobs than to change their values.

External Publics and Perceptions of the Organization   External publics are not the exclusive property of any institution. Any external public may become a target for public relations activities. For example, high-school students and recent graduates who might become college freshmen are target publics for university recruiting. Other prospective candidates for college are students in community colleges and working people who might want to return to school or enter for the first time.

Looking at the different subsets of people who constitute an organization's external publics helps PR practitioners avoid the fallacy of considering external publics as a "mass public." There is no such thing as a "mass audience or public." External publics usually consist of larger segments of people than do internal publics, but never should external publics be thought of as an undifferentiated "mass."[27]

External publics may be a constituency—like the residents of cities that have a professional sports team—or they may be an adversary—as antinuclear advocates are to electric utilities. Both types must be considered in public relations planning and communication strategies. External publics also have a great deal to do with an institution's image. When external publics and internal publics share similar perceptions of what the institution is and what it should be, the institution's image is likely to be sound because it is consistent.

The perception of an organization's image may vary from public to public, and it may change over time. Owing to significant economic, technological and demographic changes in the business environment, Stephen Downey predicts that American corporations will have to work continuously at redefining and projecting an appropriate corporate image to their external publics. As Downey, a corporate PR practitioner, observes:

> Corporate identity (in most companies still the province of public relations) will be expected to define and project—accurately, understandably, efficiently and memorably—the essence of those surviving and emerging companies. Moreover, it must do so within what is becoming truly a world economy and internationally competitive marketplace. Those companies which communicate their identity most compellingly by cutting through customer confusion and gaining the allegiance of key audiences are most likely to prosper in the new order (translate opportunity).[28]

Downey says that the organizations must reexamine their identity under the following circumstances:

▼ When public perceptions of a company do not reflect reality. Vestiges of past management mistakes, poor earnings, environmental problems, and the like may still be having a negative impact.

▼ When external forces such as a new competitor, a breakthrough product, deregulation, or an existing competitor's new identity require identification countermeasures.

▼ When competitors are slow to form clearly defined and effectively projected corporate and/or product presentation. In this sense, identity is opportunistic and can become a competitive advantage in itself.

A company that tries to impose a culture on members of its organization is headed for trouble. Corporate or organizational culture is "real and powerful," according to a *Fortune* article. "It's also hard to change, and you won't find much support for doing so inside or outside your company."[29]

In examining corporate cultures, and especially in looking at their relationship to external audiences, you should keep in mind the differences between attitudes, opinions and beliefs. Although some people use the terms *"attitudes," "opinions"* and *"beliefs"* indiscriminately, social scientists generally define each of them differently. **Attitudes** are tendencies or orientations toward something or someone—a state of mind, a manner, a disposition, a position. **Opinions** are expressions of estimates or judgments—generally something not as strongly held as a conviction, but articulating a sentiment or point of view. **Beliefs** are convictions firmly implanted in the bedrock of one's value system, embodying one's sense of truth.

Priority Publics and Planning   Tailoring public relations programs to fit various priority publics requires identifying the publics and their characteristics (through both formal and informal research methods), translating this information into a sensitive understanding of their needs, and then knowing how to communicate with them (see Example 6.14). To develop a program that is both real and realistic—not merely a facade of imagery that disillusions and alienates—you must have respect for and empathy with the target publics.

A public is a priority not only when it is centrally affected by a PR recommendation, but also when it is the most influential group in determining whether an idea, policy, event, decision or product recommendation will be accepted. Once identified as a priority public, the group must be studied for its other relationships. Insensitivity to the composition of publics, to their interrelationships and to their ideals and attitudes, may lead an organization to waste much time, effort and money on public relations programs that bore or offend the intended recipients.

For instance, an incautious communication to corporate stockholders once suggested that their dividends were high because the company had resisted the demands of employees. When an outraged employee-stockholder shared the message with other employees, a considerable loss of confidence in the company resulted. In another instance, a professional organization's newsletter announcement about its annual meeting listed recreational activities for "the ladies," not taking into account that some of the organization's members were women whose husbands might be interested in the recreational activities. After two years of protests by the women members, the wording was changed to "spouses and families." Tailoring messages to fit a designated public calls for employing the concept that clothing manufacturers use. A certain style in a certain size may not fit or please everyone for whom it was designed. But when accepted by most of a particular type of customer, it is considered a success.

The importance to successful planning of knowing a particular priority public becomes clear when you consider the variety and disparity of different publics. A PR practitioner must have the acumen of a political scientist and the instincts of a politician to work effectively (for example) with the countless

▼ **To develop a real and realistic PR program, you must have respect for and empathy with the target publics.**

government agencies that directly regulate or indirectly affect an institution. A thorough knowledge of all levels of government and of the political system itself is essential, as is maintaining open lines of communication with elected representatives and administrators. Better to receive a warning from a friend and have some time to cope with the emerging problem than to read about it in the newspaper and then have to improvise, as did cereal company executives when they learned one morning in 1972 of publicity from a government source that accused them of producing food items with no nutritional value. For weeks shoppers in grocery stores were seen clutching the "official" list of the few "nutritional" cereals. The cereal companies had known nothing of the release until they read about it in the papers; then they had to get information from their own research departments before they could respond with counterarguments. Company publicity, when finally printed, did not make the front page.

The news media are often overlooked as a target public by PR practitioners in their planning. Those who regard the press as "the enemy" generally find this attitude reflected in news coverage of their organization. In contrast, a corporation that had always cooperated with the news media continued to do so when its plant was wracked by explosions. The explosions received front-page coverage, but only for one day—and the coverage was generally sympathetic to the business. Media reports described what the company was doing to help the victims and how it was attempting to discover the cause. Clearly, the PR practitioner can benefit from keeping in close contact with both mass and specialized

EXAMPLE 6.14 ▬▬▬▬▬▬▬▬▬▬▬▬▬▬▬▬▬▬▬▬▬

Tips on Motivating Publics to Act: Advice from a Psychologist

This article, by S. Plous, Ph.D., University of Illinois, is excerpted with permission from *Animals' Agenda*, the voice of the animal rights movement. The article is intended to stimulate more effective activism by critiquing tactics often used by activists. The author bases his insights on lessons from the nuclear freeze movement and psychological research on attitudes and behavior. The advice given is a succinct text for any practitioner trying to instill behavioral change.

1. If the goal is attitude change, do not use graphic images unless they're accompanied by specific actions people can execute.

Both the nuclear freeze campaign and the animal rights movement began by relying heavily on graphic images of death and destruction. Although these images are essential to a complete understanding of the issue, they run the risk of pushing people away rather than drawing them in. *Disturbing presentations rarely lead to sustained attitude change, and they are worst when people feel unable to prevent a negative outcome*. In fact, studies show this can actually reduce intentions to act.

2. Go to the public instead of asking the public to come to you.

Most people are well intentioned but will never become directly involved. By recognizing the limits of public interest and improvement, activists can develop realistic strategies that capitalize on public goodwill without demanding more than people are willing to give.

3. Don't assume that attitude change is necessary for behavior change.

A large body of psychological research casts doubt on the proposition that the best way to change behavior is to begin with attitudes. Attitudinal change often follows changes in behavior, rather than the other way around. Yet even when attitudinal change precedes behavioral change, sustained changes in behavior are rare. Any event organizer frustrated by the discrepancy between interest and actual attendance can attest to this.

Informing smokers of the link between cigarettes and cancer is easier than persuading them to quit. Informing people how a leghold trap works is easier than persuading them to support a ban on trapping.

Assuming attitude change would lead to legislative change, the nuclear freeze movement devoted most of its resources toward education and persuasion. The result was little legislation and no nuclear freeze. Of course, changing attitudes can be a worthy goal in its own right, and there is nothing wrong with allocating resources to this end—*as long as it's viewed as an end in itself*.

4. If behavior change is your goal, use moral arguments as adjuncts rather than main arguments.

Moral views are difficult to change. It is much easier to gain support for a nuclear freeze by stressing

media such as trade, industry and association publications.

An important but seldom mentioned public is the competition. The competition is an important public to know, communicate and work with. Institutions that maintain fair and honest dealings with their competitors usually establish this relationship through trade or association organizations. It is harder to insult someone you know personally. In addition, mutual respect within an industry or profession helps prevent open hostilities that could damage everyone. For example, in 1974 a paint practical advantages of arms control than by emphasizing the immorality of the arms race. Similarly, it's much easier to convert most people to a meatless diet by discussing the health benefits of vegetarianism than by discussing whether the Bible gives people dominion over animals.

Even though the activists may be moved by moral arguments, they should not assume these arguments will affect others the same way. Moral arguments are useful adjuncts, but in most cases, they are not sufficient to change how people behave.

5. Embrace the mainstream.

It's absolutely critical that activists embrace people from all walks of life. Otherwise, [a] movement runs the risk of being discounted as radical or faddish. One problem the nuclear freeze movement encountered in building a broad constituency was that many sympathizers didn't support a nuclear freeze per se.

The animal rights movement suffers from a similarly restrictive title: many people who care about animals do not believe in animal rights. Some are uncomfortable with the arguments, or view such arguments as irrelevant to animals' welfare. It would be a tragedy to lose the support of these people based on a restrictive definition of the movement.

6. Do not offend the people you seek to change.

Research on persuasion shows that influence is usually strongest when people like the persuader and see him/her as similar to themselves. Unfortunately, animal rights activists often alienate the very people they seek to change. For example, rather than courting the cooperation of veterinarians, a recent cover article in *Animals' Agenda* characterizes the views of vets as "standard fodder," "schizoid," "pusillanimous," etc. Readers are told that "vets and animal rights advocates make unlikely bedfellows," even though it mentions prominent counterexamples.

This is not to say that the American Veterinary Medical Association has championed the cause of animal welfare—far from it. The point is more circumscribed: by using derogatory language, activists make it unlikely that others will respond positively. Inflammatory language is rarely persuasive—particularly to those who are derogated—and it's unbecoming of a movement based on compassion.

No matter how much some practices deserve criticism, activists will be more effective if they are able to understand and empathize with people whose views differ from their own. As Zen master Thich Nhat Hanh wrote in connection with the nuclear freeze movement, "The peace movement can write very good protest letters, but they are not yet able to write a love letter. We need to learn to write a letter to Congress or the President of the U.S. that they will want to read, not just throw away. The way you speak, the kind of understanding, the kind of language you use should not turn people off."

Reprinted with permission from "tips & tactics," supplement of *pr reporter*, Exeter, NH, vol. 30, No. 1, January 15, 1990.

company received an order from an important customer that it could not meet because of problems resulting from the energy crisis. It called a competitor close to the client who could fill the order, and the two competitors agreed on a commission for the first company. The second company made a sizable sale, and the first company kept an important customer. Keeping a channel of communication open benefited both companies, the industry and the customer.

▼ PERCEPTIONS AND PUBLIC OPINION

One October evening in 1982, a twenty-eight-year-old mother took her two children to a local McDonald's and was distressed by the size of the small toys included with the "Happy Meal" orders of hamburger, french fries and soft drink. She called the head of a local consumers group. The toys, plastic gun-wielding sheriffs and spear-carrying Indians, were withdrawn—10 million of them, largely as a result of events begun by that one phone call. The toys were tested by the U.S. Consumer Product Safety Commission and were found to be dangerous to children under the age of three, who would be likely to put the tiny objects in their noses, ears or mouths. As soon as officials at McDonald's learned that the toys had failed the federal test, the toys were recalled. The company, competing with at least two other major hamburger chains, Wendy's and Burger King, could not risk losing public confidence and goodwill.[30]

In 1990, McDonald's announced that it would no longer use styrofoam containers. This action came in response to complaints from environmentalists that the material is not biodegradable—although other groups said the action was not necessary because styrofoam is recyclable. McDonald's again showed a heightened level of corporate awareness and took definitive action. Others have not been so sensitive. The messages consumers get from what you say and what you do is important—as the following story illustrates.

Much to the dismay of General Motors, a common production practice suddenly backfired, resulting in a spate of consumer lawsuits. The controversy occurred when GM car purchasers discovered that many 1977 models were hybrids. GM had been routinely installing Chevrolet engines in Oldsmobiles, Buicks and Pontiacs. The Olds engine had been promoted as a rocket engine and the Chevy engine as a gas saver. The whole thing was just a misunderstanding, GM said, and made a peace offering to customers that could have cost

GM $12 million or more. However, some of the customers were too angry to accept the peace offering. GM continued to juggle motors among makes, but it stopped extolling the virtues of specific motors and began talking about the "great family of cars." The company declared that it was not doing anything wrong and characterized the whole incident as a "breakdown in communications."[31]

The breakdown, however, was between the reality and the image. The image that car dealers and sellers project is that one car differs significantly from another. The reality is that the most cost-effective mass-production techniques often result in standardization and uniformity of products. Any solution to the problem is difficult because of the differences between reality and image. A false image had been sold to the public, which was then reluctant to accept the reality. That point underlies this whole chapter.

A warning about image and reality comes from Frederick D. Watkins, chairman of the Insurance Information Institute and president of Ætna Life and Casualty Insurance Company. The age of public relations has created confusion between image and substance, he says, and PR practitioners may be tempted to settle for the role of image maker. But, he advises, public relations people should do more than serve as mouthpieces: "They can help us develop an outward-looking managerial philosophy that will be translated into actions proving our concern for the public interest."[32]

Public relations can help develop the proper management philosophy by listening and responding effectively—or as Watkins put it, in one of those dog-chasing-its-tail definitions of PR, "by working to interpret the needs of the public to the industry and by helping translate public needs to the industry and reflecting back to the public the actions taken in response to those needs."[33] When listening and responding effectively go together, the conscience of management takes on a new perspective. In an institution whose policies are inconsistent and whose management lacks integrity, no public relations effort can be effective. The role of PR is tied to acceptance of two-way communication.

Perception and Personality

Organizations attempting to disseminate public issue or public policy messages might be interested in a study finding that the meaning of political advertising rests not only in the content of the message, but also in the minds of its receivers. In other words, both the message and the perception of the message count.[34]

The role played by personality in the perception of messages has long been understood by attorneys trying cases before juries. In cases involving a great deal of property, some attorneys have asked prospective jurors questions from the Minnesota Multiphasic Personality Inventory, a psychological assessment test updated in 1989 to remove some of its racial and gender bias. Prospective jurors' responses to some questions from the MMPI often indicate how they might vote on the central issues of the case to be tried. PR practitioners now recognize and take into account the importance of personality frequently, especially when dealing with message construction and direction.

Getting a Handle on Public Opinion

Public relations practitioners function in a climate of public opinion that often conditions their own perceptions and responses. Climates of public opinion can be as broad as that of the international community with regard to a nation's presumed leadership in an arms race or as narrow as that of security analysts when a company's bonds are rerated downward.

Public opinion is what most people in a particular public think; in other words, it is a collective opinion of, for instance, what voters or teenagers or senior citizens or politicians think about a specific issue.

Bernard Hennessy says, "Public opinion is the complex of preferences expressed by a significant number of persons on an issue of general importance."[35] Hennessy, who does not distinguish between opinion and attitude, says that public opinion has five basic elements. First, public opinion must be focused on an issue, which Hennessy defines as "a contemporary situation with a likelihood of disagreement." Second, the public must consist of "a recognizable group of persons concerned with the issue." A third element in the definition, the phrase "complex of preferences," Hennessy says, "means more than mere direction and intensity; it means all the imagined or measured individual opinions held by the relevant public on all the proposals about the issue over which that public has come into existence." The fourth factor, the expression of opinion, may involve any form of expression—printed or spoken words, symbols (such as a clenched fist or stiff-arm salute) or even the gasp of a crowd. The fifth factor is the number of persons involved. The number of people in a public can be large or small, as long as the impact of their opinion has a measurable effect. The effect may be as much determined by the intensity of opinion and the organization of effort as by the size of the public. Hennessy's definition of public opinion does not deal with what could be called latent public opinion. He would reserve that term for "describing a situation in which a considerable number of individuals hold attitudes or general predispositions that may eventually crystallize into opinions around a given issue." In any case, public opinion has to be expressed in order to be measured.[36]

Public opinion expresses beliefs based not necessarily on facts but on perceptions or evaluations of events, persons, institutions or products. In the United States many people assume that "public opinion is always right." Perhaps this view should be expected in a democracy, in which elected officials must be concerned with public opinion. Long before the pollsters were on the scene, nineteenth-century essayist Charles Dudley Warner said, "Public opinion is stronger than the legislature, and nearly as strong as the Ten Commandments."

Obviously, public opinion can be misused or manipulated—as Adolf Hitler's master propagandist, Joseph Goebbels, showed. And it can be based on a lack of accurate information—as in the period before World War II when many Americans applauded Mussolini's efforts at "straightening out the

"Is there any way you PR people can improve our image without our being able to tell you anything about ourselves?"

Reprinted by permission of *Punch*.

Italians" (tourist translation: getting the trains to run on time), while many Italians were beginning to live in fear of the black-shirted fascist militia.

Public opinion also is notably unstable. Its reliability as a measurement resembles that of body temperature. For accuracy, doctors say, "The patient's temperature was 101 degrees at 7 A.M.," not "the patient's temperature is 101 degrees" (unless the thermometer has just been read). PR people would be a lot safer in their judgments if they would take the same precautions. Exposure to new information or events can quickly change public opinion, rendering recent polling research obsolete.

"Majority opinion is a curious and elusive thing," columnist Charles Frankel points out:

People's opinions on a public issue depend very much on how the issue is posed to them, and on the circumstances in which they are asked to express themselves. A minority today may well be a majority tomorrow, depending on what transpires between today and tomorrow.[37]

Frankel also discusses the nature of majority opinion on a particular issue:

[It] may not in fact express opinion on *that* specific issue. It may express a general party loyalty; it may express the individual's sense that he should go along with a coalition of interests with which he is broadly sympathetic even if he disagrees with the particular policy at issue; it may reflect simply his judgment that he does not know enough to have a reliable opinion on the specific question he has been asked, and his decision, therefore, to accept the opinion of people in authority.[38]

To keep pace with constantly changing public opinion, you must accept a few basic precepts. Not everyone is going to be on your side at any one time. The best you can hope for is a majority consensus. To achieve this, you need to retain the partisans you have, win at least provisional support from the undecided or uncommitted bloc and neutralize or win over the opposition.

Winning over the opposition is the most difficult part. Most of us read and listen for reinforcement of our own ideas. We do not like to hear ideas that conflict with our own, and we make every effort to reject them. For example, we may simply tune out and fail to hear or remember what we have been exposed to. We may discredit the source, without objectively determining the legitimacy of its evidence or argument. We may reduce the conflicting argument to a crude caricature whose fallacious elements we have no difficulty pointing out. We may distort meanings so that what we hear or read conforms to what we believe. No doubt you have seen letters to the editor of a magazine from two different people, each complimenting the publication for an editorial they interpreted in opposite ways; the readers simply read into the editorial what they wanted the publication to say. For a comprehensive list of the most important factors to consider in attempting to change public opinion, see Hadley Cantril's "laws" in Example 6.15.

Public Opinion as a Moving Target

The importance of private, individual "opinion" (attitudes and beliefs) that underlies public opinion was described as follows by Daniel Katz:

> The study of opinion formation and attitude change is basic to an understanding of the public opinion process even though it should not be equated with this process. The public opinion process is one phase of the influencing of collective decisions, and its investigation involves knowledge of channels of communication, of the power structures of a society, of the character of mass media, of the relation between elites, factions, and masses, of the role of formal and informal leaders, of the institutionalized access to officials. But the raw material out of which public opinion develops is to be found in the attitudes of individuals, whether

▼ **Public opinion expresses beliefs based not necessarily on facts but on perceptions or evaluations; it is unstable and often elusive and indirect.**

they be followers or leaders and whether these attitudes be at the general level of tendencies to conform to legitimate authority or majority opinion or at the specific level of favoring or opposing the particular aspects of the issue under consideration. The nature of the organization of attitudes within the personality and the processes which account for attitude change are thus critical areas for the understanding of the collective product known as public opinion.[39]

The capriciousness of public opinion is due to its fragile base in perceptions. For example, in September 1987, televised Congressional hearings were held over the sale of weapons to Iran and the use of that money to aid the Contra forces fighting against the Sandinista government in Nicaragua. Marine Lt. Col. Oliver North became such a popular figure during these hearings that an American doll manufacturer decided to produce Ollie North uniformed dolls for Christmas sale. But by the time the holiday arrived, the popular figure of the moment had become Mikhail Gorbachev, who had just visited the United States for a summit meeting with President Reagan. The manufacturer of the Ollie dolls responded by removing the original heads, padding the figures and attaching a Gorbachev head to each. Example 6.16 offers another illustration of commercial popularization of the Russian political leader.

Celebrities know (or soon learn) how fickle public opinion is. Influencing it requires constant effort directed toward viable—that is, credible and supportable—positioning of the organization (or person) vis-à-vis the competition. Positioning can sell a product, as Bernays proved when a promotional campaign he developed made smoking in

EXAMPLE 6.15

Hadley Cantril's "Laws" of Public Opinion

1. Opinion is highly sensitive to important events.

2. Events of unusual magnitude are likely to swing public opinion temporarily from one extreme to another. Opinion does not become stabilized until the implications of events are seen with some perspective.

3. Opinion is generally determined more by events than by words—unless those words are themselves interpreted as an "event."

4. Verbal statements and outlines of courses of action have maximum importance when opinion is unstructured, when people are suggestible and seek some interpretation from a reliable source.

5. By and large, public opinion does not anticipate emergencies—it only reacts to them.

6. Psychologically, opinion is basically determined by self-interest. Events, words, or any other stimuli affect opinion only insofar as their relationship to self-interest is apparent.

7. Opinion does not remain aroused for any long period of time unless people feel their self-interest is acutely involved or unless opinion—aroused by words—is sustained by events.

8. Once self-interest is involved, opinion is not easily changed.

9. When self-interest is involved, public opinion in a democracy is likely to be ahead of official policy.

10. When an opinion is held by a slight majority or when opinion is not solidly structured, an accomplished fact tends to shift opinion in the direction of acceptance.

11. At critical times, people become more sensitive to the adequacy of their leadership—if they have confidence in it, they are willing to assign more than usual responsibility to it; if they lack confidence in it, they are less tolerant than usual.

12. People are less reluctant to have critical decisions made by their leaders if they feel that somehow they, the people, are taking some part in the decision.

13. People have more opinions and are able to form opinions more easily with respect to goals than with respect to methods necessary to reach those goals.

14. Public opinion, like individual opinion, is colored by desire. And when opinion is based chiefly on desire rather than on information, it is likely to show especially sharp shifts with events.

15. The important psychological dimensions of opinion are direction, intensity, breadth, and depth.

SOURCE: Selections from "Some Laws of Public Opinion." Cantril, Hadley; *Gauging Public Opinion*. Copyright © 1944, renewed © 1972, by Princeton University Press. Reprinted by permission of Princeton University Press.

---

public socially acceptable for young women—a feat he no longer feels especially proud of. Positioning can also sell a person, as many elected officials can testify. In 1986, California had a heated Congressional battle during which incumbent Senator Alan Cranston, 72, talked about the "inexperience" of his opponent, Congressman Ed Zschau, 46, who for his part campaigned against "old ideas."[40]

Ideas can be sold, too. During World War II, a massive PR effort by government and industry convinced the American public that the international situation made it appropriate for large numbers of single and married women to enter the paid labor force.[41] That effort put women in jobs never before imagined as "women's work," but it also returned them to hearth and home when those jobs were needed by returning veterans. In moving from

EXAMPLE 6.16 ▪▬▬▬▬▬▬▬▬▬▬▬▬▬▬▬▬▬▬▬

Child Getting a Gorbachev Bank

Although in the spring of 1991 the Soviet Union's leader Mikhail Gorbachev was in trouble at home and his summit meeting in Tokyo was unsuccessful, he continued to enjoy international popularity. At a Seoul, South Korea, department store, this father buys his son a Gorbachev bank.

Reprinted with permission of The Associated Press. AP/Wide World Photos.

one major model of American womanhood to another—each based on American myth—the tide of public opinion was manipulated each time to suit the government's perceived needs.

Measuring Public Opinion

Because public opinion changes so often and can be influenced so easily, measuring it is big business. Most public relations people make use of published public opinion surveys as well as buy public opinion research. Published surveys, for instance, are available by subscription to the Roper Center Review of Public Opinion and Polling. Pub-

lic opinion research is offered by many groups, including SRI, which uses the VALS 2 measurement.

Various studies are also available, either without charge or at a minimal charge. And the best reason for being familiar with research methodology is to be able to apply successfully the many published surveys to a particular company, market or client.

Everyone is aware of public polls, such as those taken by Louis Harris and George Gallup, that sample the nation's moods and pass on the information to the public. Less widely known private pollsters, such as Albert Sidlinger and Jay Schmiedeskamp, measure consumer confidence. The *Wall Street Journal* describes the value of their work as follows:

> By taking frequent samples of household buying intentions, they claim to be able to determine whether the nation's consumers have enough confidence in the economy to commit themselves to such major purchases as new cars, big appliances and houses. The results of such surveys are increasingly important in government economic planning and in corporate decision making.[42]

Another private pollster is William R. Hamilton, head of Independent Research Associates, Inc., a political polling and analysis concern that "works directly, and confidentially, for political candidates who want to know as precisely as possible what the electorate thinks so they can devise an effective campaign strategy."[43]

Although attitude tests must be used promptly, because opinion is so unstable, old data should not be discarded. Information from old polls can be used later in developing simulated tests that will yield some probable responses. For instance, when John F. Kennedy was running for president in 1960, his campaign strategists used cards from the Roper Public Opinion Research Center in Williamstown, Massachusetts (depository for the old cards of the Gallup and Roper polls), to design a program simulating how people around the United States would react to various critical questions and issues, based on how they had reacted in the past. In fact, the simulation came closer to predicting the November election outcome than did the public opinion polls taken in August. The reason, Philip Meyer explains, is that the simulation, designed by Ithiel de Sola Pool,

> was acting out how the voters would react to a [campaign] strategy that had not been fully implemented. After it was implemented and the voters began to react, the polls began to reflect the results and came into closer correlation with both the simulation and the final outcome.[44]

The President's private pollsters frequently receive coverage in the news. Pat Caddell, who handled polling for President Jimmy Carter, was twenty-five the year Carter was inaugurated. Caddell has described his function as being not just to do surveys but to figure out their meaning and to contribute advice on certain issues. Caddell, also a pollster for other Democrats, got into a verbal battle with a fellow pollster during a heated U.S. Senate race in Texas in 1972, when his polling technique was publicly criticized by pollster V. Lance Tarrance. The Tarrance polling firm was being used by the incumbent Republican, John Tower, and Caddell's Cambridge Survey Research firm was being used by the Democratic challenger, Bob Krueger. Tarrance charged that Krueger's camp was using the Caddell poll as a "propaganda" device. The difficulty with private polling, especially in politics, is that—even when the pollsters make every effort to be objective about wording a questionnaire or picking a geographical area to sample—an ideological bent frequently appears.

Most political research organizations are identified with one party or the other. Yet, the private pollsters say, politics and partisanship do not prevent them from doing honest research. They use the same measurements as the public pollsters, and they report objectively to their clients. Indeed, they cannot afford to do inadequate research.

The reliability of polls has from time to time been questioned, as when Harris and Gallup predicted an overwhelming Labour Party victory in the 1970 British elections and the Conservative Party won instead. The 1992 election also was predicted incorrectly. Nevertheless, both Gallup and Harris claim that polls are generally accurate. Gallup says that, since 1948, his organization has, on the average, been off the actual balloting in important elections by a little less than one percentage point.

The problem with public understanding of any poll, but particularly political polls, was stated succinctly by authors and researchers Charles Roll and Albert Cantril:

> There is nothing immutable about the results of a poll. The way polls are treated by the press and politicians, one might be led to think otherwise. However, what a poll provides is a picture of the

public's view at only one point in time and on only the questions that were asked. Yet, inferences of sweeping proportion are frequently drawn from a poll, leading to fundamental misunderstandings of what the state of public opinion really is.[45]

Politicians are not alone in polling public opinion. Business and nonprofit associations and institutions also measure the climate in which they operate. The accuracy of such surveys is often, as one reporter noted, "a matter of interpretation." This Associated Press reporter offered as an example two reports about small business in the United States—one optimistic and the other showing conditions deteriorating. The pessimistic report was from the National Federation of Independent Business, which had an eight-year track record of surveying the climate for small business in the United States. The report represented its own summary of the current survey. The optimistic report was a public relations firm's interpretation of a survey done for Dun & Bradstreet. The survey researcher told the AP reporter that the total number of responses was 444, not "nearly 500" as the PR firm's news release had said. The release had also stated that "more than half the respondents felt that inflation would decrease"; in fact, however, the survey results actually recorded 33 percent saying it would increase, 32.7 percent saying it would decrease and 23 percent saying it would remain the same. The erroneous "more than half" assertion had come from a breakdown of companies with revenues of more than $1 million. Indeed, 52 percent of these did expect a decrease, but of the 444 respondents, only 100 were companies with revenues of more than $1 million.[46]

Another difficulty with both interpretation and process is reported by anthropologist–market researcher Steve Barnett, who notes that most opinion polls are adequate for assessing public feeling on superficial questions but says that people often behave differently from how they say they will on important questions.[47] He cites research his firm did for a group of electric utilities. Their fuel-use projections, which were based in part on poll-takers' reports of customer interviews, were falling

short of reality. To find out why, Barnett put TV cameras in the room where the thermostat was kept in 150 homes. He discovered that the discrepancy was due to "guerrilla warfare" over the thermostat between the person who paid the bill and everyone else. The constant adjusting changed the level of heat use, and the actual amount of heat used differed substantially from the poll-based projections.

Something else may be going on as well. The very act of communicating an opinion has consequences on public opinion. For example, in the 1990 election for governor of Texas, the Republican candidate, Clayton Williams, appeared to be leading until the final hours before the election, but the Democrat, Ann Richards, ended up winning without a runoff. What was going on in the pre-election polling? Two factors may have come into play. First, early polls had asked how the respondent was going to vote and what he or she thought others would do. Many women expressed their intention to vote for Richards but at the same time doubted that other women felt the way they did. Misperception of others' opinions is a common phenomenon. People often see themselves as holding different opinions from their friends or neighbors.[48]

The second element that skewed the early projections involved social relationships theory.[49] Not only were women talking with other women about the election, they were getting more ideas from these discussions than from the mass media. People often won't talk about how they feel or are going to vote if they think their friends, family, neighbors and others close to them will disagree. Many women were not saying openly (in mixed company) that they intended to vote for Richards because they didn't want to argue with male family members, office colleagues or bosses.

Some might say that another contributing factor is embodied in the Noelle-Neumann "spiral of silence" theory.[50] This theory, which assumes a "powerful effects model" for media, states that media can suppress public expression of opinions opposed to those presented in the media, creating a "spiral of silence" that grows until the media's picture of reality becomes reality itself. This might have been a factor in the miscall of the Salvadorian elections in 1990. In any case, one way to compensate for this factor in polling may be to look at alternative media, according to a study by Hernando Gonzalez.[51] He looked at the 1986 revolution in the Philippines that brought Corazon Aquino to power and found that the alternative media "broadened the context in which key events could be interpreted and influenced those segments of the audience that provided new leadership." In other words, the alternative media gave voice to opposition and helped form a media base for expressing dissident points of view.

▼ PUBLIC OPINION RESEARCH AND PUBLIC RELATIONS

The difference between public opinion researchers and PR people was stated many years ago by Fred Palmer, a partner in the PR firm of Earl Newsom and Company: "The public opinion researchers' function is to know, measure, analyze, and weigh public opinion. The practitioners' function is to help people deal constructively with the force of public opinion."[52]

The study of public opinion ties public relations research to both behavioral psychology and economics. Opinion research reflects seasonal and other types of trends in attitudes that raise questions about behavior patterns, and these in turn often require researchers to look at the economic picture to determine if the roots of the problem might be there. Anyone who questions this sort of correlation might find some adequate, if unscientific, support in simple observation. Read the front-page headlines of the newspaper, and check the Dow Jones averages. Any security analyst or stockbroker will tell you that a correlation exists between news on the AP and UPI wires and

every first-year economics student learns, the only subsequent information on the Dow Jones ticker. As thing that gives the monetary system value is confidence.

The study of public opinion is particularly important to public relations people for another reason. Information and opinion are fundamentally different. Appreciating that difference means recognizing how understanding and knowledge differ. Hadley Cantril, public opinion authority and pollster, observed that public understanding is "knowledge that is functional, that has been built up from experience, that has been tested by action."[53] Public knowledge, on the other hand, is more in the nature of intellectual data that do not play a role in concrete perception. Cantril suggested that public opinion surveys should watch for occasions when "knowledge" is used for "understanding" and should inquire into the reasons for its being linked to purpose and brought to bear on decision making.

Many public relations projects now involve behavior modification. One of these is the American Heart Association's efforts to get young people to take care of their hearts in a lifelong program. Here, as in any attempt to modify behavior, public relations people are dealing with perception versus reality. Therefore, what Cantril said about perception is particularly important.

There is still no continuing system of measurement for the "climate of public opinion." Specific tests measure public opinion on a particular issue at a given time, but no continuing study of consumers' state of mind exists to reveal, for example, how much they are willing to sacrifice in craftsmanship in return for less expensive, mass-produced products. Who knows what the real religious temper of the nation is, what spiritual values are held and by whom, and why and when these values change? Such attitudes can have political consequences, as the Italians demonstrated in 1974, when they finally voted to provide a legal process for divorce in that Catholic country.

How much freedom are people in the United States willing to relinquish in return for security?

This is a question politicians and businesspeople alike would benefit from knowing. The Opinion Research Corporation makes such probes, and *Collectivist Ideology in America* is its most comprehensive study to date. One of the few long-term series of public opinion polls in the United States is the Link Audit, by the Psychological Corporation, which tests attitudes toward eight large U.S. companies. This kind of continuing research has considerable application potential.

In recent years the advertising industry has shown an awakened responsiveness to public opinion. As advertising commentator Herbert D. Maneloveg noted in *Saturday Review* back in 1970, the brightest marketing people move to the client's side rather than to the agency's, and the brighter clients seek help from people more in tune with the times—people oriented to new needs and lifestyles. The ad agencies have been forced to meet the mood of consumerism, which demands that ads tell what the public wants to know about a producer or service, rather than what the company wants to tell.

Campbell Soups is a good example of a company that works very hard to be responsive to public opinion. Instead of developing a single set of products and a single marketing program for the entire United States, Campbell has tailored its products, advertising, promotion and sales to fit different regions and even individual neighborhoods within a city. In Campbell's case, target markets have affected the product. Even such long-established marketing arrangements as branch management are being replaced with more comprehensive planning that will respond to the company's need for a cohesive public image.[54]

Dealing with Public Opinion

Many publics share knowledge or work together on various issues. Hence, organizations sometimes find, to their dismay, coalitions of unlikely political partners involved in a boycott or other hostile action against them. Computerized information banks, electronic mail, facsimile (FAX), video-

▼ **Many subsets of fragmented publics are tied together into coalitions by common experiences, situations or interests.**

teleconferencing and special interest organizations create loosely affiliated publics with strong emotional ties to particular issues. Because of crossover of communication among these loosely connected publics, it pays to make sure that a message designed to respond to one public doesn't offend another.[55] Many subsets of very tightly woven communities are tied together by common experiences (children of alcoholics, COAs) or situations (disabilities or illnesses) or interests (animal rights). These webs of relationships are interlocking even for a single individual.

Even though different publics often share some common interests and values, it is increasingly dangerous to assume that people share common sets of values. As *Wall Street Journal* writer John Koten put it, "There is no longer one set of values that broadly fits the bulk of the middle class. There are fewer things that everybody wants and fewer things that everybody feels compelled to do."[56] Thus an organization trying to determine a socially responsible course of action must simultaneously try to respond to special interest groups interested in changing broader public opinion. An example is a revision of a high-school history textbook that discusses Abigail Adams' role in the American Revolution at greater length than that of her husband. The book's author, Henry F. Groff, says the changes resulted from his having raised two daughters and from recent scholarship that has illuminated the historical role of women (women's studies and the women's movement).[57]

The PR manager often feels caught in the force field of special interest groups. But allegiance to a mission statement can keep PR efforts from being scattershot and can work, instead, to strengthen the organization's image and the public's perception of its organizational values.

The late Kerryn King, a corporate public relations director and a counselor said:

And if your company wants to be successful, you've got to identify with the interests of your consumers, the people who buy your goods and services. And your employees, your shareholders, and the community in which you live. That's why you're building values all the time.

You may ask "What about that bottom line?" In public relations, building values constantly by winning the loyalty of employees, shareholders, the media and community—all the people you have to deal with, all the external relationships you have— is the bottom line. That's what public relations is all about. You must think "What are the public policies that are going to impact my company?"

Whether it is in Muncie or in Washington, or in Indianapolis, you've got to be aware what's going on that's going to help or hurt your organization. If it's going to help your organization, encourage it. If it's going to hurt your organization, then you'd better find out why and do something about it.[58]

Public opinion results from relationships formed between individual organization representatives and those with whom they come in contact. According to *pr reporter*, the failure to develop positive relationships led to the breakup of the AT&T/Bell companies. Although one of PR's pioneers, Arthur W. Page, set the standards for PR practice at AT&T, things had changed:

In her daily actions, Ma Bell had become the monolithic monopoly incarnate. Other rationalizations may have been used for the actual breakup, but fueling it was a long-held sense of outrage at years of bad treatment by too many telephone company personnel.[59]

Melvin L. Sharpe delineated the following set of principles to help organizations maintain favorable public opinion:

1. That the economic and social stability of an organization of any type depends on the attitudes and opinions of the publics within its total operational environment.

2. That all have the right to voice opinions in relation to decisions that will directly affect them and, therefore, have the right to accurate information about pending decisions relating to them or their welfare.

3. That an organization's management of communications is essential to ensure accurate and adequate feedback from both internal and external publics, in order to ensure the organization's adjustment and adaptation to the changes necessary for longevity.

4. That, although technology may be responsible for the fractionalization of today's society, technology can be used to reach out to these various publics.[60]

▼ SUMMARY

A public relations practitioner cannot successfully put a public relations plan in place until *all* of an organization's publics have been identified, prioritized and described—both demographically and psychographically. The organization is not likely to be communicating with all (or even most) of these publics most of the time, but understanding all publics is critical to framing messages that, while intended for a priority public, may nevertheless appeal to and be useful for other publics. How these publics receive and respond to communication is critical to relationships.

Anticipating responses from all publics is part of issues evaluation and management. A public that is seldom a priority public may become one overnight if its issues and concerns—as well as outside events that may have an impact on it—are not carefully monitored. Again, a positive, proactive approach, rather than a reactive one, is preferable, although even the best PR people and most thoughtful managements can sometimes be caught off guard. The role of public relations practitioners is to see that this doesn't happen often and to ensure that potential problems with issues are turned into opportunities to work with constituencies that seldom become priority publics.

Public relations practitioners must seize the opportunity to explain issues and concerns in which their organization is involved to internal publics first. Internal publics have the strongest sense of what the organization is, and they have an ego involvement in it. They constitute part of a corporate culture that is reflected to external audiences. In addition, internal publics interact directly with external publics, and consequently they can act as an extension of public relations efforts to reach other publics.

All of an organization's publics have perceptions of it and of its key leadership. The manner in which the perceptions of an organization's various publics fit or overlap constitutes the organization's image. Public relations practitioners cannot create an image for an organization, but they are vital in improving the way publics perceive the organization. Measuring what people think about an organization must be done continuously because public opinion is always in flux and reacts sensitively to events—many of which are outside the organization's control. In measuring what publics think about an organization, PR practitioners are usually examining attitudes and opinions; however, beliefs held by publics are critical, since these are based on values that are less susceptible to change. What an organization says and does and what others think about its words and actions provide the public relations person with the opportunity and material to influence the opinions of an organization's publics.

▼ NOTES

[1]Wilbur Schramm, *Men, Messages, and Media: A Look at Human Communication* (New York: Harper & Row, 1973), pp. 243–45.

[2]Otto Lerbinger, ed., "Relationships Are Refined and Strengthened by Modern Corporations," *purview*, 275 (January 22, 1990). From George Lodge and Richard Walton, "The American Corporation and Its New Relationships," *California Management Review*, 31 (Spring 1989), pp. 10–24.

[3]"Audience Targeting Gets Ever More Critical," *pr reporter*, 25(32) (August 16, 1982), p. 1.

[4]SRI International, VALS Program, 333 Ravenswood Ave., Menlo Park, California 94025.

[5]Betsy Morris, "Study to Detect True Eating Habits Finds Junk-Food Fans in the Health Food Ranks," *Wall Street Journal* (February 3, 1984), p. 19.

[6]Alexis S. Tan, *Mass Communication Theories and Research*, 2d ed. (New York: John Wiley, 1985), pp. 217–218.

[7]Joanne Lipman, "Readership Figures for Periodicals Stir Debate in Publishing Industry," *Wall Street Journal* (September 2, 1987), sec. 2, p. 12.

[8]Dennis Kneale, "Fuzzy Picture, TV's Nielsen Ratings, Long Unquestioned, Face Tough Challenges," *Wall Street Journal* (July 19, 1990), p. 1, A12.

[9]"Communicate," brochure from MagnaTex International, 508 State St., Annapolis, Maryland 21403.

[10]Eugene Carlson, "Why the Experts Don't Agree on Future Population Figures," *Wall Street Journal* (June 3, 1986), sec. 2, p. 31.

[11]*pr reporter*, 26(36) (September 12, 1983), p. 2. Also see Merrill Rose, "Activism in the 90s, Changing Roles for Public Relations," *Public Relations Quarterly* (Fall, 1991), pp. 28, 30, 32.

[12]W. Lloyd Warner and J. O. Low, "The Factory in the Community," in William F. Whyte ed., *Industry and Society* (New York: McGraw-Hill, 1946), pp. 21–45.

[13]John Bitter, "A Basic Training Document: Following a Problem Solving Cycle Steadies the Course in a Crisis," *pr reporter*, "tips and tactics" (January 24, 1983), pp. 1–2.

[14]Philip Lesly, "Checklist on Issues and Opportunities," *Managing the Human Climate*, 68 (May–June 1981).

[15]Otto Lerbinger ed., "Issues Management Strategies Suitable for Different Lifecycle," *purview*, 277 (March 26, 1990). From John F. Mahon, "Corporate Political Strategy," *Business in the Contemporary World*, 2 (Autumn 1989), pp. 50–62. For a comprehensive look at issues management and its implications, see Robert L. Heath, "Corporate Issues Management: Theoretical Underpinnings and Research Foundations," in Larissa A. and James E. Grunig eds., *Public Relations Research Annual*, vol. 2 (Hillsdale, N.J.: Lawrence Erlbaum Associates, 1990), pp. 29–65.

[16]Richard K. Long, "Understanding Issue Dynamics," ed. Darden Chambliss, *Public Affairs in the New Era* (New York: PRSA, 1986), pp. 22–24.

[17]Richard Claeys and J. Sherman Feher, "Research in a Short-sighted World: Lessons from EPRI's Experience," in Chambliss, *Public Affairs in the New Era*, pp. 25–29.

[18]Jim Morrissey, "The Dilemma of International Trade," in Chambliss, *Public Affairs in the New Era*, pp. 20–21.

[19]John Merriam, "Globalization of the Issues Process in America," in Chambliss, *Public Affairs in the New Era*, pp. 17–19.

[20]Jay S. Mendell, "The Practitioner as a Futurist," *Public Relations Journal* 36(12) (December 1980), p. 15. Professional futurists belong to the World Future Society, 4916 St. Elmo Avenue, Bethesda, Maryland 20814. The Society publishes an annual directory. Single practitioners might benefit from a computer program that has a strategic planning module: Ideafisher V.3.1 with Strategic Planning Module. Ideafisher is available in MS-DOS and Macintosh versions. (Fisher Idea Systems, Inc., 2222 Martin #110, Irvine, CA 92715.)

[21]Wayne A. Danielson, speech to Sigma Delta Chi, University of Texas at Austin, October 26, 1967.

[22]Andrew P. Garvin quoted by Sanford L. Jacobs, "Using Official Data Often Helps Avoid Mistakes, Find Customers," *Wall Street Journal* (January 5, 1981), p. 15.

[23]"NSF Study Finds 'Cultural Revolution' Inside Management Necessary to Compete Today," *pr reporter*, 25(34) (August 30, 1982), p. 1.

[24]Harry Levinson, "How to Undermine an Organization," *Public Relations Journal*, 22(10) (October 1966), pp. 82–84.

[25]Ibid., p. 84.

[26]Philip Lesly, "Turning Over an Elephant with a Shoehorn," *Managing the Human Climate*, 90 (January–February 1985). For the ethnoecology approach to corporate culture, see James L. Everett, "Organizational Culture and Ethnoecology in Public Relations Theory and Practice," in Larisse A. and James E. Grunig, eds., *Public Relations Research Annual*, vol.

2 (Hillsdale, N.J.: Lawrence Erlbaum Associates, 1990), pp. 235–51.

[27]Melvin L. DeFleur and Sandra Ball-Rokeach, *Theories of Mass Communication*, 5th ed. (New York: Longman, 1989), p. 159. "Mass society refers to the relationship that exists between individuals and the social order around them. In mass society . . . individuals are presumed to be in a situation of psychological isolation from others, impersonality is said to prevail in their interaction with others, and they are said to be relatively free from demands of binding social obligations."

[28]Stephen M. Downey, "Corporate Identity's Role in Economic Recovery," *PRSA Newsletter*, 11(4,5) (April–May 1983), p. 1.

[29]Bro Uttal, "The Corporate Culture Vultures," *Fortune* (October 17, 1983), pp. 66–72.

[30]Molly Sinclair, "Recall Without Injury: McDonald's Says You Shouldn't Get a Break Today," *Fort Worth Star-Telegram* (November 9, 1982), sec. 1B, p. 12.

[31]Terry P. Brown, "Bizarre Backfire, Engine Switch Brings 125 Suits Against GM, and Practice Continues, but Ads No Longer Eulogize the Olds Rocket Engine; Is There Any Difference?" *Wall Street Journal* (July 27, 1977), p. 1.

[32]Frederick D. Watkins, "Top Insurance Men Meet to Discuss Industry's Public Relations," *pr reporter*, 17(5) (February 4, 1974), p. 2.

[33]Ibid.

[34]Deirdre D. Johnston, "Image and Issue Political Information: Message Content or Interpretation?" *Journalism Quarterly*, 66(2) (Spring 1989), pp. 379–82.

[35]Bernard Hennessy, *Public Opinion*, 4th ed. (Monterey, Calif.: Brooks/Cole, 1981), p. 4. Social scientist Ithiel de Sola Pool also said: "An opinion is a proposition, while an attitude is a proclivity to be pro or anti something." For his discussion of public opinion, see "Public Opinion," *Handbook of Communication* (Chicago: Rand McNally, 1973), pp. 779–835.

[36]Hennessy, *Public Opinion*, pp. 4–8.

[37]Charles Frankel, "The Silenced Majority," *Saturday Review* (December 13, 1969), p. 22.

[38]Ibid.

[39]Daniel Katz, "The Functional Approach to the Study of Attitudes," *Public Opinion Quarterly*, 29 (1960), p. 163.

[40]Doug Willis, "Politicians Wage War of Words," *Fort Worth Star-Telegram* (September 21, 1986), p. 6AA.

[41]Maureen Honey, *Creating Rosie the Riveter: Class, Gender and Propaganda During World War II* (Amherst: University of Massachusetts Press, 1984), p. 212.

[42]Jack H. Morris, "Pollsters Gamely Try to Measure the Moods of Volatile Consumers," *Wall Street Journal* (October 4, 1972), p. 1.

[43]Fred L. Zimmerman, "How Political Pollster Influences Candidates, Stays in Background," *Wall Street Journal* (October 5, 1972), p. 1.

[44]Philip Meyer, *Precision Journalism* (Bloomington: Indiana University Press, 1973), p. 184.

[45]Charles W. Roll, Jr., and Albert H. Cantril, *Polls: Their Use and Misuse in Politics* (New York: Basic Books, 1972), p. 117.

[46]John Cuniff, "Accuracy of Surveys a Matter of Interpretation," *Fort Worth Star-Telegram* (November 20, 1981), p. 5C.

[47]Frederick C. Klein, "Researcher Proves Consumers Using Anthropological Skills," *Wall Street Journal* (July 7, 1983), p. 21.

[48]Carroll J. Glynn, "The Communication of Public Opinion," *Journalism Quarterly*, 64(4) (Winter 1987), pp. 688–97. Also see Charles T. Salmon and Hayg Oshagen, "Community Size, Perceptions of Majority Opinion, and Opinion Expression," in *Public Relations Research Annual* vol. 2, pp. 157–71.

[49]Melvin DeFleur and Sandra Ball-Rokeach, *Theories of Mass Communication* (New York: Longman, 1989), p. 192.

[50]Elizabeth Noelle-Neumann, "Turbulences in the Climate of Opinion: Methodological Applications of the Spiral of Silence Theory," *Public Opinion Quarterly*, 40 (1977), pp. 143–58 and *The Spiral of Silence—Public Opinion Our Social Skin* (Chicago: University of Chicago Press, 1984).

[51]Hernando González, "Mass Media and the Spiral of Silence: The Philippines from Marcos to Aquino," *Journal of Communication*, 38(4) (Autumn 1988), pp. 33–34.

[52]Fred L. Palmer, "Opinion Research as an Aid to Public Relation's Practice," address at International Conference in Public Opinion Research, Eagles Mere, Pennsylvania, September 13, 1948.

[53]Hadley Cantril, *Understanding Man's Social Behavior* (Princeton, N.J.: Office of Public Opinion Research, 1947), p. 31.

[54]Anthony Blanco, "Marketing's New Look, Campbell Leads a Revolution in the Way Consumer Products Are Sold," *Business Week* (January 26, 1987), pp. 64–69.

[55]Jolie Solomon and Carol Hymowitz, "Team Strategy: P&O Makes Changes in the Way It Develops and Sells Its Product," *Wall Street Journal* (August 11, 1987), p. 12.

[56]John Koten, "The Shattered Middle Class: A Once Tightly Knit Middle Class Finds Itself Divided and Uncertain," *Wall Street Journal* (March 9, 1987), p. 21.

[57]Bob Davis, "Scholastic Work, Many Forces Shape Making and Marketing of a War Schoolbook," *Wall Street Journal* (January 3, 1985), p. 1.

[58]Kerryn King, "Public Relations: A Lifetime Career," a Vern C. Schranz Distinguished Lectureship presentation, Ball State University, Muncie, Indiana, 1985.

[59]"Real Lesson of AT&T Breakup, Bad Money Laundering and Related Cases Is That Public Relations Should Change Its Focus," *pr reporter*, 28(16) (April 22, 1985), p. 1.

[60]Chester Burger, "30 Years After Sputnik—The Revolution in Communications," speech to Public Relations Society of America Detroit Chapter, Detroit, Michigan, Feb. 3, 1987.

Selected readings, activities and assignments appropriate to this chapter can be found in the *Instructor's Guide*.

▼

PR'S ETHICAL AND LEGAL ENVIRONMENT

Some ways to persuade others have ethical implications. In some cases the act of persuasion itself is an ethical issue. Some actions, although legal, may not be ethical. What is legal is easily defined, but what is ethical calls for moral judgments that often must be made with little or no guidance from precedent. Chapter 7 deals with persuasion and communication theories. Chapters 8 and 9 raise important questions regarding ethics and the law and their impact on the public relations practitioner.

CHAPTER 7

▼

PERSUASION AND
COMMUNICATION THEORIES

Public relations embraces what I call the engineering of consent based on Thomas Jefferson's principle that, in a democratic society, everything depends on the consent of the public.

Edward L. Bernays, public relations counsel

Thank God, communication isn't a disease, because we know so little about it.

Bill Marsteller, former chairman and chief executive officer, Marsteller, Inc. (now Burson-Marsteller)

As you learned in Chapter 6, public opinion is the collective opinion of groups of people. You can count on two things about public opinion: first, it will change; second, those who hold an opinion were somehow persuaded to think as they do. Although people do sometimes respond collectively, as when they applaud or join in a boycott of a product or store, they always initiate their responses individually. These individual responses indicate attitudes that reflect feelings or convictions. Each person individually decides to clap or not to clap, to buy or not to buy and to patronize or not to patronize. Consequently, we must look at individual reactions first. Then we try to figure out how these reactions of individuals affect the reactions of other individuals to produce a collective response.

It is important to keep in mind that responses are always individual before they are collective. Many faulty mass communication theories have been based on the mistaken idea that there is only a mass response. Looking at publics collectively can create a number of difficulties for public relations practitioners, as can looking at what publics say without explaining what they *do*.

▼ SOME MODELS TO CONSIDER

The attitudes and opinions of publics greatly interest the PR practitioner, but even more important is what these publics are *doing*. This point is reflected in the replacement of the communication model by the behavioral model as the theoretical underpinning of public relations (see Example 7.1).[1]

Edward L. Bernays has held this view all along, which is why he insists that public relations be viewed as a social science. The communication model encompasses publicity, publications, advertising and special events that attract attention, but all of these serve either to create or to maintain levels of awareness. All of these practices emphasize messages designed to affect attitudes and opinions, but as *pr reporter* notes, "Every dieter facing the dessert tray understands the difference between attitude and behavior."[2] The behavioral model also suggests that communication in public relations should focus less on "mass" appeal and more on direct, personal impact. Still, the behavioral model suggested here does not allow for the type of reciprocal action envisioned in the symmetrical model for public relations. The behavior model is clearly asymmetrical, although it could be modified to accommodate symmetrical behavior (see Example 7.2).

▼ PERSUASION AND CHANGE

When someone holds a strong opposing opinion, you are probably wasting your time trying to win that person over to your view. All you can hope to do is to limit whatever effects the person may have on others who are undecided or uncommitted. In particular, you should not waste time on recent converts to the opposition, since new converts to anything react with more emotion than reason and are almost impossible to reach with factual materials, much less with a persuasive argument. You should concentrate your efforts, then, on preserv-

▼ **The four steps of the behavioral model of public relations are awareness, latent readiness, triggering event and behavior.**

ing what favorable opinion exists and on winning over undecided individuals to your point of view.

There are three basic ways to get people to do what you want: power, patronage and persuasion. Power involves the use of authority and the implied or overt threat of compulsion. One obvious source of power is the legal system, which has laws that demand compliance. Other sources of power may be more subtle, but they are equally binding. For example, employees may not be legally bound to follow a supervisor's suggestions, but if they don't they may soon be looking for other jobs. Because groups can exert substantial pressure internally, peer groups are also a strong source of power. (If you don't believe that, consider how often you hear, "But I must have one. Everyone else has.") Public relations practitioners use power, for example, in planning for blood donation drives, where they rely on the tactic of asking employers to get commitments from their employees. The request is for a good purpose—an honest cause, certainly— but it still involves the use of power.

Forms of patronage used as a means of changing people's behavior may be as crude as bribery, or they may be quite delicate, particularly if a favorable opinion is sought or if there is an implied threat of denial. Patronage may involve paying a celebrity money to make advertising endorsements or public appearances on behalf of a campaign, or it may involve making a substantial contribution to a civic improvement project in a key neighborhood or area.[3]

Persuasion involves using communication to win people over. Whatever the good of the persuasion, there are essentially six steps in the persuasion process—not that each act of persuasion necessarily follows these sequentially.[4] The first step is *presenting*. A person must be in a position

EXAMPLE 7.1

Two Theoretical Models Underpinning Public Relations Practice

Communications Model

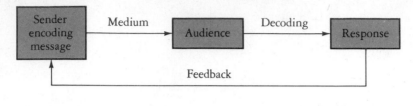

Behavioral Model

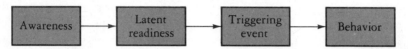

According to *pr reporter*, the behavioral model "basically shifts the objective, and with it the focus of thinking, strategizing and planning, away from the traditional model's emphasis on creating or retaining awareness."* Step 1, **awareness**, may involve creating awareness, changing levels of awareness or maintaining awareness, but in every case relevance to the individual is the key to getting attention. In this step, the diffusion process of communication—the two-step flow—contributes either positively or negatively to the next step. Step 2, **latent readiness**, precedes ac-

tion and involves referencing existing experiences, information, attitudes, values and beliefs and every other resource. The mental computer of each member of the target public is checking and matching, confirming or rejecting. In step 3, the **triggering event**, some circumstance arises, accidentally or intentionally, that causes action. Step 4, **behavior**, is that action. The initial action may only be preliminary to the final action—the ultimate, the desired behavior. This is a modification of the six-step persuasion model (see page 197).

*"Behavioral Model Replacing Communications Model as Basic Theoretical Underpinning of PR Practice," *pr reporter*, 33(30) (July 30, 1990), pp. 2–3.

SOURCE: Reprinted with permission of *pr reporter*, Exeter, NH, 33(30) (July 30, 1990), p. 1.

to receive a persuasive message—that is, both physically accessible and mentally receptive. You can present something and have the presentation ignored, however, so the second step in the persuasion process is *attending*, which means that the receiver must pay attention to the persuasive message. Beyond attending to the message, the receiver has to understand it. Therefore, the third step is *comprehending*. To satisfy this step, the

message must be presented in symbols the receiver can understand. The fourth step is *yielding*, in which the receiver accepts the message and agrees with the point of view it expresses. The next (fifth) step is *retaining* the transmitted information, which explains why repetition is so fundamental to the persuasion process. People have to be reminded of the message, even after they have accepted it. The sixth and final step is *acting*. The

EXAMPLE 7.2

Symmetrical Process Model

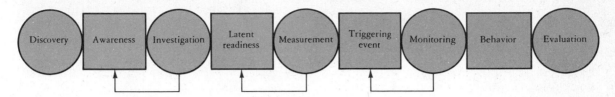

The symmetrical behavioral model involves five steps: first, **gauging** existing levels of awareness and discovering conditions under which publics are likely to respond positively to an effort to create, enhance or increase awareness of some desired behavioral goal; second, **investigating** responses to the attempt to create, raise or sustain awareness, to determine any problems with the desired behavior goal that may already be apparent and should cause goal modification (or even abandonment) with respect to one or more publics; third, **measuring** latent readiness to act, so that the action's direction can be anticipated, depending on certain conditions; fourth, **monitoring** responses to

the triggering event, to anticipate the level of resulting behavior, and interceding with action or communication or both if the behavior seems likely to be undesirable; fifth, **evaluating** behavior to determine why that particular action was taken, whether it is likely to be sustained and (if it is desired) what is needed to sustain it. Each of these five stages builds in the opportunity for publics to communicate their desires, needs and concerns so that goals can be adjusted or at least a mutual understanding can be negotiated.

SOURCE: Reprinted with permission of *pr reporter*, Exeter, NH, 33(30) (July 30, 1990).

---

persuader must be able to observe the results of persuasion in the receiver's behavior.

Some strategies that will get receivers to one point in the process will not carry them all the way through to the final step.[5] So persuasion strategy has to be planned and monitored to ascertain whether it is having the desired effect at each stage, and if it is not, why not. Parallels between the persuasion model and the behavior model are easy to see. The behavior model's awareness stage incorporates the persuasion model's presenting and attending. The latent awareness stage corresponds to comprehending, yielding and retaining. The triggering event essentially offers a demonstration of the receiver's retention, resulting in some sort of behavior. If this behavior matches the desired action, the persuasion process has succeeded.

Despite the protestations of some practitioners to the contrary, public relations frequently involves persuasion. Examples include public relations or advertising campaigns, which are generally highly visible because of the attendant publicity. In persuasion, the critical factor in opinion change usually is information or the lack thereof and how this information is presented or withheld. Information is power, as social scientist Herbert I. Schiller points out, and information resides in controllable sources—among the upper echelons of government, business and education. It tends to be made available to the public, Schiller says, through public relations people who have the power to control its flow. Their access to information and their selective use of it combine the tools of power and persuasion. Schiller rails persuasively against such "mind

▼ **In persuasion the critical factor in opinion change usually is information or the lack thereof and how the information is presented or withheld.**

---

managers," but his arguments fail to take into account the social responsibility exercised by these institutions or their representatives, plus the social responsibility assumed by news and advertising personnel in the media.[6]

Public relations persuasive strategies are planned around three elements: media, message and source.

Media Orientation

PR people use no black magic in their efforts to win over public opinion. First and foremost, public relations involves deciding what to tell, whom to tell it to, how to do it and through what media. The choice of medium is critical. It must be a believable source, able to reach the priority public and technologically capable of carrying the message. Television, for example, has high credibility and mass penetration. Safety officials who want to alert residents about an impending hurricane invariably take to the airwaves. But something complicated like a change in Social Security benefits cannot be communicated through this medium. All television can do is alert people to the change and tell them where to find the information; explaining the details requires a print medium.

People also turn to different media for different types of gratification and rewards. Many different measures have been used in examining *media use* and *gratification* motives but three seem especially well-suited: environmental surveillance, environmental diversion and environmental interaction.[7] According to these measures, people use media to see what's going on that might interest them or for sheer entertainment or to prepare for anticipated conversations or interactions with others.

How people use media for gratification may change as they change, as their circumstances change and as their relationships change. A young woman might become an avid reader of the sports pages while she is dating a sports enthusiast. A young man might begin to subscribe to art publications if he becomes interested in a young woman who is an art major. In either case, the individual's interest in the specialized medium may not outlast his or her enthusiasm for the human relationship being pursued.

Message Orientation

In selecting a persuasive strategy you must also evaluate the message itself. We do not always act as rational beings, relying on calculated judgments. We know that too much coffee is not good for us, but we may drink six cups a day anyway because we like it. Yet we may proceed cautiously in deciding about buying a car. Thus, to be effective, persuasive appeals must combine the rational and the emotional.

Think about an effective speaker you have heard recently. No doubt he or she illustrated the facts in the talk with examples—anecdotes that entertained you and helped you recall the major points. Compare that with a talk in which you took notes furiously to get down the flurry of facts. How much of the latter presentation do you remember? Unless you were compelled to take notes and to review them later, you probably don't recall a single significant fact. When given choice, as you are in most instances involving public relations material, you probably would not choose the straight facts over the fact-story.

The complexity of the individual in the audience or public has been addressed by William McGuire (see Example 7.3).

As McGuire's chart indicates, to be persuasive a message has to present something of value to the target public. It must also be compatible with that public's motives. If your public has to make some adjustments to accept a new or different idea, you must provide that adjustment and the rationale for

EXAMPLE 7.3 ▮▮▮▮▮▮▮

Motivational Theories Behind Communication/Persuasion Research

Initiation of Action / Need		Stability		Growth	
Termination of Action / Provocation		Active	Reactive	Active	Reactive
State / Relationship					
Cognitive	Internal	1. Consistency	2. Categorization	5. Autonomy	6. Problem-solver
	External	3. Noetic*	4. Inductional	7. Stimulation	8. Teleological
Affective	Internal	9. Tension-reduction	10. Ego-defensive	13. Assertion	14. Identification
	External	11. Expressive	12. Repetition	15. Empathy	16. Contagion

To use McGuire's chart, look first at what caused a response—a seeking (need) or a reaction to some stimulus (provocation). Then observe the likely effect in a stable (status quo) environment in two categories—an active response and a reactive response. Then check the growth category in both the active and reactive columns. Trace these back to the cognitive (intellectual) response and the affective (emotional) response. Consult the internal versus the external to get some idea of demonstrable effects.

tual) response and the affective (emotional) response. Consult the internal versus the external to get some idea of demonstrable effects.

SOURCE: William McGuire, "Theoretical Foundations of Campaigns," in *Public Communication Campaigns*, Ronald E. Rice and William J. Paisley, eds. (Beverly Hills: Sage, 1981), p. 55.

*abstract

it. In a free society where communication is open, the person being persuaded chooses which messages to attend to. If your message challenges your public's sense of security or self-image, you must provide an ego defense; otherwise, members of the public will repel the argument, instinctively defending their ego. If you are suggesting acceptance of something that has been rejected before as socially taboo, you must offer a value that can be adopted to replace it or rationalize it. For instance, although it may be difficult to get white Americans to adopt American-born children of other races,

they may adopt *foreign* children of other races—as they did in the 1975 Vietnam "babylift"—because of an emotional appeal to guilt or conscience. Some of this can be explained by the theory of *cognitive dissonance*. When something we are persuaded to do collides with what we think we should do, we resolve the conflict by justifying our action, rationalizing our behavior and modifying our opinion.[8]

> ▼ **A persuasive message must present some-thing of value to its intended public and must be compatible with the motives of that public.**

News media often are credited with the ability to bring about change in a free society, but agenda-setting theory studies suggest that all the news media can do is give importance or significance to a message or to an issue by giving it news coverage. Sometimes the news media are so out of touch with the "average" citizen that real public opinion on an issue grows independently, despite its being totally ignored by the news media. Such was the case in the groundswell of public opinion against 1983 legislation to withhold tax on interest and dividends. When Congress was pressured to repeal the law by an outraged electorate, the news media attributed the repeal to sudden pressure from the banking lobby. Actually, the banking industry had always opposed the legislation. The news media were relying entirely on news releases from the administration in Washington.[9]

Some useful guidance on the effects of source and message on receivers is available in secondary research (see Example 7.4).

Source Orientation

The source of information has such a big effect on persuasion that producers of commercial advertising go to great lengths to decide what qualities the person or persons featured in the commercial should have. Organizations take the same care, especially in times of crisis, to select the best spokesperson for the effect that is sought. The whole premise of Gary Hart's reentry into the 1987 presidential campaign was that he had been forced out earlier by the news media and he was going to let the voter, not the news media, decide. The concept of taking the message to the people is what twice won the presidency for Ronald Reagan. But it also contributed significantly to his fractious relationship with members of Congress during both of his terms.

People tend to believe sources that are like them, like they want to be or like they perceive themselves to be. People also seek authority in sources, most of the time. But they can be emotionally swayed into accepting someone else's advice. For example, the U.S. Surgeon General's appeal to people to use condoms to avoid possible contagion from the AIDS virus had only a marginal effect. Planned Parenthood could have told him that. It has been trying for years to prevent unwanted pregnancies, but it often has to compete with someone emotionally close to the decision maker. Part of the acceptance of authority is credibility, much of which is based on trust. People almost always trust someone close to them more than they do any authority figure.

▼ PERSUADERS AND THEIR APPEALS

We have all practiced persuading others to do our bidding since we discovered as babies that crying brought us a rescuer. As adults, we persuade people to come with us to see a film they don't want to see, or to take us to pick up our car at the shop or to come for us when the car breaks down. Although these may be considered acts of friendship, they really are negotiations. We used something in the bargaining process, stated or unstated. If you doubt that, think of the times you have heard, "I'd have to call in some chits [favors granted and not yet returned] to get that done," or "I don't have any leverage with her. You're in a better position to ask." You might even say in response, "I'll ask. She owes me one." You've probably been doing this for a long time.

Personal Persuaders

Organizations and authorities, family members and what sociologists call "significant others"—people you care about—exercise leverage over you. Organizations that you belong to ask for money regularly, and you usually give. They ask you to obey certain codes of conduct and to be present for certain events, and you comply. You may belong to the organization for social, religious or poiltical reasons, or for economic reasons (as with the organization that employs you). In the workplace, certain people are in positions of authority—those who have special responsibilities. When you work for someone or when you are a conscientious member of an organization, you generally comply with the requests of those in authority. You also generally do what close friends and members of your family ask you to do. Recognition of authority in families is long-lived when it grows into respect or when someone has the leverage of purchase (that is, inheritance). Often personal persuaders can get you to do things contrary to your own desires, best interests or values. Their persuasive control is potent.

Impersonal Persuaders

Less potent and influential are the impersonal persuaders. These are found in the mass media in the forms of editorials and advertisements. They are found in the content of various types of entertainment and among those who perform. They are found as well in educational and governmental institutions and in the commercial institutions that we depend on for goods and services. In some countries all of these may be government-operated or -controlled. These impersonal institutions may persuade you through your fear of the punishments that they have available or because of the personal persuasiveness of their representatives. A specific teacher in a school or a specific sales clerk in a favorite store moves the relationship beyond the impersonal and into the personal.

Some of these impersonal persuaders qualify as opinion makers because they influence significant numbers of people. Some are opinion makers because of their public status (as in the case of celebrities and other newsmakers), and others because they manage the news. Some of the most visible opinion makers are both public figures and news managers.

▼ **Persuaders are either personal or impersonal; personal persuaders have much more impact.**

Opinion Makers and News Managers

A news manager may be someone who creates an event that becomes news when it is made to happen, usually on a carefully detailed and prearranged schedule. The event may be Mickey Mouse's visit to a children's hospital or an IRA (Irish Republican Army) bomb threat. It may continue over an extended period of time, as did the 1979–1980 hostage crisis at the American Embassy in Tehran, Iran. A news manager may also be someone who focuses media attention on an event that might otherwise be overlooked. In addition, a news manager may attempt to control information, as many tried to do in the Nixon White House. This is not new, however. As media critic William L. Rivers notes, "Nothing is quite so absurd as thinking of news control by government as a modern phenomenon. . . . Information policy has been at the very center of governing the United States from the beginning."[10]

Public Relations and Opinion Molding

What is true of news management by government is true of any group in business, science, education or other fields that possesses specialized information: Those in command of information control its dissemination. The public's only defense is in being aware that someone is always trying to influence its opinion. A sophisticated person will ask, "What am I being asked to think? What am I being asked to do? By whom? Why?"

In a democracy these questions often are raised by members of some opposition, resulting in a struggle for public opinion. That struggle confounds some other nations whose form of government makes it possible to ignore public opinion.

EXAMPLE 7.4

What Research Tells Us About Sources, Messages, Media and Receivers of Persuasion

SOURCES

1. Self-persuasion (internalization) seems to be the most permanent source of persuasion, followed by identification and compliance.

2. High-credibility sources, when recalled, produce more opinion change.

3. Credibility of source does not affect message recall.

4. Information from low-credibility sources does not increase over time.

5. Powerful, attractive, biased sources can be more effective than unbiased sources in reinforcing opinions.

6. Biased sources are less likely to be believed if they are also perceived to be experts.

7. Expertise adds more to persuasive impact than trustworthiness, and we are more likely to be influenced by experts than by peers.

8. Attractive sources are more effective than unattractive ones, but source credibility has more impact.

9. Unattractive sources are more effective when they advocate unexpected positions.

10. Retention of a message is higher if the message was not expected from that source.

11. Sources offering rewards are more effective than sources that threaten.

12. Mild threats may be internalized and lead to compliance, while strong threats stimulate defiance.

13. A source that threatens one of several punishments for noncompliance may be as persuasive as one that promises rewards.

14. Source credibility may not matter if the messages themselves present reasonable arguments.

MESSAGES

1. Messages with explicit conclusions are more effective than messages that allow the recipient to draw her or his own conclusions.

2. Good news presented first increases acceptance of a message, even if the message also contains bad news.

3. Information at the beginning and end of a message is recalled better than information in the middle.

4. Telling both sides in a message (telling the other side and refuting it) is advisable if the recipient is educated, is likely to hear the other side anyway, is familiar with the issue or is opposed to the side being advocated.

5. High-fear appeals can be more effective than low-fear ones when receivers have low chronic anxiety or don't see themselves as vulnerable and when the recommendations are specific, clear and easy to follow.

6. Generally there's no difference in the persuasive impact of emotional over rational appeals.

7. Increased comprehension of a message increases agreement.

8. Learning increases with message repetition, but repetition can eventually cause an increase in counterargumentation and a decrease in favorable thoughts.

9. Repeated exposure to a message can increase agreement, but too much can lead to boredom and reduce agreement. A period of nonexposure can overcome effects of overexposure.

10. Generally, comparative and noncomparative ads are equally effective, but comparative ads are more effective on television than in print or on radio. Comparative ads are most effective when used with new or novelty products, when market share is small or when the desired public doesn't have established preferences.

BOTH SOURCE AND MESSAGE

1. If there's little supporting evidence for a message, the importance of source credibility is more pronounced.

2. Communicators are evaluated more favorably to the extent that their messages have the following qualities: listenability or readability, human interest, vocabulary diversity and realism.

MEDIA

1. Live or videotaped messages are most effective in changing attitudes, followed by oral (audiotaped) messages. Written messages are least effective.

2. Television involves its audience more than does radio, which is more involving than print.

3. Written messages—especially complex ones—are more easily learned and remembered than either videotaped or audiotaped messages.

4. When the message is simple, videotapes are more effective than written presentations.

5. Trustworthy sources are more effective in changing attitudes when they use television rather than print or radio media, both of which may give untrustworthy sources an advantage.

RECEIVERS

1. A message that contradicts an existing opinion will not necessarily be rejected if it appears to reward the receiver.

2. Perception is often subjective. Even when information is not adequate, receivers tend to use what is there (or what they perceive is there) to serve an immediate need or purpose.

3. Accurate and favorable perceptions of a message can be facilitated by establishing early bonding with the target public, by using familiar objects and categories and by using message cues that the public can easily recognize.

4. There is no evidence of selective retention of information based on the receivers' attitudes and behaviors.

5. Publics tend to disregard supportive messages that are easy to refute and nonsupportive messages that are difficult to refute.

6. Most mental and personality traits of receivers have diametrically opposed effects on message reception and yielding. Intelligence, for instance, facilitates reception but inhibits yielding.

7. Adjusting messages to minimize differences between the source and extreme receivers facilitates greater acceptance.

SOURCE: Adapted from Alexis S. Tan, *Mass Communication Theories and Research*, pp. 141–43, 164–65, 176–77, 204–5. Reprinted with permission of Macmillan Publishing Company from *Mass Communication Theories and Research* by Alexis S. Tan. Copyright © 1985 by Macmillan Publishing Company.

▼ **PR people, like managers in government, business and other institutions, are opinion makers through their control of the dissemination of information.**

But the freedom to compete for public opinion is inherent in our concept of democracy. PR practitioners become involved in such struggles because each side in a controversy employs them as professional advisers or spokespersons. Practitioners usually represent the side corresponding to their own beliefs, although some ethical practitioners will, (like lawyers), serve any client with loyalty whether or not they personally subscribe to the client's position. What differentiates the professional practitioner from the unprofessional news manager—who unfortunately is often mistaken for the PR person—is a strict adherence to a code of ethics that endorses a sense of social responsibility. Professional public relations practitioners never lie to the news media, although in the interests of a client they may sometimes have to say to the press, "I know, but I cannot tell you." The success of those who control certain areas of information in affecting public opinion is only as strong as their credibility. A professional public relations practitioner cannot afford to risk losing credibility.

Propaganda and Persuasion Appeals

People who want to sway opinions use a variety of persuasion appeals—not all of them honest. The following list identifies some of the propaganda devices commonly used to mislead publics:

1. *Name calling:* The characterization can be positive or negative. Someone can be called "wise and conscientious" or "a liar and a cheat" (or the matter can even be left open to interpretation, as with "He's a character!").

2. *Glittering generalities:* Many nebulous words can be used here—for example, "enthusiastic crowds," or "throngs of greeters."

3. *Transfer:* This occurs when a movie star or other celebrity campaigns for a politician or product, and some of the famous person's aura is transferred to the less well-known person or product.

4. *Testimonial:* This is an actual endorsement, as opposed to a transfer device. A common advertising technique, it involves having professional athletes and other celebrities encourage consumers to buy a product by saying that they use it.

5. *Plain folks:* A favorite of politicians, this device involves using homey language or appeals to down-to-earth concerns to convince a public that, despite their high office or aspirations thereto, the politicians are still "one of us."

6. *Bandwagon:* This compelling device is used to sway undecided people to go with the majority, however slight the majority might be. The bandwagon device is considered so powerful that networks avoid telecasting projected results of election returns in the East until polls close in the West. Some research evidence indicates, however, that such coverage has no impact on people who have not yet voted.

7. *Card stacking:* Telling "one side of the story" involves selecting facts that represent one point of view, while obscuring other facts. The result is distortion and misrepresentation.

8. *Emotional stereotypes:* These evoke all kinds of images, and are so designed: "good American," "housewife," "foreigner," and so on.

9. *Illicit silence:* This device is a subtle form of propaganda, like innuendo, suggestion and insinuation. It involves withholding information that would correct a false impression.

10. *Subversive rhetoric:* An offshoot of card stacking is the device of discrediting a person's motivation in order to discredit the idea, which may be good and useful. For example, someone may discredit the mayor's plan to build a bridge on grounds that the mayor owns property on the other side of the river. In the meantime, viewed objectively, the bridge-building plan may still be a good one for opening up commerce, traffic or tourism.

Obvious forms of these propaganda devices are easily recognizable, but their application by skillful users often is not. Anyone who communicates may employ propaganda devices—spoken, written, pictorial or whatever. Such devices also may take the form of synthetic events. The 1960s were filled with "demonstrations"—all of them propaganda devices. And among the most skillful of that era's news managers were the youths. Reared on television and other media, they knew how to use propaganda devices *and* media effectively.

Despite encompassing some techniques that are used to mislead, the word *propaganda* should not be thought of as totally negative. Propaganda can be used to change attitudes and behavior in a constructive way, too. Propagandists differ from educators in that educators teach people how to think, but propagandists try to teach people what to think.[11] Propaganda also has been used to appeal to basic human emotions in order to effect opinion changes in the public interest (see Chapter 9).

Social legislation, income tax, Medicare, civil rights laws and other public policy initiatives all reflect changes in public opinion that were sensed and acted upon by politicians. Generally, such public opinion is an emotional response to information or events. Social psychologist Hadley Cantril developed some "laws" purportedly governing this emotional response (see Example 6.15). Although critics say that no law can account for something with as many variables as public opinion, Cantril's laws do suggest five basic ideas that seem common to all studies of opinion expression: (1) events are most likely to affect opinion; (2) demands for action are a usual response; (3) self-interest must figure heavily if people are to become involved; (4) leadership is sought, and not always objectively and critically; (5) reliability is difficult to assess.

Another five elements have been isolated by psychology professor Robert Cialdini, who identifies these as being elements of self-persuasion, the strongest and most effective type of persuasion. All are tied to the social persuasion strategy discussed earlier. Cialdini explains the elements as follows:

▼ **Propaganda, an effort to teach people what—rather than how—to think, is often used to mislead.**

_____

1. *Consistency:* After committing themselves to a position, even in some trivial way, people are more likely to agree to perform behaviors consistent with that position. When people decide to comply with a request, they check to see if they have already done something that is consistent with the request. For example, in one Cancer Society charity drive it was found that homeowners who had previously gone on record as supporting the Cancer Society (by accepting and wearing a small lapel pin for a day) were nearly twice as likely as others to give a monetary donation a week later when the charity drive began. However, not all small, initial commitments are equally good at producing consistent future behavior. They are most effective in this regard when the commitments are active, public, and not coerced.

2. *Reciprocity:* One question people ask themselves before agreeing to another's request is, "Do I owe this person something?" If the answer is yes, they are more apt to comply, often when they would have otherwise declined and even when what they agree to do is more significant than what they received earlier.

3. *Social validation:* People are more influenced to perform an action or hold a belief when they see that others are doing so. An important piece of evidence people inspect in deciding what is appropriate conduct for themselves in a situation is how others are acting. For this reason, advertisers love to include the words "fastest growing" or "largest selling" in their product descriptions. They don't have to say directly that the product is good; they only need say that others think so, which seems proof enough.

---

4. *Authority:* People are more willing to follow the suggestions of someone they consider a legitimate authority in terms of knowledge and trustworthiness. Demonstrating knowledge can usually be accomplished by showing evidence of superior experience, training, skill, or information. Establishing trustworthiness is trickier. One device, in pitching a story to an editor, is to back off from this week's story but promise real newsworthiness with the following week's item—for example, "I know this item isn't exactly what you want, but wait until you see what we have for you next week!"

5. *Scarcity:* People try to seize those items and opportunities that are scarce or dwindling in availability. This accounts for the success of the "deadline," "limited number," and "can't-come-back-later" sales tactics. Research indicates that people want a scarce item more than ever when they are in competition with others for it, or when they believe they have an exclusive.[12]

Earl Newsom's four principles of persuasion build on the concept of personal identification with an idea or problem, and suggest actions that people will take in response to a personal appeal:

1. *Identification:* People will relate to an idea, opinion or point of view only if they can see it as having some direct effect on their own hopes, fears, desires or aspirations.

2. *Suggestion of action:* People will endorse ideas only if the ideas are accompanied by a proposed action from the sponsor of the idea or if the recipients themselves propose it—especially a *convenient* action.

3. *Familiarity and trust:* People are unwilling to accept ideas from sources they don't trust, whether the sources are people or institutions. Thus a goal of PR is to ensure that an institution deserves and obtains such confidence, that it increases the trust of many people and that it keeps the trust of those it counts as friends.

4. *Clarity:* The meaning of an idea in an event, situation or message has to be clear in order to be persuasive.[13]

Successful advertising copywriters certainly know the importance of the last two principles—namely, that the people doing the buying have to trust those doing the selling and that those doing the selling must communicate clearly to have any effect at all.

The element of trust needs to be emphasized in any study of opinion change. All of us are more likely to assume attitudes and accept ideas uncritically from those we love and trust. Observers predicted all kinds of voting patterns for eighteen-year-olds in the United States before they were given the right to vote. What actually happened? Most youths voted like their parents—probably because they loved and trusted them. However, even if they did not love and trust their parents, they did receive information from them over a long period of time. One communication theory—called the "sleeper effect"—suggests that the source of a persuasive message, even if it is a distrusted source, is apt to be forgotten after a long period of time, leaving a residue of information accepted as fact.

Identification and suggestion of action are also important. As for identification, most of us feel an association with others—by education, religion, occupation, social or economic status or other category. What our identification groups say and do suggest courses of action for us. These associations have potential power because, when events so demand, opinion can be mobilized along lines of self-interest. According to Philip Lesly, such mobilization can be activated by highly visible leaders. Lesly says that at least three separate groups are discernible in the "leader" category:

1. *Vocal activists* who devote themselves to high-profile advocacy of cause.

2. *Opinion leaders*, both mass-media and individual thought leaders throughout society.

3. *Power leaders*—legislators, government officials, judges and regulators who have the power to take actions that affect organizations and society.

Increasingly, the focal group in persuasion is the power leaders. They have the ability to make things actually happen. Vocal activists, media, influential individuals and groups, and the general public provide input to the power leaders, but they have little power themselves. The input that reaches the power leaders is much greater from vocal activists and from opinion leaders than from the public and from most private organizations.[14]

Opinion mobilization by a leader creates a pressure group. Even if we are not directly involved in a particular controversy, we are still likely, because of our personal loyalties, to side with the pressure group that claims to represent us. For example, during the 1970s strife in Ireland, international problems resulted when Americans of Irish descent became involved in gunrunning.

Persuasion Strategies

Persuaders use one or more of five specific strategies to enlist compliance: stimulus-response, cognitive, motivational, social appeal and personality appeal.

The *stimulus-response* (S-R) strategy, borrowed from behavioral research, presupposes that audiences can be conditioned to respond automatically to certain stimuli, such as answering the phone when it rings. But sometimes S-R doesn't work as planned. For example, capricious association may occur, in which the stimulus elicits a different response from the one desired because the mind makes a different (and unexpected) connection. Another problem arises from the need for repetition before learning can occur. If not enough repetition takes place, the response can differ markedly from the one anticipated. A third problem is that the exposure necessary for repetition is usually expensive and is not always cost-effective, because the association may be forgotten. Nonetheless, long-term payoffs from embedded recall do result when S-R works.

▼ **Persuasion strategies include stimulus-response, cognitive, motivational, social appeal and personality appeal.**

Anticipating an S-R response of some kind can affect the type of message sent, according to *Glimpse*, the newsletter of the International Society for General Semantics. The newsletter notes that this anticipation can lead to another propaganda technique:

> Once told that an event or action *signals* a particular response, we may assume uncritically that earlier learning has established such a connection, as the word *signal* suggests. Unaware how we do so, we may come to believe that a particular event or action serves as a signal because someone labels it a "signal."
>
> Thus our reasoning and conclusions may be shaped by this propaganda ploy.[15]

The newsletter offers some example of this ploy from columns and letters in the *New York Times*, including this one: "It would send the wrong signal to the Russians if [Defense Secretary Caspar] Weinberger is not included in the Geneva delegation [to the summit]," a Pentagon official said. "It would make it look like we're too eager for a deal."[16]

The *cognitive* strategy reasons that learning factual information in the context of a message can persuade if the information is retained. However, this strategy works only with individuals who have no stake in the outcome or who have no negative preconceptions about what they are being persuaded to do. Additionally, because it is cognitive, suitable alternatives have to be proposed, and the persuasion has to be presented in a context, as part of a bigger picture. For example, the purpose of exercise is not just to lose weight; it may also make you feel and think better.

The *motivational* strategy involves creating a need or stimulating a desire or want. It relies on a learned behavior, and not everyone that you want to reach can be motivated. To succeed, this strategy must offer a real or perceived reward.

The *social appeal* strategy concentrates on calling attention to social conditions. Many appeals to alleviate conditions for the poor and needy use this strategy, as do appeals designed to correct behavior like those sponsored by Mothers Against Drunk Driving. Often the appeals are tied to job-related norms.

The *personality appeal* strategy is designed for people who are outer-directed rather than inner-directed. It is based on tolerance (as opposed to intolerance) levels. Some nonsmoking and smoking appeals are personality-based, as is the appeal that promotes self-employment: "Own your own business; be your own boss."

Effectiveness of Persuasion

In making persuasive appeals to various human motives, you must consider two possibilities: that cognitive dissonance could occur, and that truth may be personal.

A theory of cognitive dissonance by sociologist Leon Festinger describes what people do when they act inconsistently with their own beliefs—as a result of pressures from power, patronage or persuasion.[17]

According to Stanford University psychology professor Philip Zimbardo, subtlety is sometimes the best persuader. He believes that more attitude change can sometimes be produced by *less* social persuasion. If people think themselves free to make decisions that run counter to their values, they sometimes need only a gentle push to take the plunge. Some smokers, for example, abandon their habit when subtly persuaded that smoking impairs the health of others, such as expectant mothers and small children. No one had to pressure them to abandon the habit; they simply became aware of the health hazard through media reports. They view themselves as having made a free choice and remain unaware that they were coaxed into changing by gentle social persuasion.

To see that truth is personal and value-oriented, we need only look at the religions of the world. All disciplines claim that their religion represents *the truth*, yet there are obviously many conflicts in doctrine among different sects or denominations. Certain objective truths are generally accepted—such as that "football is a contact sport"—but many less definitive "personal truths" exist as well, and these are often circumstantial, such as what level of propriety a person can afford to be concerned about.

Is manipulation of public opinion only a matter of communication skills and knowledge? Not always. PR practitioner Earl Newsom pointed out an example of a major failure in a six-month "skilled-persuasion" effort in an Ohio city. The campaign distributed 59,000 pieces of literature aimed at getting people to view the U.N. in positive terms. But it failed miserably because, during the campaign, the U.N. itself was particularly ineffective. It is not true, Newsom said, "that if you have enough money to pay for printing, advertising, and 'propaganda,' you can change people's minds."[18] It is also possible to overcampaign, arousing suspicion and backlash when people notice that a lot of money is being spent on the media.

Such overcampaigning may have been part of the problem with the U.S. government's unsuccessful seven-year (1971–1978), $5 billion war on cancer. A cure for cancer is not yet in sight, and public support for the battle lags. Some government officials feel that too simplistic an approach to the disease was taken originally, stimulating false hope. Others believe that the source of disillusionment and confusion was the government's decision to ban various products that cause cancer in animals[19] but have not been tested adequately on humans. Ultimately, the public's increasing refusal to join the "war on cancer" may be attributable to disillusionment over the false promise implicit in its initiation. Some legislators talked of having the battle won by the 1976 bicentennial. But "actions speak louder than words"—which was also the real lesson of the U.N. effort.

Overcampaigning probably also occurred in the effort to control smoking. Smokers clearly understood that their addiction caused cancer, but after a certain point the campaign against smoking began to falter. Then coalitions of antismokers began to obtain results that the original campaign could not produce. These groups brought about restrictions on smoking in public places by pressuring airline management, government officials and private business owners.

Persuasion occurs face to face and through mass media. But while interpersonal persuasion can result in cognitive changes, mass media tend to focus their efforts on channeling attitudes and existing behavior changes in a particular direction.[20]

▼ COMMUNICATION CONCEPTS AND THEORIES

Many theories about communication are borrowed from the social sciences. A theory, according to sociologist George Homans, is something that enables researchers to derive a wide variety of findings under a number of different conditions from "a few higher order propositions."[21]

Another definition states that a theory is "an abstract, symbolic representation of what is conceived to be reality... a set of abstract statements or rules designed to 'fit' some portion of the real world."[22] This definition appears with two sets of rules for using "a theory (a set of symbolic statements)." One set, called the *correspondence rules*, states that some of the symbols (called "conceptual independence variables") must relate with others (called "conceptual dependent variables") and to what occurs (behavior of an object or person in a situation). The other set of rules, called *functional relationships*, describes how to manipulate the symbols of the theoretical concepts to derive testable hypotheses.

In communications, the propositions resulting from various theories are constantly undergoing examination, testing and revision. They will continue to do so as we get more deeply into new media, such as VCRs and expanded cable TV choices.

▼ **The four general communication theories are structural functionalism, evolutionary perspective, social conflict and symbolic interactionism.**

The propositions that have survived testing so far suggest certain principles that may provide a useful framework, both practical and theoretical, for the day-to-day operations of public relations.

When you do research, your hypothesis testing always proceeds within some theoretical framework—usually a communication or persuasion theory. There are four commonly accepted frameworks for communication theories and two general persuasion models.

The four general communication theories are as follows:

1. *Structural functionalism* (Plato's *Republic*, Durkheim, Merton, Parsons): This theory holds that the organization or structure of society provides its stability. As a result, the forms of media and mass communication depend on their society and contribute to social equilibrium.

2. *Evolutionary perspective* (Darwin, Spencer): This theory holds that social change follows a set of natural laws and that mass communication systems have grown and developed with technology and with decision makers' needs for communication.

3. *Social conflict* (Hegel, Marx, Engels): This theory holds that social struggles occur between groups with competing needs and goals. The mass media are competitive and active in a number of areas of conflict, such as being a watchdog over government.

4. *Symbolic interactionism* (Charles Horton Cooley—environment over genes—and George Herbert Mead—language symbols in collective and individual life): This theory holds that the media present constructs of reality that offer information from limited sources, resulting in individual and collective creations of reality.

These general theories are social paradigms (sets of assumptions). Some competing psychological theories are usually discussed as a single framework, chiefly because in the study of mass communication the first four theories provide a good launching pad for discussions of collective action or effects. Nevertheless, we have to turn to a psychological paradigm for the effect of communication on the individual. Several approaches can be isolated within the psychological framework. One is the neurobiological approach, which concerns itself with the effects of communication on the nerves and the brain. Another is the comparative approach, which focuses on the effect of communication on humans versus its effect on other living creatures. A third focus is the behavioral approach, which derives from stimulus-response psychology and is closely related to the neurobiological and the comparative. A fourth is the psychoanalytic approach, which studies unconscious reactions. A related fifth orientation is the cognitive approach, which examines what people do to and with sensory input. This is the most commonly used approach in studies of the effects of mass communication.

The two general persuasion models are as follows:

1. *Sociocultural paradigm:* This model attempts to account for sociocultural variables that enable a particular individual to interpret or present reality as in the mass media.

2. *Psychodynamic model:* This model, based on the cognitive paradigm, studies how an effective message makes a person do something (deliver an overt response) that the communicator desired as an effect. One of the most valuable theories drawn from this model is Ball-Rokeach's Theory of Value Change. People who are given a value test and who are then compared with others like them or whom they want to be like will change specific values to accommodate the others' values.

If you keep these various paradigms in mind as you develop a hypothesis, you will maintain a consistent theoretical framework. Developing a sound

hypothesis has three benefits: it gives focus to the research; it eliminates trial and error research; and it allows you to quantify variables. Words that you can't quantify don't belong in a hypothesis.[23]

How We Communicate

Much public relations theory about communication rests on Carl Hovland's idea that to change attitudes you must change opinions, and that attempting to do this requires communication. For a communication to be effective, the object of the communication effort must pay attention to the communication, understand it, accept it and remember it. Once a communication reaches the level of acceptance, the question of credibility enters in. Earl Newsom made the following comment about credibility:

> It *does* seem to be true that the attitudes of people are formed by what they see us do and say—not by our insistent attempts to tell all about ourselves and persuade them that we deserve their confidence. It *does* seem to work out in practice that before we can move people to have confidence in us we must appear to them to be solving the problems *they* want to see solved—to be headed where the people are headed.[24]

The second part of the Hovland approach is raised in the question posed by H. D. Lasswell: "Who said what to whom with what effect?"[25] The "Who" here is the source of the communication. If the source is a PR practitioner, that person speaks for an entire institution whose credibility depends on the public's perception of its power, competence, trustworthiness, goodwill, idealism and dynamism, as well as on the similarity between the source and the public's self-perception. (A source can be either a person or a medium of communication, as in the expression "the *New York Times* said today.") The medium used for a communication conveys information, either factual or emotional, intended to cause an opinion change in the public.

The final part of Lasswell's question is critical for public relations people: "to whom with what effect?" That is, who was the public, and what effect did the communication have on it? We will examine these questions in the following subsections. But keep in mind that trying to change attitudes is complicated; it involves convincing a person to relinquish one way of looking at the world (or part of the world) in exchange for another. What publics do with a message defines its effect.

Reception Test for Media   Although media research departments can show tables of statistics that theoretically profile their publics, you should still ask some probing questions. For example, are the selected "receivers" chosen from a physical or from an intellectual base? A university (for instance) may define all those to whom it mails its alumni magazine as "readers," yet a substantial number are probably "nonreceivers" (they throw the publication away without ever lifting the cover) and another segment may be "lookers" (they thumb through the magazine but never read anything except photo captions). The real readers are those who read at least one article per publication in the time period sampled. The same applies to news releases. To quote former Ohio State University PR professor Walter Siefert:

> Dissemination [of news releases] does not equal Publication, and Publication does not equal Absorption and Action! Which means, in simpler words: All who receive it won't *publish* it, and all who read or hear it won't understand or *act* on it.[26]

Credibility Test for Media   Another relevant question concerns a medium's credibility. How much do surveys couched in terms of numbers reached tell you about reception? If you send out a news release to the media, not all of them will publish it, and many who do read or hear it will not pay any real attention to it. For instance, a presentation designed by the Magazine Publishers Association to show the impact of magazine advertising claimed that certain ads reached women in the twenty-five to thirty-five age bracket who, it was asserted, do most of the buying. The presentation offered supporting data to show such women's response to and recall of specific advertising messages, but it did not state the *proportion* of readers recalling these

▼ **To change attitudes, you must change opinions; and this process involves communication.**

messages. And just as some people read editorial content and ignore advertising, others do just the opposite.

Thus, in talking about public reception of media, we first have to talk in broad terms of publicity and advertising. Many studies are available on the subject of receptivity of advertising, because of its ties to marketing. Publicity is more difficult to measure because the use (much less the reception) of publicity materials released to the mass media is almost impossible to evaluate. Publicity is assumed to have a higher degree of credibility than advertising because it appears as a nonbiased "news" source—one often referred to as third-party credibility.

Studies bear out these generalities. Ethnic and religious publications have a higher credibility with their readers than other media do with theirs. Industry, trade, association and professional print media also rank high with their selected audiences. Suburban and small-town weekly publications (generally newspapers) rate next highest in credibility. Specialized magazines also rate high—again, perhaps, because their readers have a concentrated interest in the subject matter. Among mass (as opposed to specialized) media, television dominates. Possible reasons for this are the widespread belief that "seeing is believing" and TV's capacity to disengage the critical senses. Daily newspapers have more credibility than their critics often are willing to concede and a higher persuasive impact than their publishers and editors may be willing to admit. Radio stations, owing to their specialized appeal and the emotional impact of the medium, significantly affect their own loyal audiences, but these are comparatively small. At the bottom of the credibility ratings come company publications, which get mixed reviews for credibility, perhaps because they are so diverse in quality. In an era when everything else about the government seems suspect, government publications consistently get rather high credibility ratings—particularly those that include consumer-oriented studies.

Although the narrowness of their appeal makes the specialized media and the smaller mass media (suburban papers, radio) easier to evaluate, the mass media present a complex study. Studies among young people show television news rated higher in credibility than newspaper news. A college sample gave newscasts a 3-to-1 lead over newspapers.[27] A high-school sample rated TV as the preferred news source because viewers could see the news happening. Radio and newspapers almost tied for second place with this high-school audience, but newspapers were cited as more believable; news magazines rated last.[28]

The term *agenda setting* refers to the variable degrees of attention the mass media give to certain ideas, issues or themes, lending them more or less significance. A symbiotic relationship (mutually beneficial coexistence) seems to exist between message source and medium, in that mass media may pick up ideas that seem likely to represent broad appeals and then popularize them. The media agenda may also suggest to leaders some exploitable public concerns, although some evidence suggests that the power of agenda setting is diminished when the issue is abstract (federal budget deficit) rather than concrete (drug abuse).[29] There is no clear-cut "cause and effect" in agenda setting, but the impact of the mass media in calling attention to an idea, regardless of its source, is considerable.

How to Choose the Right Message

Communication theory states that, after you estimate a medium's reception and credibility, you must plan the correct message for it. If you are us-ing billboards, you must do more than simply conclude that someone driving at 55 miles per hour cannot possibly read twenty words of copy and still be a safe driver. You also have to consider the purpose of the message, as well as its form, its color and its language.

The Purpose of a Message   The purpose of a message depends on the objective of the communication. What do you wish to accomplish? The goal should be something tangible, such as increasing the enrollment of a university, and not something nebulous, such as improving the image of the institution. PR pioneer Edward L. Bernays is adamant about refusing to use the word *image* in a public relations context. According to Bernays, the word suggests that PR deals with shadows and illusions when in reality it deals with changing attitudes and actions to meet social objectives.[30]

The reality of the PR practitioner's job is reduced to basics—experience not imagery—by former Southwestern Bell Telephone area public relations director Jim Pattillo. Pattillo is blunt and very specific: "All the image building goes down the drain for the telephone industry the very first time the customer starts having a hard time with his telephone service or with company representatives."[31]

Some problems of institutional credibility cited by PR practitioner Philip Lesly can be attributed directly to peddling images instead of dealing with realities. Examples include the handling of information about the Vietnam War—a foreign policy issue—and about the New York financial crisis of the 1970s—a domestic policy issue.[32] Some data indicate that deceptive persuaders are more likely to use rationale or explanation than truthful persuaders, who tend to employ positive and negative attributes of a situation.

Once the purpose of the message has been clearly defined, the motivation and inspiration decisions are easier. Psychologist Abraham H. Maslow has devised a hierarchy of human motives (see Example 7.5).[33] You should try to frame your message to appeal to the appropriate need.

EXAMPLE 7.5

Maslow's Hierarchy of Human Needs

Physical Needs	Safety Needs	Love Needs	Self-Esteem Needs	Self-Actualization Needs

Food
Sleep
Health
Body needs
Exercise
Rest
Sex
	Safety
	Security
	Protection
	Comfort
	Peace
	Order
		Acceptance
		Belonging
		Group
		  membership
		Love, Affection
			Recognition
			Prestige
			Confidence
			Leadership
			Success
			Knowledge
				Self-fulfillment
				Creative
				  challenge
				Reality
				Intellectual
				  curiosity

Secretarial	Organizational Maintenance	Services	Programs	Advocacy

Organizations →

"Hierarchy of Needs" from *Motivation and Personality* by Abraham H. Maslow. Copyright 1954 by Harper & Row, Publishers, Inc. Copyright © 1970 by Abraham H. Maslow. Reprinted by permission of HarperCollins Publishers.

▼ *Physiological* needs—for food, drink, sex, rest and such—are the most fundamental motivations.

▼ *Safety* is the need for protection against violence, economic hazards and unpredictable reality.

▼ *Love* is more than a need for affection. It encompasses the need to belong to a group and the longing for a friendly social environment. The strength of this motivational need pulls young people, particularly teenagers, together into a seemingly impenetrable peer group.

▼ *Esteem* includes the needs for achievement and for recognition of that achievement by others. It also involves the face-saving compromises we often engage in to rescue our self-regard, such as settling for a fancier title instead of a salary increase.

▼ *Self-actualization* is the need to develop individuality and to make constructive use of one's abilities. This extends to creativity and aesthetic appreciation. One subtle aspect of this motive is the need to know and to understand.

Some principles go along with these needs. One is *homeostasis*. People constantly make an effort to maintain their own status quo. Another is the principle of *deprivation*. Related to physiological needs, it never wanes in intensity. If people are deprived of a physiological goal (for instance, food), they will continue to seek it. (One compulsive chocolate eater explained that a childhood allergy had deprived her of the pleasure of eating chocolates when very young!) When deprivation involves social goals, however, it often retains its effectiveness as a motivation only up to a point. Beyond that point it loses intensity and people may abandon a

▼ **The texture of a message—its color, movement and sound—is chosen for its persuasive appeal.**

---

goal; for instance, they may resign themselves to a certain social class or status. The principle of *satiation* weakens physiological drives and can weaken social motives, but it seems to have no effect on emotions—good news for lovers, perhaps. The principle of *goal evaluation* is based on tension, as in a straining to achieve something—to earn a karate black belt, to be a master at bridge. Goals that are not socially acceptable, however, either must be abandoned or must find support from another principle. This occurs also when certain goals prove impossible to achieve. For example, if you can't be an "A" student, perhaps you can be a "solid B" student. One other principle works in these basic motives, the *barrier* principle. A barrier placed between people and the fulfillment of their goals will enhance the appeal of the goal unless the barrier proves too great, in which case they will probably change goals.

Our goals are tied closely to what we want to be. An advertising creative director, for example, may steadfastly maintain that everyone is a snob of one kind or another—for example, if well educated, probably an intellectual snob. The promoter of a national magazine keyed to intellectuals (*Harper's*) adopted that very thesis in a mailing piece sent in a "plain brown envelope" that carried this question in the lower left corner: "Should you be punished for being born with a high IQ?" The envelope probably was opened by most recipients. What we value is often a key to our personality.

The Texture of a Message   Once you know which needs and values you want to appeal to, you understand the purpose of your message and which persuasive appeal is likely to work; then you can choose the texture of the message for its persuasive effect. The medium dictates to some extent

the range of textures. Television has the widest range—color design, movement and sound. In print the size, shape and feel of an object—as people trained in graphics know—may determine whether a brochure is picked up (much less read), whether a package is taken off a supermarket shelf, and whether an ad catches people's attention.

Motivational studies involving texture need to be interpreted by both public relations and marketing people in approaching particular problems. Regarding color, for instance, most businesspeople will not respond to a questionnaire printed on hot pink, will make little response to one on blue, but will give many answers to a questionnaire printed on green, beige or white. Label colors that look dramatic on clear glass may look unappetizing, even sickening, when the product is visible through the label.

Most of us psychologically favor certain colors. This is likely to manifest itself in our choice of colors for clothes, cars and furniture. The public relations person needs to know which colors will appeal to a particular audience and how well those colors reproduce in the medium chosen for communicating with that audience. One despairing art director, after having to change colors for a campaign owing to problems in reproducing them in different media, said with some resignation, "I'm ready to go back to the basics: red, white and blue."

Nonverbal symbols are also part of a message's texture. Be particularly careful to avoid those that suggest bias, such as a woman standing beside a man seated at a desk or an ethnic or racial minority in a subservient posture in relation to a majority figure. Nonverbal cues say things that words do not. Be sure that the symbolism your message projects matches your intentions. Well-chosen nonverbal cues can greatly enhance the message communicated by the accompanying words. Carelessly chosen cues can completely destroy an intended message.

The Language of a Message   Problems in communication are often caused by semantics. The words you use must mean the same thing to the receiver that they do to you. It doesn't matter whether the words you use to say something are the ones that *you* think sound the best or most authoritative; rather, you must focus on what words have the most forceful and desirable impact on the viewer or listener.

Only people can bestow meanings on words, says communications specialist Don Fabun, adding, "When we act as if we believed that a word symbol is the event that was originally experienced, we ignore all the steps that have made it something else."[34]

The English author Samuel Johnson once made a bet with his companion James Boswell that he could go into the fish market and reduce a Billingsgate stall tender to tears without saying a word she could understand. Here is what took place:

> Johnson began by indicating with his nose that her fish had passed the stage in which a man's olfactories could endure their flavor. The Billingsgate woman made a verbal assault, common enough in vulgar parlance, that impugned the classification in natural history of Johnson's mother. The doctor responded with, "You're an article, ma'am." "No more an article than yourself, you bloddy misbegotten villain." "You are a noun, woman," "You . . . you," stammered the woman, choking with rage at a list of articles she could not understand. "You are a pronoun," said Dr. Johnson. The woman shook her fist in speechless rage. "You are a verb . . . an adverb . . . an adjective . . . a conjunction . . . a preposition . . . an interjection!" the doctor continued, applying the harmless epithets at proper intervals. The nine parts of speech completely staggered the old woman and she dumped herself down on the floor, crying with anguish at being thus blackguarded in a set of terms unknown to her and which, not understanding, she could not answer.[35]

Jargon and obfuscation abound in government, education and elsewhere. Sometimes even attempts to clarify go wrong. In 1972 Pennsylvania's education secretary reportedly exhorted his underlings in a memo to write English instead of bureaucratese. Ironically, he wrote the memo in the sort of language he was out to eliminate: "A determination has been made that the communications effective-

▼ **Clarity, emotional impact and context are important factors in language choice; repetition and consistency are also significant.**

ness of department personnel suffers from low prioritization of clarity and correspondingly high thresholds of verbosity and circuitous phraseology."[36]

Important factors in language choice include clarity, emotional impact and context. A message's consistency with other messages from the same source and its level of repetition are also significant.

Clarity Obscurity in language has reached ridiculous proportions in American usage. And since PR practitioners are not around to explain what their messages mean, the language they use had better be self-explanatory. You must choose your words with a feeling for the associations the receivers will make, based on their individual frames of reference; the images the words will conjure up for them, based usually on stereotypes they hold; and the simple fitness of the word itself. As an instance of clarity, John F. Kennedy's inaugural address ("Ask not what your country can do for you . . .") was written almost entirely in single-syllable words and was comprehensible, as well as elegant and eloquent, to almost all who heard it. Readability can be tested. Computer programs are available to help you check the clarity and reading level of your writing.[37]

Emotional Impact This element of language has nothing to do with clarity; it depends on emotional association. Emotional impact is, of course, a significant weapon in all propaganda battles. In World War II, Axis Sally and Tokyo Rose tried to entice American defections; and two incomparable commanders of the English language, Winston Churchill and Franklin Roosevelt, urged their countrymen on with eloquent propaganda.

ARMED FORCES DOUBLESPEAK:

Military Intelligence

"Information" Officer

Reprinted with permission of Copley News service.

Context   The context of messages—their verbal settings—is also important. As one writer advises:

> There is no easy way of choosing words. They must not be so general in meaning as to include thoughts not intended, nor so narrow as to eliminate thoughts that are intended. Let the meaning select the word.
>
> A word is ambiguous when the reader is unable to choose decisively between alternative meanings, either of which would seem to fit the context.
>
> A great deal of unclear writing results from the use of too many broad, general words, those having so many possible meanings that the precise thought is not clear. The more general the words are, the fainter is the picture; the more special they are, the brighter.[38]

Repetition and Consistency   Because people both seek and avoid messages, it is important to consider the significance of *repetition* and *consistency* in public relations messages. Repetition increases the opportunity for exposure. Consistency helps increase credibility. Communications scholars who have conducted experiments on cognitive discrepancies and communication call the act of seeking "information search" and the act of avoiding a message "information preference."

Making sure that a message gets through to an intended receiver is the first goal, and repetition increases your chances of accomplishing this. Making sure that the message is believed is the next goal, and consistency helps here. But both of these techniques are based on a time element, and com-

Peanuts reprinted by permission of UFS, Inc.

munications scholars have made some disquieting discoveries in this area. First, they found that, when pressed for time, people often make decisions based on less information than they would normally require (an especially significant fact in political PR). Second, writers must decide whether their target public needs information piece by piece (which is all right if members of the public already have made their decisions) or whether they need an evaluative structure or frame of reference to permit making comparisons between alternatives.[39]

Receiving and Accepting Messages

Evidence suggests that people who have grown up with lots of television (which means most readers of this book) learn to tune out messages they do not wish to receive. Everyone does this to some degree—otherwise we would all be drowning in noise. But the high degree of unconscious selectivity exercised by members of the electronic generation poses particular challenges to the PR person trying to reach them.

Great stock was once put in the two-step flow theory, which holds that ideas flow from opinion makers down to the public at large.[40] The theory suggests that opinion leaders attending to mass or specialized media are early adopters of new ideas. Their adoption influences others, starting with people who are like themselves—those in the same occupations or social/economic class. In the past several decades, however, politicians have successfully conducted public opinion studies to see what people are interested in and concerned with and then enunciated those feelings as ideas or policies.

Presidential programs reflecting this upward flow are John Kennedy's War on Poverty, Lyndon Johnson's Great Society and Jimmy Carter's New Foundations.

Sources of a Message   How publics perceive the source of a message is a significant factor in whether they accept the message. One effective source is people. We are in almost constant conversation with people, and the information we get in this way has a higher credibility than any other— depending on the attitude we hold toward the speaker. Is it someone we like? respect? consider smart? Is it someone who resembles us or who accepts and likes us?

The credibility of "people" sources fluctuates. Recent polls show clergy, educators and physicians at the top of the credibility list, winning back the position they had relinquished for a while to celebrity sports or television figures. We tend to seek out as sources not only people but media that reflect our opinions and attitudes. For this reason, many PR veterans recommend not trying to persuade vehement opponents to change their minds, but instead try to neutralize them so they will do minimal harm.

Everyone seems to recognize that a sender must encode messages—that is, translate information into something personally meaningful to an intended receiver. However, we tend to forget the static and interference created by competing messages, credibility disturbances and the interference of selectivity on the part of the receiver. If the receiver does accept the message, it must be decoded and some response encoded.

Considering the environment of distortion that exists in our family, social, educational, religious and ethnic life, it is a wonder any communication gets through to us at all. And of course, many messages do not get through. In other instances, our intended messages are contraindicated by our "body English" or other symbols.[41] Indeed, symbols are important, whether in advertising or in art, whether as trademarks or as company logos, in conveying the meaning we intend.

In utilizing symbols we often resort to stereotyping, a mental shorthand that can be useful in processing information. The word *chair* makes you think of a certain type of chair because you have *all* chairs filed under that mental image. Often this is adequate for communication and for understanding a situation. However, the context may make you seek a particular symbol. Thus your mental image may go from your basic chair to a desk chair in a classroom setting.

But stereotypes—the pictures in our heads— are personal and may misrepresent reality. As a result, communication, imprecise at best, takes on an even greater risk when using stereotypes.[42] If you were dealing with a clearly defined target public and you had a well-grounded knowledge of which stereotypes you could use effectively and appropriately with this audience, you might proceed with some confidence. But there are some monumental examples of stereotyping.

For example, look at various situations where ways of representing women resulted in boycotts, demonstrations and even loss of elections. The stereotyping of females in advertising, television programming and news columns and by public speakers (especially politicians) has lessened in the face of activity by women's groups, but it is still in evidence. The main criticism of using stereotypes to represent roles people perform or views groups of people share is that for many, the image becomes the reality. During the civil rights movement in the United States, for example, objections by blacks to racial stereotyping were based on concerns that people who had limited contact with blacks accepted the representation as the reality.

Effects of Stimuli Public interpretation of different message stimuli is constantly being measured. Advertisers are not the only ones to take advantage of the capability to add scent to print. McCormick Foods scents its annual report. Many greeting cards offer scent, sound and optical effects from special treatment and design.

Responses to a Message

Information processing is critical in evaluating the impact (or potential impact) of communication. Carl Hovland established the idea of changing attitudes in order to change opinions, and this became known as the Yale approach to persuasion. He pointed out that effective communication involved attention, comprehension, acceptance and retention. Using Lasswell's model of who said what to whom with what effect, Hovland identified source, message, audience and audience reaction as the elements of the processing cycle. The source had to evidence power, competence, trustworthiness, goodwill, idealism, similarity (to audience) and dynamism. The credibility (trust, goodwill, idealism, similarity) and authority (power, competence, dynamism) of the source are the major conceptual factors in the Yale model.

William McGuire saw a flaw in the Yale information-processing theories. Hovland and his associates, McGuire felt, had ignored the relationship between comprehension and acceptance. Instead of emphasizing the *source*, McGuire focused on the *receiver*. His modifications clarified the relationship between comprehension and acceptance, indicating their separate effects on a persuasive message's impact. Personality traits of message recipients, he said, affected comprehension, acceptance of messages and persuasibility in general. McGuire reduced the steps of the Yale model to two—receiving message content and yielding to what is comprehended—arguing that a person has to receive a message effectively and then yield to its point in order for an attitude or opinion to change.

McGuire, like Hovland and associates, assumed that new cognitive information was learned from the content of the messages. That supposition was challenged by Anthony Greenwald, who said that people did not learn message content, but rather created their own covert messages idiosyncratically in response to the original message. However, Greenwald's cognitive response approach tells more about "the *covariation* between self-generated messages and their effects than it does about *why* covert conditions generate cognitive realignments and behavior changes."

Other theories of social and cognitive behavior also help explain message effects. Social psychologist Kurt Lewin observed that people process information and "compute" attitudes to make logical combinations.[43] *Group dynamics* are important in this process because individuals try to adjust their opinions and perceptions in response to group norms and pressures toward uniformity. Motivation, said Lewin, is socially based, which means that the group has the power to reward for compliance or to punish for deviation.

Leon Festinger's *theory of cognitive dissonance* states that people strive to reduce discrepancies that exist within their own cognitive system. Experiences may be consonant (compatible with values), dissonant (conflicting with values) or irrelevant. The greater the ratio of dissonance to consonance, the more deeply the dissonance is felt. Of course, for cognitive conflict to occur, the opposites have to be important to the person. *Cognitive overlap* occurs when more than one choice is available; the choice closest to compatibility creates the least dissonance. J. W. Brehm and A. R. Cohen suggested that the dissonance would be greater if a person committed him- or herself to a course of action while recognizing that another path was possible, whereas Eliot Aronson said that becoming aware of dissonance was a consequence of violating expectancies or rules, especially regarding one's self-concept. Hence, for example, honest persons are presumably more bothered by lying than thieves are.

Explaining people's efforts to make sense of others' behavior is called *attribution theory*. According to Fritz Heider, two types of causes are used to explain behavior: situational (external) causes and dispositional (internal) causes. The type we choose depends on some suppositions. If people often do unusual things in different situations for reasons we can't discern, we may attribute their behavior to an internal or dispositional cause. The problem with such assumptions is that analysts tend to oversimplify and overestimate people's consistency in behavior and tend to see an internal reason when the external situation might have had more bearing. Clearly people do take behavior cues from their environment, and they also have some reason to explain their behavior. The question is which comes first: the reason or the behavior?

Social learning theory holds that continuous reciprocal interaction and continuous feedback occur between a person's internal cognition and the situation. What we learn through experience, observation, listening or reading and establishing symbolic relationships teaches us to expect different consequences in different situations for the same behavior. In addition, according to the theory, reinforcements are different for various people, depending on such factors as value systems. Another element of social learning theory states that in order for learning to occur, a person must remember and expect something to occur again. Extinction is one way to change behavior. Extinction may occur when the anticipated result of an action is withheld (for example, when a parent does not respond with attention to a child's tantrum as the child expects). Rules, instructions or communications can also be used to change behaviors.

The public relations practitioner thus has a choice of several theories to apply in planning message strategy to reach a goal. The option selected may be to encourage people to belong (Lewin). It may be to avoid a message that conflicts with values or—if people are already in a state of cognitive dissonance—to help them reconcile the value conflict through rationalization (Festinger). Self-persuasion, remember, is the most successful form of persuasion. The strategy might also be to provide environmental cues (Heider) that are likely to appeal to a target group (such as using an impressive setting—

for example, a black tie event—to mark the opening of a new building). Or it may be an ongoing educational program to develop expectations (as in the case of antismoking campaigns that aim at making smokers feel uncomfortable whenever they light up in a public place).

Some researchers feel that a model devised by Martin Fishbein is useful in predicting group attitudes. The Fishbein model can be used to identify and categorize consumers according to criteria that are significant to the consumers themselves, and for this reason it may have practical implications for marketing specialists in particular.[44]

Fishbein himself contends that his model can measure both a person's emotional evaluation of a concept or object and his or her beliefs about that object. He asserts further that it can be used to demonstrate that a person's belief can change independently of attitude, with the result that two people may differ in belief but have similar attitudes.[45]

For example, two people might be against school busing to achieve integration; that is, they might have the same attitude. But one may actually favor integration through other means— desiring to integrate schools by integrating neighborhoods—while the other may oppose any measure that promotes forced socialization.[46]

Some researchers say that both opinions and facts represent answers to questions, so that it is impossible to draw a sharp line between them. A fuzzy line may separate opinions and attitudes as well, although opinions can be verbalized, while attitudes often cannot (they may be unconscious).

The opinions, attitudes and actions of people are all affected by family, friends, informal work groups and formal groups such as clubs and organizations. Group influence and pressure become particularly apparent during controversy, according to this research evidence. When issues are clear, group pressure influences at most only a third of the people, with two-thirds standing firm. If even a small countervailing voice comes in, the third shrinks away. Only when ambiguity and confusion reign can you count on a bandwagon effect, which

means that factors other than the propaganda device itself are determining media effectiveness.[47]

Getting people to believe something is easier than keeping them from accepting something you don't want them to believe. One popular idea is that early exposure to some opposing arguments will inoculate hearers against future belief in the opponents. Other evidence suggests, though, that any preliminary message may weaken the impact of a persuasive opposing attack that might follow. Some evidence also suggests that trying to elicit a critical viewpoint in a public can either inhibit or enhance the effect of a message that is to come. If you try to turn people against a message or against the messenger, your efforts could have the opposite effect of inoculating them against further negative criticisms. The effect could be to make them more vulnerable to future persuasive appeals by opponents. But reception and acceptance of a later persuasive appeal are determined by both the target of criticism and the nature of the critical act. Therefore, the situation could be manipulated to have some bearing on the outcome.

The purpose of a persuasive communication is often concealed, becoming apparent only after careful examination. Comparing the obvious content with its intent may be done in examining such organized propaganda campaigns as those launched internally by a government or directed by one government against another, as in psychological warfare. Psychological warfare is as old as war itself. Although it has become sophisticated, its goals remain basically the same: first, to convert subjects from one allegiance to another; second, to divide the opposition into defeatable groups; third, to consolidate existing support; and fourth, to counteract or refute another propaganda theme.[48]

Regarding retention of information, researcher Carl Hovland finds that during an initial period people forget verbal material rapidly; this forgetfulness gradually decreases until little further loss is noticeable. (Sometimes, in fact, the amount remembered over a period of time actually increases.) He also has found that people retain meaningful material better than obscure material, but that overusing even good material in order to emphasize it can have a boomerang effect. Moreover, the more completely people learn material initially, the longer they will remember it. Hovland also found that repeating a message up to three or four times usually increases the degree of people's attention, but that too frequent repetition without reward is likely to lead to inattention, boredom and disregard of the communication.[49]

Communications researcher Steuart Henderson Britt developed a whole set of learning principles that apply to consumer behavior:

1. Unpleasant appeals can be learned as readily as pleasant ones.

2. Appeals made over a period of time are more effective.

3. Unique messages are better remembered.

4. It is easier to recognize an appeal than to recall it.

5. Knowledge of results increases learning of a message.

6. Repetition is more effective when related to belongingness and satisfaction.

7. Messages are easier to learn when they do not interfere with earlier habits.

8. Learning a new pattern of behavior can interfere with remembering something else.[50]

One thing is certain about communication: You can never tell whether you have achieved understanding of your message unless you provide the recipient with a way to respond. Measuring understanding—rather than just message reception—was the task undertaken by two researchers, M. Beth Heffner and Kenneth Jackson.[51] They used pictures and verbal descriptions of the pictures to see whether the verbal descriptions resulted in the same mental impressions on readers as the pictures. Results showed that understanding seems to occur independently of the messages received verbally (which can occur without their being understood). Conversely, understanding can occur when messages are altered. The researchers also found that having a cognitive frame of reference helped students determine meaning. If students had the same basis for organizing information, it increased their comprehension of the messages' meaning. Some verbal descriptions were more reliable than the picture themselves. Another thing noticed was that symbols can be misunderstood. This has happened occasionally when American advertising has been "exported" without due research into the culture or mores of another country.

The complexities of operations in an international community are heightened by the sophisticated technology of instantaneous satellite communications. This increases the communicators' responsibility to ensure the fidelity of message reception through conscientious research and attention to research findings.

Because information processing is such a critical factor in communication, models that predict behavior successfully are important in planning a communication campaign. Grunig's model (see Example 7.6). attempts to illustrate the importance of audience potential to cost-effective communication. Of the four independent variables Grunig identifies, three explain when a person will communicate: problem recognition, constraint recognition and the presence of a referent criterion. The fourth variable is the controlling variable, which explains when and how a person will communicate; the level of involvement here will result in either information processing (low level) or information seeking (high level of involvement). Beyond that, recognition of a problem and awareness of some constraints yield four types of perceived situations: problem facing, constrained behavior, routine behavior or fatalistic behavior.[52] The result anticipates that, in a communication effort, four of the sixteen possibilities will be so low in cost-effectiveness as to be scarcely worth any investment: those that combine low-level (information-processing) routine behavior and fatalistic behavior. Twelve will be fairly high in cost-effectiveness.

EXAMPLE 7.6

Grunig's Theory of Message Receptiveness
Conditional Probabilities for Information Processing and Information Seeking

Audience potential is important to cost-effective communication. This diagram of Grunig's theory of message receptiveness in communication behavior attempts to illustrate that importance.

Publics:	Active	Active	Active	Active	Active rein-forcing	Latent	Aware	Aware	Latent/ Aware	Latent/ Aware	Inactive/ Latent	Inactive/ Latent	Latent	Latent	Latent	Inactive	Inactive
Behaviors:	Problem facing	Problem facing	Con-strained	Con-strained	Routine	Routine	Problem facing	Problem facing	Con-strained	Con-strained	Routine	Routine	Fatalistic	Fatalistic	Fatalistic	Fatalistic	Fatalistic
Variables:	Problem recog-nition	Problem recog-nition	Con-straint recog-nition	Con-straint recog-nition			Problem recog-nition	Problem recog-nition	Con-straint recog-nition	Con-straint recog-nition							
	Referent criterion		Referent criterion		Referent criterion		Referent criterion		Referent criterion		Referent criterion		Referent criterion	Referent criterion		Referent criterion	Referent criterion
	High involve-ment	High involve-ment	High involve-ment	High involve-ment	High involve-ment	High involve-ment	Low involve-ment	Low involve-ment	Low involve-ment	Low involve-ment	Low involve-ment	Low involve-ment	High involve-ment	High involve-ment	High involve-ment	Low involve-ment	Low involve-ment
Information seeking:	High	High	Mod-erate	Low	High	Low	High	Mod-erate	Low	Low	Low	Low	Mod-erate	Low	Low	Low	Low
Information processing:	High	High	High	High	High	High	High	High	Low	Low	Low	Low	Low	Low	Low	Low	Low
Cost-effective-ness scale, 1–10 (10 best)	5	4	7	6	3	8	10	9	2	1							

Among these, the active publics constitute a *second* target audience because an active public needs organizing communication and the active reinforcing effort needs maintenance communication. The primary publics to win are the latent, aware and latent/aware publics.

Recent research supports two aspects of Grunig's model. The research shows that individuals are more likely to seek and process information if they anticipate that it will help them solve a problem and if they are personally involved in trying to solve the problem. The research also supports the prediction that people who are constrained (and therefore would not be free to implement a solution if they had one) are less likely to seek or process information, although this relationship was largely explained by other independent variables. Contrary to the Grunig model, an individual's knowing a solution to the problem (or a "referent criterion" in Grunig's terminology) was negatively related to information seeking and processing.

Much of a public's response to persuasive information in a situation that requires a behavioral change has to do with where it lies in the diffusion cycle. The diffusion cycle has six phases:

Phase I: Awareness (also called *presenting*, as in presenting information)—The public learns about an idea or practice but lacks detail.

Phase II: Information (also called *attending*, as in getting someone's attention)—The public gets facts, develops interest, sees possibilities.

Phase III: Evaluation (also called *comprehending*, an understanding of the appeal)—The public tries it mentally, weighs alternatives.

Phase IV: Trial (also called *yielding*)—The information achieves social acceptability, experimentation.

Phase V: Adoption (also treated as one aspect of *retaining*)—The public adopts the information for full-scale use.

Phase VI: Reinforcement (also treated as the other aspect of *retaining*)—The public displays continued, unswerving commitment.[53]

▼ **Grunig's information-processing model includes some indicators of cost-effective communication for different target audiences.**

Discussions about how people's behavior can be affected through persuasion make many of us uncomfortable, even though most of us have been doing it all our lives. You learned as an infant what kind of behavior gained attention. As you got older, you learned the right words and the best timing to use in asking for money from a parent.

Behavioral psychologist B. F. Skinner made the following observation about the positive aspects of affecting what people do:

I am concerned with the possible relevance of a behavioral analysis to the problems of the world today. We are threatened by the unrestrained growth of the population, the exhaustion of resources, the pollution of the environment, and the specter of a nuclear holocaust. We have the physical and biological technology needed to solve most of those problems, but we do not seem to be able to put it to use. That is a problem in human behavior, and it is one to which an experimental analysis may offer a solution. Structuralism in the behavioral sciences has always been weak on the side of motivation. It does not explain why knowledge is acquired or put to use; hence it has little to tell us about the conditions under which the human species will make the changes needed for its survival. If there is a solution to that problem, I believe that it will be found in the kind of understanding to which an experimental analysis of human behavior points.[54]

Not only did Skinner point to a critical flaw in the effort to use today's theoretical knowledge to determine what people will actually do, he also alluded to another difficulty. Today's problems are global, but today's theories are culture-bound. Most research has been done in Western societies; and even within them, little attention has been paid to minorities. Much remains to be discovered.

▼ SUMMARY

In studying how to influence people, we have to look first at individual reactions and then at how these affect the reactions of other individuals to produce a collective response. Public relations as it is practiced today is less involved with publics conceived as a mass and with communication through mass media, although these remain important. The communication model for public relations practice has been replaced by a behavioral model that looks at what people do. People's attitudes and opinions are still important as indicators of what they may do and as feedback to let PR practitioners know when policy adjustments need to be made. However, there is some risk that the behavioral model will function asymmetrically.

There are three basic ways to get others to do your bidding: power, patronage and persuasion. The persuasion process involves six steps: presenting, attending, comprehending, yielding, retaining and acting. Among the persuaders (who include opinion makers) are public relations people who plan their persuasive strategies around three elements: media, message and source. People use media that meet their needs and are gratifying to them, and they accept messages that are meaningful and useful to them. They turn to sources of information that they consider attractive, trustworthy and knowledgeable. Research has yielded a number of observations in all three strategy areas—media, messages and sources—that are useful to public relations practitioners.

Many communication theories indicate the effectiveness of persuasive appeals and strategies. Persuaders are either personal or impersonal, with the personal having the greater impact. One form of persuasion is propaganda, an effort to teach people what to think but which is often used to mislead. It is also used to affect public opinion. Self-interest is a major factor in accepting persuasive messages, and self-persuasion is the most effective of all strategies.

Communication theories are borrowed largely from the social sciences, and both sociology and psychology offer paradigms that can serve as the framework for PR research. Much of the theoretical base for public relations originates in Carl Hovland's idea that to change attitudes you must change opinions, which means using communication effectively. Therefore public reception of media and their credibility to receivers become important considerations, as does choosing the right message for the medium and the receiver. The purpose, texture and language of the message all need to be based on sound communication principles. Receivers of messages don't necessarily accept them, which is why the sources of the message and the effects of message stimuli need to be evaluated to estimate responses. Learning theories and information-processing research have also provided insights into message response patterns. The manner in which information gets from the individual to a larger group generally is through a diffusion process that provides the basis for most PR campaign planning.

▼ NOTES

[1]"Behavioral Model Replacing Communications Model as Basic Theoretical Underpinning of PR Practice," *pr reporter*, 33(30) (July 30, 1990), p. 1.

[2]*Ibid.*, p. 2.

[3]Somewhat different motivational patterns are given by Daniel Katz and Robert Kahn in *The Social Psychology of Organi-*

zations (New York: John Wiley, 1966), p. 341. Given as "motivational patterns for producing various types of required behaviors" are the following: (1) legal compliance; (2) the use of rewards or instrumental satisfactions—either individual rewards or "system" rewards such as earned memberships or seniority, earned approval of leaders or affiliations with peers that win social approval; (3) internal patterns of self-determination and self-expression; (4) internal values and self-concept.

[4]William J. McGuire, "Persuasion, Resistance, and Attitude Change," in *Handbook of Communication*, ed. Ithiel de Sola Pool et al. (Chicago: Rand McNally, 1973), p. 221.

[5]Ibid., p. 223.

[6]Herbert I. Schiller, *The Mind Managers* (Boston: Beacon Press, 1973), pp. 134–35.

[7]Gregg A. Payne, Jessica J. H. Severn and David M. Dozier, "Uses and Gratification Motives as Indicators of Magazine Readership," *Journalism Quarterly*, 65(4) (Winter 1988), p. 909.

[8]Leon Festinger, "The Theory of Cognitive Dissonance," in *The Science of Human Communications*, ed. Wilbur Schramm, (New York: Basic Books, 1963), pp. 17–27. Also see Festinger's *A Theory of Cognitive Dissonance* (Stanford, Calif.: Stanford University Press, 1982); and Philip B. Zimbardo, Ebbe B. Ebbesen and Christina Maslach, *Influencing Attitudes and Changing Behavior: An Introduction to Theory and Applications of Social Control and Personal Power*, 2d ed. (Reading, Mass.: Addison-Wesley, 1977).

[9]Fritz M. Elmendorf, "Press Ignored Power of Public in Withholding Revolt," *Business-Economic News Report*, 2(8) (September 1983), pp. 1, 5.

[10]William L. Rivers, *The Opinionmakers* (Boston: Beacon Press, 1965), p. 1.

[11]Zimbardo et al., *Influencing Attitudes*, p. 156.

[12]Robert Cialdini, *Psychology*.

[13]From Earl Newsom's published speeches: "Elements of a Good Public Relations Program," presented to public relations conference of Standard Oil (New Jersey) and affiliated companies, December 3, 1946; "A Look at the Record," presented to Annual Public Relations Conference of Standard Oil (New Jersey), December 16, 1947; "Our Job," presented to Reynolds Metal's executives, March 21, 1957.

[14]Philip Lesly, "Guidelines on Public Relations and Public Affairs," in "Managing the Human Climate," no. 24, adapted from *The People Factor: Managing the Human Climate* (Homewood, Ill.: Dow Jones-Irwin, 1974).

[15]"Another Propaganda Technique," *Glimpse*, 39 (March 1987), p. 2.

[16]*Glimpse* (October 14, 1985).

[17]Leon Festinger, "The Theory of Cognitive Dissonance," ed. Wilbur Schramm, *The Science of Human Communications* (New York: Basic Books, 1963), pp. 17–27. See also Festinger's *A Theory of Cognitive Dissonance*, and Philip Zimbardo et al., *Influencing Attitudes*.

[18]Earl Newsom, "Elements of a Good Public Relations Program."

[19]Rich Jaroslovsky, "Elusive Quest, Cancer Research Drive, Begun with Fanfare, Hits Disillusionment," *Wall Street Journal* (October 24, 1978), p. 1; and "Elusive Quest, War on Cancer Is Hurt by Animal Test Fight, Moves to Ban Products," *Wall Street Journal* (October 26, 1978), p. 1.

[20]Mary John Smith, *Persuasion and Human Action* (Belmont, Calif.: Wadsworth, 1982), pp. 320–22.

[21]George C. Homans, "Contemporary Theory in Sociology," in *Handbook of Modern Sociology*, ed. Robert E. L. Faris (Chicago, Ill.: Rand McNally, 1964), pp. 951–52. Also, Wilbur Schramm's definition of *theory* is helpful: "a set of related statements, at a high level of abstraction, from which propositions can be generated and tested by scientific methods the results of which help explain human behavior." This definition appears in "The Challenge to Communications Research," in *Introduction to Mass Communication Research*, eds. Ralph O. Nafziger and David M. White (Baton Rouge: Louisiana State University Press, 1972), p. 10.

[22]Zimbardo et al., *Influencing Attitudes*, p. 53.

[23]Melvin L. DeFleur and Sandra Ball-Rokeach, 5th ed. (New York: Longman, 1989), pp. 29–43.

[24]Earl Newsom, "A Look at the Record."

[25]H. D. Lasswell, "The Structure and Function of Communication in Society," in *Communication of Ideas*, ed. Lyman Bryson (New York: Harper & Row, 1948), pp. 37–51.

[26]Walter Siefert, personal communication.

[27]Raymond S. H. Lee, "Credibility of Newspapers and TV News," *Journalism Quarterly*, 55(2) (Summer 1978), pp. 282–87.

[28]Paul A. Atkins and Harry Elwood, "TV News Is First Choice in Survey of High Schools," *Journalism Quarterly*, 55(3) (Autumn 1978), pp. 596–99. Also the Roper poll study for the Television Information Office showed TV having better than a 2-to-1 advantage over newspapers for credibility (*Trends in Attitudes Toward Television and Other Media* [New York: Roper Organization, 1983]).

[29]Aileen Yagade and David M. Dozier, "The Media Agenda-Setting Effect of Concrete Versus Abstract Issues," *Journalism Quarterly*, 67(1) (Spring 1990), p. 3. For a good summary of

agenda-setting theory and an insight into the role of persuasion, see Ellen Williamson Kanervo and David W. Kanervo, "How Town Administrator's View Relates to Agenda Building in Community Press," *Journalism Quarterly*, 66(2) —Summer 1989), pp. 308–15.

[30]Edward L. Bernays, "Down with Image, Up with Reality," *Public Relations Quarterly*, 22(1) (Spring 1977), p. 12.

[31]Jim Pattillo in a speech for a public relations workshop in New York City, January 1977; taken from a copy of his address printed by American Telephone and Telegraph (1977), p. 8.

[32]Philip Lesly, "Another View of the Communications Gap," in *Managing the Human Climate*, newsletter published by the Philip Lesly Company, Chicago, Ill., no. 44 (May–June 1977). For the information on truthful and deceptive persuaders, see James W. Neuliep and Manfran Mattson, "The Use of Deception as a Compliance-Gaining Strategy, *Human Communication Research*, 16(3) (Spring 1990), pp. 409–21.

[33]Abraham Maslow, *Motivation and Personality* (New York: Harper & Row, 1954). See also Maslow's *Toward a Psychology of Being* (New York: Van Nostrand Reinhold, 1962).

[34]Don Fabun, *Communications: The Transfer of Meaning* (Encino: Calif.: Kaiser Aluminum and Chemical Corp., distributed by Glencoe Press, 1969), p. 19. Copyrighted 1968 by Kaiser Aluminum and Chemical Corp., and reissued in 1987 by Macmillan Publishing Company.

[35]Herbert R. Mayes, "Trade Winds," *Saturday Review* (October 19, 1968), p. 12.

[36]Reported in *El Dorado* (Kansas) *Times*, July 13, 1972.

[37]For further information about readability indexes, see (1) Robert Gunning, *The Technique of Clear Writing*, rev. ed. (New York: McGraw-Hill, 1968); (2) Rudolph Flesch, *How to Test Readability* (New York: Harper & Row, 1951); *The Art of Plain Talk* (New York: Harper & Row, 1946), p. 197; and "A New Readability Yardstick," *Journal of Applied Psychology*, 32 (June 1948), p. 221; (3) Edgar Dale and Jeanne Chall, "A Formula for Predicting Readability," *Educational Research Bulletin*, 27, Ohio State University (January–February 1948); (4) Wilson L. Taylor, "Cloze Procedure: A New Tool for Measuring Readability," *Journalism Quarterly*, 30 (Fall 1953), pp. 415–33; and "Recent Developments in the Use of 'Cloze Procedure,'" *Journalism Quarterly*, 33 (Winter 1956), pp. 42–48. Also you might want to read Irving E. Fang, "The Easy Listening Formula," *Journal of Broadcasting*, 11 (Winter 1966–67), pp. 63–68; B. Aubrey Fisher, *Perspectives in Human Communication* (New York: Macmillan, 1978); Rudolph F. Flesch, "Estimating the Comprehension Difficulty of Magazine Articles," *Journal of General Psychology*, 28 (1943), pp. 63–80, and "Measuring the Level of Abstraction," *Journal of Applied Psychology*, 34 (1950), pp. 384–90; Davis Foulger, "A Simpli-

fied Flesch Formula," *Journalism Quarterly*, 55(1) (Spring 1978), pp. 167, 202.

[38]"The Discipline of Language," newsletter, Royal Bank of Canada.

[39]Steven H. Chaffee, Keith R. Stamm, Jose L. Guerrero and Leonard P. Tipton, "Experiments on Cognitive Discrepancies," *Journalism Quarterly Monograph* (December 1969). Illustrations are as follows: (1) Deadline pressures affect the selection of wire copy by wire editors; when under such a constraint their biases affected the selection of material whereas on other occasions, with no time pressures, they were impartial. (2) In an election campaign there are one-sided exposures early and late that attempt to persuade voters of the opposition to cross over; these should be timed to coincide with the period when they are likely to listen to arguments that run counter to their loyalties—certainly not at the last minute, however, such as an election eve telethon.

[40]For the evolution of the two-step flow theory, see Elihu Katz and Paul Lazarsfeld, *Personal Influence: The Part Played by People in The Flow of Mass Communications* (New York: Free Press of Glencoe, 1955), pp. 15–42; Katz, "The Two-Step Flow of Communication: An Up-to-Date Report on a Hypothesis," *Public Opinion Quarterly* 21 (Spring 1957), pp. 61–78; Paul Lazarsfeld and Herbert Menzell, "Mass Media and Personal Influence," in *Science of Human Communication*, ed. Wilbur Schramm (New York: Basic Books, 1963); Johan Arndt, "A Test of the Two-Step Flow in Diffusion of a New Product," *Journalism Quarterly*, 45 (Autumn 1968), pp. 457–65; Melvin L. DeFleur and Sandra Ball-Rokeach, *Theories of Mass Communication*, 5th ed. (New York: Longman, 1989), pp. 192–95, 318.

[41]Albert Mehrabian, *Silent Messages*, 2d ed. (Belmont, Calif.: Wadsworth, 1981).

[42]Walter Lippmann, "Stereotypes," in *Reader in Public Opinion and Mass Communication*, eds. Morris Janowitz and Paul M. Hirsch (New York: Free Press, 1981), pp. 29–37.

[43]Kurt Lewin, "Studies in Group Decision," in *Group Dynamics*, eds. Dorwin Cartwright and A. F. Zander (Evanston, Ill.: Row Peterson, 1953); and *Group Dynamics, Research and Theory*, 3d ed. (New York: Harper & Row, 1968).

[44]Jose L. Guerrero and G. David Hughes, "An Empirical Test of the Fishbein Model," *Journalism Quarterly*, 49 (Winter 1971), pp. 684–91.

[45]Martin Fishbein, "Investigation of Relationship Between Belief About an Object and Attitude Toward That Object," *Human Relations*, 16 (1963), pp. 233–39.

[46]While the illustration used here for simplicity involves individuals, the validity of the Fishbein model as a predictive tool for *individual* attitudes is disputed by Guerrero and Hughes, op. cit., who see its best application to *group* attitudes—certainly a significant observation for PR.

[47]Solomon E. Asch, "Effects of Group Pressure upon the Modification and Distortion of Judgment," in *Groups, Leadership and Men*, ed. H. Guetzkow (Pittsburgh, Pa.: Carnegie Press, 1951), pp. 177–90; R. S. Crutchfield, "Conformity and Character," *American Psychologist*, 10 (1955), pp. 191–98. See also Asch and Crutchfield, quoted in Rex Harlow, *Social Science in Public Relations* (New York: Harper & Row, 1957), pp. 64–69.

[48]Michael Burgoon, Marshall Cohen, Michael D. Miller and Charles Montgomery, "An Empirical Test of a Model of Resistance to Persuasion," *Human Communication Research*, 5(1) (Fall 1978), pp. 27–39.

[49]Carl I. Hovland, Irving L. Janis and Harold H. Kelley, *Communication and Persuasion: Psychological Studies of Opinion Change* (New Haven, Conn.: Yale University Press, 1953), p. 270.

[50]Steuart Henderson Britt, "Are So Called Successful Advertising Campaigns Really Successful?" *Journal of Advertising Research*, 335 (June 1969), pp. 3–9. Also in Britt's *Consumer Behavior in Theory and Action* (New York: John Wiley, 1970), pp. 46–48.

[51]M. Beth Heffner and Kenneth M. Jackson, "Criterion States for Communication: Two Views of Understanding," paper presented to Theory and Methodology Division, Association for Education in Journalism convention, Carbondale, Illinois, August 1972.

[52]James E. Grunig, "Communication Behaviors and Attitudes of Environmental Publics: Two Studies," Association for Education in Journalism and Mass Communication Monograph 81 (March 1983).

[53]*pr reporter* (January 6, 1986), p. 2.

[54]B. F. Skinner, "Origins of a Behaviorist," *Psychology Today* (September 1983), p. 31.

Selected readings, activities and assignments appropriate to this chapter can be found in the *Instructor's Guide*.

CHAPTER 8

▼

PR ETHICS AND SOCIAL
RESPONSIBILITIES

The "morality" or "ethical" nature—the correctness or rightness—of any action . . . is to be judged in terms of the degree to which it includes and integrates the purposes, and provides for the potential development of those purposes, of all other people concerned in the action or possibly affected by it.

Hadley Cantril

Lend to every man thine ear, but few thy voice.

Shakespeare (Polonius to Laertes in *Hamlet*)

In a general sense, ethics is the name we give to our concern for good behavior. We feel an obligation to consider not only our own personal well-being, but also that of human society as a whole.

Dr. Albert Schweitzer

Ethics are founded on moral principles that are themselves grounded in effects. This holds true whether you subscribe to the idea that a moral judgment must fulfill only *formal* conditions that are universal and prescriptive or whether you think it must also meet a *material* condition for the welfare of society as a whole. In either case, "ethical behavior recognizes and rests within a shared interest," according to Ivan Hill, writing for the Ethics Resource Center.[1]

Judgments about an organization's standing are made in three areas: ethics, social responsibility and financial responsibility. An organization's sense of commitment toward its publics (which often have conflicting interests) has to be articulated and demonstrated. When Arthur W. Page was hired by AT&T in 1927 as the first corporate vice-president of public relations ever in the United States, he advocated this philosophy: "Be sure our deeds match our words"—and vice versa.[2]

Ethics and responsibilities are public relations concerns on two levels. We have to consider the behavior of the individual practitioner and that of the institution she or he represents. Public relations has been called the "conscience" of management, which underscores PR's role in reminding an organization of its social responsibility to all of its publics. But no PR person wants to work for a firm that is unethically managed. Would you? There's no hope for financial and social responsibility in such an environment. In fact, most codes of ethics for public relations don't allow practitioners to represent unethical behavior. As an advocate of social responsibility, the PR person simply can't function as a conscience for a management that lacks such responsibility. That's where many PR difficulties begin.

"The choice, it seems to me," says Bank of America's senior vice-president Ron Rhody, "is either to be a 'professional manager,' or a 'managing professional.' That is, to be an employee . . . or a professional."[3]

To be a professional maintaining the standards embodied in a code of ethics takes courage, as well a strong set of personal values. In recent years, observers have expressed some concern about the sense of moral values preprofessionals—students—are bringing to their studies. The author of *The Moral Dimension*, Amitai Etzioni, wrote of his efforts to teach ethics to Harvard University MBA students, "I clearly had not found a way to help classes full of MBAs see that there is more to life than money, power, fame and self-interest."[4]

Etzioni need not have been so discouraged. Perhaps he just got to his students a little late. Concerns about the morality (or lack thereof) demonstrated by public school children have generated some pressure on their teachers to teach moral values in the classroom—a task teachers generally resist.[5] California, New York, New Jersey and New Hampshire ask their teachers to teach separate classes in morality and to include moral values in other classes, such as history, social studies and language arts. Efforts are not always successful, although relevant teaching materials are available. Many teachers worry that such lessons will merely stir up controversy in ethnically and economically diverse classrooms. They probably are correct. In practice, ethics is susceptible to many interpretations, cultural and otherwise, and students already make questionable decisions in response to the moral choices that face them (see Example 8.1).

▼ **PR involves ethical behavior on two levels: that of the individual practitioner and that of the person's employer.**

▼ COMPLEXITIES IN PR's ROLE AND FUNCTION

Davis Young of Young-Liggett-Stashower Public Relations in Cleveland, Ohio, says the problems of individual ethical behavior and social responsibility are caught up in the fact that "public relations people are persuaders. They are advocates. *But* they are also educators. They are facilitators of information."[6] Perhaps, if the ideal two-way symmetric model were strictly followed, unethical behavior would not occur. That model, discussed in Chapter 1, specifies that an organization should try to act in such a way that, even when its actions negatively affect one or more of its publics (such as through the closing of an uneconomical facility), those who are affected will understand and accept the decision, even if they don't like it. The example most often cited is a public utility; but public utilities are regulated, so the outside negotiator for the organization's publics is usually an elected or appointed commission.

Although all business is highly regulated, the federal government has tended over the past decade to favor deregulation to let business regulate itself. Even with deregulation, however, most business transactions are governed directly or indirectly by laws of commerce. Problems often arise because people don't see government regulations as *their* voice in the marketplace. Davis Young notes that prominent among the ethical problems PR must face are difficulties arising from competitive issues and conflicts of interest (the rights of smokers versus the rights of nonsmokers, for example), as well as from advocacy—what he calls the seller's truth versus the buyer's truth. He asks where the sell stops and the information begins.[7]

EXAMPLE 8.1

Survey of Student Attitudes About Ethical Choices

This Louis Harris & Associates survey of 5,000 students was done in 1989 for the Girl Scouts. Note that only 13 percent said that they would use internalized codes, such as conscience or religion. A full 9 percent said they didn't know what they would do when faced with a moral dilemma. The influence of peers is strong; 43 percent said that friends were their first choice for advice. Reprinted with permission.

Telling Right from Wrong

Moral Dilemmas

- 47% of students would cheat on an important exam–copying answers directly (12%) or glancing for ideas (35%).

- 5% would take money from their parents without asking if given the opportunity.

- 36% would lie to protect a friend who has vandalized school property, compared to 24% who would tell the truth.

Moral Guidance

- 64% say they would turn to parents for moral advice.

- 33% say that teachers and coaches really care for them, but only 7% would go to them for advice.

- 43% say friends are their first choice for advice.

Making Choices

If you were unsure of what was right or wrong in a situation, how would you decide what to do?

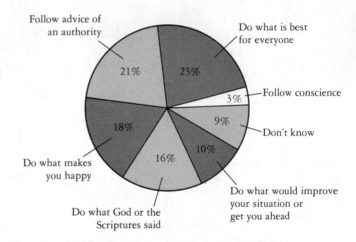

Follow advice of an authority — 21%
Do what is best for everyone — 23%
Follow conscience — 3%
Don't know — 9%
Do what would improve your situation or get you ahead — 10%
Do what God or the Scriptures said — 16%
Do what makes you happy — 18%

Not everyone agrees that PR people answer this question satisfactorily. Indeed, some say that PR doesn't even try. One of the biggest critics of PR practice is a former practitioner, Marvin Olasky, now an educator at the University of Texas at Austin. His writings often create a furor in the PR world. Albert Abend of Aetna Insurance responded to one Olasky piece by saying,

> Please let this much be clear: Executives in the public relations business do not simply articulate a

client's point of view, as Olasky seems to believe; rather, they help the client *form* a point of view, and they work to change this over time as new evidence and circumstances warrant.[8]

Considerable evidence exists of a gap between what people outside PR and what PR executives in the field see as an ethical concern. The 1980s, like the 1960s, offered a daily diet of trespasses; and the 1990s began much the same way. American business comes under attack on many fronts, and it seems always to react with surprise at the public's condemnation of its actions. Interestingly enough, in a survey of 1,000 upper-level corporate executives, two-thirds of them said they thought their peers were "occasionally" unethical. Nearly one in four of the executives believed that ethical standards could impede successful careers. Slightly more than half of their acquaintances, they said, would "bend the rules" to achieve success as long as no one was hurt.[9]

The public seems to define poor or weak business ethics as any form of "wrongdoing."[10] Faced with public outcry and the threat of legal action, companies have developed ethical codes, committees on ethical behavior and ethics training programs. University of Georgia professor Archie Carroll argues that the problem involves amorality more than immorality. He claims that, on a distribution curve between amoral and moral, most managers fall in the middle. "Ethical considerations," Carroll says, "do not get factored into management decisions, even though there is no active intent to be unethical." Carroll urges public relations people to examine their publics in order to identify and evaluate moral issues, to recognize the ambiguity within these issues, and to develop from them a sense of moral obligation.[11]

The importance to top management of making ethical decisions is shown in another survey of business, educational and legislative leaders. Three-fourths of those polled said that chief executive officers play the most significant role in setting ethical standards for employees.[12] If this is so, it clearly becomes the responsibility of CEOs to set the standards of ethical performance in their organizations. If they do not, they risk losing public credibility. The only possible explanation for CEOs failing to act is that they themselves are willing to bend the rules in order to succeed. Such individuals apparently fail to see a correlation between ethical behavior and success; and the leadership role in this area therefore falls to the public relations person.

As a practical matter, Arthur Page offered six management principles:

▼ **An organization's good standing depends on its acting in an ethical manner; an organization is judged on how ethical its publics *perceive* it to be.**

---

1. Tell the truth. Let the public know what's happening and provide an accurate picture of the company's character, ideals and practices.

2. Prove it with action. Public perception of an organization is determined 90 percent by doing and 10 percent by talking.

3. Listen to the customer. To serve the public well, you need to understand what it needs and wants. Keep top decisionmakers and other employees informed of public reaction to company products, policies and practices.

4. Manage for tomorrow. Anticipate public reaction and eliminate practices that create difficulties. Create goodwill.

5. Conduct public relations as if the whole company depended on it. It does. Corporate relations is a management function. No corporate strategy should be implemented without considering its external and internal public relations impact. The PR practitioner is a policy maker, not just a publicist.

6. Remain calm, patient, and good-humored. Lay the groundwork for public relations miracles with consistent, calm and reasoned attention to information and contacts. When a crisis comes, you will be prepared and know exactly what to do to defuse it.

These principles underscored the Page philosophy: "Real success, both for big business and the public, lies in large enterprise conducting itself in the public interest and in such a way that the public will give it sufficient freedom to serve effectively."[13]

An organization's standing depends on its actions, and an organization's *good* standing depends on its acting in an ethical manner. An organization also is judged on how ethical its publics *perceive* it to be. For example, if your organization's board of directors adopts an antitakeover device—a poison pill—and your news release says that the pill is not to prevent takeovers, who do you think you are kidding? If your organization is a bank that is reported to be failing, and you deny that you are looking for help to avoid failing, how do you think you look to the people who are considering helping you? Depositors fearful of losing their money will withdraw funds immediately because you obviously can't be trusted.

Once again, beliefs are important to the public perception of an organization. When you measure a public's view of your ethics, you are asking if it thinks you deserve to exist. Don't be surprised if your organization is seen as undeserving.

The view of an organization's ethics is likely to be based not so much on a definition of morality as on an understanding of the consequences of what the organization says and does, which are seen as either moral or immoral by its publics. Beliefs about social responsibility strongly influence whether and to what extent publics see the organization as being a good citizen, either locally or globally.

Social responsibility or good citizenship means producing sound products or reliable services that don't threaten the environment and contributing positively to the social, political and economic health of society. It also means compensating employees fairly and treating them justly, regardless of the cultural environment in which you operate. Clearly translated, this means no slave labor and no discriminatory practices. It means never offering overpriced or potentially dangerous junk in the guise of a high-quality product. It means refusing to misuse this small planet and its creatures. It means restoring and protecting anything your organization might damage or threaten during normal business operations.

Financial responsibility generally refers to an organization's fiscal soundness, as indicated by such measures as market or audience share; but it also includes how the organization interacts with investors and investment advisers. Public relations also has a financial responsibility: accounting in de-

tail for how it has contributed to the bottom line (an organization's profit margin).

These traditional measures of responsibility are important, of course, but just as significant are the perceptions people have about how a profit or nonprofit organization gets and spends its money. These facets of financial responsibility are too often overlooked in attempts to measure public images. Yet beliefs about an organization in these areas are strongly tied to confidence, trust and loyalty. For example, should we try to measure loyalty? If our organization becomes embroiled in a takeover fight, investors' loyalty may be absolutely critical. How many of our large individual stockholders will retain their holdings in the face of escalating offers?

As public relations people, we hope that our organization's image will influence our stockholders to retain their confidence in the organization's leadership. And the same goes for "stakeholders." Suppose that you represent a nonprofit organization, like a museum, and you are trying to recruit volunteers to serve in it at a time when it is receiving heavy public criticism. You must rely on the long-standing goodwill of the public toward the museum and on the ability of current volunteers to reinforce this in the community. The goodwill must be a strong resource, however, because you'll need it to bolster current volunteers' morale. The key point here is that traditional measures of financial responsibility most often are *not* adequate.

In all three areas—ethics, social responsibility and financial responsibility—publics are likely to believe that public relations people may, on occasion, be trying to influence them. The fact that PR does work to change people's views causes the individual practitioner's ethics to be closely entwined with the organization's social responsibility. The frequent tension inherent in the role is clearly articulated by Olasky. He says that free-market competition forced PR practitioners (as voices for corporate America) to seek government regulation as a means of eliminating competition while they spoke publicly of supporting free enterprise. But the very pursuit of "social responsibility," Olasky says, has fostered the popular notion that there are no "private" areas of business—that is, no areas that are off-limits to public scrutiny. In attempting to say *something* while at the same time protecting an organization's business, the PR person often deceives. Olasky also asserts that the closer business moves toward government, the more likely it is to try to affect the political process.[14]

While corporate PR poses serious hazards for the practitioner, political PR can be even worse. Political PR people often find themselves caught in the middle of conflicts resulting from use of news media by public officials and vice versa.

▼ PUBLIC CONSENT

PR pioneers Arthur Page and Edward Bernays both emphasized that organizations in democratic societies exist with the consent of their publics. These publics constantly evaluate organizations, both corporate and nonprofit, along three ethical lines: credibility, accountability and responsibility. We have already discussed these three elements in general terms, but it is appropriate now to look at the issue of responsibility in detail.

▼ RESPONSIBILITY TO WHOM?

There will always be some people in the business world who are convinced that all they need is a lawyer to keep them out of jail and a PR practitioner to keep bad news out of the paper. Indeed, one survey found that corporate executives and nonbusinesspeople differed rather markedly on whether particular marketing practices were ethical. In response to statements like "A well-known magazine, very popular with teenagers, obtains a large portion of its revenues from cigarette companies," 62 percent of corporate executives saw nothing wrong with the practice, compared with 31 percent of nonmanagement workers and 29 percent of homemakers queried.

▼ **In the areas of ethics, social responsibility and financial responsibility, publics are likely to believe that public relations people may, on occasion, be trying to influence them.**

Even today, with renewed public attention on ethics, something that David Finn observed in 1959 still rings true:

> Ethics is, unfortunately, a bad word to use when executives are sitting around a table struggling with practical problems of the day. Any public relations man who has ever had the experience of counseling his client to do something because it is "ethical" knows this to be true. It is considered a *foreign*, if not embarrassingly *naive*, word. Most businessmen react more positively to such phrases as "better from a long-range point of view," "sounder business policy," or even "good public relations" than to the idea of doing something because it is "more ethical."[15]

The result, Finn says, is that public relations, in one or another guise, performs the role of keeping management in line: "When functioning well, it acts as the anvil against which management's moral problems can be hammered." Thus, when executives establish a public relations policy for their company, "they are really concerned with significant ethical questions—without quite realizing it."[16]

In the same vein, Ed Block, former public relations executive for AT&T in New York, says:

> Counseling does not mean whining, preaching, hairshirting, pontificating or conducting ceremonial benedictions to the corporate conscience. Counseling means doing. It means action. It means wading into real problems in real time and implementing solutions that are right—and will work. Occasionally it means putting yourself and your reputation at risk in contests of contending viewpoints. I can't imagine myself calling the chairman of the board every morning and saying, "John, it's

time for your daily sermon from Ed the tribal wiseman. Please lean back and listen and when I'm through you'll be a wiser and better person." I can't imagine myself calling one of the other vice presidents and saying, "Tim, you and your staff—conscientious and highly motivated though I know you to be—are about to commit a mindless atrocity on our lovable customers and so you must listen to me before it's too late!" Of course not.[17]

The kind of corporate conscience Finn and Block say public relations must create involves constant awareness by management of the institution's responsibility to all its publics. Most professional PR practitioners recognize that they and their organizations have ethical responsibilities to ten different publics:

1. *Clients:* Being responsible to a client means not only being judicious with his or her money, but also (sometimes) saying no, because the customer is *not* always right. When a client is wrong, it is important to say so—to tell truths substantiated by facts discovered through honest research. You may have to spend up to 75 percent of your time convincing a client or management to do what is imperative for sound relations with a public.

2. *News media:* These deserve honest and valid use of their channels; that is, you should not involve them in compromising situations, such as by lying or feeding them insignificant or incomplete information. PR practitioners are accused by news media more often for sins of omission than of commission. A PR person's responsibility is not to call news media attention to bad news, but to respond with a straightforward presentation of the facts

when the news media have an unfavorable story. Exceptions might occur in legal cases where disclosure is required (for example, SEC rules) or prudent (where events are matters of public record.)

3. *Government agencies:* The PR person should be a source and resource for substantive information; this means giving facts, not fantasies.

4. *Educational institutions:* There should be a good two-way system for sharing research, ideas and resources and for offering opportunities. Both sides can enhance their riches through close, professional cooperation.

5. *Consumers of information:* An increasingly skeptical and demanding public can be exasperating, especially to those watching the profit-and-loss sheet, but sincerity and quality go a long way here. They have a right to expect goodwill and integrity in products and services.

6. *Stockholders and analysts:* Many PR practitioners owe their jobs to investors in their business and to those who counsel such investments, since they provide the economic framework and the overall climate of confidence. Both need adequate information to make good decisions; and this calls for lucid interpretations of financial status, reliable annual reports and full explanations of company developments.

7. *Community:* Because it often provides critical elements such as utilities, tax breaks, cooperative zoning plans and chamber of commerce promotion, a community has a right to expect environmental protection, a fair tax return, employment of local people and corporate contributions of funds and executive time to community projects.

8. *Competitors:* Other businesses have a right to expect from PR-advised firms a fair fight that stays within the limits of the law and does not violate individual rights or privacy. The obligations of PR practitioners are set forth in the codes of ethics or standards for behavior promulgated by various professional PR organizations. (The Public Relations Society of America's Code of Professional Standards for the Practice of Public Relations, with

Interpretations, the IABC code and the IPRA code are in the *Instructor's Guide* for this text.)

9. *Critics:* Public relations practice is likely to generate criticism from all of the preceding publics, but its very existence stimulates criticism from at least two philosophical points of view. One set of critics complains that public relations practitioners impede rather than facilitate corporate social responsibility by rationalizing corporate actions and manipulating public opinion. For these reasons, they add, corporations do not bear the full measure of hostility they deserve from their various publics for ignoring quality-of-life factors that economic indicators do not reflect. These critics are usually not fundamentally opposed to the capitalistic system, only to what they consider its abuses. They think the institutions of our society should voluntarily provide improvements in quality of life as well as economic well-being. They see public relations people as a cushion between management and the public's demand for social responsibility.

Another philosophical set of critics might be categorized as human rights defenders. This group tends to speak out against public relations practitioners who represent oppressive countries or go to other countries to work for the election of reputedly repressive leaders.

10. *Public Relations Practitioners:* Other practitioners in the field itself expect practitioners to uphold standards of behavior that will win respect for the practice of public relations. This impulse provides the basis of the PRSA and IABC codes and lies at the root of the discussions of licensing.

These codes of ethical behavior or standards of practice have been called self-serving, but they do provide guidelines and, in some cases, an argument against pressures in the workplace.

Hadley Cantril succinctly identifies the basis for appraising ethical public relations conduct:

> The "morality" or "ethical" nature—the correctness or rightness—of any action . . . is to be judged in terms of the degree to which it includes and integrates the purposes, and provides for the potential development of those purposes for all other

people concerned in the action or possibly affected by it.[18]

The study of ethics falls into two broad categories: comparative ethics, which is the purview of social scientists; and normative ethics, generally the domain of philosophers and theologians. Comparative ethics, sometimes called *descriptive ethics*, is a study of how different cultures observe ethical standards. Both diversity and similarity are of interest to social scientists. However, the social scientist looks for evidence that can be verified, and in a study of ethics such questions as whether ethical behaviors are a part of human nature spill over into other areas, such as theology and philosophy.

According to PR educator Hugh Culbertson, the philosopher and author Sissela Bok takes a near-absolute position that decisions are either morally right or wrong.[19] But there is another basis for decision making—the technique often referred to as situational ethics, which sees ethical standards not as constant but as varying or flexible in application to specific occasions or situations. Culbertson's observations of students suggest that they lean more toward situational ethics. Bok too recognizes that lies can sometimes serve a good purpose, says Culbertson. (One example is protecting Jewish house guests from discovery by Nazi storm troopers by lying about their presence. A more ordinary example might be telling a friend who asks your opinion that you think her new and expensive outfit is becoming when you think it isn't.) But, Bok asserts, in choosing between lying and truth telling, the presumption is always against lying, for the following reasons:

1. Dishonesty leads to lack of trust and cynicism—such as when a reporter discovers that a PR person has told half-truths resulting in an innaccurate story.

---

2. Lying is an exercise in coercion, forcing someone to act differently from the way he or she would have behaved if given the truth.

3. Lying is resented by those deceived, even if the deceived are liars themselves.

4. Dishonesty is likely to be discovered, and no climate for credibility can be reestablished.

5. Decisions about when to lie are often made without calculating either alternatives or consequences.

6. A lie often demands another lie to cover it up, and then others to maintain the prevarications.[20]

Dishonesty is seldom ambiguous, but some public relations actions are.

▼ RESPONSIBILITY IN PRACTICE

Some areas of public relations practice considered legitimate by most practitioners nonetheless cause public concern and arouse criticism. Among the most obvious of these are research (and how to use the resulting information), how to handle internal battles you lose with management and what to do about international activities when these involve working with foreign governments that operate according to different codes of ethics.

Research and Persuasion

Research is critical in all areas of public relations. (Chapters 4 and 5 of this book were devoted to the subject.) Finding out all that you can about the demographics and psychographics of your publics enables you to reach and communicate with them effectively. However, the uses of PR research and the purposes of persuasion must be examined by

the practitioner to minimize opportunities for abuse.

The first ethical problem to resolve is how to collect the data. Whether you do the research yourself—in-house, so to speak—or buy research services, you have to maintain certain standards toward the subjects used in the research. Earl Babbie, a well-established social science researcher, identifies the following practices that must be safeguarded in a research study: (1) ensuring the voluntary participation of all subjects, including employees when the research is of internal publics; (2) preventing harm to the subjects, either psychologically (through participation itself or as a result of facing issues they would prefer to avoid) or through analysis and reporting (when self-identification could cause damage to self-image); (3) protecting participants through anonymity and/or confidentiality, the latter occurring when the researcher identifies the participant but does not reveal the information; (4) avoiding deceiving participants, something not always possible but highly desirable; (5) reporting and analyzing results fairly and accurately so that others are not misled by the findings. Incidentally, when you buy research, you should know that members of the American Association for Public Opinion Research are pledged to uphold a code of professional ethics and practices.[21]

The second ethical problem in research involves the actual accumulation and storage of information. Probably no PR practitioner can match any level of government in its accumulation of data on an individual. Most people are in ten to thirty local and state files as individuals. In addition, the U.S. government classifies individual citizens according to more than 8,000 separate record systems, 6,000 of which are computerized. However, more and more PR people employ pollsters and market surveyers. Furthermore, accumulated lists are often sold and compilations of information are developed about respondents.

During the 1960s and 1970s, concern increased about the use of data banks containing information on individuals. As a result, the Freedom of Information Act and a consumer credit bill were passed to allow people to see just what information government and business had compiled on them. Nevertheless, both public and private institutions continue to gather substantial data, owing to the many different types of public registration (auto and boat licenses, building permits and so on) and mailing lists that are maintained. One software manufacturer, Lotus, recently responded to public pressure by canceling its "Marketplace" software that allows consumer data to be collated by categories.

The existence of the information is a problem, not only as an invasion of privacy, but also because it possesses enormous potential for misuse. Social scientists' most recent cause for alarm has been the purchase by the Internal Revenue Service of lists drawn from surveys in which people have revealed their level of income. IRS uses these lists to look for tax evaders. Social scientists (and marketing researchers) are afraid such use will discourage participation in surveys.[22]

But market research in and of itself is a cause for some concern. Purchases are monitored and even cable subscribers' use of electronic data banks is watched. Another important issue involves how you represent yourself in gathering facts. Some market survey techniques call for researchers to represent themselves as "clients" for a company's service, which is tantamount to lying to get information. One responsible market researcher who was asked to use this approach declined, saying, "I can get better data honestly." This researcher was alluding to the fact that research data are frequently misrepresented to a client.

A third problem has to do with how research information is used. A metropolitan newspaper's managing editor observed how public relations had changed between the 1950s (when its function was largely to perform publicity) and the 1980s (when its function seemed to be to provide information for manipulative use by, among others, political figures). He cited a local mayoral race in which attitudinal studies were done before a candidate announced that he was running for the office.

Then the candidate's strategists couched his position statements in terms consonant with the attitudes the polls had reflected. "That's scary," the editor said.

In public relations you become a consenting agent of attitude change. What sorts of questions should you ask yourself before you get involved in a persuasive effort?

First, you need to consider what you are trying to change. If behavior change is your objective, is it something people must be aware they are changing (as in stop-smoking campaigns waged by several of the national health agencies), or is it something people will change without being aware of it (such as automatically turning out lights without thinking consciously of energy conservation)? Second, you must ask whether the attitude change is one that will benefit the involved publics. Do you believe in what you are doing? Then you need to look at how specific the change needs to be. Will it involve a particular attitude (such as how the public feels about the hospital you are working for) or a general set of attitudes (how the public feels about health care in the United States, in general)? You need to examine how long the change will have to last and how many people are involved in it.

Some measure of the effect of your effort must be built into the program, since the effect might not be what you anticipated. In addition, you might have to consider here how your role will be perceived and whether your public constitutes a captive audience. Is it an audience with whom you will be having other dealings? Do you have misgivings about being identified as a persuader on this particular issue? What is at stake for you in the effort: personally? professionally? You may find that some roles put you in conflict with others you perform. As a volunteer public relations person for the American Cancer Society, for example, you could find yourself at odds with your professional duties of effectively representing a tobacco company client.

▼ **Ethical conflict over policies may arise between PR practitioners and management; the alternatives available for the practitioner who is overruled are to compromise or to leave.**

Internal Battles and Defeat

Public relations people generally try to persuade management to act in socially responsible ways toward all publics. Occasionally, though, the interests of two or more publics conflict, or the profit interests of the company conflict with the interests of one or more of its publics. Management decisions are not always in line with what the PR person recommends. What happens then? The PR person can first try to reach a compromise. If that doesn't work, he or she must review the situation to decide just how serious the conflict is.

Public relations practitioners are constrained in their efforts to influence management by at least four factors: (1) lack of access to management; (2) restraints on information collection; (3) roadblocks to dissemination of timely, accurate information; (4) a narrow definition of the role of public relations.[23] Of these factors, the first two pose the most serious problems. Researcher Michael Ryan concludes that practitioners need to find environments suitable to them. The most innovative practitioners should seek the most constraint-free environment; those who prefer routine tasks may be able to function well in an environment where management imposes constraints on employees' behavior.[24]

Some practitioners label themselves "team players" and carry out each management's decision as though it were their own. Others may carry out decisions imposed from above, but not as effectively as they would have worked on their own—a subtle form of sabotage that raises an ethical question in itself. The alternative is to move on to another place where the ethical climate is more compatible.

One practitioner asserts that leaving is difficult to do. "Your ethics may be as good as your credit rating. No one with a big mortgage and lots of bills takes too many risks for a 'cause'." But this is not always a valid rule. Doing something you feel is wrong is often worse for you personally and professionally than having to go job hunting. Moreover, if the action taken violates the PRSA or IABC code, you have to leave. If you don't, you risk being reported for the code violation by another practitioner. Fortunately, crises of confidence rarely occur because most people gravitate toward managements with goals compatible with their own.

Foreign Governments and Locations

Working within, with or for foreign governments poses some complex ethical questions because of different cultural patterns. One CEO from a multinational corporation said, in confidence and with some degree of exasperation:

> I wish each nation's government would make paying bribes explicitly illegal. We pay bribes abroad—all kinds—to do business. Those crooks just soak us—all the way from border guards to get materials moved among the countries to the heads of state. We have to pass the costs on to our customers. I hate it. It makes me sick. But there is simply no other way to get things done abroad.

Anyone who has lived in such an environment can appreciate his comments, even without agreeing that bribery is necessary.[25]

In response to the surfacing of "questionable payments" by corporations doing business abroad, legislation was passed in the United States making bribery illegal. But where do you draw the line between bribes or kickbacks and such traditionally acceptable practices as tips, gratuities and gifts? When do these become conditions for doing business? Even in foreign countries where bribes and kickbacks are illegal, such practices may exist in custom, which is difficult to work around.

Some companies, like multinational Ingersoll-Rand, have tried to protect themselves by establishing a committee of outside directors charged with investigating all business practices. From an outside director's point of view, the role of adviser is probably preferable to that of police inspector. However, all companies—multinationals, in particular—are trying codes of conduct, outside directors and anything else they can think of to undergird corporate morality. Multinationals have a social responsibility to all of their publics, not just to the national in which they were originally chartered.

With globalization, the culture-based aspect of ethics will become increasingly important as a business condition and a source of problems. At the root of culture lie values, which manifest themselves in such forms as social customs, family life, housing, clothing and food, recreation and leisure, education, class structure, political patterns, religion and folk beliefs, economic institutions and the arts.[26] Ethical conflicts in these areas can arise over the status of women and children, hiring practices (especially where sex, class or caste are factors), job descriptions (especially ones that might violate some religious observances), conditions for promotion, the treatment of animals, and contracts or agreements with suppliers or the government, just to name a few.

Working directly for foreign governments poses even more ethical questions. Some questions have been raised about U.S. political strategists, pollsters and political PR campaign managers who handle candidates in other countries—even when the elections are free and open. Although attorneys represent clients with public and professional impunity (in fact, their services are supposed to be available to all), public relations firms share the image of their clients. Not only the firm, but also the individual handling the PR account, may find it difficult to defend working for a country that has a reputation for being repressive.

Many countries with records of human rights violations have turned to U.S. public relations firms for help. And the desire to look good in world public opinion is not the only reason for doing so. U.S. aid payments are bigger to nations with better rep-

▼ Conflicts may occur when the PR person works for or in foreign countries with different codes of ethics.

utations in this area. Tourism may increase as well. Some companies accept only foreign clients with reputations as responsible world citizens; but as one said in discussing the Iranian turnover of 1979, such a judgment gets more and more difficult to make.

Burson-Marsteller chairman Harold Burson made no apology for his firm's agreeing to take on Argentina as a client before the 1983 installation of a civilian regime in that country. The firm told the government it had an image as a dictatorial institution and warned it to halt any campaign that denied civil liberties or human rights. The agency's counsel can play a beneficial role in such situations—if the client heeds the advice it is paying for. If the advice is not heeded, practitioners representing that nation in the United States as a foreign agent are sure to be criticized, as Burson has been.

Foreign governments rely increasingly on U.S. (and British) public relations firms for both government contracts and media relations. An example of media relations use was cited by the *Washington Journalism Review:*

> When a socialist government came to power in Greece in 1981, replacing nearly a decade of right-of-center governments, Prime Minister Andreas Papandreau swiftly hired the New York PR firm Fentom Communications, Inc., at $6,000 a month, to get word to the American press that socialist governments aren't all bad.[27]

Some media people say that the PR firms aren't effective and that the embassies of the countries could do the same job. Others consider the embassies less skilled at media relations. Apparently the only effective PR people are those whom media people accept as credible sources. When their own media contacts haven't worked, foreign countries have often turned to advocacy advertising.

▼ RESPONSIBILITY IN ADVERTISING AND SPONSORSHIPS

During a casual, informal conversation of the type that sometimes follows a business conference, a young advertising executive was interrupted by a phone call from one of his clients. Answering, the ad executive smiled and responded enthusiastically, "I *am* glad you got over to see the sign. We thought it was handsome, too!" Then he added somewhat cautiously, with a serious expression crossing his face, "Well, it is effective, of course, but we don't know how much more so than some of the other things we are doing, and according to the budget we worked out together, I just don't think we can afford another right now. Let's talk about it and if it really does work out as well as we anticipate, we can plan for others like it in the next year's budget. Okay? Thanks for calling."

The young executive hung up and turned with a big smile to his two associates: "Our client just saw that sign we put up yesterday and wants six more." "Six!" one of the associates gasped. "He can't afford it!" The advertising man nodded in agreement and explained to his other visitors: "We got one of those new multidimensional, lighted, revolving signs for one of our clients, and he's so in love with it he's forgotten how much it cost." Someone asked if he was going to recommend more signs for the client. "I don't think so. He really doesn't have that kind of money, and advertising that causes a business financial problem is sort of defeating its purpose, isn't it?"

Perhaps it's because that young executive makes decisions with his client's best interests in mind that he is in great demand in the metropolitan area where he owns and manages his own advertising agency. He clearly understands that the first responsibility in advertising is to an agency's clients.

Another advertising executive, the vice-president of a locally owned agency in another metropolitan area, called one evening to put off a dinner conference for another hour. She is her agency's time buyer and had stayed at her desk all day trying to work out the best broadcast buys for a client. Experienced in all media, she is particularly suited for the latitude her agency's owner and president has given her: "Change the schedules any way you want. What we are after is the best media buys for our customers." She is liked and respected by the media salespeople, who know she will give them a polite hearing and examine their contract suggestions carefully and considerately. She is trusted by the agency's clients, who know there is no competition within the agency to place the ads in a particular medium in order to increase personal commissions. They also know the bills they get have been carefully checked and the time purchases monitored. That kind of service is worth at least an agency's traditional 15 to 20 percent!

What about so-called kickbacks? This is a source of confusion to many who do not know the difference between a legitimate agency discount and unethical practice. When a client buys time or space directly from the media, the time or space is sold according to the rate for which the client qualifies—local, national, nonprofit and such. The media then prepare the ads or commercials and charge the client for the time or space and (usually) for any production costs. If the client wants to preserve some kind of uniformity in advertising, the advertising then goes to the media ready for instant use. The agency therefore receives a commission—from the media—which theoretically covers the convenience of their having prepared materials (instead of leaving this task to the media) and of their having brought the media some business.

To receive such a commission, though, the person placing the ads must represent a recognized agency. Unethical practitioners, sometimes working as staff PR, have been known to accept the commissions from the media—and pocket the money themselves. Since PR staffers work on a salary, they should not personally benefit from media discounts.

The second responsibility in advertising concerns the message itself. Subliminal advertising comes up for discussion from time to time, often in a classroom setting. Books have been written on the subject. However, most social scientists discount the effectiveness of such advertising and mass media gatekeepers (advertising dirctors in particular) deny that such ads, if submitted, would be published. Nevertheless, subliminal suggestion is possible. You can buy tapes that supposedly help you learn while you sleep, relax or are otherwise occupied. The eye can physically detect and relay to the subconscious symbols (words and art) that the conscious mind doesn't react to at the time. But it is unlikely that subliminal advertising is created on any significant scale, much less that it abounds.

What about advertising that doesn't tell the whole story? A full-page ad that ran in the four Rochester (New York) newspapers in the fall of 1986 asked, "Are Super Absorbent Diapers Safe for Your Baby?" The ad was an interview with toxic shock specialist James K. Todd, who said he would let his own child wear the diapers. The ad announced that the message came from Manning, Selvage & Lee, Inc. The *Wall Street Journal* asked: Why would a public relations firm run a newspaper ad about diapers? The ad, it seems, was really from client Procter & Gamble, which had been getting a lot of calls about the super absorbent diapers after the problem of TSS (toxic shock syndrome) was related to the use of super absorbent sanitary napkins.[28] The company spokesperson told the *Wall Street Journal* that the omission of Procter & Gamble's name from the ad was merely an oversight. Perhaps.

In another instance, the *Wall Street Journal* rapped the Tobacco Institute (an association of cigarette manufacturers) for giving money to the National Association of State Boards of Education to produce booklets called "Helping Youth Decide." The president of the State Education Boards said a brochure about drinking was being produced by the U.S. Distilled Spirits Council. Now, are these examples of an enlightened sense of social responsibility or what the *Journal* suggested in its story headlined "Foxes in the Coop"?[29]

Similar criticisms of advertising are also leveled at sponsorships, such as the Virginia Slims women's tennis tournament or the Marlboro cigarette and Burgermeister beer sponsorship of a Monkees'

rock concert in the Portland, Oregon, civic stadium during the summer of 1986. Although cigarette advertising is outlawed on television, a local cable system carried the concert, showing its youthful crowd, many of whom were wearing Marlboro jerseys.

The harshest critics of advertising say that it does not need to be subliminal to damage. Stimulating people to buy what they do not need or to buy something instead of spending or saving prudently is also unethical. These kinds of choices, though, seem to be a permanent feature of the free marketplace.

Protecting the Client

Just as a client's name should be respected, so should its rights to a trademark, logo or trade name. Protecting these forms of property can be difficult. For one thing, only the name of the specific design may be protected; there is no law against stealing ideas. This may explain the similarities often found in symbols, names, and even in advertising ideas.

The only recompense for a copied idea is the realization that imitation is the sincerest form of flattery. If your trademark or logo is copied, you may be able to sue for damages, but only if the *precise* design is used. It does not make any difference legally that the public might fail to distinguish between your design and the thinly disguised copied one. For instance, the symbol of the famous Texas Boys Choir, a silhouetted choirboy in bow tie holding an open music book, was appropriated by a civic girls' chorus. In the altered design, the choir boy's ears were covered with shoulder-length hair and the pants legs were filled in to resemble a skirt. A copyright authority stated that the changes were sufficient to prevent a suit. The alternative was simply for the Boys Choir to stop using the symbol it had created, which it did for several years until the other group's use of it declined.

If you are watchful, you can find numerous examples of close copies, especially with logos or creative advertising concepts and designs. Look, for example, at the logos for Minolta, AT&T and Sun-Belt Savings. Other packaging similarities are found in bleaches (white plastic container with predominantly blue label) and corn chips (red and yellow packaging)—both prompted by imitation of very successful brand-name products.

Trade names are also legally entitled to protection, but this often becomes virtually impossible to enforce when they fall into generic use, such as "Kleenex," "Band-Aid" and now (almost) "Xerox."

Protecting the Consumer

Efforts to protect the consumer cover a wide range of areas, but we will focus on three: products, politics and promotions.

Products   A PR person should warn a client when his or her product is being erroneously confused with another (thus violating consumer confidence) or when the product itself is creating a consumer problem.

When RJR Nabisco, Inc., decided to come out with a new cigarette called Dakota to compete with the Marlboro man, the company initially targeted women. The project's code name, "Project Virile Female," and other details of the marketing proposal were leaked to the media, presumably by a disgruntled company employee.[30] The disclosure was made to the Advocacy Institute, a Washington, D.C.–based anti-smoking group, which timed a release to coincide with a Senate hearing on cigarette advertising targeting specific groups. This RJR Nabisco promotion came just after the company was involved in a plan to promote a cigarette called Uptown to blacks. Dakota's target public was a white female, 18 to 24 years old, with a high-school degree, a job instead of a career and the chief aspiration of having an "ongoing relationship with a man." The cigarette never made it to the marketplace!

Criticized for using the cartoon character Joe Camel to sell cigarettes, RJR Nabisco launched an educational campaign advising children not to try the product until they were old enough to make a "mature" decision about smoking. The company refused to stop using its popular character (which has high recognition and appeal among youngsters) in advertisements.

Compare that with the actions of Pepsi-Cola, which in 1991 canceled its plans to broadcast a Super Bowl giveaway game that involved call-ins. The company's concern was that its promotion would overload the phone networks, which might be needed in an emergency, since the war in the Persian Gulf was in progress. The company had planned to flash a number on the TV screen during its Super Bowl commericals, and callers could qualify for three $1 million prizes to be given away at the end of the game.

Responsible behavior also came from a glue manufacturing firm, Testor, which took direct action when youngsters began sniffing glue for chemically induced elation. Testor had not run an ad in five years; but when glue-sniffing exploits began to make news, Testor began putting an ad in hobby trade magazines that read: "You can be sure it's the model—not the kid that's gonna fly. Because . . . you can't sniff Testor's, there's something in it." The ad was the result of a decision made by the company's president, Charles D. Miller, who got a grant for an independent research laboratory to find an additive that would make it impossible for youngsters to sniff glue. Testor made the new formula available to all its competitors and also made the lab research available to every manufacturer using solvents in retail products.

Standards of ethical behavior in advertising are set forth in the advertising profession's own code and in an elaborate two-tiered mechanism to deal with truth and accuracy in national advertising—although, of course, there is nothing to prevent those who do not subscribe to it from plying their trade. But even if advertisers ignore their own code, the media may provide the restraint—at least in matters of taste.

Politics   Late in the afternoon of November 21, 1963, a full-page ad, headlined "Welcome Mr. Kennedy," was given to the *Dallas Morning News*. It read, in part:

Mr. Kennedy, despite contentions on the part of your administration, the State Department, the Mayor of Dallas, the Dallas Chamber of Commerce, and members of your party, we free thinking and American thinking citizens of Dallas still have, through a Constitution largely ignored by you, the right to address our grievances to you, to disagree with you and to criticize you.

This was followed by a dozen questions regarding government policy, each addressed to the president with a boldface "Why?" The ad was signed by "American Fact Finding Committee, an unaffiliated and nonpartisan group of citizens."[31] In the case of all political advertising, payment with copy is required. A check for more than $1,000 was presented and the ad was accepted.

The advertiser had another $1,000-plus check for the city's other daily newspaper. By the time the advertiser reached the fifth-floor offices of the *Dallas Times Herald*, some ten blocks away, most of the advertising staff for that afternoon paper had already left for home, since they usually checked in at 7 or 8 A.M. A young salesperson read the copy and refused the check, saying, in effect, "We don't accept advertising like that at this newspaper." Although newspapers have the prerogative as private institutions to accept or reject advertising, the timing of the ad was unfortunate for the *News*. It appeared in the newspaper the morning of November 22, the day President John Kennedy was assassinated.

Broadcast stations have less flexibility in rejecting political advertising because of the *equal-time provision*. This provision appeared in the 1934 Broadcast Act through the incorporation of language from the 1927 Radio Act stating that, if a licensee permits any person who is a legally qualified candidate for any public office to use a broadcasting station, the licensee has to give equal opportunity to all other such candidates. Furthermore, the licensee (broadcast station) has no power of censorship over the material broadcast. This stipulation was regarded somewhat ruefully by Atlanta, Georgia, broadcasters who in 1974 had taken the advertising of one political candidate and then, under FCC regulations, had to accept the spots of

his opponent, Democratic candidate J. B. Stoner. Stoner's taped messages said: "I am the only candidate for the U.S. Senate for white people. The main reason why niggers want integration is that niggers want our white women. I am for law and order. You can't have law and order and niggers." The messages, broadcast over radio station WPLO and WSB-TV, evoked a deluge of protesting phone calls, but the spots ran for a week anyway.

The equal-time provision was amended in 1959 by the *fairness doctrine*, which stated that legally qualified candidates can appear on bona fide newscasts, news interviews, news documentaries or on-the-spot coverage of news events without the licensee's having to provide equal time to opposing candidates. But another clause proved more difficult to interpret: because stations are supposed to operate in the public interest, they must afford reasonable opportunity for the discussion of conflicting views on issues of public importance. The fairness doctrine had been interpreted to include advertising as well as program content and was the basis on which two networks, ABC and CBS, refused Mobil's explanatory advertising on the energy crisis.

The FCC discontinued the fairness doctrine in 1987. Print media supported the broadcasters in their effort to get rid of the requirement. Congress then tried to enact the fairness doctrine as law, but the bill was vetoed by President Reagan. Some members of Congress say the issue is not dead yet.

The 1990 elections in the United States were characterized by negative campaigning and low voter turnout. There's no proof of a cause-and-effect relationship between these events, but many voters said they just couldn't bring themselves to vote for anyone who resorted to using half-truths and outright lies to discredit an opposing candidate. Negative campaigning is certainly not new in U.S. politics. But today people rarely have an opportunity to meet touring candidates. Instead, candidates tend to focus on appearances in television studios and meetings with newspaper editorial boards. Furthermore, the candidates must use the media to campaign effectively, expensive though it might be. But they don't have to launch negative campaigns concentrated in costly television spots that are models of propaganda devices.

Because the candidates are really known to only a few, the electorate inevitably votes for "images" rather than for men and women. In addition, "issues" change, resist any very riveting response and are impossible to present in 15 or 30 seconds. Traditionally, party platforms provided a more philosophical and coherent summation of candidates' views. But some party members find it difficult to stand on their party's platform, as candidates in 1990 indicated with their diverse stands on abortion, regardless of party affiliation.

Therefore, to distinguish themselves from their rivals, many candidates use negative advertising—perhaps not early in the campaign, but as election time nears. Results show that negative advertising works, but it does so most effectively when there is a deadline for something to happen, like balloting. In 1990, most of the personalized attacks took place in the last few weeks of the election. Many candidates held back money in their "war chest" and some bought blocks of media time to use in case of a last-minute attack.

The problem for public relations people involved in politics is that people tend to see all campaigns as "public relations" efforts, regardless of who actually runs them. The campaign for a risky candidate usually involves strict control of exposure, limited access to media and voters, no discussion of issues or philosophy of governance, and as much television commercial time as available money allows. The unfortunate consequence of the last feature is that only candidates who have money or the ability to raise it can even compete. This narrows the field.

During an election campaign period—which now lasts at least a year, and sometimes extends to eighteen months, the "public relations" tactics employed by various candidates arouse a great deal of resentment toward public relations practice. In fact, however, many political election campaigns are not handled by public relations practitioners. There

may be several reasons for this. First, if the PR practitioner is a member of PRSA, he or she must comply with specific standards governing the practice of political public relations. These standards state, among other things, the following:

> It is the responsibility of PRSA members practicing political public relations ... to be conversant with the various statutes, local, state, and federal, governing such activities and to adhere to them strictly. This includes, but is not limited to, the various local, state and federal laws, court decisions, and official interpretations governing lobbying, political contributions, disclosure, elections, libel, slander and the like. It also is the responsibility of members to abide by PRSA's Code of Professional Standards.[32]

The PRSA code itself requires, among other things, conducting business in the public interest, dealing fairly with the public, adhering to standards of accuracy and truth and not knowingly disseminating false and misleading information or corrupting the integrity of the channels of communication.

There's more. PRSA members must represent their clients:

> in good faith, and while partisan advocacy on behalf of a candidate or public issue may be expected, members shall act in accord with the public interest and adhere to truth and accuracy and to generally accepted standards of good taste.[33]

Furthermore, members are forbidden to:

> issue descriptive material or any advertising or publicity information or participate in the preparation or use thereof that is not signed by responsible persons or is false, misleading, or unlabeled as to its source, and are obligated to use care to avoid dissemination of any such material.[34]

Beyond that, PRSA members cannot use campaign posts to garner commissions from suppliers or media without their client's consent. Nor are they allowed to use their post as a step toward government employment. PRSA members are to "avoid practices that might tend to corrupt the processes of government," and they "shall not make undisclosed gifts of cash or other valuable considerations that are designed to influence specific decisions of voters, legislators, or public officials on public matters."

Other restrictions are included in the code, as well, but one more deserves specific mention here: "Members shall not, through use of information known to be false or misleading, conveyed directly or through a third party, intentionally injure the public reputation of an opposing interest." It's hard to play in the election ball game—at least the way it was played in 1990—following those rules. Yet many did, or tried to.

Unfortunately, everything that went on was called "public relations." Public relations counselors now find themselves wondering how to deal with the problem of negative campaigning itself, the popular perception that public relations people are responsible for it and the notion that these are "legitimate" public relations practices. Another worthwhile item to put on the agenda might be an effort to make individuals who hold the nation's top public relations jobs (such as "press secretaries") accountable to a code of professional practice.

Promotions The "gatekeeping" role played by values can work in favor of some questionable practices. Advertising man George Lois, principal at Lois/GGK ad agency, had a client (New Retail Concepts) with a new product ("No Excuses" jeans) and a small ad budget. A commercial with Marla Maples of Donald Trump fame was made for the product. The commercial was subsequently rejected by NBC and CBS; ABC asked the jeans company for more information about their intentions to buy time. New Retail Concepts then issued a publicity release to all major media, declaring that all three networks had rejected the ad (which was not precisely true). In any case, the president of New Retail Concepts, Neil Cole, says the commercial wasn't created just so the networks would reject it, but he did say that the more publicity the stunt or situation (depending on your interpretation) generated, the less air time he would have to buy for marketing the jeans.[35]

An old controversy may finally have been laid to rest when the second major producer of infant formula, American Home Corporation, announced that it, like Nestlé, would stop giving free infant formula to hospitals in Third World countries. Both companies had been supplying the formula, which discourages breast feeding and had been blamed for infant deaths outside the hospital that occurred after mothers mixed the formula with unsterilized water or excessively diluted it to save money. Children subsequently died from dehydration caused by stomach upsets or malnutrition. Both companies are still under a boycott from an advocacy group, Action for Corporate Accountability, which accuses them of using dangerous methods to sell their products.

A controversy has developed over drug makers' addressing promotional advertising directly to consumers. Formerly, drug companies advertised only in medical journals. But people are demanding more control over their health-care options and are choosing generic drugs, often from a mail-order catalog, to avoid higher costs. Because of consumer changes, drug companies are going directly to the marketplace. Consumer activists, who might have been expected initially to support such a direct approach, are actually against it. They believe that the more extensive public campaign will cause drug prices to rise. Some activists who oppose direct sales of drugs to the consumer point to practices that they consider misleading, such as the promotion of calcium to women as a preventive for osteoporosis.[36]

Women were also the principal target public in another drug promotion controversy, Retin-A. Ortho Pharmaceutical took a sixteen-year-old product and presented it at a press conference as a wrinkle remover.[37] The drug is only available by prescription in the United States, but it can be bought over the counter in some other countries. Nevertheless, product advertising, promotion and publicity began before the Food and Drug Administration ruled on whether it was safe and effective when used as a wrinkle remover. As a result of investigating the Retin-A story, *Money* magazine arrived at these conclusions:

1. The pharmaceutical industry is bypassing physicians and going directly to consumers through the popular press, without explaining the product's limitations and dangers.

2. "Company publicity efforts, backed by million-dollar budgets and aided by *public relations firms*, [our emphasis] sometimes take place long *before* the drug has been approved by the FDA" for the specific use the manufacturer is encouraging.

3. Medical researchers funded by the companies for the initial research also receive fees for consulting and helping stage special public information events to promote the product. This compromises their objectivity, and yet these relationships are seldom disclosed.

4. The popular press doesn't probe beyond the publicity releases.

5. The FDA is too understaffed, overworked and tied up by laws to respond effectively in the media-dominated environment.[38]

Consumer abuse resulting from car rental agency promotions reached such a high level that the *Wall Street Journal*'s lead read: "Rent a car and you may get taken for a ride." The problem is "bait and switch" advertising that neglects to mention rather critical points like the fact that the quoted price is only for cars with manual transmissions, uses scare tactics to get customers to buy the "collision damage waiver" although most auto insurance policies cover the driver in a rental car in any case, and on and on. In fact, it's so bad that a Florida restaurant ran commercials lampooning the rental agencies: "The car is cheap, but the keys are extra."[39]

Compare that with the quick demise of a promotion that was causing consumers problems, despite the fact that it was the largest advertising campaign in the company's history. Coca-Cola Company initiated a $100 million summer promotion in 1990 that involved putting money and certificates for prizes in regular cans of Coca-Cola Classic. Plans were to distribute 750,000 "MagiCans" through August 15, but Coke officials ended the promotion with only about 200,000 cans distributed. The problems varied from broken prize delivery mechanisms to a boy in Massachusetts who drank some foul-smelling water from a can. (The cans with the prizes were weighted with water.) The company took out full-page ads to warn consumers and to tell them how to distinguish between a broken prize and a working one. It also advised against drinking the filler water, although health officials who tested the water said it wasn't harmful. A company spokesperson said, "Given that there are no health or safety issues involved here, legal considerations played no part in our decision."[40]

PR persons have been reminded of their own ethical responsibilities by the rise of the consumer movement and by citizens' complaints about puffery or exaggerated claims in advertising. As a result, the Federal Trade Commission now requires that advertising claims be substantiated by scientific or otherwise reliable proof. In response to an offending advertisement, the FTC can levy a fine, order withdrawal of the ad or sometimes compel the offender to present "corrective" advertising—as Profile Bread had to do to refute its earlier claims that its bread provided substantial help in weight reduction, and as Listerine had to do to compensate for its earlier claims that its preparation killed germs.

Advertising agencies are concerned that they as well as the client may be held responsible for such deceptions and exaggerations, but perhaps both should be more worried about their audience than about their legal culpability. A study by Scott Ward, Harvard Business School behavioral scientist, reveals that youngsters start to develop "somewhat cynical attitudes" toward TV ads between the second and fourth grades. That's when children begin to say things like "This commercial is funny, but it isn't true," and what they say is based on their personal experience with the product. By the time they reach junior high school, kids think ads are something to laugh at, not to believe. Next, they begin to pay attention only to the program and tune out commercials when these come on. Later, Ward says, they become more and more "jaded to commercial exposure"—to the point where, if they watch commercials at all, they focus their attention on the commercial itself rather than on the product advertised.[41]

Should there be counteradvertising (that is, ads presenting the opposite point of view)? The first counterads to attract significant attention were the antismoking ads, which appeared on TV before broadcast cigarette advertising was prohibited. Counteradvertising has also been placed by environmental groups. In some cases, broadcast stations have been required to run counter-commercials without charge as public service announcements. All stations are alarmed at the prospect of rulings requiring "equal time" across the board, which they worry might mean financial disaster.

An elaborate mechanism was set up in 1971 by the advertising industry to deal specifically with accuracy and truth in advertising. The National Advertising Divison (NAD) of the Council of Better Business Bureaus (CBBB) first investigates the case and makes a judgment. NAD's judgment may be appealed to the National Advertising Review Board (NARB), which makes a final judgment. Complaints from outside the system can go directly to NARB, with the permission of the NARB chairman.[42]

Regulatory boards can give consumers some protection when promoters and advertisers play on public greed by making frequent use of the word *free*. Brown & Williamson Tobacco Corporation was pressured by NARB, upholding a prior NAD decision, to stop using the word *free* in ads promoting the bonus of five extra cigarettes in packs of Richland. These cigarettes were packed twenty-five to the pack, not the more customary twenty to a pack, so NARB concluded that the price of a pack simply reflected a lower price per cigarette—not an equal price plus five free cigarettes. NAD also challenged

New York Air and United Air Lines for referring to their food, beverage and baggage checking as "free," since no other carrier charges for these services.[43]

Even with the trend toward self-regulation, such matters as the number of commercials in a time segment have stirred controversy. Although the time allotment has not changed, most of the major networks now allow advertisers to promote multiple products in a time segment. For example, a 30-second time spot can be used to run two 15-second commercials for different but related products. Only CBS is holding out on its restriction that commercials in the time slot must be unrelated and that no video bridge between the two may be used. Until 1967, the networks sold only 60-second spots; and Alberto-Culver led the fight for making 30-second segments available. The same company pushed hard for the split 30s that have now become very common in broadcast advertising.

Still another question arises when sponsorship really constitutes advertising. Public television is supposed to be devoid of advertising, but programs are openly sponsored. In the early days of public broadcasting, no company could sponsor a program that related to its product or cause. Later, however, sponsored films began to be shown on public television, and then outright sponsorship of programs related to the sponsor were permitted. For example, a computer software company carried in its print ads a line about its upcoming public TV show on computers.

The most recent controversial decision changed underwriting rules for Public Broadcasting Service (PBS), which allow a company that makes or sells liquor to underwrite programming production. Commercial television is prohibited from running liquor or cigarette commercials, and government regulation prohibits cigarette advertising on television. However, RJR Nabisco, which handles both tobacco and liquor products, among others, can sponsor PBS programs.

▼ RESPONSIBILITY IN PUBLICITY

The ethical question of when and how to acknowledge the PR source of news is extremely important. Critics question the ethics of having news appear in the mass media precisely in the form submitted by a PR person. They feel that PR-originated news should carry some identifying label to alert the reader or viewer. Many PR and media people regard this as impractical and (for different reasons) undesirable. They argue that it is the job of newspeople to know the source of the information they use and to employ discrimination and good editorial judgment about what is disseminated and whether attribution is needed.

In the *Columbia Journalism Review*, Jeanne Edwards, a critical observer of news media, made the *Wall Street Journal's* use of news releases the subject of a 1980 story in which she charged that some of the press releases were passed off as original material or given *WSJ* bylines. *CJR's* story reported on seventy companies queried. According to Edwards:

> In 53 cases—72 percent of our responses—news stories were based solely on press releases: in 32 of these examples, the releases were reprinted verbatim or in paraphrase, while in 21 other cases only the most perfunctory additional reporting had been done. Perhaps most troublesome, 20 of these stories (29 percent) carried the slug "By a *Wall Street Journal* Staff Reporter."[44]

In response, Frederick Taylor, then executive editor of the *Wall Street Journal*, said, "Ninety percent of our daily coverage is started by a company making an announcement for the record. We're relaying this information to our readers." And those slugs (bylines)? "A staff written piece is a staff written piece—and that's what the slug means."[45] A study of less specialized papers suggests that direct use of PR-generated copy is normal (see Chapter 12).

Responsibility extends to pictures, too (see Example 8.2). There's little comfort in the fact that misleading art is not new.

PR as a Source

To investigate how public relations is practiced in institutions where it is taught, Frank Wylie conducted a survey of randomly selected colleges and universities in five western states.[46] He queried the public relations department of each educational institution, the president's office and key news media in the area where the institutions were located. He discovered that only 53 percent of the people running PR departments had any experience in either public relations (13 percent) or journalism (40 percent). Among the types of unethical conduct they reported being asked to perform were the following: put out material that was not newsworthy (53 percent); release inaccurate information (15 percent); intervene with the student newspaper (21 percent). Only 72 percent reported having "complete confidence" in enrollment data, 61 percent in fund-raising information and 55 percent in athletics information. More than 25 percent have worked to kill one or more legitimate news stories that would have adversely affected their university, and 52 percent saw this as a common practice in college public relations. Finally, 35 percent acknowledged having communicated false or misleading information, either knowingly or unknowingly, and 38 percent viewed this as a common practice.

These data don't quite match the picture of public relations given by the presidents of the same educational institutions, 88 percent of whom believed that all news releases from their institution were newsworthy and that nothing sent from their universities was false and/or misleading. Only 7 percent of the presidents said that they had asked the PR person to try to kill a legitimate news story, and none reported having asked the PR person to distribute a story that was "inaccurate, misleading or false."

EXAMPLE 8.2

Composite Art as a Deceptive Practice

AP Log

The Associated Press
50 Rockefeller Plaza
New York, N.Y. 10020
September 11, 1989

TV Guide Composite Not Without Precedent

By HAL BUELL
Assistant General Manager for Newsphotos

When TV Guide placed the head of Oprah Winfrey on the body of Ann-Margret to produce art for the cover of its Aug. 26 issue it caused a minor media flap.

It wasn't really a photograph, a TV Guide spokesman contended in a story transmitted by AP. But at the same time it was conceded that the casual reader could mistake it for a photo.

Representatives of the two women who commented on, discussed or otherwise gossiped about the unlikely mix and match artifact gasped in mock or real horror.

No one mentioned that the stunt was not new. It was at least 100 years old.

Consider the case of Abraham Lincoln. Shortly after he died, entrepreneurs of the time, in an effort to capitalize on the news, produced a fresh engraving of the great emancipator. But none of the available "art" was just right. So they took a headshot made by Mathew Brady, reversed it and put it atop the body of John C. Calhoun.

The photographic evidence is printed here.

Their misdeed was discovered much later by scholars who noted that Lincoln's famous mole was on the wrong side of the image. Additional research showed that the papers next to Calhoun's left hand were changed from Southern slogans such as "Strict construction, free trade, sovereignty of the state" to "Constitution, Union, Proclamation of Freedom."

It wasn't the only time that Lincoln's head was seen on another body. Other research revealed that it also appeared on the body of Andrew Jackson.

That portrait survives today — on the $5 bill.

Reprinted with permission.

Among media respondents, 35 percent believed that news releases from educational institutions in their area were sometimes *not* newsworthy, but only 26 percent said that university and college PR people had attempted to kill a story (a figure corresponding closely to the 25 percent of PR people who admitted to having done this).

On balance, there appears to be cause for concern. Surely instructors find it more than usually challenging to try to teach students the contours of ethical public relations practice at an institution where such practice is not routinely upheld.

The relationship between PR people and newspeople is rarely the kind of contest in which the PR practitioner plots to sneak misleading or non-newsworthy material into print, and the reporter tries to "get" the PR practitioner's client. Publicity is supposed to *facilitate* the news-gathering process.

This does not mean that abuses never occur. For instance, the U.S. government sometimes arranges to have opinion-making "policy" books printed by a commercial publisher (for example, Ralph P. Slater's *The Sword and the Plow* [New York: Praeger, 1965]) so that the reader not only has no idea of the actual source of the book but also pays for it three times: (1) through the subsidy given by the government to the freelance writer to research and write the book; (2) through the subsidy given to the commercial press to print the book; (3) through the retail cost of the book. Meanwhile, readers are also paying for a national printing service, the U.S. Government Printing Office, which can produce books relatively inexpensively.[47]

During any election year, look for books about candidates who are already officeholders, and watch out for any heavily promoted books that seem to support a principal plank in a party platform, especially when that party is currently in power. This became an issue in the confirmation of Nelson Rockefeller as Vice President in 1974, when it was learned that his brother Laurance had paid for the writing and publication of a book attacking Arthur Goldberg during a New York gubernatorial contest. This sort of subversive publication is, of course, unethical, irresponsible and yet another

factor contributing to the overall distrust of publicity.

One deceptive publicity practice that has invaded the magazine field (coming perhaps from small newspapers) involves specialized magazines, and is relatively transparent. A company that buys an elaborate ad—always four-color, usually double-truck (two pages side by side), and sometimes with a foldout—is almost always featured in an article with several pictures in the same issue. Sometimes the article carries no byline. When it does, the professional identity of the writers is seldom disclosed. In all likelihood, the writers are publicists for the advertisers. In one case, an aviation magazine that carried a prominent four-color advertisement for an airplane manufacturer's new model also published an illustrated four-page article on the plane and gave it the cover.

Xerox got into trouble with something not nearly as devious. As a sponsor of such television series as Alistair Cooke's "America" and Kenneth Clark's "Civilization," the company had been widely applauded. Nothing seemed wrong with doing the same thing in another medium, so Xerox approached *Esquire* about underwriting a special piece. *Esquire* chose the topic and the author with approval from Xerox. The result was a twenty-three page personal essay by Pulitzer Prize winner Harrison E. Salisbury, "Travels through America." It appeared in the February 1976 issue of *Esquire*, bracketed by modest Xerox ads. The front ad began, "First a word from the sponsor." Xerox paid Salisbury a $40,000 retainer for his six-months' work on the piece, plus $15,000 in expenses, and the company brought $15,000 worth of advertising in *Esquire*. *Esquire* saw nothing wrong with the arrangement, because it had final editorial control; had Xerox not approved of the finished piece, *Esquire* was free to publish it anyway and keep the money too. But criticism of the piece came from prestigious author E. B. White, who argued that selling editorial space represented a serious erosion of the free press. His criticism was not of the particular piece but of the possibilities for abuse that such an arrangement offered. The company listened to its critic and canceled two other projects similar to the *Esquire* essay.

Some magazines that compete with commercial publications for readership and advertising are actually public relations tools themselves. Among these are American Express's publications *Travel and Leisure* and *Departures*. Others are Ford's (one of the oldest) and Philip Morris's (the company magazine with the largest circulation, which began considering advertising in 1987). *Smithsonian* is actually a government publication because the Smithsonian Institution, which publishes it, is a government entity. Old hands at distributing magazines to customers are DuPont, Volvo, Peat-Marwick, Mercedes-Benz and, of course, the airlines. Among the newest giveaway magazines are those published by AT&T and Federal Express.[48]

Although professional communicators express concern over the lack of a clear division between news and advertising copy, the public seldom seems to give it a thought. Study after study has indicated attention to *content*, with little understanding of the difference between commercial content and editorial content. Or perhaps this just shows an advanced level of calloused disbelief.

Interconnections among advertising, marketing and public relations are impossible to sever. It is best to accept that at the outset. Just as people don't separate the content in publications, they don't discriminate between the separate "voices" of an organization's advertising and its publicity. In their promotion of discount fares and on-time service, airlines discovered that their marketing promises were being taken seriously, even literally. This created unfortunate consequences when customers did not receive what they thought the commercial message had promised. The public's reaction was serious enough to warrant complete revision of flight schedules for all the major airlines.[49]

Matters of Taste

Judgment calls are the name of the game in matters of taste. Even a PR effort that seems to be performing a public service can be criticized. For example,

an effort to dramatize heart disease by presenting a live telecast of heart surgery resulted in controversy.[50] One hospital PR person compared the event to a circus in the Roman Colosseum. Healthcare communicators surveyed generally responded favorably to the broadcast but were split almost evenly on whether it should have been done live or taped. One hospital PR person noted that a separation of Siamese twins had been telecast live, but without an announcer in the operating room whose voice might have distracted the medical team. She said that it would have been just as effective taped and that, in any case, nothing should have been done to put pressure on the doctors during surgery.

In California, the American Cancer Society's public service announcement that showed a fetus smoking inside its mother's womb had to be withdrawn because of public outcry. Others saw the announcement as a dramatic image for what actually happens to the unborn when the mother inhales cigarette smoke.

Money Matters

What happens when you, as a publicity writer, have a story accepted by a publication? Are you entitled to compensation for the story or pictures? No! Publicity is free; magazine editors know it and won't offer payment. Many will give you a byline, and some will identify you as a guest author in that issue. But make sure your identification carries your relationship to the piece you are writing.

What if a magazine staff writer writes a story suggested by a PR firm and allows his or her expenses to be paid by the firm? What if the writer accepts a fee as well as expenses from the firm? The ethical problem here is not only that the magazine staffer is "on the take" but also that the PR people are inducing the misconduct. It is permissible for a public relations practitioner to suggest a story to a publication; and if the idea is accepted and a writer assigned, the practitioner may make arrangements for accommodations and may see that all expenses involved in getting information for the story are covered. Almost all publications permit such arrangements on expenses, but many want to pay for transportation and accommodations themselves. Some are flexible about the accommodations.

Increasing criticism has been voiced about junkets—all-expenses-paid excursions for movie reviewers to the location of a filming, for travel editors to the opening of a new resort hotel or amusement park, for fashion editors to the site where a new line (cosmetics, shoes, sportswear, anything) is being introduced, or for real estate editors to the opening of a new luxury development in a remote area. Critics charge that such junkets amount to the purchasing of editorial talent. Most PR practitioners see nothing wrong with them, however, particularly since there is no control over what the wined and dined reporters write. And most practitioners use a careful screening process to separate the professionals from the freeloaders. Sometimes a strict publication will allow its reporter to go but will insist on paying for the transportation and accommodations. Others permit these to be paid for if the reporter acknowledges the fact in his or her copy. Still others permit reporters to accept trip packages because they believe the gratuities will not affect how the reporters handle the story.

Some publications give such trips as rewards to staffers. A flurry of criticism arose in 1986 over Walt Disney World's invitation to more than 14,000 representatives from broadcast and publishing to attend a three-day event observing the amusement park's fifteenth birthday. Backers included seventeen airlines and twenty-six hotels plus local (the city of Orlando and Osceola County in Florida and Orange County in California) and state (Florida) government. Disney offered the journalists three choices: all expenses paid, a token payment of $150 or no payment at all. Some 5,000 to 6,000 media people plus their guests (about 10,000) accepted the invitation. Disney said no effort was made to control the slant or the coverage. Most who accepted the $150 package said that the trip clearly cost them considerably more. Many travel editors said that they couldn't afford to cover travel news without such packages. Some media did refuse. The debate goes on.[51]

Some observers feel that this debate should be extended to the situation where the information source (sometimes a public relations person and sometimes not) pays the expenses of a freelance travel writer.[52] News media tend to ignore this situation and treat the article as a submission by a freelancer who used her or his own resources to get the story. At least three major newspapers (*New York Times, Chicago Tribune* and *Boston Globe*) will not take any subsidized travel stories and insist on documentation. On the other hand, Barry Anderson, former president of the Society of American Travel Writers, says he doesn't think freelancers can survive without some travel assistance, and the PRSA Code of Professional Standards permits practitioners to provide free trips for media representatives, including travel writers, if the purpose is to allow coverage of a story with legitimate news interest, if the trip is made available to all writers, and if no preferential treatment or guarantees are expected or implied. Some public relations people compare this to the free access to events provided to sportswriters and theater and music critics, although some news media insist on paying for these as well.

Broadcasters appear to have more flexibility, especially in situations where it's clear to the viewer that the resort area featured in the travelogue obviously cooperated in the production. These features are usually broadcast on special channels or in quasi-commercial programming. But how do these TV magazine format features differ from newspaper travel sections?

The Society of Business Writers was the first to respond to this problem. It adopted a code of ethics that specifically outlaws junkets and "freebies." A member may not accept any special treatment or any gift of more than token value; all out-of-town travel must be paid for by the writer's employer. Other professional journalism organizations followed suit, as did individual newspaper corporations. Most publications had already prohibited outright gifts to their editorial staff members, either directly or through people in their own advertising departments. Some specialized publications, though, such as *Car and Driver*, only ended staff freebies in 1991.

Newspapers always seem to watch this practice especially closely. Some will not allow their reporters to accept any gifts whatsoever; others are aware that their reporters often receive small gifts from PR sources but only worry when many stories appear from a single source or when a gift seems large enough to be potentially compromising. One relevant consideration is a ruling by an administrative law judge for the National Labor Relations Board in a case involving the Madison (Wisconsin) *Capital Times* that gifts to newspeople were part of a news employee's wages and could not be prohibited by the newspaper. Editorial publisher Miles McMillan appealed the decision to the full NLRB, which upheld the newspaper's right to establish a code of ethics preventing freebies. One fashion editor often receives free cosmetics, gimmicks and gadgets of all descriptions—but at the risk of the givers. She reports on such gifts and doesn't hesitate to point out bad features. Her editor doesn't worry about news sources compromising *her* integrity.

There is another side to this, though. Public officials are also on PR gift lists. Many companies have certain public officials they want remembered and tell their PR person to "buy something." Many city, county and state governments have strict regulations about what public officials may accept, but just as many don't. Common prudence suggests that all gifts should be "token" rather than substantial. One executive who shops the catalogs every year for gifts to suggest to his clients offers this rule of thumb: "When I choose something, I always think, how would I feel if I suddenly saw this on the 6 P.M. news? That curbs my buying sprees considerably."

Another kind of remuneration—one that inflates the ego as well as the pocketbook—is the awarding of prizes, and this affects both press and public officials. Does a reporter embark on a series about arthritis to enlighten the newspaper's readers or to increase the writer's chances for tangible recognition from the Arthritis Foundation? Does a local television station do a documentary on possible fire hazards during the summer to warn its viewers or to receive recognition from the Firefighters' Association? Does a network choose its documentary for overriding public interest or a chance to win an Emmy or Peabody? Does an ambitious lawyer offer to head the local symphony drive for the arts out of love of music or because his eye is on a civic club's annual outstanding citizen award? Commercial as well as nonprofit institutions engage in these incentive programs, but these seem to meet with greater editorial acceptance than junkets, even though many awards are cash prizes.

A more blatant type of remuneration is the moonlighting that some reporters and photographers do at part-time publicity jobs. Although most media executives do not condone the practice, few make serious efforts to stop it. As one newspaper's photo chief said, "Are you kidding? All my good people would quit. They can't live on what this paper pays them." Nevertheless, there are all sorts of ethical ramifications. Certainly it encourages the newsperson to ensure that the publicity gets in—to keep a paycheck coming.

Keeping the public and private sectors separate caused particular concern in 1978 when attention became focused on the facilities provided for news media in public places (government centers), such as courthouses and state capitols. In many of these places free parking spaces, a paging system and a complete writing facility with desks, typewriters, telephones and even attendants were provided. The taxpayer was picking up the tab, of course. Much of the furor over such perquisites ("perks") originated in the Washington, D.C., news media's criticism and exposure of congressional perks. Congressman David Obey, (D–Wisc.) responded by suggesting that this was a case of the pot calling the kettle black. Suddenly government perks for reporters came under scrutiny everywhere, much to the consternation of some government people hired to handle the news media. When the reporters moved out, the working relationships of these staffs with the news media became a lot more complicated. News agencies could preserve their integrity by paying rent for the facilities and furnishings.

Some state governments, whose constitutions bound them to provide the media with free space and prevented reimbursement, were caught in a bind. However, few people working in the public relations role for government saw the facilities issue as a threat to the free press system, and several pointed to an observation made by some newspeople themselves—that lack of facilities really inhibited news coverage. The bigger organizations could afford to foot the bill, but some of the smaller media, whose reporters tend to look carefully at what their constituents' representatives are doing, were forced to abandon coverage and use the more general wire-service copy.

Public relations people often control more than their budgets. Generally the corporation's investments in the community—gifts to civic, social, even national organizations—are within the control of the PR department. This is especially true of national organizations to whom the company gives its support. These relationships are scrutinized by special-interest groups that monitor such gifts to be sure minorities and other disadvantaged groups are not excluded. Their reviews can also put an institution in a bad position if its funds go to groups that do exclude minorities or that practice discrimination or that have labor policies that could be criticized as unfair.

A critical review of where an institution's dollars go extends beyond the budget for social and community affairs, to cover investments of all kinds—including the employee pension fund. At least one company refuses to buy South African rands because of that country's racial policies. Many mutual funds have also been criticized for their investments in South Africa, in defense industries, in nuclear energy and in other companies with problematic records in relation to health and safety. One fund manager said, "If you look deep enough, you'll find a problem with any campaign." He also noted that "different people have different interpretations of what is a socially responsible investment."[53] A national church group called for review of investments in its funds because of stock bought in Nestlé, which has been criticized for its marketing practices in some Third World countries.

The timing and content of PR announcements can also cause problems, as Warner-Lambert found out in announcing its drug for treating heart attacks. The pharmaceutical house and the *New England Journal of Medicine* called a joint news conference in November 1987 for security analysts and news media, but they embargoed the news releases. Of course the security analysts went back to their offices and got a head start for their regular customers before the news media could alert the investing public at large. This was unethical, but it was not illegal.

The Puppet Show

When governments offer space to newspeople, the relationship between the two groups is direct, at least. But less obvious connections exist between many organizations and special interests in our society. For example, the false front organization is an old public relations gimmick that hurts PR credibility and violates the PRSA code of ethics. When a product or a person needs a forum, a club (which appears to be a collection of people with a common interest) is created. Best recognized is a fan club for a star. But such clubs seldom begin spontaneously. More sophisticated creations have a stated generic rather than specific intent. Not uncommon is the tactic of establishing information centers. Ayerst, which produces Premarin, an estrogen hormone, also sponsors the Information Center on the Mature Woman. The *New York Women's Liberation* newspaper accused Ayerst of forming the information center specifically to promote its drug. Ayerst denied the charge, stating that "Funded by Ayerst Laboratories" appeared at the bottom of the center's letterhead, although in small type. However, stories from such centers often find their way into the news media without the explicit tie being shared with readers or listeners. In such cases, who is at fault if the consumer is misled?

Criticism arose during the late 1970s on another front when PR people developed "brokers' clubs." Trying to reach stock analysts has always been difficult, so some companies began making their pitch directly to the brokers, who are the salespeople anyway and who greatly influence purchases by investors. Clubs for stockbrokers sprang up all over the country, but they were convened only when they had a speaker—usually the president of a public corporation. The appearance of the president was then arranged by, you guessed it, the corporate PR director.

PACs: Political Action Committees

Political action committees (PACs) are clearly identifiable, legal organizations registered and incorporated in states to raise money for politicians whom they favor. The corporate political war chests they command are sizable. For example, a law firm's PAC fund contributions may exceed $100,000, and one state's professional organization for CPAs has a political fund of more than $200,000. PACs are also developed by unions and by activist groups such as anti-abortionists and homosexuals. Most states require that PACs maintain public records of their names, affiliations and assets and the names of those who make donations to them above a given amount. However, in some cases the information is not easy to get. Public relations ethical questions arise over how the money is raised (through pressure put on employees, for example), how the money is spent (on political candidates who may not behave in the best interests of society), how

much information is made public about the institution's PAC and whom it supports. Although big business and big labor dominate PAC activity, many professional and trade associations are also involved. These institutions defend their right to bankroll the candidates they feel will support them most staunchly when in office. Critics of PACs insist that they invite abuse of the electoral process.

News Media and Political PR

Politicians and the news media are natural adversaries. The cause for conflict, as William Blankenburg identifies it, is that "undefinable thing called news that mixes two combustibles, timely disclosure and objective truth, one of which is chaotic and the other coercive."[54] Caught in the middle of the conflict is the political PR person. Although government officials are public servants and should respond to the public (represented by news media), the Pentagon's distrust of such responsiveness has gone to the extent of administering lie detector tests even to top-level officials to make sure that no "unauthorized information" goes to a reporter. Often the problem with unauthorized information is that its release would be inconvenient. The PR person is always suspect and therefore occupies a high-tension spot. The tension is heightened by the way public officials use the news media and vice versa. *TV Guide* reported on an interview with Henry Kissinger, former secretary of state and renowned power broker, in which Kissinger made several illuminating comments.

The news leak is one of Washington's most famous specialties, regardless of the Administration in power. Henry Kissinger told *TV Guide* magazine (April 2 issue) that he discovered how the leak works when President Nixon was considering elevating him from National Security Adviser to Secretary of State.

The President had never discussed the job possibility with Kissinger, so he assumed the news leak reported by Dan Rather of CBS "Evening News" came from an ally trying to secure the Cabinet post for him, or a foe eager to block the appointment.

Kissinger called Rather. "I asked him whether the thing had come from a friend or from a critic, and he very decently told me it was not from a friendly source. He didn't tell me, obviously, who the source was," Kissinger explained.

"There is absolutely no doubt that when an official deals with the press he is trying to 'use' the press," Kissinger said. "And there is no doubt that when a reporter deals with an official, he is trying to 'use' the official. That has to be faced from the beginning.

"An official is very unwise—in addition to being morally wrong—if he deliberately misleads the press. But the press must understand that the official is there not to please them but to achieve his objective," he continued.[55]

In international PR practice, media play by different rules. In mainland China, for example, newspaper space is limited, since most papers may print only four pages. A PR person seeking publicity must therefore go to the China News and Culture Promotion Committee and buy the services of its members in order to get into either print or broadcast news. Advertising is another problem, since space is so limited that an advertiser may have to wait weeks or months for an opening. Cash up front and freebies are the standard cost of getting media time and space.[56]

Leaks compromise the integrity of news channels. In countries where the integrity of news channels is taken seriously, that integrity can be jeopardized when a spokesperson takes his or her role too literally and issues quotes from conversations that never took place. Although "creating quotes" is routine in public relations, it is done only when statements are prepared prior to an event and approved by the person to whom they are ascribed. Later, when a news-making event occurs—when, for example, a speech is given—the person frequently uses the prepared remarks, making them his or her own by conveying the information they contain in his or her own words. In April 1988, however, former presidential press secretary Larry Speakes, while promoting his book *Speaking Out*, claimed that he manufactured some quotes and attributed them to President Reagan when Reagan met with General Secretary Gorbachev in Washington. Here was a situation where the Russians knew the words were never said. Speakes said he was relieved that the Russians didn't say anything. The president denounced the "kiss and tell" tenor of Speakes's book but did not deny the substance of the allegations. In the midst of the furor that the incident sparked, Speakes resigned from his public relations position at Merrill Lynch.[57] He has since returned to PR work in Washington, D.C.

Henry Kissinger himself came in for some criticism for an appearance he made on ABC.[58] At the time, Kissinger had a fee arrangement with the network specifying that in breaking news events ABC had first call on his services. On June 4, 1989 when the Chinese government began to kill student protesters in Beijing's Tienanmen Square, ABC sent a news crew to Kissinger's weekend home in Connecticut for a live interview. In that interview Kissinger stressed the relationship between the United States and China and said that he would not recommend sanctions. A month later in his op-ed column for the Los Angeles Times Syndicate, he praised Chinese leader Deng Xiaoping for his economic reforms. In each instance, TV viewers and readers were not told that Kissinger, through his business consulting firm (Kissinger Associates) and a subsidiary (Kent Associates), had extensive ties to China—nor that 8 percent of the revenue from both firms comes from businesses wanting to do business in China. (In September 1989, Kissinger joined the board of directors of CBS, ending his seven-year stint as a commentator and source for ABC.)

The public relations firm of Hill & Knowlton has drawn criticism from other public relations people for presenting to the Congressional Human Rights Caucus a Kuwaiti girl (later identified as the daughter of the country's ambassador to the United States) who told a story of Iraqi soldiers taking infants out of incubators and leaving them on the hospital floor to die. When no direct evidence such as eyewitnesses to these atrocities could be found after the war, H&K was accused of creating the story for its client. Finally, a year and a half after the incidents alleged, Kuwaiti officials presented news media with a nurse who claimed to have witnessed the atrocities; no explanation was offered for the delay by the nurse in coming forward. In another alleged breach of ethics, H&K is accused of representing the Bank of Credit and Commerce International (BCCI) as a respectable, legitimate institution. Even if H&K was deceived by its clients, it remained responsible for learning the truth before spreading the information. The BCCI case has resulted in legal action against the PR firm.

The Public's Right to Know

The media's right to know is related to the public's right to information. The Freedom of Information Act has given individuals access to certain types of information, and the media derive their right to that information from the public's right. The act, however, does protect certain kinds of information from public exposure. Information that the government believes is important to national security remains confidential, as does information that pertains to ongoing criminal investigations. Of course, the act has nothing to do with financial and commercial information generated by private sources. Other state and local regulations, such as the open-meeting laws, also protect certain kinds of information. Governmental bodies still have the right to discuss such things as collective bargaining and certain personnel matters in executive session.

Although some information remains hidden from the media, some critics believe that the media are now privy to too much information. Other critics maintain that the media do not treat privileged information with sufficient discretion or respect.

Many problems that the news media encounter are attributable to the fact that we as a public do not agree on what we want to know. We do not agree because our basis for deciding what we want to know is a value system; since we have different value systems, complete agreement appears to be impossible. Nevertheless, the law says we have a

▼ **The nature and extent of the public's right to know remain subjects of considerable dispute.**

---

right to know everything that does not invade an individual's privacy—and the privacy of public figures in some instances—and everything that does not defame a person or a group.

The limits on these two crucial freedoms—to be informed and to be left alone—have been set, but they continue to evolve in court cases, because these rights come with obligations. The news media are not the only ones who fail to uphold their obligations to tell the public what they need to know in order to make rational decisions. In the past, the commercial sector has often withheld health and safety information from consumers and employees. Additional examples continue to come to light.

In a 1981 survey conducted through the American Management Association, David Finn found that 15 percent of CEOs were always accessible to news media representatives and that 56 percent of them usually were.[59] The first major difficulty for PR people and journalists was not the CEOs' lack of accessibility in general; it was their failure to understand how important deadlines were to the news media. The second major difficulty for the news media was that CEOs did not understand what "off the record" meant.

The third difficulty Finn uncovered was that PR people and journalists agreed that, during interviews, CEOs are defensive and don't give reporters a chance to ask questions. Almost three-fourths of the reporters and over half of the PR people faulted CEOs for viewing all negative stories as biased. The journalists cited two other problems PR people tended to minimize. More than half of the reporters thought CEOs were not honest with their own PR departments, and almost half of the reporters thought CEOs viewed all reporters as being "out for blood."

Finn's survey results showed that 47 percent of the PR people responding admitted that they had deliberately and personally withheld information from the news media. Moreover, they viewed their actions as acceptable behavior. Most of the public relations people said they withheld information primarily for legal reasons, and 93 percent of the journalists who participated in the study agreed that legal considerations justified withholding information.

The next most frequently cited reason for withholding information was competitive considerations. Over three-fourths of the journalists agreed that this was legitimate. The next most common justification for withholding information in order of importance for PR people was governmental restrictions. Just 57 percent of the journalists thought that this was a good reason. The difference here suggests that the journalists didn't exactly understand what the restrictions were; or perhaps they thought that the PR people were hiding behind those restrictions. A fourth reason for withholding information was a feeling of responsibility to stockholders. Only a little more than half of the journalists thought that this feeling of responsibility justified withholding information.

Ethical reasons were also important to PR people as a basis to justify withholding information. Less than three-fourths of the journalists agreed that this was legitimate. Well over half of the PR people in the survey also believed that protecting privacy and avoiding a negative effect on a company's image were legitimate reasons for withholding information. More than half of the journalists concurred that protecting personal privacy was a valid reason, but less than a fourth considered the desire to protect the company image a valid excuse. Over a fourth of the PR people also admitted that they had withheld information for fear of their jobs. Almost half of the journalists were sympathetic to that reason.

Both the PR people and the CEOs said that incorrect stories were almost always caused by the journalists' failure to understand business. PR peo-ple also felt that journalists were not properly trained and that incomplete information was given to them. A little more than a fourth (29 percent) felt that reporters were biased. On the other side, the journalists believed that they could do a better job if they learned more about reading a balance sheet, better understood the general practices of management and economic theories affecting free enterprise, fully comprehended the working of the stock market and knew how profits were used. If that is indeed the case, the source is obliged to help the journalists tell the story accurately, not in a self-serving way.

The AMA survey resulted in Finn's offering a list of suggestions for PR people, business CEOs and journalists. In all of them, he pleads for more interaction, not less; more openness, not less. To that plea we might add the need for a more highly developed sense of responsibility by business and the news media toward the public, who must base their decisions on what they can discover in the news media.

Journalist Tom Wicker observes that journalists tell a story well when they report on what is actually happening, but they do less well when they report on an event they have not witnessed first-hand:

> When it [the press] does venture beyond its fixation on events and spokesmen, the press itself often is ill-informed, and what's printed and broadcast as news is frequently confusing and misleading or just plain wrong. One reason is the supposed need to simplify things for a public presumed to be hurried and none too interested. Complex economic matters, say, or arcane questions of nuclear strategy and arms control are difficult enough to understand and harder to explain, particularly under pressures of time and space, without trying to reduce them to the level of a first-grade primer.
>
> All too many reporters, moreover, get their information about these and other matters "on the beat"—from sources, such as the Pentagon, likely to be self-serving. Few reporters, fighting their deadlines, have the time or perhaps the inclination for outside study of more even-handed and sophisticated documentary or academic material, or for

pursuing sources with a different point of view and no vested interest.[60]

Most of the criticism that organizations receive is from the mass media. Organizations are likely to counter that criticism by observing that the media are not above reproach themselves. The American Heart Association has documented the fact that publications (primarily magazines) and broadcasters (primarily networks) will not accept editorial matter that claims smoking is a factor in causing cardiovascular disease. This, of course, is contrary to journalistic codes of ethics; but codes are standards, not law.

Promotions and Public Opinion

Although many organizations climbed on the environmental bandwagon in the 1990s, not all of the tie-ins have been successful. For example, Procter & Gamble advertised its Pampers and Luvs brand diapers in an Earth Day magazine to be sold at Hardee's restaurants. The purpose, P&G said, was to educate consumers about new technology for composting the diapers. Critics responded that the ad was misleading because the technology for the composting was not widely available.[61]

Some organizations have been criticized for promoting environmental sensitivity while continuing to pollute with other products or operations. The irony of some corporate efforts was pointed out by *National Wildlife* magazine, which noted that the nation's eight largest petrochemical manufacturers had contributed $2 million each in seed money for plastic recycling centers that now produce polystyrene pellets used in beach park benches from which visitors can watch "waves of tar balls washing up."[62]

One company that decided its environmental efforts should be more than hype is McDonald Corporation. The company is working with the Environmental Defense Fund on its waste-reduction effort. The effort goes beyond McDonald's announced abandonment of the plastic box for take-outs. The joint task force of the advocacy group and the company has arrived at forty-two initiatives to help McDonald's reduce by 80 percent the 238 pounds of waste each of its 11,000 restaurants generates daily.[63]

▼ INDIVIDUAL RESPONSIBILITIES

Ethical performance amounts to doing what's right to preserve your integrity, in accordance with your value system. But values are culture-bound, which is why difficulties often arise across cultures. In the United States, honesty is valued, but it isn't rewarded very well. In short, as any "whistle-blower" can tell you, there's not much reward for ethical behavior. (Whistle-blowers are individuals who call public attention to problems within their own industry, business or organization. As a result of their revelations, they often lose their jobs and have trouble finding other employment. Women and minorities who file anti-discrimination lawsuits often encounter the same difficulties, even when they win.)

Two Columbia business school professors investigated the material value of ethics training by surveying 25 years of alumni experience.[64] They discovered that, of the 1,070 alumni from the classes of 1953–1987 who responded, 40 percent said they had been implicitly or explicitly rewarded for taking some action they considered to be ethically *troubling* (emphasis ours), and 31 percent of those who had refused to take some ethically troubling action said that they had been directly or indirectly penalized for their choice.

Two writers for the *Harvard Business Review*, seeking to prove the thesis that "honesty pays," found the opposite to be true. Their study led them to conclude that "power can be an effective substitute for trust." According to these researchers, "Trustworthy behavior does provide protection against the loss of power and against invisible snipping. But these protections are intangible, and their dollars-and-cents value does not make a compelling case for trustworthiness." Then why be trustworthy? The authors say, "Only our individual wills, our determination to do what is right, whether or not it is profitable, save us from choosing between chaos and stagnation."[65]

There may be faint comfort in that. Their research suggests that conscientious public relations practitioners must attempt to function ethically and responsibly in settings where a different culture may support different values, in a larger society in the United States that lauds ethical behavior but seldom rewards it, and in situations where others are using entirely different standards reflecting divergent underlying values. In fact, the student views expressed in Example 8.1 may signal that values in American society are changing. You might want to test your own business ethics in Example 8.3.

No wonder, then, that headlines like the following provoke little shock or outrage:

In Public Relations, Ethical Conflicts Pose Continuing Problems

Lies, Stonewalling, Cover-ups to Protect the Company Often Are a Way of Life

Indecent Burial of Bad News

The succinct prose of these *Wall Street Journal* headlines summarizes most of the problems public relations has with its own image; the story under the headlines described the activities of some people with the PR title who have contributed to that image.[66] PR's image also is tarnished by those who usurp the title:

> Chicago police picked up a prostitute in a bar for soliciting. She had been handing out cards with her name, phone number, and address. Below her name were printed two words: Public Relations.
>
> A minor Tammany Hall clubhouse politician in New York, with ties to a former local political leader, acted as the go-between in shady operations. On the door of his office appeared these words: Public Relations.
>
> In Washington, a former administrative assistant to a congressman entertained politicians and tried to influence their views on pending legislation without registering as a lobbyist. His letterhead carried the words: Public Relations.
>
> A former newspaperman in Los Angeles was the liaison between the head of a corporation and pol-

iticians in the California Legislature, arriving with his little black bag at the right moment before campaigns. He listed himself as a public relations counsel.

> There is no restriction on the use of the words "public relations." Anyone can use them. And all sorts of characters do, without performing any of the functions normally associated with the practice of public relations. They are usually the fringe people who, for the lack of another title for their work, are happy to use "public relations."[67]

If a client wants to hire a PR practitioner, what assurance does the client have that the practitioner is ethical and responsible? Should there be a licensing procedure for PR, with education, testing and preliminary practice as prerequisites, as in the legal and medical professions? Or should there be something similar to the accounting profession's certification (CPA—Certified Public Accountant)? The advantage of licensing is that it would establish a level of competence or professionalism among public relations practitioners.

Just as the CPA has not eliminated the uncertified public accountant and auditor, so there could be licensed and unlicensed PR people, with the qualifications for each being vastly different. Edward L. Bernays's argument for licensing is that only through controlled entry into and exit from the practice of public relations can PR become a profession:

> Licensing can be accomplished with ease, without in any way infringing on the rights guaranteed by the First Amendment. Lawyers, for instance, are licensed and their freedom of speech is guaranteed by the United States Constitution. So are medical doctors free to speak their minds on any subject. I have taken this question up with lawyers and they assure me that this amendment in the Bill of Rights cannot be infringed upon.
>
> Self-licensing is of no use in assuring that standards be maintained. Self-licensing carries no legal sanctions with it. In the case of doctors and lawyers, misbehavior brings legal sanction by the state, disbarment or other sanctions.
>
> As for the licensing, the same procedure would be followed as is the case with doctors and law-

yers. The state appoints a committee of a Board of Examiners chosen from the profession. The law would stipulate that this group draw up an examination which a practitioner would have to pass. This same board from the profession would, as in the case of doctors and lawyers, serve as the body to inflict punishment as necessary.

As far as the practitioners now practicing, they would have the right to continue to practice. Under the circumstances it would take a generation to change the present situation. But all new practitioners would have to go through the formal procedure. The various educational programs now in existence would, however—in deference to the examinations taking place in each state—obviously have to change their course so that the graduating students would be able to pass the examination.

I have read several good books on the history of the professions. They state that in the early nineteenth century a number of new professions, like civil, electrical, other engineering, needed to protect the public from imposters as well as to ensure standards within their own profession. They asked the state for licensing, registration and legal sanctions. Thus, licensing, registration and legal sanctions became the practice in England and spread to the U.S. Today there are no standards set for public relations practitioners. Any paper hanger can call himself or herself a public relations practitioner. And often does.

Licensing, registration and legal sanctions set up standards and protect the profession and the public alike.

It would be easy for one state to adopt the practice, and it would spread to the satisfaction of profession and public alike.[68]

However, many people who come into PR from a news media background feel that, if public relations were licensed, a move to license newspeople would not be far behind. Moreover, they argue that an accreditation format already exists in the Public Relations Society of America's program requiring experience, testing and the approval of other professionals. And they point out that even that program has resulted in few members being accredited. (Somewhat more than 3,700 current members of PRSA are accredited, and through the

▼ **Lack of formal control over use of the title** *public relations* **leads to abuses and raises the question of licensing.**

years more than 4,500 have been accredited. Currently PRSA membership is over 15,000.)

Most significant in terms of ethics is the fact that few cases of censure and suspension have occurred, although nearly eighty grievances have been filed. Members of PRSA are governed by a Code of Professional Standards. Violations of that code may be called to the attention of the association's Grievance Board for action to be taken against the offender. Since the PRSA code was adopted in 1954 (revised from a 1950 Code of Ethics), only four people have been suspended (although two others resigned while being investigated). Four others have been censured and nine have been reprimanded, as of 1990.

Additionally, the International Association of Business Communicators (IABC), which also includes many PR practitioners, has an accreditation process. The merits of the two accrediting processes have been examined by committees in both organizations and found wanting; but as one executive put it, "It's all we have." Accrediting processes serve to identify practitioners recognized by their peers through written and oral examinations to be qualified to practice public relations. Policing members' standards of practice provides an internal check against malpractice. Even if members are denied continued association status, however, they still can practice public relations.

Not everyone in the field, of course, argues for licensing. Many, indeed, oppose it. According to critics of licensing, it would have various damaging effects on the best interest of the public: the power to deny or revoke a license would be abused; state licensing would deprive people in less populated areas of public relations practitioners; state licensing would stifle out-of-state competition, lead to parochial practices, create boundaries where none now exist and complicate the national practice of

EXAMPLE 8.3

Business Ethics: What Are Your Personal Standards?

Hard work, fairness and honesty were the values we grew up with, but do they exist today? Influence peddling in Washington, insider-trading scandals and fraud among TV ministers are common headline themes. Are there similarly unsavory developments in the average office, store or hospital? This confidential questionnaire was used by *Working Woman* magazine to measure how its readers would make the tough choices business people make on a daily basis.

OFFICE DILEMMAS: WHAT IF . . .

1. *One of your associates obtains a confidential report from a competitor. It contains information crucial to your sales effort. You . . .*

Return it to your associate, saying it is unethical to take such information □
Read it and use it □

2. *Some of the doctors you work with prescribe an expensive brand of medication even though cheaper ones are available. You suspect it is because the manufacturer regularly treats them to expensive entertainment. You . . .*

Blow the whistle to the local standards board □
Say nothing □

3. *One of the purchasing agents you sell to makes very sexist comments to you. He buys more of your product than other companies do and gives you a good price. You . . .*

Stop selling to the sexist purchasing agent □
Sell to the sexist purchasing agent □

4. *You have to pick up your child from school early even though you have an important meeting at work. This has happened four times in the last month. You . . .*

Make up an excuse □
Tell your boss the truth □

5. *The doctors in your unit routinely overcharge for their services. The government makes them resubmit many bills, but some get through. You . . .*

Do nothing □
Report them □

6. *You've been working late and on weekends. Recently you had lunch with an old friend and picked up the tab. When the bill comes you . . .*

Put it on your next expense account □
Write a personal check □

7. *Your boss confides that your company will relocate to another state. Fellow employees ask you to confirm or deny rumors. You . . .*

Tell them the truth in confidence, even though the company may suffer and you could be fired □
Keep quiet until the official announcement □

8. *One of your employees is a heavy drinker. You have never seen her drunk at work, but it could be a problem. You . . .*

Fire her rather than risk insurance problems □
Tell her to stop drinking or else risk dismissal □

CODES OF ETHICS

1. *Do you feel business ethics have become worse, improved or stayed the same over the last ten years?*

Become worse □
Improved □
Stayed the same □

2. *In your opinion, do the huge sums of money on Wall Street corrupt people?*

Yes, money corrupts □
No, the people were originally corrupt □

3. *Which of the following kinds of ethical violations have you observed where you work?* (Check as many as apply.)

Lying to employees □
Expense-account abuses □
Violating confidentiality □
Bribery □
Sexual harassment □
Lying to make a sale □
Taking credit for others' work □

Favoritism/Nepotism ☐
Discrimination ☐

4. *How do you react when you see unethical behavior at work?*
Report it to superiors ☐
Report it anonymously ☐
Confront the person but don't report it ☐
Do nothing ☐
Never happens ☐

5. *How often are the ethics of business decisions discussed where you work? Are they informal or formal discussions?*

	Informal	Formal
Very often	☐	☐
Sometimes	☐	☐
When a problem arises	☐	☐
Seldom/Never	☐	☐

6. *Is there a written code of ethics where you work?*
Yes ☐
No ☐
Don't know ☐

7. *If there is no written code of ethics, do you think one would be useful?*
Yes, it would be useful ☐
No, it would not be useful ☐
No, it is not necessary ☐

8. *Please indicate where you learned to make ethical decisions on the job.* (Check as many as apply.) *Which one* was most influential?

	Where Learned	Most Influential
Family	☐	☐
Religion	☐	☐
College (general)	☐	☐
College business class	☐	☐
Friends	☐	☐
Business colleagues	☐	☐
Books, magazines or newspapers	☐	☐
Special course on ethics	☐	☐
Boss	☐	☐
Nowhere in particular	☐	☐

9. *Have you ever worked for a company or institution that got into trouble over ethical violations?*
Yes ☐
No ☐
Don't know ☐

YOUR VALUES

Here are some statements people sometimes make about business. Please circle the number that indicates how strongly you agree or disagree with each statement.

a. *The question of right or wrong depends on the particular business situation.*

Strongly agree		Neither		Strongly disagree
1	2	3	4	5

b. *Sometimes it is necessary to break the rules to get ahead.*

1	2	3	4	5

c. *Most successful people occasionally have to compromise their principles.*

1	2	3	4	5

d. *If business cannot operate ethically, it should be regulated by government.*

1	2	3	4	5

e. *Most women are more ethical than most men.*

1	2	3	4	5

f. *Most business people basically are honest.*

1	2	3	4	5

g. *The bottom line is the only standard for judging a business.*

1	2	3	4	5

h. *There are absolute ethical standards that every business should adhere to.*

1	2	3	4	5

(Continued)

EXAMPLE 8.3

Business Ethics: What Are Your Personal Standards? (*continued*)

INDUSTRY STANDARDS

1. *Here is a list of various occupational groups. Which ones do you feel have the greatest incidence of unethical behavior?* (Check up to three.)

Banking ☐ Manufacturing ☐
Finance ☐ Media ☐
Government ☐ Medicine ☐
Law ☐ Sales ☐

2. *Suppose you are job hunting. Would you work for any of the following?*

	Yes	No	Maybe
An energy company with a history of environmental accidents	☐	☐	☐
A manufacturer with a bad worker-safety record	☐	☐	☐
A financial company indicted for insider trading	☐	☐	☐
A law firm that defends known racketeers	☐	☐	☐
A cigarette manufacturer	☐	☐	☐

3. *One of your employees has purchased a top secret report from a competitor's company without your knowledge. What do you do when you find out?* (Check as many as apply.)

Fire the employee ☐
Reprimand the employee ☐
Reward the employee ☐
Do nothing ☐
Send back the report ☐
Keep the report ☐

4. *You have a close friend in a competing company. You occasionally trade information about company products and plans. This is . . .*

A major ethical violation ☐
A minor ethical violation ☐
Not a problem ☐

SEX AND THE WORKPLACE

Here are some situations involving sexual behavior. Please indicate which ones you are aware of in your workplace. Also tell us whether they are major or minor violations or if they have nothing to do with business ethics.

	Aware of	Major	Minor	No Problem
Flirting to make a sale	☐	☐	☐	☐
Having sex with clients to make a sale	☐	☐	☐	☐
Doing business with clients who are sexist	☐	☐	☐	☐
Having sex with co-workers on company time	☐	☐	☐	☐
Becoming sexually intimate with the boss	☐	☐	☐	☐

THE PROBLEM WITH PERKS

1. *Please indicate whether you consider each of the following a serious problem, a minor problem or not an ethical problem at work.*

	Serious	Minor	No Problem
Taking office supplies home	☐	☐	☐
Copying computer software for personal use	☐	☐	☐
Making personal calls on a company phone	☐	☐	☐
Calling in sick when you need a mental-health day	☐	☐	☐

Sharing company
   discounts with a friend ☐ ☐ ☐
Padding expense
   accounts ☐ ☐ ☐

2. *At what level does entertainment or a gift become a bribe?*

$25 to $49 ☐
$50 to $99 ☐
$100 to $499 ☐
$500+ ☐
None; any gift that achieves its purpose is
   acceptable ☐

WHAT IS ETHICAL?

Please indicate how you feel about each of the following situations. (Circle the appropriate number.)

a. *Your boss secretly treats her best clients to cocaine.*

Illegal	Unethical	Neutral	Acceptable Practice	Good Idea
1	2	3	4	5

b. *An account exec refuses to attend an important client's party because she feels uncomfortable about the amount of drinking.*

1   2   3   4   5

c. *An administrative assistant routinely makes up excuses for her boss when he takes long lunches with his secretary.*

1   2   3   4   5

d. *A public-relations officer makes the financial picture of her company appear rosier by withholding critical information.*

1   2   3   4   5

e. *A real-estate agent is showing a house. She doesn't point out that the basement floods.*

1   2   3   4   5

f. *A manager has accumulated many sick days. She takes a few days off and calls in sick.*

1   2   3   4   5

g. *A procurement officer recommends her brother-in-law's company for one of her projects without revealing the connection to her boss.*

1   2   3   4   5

h. *A book publisher gives his college-age niece a highly sought-after unpaid summer internship.*

1   2   3   4   5

i. *An executive learns that his company is about to be sold, which is bound to send its stock price soaring. He leaks the information to two of his biggest clients as well as to several friends.*

1   2   3   4   5

j. *After a year of poor sales, a sales representative convinces her boss to let her give expensive gifts to prospective clients. The tactic works, and sales increase.*

1   2   3   4   5

k. *Company policy forbids employees to discuss their salaries. But two people trade information to negotiate better with their boss.*

1   2   3   4   5

l. *A job applicant finds out the morning before her job interview that she is pregnant. She decides not to say anything rather than jeopardize her chances.*

1   2   3   4   5

(Continued)

EXAMPLE 8.3

Business Ethics: What Are Your Personal Standards? (*continued*)

SUCCESS AND SATISFACTION

1. *Altogether, how many years have you worked full-time?* _____

2. *Overall, how successful have you been over the course of your career?*

Consistently successful	☐
Mostly successful	☐
Some ups and some downs	☐
Mostly unsuccessful	☐
Consistently unsuccessful	☐

3. *Please circle the number that indicates how satisfied you are by your job.*

Very unsatisfied   **Very satisfied**

1   2   3   4   5

4. *How successful are you at your current job?*

Very unsuccessful   **Very successful**

1   2   3   4   5

5. *Overall, how satisfied are you with your life?*

Very unsatisfied   **Very satisfied**

1   2   3   4   5

6. *Have you ever taken an ethical stance that has affected your career? If so, was the effect positive or negative?*

Yes–positive	☐
Yes–negative	☐
No	☐

7. *Have you ever been accused of making a bad ethical decision at work?*

Yes, I was fired	☐
Yes, I was given a hard time	☐
No, never happened	☐

8. *What kinds of ethical decisions in your job make you most uncomfortable?*

_____

_____

_____

INFORMATION, PLEASE

1. *How old are you?* _____

2. *Your sex?*   Female ☐   Male ☐

3. *What is your marital status?*

Single	☐
Single, living with partner	☐
Separated, divorced, widowed	☐
Married or remarried	☐

Your age at first marriage: _____

4. *What is the highest level of education you have completed?* _____

5. *Are you employed . . .*

Full-time?	☐
Part-time?	☐
Not currently employed	☐

6. *What is your occupation?* _____

7. *What is your title?* _____

8. *Do you work for yourself or someone else?*

Self-employed	☐
Partnership	☐
Work for others	☐

9. *What is your total annual income? If you are married or living with someone, what is your partner's total annual income?*

	Mine	Partner's
Less than $9,999	☐	☐
$10,000 to $19,999	☐	☐
$20,000 to $29,999	☐	☐
$30,000 to $44,999	☐	☐
$45,000 to $59,999	☐	☐
$60,000 to $74,999	☐	☐
$75,000 to $99,999	☐	☐
$100,000 to $149,999	☐	☐
$150,000 or more	☐	☐

10. *What is your zip code?* _____

Reprinted with permission from *Working Woman* magazine. Copyright © 1990 by WWT Partnership.

public relations; people would take other titles to avoid the licensing laws. There are several major practical barriers to licensing, such as defining and enforcing what is permissible, agreeing on a definition of PR practice and a body of knowledge, deciding who will do the enforcing and deciding who needs to be licensed. Licensing would hurt the growth of the field by restricting and confining entry into the profession, and it wouldn't necessarily keep out unethical practitioners.

Meanwhile, public relations and its practitioners continue to attract public attention. One public relations practitioner attracted *Newsweek*'s attention with his client charges: no publicity, no charge. But rates for articles varied, according to the prominence of the medium: a *USA Today* piece would cost a client $7,710, while a piece in the *New York Times* would run $8,830. Since his charging philosophy violates several ethical codes, Reed Trencher's firm, Primetime, gets bad marks from PR practitioners. *Newsweek*'s writers, though, took a different view:

> Primetime's fee scale is a reminder of how easily they [journalists] can be manipulated. By some estimates, half of all stories are pitched by publicists, though it's impossible to get journalists to admit to a fraction of that . . . Perhaps the best thing to be said for the Trencher system is that it could weed out the overgrown PR industry . . . Even a minor league reporter has a desk jammed with unopened mail. If more clients started billing for performance, many publicists—no longer paid for just "trying"—might go out of business, and the appalling undergraduate courses in PR at universities would wither. Without the clutter, the good stories peddled by publicists might make it through. More important, lazy journalists would be forced to think of more on their own.[69]

Some PR firms deal in influence peddling rather than in information peddling. The most visible person in this category during 1987 was President Reagan's former chief of staff Michael Deaver, who was charged with lying to Congress. In a separate case, he was charged by a grand jury with illegal lobbying activities. The 1978 Ethics in Government Act bars any high-ranking government official from trying to influence former associates for one year after leaving office.

Because of Deaver's prominence, the indictment was embarrassing to the public relations industry. But the worst had already happened: the president of the Public Relations Society of America had been accused of insider trading. To make matters even worse, most PRSA members heard of it for the first time on the front page of the September 26, 1986, edition of the *Wall Street Journal* (see Example 8.4).

Canadians had a similar problem in 1987 when the former president of the Canadian Public Relations Society, William W. Wall, was accused by the Ontario Securities Commission of violating the Ontario Securities Act. He was responsible for news releases indicating that Calgroup Graphics Corporation would get $18 million in financing from the U.S.-based Midata Management Corporation for the production of two films. When no more information about the deal arrived, trading was stopped.

Reciprocal Trust

An area of major importance in PR involves keeping confidences with the media and with other publics. For example, a reporter on the trail of a story deserves the exclusive he or she is ingenious enough to seek; a PR practitioner should not pull the rug out by offering a general release before the reporter has had an opportunity to use the material. Also, a news medium has the right to expect a practitioner to be entirely aboveboard in offering information. Feature ideas, suggestions and pictures should be offered on an "exclusive use" basis. Certainly magazine editors expect stories and pictures submitted to be exclusives. A magazine editor who finds the same or a similar story in another magazine will never trust you again.

A story issued in printed form "for general release" notifies an editor that other news media have the story. However, a story marked "Special to the Banner" should be just that. No other news medium in that circulation area should receive the

EXAMPLE 8.4

The Tony Franco Affair

This is a story, to borrow from from the *Wall Street Journal* account, of "how PRSA, perhaps the nation's premier organization of communicators, and Mr. Franco, the top-dog flack of them all, somehow failed to communicate."

Anthony Franco, president of Michigan's largest PR firm, based in Detroit, met in his office June 11, 1985, with executives of a Detroit department store, Crowley, Milner & Co., which was about to be bought by a private investment company, OAC, for $50 a share. Franco was helping prepare an announcement of the sale.

A complaint (a civil and criminal action) from the Securities and Exchange Commission says that when Franco knew the sale was going through and would be announced publicly, he called his broker and told him to buy 3,000 shares of Crowley stock. The stock was bought the next day, June 12, at $41 a share, before the public announcement. It was the order's size that caught the attention of the American Stock Exchange, which then notified Crowley. When Crowley confronted Franco, he denied responsibility for the purchase, called the broker and asked him to rescind the trade, which the broker did. The SEC says Franco discussed with the broker how he "might avoid having to take responsibility for the media," but the broker declined to follow such an action.

The SEC investigation began on October 1985, but Franco did not tell PRSA or the Board of Ethics. He took office on January 1, 1986. In the spring he learned that the SEC was going to file charges. He told one PRSA associate but neither the associate nor Franco told other PRSA officers or members. In early August, Franco finally did tell David Ferguson, his immediate predecessor as PRSA president. Franco says he later told the two other PRSA officials that the SEC might file the charges. They say he swore them to secrecy on grounds that he and his family might be hurt if there were a leak. They were concerned about the legal implications. On August 26, the SEC formally filed charges. Some PRSA leaders found out that day; others read it in the newspapers. The next day, Franco resigned after signing a consent decree with the SEC.

No news release was ever issued because, according to PRSA leadership, Franco agreed to appear before PRSA's Board of Ethics on September 19, and that proceeding had to be kept confidential. Franco, however, resigned from PRSA that day.

On September 11, president-elect Jack Felton did send a letter to PRSA's membership saying he that was president and telling them about Franco's resignation, but he had asked Ferguson to take over until the crisis was resolved so that he could learn his work obligations.

The whole story serves as an example of how difficult it is to practice what we preach, and a lesson in how dreadful the results can be (in the news media and in loss of credibility) when we don't.

SOURCE: Drawn, in part, from Joanne Lipman, "PR Society Receives Some Bad PR from Ex Chief Anthony Franco, *Wall Street Journal* (Sept. 26, 1986), pp. 1, 16.

---

story. (If you send it to other newspapers, you should let the editor know.) The quickest way to destroy your welcome in the newsroom is to plant the same story all over the place. Even if the same story is given to the morning and evening editions of the same newspaper, you are in trouble.

Each deserves different stories with different approaches. The best way to do this is to take separate stories to one person at each newspaper. Decide where each story would most appropriately appear or who on the paper would most likely be interested. If it is a column item and more than one newspaper is involved, you should determine which columnist would be most likely to use the piece and plant it there—only there.

News media should also be able to trust you to have cleared publicity pictures submitted to them by securing a release from those who posed. They should also be able to trust you to protect them from copyright complications and libel and lottery laws that can be violated in publicity copy.

When you supply news to the media, you are bound, ethically and morally, just as they are, by the codes to which their members subscribe. By the same token, the news media owe public relations practioners a responsibility to honor agreed-upon release dates and times. Most do. If a story breaks earlier than designated, try to discover why. Often it is an accident. However, if a publication frequently has "accidents," don't give future stories to that publication until there is no jeopardy to your client. Do this quietly, without any warning and certainly without threats. It won't take the publication long to figure out what is happening and why.

Crisis situations are the most trying for relationships because both sides are under pressure and both sides are generally frustrated. Journalists accuse PR people of misrepresentation and covering up information. PR people accuse reporters of bias and inaccuracies. Part of the problem resides in how the "truth" appears to each side. PR commentator and practitioner David Finn has observed:

> One of the most disturbing discoveries public relations people can make about themselves is that learning "the facts" doesn't always tell them what

they should believe. As citizens and readers of newspapers and television viewers, they have opinions on as many things as anybody else.

But sometimes their convictions run counter to positions held by a client. Then they study "the facts" and listen to what their client's experts have to say, and those passionate convictions become surprisingly less convincing. They see another point of view and find it more persuasive than they imagined.

The first time this happens, public relations people don't mind admitting they might have been wrong. But when it happens again and again they begin to wonder whether any point of view can be supported by a given set of facts and a particular group of experts. And they fear that a lifetime of listening to all the experts who support their clients' positions weakens their capacity to make independent judgments.[70]

The question of corruption of judgment is a serious one for public relations people. Often the heart of a dispute is not over facts but over the interpretation of facts and over conflicting value systems. In these situations, the best guide for the PR person is to return to the formula for socially responsible public relations decision making. Who are the publics? What are the interests of each in the decision or situation? How will an institution's policy, position or action affect each of these publics? What social values are involved? What values are in conflict? What will the effects be? Can the effects be defended? The PR person who loses the public's perspective has forgone public responsibility and become the persuaded instead of the persuader.

▼ SUMMARY

Ethics are founded on moral principles that are themselves grounded in effects—what happens as a result of what you do or don't do. You and the organizations you work for are judged in three areas: ethics, social responsibility and financial responsibility. An organization's sense of commitment to its publics (which often have conflicting interests) has to be articulated and demonstrated. But the idea that an organization should be held accountable to its publics is not new. The nation's first corporate vice-president of public relations, Arthur Page of AT&T, set forth some ethical guidelines as early as 1927.

The notion that public relations counsel should be the conscience of management is unfortunate, because public relations has a difficult time functioning effectively and ethically if management creates and sanctions a poor moral climate. Unfortunately, many people feel little obligation to ethical standards, and some studies of young people's principles of conduct suggest that they fall below generally accepted American standards for moral behavior.

Some managements are not much better. They tend to ignore problems until publicity calls attention to them in such a way that they can't be ignored. Then, when the public takes the problem to lawmakers, the managements complain that they are being unfairly treated. Finally, when laws are passed, they resume their role as "good citizens" and announce that they will obey the new rules.

As a result of public attention to unethical behavior, many organizations began writing codes of ethics, but some authorities believe that the CEO sets the management tone for ethical behavior, for better or worse. In a democratic society organizations exist with public consent, and their publics generally observe their credibility, their accountability and their responsibility.

The question is, "Responsibility to whom?" Public relations people can identify at least ten publics: clients, the news media, government agencies, educational institutions, consumers of information, stockholders and analysts, the community, competitors, critics and other public relations practitioners. Guidelines for a public relations person's own performance are provided in codes of ethical practice or professional standards.

Responsibility in practice includes dealing with research and persuasion, internal power struggles and foreign contacts whose cultural codes for ethical behavior might be quite different. The practitioner's responsibility in advertising and sponsorships includes protecting the client and the consumer—the latter in terms of products, politics and promotions. Closely related is the practitioner's responsibility in publicity, which includes behaving properly as a source, determining matters of tastefulness, handling financial relationships and maintaining clear lines between source and action. Political public relations presents some difficult challenges and includes areas of ambiguity, like handling PACs and working with news media, but codes offer professionals guidance in those areas.

Not all people who practice public relations are professionals, and in any case individuals have different interpretations of ethical responsibilities. Clearly, however, ethics and honesty don't offer the fast track to rewards. Instead, they must be seen as an investment in personal integrity and as a sign of professional performance.

▼ NOTES

[1]Ivan Hill, *Common Sense & Everyday Ethics* (Washington, D.C.: American Viewpoint, Ethics Resource Center), p. 5.

[2]John A. Koten, "Moving Toward Higher Standards for American Business," *Public Relations Review*, 12(3) (Fall 1986), p. 3.

[3]Ronald E. Rhody, "The Matter of Survival," speech to Public Relations Society of America Seminar, Palm Springs, California, June 26, 1990. (Reprinted by Bank of America Corporate Public Relations #3124, Bank of America, Box 37000, San Francisco, California 94127.)

[4]Amitai Etzioni, "Money, Power and Fame," *Newsweek* (September 18, 1989), p. 10.

[5]Sonia L. Nazario, "Schoolteachers Say It's Wrongheaded to Try to Teach Students What's Right," *Wall Street Journal* (April 6, 1990), p. B1.

[6]Davis Young, "Confronting the Ethical Issues That Confront You," presentation at PRSA National Conference, Professional Development Seminar, November 9–10, 1987, Los Angeles, California.

[7]Ibid.

[8]*pr reporter* (May 13, 1985), p. 2.

[9]Timothy D. Schellhardt, "What Bosses Think About Corporate Ethics," *Wall Street Journal* (April 6, 1988), p. 21.

[10]Archie B. Carroll, "Crisis in Ethics Faces American Business: Amorality No Longer Tenable in Modern Society," and "Amorality Distinguished from Immorality," *purview*, supplement to *pr reporter* (February 19, 1988), p. 1.

[11]Ibid.

[12]"Ethical Concerns of U.S. Business Offer Openings for PR Leadership but One-third Say Issue 'Overblown,' " *PR Strategies USA*, 1(1) (February 1–15, 1988), p. 2. (1545 New York Avenue, NE, Washington, DC 20002).

[13]Arthur W. Page, "The Page Philosophy" (Arthur Page Society, Inc., Room 19A, 225 West Randolph St., Chicago, Illinois 60606).

[14]Marvin Olasky, "Public Relations vs. Private Enterprise: An Enlightening History Which Raises Some Basic Questions," *Public Relations Quarterly*, 30(4) (Winter 1985–1986), pp. 6–13.

[15]David Finn, "Struggle for Ethics in Public Relations," *Harvard Business Review*, 12 (January–February 1959), pp. 9–11.

[16]Ibid.

[17]Ed Block, address to the Texas Public Relations Association, Kerrville, Texas, July 22, 1978.

[18]Hadley Cantril, *Understanding Man's Social Behavior* (Princeton, N.J.: Office of Public Opinion Research, 1947), p. 60.

[19]Hugh M. Culbertson, "How Public Relations Textbooks Handle Honesty and Lying," *Public Relations Review*, 9(2) (Summer 1983), pp. 65–73 (especially pp. 67, 68, 72).

[20]Sissela Bok, *Lying: Moral Choice in Public and Private Life* (New York: Pantheon Books, 1978).

[21]Earl Babbie, *The Practice of Social Science Research*, 5th ed. (Belmont, Calif.: Wadsworth, 1989), pp. 472–78.

[22]John Koten, "IRS Use of Mail-Order Lists Concerns Market Researchers," *Wall Street Journal* (March 8, 1984), p. 29. Also see Michael W. Miller, "Data Mills Delve Deep to Find Information About U.S. Consumers," *Wall Street Journal* (March 14, 1991), p. 1, A12.

[23]Michael Ryan, "Organization Constraints on Corporate Public Relations Practitioners," *Journalism Quarterly*, 64(2 & 3) (Summer–Autumn 1987), pp. 473–82.

[24]Ibid.

[25]For an interesting alternative view of the bribery problem in international business, as well as numerous cases highlighting other conflicts in overseas business (and PR) rela-

tions, see Lane and DiStefano, *International Management Behavior* (PWS-Kent, 1992).

[26]U.S. Department of State (1979), *Foreign Service Notebook*, Section xii, p. 1.

[27]James Buie, Maura Casey, Gregory Enns, Vandanna Mathur and Mark Williams with Richard T. Stout, "Foreign Governments Are Playing Our Press," *Washington Journalism Review* (October 1983), p. 23.

[28]"This Ad Is Brought to You by . . . ," *Wall Street Journal* (November 21, 1986), p. 31.

[29]*Wall Street Journal* (September 26, 1984), p. 31.

[30]Alix M. Freedman and Michael J. McCarthy, "New Smoke from RJR Under Fire," *Wall Street Journal* (February 20, 1990), pp. B1, B6.

[31]Hearings Before the Presidential Commission on the Assassination of President Kennedy, Vol. 18, Exhibit 1031 (Washington, D.C.: U.S. Government Printing Office, 1964), p. 835.

[32]Public Relations Society of America, *Code of Professional Standards for the Practice of Public Relations: An Official Interpretation of the Code as It Applies to Political Public Relations*, Precepts 1 and 2.

[33]Ibid., Precept 3.

[34]Ibid., Precept 4.

[35]Joanne Lipman, "Ads Convert Rejection into Free Publicity," *Wall Street Journal* (July 30, 1990), p. B4.

[36]Kelley Griffin, "Calcium Supplements. Boon or Boondoggle?" *Graduate Woman* (newsletter of American Association of University Women), 81(6), p. 12.

[37]Leslie N. Vreeland, "The Selling of Retin-A," *Money*, 18(4) (April 1989), pp. 75–87.

[38]Ibid.

[39]Jonathan Dahl, "Car-Rental Firms Leave Drivers Dazed by Rip-Offs, Options, Misleading Ads," *Wall Street Journal* (June 1, 1990), pp. B1, B8.

[40]Michael J. McCarthy, "Coca-Cola 'MagiCans' Go Poof After Just Three Weeks," *Wall Street Journal*, (June 1, 1990), pp. B1, B8.

[41]Scott Ward, "How Children Learn to Buy: The Development of Consumer Information-Processing Skills," People & Communication Series No. 1, Books on Demand, UMI.

[42]Eric J. Zanot, "The National Advertising Review Board, 1971–1976," Journalism Monographs 59, Association for Education in Journalism, February 1979.

[43]Ronald Alsop, "Advertisers Get Reprimanded for Saying 'Free' Too Freely," *Wall Street Journal* (March 26, 1987), p. 33.

[44]Jeanne Edwards, "Journalists and Public Call for Higher Ethical Standards," *Press Women*, 46(4) (April 1983), pp. 2–4.

[45]Ibid.

[46]Frank Winston Wylie, remarks at CASE conference, Los Angeles, January 30, 1989.

[47]William L. Rivers, *The Adversaries* (Boston: Beacon Press, 1969), pp. 157–64.

[48]Ronald Alsop, "Line Between Articles and Ads Is Fuzzy in These Magazines," *Wall Street Journal* (September 17, 1987), p. 31.

[49]Cynthia F. Mitchell, "The Big Promises of Some Air Fares Get Lost in a Tangle of Restrictions," *Wall Street Journal* (Nov. 7, 1985), p. 31.

[50]"Was Life/Death Drama Lure of Live TV Operation? Is That Voyeurism?" *pr reporter* (April 11, 1983), p. 1.

[51]James C. Clark, "Are Media Living an Illusion with Junket to Fantasyland?" *Fort Worth Star-Telegram* (September 20, 1981), p. 14A.

[52]Mac Seligman, "Travel Writers' Expenses: Who Should Pay," *Public Relations Journal* (May 1990), pp. 27, 28, 34. Also see Ed Avis, "Have Subsidy, Will Travel," *The Quill*, 79(2) (March 1991), pp. 20–25; Eric Hubler, "Freebies on the Tube," *The Quill*, 79(2) (March 1991), pp. 26–27.

[53]Elliot D. Lee, "It's All Relative: Mutual Funds Discover 'Socially Responsible' Is in Eye of Beholder," *Wall Street Journal* (May 20, 1987), p. 33.

[54]William B. Blankenburg, "The Adversaries and the News Ethic," *Public Relations Quarterly* 14(4) (Winter 1970) p. 31.

[55]James F. Haughton, *TV Guide* news releases, March 28, 1983.

[56]James McGregor, "Chinese Journalists Learn Value of PR, and Foreign Firms Use the Opportunity," *Wall Street Journal* (October 21, 1991), p. A17.

[57]Owen Ullmann, "Speakes Quits at Brokerage in Wake of Flap over Concocted Quotes," *Dallas Morning News* (April 16, 1988), p. 3A.

[58]John L. Fialka, "Mr. Kissinger Has Opinions on China and Business Ties," *Wall Street Journal* (September 15, 1989), pp. 1, A7.

[59]David Finn, "The Business-Media Relationship, Countering Misconceptions and Distrust" (New York: AMACOM, 1981).

[60]Tom Wicker, *The Right to Know: An Unending Battle* (Tucson, Ariz.: University of Arizona Press, 1984).

[61]Alecia Swasy, "Commercial Tie-ins Muddy Earth Day Observance," *Wall Street Journal* (April 15, 1991), p. B1.

[62]Ginny Carroll, "Green for Sale," *National Wildlife*, 29(2) (February–March 1991), p. 24.

[63]Frank Edward Allen, "McDonald's to Reduce Waste in Plan Developed with Environmental Group," *Wall Street Journal* (April 17, 1991), pp. B1, B6.

[64]Amanda Bennett, "Doing the 'Right' Thing Has Its Repercussions," *Wall Street Journal* (January 25, 1990), p. B1.

[65]Amar Bhide and Howard H. Stevenson, "Why Be Honest if Honesty Doesn't Pay?" *Harvard Business Review*, 67(5) (September–October 1990) pp. 121–29.

[66]Jim Montgomery, "The Image Makers: In Public Relations, Ethical Conflicts Pose Continuing Problems," *Wall Street Journal* (August 1, 1979), p. 1.

[67]L. L. L. Golden, *Only by Public Consent* (Melbourne: Hawthorn Books), p. 327.

[68]Edward L. Bernays, letter to Doug Newsom, August 1984.

[69]Johnathan Alter, with Pamela Abrahamson, "Is This Article Worth $19,260?" *Newsweek* (April 20, 1987), p. 77.

[70]David Finn, "Medium Isn't Always the Message," *Dallas Morning News* (May 21, 1981), p. 4D.

Selected readings, assignments and activities appropriate to this chapter can be found in the *Instructor's Guide*.

▼

Laws Affecting PR Practice

Law: a mousetrap easy to enter, but not easy to get out of.

Francis Maitland Balfour

The law is the last result of human wisdom acting upon human experience for the benefit of the public.

Samuel Johnson, *Miscellanies*

You've been asked to write a publicity release that downplays your organization's financial crisis. Can you do that?

One of your clients spent a lot of money for a distinctive logo that you promoted with stories in the trade press describing its development. Now you find an advertisement in *Wall Street Journal* for an organization with a logo very similar to your client's. What can you do?

You've been asked to write the script for an infomercial (a program-length commercial) that mimics a talk show program to the extent of simulating "commercial breaks." You don't know anything about the product or the doctor being "interviewed" on this infomercial—other than what you've been given by your boss. Can you write the script?

Your lawyer client calls to tell you that she's just completed a week of special seminars and received a certificate. She wants to know if she can add the certification to the letterhead of the stationery you helped design for her. What do you tell her?

You're trying to create a full-page ad for a special newspaper section that will call attention to the annual outdoor sports event you handle. Thus, you need a photo of people attending an event that has yet to occur. Last year's news coverage included a good picture of a couple inflating a raft. Can you use the picture?

Your organization's human resources person calls to ask if you have model releases for the pictures of employees used in the last magazine. One

▼ PR people's involvement with law may be categorized as normal legal exposure, work-oriented legal exposure and extraneous legal exposure.

of those pictured doesn't work for your organization any more. You don't have a release. Is this a problem?

These are all legal questions that PR practitioners encounter. Because such questions sometimes catch them unaware, it's wise to have a close working relationship with the organization's attorney. Indeed, most public relations practitioners in independent practice have their own attorneys. Of course, sometimes the legal difficulties PR people encounter are of their own making.

In the late 1980s the president of PRSA was accused of insider trading, and the first PR firm in history was charged with the same offense. Because PR people are faced with countless temptations, the practice of public relations is a legal minefield.

▼ THE LIABILITIES OF PRACTICING PR

PR practitioners are more conscious than ever of their legal exposure. An Oklahoma City counselor says he now buys malpractice insurance, a business expense he never considered until the mid-1970s. The policy is his reponse to three areas of exposure identified by attorney Morton Simon: (1) *normal legal exposure*, like that encountered by any other person, encompassing civil and criminal matters, including conspiracy; (2) *work-oriented legal exposure*, such as that found in the course of normal PR or publicity activities; (3) *extraneous legal exposure*, including everything from testifying as an expert witness to getting sports event tickets for a client to lobbying without registering as a lobbyist or reporting income and expenses from such activities. This third category also includes allowing the corporation to use the public relations office as

a conduit for illegal corporate political contributions and, in the international arena, allowiing it to use the PR office as the locus for bribes or other illicit activities.[1]

Legal Problems: Civil and Criminal

Civil suits involving PR practitioners may occur in relation to communication activities—for example, copyright infringements—or physical activities, such as accidents during plant tours. In addition, the practitioner may have statutory and administrative liability in connection with dealings with government administrative agencies (SEC, FTC, FDA, ICC and others). A publicity release, for example, may violate SEC regulations, cause the company's stock to be closed for trading and result in court action. A carelessly worded ad can result in fines and perhaps court action. The statutory responsibilities are substantial. Sometimes a civil case is the result of failing to do something required as a matter of compliance, rather than doing something wrong—failing to disclose information, for example. Or it might be an entirely internal matter, such as a letter to employees advocating management's position on a unionization effort. The NLRB takes a dim view of persuasive communications that sound coercive.

More so than ordinary citizens, PR practitioners are also exposed to many opportunities for **criminal** actions such as bribery, price fixing, mail fraud, securities manipulation, and even perjury. To yield to these opportunities, however, is to risk criminal charges, particularly for conspiracy. It is imperative, therefore, to understand the PR person's legal standing as the agent of the client. As Simon explains:

> Whatever the PR practitioner does, he usually does by reason of his retainer by his client and in concert with the client. Joint or multiparty action is therefore almost indigenous to the PR function. This is the root of the conspiracy charge.[2]

Simon lists five instances in which a PR practitioner can be found liable to a conspiracy charge. These occur when the practitioner (1) participates in the illegal action; (2) counsels, guides and directs the policy behind it; (3) takes a large personal part in it; (4) sets up a propaganda agency to fight enemies of it; or (5) cooperates to further it.

Legal Cases

Simon suggests that PR practitioners are usually involved in four specific kinds of cases: the big case, the human interest case, the routine case and testimony. The *big case*, as he describes it,

> may be antitrust action directed at [a company's] entire marketing program, a labor relations hearing involving thousands of employees, suits involving product liability—especially those which deal with basic safety or acceptability of a product—minority stockholders' actions charging mismanagement or fraud, and other litigation basic to the continued success of the company.[3]

The *human interest* case may not involve much money, but by its nature it has a particular appeal to the news media. Simon lists the following examples:

> a minor civil rights charge, a local zoning conflict, a right of privacy suit by a "glamour name," air or water pollution charges, suits against a company by a retired employee seeking a large pension, and myriad other kinds of litigation which may concern either an individual or some community interest.

The *routine* types of litigation are commonplace results of being in business. They include "actions for breach of contract, workmen's compensation claims, tax refund matters." Routine suits rarely involve such public relations activities as the preparation of documents, publicity releases or media conferences for executives. Therefore, most routine litigation is unlikely to need staff PR involvement or the PR firm's help (if the company is a client). Of course, the PR person who owns a firm or works as a consultant is subject as such to all the routine and normal potential litigation of being in business.

▼ **PR practitioners are more likely than the average citizen to get involved in conspiracy charges (such as for bribery, price fixing, mail fraud, securities manipulation and perjury).**

Cases calling for a PR person's *testimony* typically involve his or her participation in the company program at issue in the legal action or his or her status as an "expert" witness. These may vary from "cases growing out of preparation of the company president's statement before a congressional committee to a $200 supplier claim for tables and chairs used at a company picnic." Cases may also involve a high-profile client or a company executive accused of some illegal act.

Working with Legal Counsel

Most large institutions, businesses and news media have legal counsel. If your client retains legal help, use it. The client's own counselor is as eager to stay out of trouble as you are. One word of caution, though. Some attorneys are not knowledgeable in communications law, and their instinct is to have a client or the organization say nothing. This is usually not the best public relations response. You need to know where to go for specialized legal counsel.

Many practitioners have also built up libraries of cases and regulations relating to both public relations and their clients. In addition, many PR firms have prepared manuals for their employees to alert them to legal trouble spots. Clients, too, may have manuals; the PR person should ask for them and examine them carefully for areas where misunderstandings might create problems.

The public relations person within a corporation needs to establish a liaison with the corporate attorney, advises Morton Simon. Simon suggests that some CEOs ask PR practitioners to do "Machiavellian" things because they don't understand what a PR person is supposed to do, because so many "loose" descriptions of the PR job are floating around and because PR activities are difficult to define.[4]

David Simon, president of Simon Public Relations in San Francisco, offers another reason.[5] The top PR person now holds a seat within inner management councils, helping to formulate policy that will affect the organization's various publics, with special concern for how that policy will be understood and accepted by those publics. Therefore, the corporate PR person is in a good position to assist corporate counsel in planning strategies and suggesting how the various publics are likely to receive legal actions. The PR person also needs legal counsel's help, especially in reviewing financial materials. For these reasons, the relationship between the two needs to be complementary, not adversarial.

Ways to Stay Out of Trouble

Maintaining a good relationship with the organization's attorney is one of the best ways to stay out of trouble, but attorney Morton Simon identifies others:

1. Recognize your individual responsibility for your actions—none of this "I only did what the boss said." The law won't look at it that way.

2. Know your business.

3. Ignore the vague lines between advertising and PR, because the law often does.

4. Decide how far you are willing to go to run a risk of jail, fine, a cease and desist order or a corrective order.

5. "Know your enemy," especially which government agency is likely to go after you. It helps to get on the agency's mailing list and read all speeches its administrators give. Often these may provide the first hint of troubles for your company or industry.

Recognizing Troublesome Areas Can Keep You Alert to Potential Problems   Simon notes three general types of legal involvements. The first

consists of meeting federal, state and local government agencies' regulations on everything from antitrust matters to building permits.

The second consists of *government-related activities*—activities that hinge on laws or regulations such as libel and slander; right of privacy; contempt of court; ownership of ideas including copyright, trademarks and patents; publicity; political views, registering political activity as lobbying and representing foreign governments; contract disputes; stockholder actions; fair trade problems; use of photos of individuals and groups; preparation of publicity releases, advertising copy, games and giveaway promotions; and financial collections.

The third type consists of *contracts* with clients and suppliers of goods and services. These deal with such matters as who owns the music for a commercial jingle if the client moves his or her account from the agency that created the commercial and what recourse you have if the photographer you hired to make enlargements messes up the color negatives you provided.[6]

In any of these three types of cases, a PR person *outside* the situation is likely to be called by either side as an expert witness. When this occurs, you must devote considerable time to research—gathering facts in the case, not relying just on what you are told. (Most PR testimony consists of fact finding, in the discovery part of litigation.) Additionally, most PR people alert their own attorney, who can advise them of any legal traps or personal jeopardy. Litigants generally pay fees for expert witnesses. However, excessive fees tend to invalidate the testimony. (The opposition generally tries to get the precise sum made public, usually as a part of the deposition.)

Danger Zones   The greatest legal danger zones to a PR person are business memos, letters and proxy fights; use of photos; product claims; accusations that might be ruled libel or slander; promotions involving games; publicity that might result in charges of misrepresentation; and political campaigns. You should keep handy a checklist of laws covering areas such as contracts, releases, statements of responsibility and rights of privacy.

Most important, don't guess. Get legal assistance. Talk with the organization's legal counsel. Work closely with media and organization attorneys. The New York Stock Exchange encourages calls and other inquiries. Query any government body involved, and get a statement of legal precedent or request an informal ruling. Get advice from the Public Relations Society of America.

▼ GOVERNMENT REGULATIONS

As a practitioner, you may find yourself working with any of hundreds of government agencies. Of this multitude, five are particularly important: the Postal Service, the Securities and Exchange Commission (SEC), the Federal Trade Commission (FTC), the Food and Drug Administration (FDA) and the Federal Communications Commission (FCC).

Postal Service

Postal Service regulations prohibit dissemination by mail of obscene materials, information about a lottery (two important elements: consideration and chance) and material that would incite riot, murder, arson or assassination. A 1975 law exempts newspapers and broadcast stations from prosecution in publicizing state-operated lotteries. However, newspapers may not carry information on another state's lotteries in editions that are mailed.

Certain state laws prohibit the circulation of magazines carrying particular types of advertising, so space buyers have to beware. Furthermore, although substantial specifications exist for inserts in second-class magazines, the total reference to the subject in the *Postal Service Manual* with respect to controlled-circulation publications is one sentence: "Enclosures are not permitted."

All mailing pieces face multiple regulations regarding size, weight, thickness and where an address may appear. It is best to have the design of a piece checked by the post office, or to use standard shapes and weights already approved.

▼ **Many general PR activities fall under the purview of one or more of five government entities: the Postal Service, the Securities and Exchange Commission (SEC), the Federal Trade Commission (FTC), the Food and Drug Administration (FDA) and the Federal Communications Commission (FCC).**

A sender's freedom to reach publics by direct mail has been limited by a 1970 decision in a U.S. District Court, which has been upheld by the U.S. Supreme Court.[7] Senders may be compelled to delete an address from their mailing list and may be prohibited by law from sending or having an agent send future mailings to an addressee at the addressee's request.

The case began when a mail-order business challenged a California regulation stating that the recipient has a right not to have to receive "a pandering advertisement which offers for sale matter which addressee in his sole discretion believes to be erotically arousing or sexually provocative." If a violation occurs, the addressee may report it and the Postmaster General will inform the sender, who then has an opportunity to respond. An administrative hearing is held to see whether a violation has occurred. The Postmaster General may request the U.S. Attorney General to enforce compliance through a court order.

Three points here are significant:

1. The law allows a person absolute discretion to decide whether he or she wishes to receive any further material from a particular sender. (The material need not be erotic.)

2. A vendor does *not* have a constitutional right to send unwanted material to someone's home. A mailer's right to communicate must stop before the mailbox of an unreceptive addressee.

3. The law satisfies the due process rights of the vendor who sends the material. It provides for an administrative hearing if the sender does violate

▼ **Two documents that PR staff or firms must prepare are the annual report and the 10-K.**

the prohibitory order from the Postal Service, and a judicial hearing is held prior to issuance of any compliance order by a district court.

As a result, the Postal Service now provides two relevant forms. Form 2150 is directed to a particular sender and is usually requested when a person has received obscene or sex-related materials in the mail. Form 2201 is a request that a person's name be removed from *all mailing lists*. In an effort to counteract legislation that might be directed toward controlling unsolicited mail, the Direct Marketing Association has asked that all persons who wish to be removed from the lists of their members send their name and mailing address to the DMA (6 East 43rd Street, New York, New York 10017). The DMA then contacts individual mailers and asks that they delete the name.

Securities and Exchange Commission (SEC)

Public corporations (those whose stock is publicly traded and owned) have to be concerned with SEC regulations, and all corporations must be aware of and sensitive to personnel and financial information that might be released. The larger the company, the more likely it is to let something escape that should not have. This is particularly true when the corporation must coordinate its information dissemination with one of its clients (especially in the case of companies with government contracts) or when releases are prepared by an outside firm.

It is wise to have a procedure for clearing news releases so that no one is confused about what to do and (it is hoped) so that no one jumps the gun and releases a story before it has been cleared (see Example 9.1). Some institutions release only the information required, but a case can be made for using releases as early warning signals (such as

for possible bankruptcy filing) and as timely announcements of good news. Taking the offensive in takeover battles is a new PR tactic. However, financial abuses of the 1980s pushed SEC to take a more active role in policing disclosures.

Some suggested guidelines for disclosing information have been prepared by the American Society of Corporate Secretaries, after conferring with SEC representatives, to assist officers and employees responsible for disseminating corporate information to financial analysts and the investment community (see Example 9.2). Some companies have developed internal checks, and some advocate going beyond what is required (see Example 9.3).

The annual report and the 10-K are two documents that PR staff or firms must prepare. Annual reports have become promotional tools used by investment brokers and the company itself in presenting the company to all members of the financial public, from banks to analysts. When annual reports are distributed, a news release summarizing the main points and announcing the report's publication is also sent out (see Example 9.4). An effort to make the annual report an integrated document didn't work too well, so the SEC uses the 10-K as the best way to integrate management messages with financial reports (see Example 9.5).

Timely and Adequate Disclosure of Material Information   The timely and adequate disclosure of *material* corporate information, information affecting investment decisions, is a principal purpose of the Federal Securities Acts, as well as the stated policy of all national stock exchanges for publicly held companies. In addition to the SEC, which administers six major federal statutes in this area, other federal agencies important to financial institutions include the Federal Deposit Insurance Corp. (FDIC), which insures bank deposits, and the Federal Home Loan Bank Board (FHLBB) and the Federal Savings and Loan Insurance Corp. (FSLIC), which are responsible for savings and loan associations. Beyond formal channels, the National Associ-

EXAMPLE 9.1

Procedures for Clearing News Releases

HANDLING OF PRODUCT NEWS RELEASES

1. First draft of copy to primary sources for preliminary approval.

2. Draft of release to Corporate Secretary for approval.

3. Revised copy to Legal Department for approval.

4. Draft to division General Manager for approval in certain instances. (Group Public Relations Manager should make judgment in this instance.)

5. Copy of approved news release is then mailed to the company handling news releases along with media selection sheets for distribution.

6. Media covered will depend on the nature of the product, its importance to the various markets and industries and the marketing philosophy behind the development. (Distribution should be as broad as possible without covering media that would obviously not be interested in the development.)

7. Internal distribution of the news release to be determined by the Group Public Relations Manager.

APPROVAL CHAIN FOR AGENCY-PREPARED RELEASES

1. Clear with primary source at division.

2. Send cleared draft to Group Public Relations Manager for corporate clearance.

3. Following approvals at corporate level, distribution may be made through agency channels.

4. Copies of completed release to all involved in clearances. (News releases that must be approved at the corporate level include features, case histories, new product releases and any other product-oriented information released to magazines or other news media.)

HANDLING OF PERSONNEL NEWS RELEASES

1. First draft of copy to individual named in release to check accuracy of facts.

2. Draft of release to source requesting release.

3. Draft of release to division General Manager or individual's immediate superior at corporate level.

4. Draft to Corporate Secretary and Legal Department for legal clearances.

5. Draft to Group Vice President in cases of key promotions at divisional level. In instances of key corporate promotions, the Chairman, President, Executive Vice President, General Counsel, and appropriate Group Vice President must clear release.

6. Media coverage should include plant cities, corporate headquarter's city, individual's home town, association publications, appropriate alumni publications, as well as trade magazines covering industries served by division or group with which individual is associated.

7. Internal distribution determined by Group PR Manager and, in cases of key corporate promotions, by Public Relations Director.

8. Copies of news release should be sent to everyone included in chain of approval.

---

ation of Securities Dealers Automated Quotation, Inc. (NASDAQ), a voluntary self-regulating association of over-the-counter brokers and dealers, enforces SEC policy governing company advertising, communication and literature.

Major court cases have shown that corporate officials and employees must understand the legal obligations of proper corporate disclosure.[8] This is particularly true of the corporation's relationship with financial analysts and the investment community. In the Texas Gulf Sulphur case,[9] a federal District Court ruling that the U.S. Supreme Court let stand, an *insider* was defined as anyone who has access to information that, if disseminated, might

EXAMPLE 9.2

Guidelines for Dealing with Financial Analysts and the Investment Community

A. PRINCIPLES OF PUBLIC DISCLOSURE

1. The basic rule for corporate officials, when dealing with financial analysts and other members of the investment community, is that no item of previously undisclosed material corporate information should be divulged or discussed unless and until it has been disclosed to the public by a general press release or by an equivalent public statement. Material information as defined most recently by the [SEC] is "of such importance that it could be expected to affect the judgment of investors whether to buy, sell, or hold . . . stock. If generally known, such information could be expected to affect materially the market price of the stock." Considering the facts of the cases decided to date, material information in each instance consisted of information about the corporation or its securities, which if disclosed, could be expected to have a reasonably prompt and substantial impact on the market price of the securities involved, i.e., resulting in a market price change perceptible in excess of the usual day to day or week to week fluctuation of the stock in question.

2. The New York Stock Exchange has recommended that corporations observe an "open door" policy in their relations with the investment community. It is appropriate to communicate with stockholders, financial analysts, trust officers, investment counselors, etc., either individually or in groups to answer their questions or to volunteer information, so long as undisclosed material information is not privately divulged. It is important that information should not be given to one individual or group which the corporation would not willingly give to any other individual or group asking the same question. In other words, preferential treatment of any class of community members with regard either to fullness of discussion or to disclosure is to be avoided.

3. If it is expected that any material information, previously undisclosed, is to be revealed at a meeting or interview, a press release should be prepared in advance and publicly released to the financial press and wire services prior to or concurrently with the meeting, unless the press itself is adequately represented at the meeting. If material information is inadvertently disclosed at a meeting a press release must immediately be issued.

4. Further explanatory information within the context of a previous public disclosure may be given to financial analysts and others. Any new material information, however, should be given only in accordance with the procedures set forth in Paragraph 3.

5. Estimates of future earnings may be dealt with by either of the following methods, depending upon the policy of the individual company:

   a. Those companies which make it a practice not to issue any projections of earnings are frequently asked by financial analysts to comment on estimates made by them with respect to a future period or periods. Some companies do not comment on such estimates; others respond that such a projection is or is not "within the ball park." It may be necessary under certain circumstances to emphasize that the "no comment" implies neither an approval nor disapproval of the estimate. If, however, an independently arrived at estimate is deemed to be unreasonably high or low for the period in question in the light of responsible projections made by management, it may be appropriate to indicate that such estimate is "too high" or "too low" in order to prevent widespread dissemination of a substantially incorrect earnings projection within the investment community.

   b. Companies desiring to issue projected earnings, which are responsibly prepared and appropriately qualified, should do so only by public disclosure. Once such disclosure has been made and the projection remains materially unchanged, the company may discuss with individuals or groups the background and details of such projection. Such projection can also be compared with earnings for prior periods. If a publicly issued earnings projection becomes materially inaccurate, a new correcting public disclosure should be made.

B. PROCEDURES AND PRACTICES

1. It is suggested that the following procedures be utilized to implement the Principles of Public Disclosure set forth in Section A:

a. Only certain designated officers or employees be authorized by the corporation to speak before or with members of the investment community;

b. One or more of such designated individuals (referred to hereafter as "the designated official") be given the responsibility for approving, in advance, commitments for speeches or interviews with the press on financial matters;

c. Press releases and texts or outlines of speeches to be reviewed in advance by the designated official to insure, among other things, that they are not misleading, i.e., are accurate, balanced, and do not emphasize facts disclosed out of proportion to their actual importance when considered within the overall context of the corporation's business;

d. Answers to probable questions on sensitive matters be prepared in advance of meetings with the press or members of the investment community.

2. While it is impractical to categorize what constitutes material information, public disclosure should be considered for the following subjects prior to discussion with individuals or groups:

a. Total sales, sales by product groups, or percentage of total sales by product groups, for any period;

b. Earnings;

c. Profit margins;

d. Plans to borrow funds or to sell additional equity securities;

e. Proposed changes in dividend policy or rate, stock splits, or stock dividends;

f. Proposed acquisitions or joint ventures;

g. Proposed major management changes;

h. Contemplated major management changes;

i. Any other important development such as sale by the company of any significant asset, major contracts, pending material litigation, etc.

3. The following subjects are among those which, in the absence of special circumstances, are not ordinarily regarded as constituting material information requiring public disclosure prior to discussion with individuals or groups:

a. Total project capital or research and development expenditures;

b. Plans for construction of new plants or expansion of existing plants not falling under Paragraph 2(g) above;

c. Existing or planned inventory levels;

d. General trends of sales or other operating conditions for the industry as a whole;

e. Estimates of the corporation's effective tax rate and investment tax credit for the current and future years;

f. Depreciation policy and estimated depreciation rates;

g. General information concerning the company's business, prospects for various product groups, etc.

(Continued)

EXAMPLE 9.2

Guidelines for Dealing with Financial Analysts and the Investment Community (*continued*)

4. It may be in a company's interests to prepare a memorandum of each meeting or conversation with financial analysts or other members of the investment community, stating the names of the persons involved, the date of the meeting or conversation, and the items discussed. In addition, a complete record should be kept of all public disclosures.

5. Stricter limitations in addition to the foregoing Suggested Guidelines may apply in the event a public offering is pending or in process.

SOURCE: "Corporate Reporting Requirements," *Public Relations Journal,* 36(4) (April 1980), pp. 25–47. Reprinted with permission.

Note: Although these guidelines are still valid, an important decision was made in September 1976 in the U.S. District

Court of Judge Robert J. Ward. Judge Ward ruled that Bausch & Lomb and its chairman, Daniel G. Schuman, had not violated the antifraud provision of the federal securities law during March 1972 when they granted a series of interviews to four financial analysts who followed the company's stock after there had been some adverse publicity about the company's soft contact lens, Soflens. Schuman had been concerned about the interviews but had been candid within the bounds of proper disclosure. One of the analysts then called him, and in a telephone conversation Schuman attempted to correct the analyst's low first-quarter earnings estimate. Then Schuman called back to change his own rough estimate. The other analysts who had been at the interview were also called and given the same estimate. Then, as further protection, Schuman also gave the *Wall Street Journal* the earnings estimate. Despite his precautions, the SEC took the chairman and the company to court. Judge Ward's decision recognizes that a sincere effort was made to supply analysts with raw data that would, in effect, protect investors.

---

influence the price of a stock. A PR person who writes a news release, then, could be considered an insider. A PR firm must therefore disclose in its news releases that it is acting on behalf of an issuer and is receiving consideration from the issuer for its service (see Example 9.3). Richard S. Seltzer, former SEC special counsel, writes:

> The SEC apparently believes that fraudulent schemes initiated by corporate insiders may be facilitated by the action—or deliberate inaction— of outside professionals: the accountant who "stretches" generally accepted accounting principles; the lawyer who is willing to "overlook" material disclosures; and even the public relations practitioner who seeks to portray a convincing, but inaccurate, picture of corporate events.[10]

Ignorance of the legal requirements, of course, is no excuse, as the Carnation Company found out in 1984. Chairman of the Board H. Everette Olson

and President Timm E. Crull negotiated a sale of Carnation to Nestlé but did not tell Carnation's treasurer or the head of corporate relations because they didn't want to "compromise" those executives in their dealings with the financial press and general media. When leaks of the sale occurred and were denied by the two officers who had no knowledge of the negotiations, the SEC called their denials "false and misleading."[11] Wall Street lawyer John Ruhnka and law professor John Bagsby commented:

> Disclosure decisions—what to disclose, when to disclose and how to disclose significant nonpublic information—have become potential minefields for publicly held companies. No simple guidelines protect them from subsequent liability. But executives can reduce the possibility of mistakes if they know the requirements, current legal or regulatory issues and the kinds of problems that regularly arise, [and] then adopt some practical responses. To consult with your legal counsel is natural, but not always enough.[12]

EXAMPLE 9.3

Discretionary Disclosure

The argument is made here for using a preliminary disclosure release as an early warning or advance information system. The release is not a forecast but an announcement. The risk is that management might abuse this technique, using it to manipulate its publics, with a resulting loss in credibility.

Mr. X, chairman of the board of Ajax Company, said today that the company's board of directors intends to increase the annual cash dividend payment on the company's common stock for the coming year to $2 per share from $1.75. The company issues the release three full months before the board actually increases the dividend as described.

Issuing such an anticipatory statement creates a number of potential benefits for the company:

▼ The issuing company can control the timing of the announcement, an important consideration for companies that have learned through bitter experience that their dividend action, no matter how newsworthy, gets lost in a massive table with dividend action of many other companies. It also allows a company to give an accurate and valuable signal to investors when the timing may be right to do so.

▼ A company can show the cause-and-effect relationship linking two corporate events. For example, the above example could be linked with a report of higher earnings for the year, sale of a problem division, or even a change in control of the corporation.

▼ A corporation can respond to shareholder demands without imprudently putting itself at financial risk too early.

▼ The impression may grow that a company is well managed; the company thinks ahead, says what it plans to do and then does it.

SOURCE: Robert W. Taft, "Discretionary Disclosure," *Public Relations Journal,* 39(4) (April 1983), pp. 34–35, published by The Public Relations Society of America, New York, NY. Used by permission.

Another federal court decision also affected financial PR significantly. Pig 'N' Whistle, a Chicago-based restaurant and motel chain, was headed by Paul Pickle, who had previously been sentenced to three years in prison for misapplication of federally insured funds. Pig 'N' Whistle was brought before the SEC in February and March of 1972 to answer charges of having distributed two untrue and misleading press releases concerning stock transactions and acquisition of property in 1969. The firm was also charged with illegal stock registration.[13]

The two releases, one made on September 8 and the other on December 30, contained untrue or misleading statements about the purchases of the Mary Ann Baking Company, and the Holiday Lodge near Lake Tahoe. Pig 'N' Whistle stock shot up to $18 per share after the two releases—which came from Financial Relations Board, Inc., a public relations company—were printed. Pig 'N' Whistle had been a client of Financial Relations for eight weeks in 1969.[14] The statements released by Financial Relations were handled by only one member of the firm. The president of Financial Relations stated that Pig 'N' Whistle had not provided the firm with proper SEC registration papers for the stock. The PR firm was told by Pig 'N' Whistle lawyers that immediate disclosure of the purchase made by Pig 'N' Whistle was necessary to comply with SEC disclosure requirements.[15] Thus, the releases couldn't wait for registration papers to be filed.

EXAMPLE 9.4

SEC Requirements for Annual Report Interpretive News Releases

WHAT'S NEW

MD&A: Increased Emphasis

The SEC has furnished guidance regarding the text of the discussion of financial condition and results of operations, known as Management's Discussion and Analysis of Operations (MD&A) section of the annual report. The Interpretive Release (33-6835; 34-26831; IC-16961; FR-36/May 18, 1989) makes specific remarks concerning this section. What will the impact of this release be on the current crop of annual reports?

We believe that the spirit of this release will exert a salutary effect on the text of the annual report. On the one hand, the release opens the door to a wide range of possible topics and issues that need clarification and explanation. On the other hand, it helps define what many of those key points should be.

Specifically, the release highlights the following areas of concern:

▼ long and short-term liquidity and capital resources analysis;

▼ material changes in financial statement line items;

▼ required interim disclosure;

▼ MD&A analysis on a segment basis;

▼ preliminary merger negotiations.

Separately, financial institutions are directed to disclose information regarding their participation in certain high yield financings and highly-leveraged transactions, whether as an originator, lender, purchaser or syndicator or secured high-risk debt.

In addition to the historical overview, the release refers to a prospective or forward-looking discussion of operations and finances. This should address known trends, demands and commitments, as well as any uncertainties that are reasonably expected to have material effects on the financial condition and results of operations. Moreover, any industry-specific information which will further describe the particular nature of the company's markets should be included. Note that the SEC's "safe harbor" rule protects companies from liability if such required statements are made on a "reasonable basis" and in "good faith." Underlying assumptions, if disclosed, are also protected.

The recent Interpretive Release is an opportunity to provide additional, meaningful and contextual background. From this enhanced basis, the MD&A will better illuminate such important signals as growth trends, modernization, research and product development and marketing strategies. Note that in the effort to permit investors to more fully evaluate operations and financial resources, companies are given a wide degree of latitude in the text of the analysis and the graphic representation of the data. We recommend that the Release be consulted during the preparation of the MD&A discussion.

Reprinted with permission of Gavin Anderson Doremus & Co.

The SEC investigated the actions of both Pig 'N' Whistle and Financial Relations and ruled that Financial Relations had not exercised due caution in establishing the truth about the information furnished by Pig 'N' Whistle. The SEC said that Financial Relations should have done independent research before allowing any release to leave their offices. As a result, Financial Relations established within thirty days new procedures for reviewing the credentials of any new clients and for verifying the facts given to them for publication. This verification of facts covers any information that might affect investment decisions by stock purchasers. The

SEC also ordered Financial Relations to cease any contact with Pig 'N' Whistle.

In the 1970s, following the Pig 'N' Whistle case, the SEC began reviewing possible new disclosure regulations designed to protect the stock purchaser. The most important outcome of this from the point of view of public relations is that the kind of information released has to be more detailed and exact. Statements must be registered and must include a budget and cash flow projection for the company.[16] It is an SEC violation to issue a false and/or misleading release, whether or not a profit is realized as a result.

Public relations practitioners have to provide more information and be more certain now that the information is true than in the past. Further, the people who do the research and write the releases now assume the same liabilities as the company about which the releases are published. The information the public relations department or firm releases—the financial operations, history, future outlook, management and marketing structure of the company for which they are working—must therefore be carefully considered. The SEC has placed a heavy burden on public relations practitioners by holding them accountable. The agency has also left PR firms up in the air about how specific and detailed their information must be. The problem comes down to a matter of opinion and to the legal interpretation of "reasonable" or "ordinary care."[17] Financial releases must also be considered in the context of *other* public information put out about the company. This underscores the need to speak with one voice, to ensure that no information is misleading.

Initial Disclosures   The basic principles of public disclosure are given in the guidelines in Example 9.2. The following points are critical:

1. Unless trade secrets or competitive data are at risk and would justify a delay, publicly held companies must announce all important developments promptly. The 8-K reports must be filed within fifteen days of the event, such as an unfavorable court ruling in a lawsuit, a sale of significant assets or an acquisition.

2. A timely news release must be issued to report any event that is likely to affect the price of stock. The exchanges will stop trading in a stock when a leak occurs, but only briefly. (The New York Stock Exchange's maximum delay is three hours.)

3. A business judgment to withhold must be made in good faith—that is, not to defraud—and management must be able to demonstrate that it used reasonable care in identifying and evaluating facts in making the decision. In any case, announcements issued cannot be false and misleading. Texas Gulf Sulphur got into trouble by postponing a news release about a mineral find so that it could buy more land in the area of the discovery. The court found no fault the company for withholding information about the find while it bought additional acreage, but the court found that issuing a release that downplayed the find was false and misleading.

4. There must be no delay in reporting good or bad news.

5. Companies have what the SEC calls an implied duty to report material information between quarters so the financial markets will not be misled.

6. Formal disclosures (detailed financial documents that the SEC calls 10-K, 10-Q or 8-K) or informal disclosures (news releases) must be sufficiently accurate and complete that the information does not mislead, although every known material fact does not have to be communicated. (The Ronson Corporation was charged with misleading those who read its formal 10Q and 10K reports for not revealing that it was losing an important customer that accounted for 15 percent of its revenues.)

7. News releases are as important as formal reports. The SEC concluded that Fidelity Financial Corporation's year-end release was misleading because it didn't point out that the company's auditors had said they might need to include a "going concern" qualification on its 1981 financial statement because it was losing money at such a fast rate. The SEC said the release gave the impression of "business as usual."

EXAMPLE 9.5

SEC Requirements for Annual Reports

SEC REQUIREMENTS

Audited Financial Statements

▼ Consolidated balance sheets (2 years)

▼ Consolidated statements of income (3 years)

▼ Consolidated statements of cash flow (3 years)

▼ Consolidated statements of shareholders' equity, or footnote disclosure (3 years)

▼ Notes to consolidated financial statements

▼ Report of independent public accountants

Supplementary Financial Information

Selected quarterly financial data (2 years):

▼ Net sales

▼ Gross profit

▼ Income (loss) before extraordinary items and cumulative effect of any change in accounting policies

▼ Per share data based upon such income (loss)

▼ Net income (loss)

▼ Disagreements on accounting and financial disclosure matters

Selected Financial Data for Five Years

▼ Net sales or operating revenues

▼ Income (loss) from continuing operations (in total and per common share)

▼ Total assets

▼ Long-term obligations and redeemable preferred stock (including capital leases)

▼ Cash dividends declared per common share

▼ Additional items that will enhance understanding and highlight trends in financial condition and results of operations

(Such data may be combined with the five-year summary information on the effects of inflation and changing prices if required by FASB Statement No. 33, as amended by Statement No. 82.)

Management Discussion and Analysis of Financial Condition and Results of Operations

Discuss financial condition, changes in financial condition and results of operations; provide other information believed necessary to an understanding of the Company's historical, current and prospective financial condition. The areas to be covered include Liquidity, Capital Resources and Results of Operations; they may be combined whenever the three are interrelated.

Generally, the discussion shall cover the three-year period covered by the financial statements.

▼ Liquidity: Identify any trends, demands, commitments, events or uncertainties that will materially increase or decrease liquidity. If material deficiency is identified, indicate course of action to remedy situation. Identify and describe internal and external sources of liquidity; briefly discuss any material unused sources of liquid assets.

▼ Capital Resources: Describe material commitments for capital expenditures as of end of latest fiscal period; indicate general purpose of such commitments and anticipated source of funds needed. Describe any known material trends, favorable or unfavorable, in capital resources. Indicate any expected material changes in mix and relative cost of such resources. Discussion shall consider changes between equity, debt and any off balance sheet financing arrangements.

▼ Results of Operations: Describe any unusual or infrequent events or transactions, or significant economic changes, that materially affected reported income from continuing operations. In each case indicate extent to which income was affected. Also describe any other significant components of revenues or expenses that would enhance an understanding of results.

The discussion should use year-to-year comparisons or any other format that will enhance a reader's understanding. Where trend information is relevant, reference to the five-year selected financial data may be necessary. Known trends, demands, commitments or uncertainties that are reasonably likely to have material impact on sales or revenues, income and financial condition must be described. Any events that will cause a material change in the relationship between costs and revenues (cost increases in labor or materials, or price increases or inventory adjustments) must be disclosed. If there are any material increases in net sales or revenues, provide narrative discussion of the extent to which such increases are attributable to price increases in the volume or amount of goods or services sold, or to the introduction of new products or services.

Review the impact of inflation and changing prices on net sales and revenues and on income from continuing operations.

Discuss any uncertainties regarding the impact of recently adopted legislation.

Industry Segment Breakdown for Three Years

▼ Revenue (with sales to unaffiliated customers and sales or transfers to other industry segments shown separately), operating profit or loss, identifiable assets, capital expenditures and depreciation attributable to industry segments and geographic areas, for three years. Classes of similar products or services, foreign and domestic operations, export sales.

Financial Reporting and Changing Prices Information

▼ Five-year summary: effects of inflation and changing prices; may be combined with Selected Financial Data

Information on the Market for Common Stock and Related Security Holder Matters

▼ High and low sales prices of stock for each quarterly period in last two years

▼ Frequency and amount of dividends paid

▼ Principal market(s) in which the company's securities are traded and stock symbols.

Identity

▼ A brief description of the company's business

Directors and Executive Officers

▼ Name, principal occupation, title, employer's principal business

Litigation

▼ Cite significant cases; include any in which civil rights, ecological statutes or ethical conduct of directors or executive officers are involved.

Form 10-K

▼ Offer of free copy of Form 10-K in annual report or proxy statement in boldface type (not required if annual report is incorporated by reference into the Form 10-K and is filed with the SEC in satisfaction of disclosure requirements).

(Continued)

EXAMPLE 9.5

SEC Requirements for Annual Reports (*continued*)

Type-Size Requirements

▼ Financial statements and notes—Roman type at least as large and legible as 10-point Modern; if necessary for convenient presentation, financial statements may be Roman type at least as large and legible as 8-point Modern; all type leaded at least 2 points.

Distribution

▼ Distribution of annual report to all stockholders, including beneficial owners underlying street names, analysts, brokers, press.

▼ Annual report must precede or accompany proxy statement if proxies are solicited in connection with an annual meeting.

Signficant Accounting Policies

The SEC requires that these subjects be reported in accordance with generally accepted accounting principles:

▼ Principles of consolidation, summary of accounting policies, changes in accounting principles

▼ Inventories: valuation method

▼ Property, plant and equipment: depreciation policy

▼ Lease commitments

▼ Translation of foreign currency transactions

▼ Effects of changing prices and general inflation

▼ Long-term debt agreements, short-term borrowings

▼ Pensions: accounting and funding policies

DELIVERY OF REPORTS

Note:

Following are the delivery requirements of the annual report to your shareholders, based on where your securities are listed or traded.

NYSE

15 days before annual meeting: not later than 90 days after close of your fiscal year.

AMEX

10 days before annual meeting; not later than 120 days after close of your fiscal year.

OTC

No delivery of annual report to shareholders is necessary unless there is an annual meeting for which proxies are being solicited. State laws governing corporate activities should be checked to determine how many days before your annual meeting the annual report must be delivered.

ADDITIONAL CONSIDERATIONS

FASB Statement No. 96

New Financial Accounting Standards Board (FASB) rules will require companies to use the liability method to record deferred taxes. Such deferred tax expenses and liabilities must reflect future announced statutory tax rates beginning in 1988.

1986 Tax Reform Act (TRA) Effects on Earnings

Between 1987 and 1989, there are a variety of options for adopting the new GAAP tax rules. Companies that do not adopt the new rules in 1987 are required by a new SEC ruling to disclose the potential impact of the new rules on company earnings.

Pension Accounting

The FASB's new pension accounting rules issued in 1985 became mandatory in 1987. These rules govern determination of domestic U.S. defined benefit pension plan costs and the disclosure of pension plan assets and liabilities.

Cash Flow Statement

A Cash Flow Statement has replaced the Changes in Financial Position Statement.

Accountant's Report to Shareholders

Beginning in 1988, the Accountant's Report to Shareholders replaced the Audit Opinions.

The AICPA has clearly told auditors that they are (1) to actively search for fraud and (2) are required to evaluate whether or not there is substantial doubt about a company's ability to survive.

The Shareholder Communications Act

Since January 1, 1986 broker-dealers have been complying with SEC rules designed to help companies communicate with their beneficial shareowners.

Commercial banks, which account for about 75 percent of stocks held in "street names" including most of the beneficially owned shares of institutions, must also comply, effective December 28, 1986, with the provisions of similar SEC rules by furnishing, upon request, the names and addresses of beneficial owners.

However, bank obligations in connection with obtaining and forwarding proxy material to beneficial owners were deferred until July 1, 1987 in order to give banks sufficient time to establish workable procedures for the implementation of this system.

The Commission also adopted an amendment that changes from three to five business days the time in which a bank is to execute an omnibus proxy and provide notice of that execution to respondent banks.

The following amendments to the Shareholder Communications rules became effective in 1988:

Exclusion of specified employee benefit plan participants from the operation of the proxy processing and direct communications provision of the shareholder communications rules. The exclusion would apply only with respect to securities held by an employee benefit plan established by the issuer of the securities, or, at the option of the issuer, by its affiliate. Under the amendments, registrants would be required to cause proxy materials to be furnished in a timely manner to plan participants excluded from the operation of the proxy processing provisions.

The Commission also adopted an amendment to the definition of employee benefit plan, for purposes of the shareholder communications rules, to include those plans that are established primarily for employees but also include other persons, such as consultants.

Summary Annual Reports

A January 20, 1987 Securities and Exchange Commission ruling gives publicly-owned companies the option of issuing summary annual reports to shareholders without including the complete financial data previously required by the SEC.

However, the ruling stipulates that if a company uses the new format, every shareholder must receive in the proxy statement or in a 10K all of the financial information before the annual meeting and in accordance with previously established rules.

(Continued)

EXAMPLE 9.5

The response to the issuance of summary annual reports has been underwhelming. In a 1988 study of nearly 300 corporations, many respondents expressed concern that the effort to limit the data would be viewed negatively by shareholders and securities analysts.

Other Postemployment Benefits

The Financial Accounting Standards Board (FASB) has a new standard on Employers' Accounting for Postretirement Benefits Other Than Pensions. The standard on other postemployment benefits (OPEB) requires recording the present value of these future costs as current liabilities. The required provisions took effect in 1992.

Financial Instruments

The FASB is expected to shortly issue a standard regarding information on certain financial instruments. Specifically, companies will be required to disclose the face amount, nature and potential accounting loss for financial instruments issued for fiscal years ending after June 15, 1990. Additional information is required regarding those financial instruments that have concentrations of credit risk.

Reprinted with permission of Gavin Anderson Doremus & Co.

Follow-up Disclosures   Additional disclosure is necessary under four circumstances:

1. New information must be updated when new events make previous statements misleading.

2. Responses to outside reports must be made if these are misleading and come from people in a position to have had the information approved by the company, such as an underwriter, director or large shareholder.

3. Trading of shares held by executives and all insiders, including the company itself and company-managed pension plans, must be reported unless all material information about the stock's value already has been made available to the public. (The company is liable if it has given material nonpublic information to outsiders.)

4. Acquisition and merger information must be disclosed when negotiations reach agreement in principle.

Rumors and Leaks   When you are faced with rumors or leaks, you have three options: you can admit and disclose; you can make no comment or deny; or you can dodge and mislead. Courts have disagreed over where to draw the line clearly between exploratory preliminary talks and serious negotiations.[18] The former may be reported in a relatively leisurely manner, but the latter should be reported quickly because information about them almost always leaks. Two bills introduced into Congress in 1987 would have amended the SEC Act of 1934 on this point. One would have required a yes or no response in talks about a tender offer. The other would have made misleading statements illegal but would not have outlawed the "no comment" response, which could cause speculative buying.

Insider Information   It is just as important to understand the SEC's view of information to which there is "equal access." People who have knowledge that others do not have access to are called *insiders*. Thus, an insider, viewed broadly, is anyone who has information "everyone" else doesn't have (for example, information not generally available) that would give that person an advantage in buying or selling a company's stock. The court's rather narrow definition in the Texas Gulf Sulphur case stipulated that an insider is an "officer, director or beneficial owner of 10 percent of any class of equity or security." This definition has never been accepted by PR people, who looked with horror at headlines like "Press Release Goes to Court."

PRSA's interpretation of financial PR in the Code of Ethics was adopted in 1963 and amended in 1972 and 1977. PRSA president Tony Franco would have been charged by the organization with violating this code in 1986, had he not resigned from PRSA. Franco pleaded *nolo contendere* (which means "no denial but no admission") to the SEC charge in the case.[19]

Insider trading means using inside information to buy or sell securities or to buy puts, calls or other options on securities. This is considered insider trading whether the action is taken in the name of the person initiating the transaction or in the name of someone else. The U.S. Supreme Court upheld lower-court insider trading convictions of former *Wall Street Journal* reporter R. Foster Winans and two co-conspirators on November 16, 1987. The SEC viewed the ruling as an affirmation of its efforts to halt insider trading, efforts that had become very aggressive in the 1980s. The Court's opinion upheld the convictions of the former reporter for securities, mail and wire fraud. The Court refused to reject the misappropriation theory, which holds that information may be misused no matter how it is obtained. (In this case, the reporter had obtained it in the course of writing his "Heard on the Street" column.) The misappropriation theory strengthens the SEC's broad interpretation of insider trading.

The SEC's interpretation is expected to cover the gray areas of the insider trading law, including informed tips received directly or indirectly from or through associates; from raiders; from overheard conversation; or from prepublication access to news stories.

Even before the ruling in the Winans case, however, the SEC had charged a PR firm with insider trading. That case involved Ronald Hengen of R. F. Hengen, Inc., a financial public relations firm hired by Puritan Fashions Corporation (which was later bought by C. K. Holdings, Inc.). Andrew Rosen, Puritan's president in 1983, had issued an earnings projection of $3.25 per share on annual sales of $300 million. The SEC said in its complaint that both Rosen and Puritan's chief financial officer knew that the projection would not be met and so did Hengen, who told a stockbroker, who told another stockbroker. The two brokers allegedly engaged in $2 million worth of trading in Puritan stock before the public announcement that the earnings and sales projections were incorrect.

Handling Timely Disclosures and Inside Trading One specialist in investor relations summarized the insider and timely disclosure rulings as, "Tell as few people as possible anything, and then tell everyone everything," although it's not quite that simple, of course. Curtis Anders is more specific:

1. Remember, internal corporate communications channels are not always effective, so include internal notification in the disclosure plans.

2. Since decisions must be made in advance, it is important for the PR person to have continuing access to facts and he or she must work closely with other PR people involved (as in a merger or other type of acquisition situation, for instance). Contingency plans should be made, on the assumption that a leak will indeed occur.

3. Keep the stock exchange notified or consult it if something unexpected occurs or if an exchange ruling is not clear.

4. Notify the appropriate official in the stock exchange by telephone either before or simultaneously with the release of the information to the news media.

5. Make the announcement on the broad tape [stock exchange tape] and give the release to Dow Jones, the public relations and business news wires, national wire services, and any foreign news services that might be especially in-

terested. This is about as close as you can get to telling everyone at once.[20]

Anders offers the following advice to ensure that a company will comply with the New York Stock Exchange's *equal access policy:*

1. Make a comprehensive survey of the totality of information regarding the corporation, then establish a clear distinction between what can and should be made freely available to the public, including the facts that must be withheld and protected by the most stringent security provisions.

2. Designate certain executives to act as official spokespersons and insist that all contacts with the press, security analysts, and others be channeled through them. The corporation must speak with one voice to all.

3. Provide systems that will keep designated spokespersons informed at all times of what can and what must not be disclosed.

4. Avoid all situations that will tend to create the impression that the corporation is willing to give confidential information to anyone, or that it is willing to disclose *any* information to some recipients that it is not equally willing to provide to others or to the public generally at the same time.[21]

If new stock is to be issued, there is a registration period during which two types of publicity are forbidden: *any estimates* (dollars or percentages), even in broad or general terms, of *earnings* or *sales* for the industry or any product lines, and *any predictions* of *increases* in *sales* or *earnings* from *any* source.

Federal Trade Commission (FTC)

While the Securities and Exchange Commission looks out for the rights of investors, another equally alert agency, the Federal Trade Commission (FTC), looks out for the rights of both investors and consumers. On the investor side, it monitors antitrust legislation and has been very aggressive in monitoring proposed mergers that impinge on an-

titrust laws. On the consumer side, the FTC's scrupulous surveillance has resulted in charges of false claims relating to publicity releases as well as to advertising. As in advertising, both the client making the assertions and the PR department or firm disseminating them are legally liable. The only protection is to take prudent precautions.

Consequently, the publicist should seek some verification for product or service claims before publicizing them. One suspicious (or cautious) publicist insists on trying a product before he writes the release. "If it works, and works well, I write a better story. If it doesn't work, I don't write it!" This is fine if the thing to be publicized is tangible, but often it is not. Services must be carefully explored, too. Some professionals, such as lawyers, have been sued for deceptive ads. Since the writer is legally responsible, some PR writers, especially those in independent firms (as opposed to corporate staff), require notarized statements from research and development staff of product attributes.

The conscientious publicist is less concerned with the action of government agencies than with consumers' wrath or loss of confidence, but he or she should still be aware that fraud or misrepresentation, as it applies to advertising, is watched over by the FTC, the local Better Business Bureau and state and local law enforcement authorities. And the PR person should certainly be aware that payola and similar illegal promotional activities are grouped by the law in the category of "bribes."

Among the promotional activities monitored by the FTC are infomercials—program-length commercials that are scripted to simulate standard entertainment or educational features. The FTC now has guidelines for infomercials. Instead of attempting to prosecute the producers of the products (miraculous aging cures) or services (making $1 million in real estate), the FTC has decided to go after the producers of the infomercials. The FTC guidelines require that the infomercial producers have "reliable, scientific evidence" before making any claims for a product's efficacy or safety. The FTC also requires disclosures that the infomercial is a paid commercial if it runs longer than fifteen minutes. These disclosures have to appear at the beginning and end of the program, as well as before any ordering information.[22]

The FTC has also made some infomercial production companies more cautious. TV Inc. of Largo, Florida, says that it will no longer create infomercials for anything that has to be ingested, whether foods or medicines.[23]

The Federal Trade Commission also has a policy that holds celebrities accountable for the statements they make in advertising. The first example of that FTC policy was a consent agreement of May 11, 1980, with singer Pat Boone. Boone was a spokesman for Acne Statin, a skin preparation manufactured by Karr Prevention Medical Products, Inc. The FTC accused Boone of making false claims that the product cured acne, that it was superior to competitive products and that some members of his family had used the product with good results. Boone agreed to contribute to any restitution the FTC might order, but he didn't deny or admit the charges.[24] Under the Reagan administration, the Federal Trade Commission became less aggressive, and Boone was even quoted as saying he would go back on the air to support the product. But while Boone had personal knowledge of this particular product, many celebrities endorse products without knowing anything about them; their only contact might be in having the product shipped free to their home or office (see Example 9.6).

Food and Drug Administration

Like the FTC, the Food and Drug Administration (FDA) is active in protecting consumers. For instance, the FDA developed guidelines for consumer advertising initiated by drug companies. The first prescription drug advertising in the fall of 1983 appeared on cable TV shows aimed at physicians, but there is no way to exclude the lay public from exposure to the same advertising.

In September 1987, Sandoz Pharmaceuticals placed twenty-five full-page ads in newspapers nationwide to call attention to its antiallergy medicine Tavist-1. The *Wall Street Journal* noted, "the Sandoz

▼ **The FTC is centrally concerned with protecting the rights of both investors and consumers in relation to restraint of trade and false product and service claims.**

ads are the first to mention a prescription drug by name in general-interest publications."[25] The Food and Drug Administration reviewed the Sandoz ads and proclaimed them legal. The FDA requires that ads mentioning a drug by name be balanced and contain the sort of prescription information doctors get about side effects and possible problems.

Physicians have expressed some concern that ads such as this will show only the advantages of the product. Nevertheless, the marketing, promotion and advertising of prescription drugs already has the drug companies' PR people heavily involved.

In 1991, the FDA told doctors who serve as paid agents of the drug industry that they too would be targets of FDA surveillance. At the same time a warning went out to the pharmaceutical industry to stop touting (in promotional brochures and articles) FDA *un*approved uses for products. The FDA is developing its guidelines for what the agency considered "appropriate" promotional activities.

But the FDA doesn't just watch advertising. News releases can get you into trouble, too. Nutrasweet's fat substitute was introduced by Monsanto in 1988 at a highly publicized news conference. The company said that, because the product was made with all natural ingredients, it didn't need FDA approval. But Monsanto found out differently: the product was held up by the FDA. The lesson here is that the government agency should be included in the news release screening (preapproval) loop, because it can rule that a news release is misleading or does not give fair balance; alternatively, it can say that the product hasn't been approved, either at all or for a specific use.[26]

EXAMPLE 9.6 ▬▬▬▬▬

FTC's Policy Toward Deceptive and Unsubstantiated Claims

Advertising claims that come to the attention of the FTC staff are evaluated on the basis of the criteria contained in this protocol.

A. CONSUMER INTERPRETATIONS OF THE CLAIM

1. List the main interpretations that consumers may place on the claim recommended for challenge, including those that might render the claim true/substantiated as well as those that might render the claim false/unsubstantiated.

2. Indicate which of these interpretations would be alleged to be implications of the claim for purposes of substantiation or litigation. For each interpretation so indicated, state the reasons, if any, for believing that the claim so interpreted would be false/unsubstantiated.

B. SCALE OF THE DECEPTION OR LACK OF SUBSTANTIATION

3. What is known about the relative proportions of consumers adhering to each of the interpretations listed above in response to Question 1?

4. What was the approximate advertising budget for the claim during the past year or during any other period of time that would reflect the number of consumers actually exposed to the claim? Is there more direct information on the number of consumers exposed to the claim?

C. MATERIALITY

5. If the consumers do interpret the claim in the ways that would be alleged to be implications, what reasons are there for supposing that these interpretations would influence purchase decisions?

6. During the past year, approximately how many consumers purchased the product* about which the claim was made?

7. Approximately what price did they pay?

8. Estimate, if possible, the proportions of consumers who would have purchased the product only at some

*Throughout, "product" refers to the particular brand advertised.

price lower than they did pay, if at all, were they informed that the interpretations identified in response to Question 2 were false.

9. Estimate, if possible, what the advertised product would be worth to the consumers identified by Question 8 if they knew that the product did not have the positive (or unique) attributes suggested by the claim. If the claim can cause consumers to disregard some negative attribute, such as risk to health and safety, to their possible physical or economic injury, so specify. If so, estimate, if possible, the annual number of such injuries attributable to the claim.

D. ADEQUACY OF CORRECTIVE MARKET FORCES

10. If the product to which the claim relates is a low-ticket item, can consumers ordinarily determine prior to purchase whether the claim, as interpreted, is true, or invest a small amount in purchase and then by experience with the product determine whether or not the claim is true? Does the claim relate to a credence quality, that is, a quality of the product that consumers ordinarily cannot evaluate during normal use of the product without acquiring costly information from some source other than their own evaluative faculties?

11. Is the product to which the claim relates one that a consumer would typically purchase frequently? Have product sales increased or decreased substantially since the claim was made?

12. Are there sources of information about the subject matter of the claim in addition to the claim itself? If so, are they likely to be recalled by consumers when they purchase or use the product? Are they likely to be used by consumers who are not aggressive, effective shoppers? If not, why not?

E. EFFECT ON THE FLOW OF TRUTHFUL INFORMATION

13. Will the standard of truth/substantiation that would be applied to the claim under the recommendation to initiate proceedings make it extremely difficult as a practical matter to make the type of claim? Is this result reasonable?

14. What are the consequences to consumers of an erroneous determination by the Commission that the claim is false/unsubstantiated? What are the consequences to consumers of an erroneous determination by the Commission that the claim is true/substantiated?

F. DETERRENCE

15. Is there a possibility of getting significant relief with broad product or claim coverage? What relief is possible? Why would it be significant?

16. Do the facts of the matter recommended present an opportunity to elaborate a rule of law that would be applicable to claims or advertisers other than those that would be directly challenged by the recommended action? If so, describe this rule of law as you would wish the advertising community to understand it. If this rule of law would be a significant precedent, explain why.

17. Does the claim violate [an industry] Guide or is inconsistent with relevant principles embodied in a Guide?

18. Is the fact of a violation so evident to other industry members that, if we do not act, our credibility and deterrence might be adversely affected?

19. Is there any aspect of the advertisement—e.g., the nature of the advertiser, the product, the theme, the volume of the advertising, the memorableness of the ad, the blatancy of the violation—which indicates that an enforcement action would have substantial impact on the advertising community?

20. What, if anything, do we know about the role advertising plays (as against other promotional techniques and other sources of information) in the decision to purchase the product?

21. What is the aggregate dollar volume spent on advertising by the advertiser to be joined in the recommended action?

22. What is the aggregate volume of sales of the advertised product and of products of the same type?

G. LAW ENFORCEMENT EFFICIENCY

23. Has another agency taken action or does another agency have expertise with respect to the claim or its subject matter? Are there reasons why the Commission should defer? What is the position of this other agency? If coordination is planned, what form would it take?

24. How difficult would it be to litigate a case challenging the claim? Would the theory of the proceeding recommended place the Commission in a position of resolving issues that are better left to other modes of resolution, for instance, debate among scientists:? If so, explain. Is there a substantial possibility of whole or partial summary judgment?

25. Can the problem seen in the ad be handled by way of a rule? Are the violations widespread? Should they be handled by way of a rule?

H. ADDITIONAL CONSIDERATIONS

26. What is the ratio of the advertiser's advertising expense to sales revenues? How, if at all, is this ratio relevant to the public interest in proceeding as recommended?

27. Does the claim specially affect a vulnerable group?

28. Does the advertising use deception or unfairness to offend important values or to exploit legitimate concerns of a substantial segment of the population, whether or not there is direct injury to person or pocketbook, e.g., minority hiring or environmental protection?

29. Are there additional considerations not elicited by previous questions that would affect the public interest in proceeding?

SOURCE: Elizabeth J. Heighton and Don R. Cunningham, *Advertising in the Broadcast and Cable Media*, 2d. ed. Belmont, Calif.: Wadsworth Publishing, 1984, pp. 310–11. © 1984 Wadsworth, Inc. Reprinted by permission.

Federal Communications Commission (FCC)

In 1981, the Federal Communications Commission (FCC) deregulated broadcasting—an action that primarily affected its public affairs programming requirements and the fairness doctrine for television and radio. In 1987, the FCC did away with the fairness doctrine altogether, as discussed in Chapter 8.

The deregulation has made it more difficult to get public service time. And the demise of the fairness doctrine has made broadcasters more hesitant to accept issue advertising in any form, whether purchased time or public service announcements, because avoidable controversies can hurt advertising revenues.

The fairness doctrine required a station to provide reply time to any person or group who thought the presentation of a controversial issue had either attacked them or not presented their point of view. Still in force is the ballot rule, which requires stations to sell time to the opposing side if they sell advertising time to one side when both are represented on an election ballot. However, many stations erroneously think they don't have to do this any longer and have refused to sell time to an opposing point of view.

Many people forget that the FCC also regulates telecommunications, including telephone and computer networks and satellite communications. The newest technology to be regulated integrates voice, data, text and video into a single global network. Integrated Services Digital Network began by expanding and digitizing existing telephone networks; then data and text services were added to voice communications, with further plans to add video capacity. By using its fiber-optic cables, AT&T, (which owns the largest number of telephone lines) can transmit not only telephone calls, but also television signals and other service signals directly into the home. The interest of telephone companies in the television market continues, although a 1988 law blocks this option for the time being.

In 1988, the FCC opened the way for high-definition television (HDTV). Current policy requires HDTV broadcasts to be compatible with conventional television receivers, a policy similar to the one that required color broadcasts to be compatible with black-and-white sets.

▼ COURT RULINGS AND LEGAL RESPONSIBILITIES

Many aspects of PR are affected by court rulings and a variety of civil and criminal laws. Here we will touch on those that seem particularly important. One aspect of almost all of the legal responsibilities resulting from these is the presence of truth as a required element. Johnson & Johnson's Tylenol was the subject of a civil suit settled in May 1987.[27] Actually, what was being contested was Johnson & Johnson's slogan for the product: "You can't buy a more potent pain reliever without a prescription." The slogan was not true, said Judge William C. Conner, and he accused Johnson & Johnson of false and misleading claims in its advertising for Tylenol that exaggerated its superiority over other pain relievers. The judge reviewed all of Tylenol's ads and said the case pointed out five good lessons for consumers and advertisers:

1. Don't be fooled by headlines and pictures.
2. Beware of every word, even the smallest ones.
3. Numbers don't mean much, even the big ones.
4. Know the ingredients behind the product.
5. Repeating a slogan doesn't make it true.

Another interesting example of a company's legal responsibility comes from a 1978 case. In that year a Minnesota court ordered the Ford Motor Company to pay for repairs to a buyer's pickup truck. Ford had advertised the vehicle in a TV commercial that showed it being driven over very rough ground. When the buyer drove his truck over similar ground, he did $500 worth of damage to the cargo box. The judge ruled that Ford's advertising became an implied part of the warranty, since it led the purchaser to believe the truck could be operated as it was in the commercial. The judge did not say Ford was guilty of false advertising. However, another judge found that the makers of Listerine mouthwash were. Listerine had been advertised as a cold remedy for fifty years, but in 1978 it had to mount a $10.2 million advertising campaign publicizing the fact that the claim was not true. The advertising had to say, specifically, "Listerine will not help prevent colds or sore throats or lessen their severity."

A 1990 case involved a special event. Volvo had spent twenty-four years building a favorable image of its cars as the safest and strongest on the road. The special event was a monster truck contest in San Antonio, Texas, one aspect of which involved driving the monster trucks over several cars, including a Volvo. The other cars caved in, but the Volvo stood tall, and was hardly affected. The reason, brought to light later, was that Volvo's advertising agency had had steel reinforcing pillars placed inside the Volvo and had weakened the other cars' tops with cutting torches so they would collapse.

Footage of Volvo's "successful" performance was used in commercials. When the truth became known, however, WPP group's actions for Volvo cost them the account, Volvo suffered a serious loss of credibility, and other public relations problems resulted from this deceitful action.

Special events have also captured the attention of the Internal Revenue Service. A 1991 IRS ruling would tax, at the rate of 34 percent, donations that nonprofit organizations receive from corporate sponsors. Athletic events got the first warnings, but also liable are cultural events that enjoy corporate sponsorship. The ruling was directed at Mobil Oil Company for the Mobil Cotton Bowl and John Hancock Insurance for the John Hancock Bowl. The potential reach of the ruling rallied all nonprofit groups to seek exemptions. The repercussions of the IRS ruling are indeed broad, extending even to universities that name endowed chairs or buildings for donors.

Free Speech and the Organizational Voice

Whether or not you, as a PR practitioner, are involved in preparing your organization's advertising, you share in the responsibility for maintaining the organization's credibility. This is especially true in relation to handling the publicity resulting from any lawsuit, because it is bound to have some impact on both consumers and investors. Such situations are exactly what public relations practitioners have in mind when they argue for speaking with one organizational voice and coordinating all communication efforts.

The freedom of that organizational voice may be jeopardized by legal actions, primarily against some forms of marketing and advertising. And while all courts have long recognized that organizations, like individuals, have a "voice," some Supreme Court decisions have restricted commercial freedom of speech in ways that have threatened to muffle organizational or institutional voices.

Restrictions   The first major restriction on institutional voices involved the banning of tobacco advertising on television. (There are efforts now to ban the advertising of all tobacco products in all media.) The free speech counterargument is that, as long as the product is legal, producers should be permitted to advertise it. (In fact, farmers are subsidized to grow tobacco. There seems to be some inconsistency in government policy, at least.)

The same sort of ruling appeared in a more recent (1986) Supreme Court decision upholding Puerto Rico's prohibition against advertising gambling to local citizens, even though gambling is legal in the Commonwealth (which is associated with the United States). In another, more recent case, decided in June of 1990, the Court ruled that college students who wanted to hold a Tupperware party at a campus of the State University of New York could not do so because of a university ban on such "commercial" enterprises.[28]

▼ Speaking out on issues on behalf of an institution can result in contempt charges if the issues are currently in litigation.

The 1990s began with a flurry of legal action against artists and arts organizations—much of it centered on the National Endowment for the Arts, which had funded some exhibits and artists that provoked controversy over obscenity. The NEA was not the only focus for challenges to First Amendment rights. The rap group "2 Live Crew" was arrested while performing, and some record and tape store owners were arrested for selling the group's recordings, in both cases because the lyrics were alleged to be obscene. The eventual legal decisions in all of these most recent cases came out in favor of free speech, but the controversy is not over.

Observers see a threat to individual freedom in another case, involving a suit by the Attorney Registration and Disciplinary Commission of Illinois against a lawyer who listed his certification by a trial lawyers' group on his stationery. The American Advertising Federation has filed a brief in court supporting the lawyer, saying that the certification mention doesn't constitute advertising, and even if it did, the restriction is far too broad. In any case, they urge, restrictions can't validly be placed on speech unless the speech is misleading.[29]

Contempt of Court   Contempt may occur when you comment on a case that is pending before a court in such a way that it can be construed as an attempt to influence a jury or prospective jurors. When a case is in its pretrial stages, you should avoid putting your argument in advertising or publicity. A company with its case in court can't take it to the public by issuing releases or buying ads explaining its position. It can't send out a mailing if the judge has ordered that no public comment be made on the trial. If the news media's coverage of a trial erodes public confidence and hurts the company, it still can't respond. Failure to comply may result in a contempt citation. Even is-sue advertising can cause problems. Aetna Insurance's ads about damage suits running up the cost of insurance created problems subsequently in choosing a jury that had not been "exposed."

In another case, Sony mounted a campaign to counter adverse publicity stemming from its sale of blank videocassettes, which consumers might use to create "pirated" versions of prerecorded tapes. However, this campaign didn't begin until the case was on appeal. A lobbying effort to change the copyright law was going on at the same time Sony was arguing that current law permitted its videotapes to be made, sold and used by the public. The Supreme Court upheld Sony's position. However, the fight to change the copyright law's treatment of videotapes continues.

Publicizing Political Views   State laws cannot prevent firms from publicizing (or advertising) their position on political issues that materially affect their property, business or assets. In 1978 the Supreme Court found unconstitutional a Massachusetts state law that prohibited companies from making contributions to support a political viewpoint.[30] Thus, on referendum issues, corporations, like individuals, have the right to convey information of public interest, whether or not the issue directly affects the company.

The Supreme Court has not ruled on whether corporations can support candidates. However, since corporate campaign contributions are illegal in most states, corporations have developed political action committees (PACs), which can gather funds and do have some impact. Recently, controversy has arisen over the power of these groups, and future regulations may limit their current freedom.

In 1988, the Supreme Court ruled unconstitutional a District of Columbia code provision that had made it unlawful to display within 500 feet of any foreign embassy any sign that would bring a foreign government into "public odium or public disrepute." It also found unconstitutional a lower-court ruling that protesters could not congregate within 500 feet of a foreign embassy. The ruling came after the Soviet embassy had been picketed with signs saying "Release Sakharov" (the physicist and human rights activist), and after the group outside the Nicaraguan embassy had carried signs that said, "Stop the Killing."

In another case of free speech, *Hustler* [magazine] v. *Falwell*, the Supreme Court ruled that, as a public figure, Jerry Falwell could not recover damages from an ad that was an obvious parody. The court ruled that public figures are not entitled to recover even for emotional distress unless the publication contains a false statement of fact made with actual malice.

Individual Practitioners' Responsibilities

Public relations practitioners must register with the U.S. government when they represent a foreign government or act as a lobbyist, and they are personally legally liable for the accuracy of statements they write for advertising and publicity—regardless of who directed them to write the material. They are also responsible for material and information they provide as a news source.

Registering Political Activity   Public relations practitioners representing foreign governments must be registered with the U.S. government as foreign agents. (When the Justice Department took the PR man for the French-made Concorde SST to court for failing to register, he responded by putting a "foreign agent" identification on his Christmas cards.)[31]

Lobbyists functioning at all levels of government usually have to be registered, although laws vary. For example, New York City requires the registration of anyone who attempts to influence city legislation or is responsible for "articles or editorials designed or intended to influence directly or indirectly any municipal legislation."[32] On the federal level, lobbying activities consist of (1) payment to a legislative agent of $250 or more in a given calendar quarter to lobby; (2) making twelve or more oral lobbying communications per quarter through paid officers, directors or employees with senators

or representatives from districts other than those in which the principal place of business is located; (3) making lobbying solicitations (which means asking others to write), if the expense of solicitation on a specific issue costs more than $7,500 in a calendar quarter.

Product Liability and Publicity and Advertising   Calling consumers' attention to a product that later harms them raises liability concerns among public relations writers and advertising copywriters who handle publicity. Many writers now ask for certification of product reliability before writing news releases and ad copy, as assurance that the product will perform as claimed and will not cause harm. Agency managers and in-house managers who were previously reluctant to ask for such protection for their ad and publicity copywriters might reconsider now that many media are doing so. Media have been characterized as "conduits" for harmful product or service information in judicial proceedings, and they don't like the idea of facing expensive lawsuits.[33]

Complying with Consumer Rights

People have sought legal means to obtain information that will help them make rational decisions about their lives.

Freedom of Information Act   The FOI Act brings much government-held information within the reach of the news media and the public in general, including reams of data provided by corporate executives to meet the regulatory requirements of various government agencies, commissions and bureaus. The public relations corporate staff officers should know what information is filed with these various government offices, to anticipate any that might cause problems if released under an FOI request.

Corporate lawyers will advise you about what confidential material is protected under the law, but generally the only types of information exempted from disclosure under the FOI Act are

▼ The Freedom of Information Act exempts from disclosure trade secrets and confidential, commercial or financial information that is obtained from sources outside government.

trade secrets (narrowly defined) and confidential, commercial or financial data obtained from outside government. Competitive disadvantage is a legitimate argument for protecting confidentiality, but it must be proved; the mere possibility of harm to a competitive position is not adequate. Some portions of otherwise protected material still may have to be released if, after critical portions are eliminated, the basic confidentiality is protected. Another way to justify confidentiality is to show that release of the information will make it difficult for the government to get the same type of information in the future.

Right to Know The increasing number of state "right to know" laws patterned on the Freedom of Information Act make information available to the public regarding the presence of hazardous substances in the environment. Some of the information becoming available under these laws is being released as a result of court rulings in favor of company management against regulatory agencies such as the Occupational Safety and Health Administration (OSHA).

Open-meeting Laws PR people need to be aware of which of their organization's meetings must be announced and open to the public. "Sunshine laws" require that almost all government meetings, except those dealing with personnel matters, be open. Very unfavorable publicity can result from violations.

In many states, it is impermissible to say only "personnel matters" or "closed" on the notice of a meeting. The matters to be discussed must be specifically listed on the agenda, even though that part of the meeting may be closed. Federal law requires that governmental bodies keep a tape recording of any executive session that is closed to the public. However, anyone who makes that tape recording or a portion of it public is subject to civil and criminal penalties. (Guides to different states' access laws are often published in *Quill*, the magazine of The Society for Professional Journalists.)

In their role as a news source PR people often respond to calls from media representatives or initiate calls to share information that may or may not be about their client(s) or organization. If their statements are false or misleading, they may find themselves involved in litigation—even if confidentiality has been promised by the media.

Copyright Laws

Copyright laws protect a literary work, both in form and in style, from publication in any manner.[34] Before quoting from copyrighted works, you must ask for permission. There are some exceptions to this general rule, however.

If artistic efforts (writings, art, graphics, photos or other creative work) are done on company time by an employee using company resources, the material belongs to the organization (the person's salary constitutes his or her compensation). In some cases, an organization will make an arrangement for one-time use and permit the artist to earn extra money by subsequently selling the work elsewhere. However, the artist can only sell work done on company time when a prior agreement exists between employer and employee.

If the organization wants to use other work by the employee that is not a part of his or her regular duties or that doesn't qualify as "work made for hire," permission must be obtained. An example would be a piece of art produced by an employee privately and on his or her own time that is to be used on a company Christmas card.

When work is purchased from an outside person (as supplier), there can be confusion later unless an agreement is drawn up. Most PR people either buy file rights or one-time rights (which are non-exclusive). But even then you should make sure there is a written agreement when the work is ordered (see Examples 9.7 and 9.8).

A Supreme Court decision issued in 1989 said that written agreements between a freelancer and the commissioner of the work are valid only if the work fits under one or more of nine definitions found in the law: work created within the scope of employment; collective work (ads); part of an audiovisual work; a translation; a supplementary work; a compilation; instructional text; a test or answers to a test; or an atlas.

The transfer of ownership of the copyright is defined as an assignment—a transfer of exclusive license to reproduce the work, to prepare a derivative from it, to distribute copies by sale, rent, lease, loan or transfer of ownership, and to perform or display the work in public. A written assignment has to be filed with the Library of Congress, just like copyrights the originator would file.

Extent of Protection   Copyrights cover written and recorded (audiovisual and photographic) work, and are an intangible property right that begins when an original work is created. Copyright protects the specific expression of the idea. A person who wishes to copyright an original work must use the copyright symbol (©) on a substantial number of copies that are publicly distributed. In addition, two copies must be sent within three months of publication or recording to the Copyright Office of the Library of Congress, with a request for an application for registration for copyright. The fee can be as low as $11, but it varies with the size of the work being copyrighted. The copyright owner has exclusive rights of reproduction, adaptation, distribution, performance and display. Copyrights that were secured prior to January 1, 1978, are protected for twenty-eight years and may be renewed during the twenty-eighth year for an additional forty-seven years.[35] Copyrights secured after January 1, 1978, are good for fifty years after the author's death. Company publication copyrights are good for seventy-five years from the year of first publication or for one-hundred years from the year of its creation

▼ **Copyright laws protect a literary form or style from duplication in any manner without the owner's consent.**

if it is never published. When copyrights expire, the works they covered enter the "public domain" and become available to all for any of the previously restricted purposes.

In 1983–1984 news media contended that videotapes of news broadcasts constitute a copyright infringement. Some companies regularly supply clips of exposure to clients, and other PR people capture their own. Implicated in the same issue was the legality of home videotaping with videotape recorders (VTRs). The issue was resolved in 1984 when the Supreme Court ruled that Sony was not directly contributing to copyright infringement by making and selling VTRs, since VTRs have substantial noninfringement uses.[36]

Copying or "copycatting" is a common problem in advertising, but because *ideas* cannot be copyrighted, there is seldom a legal case in this area. The form that ideas take, not the ideas themselves, is entitled to copyright. However, a 1989 Supreme Court decision enables advertisers to copyright individual ads separately from the copyright that covers the publication in which they appear. If an advertiser brings a previously composed ad to a newspaper for publication, the advertiser owns the copyright unless there is an explicit agreement to the contrary. However, if the staff of the newspaper or magazine prepares the ad, the periodical owns the ad and can copyright it. Such an ad can't be published elsewhere without permission from (and compensation to) the publication that created it. Of course, for the copyright to be enforceable, the published ad must carry a copyright notice.

Fair Use   Violation of any copyright is an infringement, but one defense against infringement is fair use.[37] This includes use of one or more parts of the work in criticism, comment, news reporting,

EXAMPLE 9.7 ■■■■

Sample Copyright Authorization Form

COPYRIGHT AUTHORIZATION

Date: _____

A. Name of work (property): _____

B. Use (brief description of use: e.g., annual report, press kit, feature story, speech, presentation): _____
    _____
    _____

C. Ownership of copyright (check as appropriate):
    ☐ 1. We (user of form) own, because it is
    ☐ Work-for-hire because it was made by our own employee(s).
       Name of employee: _____
    ☐ Work-for-hire because:
       (i) It is a commissioned work, and there is a writing signed by the creator to that effect.
            Date agreement signed: _____
            Name of creator: _____
                                          -and-
       (ii) The work is for one of the following:
            ☐ a contribution to collective   ☐ a supplementary   ☐ a test
                work   work   ☐ answers to a test
            ☐ a part of audiovisual work   ☐ a compilation   ☐ an atlas
                                               ☐ instructional text ☐ a translation

    ☐ 2. We do not own, but we can use because:
    ☐ We have assignment of all copyright rights by written transfer, signed by copyright owner,
       that has been recorded with Register of Copyright in U.S. Library of Congress.
       Date of assignment: _____
       Name of creator: _____
    ☐ We have one or more of the following five exclusive licenses:
       ☐ 1. to reproduce (make copies)
       ☐ 2. to prepare a derivative work (sequel or prequel)
       ☐ 3. to distribute (sell) copies
       ☐ 4. to publicly perform
       ☐ 5. to publicly display
       Date of signing license: _____
       Name of copyright owner: _____
    ☐ We have the following nonexclusive license in writing and signed by copyright owner
       (briefly describe nonexclusive right; e.g., the use of photo as cover of annual report, use of
       statistical table in annual report):
       _____
       _____

    ☐ We have purchase order, unsigned by copyright owner, but received by copyright owner and
       containing the nonexclusive license thereon and paid pursuant thereto:
       Name and date of purchase order: _____
       Date of payment of purchase order and check number: _____
       Nonexclusive license (describe): _____
       _____
       _____

Sᴏᴜʀᴄᴇ: Reprinted with permission of The Institute for Public
Relations Research and Education.

EXAMPLE 9.8 ▬▬▬▬▬▬▬▬▬▬▬▬▬▬▬▬▬▬▬▬▬

Letter of Agreement

This letter will confirm agreement between _____

(contributor)

and _____ regarding the contribution of

(author)

_____

(photographs or problems or artwork, etc.)

to the work titled _____

by _____

(author)

in return for _____ .

(acknowledgment in the preface, money, etc.)

The material described above has been specially ordered, requested, or commissioned for use as a contribution to

an instructional work or as a supplementary work, and the undersigned parties agree that the material so described

will be considered a work made for hire and the property of _____

_____ .

(author)

Please sign, date and return all copies of this letter to _____

_____ .

(author)

_____   _____

Contributor's Signature   Author's Signature

_____   _____

Date   Date

Used with permission of Wadsworth Publishing Company.

teaching, scholarship or research. Many publishers filed suit against Kinko's Copies because of copyright violations in preparing "textbooks to order" for professors. Most Kinko's outlets are now extremely cautious about checking copyrights and asking professors to get permission, in writing, from the copyright holders before they will copy such materials.

Since so much public relations work is farmed out to freelancers, public relations freelancers should realize that they don't own works they were paid to produce. This includes work produced by employees within the scope of employment and work commissioned for use as a part of a collective work, if the parties agree that it is work "for hire."[38]

Copyright infringement applies also to music, which explains why more and more songs for everything from sales meetings to commercials are being written "for hire." Unless music is in the public domain, it may not be used. Even if the music itself is not copyrighted, the words may be. With regard to music, copyright infringement means using words or both—or similar-sounding versions—without express permission. And although permission may have been given to use the composition and the words, an additional copyright may exist on the specific arrangement or version of the composition. If you want to use a recording, you may have to pay for performance rights. You can't just choose music you like and use it. Furthermore, if you are determined to use a particular piece, be prepared for long negotiations for clearance and sometimes very costly permission fees, especially if you are going to broadcast it. The term *broadcast* has its own definition, which does not necessarily include using mass media. For example, sponsors of any form of public dancing in an entertainment establishment that uses records instead of live music has to pay the copyright holders a fee, and musicians who perform have to pay to use the compositions they perform in public or for recordings.

Nonprofit organizations can usually obtain permission to use music in a public relations campaign either free of charge or by paying a small fee. However, they still have to get permission.[39]

Confusions: Patents and Trademarks   Patents are often confused with copyrights. *Patents* are government grants that offer protection for inventions and novelties; *trademarks* are distinctive, recognizable symbols (word, design or a combination of the two) protected from infringement, previous claim or use without permission. In this sense, trademarks are like a company's brand name or identification (logo). To use a patent or trademark, you must check with the government registry and ask the owners for permission to use. The Patent Office of the U.S. Department of Commerce administers laws dealing with patents and trademarks.

Defamation: Libel and Slander

There are two kinds of libel: civil and criminal. Libel (written or otherwise published defamation) was originally confined to statements made in the print media, but it now applies to statements made in the broadcast media as well. The courts have interpreted libel as a more serious offense than slander (spoken defamation).

Civil Libel   *Civil libel* is defined as tortious (that is, noncriminal) defamation of character by malicious publication tending to blacken the reputation of a living person so as to expose him or her to public hatred, contempt or ridicule. It also means injuring the person in his or her trade or profession. Use of "alleged" or other subtle qualifications is of no protection. Civil libel law encompasses all forms of defamatory communication about a person's character, including headlines, tag lines and all art work (photographs, cartoons and caricatures). It also applies to errors that may result in libel, such as incorrect initials or the wrong name with the wrong photo. If the defamation occurs in an accurately quoted statement that contains a libelous statement, the person or medium publishing the statement may still be held responsible.

In libel cases involving public officials and public figures, "actual malice" must be proved. But don't count on their being held to that standard of proof. Definitions of all three designations—*libel*, *malice* and *public figures*—remain subject to individual interpretation in the courts.

Publication in libel suits is defined as dissemination of more than one copy. Consequently, office memos, letters, telegrams and broadcasting scripts are all subject to libel laws, just as newspapers, newsletters and brochures are. Anyone who takes part in the procurement, composition and publication of libelous material shares responsibility for the libel, although the original publisher is not responsible for subsequent publications by others. Even persons who bring the matter to the attention of anyone connected with possible publication are subject to being sued for libel (see Example 9.9 for a guide to determining what is libel). Copying and distributing a libelous piece could also result in additional action against the person or persons responsible in the organization.

Slander is spoken defamation. However, it does not always apply to broadcast defamations, because multiple copies of a script may have been produced; thus, even though the copy is eventually spoken, the scripts constitute publication and are therefore libelous, not slanderous.

Criminal Libel   *Criminal libel*—breach of peace or treason—involves inciting to riot or some other form of violence against the government or publishing an obscenity or blasphemy. However, charges of criminal libel are rarely pressed, and one writer suggests that such a prosecution might be unconstitutional.[40]

Defense Against Libel Charges   There are three traditional defenses against charges of libel:

1. *Truth:* substantial proof that is admissable in court.

2. *Privilege:* a fair and true report of a public, official or judicial proceeding.

3. *Fair Comment:* statements made in an honest (albeit erroneous) belief that they are true; also, statements with some element of exaggeration or irony in them that nonetheless do not overstep the

▼ **Libel laws provide for three traditional defenses: truth, privilege and fair comment; the necessity to prove "malice" can be considered an additional protection against libel suits by public figures.**

bounds of reasonable civility; however, it is up to the jury to decide the issue of "fairness."

A constitutional protection, if not a defense, is provided by the Supreme Court's 1964 decision in *New York Times* v. *Sullivan.*[41] This decision makes it necessary for a public official to prove malice in a libel suit. The court decides the question of "malice," but basically it involves an intent to harm. The primary significance of the *New York Times* v. *Sullivan* case lay in its implication that the Supreme Court could and would look at libel judgments to make sure that constitutionally guaranteed freedoms were not denied. In addition, because the defamatory statements in the case were contained in an advertisement, the court's decision signaled that the standard of proof it was imposing applied to commercial speech as well as to noncommercial speech. Finally, the Supreme Court said it was limiting the power of all states to award libel damages for statements about public officials. In the court's opinion, *actual malice* was defined as either knowledge that the libelous statement was false or a reckless disregard for whether it was true or false. Thus, what the writer thinks about the truth or falsity of the statement becomes a central question in its actionability.

A subsequent case extended this requirement to "public figures" other than officials—that is, to anyone who has put him- or herself in the public arena, such as a United Fund chairperson. However, in a 1974 decision,[42] the Supreme Court held that information conveyed by the press that falsely maligns a person—such as unprovable accusations—is still subject to a jury determination of negligence, regardless of the public figure's status or voluntary involvement. What this means to PR

EXAMPLE 9.9

A Guide to Libel

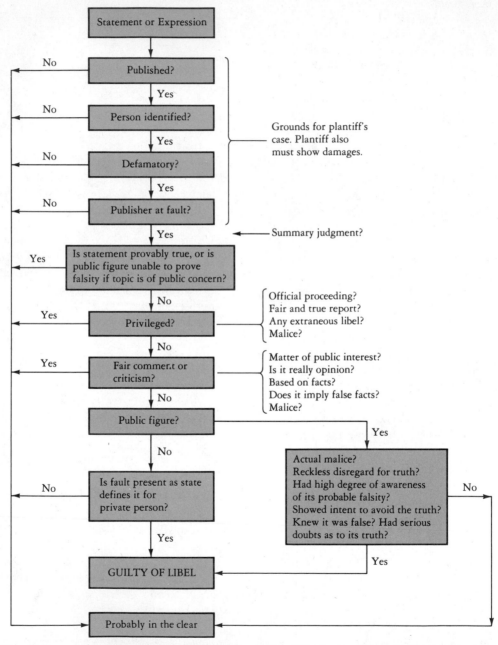

Is It Libel? Libel is the culpable (careless or knowing) publication of false information damaging to a person's reputation.

Statement or Expression

Published? — No

Person identified? — No

Defamatory? — No

Publisher at fault? — No

Grounds for plantiff's case. Plantiff also must show damages.

← Summary judgment?

Is statement provably true, or is public figure unable to prove falsity if topic is of public concern? — Yes

Privileged? — Yes
Official proceeding?
Fair and true report?
Any extraneous libel?
Malice?

Fair comment or criticism? — Yes
Matter of public interest?
Is it really opinion?
Based on facts?
Does it imply false facts?
Malice?

Public figure? — Yes

Actual malice?
Reckless disregard for truth?
Had high degree of awareness of its probable falsity?
Showed intent to avoid the truth?
Knew it was false? Had serious doubts as to its truth? — No

Is fault present as state defines it for private person? — No

GUILTY OF LIBEL

Probably in the clear

SOURCE: Albert Skaggs and Cleve Mathews, "Is This Libelous? Simple Chart Helps Student Get Answer," *Journalism Educator* (Autumn 1982), pp. 16–18. Revised chart (1992) reprinted with permission of Cleve Mathews.

people is that careless overstatements in a news release can be costly.

A recent ruling by a Duluth, Minnesota, state court, if upheld by the Supreme Court, could make it even more costly. The case involved a public figure and all the statements made in the *Duluth News-Tribune* were true, but the plaintiff claimed that he had been defamed by implication—that is, by a false impression. The Minnesota Supreme Court overturned the state court's ruling in May of 1990, but the case is headed for a Supreme Court decision.[43]

The U.S. Supreme Court has ruled that public figures must prove statements false, defamatory and published with knowledge that they were false or with reckless disregard for their truth or falseness.

Private figures in most states must prove negligence to recover actual damages; and all plaintiffs, whether private or public figures, must prove reckless disregard for the truth or calculated falsehood to recover punitive damages. Since releases typically go into more than one state, you have to assume that a private plaintiff will only need to prove negligence to recover actual damages. However, the writer of the release might be in one of a few states that imposes a higher standard of proof.

The standard itself is interpreted differently in some states. Some use the "prudent person" standard, while others use the "prudent publisher" (which applies the standard of care set by the media).[44] One defense to an action filed by a private individual is that if the person has read and approved an article about himself or herself before its publication, he or she cannot later claim to have been libeled.

Another limit to libel charges is the *statute of limitations*, which provides that a person cannot be sued after a certain period of time has elapsed. (States have varying periods of from one to five years.) In the past, if the defamed person died, the suit would often be dropped, on the theory that the dead could not be harmed by false reports. But more courts are now accepting libel suits (and slander suits) on behalf of the dead, reasoning that their name or reputation could be defamed even if they could not be materially injured.[45]

Right of Privacy

The right of privacy applies only to people, not to organizations. Violations of it take four forms: (1) intrusion into solitude; (2) portraying someone in a false light (making the person appear to be someone or something he or she isn't); (3) public disclosure of private information; (4) appropriation (using a person's name or likeness for commercial purposes without the person's consent).[46] Unlike the other three, appropriation does not have to breach decency or cause mental anguish or ridicule. It is the privacy violation that causes most PR problems. Model and photo releases are usually obtained in order to avoid these problems.

A picture, letter or name of a living person cannot be used in advertising or publicity without his or her consent. For instance, a cereal company once used an artist's representation of a woman that showed her pregnant. Because the real woman was neither pregnant nor married, she sued.

Photos taken at an event for publicity purposes may later be used innocently or ignorantly in a brochure about the event. The photo might even be used in an ad, perhaps because it just happens to be available. Using such photos in an ad poses a legal problem. Furthermore, even in a publicity situation, people may not be aware that their picture is being taken and for any number of reasons may not wish to have their photograph used.

Most attorneys for public relations people advise that releases should always be obtained. In most states, consent is the best defense; typically, newsworthiness is a more difficult rationale to defend. For example, employee pictures and names can be used internally; but if distribution is external, newsworthiness is lost as a legal defense. Even photos for internal use must be germane to the job—for example, giving information about promotions—or an employee who has not given consent may sue for invasion of privacy. Furthermore, use of an employee's name or image must end when the person leaves the organization's employment (refer to Example 9.8).

Employees must be treated both as employees and as private individuals who should not be forced to pose for annual report pictures if they don't want to. The company doesn't have the right to use their photos without permission. Furthermore, if they leave the organization and have not signed a permission form for the use of their picture, using it anyway can create a serious legal problem.

In one privacy suit, a photo became part of the product. A photograph of a prominent Chicago-area nun, Sister Candida Lund, chancellor of Rosary College in River Forest, showed her in nun's attire and seated in a chair. The photograph appeared on a greeting card produced by California Dreamers, Inc., of Chicago. The words above the photo, which does not identify Lund, say, "It's all right if you kiss me." Inside the card are the words, "So long as you don't get in the habit." The Dominican nun does not know where the card company got the photo, which certainly was used without her permission. She charged that the card demeaned her morals, violated her exclusive property rights (by using the picture without permission) and embarrassed her and the college. Apparently Rosary College alumni had seen the card in gift shops from Alaska to Texas.[47]

The courts have upheld the use of celebrity look-alikes under the First Amendment privilege, as long as it is clear that the real celebrity is not involved. A "false light" invasion of privacy suit in 1986 was ruled to state a claim similar to a suit for libel. The particular case (*Eastwood* v. *Cascade Broadcasting et al.* in the Washington State Supreme Court) was subject to the two-year statute of limitations for filing on libel.

Contracts and Consents

A PR practitioner need not get involved in a lot of permission forms and contracts, but he or she ought to know about at least five such forms: the model release, the employee contract, the photo agreement, the work for hire (usually writing) and the printing contract.

Major elements of a consent release (see Example 9.10) are identified by Frank Walsh as *written consent of all parties* (employer, employee and parent of employee if a minor); *consideration* (something of value exchanged, like $1); *scope* of the use *defined* (as photo used in brochure only); *duration* (a set time period, not forever); *words binding* (heirs also have to be considered after death of person giving consent); and *no other consideration* involved (such as some sort of inducement or promise).[48]

Contracts with celebrities should spell out exactly what the celebrity is to do and what aspect of the public personality will be used. The following considerations are significant:

1. Is endorsement for the client by the public personality a factor?

2. Does that public personality expect to be paid for the use of his or her name?

3. Are the public relations activities on behalf of the client proprietary?

4. Are there any relevant contractual provisions?[49]

Model Release   Serious legal problems can arise from failure to get a person's permission before using his or her photograph or other likeness in publicity or advertising. The photographer should always have the model sign a photo release form. Pads of model releases are available in most photo or stationery stores. If pictures of minors are used, the permission of parents or guardians must also be gained. The contract shown in Example 9.11 was used by a photographer taking pictures of a group of youngsters. Notice that the permission for use extends to publicity for the organization only. This guarantees that the pictures will not be used to en-

EXAMPLE 9.10

Model Consent Release

EXCHANGE OF VALUE

PROPER PARTIES

SCOPE

DURATION

WORDS BINDING ON PERSONAL REPRESENTATIVES

NO OTHER INDUCEMENTS, STATEMENTS OR PROMISES

PROPER PARTIES

In consideration of the sum of _____
dollar(s), the receipt I hereby acknowledge, I certify I am
twenty-one years of age and hereby give (organization's
name), its successors and assigns and those acting under its
permission or upon its authority, the unqualified right and
permission to reproduce, copyright, publish, circulate or otherwise use photographic reproductions or likenesses or me
and/or my name. This authorization and release covers the
use of said material in any published form, and any medium
of advertising, publicity or trade in any part of the world for a
period of ten years. Furthermore, for the consideration above
mentioned, I, for myself, my heirs, executors, administrators
or assigns, transfer to the organization, its successors and assigns, all my rights, title and interests in and to all reproductions taken of me by representatives of the organization. This
agreement represents in full all terms and considerations and
no other inducements, statements or promises have been
made to me.

_____   _____

(Signature)   (date)   (Signature-organization)   (date)

Note: Consent is written, but does *not include* any reference
to minors or agents; nor is it a part of a broader agreement.

Source: Used with permission of Frank Walsh.

---

dorse a product or to further any other unspecified
purpose.

Employee Contract   A client has a right to expect loyalty and confidentiality from a practitioner.
Some large PR firms have their employees sign a
restricture covenant—and that means everyone,
from the account executive to the file clerk (see
Example 9.12). Ted Baron, president of a New York
firm, recommends this "because they have access
to insider information and documents, some of
which your clients' competition or others would
love to get hold of."[50] What are the penalties for
breaking a covenant? Any sort of punishment management decrees—even firing, if the breach injures
a big client or causes the company to lose clients
unnecessarily. A covenant is a moral commitment
as well as a psychological one (for, of course, you
are less likely to do something if you publicly say
you won't).

EXAMPLE 9.11

Photo Release for a Minor

I _____ parent/guardian of _____
         (Signature)   (Name of minor)

do hereby grand permission for all photographs taken of

_____ during _____
      (Name of minor)   (Time schedule, which

_____ may be used by _____
   included on-site location)   (Name of organization)

for either publicity or advertising for _____
                                                              (Name of organization)

Employers need to be especially careful with insider information, since "tippers" as well as "traders" are penalized for using any material nonpublic information.

Photo Agreement   This is a contract between a PR practitioner or firm and a freelance photographer who is being hired to work on an assignment (see Example 9.13). Make sure that your agreement with the photographer spells out the limits of use for photographs. (Charges are usually higher when the photos will be used in ads than when they will be used in publicity.) You may want to use the photo more than one time or in different ways. Some photographers are willing to specify future use in one agreement. Many require one agreement per use. Remember that copyright protection begins for the photographer when the film is exposed. This will affect the agreement you draw up.

Work for Hire   Occasionally a public relations practitioner in an organization (profit or nonprofit) or in a firm will hire a writer or artist for a specific job. It's common for a writer to be hired to handle an annual report, for example. The "work for hire" letter of agreement sets the boundaries of the employment arrangement (see Example 9.14).

Printing Contract   In making a printing agreement, remember that no two situations are exactly alike, so the suggestions that follow will not always be appropriate. However, they may help you develop your own contract or agreement. Remember that, along with the contract, you will need to furnish the printer with specifications identifying how you want the publication to look. The following suggestions are often relevant for making a printing agreement.

1. *Dummy* a typical issue of the publication, showing the number of columns, widths of columns, page size, number of pages and estimated ratio of advertising to editorial matter (if you intend to have advertising). Ask the printer for a quote on the price for a fixed number of copies of a certain number of pages. Ask for the price per hundred for additional copies. You also need to know how much it will cost to add pages or additional color.

2. *Deadlines* for the publication must be reasonable for you and for the printer. You might vary deadlines for certain pages in a large publication like a magazine, especially if the pages have color or a great deal of statistical matter (such as charts or graphs). But make sure the deadline for the final product, as in delivery date and time, is firm.

EXAMPLE 9.12 ▮

Employee Covenant

TED BARON, INC. PUBLIC RELATIONS
104 EAST 40TH STREET · NEW YORK, 10016 · (212) 988-0517

Theodore Baron
President

> I hereby agree that during the course of my employment and thereafter for a period of two years I will not divert or attempt to divert any accounts or business of Ted Baron, Inc. either directly or indirectly for my own account or for the account of any other person or firm. Furthermore, it is hereby acknowledged that all records and other data concerning present or future clients of Ted Baron, Inc. are highly confidential and entitled to protection under the law as trade and business secrets of Ted Baron, Inc.

_____
Employee's Signature

_____
Date

Reproduced courtesy of Ted Baron, Inc.

3. *Corrections* can be costly. The printer must agree to furnish galley proofs on all copy and advertising. Usually there is an extra charge for making corrections on page proofs.

4. *Makeup* troubles are often the reason for corrections. Make sure you provide the printer with legible dummys, correctly marked, and with copy you've checked for accuracy.

5. *Paper* is sometimes a problem. You and the printer must agree on the type and quality of stock you will use, and you should insist on guarantee of continuity of supply (and price, if possible).

Photo Agreement

PHOTOGRAPHIC AGREEMENT FORM

This form will constitute our agreement with you for the services which you will render as a photographer for (Name) Corporation ("Company"). The specific terms and conditions under which you will render such services are as follows:

1. You will act as an independent contractor and will not be an employee of the Company.

2. Your duties will include photographic assignments for the _____ [corporate divisions] in _____ [countries]. You will perform your photographic assignments under the direct supervision of the Director of Public Relations of the Company or his appointed representative.

3. For each day that you render your photographic services to the Company as set forth above, the Company will pay to you the sum of _____ for your services, plus all reasonable food, lodging, and traveling expenses incurred by you in the performance of your assignment. Upon return from the countries set forth above, you will prepare and submit an expense report and the Company will reimburse you for such expenses. The Company also will pay the cost of all film and shall pay all photograph developing charges incurred by you in the performance of your assignments hereunder.

* 4. All photographs taken by you in the performance of your assignments hereunder shall be and remain the property of the Company, including prints and negatives. In addition, the Company shall have the right to use all photographs taken by you in the performance of this agreement in any manner whatsoever, without limitations or restriction.

5. This agreement will become effective on _____ [date] and shall remain effective until you have completed your photographic assignments for the _____ [corporate divisions]. This agreement may be terminated by either party at any time upon notice to the other party. Termination of this agreement shall in no way affect the terms and conditions set forth in paragraph 4 above.

If the above terms and conditions are acceptable to you, please execute the enclosed copy in the space provided and return that copy to me.

(Name) CORPORATION

By _____
Director of Public Relations

Accepted this _____ day of _____

---

*This may not be agreed to by the photographer, who will want to retain copyright.

SOURCE: From *Public Relations Manual*, Eaton Corporation. Reprinted by permission.

EXAMPLE 9.14 ∎

Work-for-Hire Form

WADSWORTH PUBLISHING COMPANY, INC.

BELMONT, CALIFORNIA 94002

FREELANCE LETTER OF AGREEMENT

This letter will confirm agreement between you and Wadsworth Publishing

Company, Inc. ("Wadsworth") regarding your services as a _____

_____

for the work_____

by_____.

Wadsworth will pay you_____

_____.

You agree that this compensation will be complete payment for all services
you perform, that any original material you submit is assigned to and will
become the property of Wadsworth, and that Wadsworth will have the sole
and exclusive right to reproduce and publish the material in this or any
other work or to use the material for any purpose whatsoever. Wadsworth
also retains the right to assign its interest, property, and liabilities
under this agreement.

Nothing in this agreement will be construed to effect an employee-employer
relationship. It is understood that you are an independent contractor and
your work will be considered a work for hire. While you will control the
means and methods of production, Wadsworth will be the sole judge of the
acceptability of the material you submit.

Please sign, date, and return all copies of this letter to Wadsworth.
One copy will be returned to you after we have signed it.

_____   _____
Your Signature   Wadsworth Publishing Company, Inc.

_____   _____
Your Social Security Number   Date

_____
Date

Used with permission of Wadsworth Publishing Company.

6. *Art* charges are usually specific. Get a list of art charges from the printer, and go over with the printer the types of art you are likely to use. Keep the information sheet on charges for reference in planning individual issues.

7. *Printing technique* is a basic decision, and usually a primary one, since few printers can handle both letterpress and offset. In deciding on a printing technique, you need to consider the quality of the job. If you have color covers, for example, with delicate shades, all the covers will not look alike when printed unless you pay extra for special handling—that is, for cleaning the press periodically to maintain color consistency. Don't put yourself in the position of demanding, after the fact, something you didn't arrange (and pay) for in the contract.

PR Services and Taxes

In some states, services such as home repair and maintenance are not subject to sales taxes. Although Florida repealed its controversial sales tax on advertising when revenues began to plummet and boycotts were invoked, service industries are growing in an economy that is no longer heavily industrial. As tax bases are sought, efforts surely will be made to tax the service sector, including professional services such as those offered by accountants, lawyers and advertising and public relations practitioners. Watch for state laws in this respect and, of course, the laws of other countries if you do business abroad.

▼ SUMMARY

Let's start by answering the questions posed at the beginning of the chapter. No, you can't write a publicity release that downplays the organization's financial crisis—unless, that is, you want to go to jail. You, individually, are responsible, regardless of who told you to do it. If you want to be cynical, the person who approached you might, when faced with a lawsuit, deny having done so. Where does that leave you?

How you handle the question of the "copycat" logo depends on whether you registered your logo as a *trademark*. If you did, you can protect it better than if you just copyrighted it. If you did nothing, you can count on its being copied. If you didn't do anything and you see something sufficiently similar in the *Wall Street Journal* that it might confuse the public, you might have a case anyway. But if a significant difference exists—say, the organization is in another field of business altogether—you don't have much of a chance.

With regard to the infomercial that you've been asked to script, you can't make it appear so much

like a program that the audience is likely to be misled. The inclusion of quasi "commercial breaks" within a larger commercial presentation is not approved by the Federal Trade Commission. Again, you'd better check to make sure that the product/service being promoted in the infomercial can do all the things you are being asked to say it can do in the script. Remember, the writer and the producer are the ones risking jail time, not the people who are offering the product/service for sale. Get a notarized statement specifying what the product/service will do. If you have problems getting documentation or verification of product/service claims, check with an attorney experienced in dealing with the FTC.

In the next hypothetical situation, if your lawyer client wants to include her certification on her letterhead, it could be interpreted as "advertising." Announcing a specialty is widely approved in medicine, but not in law, even though it is approved in some states. In fact, in some states you will find attorneys listed by state board certification of specialization in the telephone book's business section (yellow pages).

The photo you are thinking about using in the special section for the outdoor sports event may not be usable, because most news photographers don't get model releases when they take pictures. But they do get names and addresses—or they are supposed to. If you know the models' names and addresses, you can use the photo if you obtain their permission in the form of a signed release. Another reason to be careful about using such photos, even if you already have a release, is that one of the persons pictured might have died in the intervening period. You don't want to cause distress to the family by using the photo. When you have your own photographer shooting publicity pictures during a special event, give the photographer a package of release forms to have filled out as the pictures are taken. This solves a lot of questions about use, and it helps with identifications, too.

The question from human resources about pictures of employees in the last magazine should always be answerable with a "Yes, there is a model release on file." In this instance, you could be in trouble since there isn't one. You should always get model releases when you take employee pictures, because you don't know how you might use the picture later, and you don't know how long each employee photographed will be with you. If you have a publication in production, and a person whose picture you've taken leaves the company, it could cost a great deal to change the picture. In this case, since the magazine picture amounts to publicity, not advertising, you probably don't have a serious problem. But in situations like this one, a quick call to the organization's attorney is in order—to let the attorney know of a possible problem and to check the risk.

Public relations practitioners need to work closely with their organization's legal counsel because all sorts of civil and criminal cases can come up—some of them routine, but some likely to have high levels of "human interest" that attract media attention, and some that involve major issues like labor negotiations or mergers that demand media coverage.

Cases can arise in three general areas of legal involvement: failure to satisfy regulations of government agencies; violation of civil or criminal law (libel, privacy, copyright and so on); and breaches of or disputes over contracts. Almost everything you write can become a point of litigation, so you need to be cautious.

The government regulatory bodies that PR practitioners are usually involved with are the U.S. Postal Service, the Securities and Exchange Commission, the Federal Trade Commission, the Food and Drug Administration and the Federal Communication Commission. The peculiarities of an organization's (or client's) business may bring it within the purview of other agencies as well, and certainly everyone needs to be concerned about the Internal Revenue Service.

Some organizations believe that recent legal decisions have encroached significantly on the autonomy of the organization's voice—that is, on its freedom of speech. The judicial case law on this subject is not entirely clear. But an organization that attempts to influence a judge or jury by speaking out when a case is pending in court risks being charged with contempt of court. That doesn't prevent an organization or groups of people from expressing political views, although the role of PACs is being reconsidered.

As individuals, PR people are responsible for registering their own activities as lobbyists or as representatives of foreign governments, and for assuming responsibility for the truthfulness of what they present as information in any form, whether publicity or advertising.

Beyond these areas of responsibility, public relations practitioners need to be sensitive to other consumer rights such as access to information through state and federal freedom of information acts and open-meeting laws.

The areas of law to which public relations people are most vulnerable are defamation, invasion of privacy and misuse of copyrighted materials. Caution is essential when saying or writing anything that may injure the reputation of another, and individual rights to privacy must be considered, even when the individual is a "public figure."

The client or organization that the public relations practitioner works for needs to be protected by copyrighting the materials it produces, and needs to avoid violating the copyrights others hold, especially those who do work for hire. Contracts and releases protect both the organization and those with whom it works, including employees, from getting at cross purposes with each other and causing legal wrangles over rights of privacy or ownership of creations.

The most important protection for the public relations practitioner is to know where dangers exist and to work with competent legal counsel in steering the organization or client safely through dangerous situations.

▼ NOTES

[1]Morton J. Simon, speech to North Texas Chapter of the Public Relations Society of America, Dallas, Texas, August 29, 1978.

[2]Morton J. Simon, *Public Relations Law* (New York: Appleton-Century-Crofts, 1969), pp. 16–17.

[3]Ibid.

[4]Morton J. Simon, speech to North Texas PRSA.

[5]David H. Simon, "Lawyer and Public Relations Counselor: Teamwork or Turmoil?" *American Bar Journal*, 63 (August 1977), pp. 1113–16.

[6]Morton Simon, *Public Relations Law*, pp. 16–17.

[7]*Rowan* v. *Post Office Department*, 397 U.S. 728 (1970), Appeal of U.S. District Court for Central District of California, January 22, 1970, decided May 4, 1970.

[8]Two major cases are *SEC* v. *Texas Gulf Sulphur*, 344 F. Supp. 1983 (1972) and *Financial Industrial Fund* v. *McDonnell Douglas*, 474 F. 2d 514 (1973).

[9]*SEC* v. *Texas Gulf Sulphur*, 344 F. Supp. 1983 (1972).

[10]Richard S. Seltzer, "The SEC Strikes Again," *Public Relations Journal* 28(4) (April 1972), p. 22.

[11]*SEC* v. *Pig 'N' Whistle Corp.*, 359 F. Supp. 219 (1973).

[12]John Ruhnka and John W. Bagsby, "Disclosure: Damned If You Do, Damned If You Don't," *Harvard Business Review*, Vol. 64 (Sept./Oct. 1986), pp. 34–40.

[13]*SEC* v. *Pig 'N' Whistle Corp.*, 359 F. Supp. 219 (1973).

[14]Ibid.

[15]See *SEC* v. *Pig 'N' Whistle*, CCH Fed. Sec. L. Rep. (1972), pp. 34–38, 42–43.

[16]For additional information, see Bryon Burrough, "SEC Bid for Full Merger Disclosure Begs Question: What Is Disclosure?" *Wall Street Journal* (August 12, 1978) , p. 17.

[17]Alan J. Berkeley, "Stand by for Change: The Future of Investor Relations: Ripeness and the Disclosure of Significant Corporate Events," speech to Texas Public Relations Association, Houston, Texas, August 1987.

[18]See *Greenfield* v. *Heublein*, 742 F. 2d 751 (1984), a decision that did not settle the matter of whether boards of directors have to approve agreements in principle prior to the announcement. The failure to settle caused a class action lawsuit in 1985 over the RCA–GE merger. Compare *Levinson* v. *Basic, Inc.*, 786 F. 2d 741 (1986), where the court ruled that meetings occurring over a couple of months (during which time the company issued releases insisting it didn't know why trading was heavy) on a possible merger *were* material and should have been disclosed. The current Supreme Court rule is that materiality depends on the *probability* that the transaction under consideration will be consummated. (99 L. Ed. 2d, 220)

[19]Frank Walsh, "Public Relations Firm Charged with Insider Trading," *Public Relations Journal*, 42(5) (May 1986), p. 10.

[20]Curtis L. Anders, "The New Guidelines for Corporate Information," *Public Relations Journal*, 25(1) (January 1969), p. 14.

[21]Ibid.

[22]Joanne Lipman, "FTC Zaps Misleading Infomercials," *Wall Street Journal* (June 19, 1980), pp. B1, B6.

[23]Ibid.

[24]*Facts on File* (September 15, 1978), p. 22.

[25]Michael Waldholz, "Prescription-Drug Maker's Ad Stirs Debate over Marketing to Public, *Wall Street Journal* (September 22, 1987), p. 39.

[26]Joe and Losana Boyd, "Prescriptions for Preapproval," *Public Relations Journal*, 44(4) (April 1988), p. 14.

[27]William Power, "A Judge Prescribes a Dose of Truth to Ease the Pain of Analgesic Ads," *Wall Street Journal* (May 13, 1987), p. 31.

[28]Joanne Lipman, "Court Case Fans Firms' Worries About Commercial Free Speech," *Wall Street Journal* (September 12, 1989), p. B6.

[29]Ibid. For a good discussion of the issue, see Catherine A. Pratt, "First Amendment Protection for Public Relations Expression: The Applicability and Limitation of the Commercial and Corporate Speech Models," Larissa A. and James E. Grunig eds., *Public Relations Research Annual*, vol. 2 (Hillsdale, N.J.: Lawrence Erlbaum Assoc., 1990), pp. 205–17.

[30]*First National Bank of Boston* v. *Bellotti*, 435 U.S. 765, 55 L. Ed. 2d 707, 98 S. Ct. 1407.

[31]"Washington Wire," *Wall Street Journal* (January 2, 1976), p. 1.

[32]*Public Relations Society of America National Newsletter* (April 1974), p. 4.

[33]George E. Stevens, "Newspaper Tort Liability for Harmful Advertising," *Newspaper Research Journal*, 8(1) (Fall 1986), pp. 37–41.

[34]For a monograph on the implications of the new interpretation of copyright law for public relations, see Harold William Suckenik, "Copyright Rights Just Changed Forever—Do You Know What You're Buying and Why?" from the Institute for Public Relations Research and Education, 3800 South Tamiami Trail, Suite N, Sarasota, FL 34239-6913. The American Society of Journalists and Authors' Code of Ethics and Fair Practices has a position on work for hire and on model agreement. Society's address: 150 Broadway, Suite 302, New York, NY 10036.

[35]Write the U.S. Government Printing Office for copies of the copyright law that went into effect January 1, 1978 and for interpretations of the new applications. See also Kent R. Middleton, "Copyright and the Journalist: New Powers for the Freelancer," *Journalism Quarterly*, 56(1) (Spring 1979), pp. 38–42.

[36]*Sony Corporation of America et al.* v. *Universal City Studios*, U.S. Law Week 52 LW 4090, No. 81-1687 (1984).

[37]*Harper & Row Publishers, Inc.*, v. *National Enterprises*, 105 S. Ct. 2218 (1985).

[38]Marshall Leaffer, "An Overview of Copyright Law for Journalists and Other Media Artists," speech to Association for Education in Journalism and Mass Communication, San Antonio, Texas, August 1987.

[39]Ibid.

[40]Robert Sack, *Libel, Slander and Related Problems* (New York: Practising Law Institute, 1980).

[41]*New York Times* v. *Sullivan*, 376 U.S. 254, 11 L. Ed. 2d 686, 84 S. Ct. 710 (1964).

[42]*Gertz* v. *Robert Welch Inc.*, 418 U.S. 323, 41 L. Ed. 2d 789, 94 S. Ct. 2997 (1974).

[43]Amy Dockser Marcus, "'False Impressions' Can Spur Libel Suits," *Wall Street Journal* (May 15, 1990), p. B1.

[44]Susan Caudill, "Choosing the Standard of Care in Private Individual Defamation Cases," *Journalism Quarterly*, 66(7) (Summer 1989), pp. 396–434.

[45]Kyu Ho Youm, "Survivability of Defamation as a Tort," *Journalism Quarterly*, 66(3), pp. 646–52.

[46]Sondra J. Byrnes, "Privacy vs. Publicity," *Public Relations Journal*, 43(9) (September 1987), pp. 46–49.

[47]"Nun Not Laughing at Greeting Card," *Fort Worth Star-Telegram* (August 12, 1985), p. 7A.

[48]Frank Walsh, "Elements of a Consent Release," *Public Relations Journal* (November 1983), p. 8.

[49]David M. Coronna, "The Right of Publicity," *Public Relations Journal* (February 1983), pp. 29–31.

[50]Ted Baron, "Legal Protection for the PR Agency," *Public Relations Journal* (September 1971), p. 33.

Selected readings, activities and assignments appropriate to this chapter can be found in the *Instructor's Guide*.

▼

PR IN ACTION

Looked at alone, each component of PR
practice may appear to be simple and easily
mastered. But skillfully blending these components into a successful program is what
makes public relations effective.

Chapter 10 describes public relations
strategies and some of the details of public
relations work, including fees, budgets and
checklists. Chapter 11 examines the communication channels PR practitioners use.
Chapter 12 looks at PR tactics, including media expectations. Chapter 13 explains how
to launch a PR campaign, and Chapter 14
tells how to examine PR cases to learn from
others' experiences. Chapter 15 provides
guidance for dealing with crises.

▼

PROBLEM-SOLVING STRATEGIES: THE MANAGEMENT OF PR WORK

Modern education has frequently been criticized for turning out people who know a great deal more than they understand . . . it is only from concrete experience that one can really build up a capacity to discriminate, to be selective, that is, to be aware of differences.

Hadley Cantril

To be possessed of a vigorous mind is not enough; the prime requisite is rightly to apply it.

René Descartes, philosopher

Strategic management applies to public relations in two important ways. The first is the public relations department's role as part of the management team in developing problem-solving strategies for the entire organization. The second has to do with the public relations department's own efforts to integrate and coordinate its work with that of the organization.

▼ PR'S ROLE IN OVERALL ORGANIZATIONAL PLANNING

Any organization's public relations efforts exist to support the overall mission of the organization. For that reason, any public relations department's development of an annual plan, either for the organization or for the PR department, has to start with the organization's mission statement or organizational purpose. The way it develops from there often depends on the nature of the organization, but the elements of the public relations plan remain the same.

One role of the public relations department is to assist with the evaluation of an organization's mission. This may include revising and rewriting or perhaps conceptualizing and writing a mission statement. In any case it must be done as part of PR's policy-making role as counsel to management.

Mission, Descriptive and Identifying Statements

Most organizations develop their mission statement early in their existence, but at least once every ten years the statement deserves a careful and systematic review by internal and special external publics. While calling for a mission statement review is the prerogative of top management, the PR department is responsible for organizing and planning the review. One outcome of mission statement review is likely to be a rewritten or modified statement. Even if the mission statement is kept intact, internal publics and critical external publics must agree on this outcome of the review. The mission statement review is generally followed by a review of the long-range objectives by which the organization intends to implement the mission.

Mission statements set the tone for the organization, establish its character and define the parameters of its activities. They may be long, philosophical commentaries on the nature of the enterprise—as most university mission statements are—or they may consist of one or two simple paragraphs.

In addition to the mission statement, organizations write *descriptive statements* about themselves. These are more subject to change than a mission statement, but essentially they interpret that statement. As an example, look over some of the literature your university admissions office sent to you when you were considering attending the school. The way the university describes itself tells you something about its self-image. The descriptive statements of publicly held companies appear in their annual report, on the inside front cover—usually in a box. These same statements appear in reports from analysts and brokers when you inquire about the companies' stock.

Because mission statements and descriptive statements tend to be long, most organizations also write a short, snappy *identifying statement* that can be used in connection with the organization's name. These are usually not more than one sentence long. Many organizations use these as the last paragraph in news releases, knowing the copy-

▼ **The PR department helps plan, write and disseminate the organization's mission and strategy as well as its own communication plans.**

___

editor will often delete the last sentence but that sometimes it will appear. The idea is for repetition of this identification to help reinforce knowledge of the organization's role. Look for this in the last paragraph of stories about nonprofit organizations in your local newspaper.

Objectives and Goals

Organizational objectives are always tied to the mission statement, and they must be consistent with the view of the organization projected by the descriptive and identifying statements.

Depending on its type, an organization may have several sets of objectives, fitting like concentric circles. The farthest circle out represents objectives 10 years away; the next, objectives 5 years away; then 3 years away; and then one year away. Some organizations, especially nonprofit ones, develop elaborate books explaining these long-range plans. Generally they have to rely on these to raise money for the projects listed in the long-range plans, while the next year's objectives fit into an already established budget.

Unlike the mission statement, with its interpretations in the descriptive and identifying statements, objectives should have definite outcomes but remain unspecified as to time or degree. Early "management by objectives" work in the late 1950s confused goals and objectives, or used them interchangeably. Later works sorted out the two, assigning different qualities to each.[1]

Some dictionary definitions of *objective* use *goal* as a synonym. A thesaurus is likely to offer the following synonyms: goal, objective, purpose, aim, target, intention, destination, end. For planning purposes, it's better to treat an objective as the destination—where you want to go, such as a city on a road map—and goals as the achievements or incremental steps marking progress along the way—stopping points on the road map, taking you there. The goals are smaller, shorter-ranged, and easier to measure. Each one describes a set task to be accomplished within a given time period and to a specified degree.[2]

You can design and implement research to measure specific goals and to monitor your progress as you go.

Publics and Positioning

One aspect of planning for an organization involves identifying and describing all of its publics (see Chapter 7). You can then determine which are your primary publics under most circumstances—the ones you can expect to deal with directly on virtually a daily basis. You will work with secondary publics, too, but less frequently. Certainly both primary and secondary publics come into consideration in all aspects of planning. An organization's publics say something about what it is and what it does, just as surely as a person's friends and associates indicate what kind of a person he or she is and what he or she does.

The way these various publics respond to goals and objectives set by the organization directly contributes to the organization's level of success in accomplishing them. To build support for each public, you need to develop a realistic general message statement about how you'd like that group to view your organization. For example, employees are not likely to see management as "benevolent and kind," but "fair and honest" may be a reasonable view to strive for—provided that management really is, of course.

The way the organization wants to be seen by most of its primary publics, as reflected in its descriptive and identifying statements, is called *positioning*. Positioning is thus similar to the marketing strategy of differentiation, which involves emphasizing the ways in which a product or service differs from its competitors. An example is the American Heart Association's determination some years ago to position itself as "the" organization to which people would turn for information about cardiovascular disease, whether the people were physicians, reporters, science writers, government policymakers or private individuals.

Determining how to express a position and how to advance the idea the position represents to each public is central to the planning done by the organization's public relations department.

Programs and Activities

Some of an organization's programs and activities are the primary responsibility of the public relations department, but many are not. With respect to these, the public relations department serves as a source and resource. But when some of the organization's communications activities fall outside the responsibility (and authority) of the public relations department, most public relations directors feel they lack control. The least they would hope for is a "flow-through" pattern, in which all communications decisions cross their desk, even though these decisions may not be alterable. Most desirable is a consulting role in all such decisions. The role of the public relations department is often based on corporate tradition, on how management sees the public relations function and on the talents and abilities of the public relations staff, especially its leadership.

Monitoring and Evaluating

Even when many activities and countless forms of communication occur within an organization, the public relations department usually occupies the best position for monitoring what is or isn't happening and for evaluating how different publics are responding to various actions, messages and representatives of the organization.

Like other units in the organization, the public relations department is responsible for evaluating the results of its own efforts. At budget time, someone will always ask, "What did you do? How much did it cost? What did we get for the investment?

How cost-effective was it? How did it contribute to the bottom line?" However, in its evaluations, the public relations department is more interested in answering questions along the lines of: "What do our publics think of us? How does this match with what we think of ourselves? How are events, situations, attitudes, etc., going to affect us in the future?" Both types of monitoring and evaluation need to go on, and both help the organization's leadership plan and give day-to-day direction to the organization.

Commercially available computer software can be used to conduct a public relations situation analysis—setting objectives, writing a budget, developing a strategy, deciding on tactics and then evaluating results. The original program and an improvement for it were called PR Pro, and the program was developed by practitioner Don Bates and educator John Pavlik. It runs on any Apple computer that holds at least 640K of RAM memory; you'll also need HyperCard version 1.2.2, 2.0 or 2.2, as well as a mouse.

▼ PLANNING AND MANAGING PUBLIC RELATIONS WORK

Public relation's role in developing an organization's formal planning is significant. PR advisers help develop a mission statement for the organization—counseling on publics and on strategies to reach objectives, as well as on environmental monitoring—as part of determining the organization's three-year, five-year and ten-year goals and objectives. In addition, the public relations department must develop its own communication goals and objectives.

Some PR communication plans are tied directly to the organization's plans. Even if an organization does not have periodic plans, the public relations department still must have a generic communications plan that fits into the organization's annual activities. In addition, the public relations department needs a crisis communication plan, or at least guidelines for dealing with crises. Like other communication activities, however, that rely on the cooperation of other divisions in the organization and on the blessings of top management, crisis management plans must be developed jointly with other departments in the organization and must be approved by top management (see Chapter 14). Public relations managers have "vertical" jobs, in management terms, because they must function directly with all parts of the organization and at all levels.

PR is difficult to plan and manage because of high expectations, uneven levels of demand and the creative element. It calls for flexibility and entrepreneurship, often in environments that don't reward either. Many public relations problems arise from the failure of public relations practitioners to manage an internal situation, and this often turns on lacking approval to do whatever is necessary to accomplish the job. One PR practitioner whose publications were heavily criticized in a professional workshop complained that she knew what to do but couldn't convince her boss. A public relations manager for a presidential candidate resigned because, among other things, he couldn't get advance copies of the candidate's speeches. Ridiculous? Of course, but it happens all the time. Invitations to a major benefit arrived a scant four days before the event because a mailroom manager decided to send the hand-addressed envelopes third class after she opened one and saw that everything inside was printed. PR people often find it difficult to avoid drowning in details, but *not* watching the details is just as disastrous.

Strategic Planning

Strategic planning is used because traditional planning depends on a reasonably predictable environment; but due to the global nature of politics and economics, a predictable environment no longer exists. In 1980, management consultant Peter Drucker wrote in *Managing in Turbulent Times*:

> Planning as a rule starts out with the trends of yesterday and projects them to the future—using a different "mix" perhaps, but with very much the

same configuration. This is no longer going to work. The most probable assumption in a period of turbulence is the unique event which changes the configuration. Unique events cannot, by definition, be "planned." But they can be foreseen. This requires strategies for tomorrow, strategies that anticipate where the greatest changes are likely to occur and what they are likely to be, strategies that enable a business—or hospital, school or university—to take advantage of new realities and to convert turbulence into opportunity.[3]

The plan for the PR unit or department begins with its own mission statement, describing how it sees itself, its role and its contributions to the organization. This statement is necessary because the public relations department is often called on to do things or to respond to possible opportunities that really constitute temptations unrelated (or even counterproductive) to its central mission.

The mission of the PR unit helps define the job description for the whole unit—what it does in and for the organization. Changes in top-level management can cause discomfort with what the public relations department is doing unless the department can point to something that describes the department's activities and offers a clear rationale for them. New management may still want to make some changes, but it may nonetheless benefit from a better understanding of what the public relations function has been or should be—particularly if management comes to the top from another organization or from an isolated area within the organization, such as engineering.

The public relations department also needs to set its own objectives and goals with respect to managing the department. For example, one long-range objective may be for the department to produce its own presentation slides and graphics in-house. A goal for the year could be to obtain equipment, or perhaps only software, that would make such an objective more achievable.

Next, the public relations department needs to prioritize its own publics. This differs from maintaining a data base on the organization's publics, which might include description (demographics and psychographics), data (addresses, for instance), analysis (attitudes toward the organization and its products or services) and prioritization by issue or event. The PR department's own publics may include top management, other important sources of information within the organization, media personnel and special trade or government publics. The department needs to understand clearly who these publics are and what their special relationship to the unit is.

The department's relationship to the organization should also be spelled out in its own position statement, describing itself as "counsel to management" or "communications center" or whatever it intends to be within the organization.

Then the public relations department needs to schedule and prioritize the activities that traditionally fall within its sphere of responsibility. This is very important because sometimes, when special requests come or opportunities appear, other duties may not get done or may have to be postponed. The department's "calendar" of activities helps it plan its time effectively. Perhaps, too, some things the department has been doing just because "we've always done it" need to be replaced on the schedule by other, more productive activities.

Finally, the department needs to monitor everything it does to see whether the planned activities are being done correctly and whether they are eliciting the desired response. Monitoring the department's activities as they occur saves some of them from being unsuccessful and makes end-of-year reporting easier. The result of each activity should be scrutinized to determine what worked and what didn't, and recommendations should then be offered for the next year. The department must also perform a year-end review and evaluation, either as part of its overall management review or as part of the budget-making process. In any case, the public relations department's activities resemble those of other departments except that most of its activities support the organization as a whole or other specific units within the organization, rather than the department itself. This sometimes means that the department fails to get the recognition it deserves.

Along the way, the public relations department's plans for itself and for the organization may be interrupted by the need to develop special problem-solving strategies.

Problem-solving Strategies

One of the oldest formulas for problem-solving is John Marston's R-A-C-E formula—an acronym for Research, Action, Communication and Evaluation.[4] But, the concept is found earlier (without the acronym) in Scott Cutlip and Allen Center's 1952 version of *Effective Public Relations*: find the facts; establish a policy and/or plan a program; communicate the story; and get feedback from internal and external publics to help determine modifications or future planning.[5] A modification (with another acronym) appears in Jerry Hendrix's *Public Relations Cases*: R-O-P-E.[6] Like Marston, Hendrix begins with research (R) but then he moves to objectives (O), of which he sees two: output objectives and impact objectives. Output objectives are communications the public relations effort seeks to generate over the target period. Impact objectives have three divisions: informational objectives (message exposure, comprehension and retention); attitudinal objectives (creation, reinforcement and change); and behavioral objectives (creation, reinforcement and change). The P in Hendrix's formula stands for "publics," of which Hendrix offers an extensive list (see Chapter 7). The final step, once again, is evaluation (E).

The problem-solving procedure offered by Glen M. Broom and David M. Dozier is more complex.[7] The ten steps begin with defining or identifying the problem (1), followed by performing a situational analysis that involves assessing background information and data and examining internal and external factors and forces (2). Problem identification and situational analysis are followed by setting program goals (3). (Broom and Dozier use the term *goals* instead of *objectives*.) The next steps are to identify publics—who is affected and how (4)—and then to set program objectives (5) and plan action programs (6) for each public. Then each public's communication program—message and media strategies—is determined (7). These steps are followed by program implementation, in which responsibilities, schedules and budget are assigned (8), evaluation (9) and finally, feedback (10).

The Broom-Dozier process may not be as easy to remember, but it constitutes a more complete approach to problem solving. The approach taken by one of the authors of this text is presented in Example 10.1. Any problem-solving plan should take into consideration intervening situations: how others will react (especially within the existing power structure); how the organizational culture affects the approach to problem solving; and how those who are not intended publics for messages—the nimbus groups—may interpret or respond to them.

Intervening Situations

Some difficulty in handling problems may occur because of differing perceptions of the problem and of existing situations. The perceptions involved may be yours or others'. One way of understanding barriers to solving problems appears in Example 10.2. Robert L. Katz sees five major barriers: information you don't know; effects of the way you look at the problem; limitations you face (that is, restrictions on the choices the situation offers); your own personal limitations (or management's); and problems associated with upsetting the equilibrium of the organization or of others. Each barrier not only threatens to block your efforts to arrive at a solution, but presents the prospect of making the problem worse.[8]

The problems that your own biases contribute are detailed in Example 10.3, which shows how difficult it is to attempt an "objective" view of a problem, much less an "objective" presentation of the

EXAMPLE 10.1

What Do You Do When There's a Problem?

What is the procedure for handling a problem? Where do you start?

1. Assemble readily available facts and background material. Have everything at hand relative to the problem; analyze and discuss these with executives. Background materials include four areas: organizational/client, opportunity/problem, audience, research.

2. Determine which publics are involved or affected.

3. Decide if additional research is needed to properly define the problem and evaluate its scope.

Where do you go from here?

4. Once the problem is defined and the publics determined, formulate a hypothesis. Assemble facts to test the hypothesis, and revise it if it doesn't correspond.

5. Elements to consider in this initial planning:
   a. What is the object of the PR effort—what specifically do you want to accomplish? Be able to state this in concrete terms.
   b. What image of the organization do you want to present? (This should be a projection of the mission statement, but specifically adapted for this situation.)
   c. Which publics are targets? Why?

6. Who are other audiences whose opinions matter?

Now that you know who you want to talk to and what image you want your actions to reflect, what do you say to accomplish that?

7. What message do you have for each public? These messages should have a particular slant for each audience, but they should convey the same basic theme and information.

8. What media can you use to carry these messages? Which media for each group are received and are credible? Will these media carry your message? If not, what other media can you use? Can you use conventional channels of communication (magazines, newsletters, closed-circuit TV, etc.) for internal audiences?

9. What response do you want from each audience?

10. What budget can you use for this—regular allocated budget or a special fund?

---

problem to others.[9] Difficulties of perception can affect the way issues management is handled, for example.

The way various stakeholders see a problem can cause an organization to modify or change its reaction to problems. Stakeholders may not define the problem the same way management does, for example, and they may not appreciate the organizational purpose because it doesn't match their own purposes. Furthermore, they may not understand or be able to comply with the process offered as part of the solution. In that case the solution may not even strike them as reasonable.

The way various individuals within the organization perceive the problem affects the organization's responses, too (see Example 10.4). Some of this has to do with power structures, and some with organizational culture—existing situations. Power structures are a frequent source of resistance to responses. Sometimes that power resides in top management; sometimes it rests with departments within the organization that influence management decisions in certain situations. In dealing with environmental issues, for example, management is

11. What is the best timing for actions? Develop a schedule and tie-in with other events to make news when appropriate or to avoid it if news coverage might prove detrimental.

12. Review problems or obstacles that might arise and make contingency plans for these.

13. Build in monitoring devices so you'll always know how you're doing.

Once it's all over, how do you know what happened?

14. Plan for evaluation.

15. Evaluate all aspects of the situation—the impact on and response from all audiences. Evaluation includes (1) impact—informational, attitudinal and behavioral—and (2) output (media efforts and results).

16. Communicate results.

In brief:

1. Find the central core of difficulty.

2. Check your total list of publics and note all of those who are involved in the problem, both directly and peripherally.

3. Determine the problem's status in terms of potential harm to the organization.

4. List the related difficulties to be considered.

5. Explore the alternatives.

6. List the desirable objectives.

7. See how the solution fits into the long-range plans that are shaped toward what you see as the mission.

8. What are the immediate plans, and how do these fit with the long-range plans? Short-term solutions that don't fit long-range objectives and are not consonant with the mission statement are wrong. Don't do them. Start over.

Procedure for handling the problem internally:

1. Detail the plan and submit it to the policy executive for approval.

2. Get approval in writing.

3. Keep all people who are directly involved informed on a continuing basis throughout the move toward solving the problem.

likely to turn to engineering to see what is possible and how much it will cost.

Sometimes influence comes from power structures outside the organization. One powerful group is large stockholders—organizational investors such as insurance companies or pension plans—which influence decisions about dividends. Certainly institutional ownership of large blocks of stock has affected the attention paid to quarterly reports; some observers say that this has caused businesses to focus on short-term (rather than long-term) solutions to problems.

Another major factor in how an organization responds to a problem situation is the organization's corporate culture. The stronger the corporate culture is, the less flexibility the organization has in adopting solutions that are out of the ordinary or are not within the normal range of the expected behavior of the organization.[10]

The way the decision-making groups function together also affects problem solving. This is less likely to follow any specific decision-making

E X A M P L E   1 0 . 2

Barriers to Problem Solving

These barriers to arriving at a solution to a problem illustrate the complex inter- and intrapersonal difficulties you are likely to encounter.

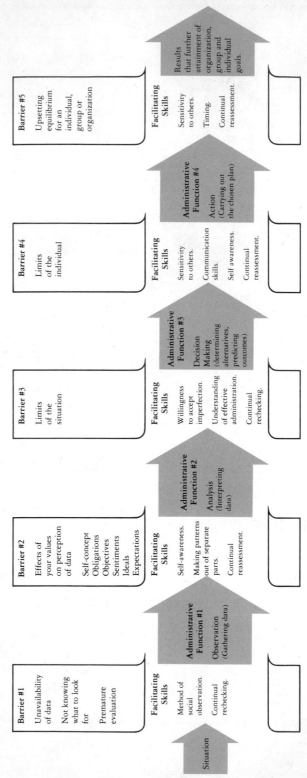

Source: Reprinted by permission of *Harvard Business Review*. An exhibit from "Human Relations Skills Can Be Sharpened," by Robert L. Katz, in *People: Managing Your Most Important Asset* (Boston: Harvard Business Review, 1990), p. 67. Copyright © 1990 by the President and Fellows of Harvard College; all rights reserved.

EXAMPLE 10.3 ▬▬▬▬▬

Personal Perceptions and Problem Situations

The way we look at a problem situation determines our approach to solving it. The complexity of our view is shown here. Other intervening factors arise when we attempt to communicate our perception—including how we want others to think of us.

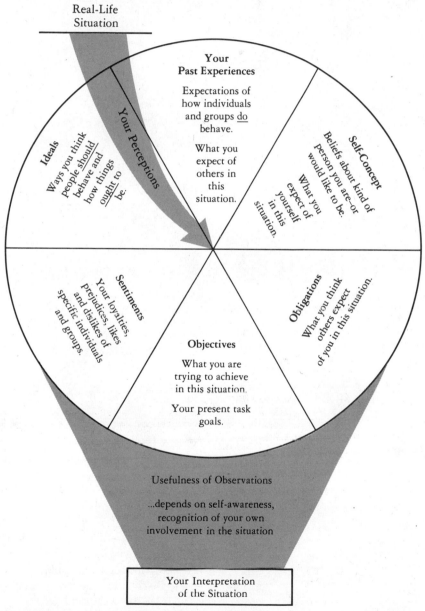

Real-Life Situation

Your Perceptions

Your Past Experiences

Expectations of how individuals and groups do behave.

What you expect of others in this situation.

Self-Concept

Beliefs about kind of person you are—or would like to be.

What you expect of yourself in this situation.

Ideals

Ways you think people should behave and how things ought to be.

Sentiments

Your loyalties, prejudices, likes and dislikes of specific individuals and groups.

Objectives

What you are trying to achieve in this situation.

Your present task goals.

Obligations

What you think others expect of you in this situation.

Usefulness of Observations

...depends on self-awareness, recognition of your own involvement in the situation

Your Interpretation of the Situation

SOURCE: Reprinted by permission of *Harvard Business Review*. An exhibit from "Human Relations Skills Can Be Sharpened," by Robert L. Katz, in *People: Managing Your Most Important Asset* (Boston: Harvard Business Review, 1990), p. 61. Copyright © 1990 by the President and Fellows of Harvard College; all rights reserved.

Difficulties with Perceptions in Solving Problems

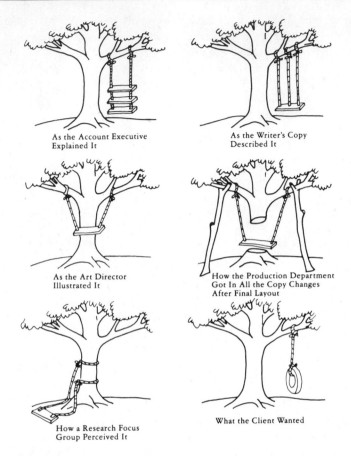

As the Account Executive
Explained It

As the Writer's Copy
Described It

As the Art Director
Illustrated It

How the Production Department
Got In All the Copy Changes
After Final Layout

How a Research Focus
Group Perceived It

What the Client Wanted

MORAL: Asking Questions Is a Sign of Strength

model, however, than it is to be related to the initiative of members of the group who are making the decisions, to their interpretation of their choices and to the effects of those choices (contingency factors).[11]

Public relations people are involved in problem-solving situations almost constantly, and a good many of the eventual solutions to these problems are arrived at by groups. Occasionally, these groups include some people from outside and some from inside the organization; but most are arrived at internally, with much of the effort being exerted by the public relations department or outside PR counsel to the organization.

▼ PR DEPARTMENTS AS SOURCES AND RESOURCES

Resources available in the public relations department are often needed by other divisions of the organization. PR can supply information on the organization's publics, on the socioeconomic and political climates in which the organization functions and on media.

A number of publications for the organization as a whole must be prepared by the public relations department. One such publication is the manual that determines how the organization's name and logo will be used by all of its departments and by anyone outside the organization, such as when it is used in cooperative promotions (see Example 10.5). In addition to having written descriptions that set out color, size, type, format and permission procedures, most organizations keep slicks available for easy use by their own divisions and by others. Another publication that public relations departments produce is the organization's staff or employee handbook, which sets forth various procedures that employees must follow. This publication also helps instill the corporate culture and standardizes many day-to-day activities.

Depending on the organization, there may be several other publications, usually dealing with processes or procedures. These include a safety handbook, a guide to handling crises, and a style manual for handling corporate letters, memos and the like.

PR often acts as the publishing division of the organization. As a result, other departments make numerous publication requests of it. Since PR is usually a profit center in most large organizations, these projects are charged to the requesting department. PR wants the business, even if it has a number of projects in progress, because it wants to control and coordinate the organization's publications so that they all seem to belong to the same "family" and to "speak with one voice." The family look of all public images reinforces the organization's identity and helps PR build the corporate image. The growing tendency of departments to send

▼ **The source of most of the organization's materials—both print and audiovisual—is the PR department.**

projects to outside suppliers or to do the job themselves with desktop publishing equipment makes the manual governing the use of logo, colors and corporate style increasingly important.

In addition to acting as the publications division, the PR department usually serves as the presentations division, too. This means writing speeches and making slides, electronic visuals or full-blown videos for internal and external use.

Internally, the unit may produce or coordinate video news releases and (if nonprofit) public service announcements for radio and television. It may also be in charge of setting up satellite coverage of events or handling teleconferences or other meetings that need to be scripted and videotaped, such as the annual meeting.

While the "clients" for these presentations are generally management or principal officers, the calls may come from a subdivision of public relations such as investor relations, public affairs, consumer relations, industrial relations, labor relations or—in the case of universities and some other nonprofit organizations—development (fundraising); alternatively, they may come from marketing, personnel (usually for training videos or presentations of benefits changes) or any special unit of the central organization or its subsidiaries. Requests from public relations subdivisions may be for production only, but requests from other divisions generally involve research as well as production, and they carry the possibility of extensive revision because of communication problems that often arise between the specialists and the communicators.

Charging for PR Services

Public relations departments in organizations must figure out how to charge for what they do for other units against the budgets of those other units. The

EXAMPLE 10.5

Standards for Logo Use from the American Heart Association

Internally and externally, you'll need standards for using the organization's symbol—size, shape, color and variation. Control in these areas promotes organizational identity.

SIGNATURE CONFIGURATIONS

There are seven acceptable configurations of the American Heart Association signature. These configurations have been designed for maximum flexibility and allow for application to various formats.

The symbol of the American Heart Association is a solid red heart, inset with a white torch, and a red flame above. The red used for the heart and flame must be matched by your printer to a color swatch of PANTONE* 485 (PANTONE Matching System—an ink formula available nationwide). White is the preferred background color for the symbol.

*Pantone, Inc.'s check-standard trademark for color reproduction and color reproduction materials.

One line—Flush left

American Heart Association

One line—Flush right

American Heart Association

Two line—Flush left

Two line—Flush right

Three line—Flush left

Three line—Flush right

Two line—Centered

COLOR

The heart-and-torch symbol should be matched by your printer to PANTONE® 485. This color was selected for the AHA symbol because of its warm, vibrant tone. Adopting it for all Association materials will promote and enhance the image we are seeking to project. In some instances, such as black and white newspaper advertisements, the symbol may be used with a 60% screen of black.

The logotype may appear in black with a red (PANTONE 485) symbol, charcoal gray (PANTONE 411) with a red symbol, or in red with a red symbol. In black and white reproduction, the logotype should be black with the symbol in 60% black.

The signature should normally appear in two colors — the symbol in PANTONE 485 and the logotype in black. When using 4-color process printing, the symbol should be printed in 100% magenta and 100% yellow.

The signature may also appear in two colors with the logotype in PANTONE 411 (charcoal gray) and the symbol in PANTONE 485.

In certain situations where red (PANTONE 485) is the only available color or you wish to use red and a color other than black, you may print the logotype in red as well as the symbol.

When black is the only available color, the symbol should be printed in a 60% screen of black. This is normally reserved for newspaper reproduction, forms, throw away flyers, and program covers printed on paper other than white.

SOURCE: Reproduced with permission. © *Graphics Standard Manual*, 1983, 1985, 1989. Copyright © American Heart Association.

▼ **Budgeting the PR operation includes plan-ning for people costs and operations costs.**

tasks that the PR unit has as its primary responsibil-ity are paid for out of the PR budget, but funds for service projects for other units are not built into this budget. Consequently, service projects can drain away resources (people and money) from the department's own budgeted needs unless the costs (for both people and operations) are charged back to those who requested the services.

Two systems are commonly used to handle this problem. In the first, the public relations depart-ment gives an estimate to the requesting unit, and that unit determines how elaborate it can afford the production to be and still stay within its own budget. Then, generally, funds are transferred from the other unit to public relations in accounting. No money actually changes hands. If the public rela-tions department has to go outside the organization for some services, these bills are submitted directly to the other unit for payment. (Occasionally, the public relations department may want to pay these bills and ask for reimbursement because, if the other unit doesn't pay promptly, it can damage the relationship between the PR department and a sup-plier it works with on a continuing basis.)

The second system involves having the public relations division function as a profit center for management. In such cases, the unit may be elabo-rately equipped, but it is expected to earn money. For that reason, it takes outside jobs—either from the organization's subsidiaries or from unrelated organizations. Thus the public relations division, al-though internal, functions like an agency; and strict accounting of time, talent, supplies and other re-sources becomes critical. If the public relations di-vision doesn't turn a profit, it may find itself "out of business," regardless of how much the organization itself may have used the PR function. Often when this type of arrangement is used, management sees the PR function as oriented less toward counseling and more exclusively toward communication.

Setting Fees   Most of the costs of a PR person, firm or department are for personnel time. Thus systematic ways must be developed to keep track of the time spent and to charge for it. Three basic methods can be used for determining client charges:

1. The *fixed fee*, seldom used now because it is a bit risky, sets a specific fee in advance for all work *and* expenses on a particular project. (Example 10.6 presents a simple method for estimating costs.)

2. The *fee for services plus out-of-pocket expenses* is a more popular form of billing. Out-of-pocket costs include such items as travel for a client, hotel rooms and meals, taxis, gratuities, telegrams, long-distance phone calls and entertainment.

3. The *retainer* covers counseling, supervision, profit and overhead. Overhead costs include all indirect expenses of doing business: utilities, secretarial and clerical costs, office supplies, amortization of equipment and so on. Additional charges are made for services at hourly rates that reflect payroll costs plus out-of-pocket expenses. Many firms charge a retainer that covers counsel-ing, supervision and profit, with an additional charge covering payroll and overhead expenses. All out-of-pocket costs are extra and are billed as such.

Firms   The cost of staff time spent on a project is measured in staff salaries, usually prorated to the nearest hour of time spent. The cost of executive time and supervision depends on the size of the agency: large agencies have executive oversight: small ones include the executive in the staff part of the time.

A PR business incurs chargeable and noncharge-able expenses. The following expenses can be charged to a client: (1) meetings with clients to prepare account material; (2) interviews, surveys and placement of materials; (3) supervision of mailing and distribution of releases, photograph as-signments and other visual material prepared for the client; (4) travel time, including going to and from client's office, as well as time spent in off-

EXAMPLE 10.6

Costing an Activity

You plan for what you think each activity will cost, based on previous experience or actual bids. The total of the estimates should give you an idea of how much of your project budget (or departmental budget, if it's coming from that) the activity will consume. Then you have to decide first whether or not to do it; and second, if it costs too much, how much (if at all) you can scale it down. Some projects lose their effectiveness when scaled down, and you are better off not doing them at all.

For example, suppose that your activity sheet reads as follows:

Activity	Due Date	Budget	Responsibility	Cost
Poster	*November 1*	*$175,000*	*A. J. Smith*	*$174,700*
	due October 15		*Art Department*	
design	August 15	2,000	freelance (name)	1,700
copy	August 15	500	(in-house) (name)	350
finished art	September 7	5,000	freelance (name)	5,150
printing	September 20	35,000	printing co. (name of person)	
space buy	August 1	50,000	outdoor adv. co. (person)	
posting/removing	December 30	75,000	outdoor adv. co. (person)	
monitoring	November 1	2,000	research agency (person)	
evaluation*	January 30	3,200	(piggybacked research)	3,000
poster publicity	October 15	2,000	(in-house) name	1,000
supervision	August 1	1,000	(Smith project supervision)	
department overhead		500		
TOTAL:		$176,200	(overbudget, so needs trimming)	

*Eval: exposures, recognition, unaided recall, positive
    awareness
    percentage of attendance attributed to poster alone
    percentage of attendance attributed to poster and
    broadcast adv.
    percentage of attendance attributed to poster and print
    adv.
    percentage of attendance attributed to newspaper
    stories
    percentage of attendance attributed to newspaper and
    mag.
    percentage of attendance attributed to television
    coverage
    percentage of attendance attributed to radio coverage

Evaluations help show how cost-effective the posters were,
so you'll know whether they contributed to attendance. (This
is only one measure of their overall effectiveness, though.)

hours (evenings and weekends) with client personnel on client matters. Nonchargeable expenses include the following: (1) keeping up contacts with media representatives; (2) meetings with office and staff and other group conferences related to PR business; (3) new business solicitation and preparation of materials for potential clients; (4) professional activities such as seminars, meetings and time spent on professional/firm matters; and (5) leisure time spent away from home in hotels, as well as purely social activities with clients, whether or not these occur in the evening or on weekends. Example 10.7 shows a typical budget.

This type of cost accounting makes it necessary for employees and executives to keep an accurate record of time spent on a project. Time segments are broken down in small sections, such as five minutes or fifteen minutes. To simplify matters, clerical, secretarial and mailroom salaries are ordinarily billed as overhead. This means that only the executives have to keep detailed records of how their time is spent. To facilitate this, most executives keep diary sheets (see Example 10.8) and weekly expense reports.

Many firms use an electronic software system to help them monitor and record time. One such system is PR Wizard Software from Data Directions, which consists of two modules. The Back Office module includes production, accounting, fee billing, production billing, integrated accounting, time reports and profitability. The Front Office module includes writing/editing, electronic mail, telephone messages, administration and research.

Most companies determine their profit objectives before setting hourly wages. *Small firms* do a lot of networking and rely on outside suppliers for advice, skills and services. They also rely heavily on freelancers and other contract workers. The highest fees these firms earn are for counsel and for strategy sessions, which are usually handled by the principal. Lower fees are paid for writing and producing materials. These tasks are most often farmed out. Most firms count on a 20 to 75 percent return before taxes, based on a 70 to 75 percent billable portion of a 7.5-hour day and a 1,550- or 1,660-hour year, including vacations and holidays. Higher fees are generally charged for emergencies, special projects and delinquent accounts. Most give their retainer clients quarterly reports, with charges for extra services or credit carried over to the next quarter.

Medium-size firms set aside a specific amount from profits to attract new business. Most hire people only when they get a new account. They use teams to work on accounts, but generally use only part of a team member's time for a specific account. Sometimes a new businessperson is hired just to get new accounts and is paid a commission to do so. Many of these firms are made up of generalists who rely on specialists to handle certain accounts.

Large firms are generally organized into groups composed of people who have the special expertise needed to handle a particular client's requirements. Larger firms normally have departments, such as media relations, that serve all groups. Groups usually make their own presentations, so the firm's principals are less in demand by the client than they are in the smaller and medium-size firms. Large firms hire generalists and specialists and are more likely to hire outstanding people and then find work for them. New people are usually tested at skills-level jobs (such as writing releases or managing a news conference) to see what they can deliver, before they are given the chance to try management jobs.

The Small Client   Making small accounts earn their keep is sometimes a problem. One difficulty you are likely to encounter is that, because smaller companies have little experience in using public relations services, they often make unreasonable demands and expect extraordinary results. It helps if you concentrate your efforts where you are most likely to get demonstrable results: trade publications, weeklies, locally produced Sunday supplements and other regional media. See if the client has a feature appropriate for a local television "magazine" program. You will probably have to do

Typical Budget

Expenditures:	Jan	Feb	Mar	Apr	May	Jun	6 Mo. Totals	Jul	Aug	Sep	Oct	Nov	Dec	12 Mo. Totals
Staff:														
Salaries														
Benefits														
Expenses														
Part-time help														
Office:														
Rent or space allocation														
Utilities														
Equipment:														
Maintenance & Repair														
Purchases														
Rental														
Communications:														
Telephone														
Telegraph, TWX, Telecopier, etc.														
Messenger service														
Postage														
Production:														
Design services														
Typesetting														
Photography														
Printing														
Media space														
(Other)														
TOTALS														

SOURCE: Reprinted with permission by Jim Haynes, "Organizational Budgeting Techniques," in Carol Reuss and Donn Silvis, eds., *Inside Organizational Communications* (New York: Longman, 1981), p. 72.

EXAMPLE 10.8

Executive Weekly Time Report/Diary Sheet

Burson·Marsteller Weekly Time Report

Week Ending Sunday (or the 16th)

| Employee Name | Employee Number | Office Name | Group Name | Month | Day | Year 19 |

	Client Number	Division Number	Job No.	Client Name	Mon	Tues	Wed	Thurs	Fri	Sat	Sun	Total Hours
1													
2													
3													
4													
5													
6													
7													
8													
9													
10													
11													
12													
13													
14													
15													
16													
17													
18													
19													
20													
21													
22	9 9 9 9 9			New Business									
23		0 3 3		Administrative									
24		0 3 4		Company Meetings (Non-Client)									
25		0 3 5		Outside Meetings, Conventions, etc. (Non-Client)									
26		0 3 8		Company Promotion									
27		0 9 0		General									
28		0 9 1		Absence									
29		0 9 2		Vacation/Holiday									

Total Items [ ]   **Total Hours** | | | | | | | | | |

For Accounting Use Only: Batch Control # _____   Date Input: _____   Input By: _____

SOURCE: Reprinted with permission of Burson-Marsteller.

---

a better selling job to the print and television media on such features because of their limited scope and appeal.

Be sure all your efforts are related to the client. Tell every success story to the client, even if it is just a column item. Help the client develop programs that will generate publicity. You may want to help the client start a simple internal communications program, like a newsletter. Help the client use advertising economically. Small clients need the effectiveness of a paid-for message. Watch the client's costs carefully. Small budgets can't absorb things like printing overruns or expensive mass mailings. Probably most important, be sure you have a contract that spells out obligations and provides for prompt payment, such as ten days after billing. If you are dealing with a new client you don't know much about, it is not a bad idea to require some prepayment.

The Large Client   Large clients can be habit-forming. They supply needed capital and often prestige. But if they pull out, your financial health and your credibility can be damaged. Diversification offers the best defense against such damage. You need to guard against relying too much on one account. At the same time, that account may give the firm a great deal of expertise in one area, such as public affairs, or in one industry, such as investments or fashions or automobiles. You can't ethically handle competing clients at the same time, but if you lose one account and have built a reputation in a field, it makes sense to find other clients in that same field to match your expertise. Large clients often demand involvement by the principals in the firm, and they sometimes consume more time than you can reasonably bill for if you're not careful.

Personalities are always important in client relations, but they are critical with a superclient. You need to be sure of the people skills of those working on the account who are in close contact with the client. You may be dealing with the client's middle-level management, whose power to make critical decisions may be quite limited. You may have to work with someone who is out of the policy mainstream and who may therefore mislead you concerning top management's wishes. This can cost you the account. Sometimes when a budget gets very large, expectations grow unrealistically high.

Budgeting a PR Operation

In a PR office, salaries and fringe benefits amount to approximately 80 percent of the total expenses, leaving 20 percent for profit, new business development and company (as opposed to client) costs. Thus, 20 percent of the costs cannot be billed out. Since some of these costs are discretionary, it occasionally works best to have a set budget for them so that no misunderstandings ensue over travel and entertainment allowances, membership dues, long-distance phone calls and other nonbillable expenses. The other company expenses are usually predictable, since they involve rent, insurance and utilities. Such variables as office supplies and postage have to be estimated roughly.

The amount to invest in seeking new business must also be calculated rather roughly, based on the rate at which the firm desires and needs to grow. PR practitioner Alfred G. Paulson, author of articles on fiscal planning, suggests that a 20 percent anticipated or planned annual growth rate is not realistic and might prove taxing for a company that already handles a large volume of business.[12] The costs of attracting new business and of acquiring the staff to handle it are real considerations. If too rapid an expansion takes place, problems with limited facilities might also enter the picture. However, Paulson warns than an anticipated growth rate of 10 percent or less would be too low to stimulate the action and enthusiasm needed to develop new business contacts and clients. A growth pattern of roughly 15 percent, he says, allows a realistic profit return expectancy of 25 percent before bonuses, profit sharing and taxes.

Would it ever occur to you to put in your PR budget the cost of responding to news media requests, in case your institution suddenly became the focus of news? Perhaps you should. Consider what happened to Washington Public Power Supply when its failure to pay on bonds became news, according to Gary Petersen, its information services director:

> "WPPSS is averaging 1,500–2,200 news clips a month just from the Pacific Northwest. Our twice-a-month executive board meetings are regularly covered by 5–7 TV stations, usually at least one national, and some 30 reporters including the *NY Times* and the *Wall Street Journal*. *Time* magazine has reported on the Supply System in 3 of its 4 last issues. Three members of my staff regularly handle some 150–200 media inquiries per week (and sometimes 150/day) from all over the U.S. And in

a usual week we will have at least 1 or 2 national media visit our sites for 1–3 days. It goes on, but suffice to say that, to my knowledge, there is no other single company that has this kind of consistent news coverage other than perhaps G.P.U. & Three Mile Island."

Washington Public Power Supply System's (WPPSS) effort to "recover costs" by charging media for document requests elicited some disagreements (see *prr* 6/13). Responding to *prr*'s article, information services director Gary Petersen explains:

"To give you a feel for the volume of requests we have been getting, in 1982 we charged 10¢ a page and received $12,740 for all the records provided. 127,400 pages of text had to be located, copied, packaged & mailed.

"It was only when the total WPPSS staff was reduced by more than 25%, and when the document requests began involving extensive staff & legal research that our records management group suggested a fee to recover costs. If a request was for a specific document (which required no research), we made only the 10¢ a page charge."[13]

In an organizational setting, PR department budgets vary dramatically depending on management's perception of the importance of the function. Nonprofit organizations value the PR function more highly than do many commercial enterprises, since so much of the total organizational operation is PR-related. PR budgets can therefore account for from 5 to 10 percent of the nonprofit's total budget. Corporate PR budgets are anywhere from 0.1 percent to 1 percent of the total budget, although a few are as high as 3 percent. Many corporate PR departments keep slim staffs and farm out many jobs to suppliers. In any case, as prices change and costs increase, you will have to defend your budget decisions and campaign vigorously for additional money simply to continue functioning at current levels. Consequently, you will have to prove the effectiveness of your function. Although your budget must conform to the organization's for accounting purposes, you have some leeway within those lim-

its. Jim Haynes, a seasoned practitioner and educator, offers a series of guidelines for developing a budget. Remember, Haynes says, to add in overhead, which is what the organization charges back to you as your portion of operating costs for space plus the services of the people who work there plus equipment purchases and maintenance.

Haynes says:

Everything that's worth doing costs money, just as everything that's *not* worth doing costs money. The trick is to decide *what* is worth doing. List those things in order of importance, and do *only* those important things you can afford to do. Simple, right? Perhaps not, but it's the most *logical* approach to budgeting I've ever heard of, since it's based upon *what needs to be done*, rather than "what we did last year."

How do we do that?

After you have studied your organization's objectives and determined how communication can assist in their accomplishment, do the following:

▼ List all your audiences in order of importance, with the most important at the top of the list.

▼ For *each* audience, list the communication media you plan to use during the next 12 months to reach that audience.

▼ Put a price tag on what it costs to use that medium one time.

▼ List the number of times during the next 12 months you plan to use the medium. (How many newsletter issues will you print? Etc.)

▼ Multiply the number of times by the unit cost to reach a total cost for the year for each medium.

▼ Do the same thing for each communication medium, audience by audience.

▼ Add up the total cost for the year for *each* audience, dropping out the costs for media that repeat from one audience to the next. (For example, a newsletter might be distributed to several different audiences, but include its cost only once, the first time it appears.)

▼ Add *all* the totals for all the audiences. That's your *desired* communication budget for the year.

▼ If the total is too big, you have two choices:

    ▼ Eliminate audiences, starting at the bottom of the list with the least important audience.

    (or)

    ▼ Eliminate media, starting at the bottom of the list for *each* audience.

▼ Add to your total the cost of overhead expenses which cannot logically be appropriated to the cost of communicating with individual audiences. Overhead items will vary from organization to organization but might include such expenses as rent, utilities, equipment, supplies, salaries, etc.

▼ Be sure to make a comparison with present expenditures. Many organizations have never prepared an overall communication budget and they are frequently surprised to find out how much money they're spending on ineffective materials![14]

If the advertising/marketing section reports to your communications department, your budget must include a line item for advertising. How much you budget for advertising is a subjective management decision. However, some variables have been identified by the Strategic Planning Institute of Cambridge, Massachusetts, which has compiled these variables into a data base, Profit Impact of Market Strategy (PIMS). In 1983, the Cahners Publishing Company commissioned a study using PIMS to identify the factors most frequently considered in determining product ad budgets. These "decision rules" are (1) setting the ad budget as a percentage of total industry sales; (2) raising ad budgets to get or sustain a high market share; (3) increasing ad budgets in faster-growing markets; (4) increasing ad budgets for lower deliverability (that is, lower plant capacity); (5) spending more for advertising at lower unit prices; (6) spending more for advertising if customers typically spend less of their income on the product; (7) planning to spend more for advertising for the very highest-quality products; (8) spending more for advertising if there are many products in the line; (9) diverting more advertising dollars to standard products.

If you are not dealing with the product line but are handling corporate or image advertising, you need to follow these additional decision rules:

1. Spend more if you are new to the field or need to clarify your image because of a name change, a merger or a previously low image in the field.

2. Spend more if you have *no* consumer products or services.

3. Spend more if you wish to increase recognition as an industry leader.

4. Spend more, and certainly not less, in a recession when product or service advertising is reduced in order to hold market identity and market share.

5. Spend more for before-and-after research to pretest and to evaluate product impact.

Sometimes the PR department is responsible for an organization's philanthropic efforts (usually for publicity or goodwill). Corporate giving and sponsorships, as well as cause-related marketing, have to be evaluated at the outset for consistency with the donor's organization mission. A way must be devised to measure the efforts' impact in publicity or goodwill. Unobtrusive measures (such as number of applicants for a grant or scholarship) and formal evaluations (such as surveys for recognition of donor and gift) may be used for this purpose.

Defending the Budget

The same research you use to evaluate the effects of public relations efforts can be used to defend the budget and to ask for increases. In addition, as in all other units, equipment has to be repaired, updated or replaced, and this calls for budget documentation of the equipment's usefulness to the public relations department in achieving its own goals and in furthering the organization's goals.

Budget officers want evidence of cost effectiveness, but success with people is difficult to document, and much of what public relations departments and firms do involves people. You have to find creative ways to make your case for success.

You'll also have to defend the public relations talent in your department, and you may have some difficulty in explaining how you use people there. Many creative people are not interested in being promoted to management tasks. In fact, in some cases, such promotion would be a disaster for them and for the department. They need to be compensated, however, and they need to receive salary increases to stay in the department. You have to find a way to explain the value of what they do, without changes in title or job description.

Managing PR People

To manage PR people effectively, you must first recognize that they are creative people who work under continuous pressure and face criticism from all fronts for whatever they do. Next you must realize that they are individuals with professional attitudes that tend to make them more committed to their field than to the particular place where they may be working. Finally, although most PR people are highly trained communicators, they often don't communicate as effectively with their colleagues as they do when they are working either with other departments or with outsiders at a communications task.

An organized and systematic plan is necessary to accomplish tasks, but PR employees are generally less tolerant of inflexible rules and routines than other employees. They often face criticism from other employees who don't understand the nature of public relations jobs but do know that PR people come and go with more freedom than many other employees. In addition, other employees know that PR people work with the (often unpopular) media. Perhaps worst of all, PR people are spokespeople for management.

Cultivating personal growth and keeping PR employees from getting bored with routine chores are challenges for PR managers. PR managers must also see to it that their employees learn the organization's business thoroughly. They also must see to it that their employees keep up with developments in their own field.

You will probably not have management responsibility right away; but while you are laboring at low levels, consider keeping a list of things to recall when you do assume management responsibilities. Remember, employees look to the manager or supervisor for leadership and for knowledge of the rules. The manager is expected to provide a good working environment for employees and to support them in their dealings with top management. Employees look to the manager for counsel (sometimes even on personal matters). They expect the manager to listen, to do more than they do and to do it better. Finally, they expect the manager to help gain recognition for them and for the department. Employees are the public relations "front-line" of any organization, and that holds especially true for the PR department's own employees.

Cultural Values and Social Conflict in a Global Society

With the internationalization of business, some of an organization's public relations employees may be sent abroad, either for brief periods or to live and work in another culture. Large public relations agencies have offices all over the world, and these tend not to be entirely staffed by nationals of the country where the office is located. Consequently, PR people need to consider how the cultural values of the parent organization can cause conflict in the resident culture.

Accompanying employees on foreign assignments is some of the organization's own culture—often called *corporate culture*, although it exists in nonprofit organizations as well. While this culture often helps give the organization a recognizable identity and an implicit "code of conduct," it also conveys a value system. *Value* is used here in its sociological sense: societal ideals, customs, institutions and traditions that the people of that society hold in high regard. Some organizational cultures are responsive to their environment, assimilating quickly by adapting to the resident culture while maintaining some of their own culture. This happens most readily when the employees are able to assimilate and when the parent company allows offices in the foreign community to adapt to the resident culture.

Value conflicts can occur over such concepts as time, status of women, regard for animals and ecology. All of these can put the organization at odds with its environment and can be sources of misunderstanding and resentment.

An organization may not be willing to compromise on some values, such as cleanliness, education, personal freedom and egalitarianism. Moreover, some ways of doing business in other parts of the world may conflict with laws governing the parent company—anything from standard bribes or kickbacks to the subordinate status of women to the employment of children. In these situations, some understanding must be reached with the host nation, and this can only be accomplished when the organization's employees act with flexibility and sensitivity. While the organization faces unique challenges abroad, it also gains opportunities to learn and to incorporate new ideas from the host culture. Particular care must be exerted to ensure that internal publications and audiovisual presentations—some of which may be prepared at home but distributed to offices abroad—don't offend or violate cultural norms.

Of course, you don't have to go abroad to get into trouble by offending a cultural group. The stereotyping of people in any medium is likely to cause trouble, even when it's intended to be amusing; and language can offend, as General Motors discovered at home. GM's situation involved nimbus groups—unintended recipients of a message. Often this occurs internationally when mass media (publications and broadcasts) cross borders to reach publics who are not intended recipients. In the GM case, an internal video—and not the video's effect on its intended (internal) public, but its effect at second hand on external publics who learned of it through news reports—caused the problem.

The video, presented by GM's Chevrolet division at an intenal marketing show in Detroit during September of 1990, contained interviews with customers who explained why they preferred the Chevrolet product. At one point the video showed a foreign competitor's product while one of the customers referred to it as "that little faggot truck."

News reports of the video reached the city of San Francisco, which has a politically powerful gay community. The city threatened to rescind its contract with GM to buy about $500,000 per year in cars and trucks unless GM showed how it would avoid discriminating against gays in the future. The city's officials were acting under a city ordinance that bans discrimination against homosexuals.

GM's response was to issue a corporate directive barring discrimination or insults against homosexuals, and GM Chairman Robert C. Stempel sent a letter of apology to the city of San Francisco. The company included a notice about the directive in its December 1990 company newsletter. Although the company already had an anti-discrimination policy, the new directive extended its protection to cover sexual orientation.

The nationwide directive issued on November 29, 1990, to GM managers stated that each employing unit would be responsible for implementing the policy. San Francisco officials wanted to see how GM implemented the policy before they agreed to lift their boycott, and they wanted GM to donate to a national organization that fights discrimination against gays.[15]

As GM discovered, problems often arise not out of carefully considered situations but out of careless, off-handed ones. Every word, every gesture, every representation of the organization is important.

▼ SUMMARY

The public relations department must help the organization develop a mission statement, if one does not exist; if one does, the PR department must help update or reevaluate it. Public relations people then use the mission statement to develop descriptive and identifying statements for the organization to use repeatedly in order to establish how it sees itself. The PR department also helps management develop and interpret the organization's objectives and goals. The organization's publics and how they see the organization are additional concerns of the public relations department, as is the need to develop programs and activities to help the organization realize its objectives and goals. The involvement of the public relations department in these activities usually depends on how management sees the role of the public relations department—as counsel to management or as primarily supplying a communications function. And finally, the public relations department is responsible for monitoring the organization's activities, its projects and its relationships with its publics and for helping to evaluate the organization's progress toward achieving its goals.

Besides fulfilling its support role for the organization, the public relations department must develop its own mission statement describing its contribution to the organization, and must set its own objectives and goals as a department. Furthermore, it has to define and prioritize its publics as well as the organization's publics. As a department, it has to plan its own activities and develop plans for its role in the organization. Such plans are both long-range and short-range. The department needs to monitor its own activities as well as those of the organization, and it must evaluate its own successes in order to be successful in the organization.

The public relations department is also involved in identifying and solving strategic problems for the organization. Many formulas have been used, but the best technique for addressing problems is a multiphase activity that can't be reduced to an acronym. In the process of problem solving, the public relations department is likely to encounter many complicating circumstances, the first of which is perception of the problem—by the individual PR practitioner and also by others. The other area of difficulty involves existing situations such as the power structure of the organization, the prevailing corporate culture and the extant decision-making processes within the organization.

The public relations department of an organization participates in a great deal of decision making with other units, since it functions as a source and resource for the organization. It may even be set up as a profit center, accepting outside clients much like an independent PR firm. In any case, it usually charges, if only for purposes of internal accounting, for its work.

The fees set by public relations groups are figured in one of three ways: as fixed fees, as fees plus expenses or as a retainer. Firms incur noncharge-able fees that can be expensive. For this reason some firms look for large clients to help cover these costs through the large volume of activity they generate. The problem is that loss of a large client can force a PR firm into financial difficulty. On the other hand, some small clients cost the firm more than they return in fees. Budgeting a public relations operation means keeping strict accounts of people's time, because that's where the greatest loss can be. Some computer software programs can help with this, and even electronic devices are available to help with monitoring.

As important as setting and living within a budget is defending that budget to financial officers. Inside the organization, some public relations departments face zero-based budgeting, so they have to prove their worth annually. Clients also look for dollar value in their public relations services.

While people constitute the greatest cost in a public relations operation, they are also the greatest asset. Managing creative talent isn't easy, nor is it easy to explain to organization executives that an artist doesn't want to be promoted to a management position but does want to get more money for continuing to do the same job well.

Since employees of public relations firms and PR corporate offices are often stationed abroad, public relations managers must consider how their own cultural values can lead to conflicts in the resident culture. Avoiding conflicts requires both strategic planning and sensitivity.

▼ NOTES

[1]Russell L. Colley, *Defining Advertising Goals for Measuring Advertising Results* (New York: Association of National Advertisers, 1961).

[2]The widely used Colley DAGMAR process clearly positions goals, separating them as measurable. See also Michael L. Ray, *Advertising and Communication Management* (Englewood Cliffs, N.J.: Prentice-Hall, 1982) for a complete discussion of the *measurable* goals principle.

[3]"Developer of 'The Strategic Management Process' Questions Traditional Planning: Sees Limitations, Need for Line Management Involvement," "tips and tactics," *pr reporter*, 23(6) (April 15, 1985), p. 2.

[4]John E. Marston, *The Nature of Public Relations* (New York: McGraw-Hill, 1963), pp. 161–73; also in his *Modern Public Relations* (New York: McGraw-Hill, 1979), pp. 185–95.

[5]Scott M. Cutlip and Allen H. Center, *Effective Public Relations* (Englewood Cliffs, N.J.: Prentice-Hall, 1952), p. 87.

[6]Jerry A. Hendrix, *Public Relations Cases* (Belmont, Calif.: Wadsworth, 1988), p. 19.

[7]Glen M. Broom and David M. Dozier, *Using Research in Public Relations* (Englewood Cliffs, N.J.: Prentice-Hall, 1990), p. 25.

[8]Robert L. Katz, "Human Relations Skills Can Be Sharpened," in *People: Managing Your Most Important Asset* (Boston: Harvard Business Review, 1990), p. 67.

[9]Ibid., p. 61.

[10]C. A. Bullis and P. K. Thompkins, "'The Forest Ranger Revisited: A Study of Control Practices and Identification," *Communication Monographs*, 56(4), pp. 304–5.

[11]Marshall Scott Poole and Vonelle Roth, "Decision Development in Small Groups V Test of a Contingency Model," *Human Communication Research*, 15(4) (Summer 1989), p. 588.

[12]Alfred G. Paulson, "Cost Accounting in the Public Relations Firm," *Public Relations Quarterly*, 16(3) (1972), pp. 14–15. See also "Budgeting in the Public Relations Agency" and "Accounting Reports in Public Relations," *Public Relations Quarterly*, 9(4) (1972). These also are contained in a brochure, "Budgeting and Accounting for Public Relations Firms," with Paulson's article on fee billing and one by Farley Manning on "How to Charge a Client." Copies available on request: A. G. Paulson, 103 Park Ave., New York, NY 10017.

[13]"Being in the News Proves Costly," *pr reporter* (July 18, 1983), p. 3. (Some companies handling high-volume products like automobiles routinely get similar attention.)

[14]Reprinted with permission of Jim Haynes, public relations counselor, Dallas, Texas.

[15]Jim Carlton, "An Apologetic GM Bars Discrimination, Insults Against Gays," *Wall Street Journal* (December 31, 1990), pp. 3, 28.

Selected readings, activities and assignments appropriate to this chapter can be found in the *Instructor's Guide.*

▼

Communication Channels
and Media

What you are stands over you the while, and thunders so that I cannot hear what you say . . .

Ralph Waldo Emerson

Even the most helpful editor does not look at the problem from the viewpoint of the publicist, and it simply does no good for the publicist to have a perennial chip on his shoulder.

Richard Weiner, PR practitioner and author

Channels of communication are public or private paths for messages to and from various publics. Media are conveyances for messages in those channels. Public channels are dominated by mass or specialized media available to anyone who chooses to subscribe or tune in. Private channels are more commonly used by media directed to a particular chosen individual or group. It's important to remember that, while a medium may be a person, media generally are either print or electronic.

Print and electronic media may be classified as either internal or external, depending on the audience to whom the message is directed; however, the audience, and not the medium itself, is actually internal or external. In public relations, media are viewed as either controlled or uncontrolled. When a message is controlled, you can be reasonably sure that it reaches its intended receiver exactly as you sent it.

The PR practitioner chooses the appropriate means of communication based on four things: purpose of communication; knowledge of intended audience; knowledge of message to be delivered; and awareness of resources available. For external audiences, the communication media are usually newspapers, magazines, television and radio, although they may also include electronic message systems, facsimile, billboards, posters, signs on transportation carriers, flyers, window displays, bill stuffers, films, skywriting, trade fair exhibits and public newsletters. In addition, unique items such as campaign buttons and an organization's clothing—T-shirts, windbreakers or corporate ties—present limited messages.

Internal audiences are reached by special magazines and newsletters; closed-circuit TV programs or special videotape presentations; speeches and meetings; in-house displays, exhibits and posters; flyers; memos; and paycheck stuffers.

The PR practitioner must select the communication medium that will best reach the target audience and be received by it as credible. Television is regarded as the number one source for news, and it is also considered the most believable medium.

How different audiences use different media dictates how, when and under what circumstances the audience will be exposed to the message, and therefore what the life span of the message might be. The medium itself offers clues. For example, certain types of advertising appear in specific sections of the newspaper and in certain types of publications. However, advertising agencies have determined that the intrusion of an ad into "foreign territory" can make it stand out successfully if other elements are right for acceptance of the message—in other words, if the audience is there. For instance, Burson-Marsteller was the first to use the *New York Times Book Review* for a nonbook ad and the first to use local radio to sell small computers (for IBM).

▼ CHOOSING THE MEDIUM

All public relations efforts should have a specific objective. That objective, together with the audience, the message itself, the element of timeliness and your budget, should determine your choice of media. Generally, a mix of media is used; and one important consideration in this regard is the choice between controlled and uncontrolled media.

A billboard is an example of a controlled medium. You have complete control over its content and its appearance. Television, on the other hand, is an uncontrolled medium, since—even when you

▼ **How an audience uses a medium dictates how, when and under what circumstances the audience will be exposed to the message and what the life span of the message might be.**

control the content of a message (because it is an ad or PSA)—you do not control its context (what spot is shown immediately before or after it, and what content the surrounding program will have. Still, an advertisement or public service announcement does constitute a controlled communication; other forms of communication are uncontrolled. For example, a news conference or a groundbreaking ceremony that receives TV coverage is an uncontrolled communication, since the PR person has no assurance that the cameras will film the event or focus the coverage in the desired way.

Of course, there is an element of uncontrollability in every aspect of communication. There is no guarantee that the audience to whom a message is directed will pay attention to it or respond to it. You must carefully weigh the advantages and disadvantages of each medium before investing time, creativity and money. However, avoid the temptation to consider *production costs* instead of *cost-effectiveness*.

You should consider three questions in selecting the proper medium for your message:

1. What audience are you trying to reach, and what is its credibility rating for each medium?

2. When do you need to reach this audience, and by what date does it need to receive a message in order to respond to it?

3. How much do you need to spend, and how much can you afford to spend?

After you have answered and evaluated these questions, you need to ask four additional questions:

1. Which medium reaches the broadest segment of your target audience at the lowest cost?

2. Which one has the highest credibility, and what is its cost?

3. Which medium can you count on to deliver the message within the necessary time constraints for the message to be effective?

4. Should a single medium be used? If a media mix is desirable, which media should be used to complement one another?

To make effective use of the media selected, you must know enough about the mechanics and technology of each medium to prepare the copy properly. Most students are surprised by the amount and different styles of writing demanded of PR practitioners. PR professors are not surprised, however, because in recommending students for jobs after graduation, they find the most frequently asked question is "Can they write?" The question implies "for all media." In preparing messages for all media, you must consider the differences and the advantages and disadvantages of various media (see Examples 11.1 and 11.2).

▼ TYPES OF ADVERTISING USED IN PR PRACTICE

As we noted earlier, advertising and publicity are often confused, even though they differ significantly. Advertising is *paid-for* broadcast time or print media space; publicity is *news* about a client, product or service that appears in broadcast or print media. Perhaps the confusion over the two occurs in format, as when ads in newspapers or magazines are designed to look like articles. Or

perhaps the problem is that people fail to distinguish between the nature of advertising as a fundamentally controlled form of communication and the nature of publicity as an uncontrolled form subject to editorial alteration.

It is the implied exercise of editorial judgment over a piece—even when the piece remains unchanged from how it was originally presented by its source—that sets a publicity item appearing in a medium apart from an advertising item appearing in the same medium. Thus, when John Fischer was editor of *Harper's* magazine, he turned down a lucrative proposal for paid space because the ad would have appeared in the same format as *Harper's* articles, with nothing to identify the supplier of the copy and nothing to tell readers the space was purchased. Fischer thought the public might be misled, and he was probably right.

Before we discuss advertising as defined, we need to look at two deviations from the definition that nevertheless qualify as advertising: house ads and public service announcements (PSAs). Further, we need to understand the more commonly accepted form of "PR advertising"—institutional advertising—and how it is used for issues, advocacy and identity. Also discussed in this section are specialty, cooperative and professional advertising.

House Ads

A house ad is an ad that an organization prepares for use in its own publication or in another medium controlled by the same owner. When these messages appear in broadcast media they are called "promos," for promotional announcements. For instance, a newspaper that is part of the Scripps-Howard chain might promote a special subscription offer or announce a new "Lifestyles" section by running an ad on the local Scripps-Howard television station (see Example 11.3). No money is exchanged, although space allotments or "budgets" are established. House ads are one exception to the definition of advertising as paid-for time or space.

EXAMPLE 11.1

Principal Media: Advantages and Disadvantages

TELEVISION

ADVANTAGES

1. Combines sight, sound and motion attributes
2. Permits physical demonstration of product
3. Believability due to immediacy of message
4. High impact of message
5. Huge audiences
6. Good product identification
7. Popular medium

DISADVANTAGES

1. Message limited by restricted time segments
2. No possibility for consumer referral to message
3. Availabilities sometimes difficult to arrange
4. High time costs
5. Waste coverage
6. High production costs
7. Poor color transmission

RADIO

ADVANTAGES

1. Selectivity of geographical markets
2. Good saturation of local markets
3. Ease of changing advertising copy
4. Relatively low cost

DISADVANTAGES

1. Message limited by restricted time segments
2. No possibility for consumer referral to message
3. No visual appeal
4. Waste coverage

SOURCE: Leon Quera, *Advertising Campaigns: Formulation and Tactics* (Columbus, Ohio: Grid, 1973), pp. 71–74. Used by permission.

MAGAZINES

ADVANTAGES

1. Selectivity of audience
2. Reaches more affluent consumers
3. Offers prestige to an advertiser
4. Pass-along readership
5. Good color reproduction

DISADVANTAGES

1. Often duplicate circulation
2. Usually cannot dominate in a local market
3. Long closing dates
4. No immediacy of message
5. Sometimes high production costs

NEWSPAPERS

ADVANTAGES

1. Selectivity of geographical markets
2. Ease of changing advertising copy
3. Reaches all income groups
4. Ease of scheduling advertisements
5. Relatively low cost
6. Good medium for manufacturer/dealer advertising

DISADVANTAGES

1. High cost for national coverage
2. Shortness of message life
3. Waste circulation
4. Differences of sizes and formats
5. Rate differentials between local and national advertisements
6. Sometimes poor color reproduction

EXAMPLE 11.2

Supplemental Media: Advantages and Disadvantages

DIRECT MAIL

ADVANTAGES

1. Extremely selective
2. Message can be very personalized
3. Little competition with other advertisements
4. Easy to measure effect of advertisements
5. Provides easy means for consumer action

DISADVANTAGES

1. Often has poor image
2. Can be quite expensive
3. Many restrictive postal regulations
4. Problems in maintaining mailing lists

POINT-OF-PURCHASE DISPLAYS

ADVANTAGES

1. Presents message at point of sale
2. Great flexibility for creativity
3. Ability to demonstrate product in use
4. Good color reproduction
5. Repetitive value

DISADVANTAGES

1. Dealer apathy in installation
2. Long production period
3. High unit cost
4. Shipping problems
5. Space problem

OUTDOOR POSTERS (ON STATIONARY PANELS)

ADVANTAGES

1. Selectivity of geographical markets
2. High repetitive value
3. Large physical size
4. Relatively low cost
5. Good color reproduction

DISADVANTAGES

1. Often has poor image
2. Message must be short
3. Waste circulation
4. National coverage is expensive
5. Few creative specialists

TRANSIT POSTERS (ON MOVING VEHICLES)

ADVANTAGES

1. Selectivity of geographical markets
2. Captive audience
3. Very low cost
4. Good color reproduction
5. High repetitive value

DISADVANTAGES

1. Cannot be employed in all theaters
2. Waste circulation
3. Surroundings may be disreputable
4. Few creative specialists

MOVIE TRAILERS

ADVANTAGES

1. Selectivity of geographical markets
2. Captive audience
3. Large physical size
4. Good medium for manufacturer/dealer advertising

DISADVANTAGES

1. Cannot be employed in all theaters
2. Waste circulation
3. High production costs
4. No possibility for consumer referral to message

ADVERTISING SPECIALTIES

ADVANTAGES

1. Unique presentation
2. High repetitive value
3. Has a "gift" quality
4. Relatively long life

DISADVANTAGES

1. Subject to fads
2. Message must be short
3. May have relatively high unit cost
4. Effectiveness difficult to measure

PAMPHLETS AND BOOKLETS

ADVANTAGES

1. Offer detailed message at point of sale
2. Supplement a personal sales presentation
3. Offer to potential buyers a good referral means
4. Good color reproduction

DISADVANTAGES

1. Dealers often fail to use
2. May have a relatively high unit cost
3. Few creative specialists
4. Effectiveness difficult to measure

COMPUTERS

ADVANTAGES

1. Highly personalized
2. Creativity and flexibility
3. Home, office and remote site use

DISADVANTAGES

1. Restricted group of users
2. Costs high

EXAMPLE 11.3

House Ad

TRUE CHU

Mike Chu. Founder of Synergie, one of the hottest agencies in the history of Hong Kong advertising—and since a 1988 merger, chairman and executive creative director of The Ball Partnership, Hong Kong, voted 1989 Ad Age International Agency of the Year, Runner Up. Here, from a recent conversation, are Mike Chu's true views.

On beginnings:

I was born in Hong Kong, son of Chu Yuk-wa—one of the last great Shanghainese film producers. So I grew up with film stars, directors and writers. As a teen-ager, I wanted to be a film director—but my parents wanted me to be an architect, an engineer, a doctor or a lawyer. Out of those options, I chose architecture. Then I met some friends who were studying art at the California College of Arts and Crafts. They seemed to be having so much fun. I enrolled on an urge—and never looked back!

On early jobs:

After I'd earned my degree in 1975, I worked in several advertising and design related jobs in the Bay Area. In 1977, I came home and joined Benton & Bowles and later Bozell. During those years I put in 80- to-100-hour work-weeks. I ate and breathed advertising. And I learned my craft during these years. Three years later, at 25, I joined Ted Bates/Hong Kong as the agency's creative director. And then a year after, I was proud to become the youngest board director in all of Bates's worldwide network.

On success—and dreams:

After several years at Bates, I became discontented. I wanted to do the best creative work possible and I knew that the place to do it was in an agency committed to excellence, with people who shared my dream. It meant starting an agency from scratch, as there were none around that met my requirements. Ronald Yue, whom I'd met in my first job, became my partner and when Bozell agreed to put up 65% of the capital, we were in business.

On Synergie—and synergy:

We opened Synergie Communications with zero billings in 1983. When we merged with the Ball Partnership four years later, we were billing HK$100 million. Today, we're at HK$360 million, more than twice what the two shops were billing when we merged. Obviously the synergy was good.

On the creative environment:

The key word is respect. Respect your staff and respect will be reflected in the look and feel of your working environment. I've worked in places where I *hated* my office—how can anyone perform under those conditions?

On the agency's personality:

Our agency is populated with people who are young, energetic, creative. Obviously, that has shaped the way we work, the way we live, the way we think. And thus, it has defined our personality.

On the agency as educator:

Many agencies are content to produce ads to be seen by the client, not by the consumer. But great agencies must be educators, not simply communicators. We teach our clients that ads must be single-minded with strong and memorable ideas; powerfully expressed so they come across in a split second, but are remembered for a long time.

On the essence of a good ad:

There is no gimmick to it; an arresting visual, a grabbing headline, a unique proposition. But make sure it is all relevant to the product or the service. And I would add another requirement—style. In today's cluttered media marketplace, you can't win unless you establish a brand personality. Products, like people, each have their own style and personality. I like to think I do not create ads, but rather personalities for products.

On the Hong Kong way:

Hong Kong is a worldclass, cosmopolitan city. Our Hong Kong skyline even *looks* a bit like New York's. But inside those high-rises, Hong Kong is the business capital of Asia. Our way of doing business is based on honor, trust and respect. In America, it is all contracts and lawyers. If a contract is necessary to protect yourself in a relationship, why have the relationship?

On hiring:

I look for some eccentricity in the people I hire. It's difficult to create great advertising unless you have people who think differently. "Normal" people produce "normal" advertising—and that's dull.

On the ultimate deadline:

The year 1997 is the ultimate deadline. In any other country, companies can make long-range plans. You can't do that here—not when you know everything will be handed over to the People's Republic of China in 1997; not when our government is the greatest bastion of free enterprise, and the Chinese government is the greatest bastion of communism. Over the next five years, nearly everyone in this agency will change jobs and probably half will move to Australia, Canada, the UK —a sad thing. So far, I have no plans to leave Hong Kong.

On The Asian Wall Street Journal:

The Asian Wall Street Journal is the right publication, at the right time, in the right place. Over the past decade or so, the business capitals of Asia have become closer— in both a real and a psychological sense— than ever before. You can't do business in Asia unless you think of Asia as one region. The Asian Wall Street Journal is the only publication with that point of view. That's why it attracts such a select audience: executives, decision-makers, managers. Every creative person knows it's important to know your target—and nowhere is the target as well defined as it is in The Journal. Throughout Asia, English is the language of business— and throughout Asia, The Asian Wall Street Journal is *the* daily of Asian business!

THE WALL STREET JOURNAL.
IT WORKS—AROUND THE WORLD!

SOURCE: Reprinted with permission of Dow Jones & Co., Inc., publisher of *The Wall Street Journal*. *The Wall Street Journal* is a trademark of Dow Jones & Company.

Public Service Announcements

The second exception to the advertising rule of paid-for time or space is the public service announcement (PSA). PSAs are sales or promotional pieces—not news stories—in the form of announcements. Unfortunately, promoters of civic events or nonprofit organizations that qualify for PSAs are often unaware of exactly what a PSA is.

Generally, broadcast stations give air time for PSAs, which are prepared just like commercials, from organizations such as the United Way, the American Heart Association or the local symphony. No money is exchanged, but the station may send the nonprofit organization an invoice for the amount of air time given, listing the number of hours and the commercial rate and bearing the notation "paid in full."

One word of warning if you work for a non-profit advertiser: Just because your free public service time leaves some money in your advertising budget, don't splurge on sizable ads in print media. Broadcasters can read. If a station is running your spots free of charge on public service time and you buy sizable ads from a print space salesperson, you are likely to get a bill instead of a complimentary credit slip from the broadcaster.

PSAs have also found their way into cable systems. A public service/cable service now periodically distributes PSAs to 100 of the country's largest cable systems.[1]

Print PSAs are generally, but not always, found toward the back of magazines and occasionally in newspapers. Leftover space is made available for free display ads (see Example 11.4).

Institutional Advertising

The objective of some institutional advertising is to convey a particular message. *Issue ads* are used by an organization as a forum for its views on a topic or problem. When the issue affects the organization directly, the advertising almost amounts to "position" statements directed to the public. Companies seeking public support for corporate policies and programs have begun to invest more in this type

of advertising, called *advocacy advertising*. Advocacy ads are a form of lobbying to influence public opinion. Another type of institutional ad, which can be considered less a persuasive message and more a reminder, is the type some companies call *sustaining* or *image ads*. A similar device is the *identity ad,* often used by nonconsumer product companies, or by consumer-oriented companies when takeovers or spinoffs have blurred public recognition.

Issue Advertising   Issue ads give organizations a forum for expressing their opinions and views on a controversy or issue that is receiving public attention or scrutiny.

International concern over the rapid decline in numbers of elephants in eastern Africa has led many governments (including the United States) to ban the importation of even antique elephant ivory. Nevertheless, the poaching continues. The ad in Example 11.5 was created as part of an international campaign to preserve the animals.

Advocacy Advertising   Advocacy ads go beyond offering a general comment on issues to urging support for a position that benefits the organization specifically. (See Example 11.6). Advocacy advertising in the broadcast media has traditionally been called *advertorials,* but this term now is applied to long magazine supplements, as well. The long copy provides more information about a product or service and generally appears in magazines carefully chosen to reach audiences likely to be interested in learning more about the organization than a single-page ad could convey.

Corporate advocacy advertising often looks like editorial copy, although it may be clearly identified as an ad. Some product advertising done by specialty houses looks like features or columns. The "Homes" section of Sunday papers, for example,

EXAMPLE 11.4

Public Service Announcements

Look closely and you can see the scars.

There are no bruises.
And no broken bones.
She seems the picture of the perfect child.
But if you look closely you can see how rejection, fear and constant humiliation have left scars that have tragically affected her childhood.

So now only a shattered spirit remains.
And the light of laughter has gone out.
Remember that words hit as hard as a fist.
So watch what you say.
You don't have to lift a hand to hurt your child.
Take time out. Don't take it out on your kid.

SOURCE: Reprinted by permission of the National Committee for Prevention of Child Abuse.

EXAMPLE 11.5

Issue Ad

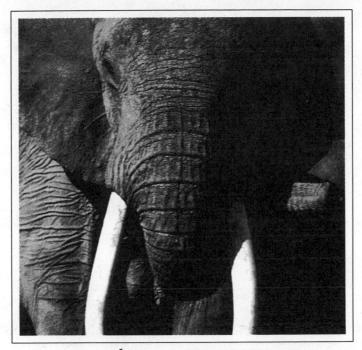

YOU'RE LOOKING DEATH STRAIGHT IN THE EYE. RUN FOR YOUR WALLET!

You are in no immediate danger. Unfortunately, the same cannot be said about the African elephant. Until recently, armed poachers would have made this elephant just another statistic of Kenya's killing fields.

This once proud animal would be horribly mutilated, his face hacked off with an axe, sometimes while the poor creature is still alive. His lifeless body left in a crumpled heap to rot under a burning sun.

A bloody high price to pay for ivory.

This wanton destruction of a majestic, intelligent animal must end. The Kenya Wildlife Fund supports the efforts of Dr. Richard Leakey and his anti-poaching campaign. It's working, but they need your help.

If our generation doesn't put a stop to this senseless slaughter, there won't be elephants for the next generation.

Don't be part of this annihilation. Never buy or wear ivory. And give what you can to The Kenya Wildlife Fund.

For more information on how you can help contact:

THE KENYA WILDLIFE FUND,
P.O. Box 2445, Station "B",
Richmond Hill, Ontario L4E 1A5
Tel. (416) 841-3999

THE KENYA WILDLIFE FUND

Reprinted with permission.

EXAMPLE 11.6

Advocacy Ad

IT'S ONLY A MATTER OF TIME.

We now import more than 40 percent of all the oil we use. And that percentage is growing. Our excessive dependence on foreign oil could blow up in our faces at any moment if our supply were somehow disrupted.

But the more we use nuclear energy, instead of imported oil, to generate our electricity, the less we have to depend on uncertain foreign oil supplies.

America's 112 nuclear electric plants already have cut foreign oil dependence by 4 billion barrels since the oil embargo of 1973, saving us $115 billion in foreign oil payments.

But 112 nuclear plants will not be enough to meet our rapidly growing demand for electricity. We need more plants.

Importing so much oil is a danger we must not ignore. We need to rely more on energy sources we can count on, like nuclear energy.

For a free booklet on nuclear energy, write to the U.S. Council for Energy Awareness, P.O. Box 66080, Dept. BB01, Washington, D.C. 20035.

U.S. COUNCIL FOR ENERGY AWARENESS

Nuclear energy means more energy independence.

Reprinted with permission.

looks like editorial copy but is clearly labeled as advertising. The line between advertising and publicity will blur further as traditional media are used in more and more exotic ways.

Image Ads   Image ads are often used by companies seeking to modify their public image (see Example 11.7). They may present a redesigned logo or a change in policy. The image ad is also used by monopolies that wish to represent themselves as public servants. Utility companies frequently use this type of advertising to win favorable public opinion before requesting rate increases or attempting to ward off restrictive legislation.

Nonprofit organizations, especially trade and professional organizations, may use image advertising, too (see Example 11.8). Because of an image ad's tone and content, it may be mistaken for publicity.

Some image advertising looks like product advertising and vice versa (see Example 11.9). A company may relate image to product if it is important to the company's reputation that its name be associated, in the public's mind, with a certain product. When image ads are not used, the company may begin to suffer a decline in public approval and market share; after two years, the decline is quick and dramatic. If image ads are stopped when money is tight, the results can be disastrous.

Advertising in Other Formats

Sometimes the artwork for a print ad can be used in other formats. The most common of these is the *poster,* which in smaller form is called a *flyer,* and in larger form a *billboard.* Other versions are *transit* or *in-store* advertising. Some versions, usually of flyer size, are even sent as *fax* advertising. Fax advertising, which is usually from suppliers or service industries, has encountered some problems because the receiver pays for the paper on which the unsolicited message is printed.

There should be continuity between poster or billboard art, the packaging for a product and the store displays. An opera association, for example, may have a table flanked by posters set up in the lobby at performances to sell cups, tote bags, umbrellas and other items bearing the opera's logo. The purpose in this case is to raise money for the nonprofit organization. Some of these items, like pens with the opera logo, are the types of materials that profit-making organizations give away as advertising specialties.

Specialty Advertising   Without looking, can you recall the company whose name is on the pen you use or on your desk calendar? Advertising specialties are useful, inexpensive items, such as pens or calendars, imprinted with an organization's name, logo or message. These items are given free to customers or perhaps as souvenirs to those who attend a special event.

Cooperative Advertising   Cooperative advertising offers almost as many advantages as advertising placed by a single organization. When one advertiser shares a message with another—such as when a cheese dip manufacturer combines with a potato chips manufacturer to buy advertising space and time—it also shares the production and space/time costs. This enables each to participate in both the production and the exposure. Sometimes creative compromises are necessary, but it still is a controlled situation (see Example 11.10).

Advertising by Professionals

Both advertising agencies and PR firms are now learning to deal with a form of advertising and promotion that involves lawyers, dentists, doctors and other professionals, who until recently were prohibited by their professional codes of conduct from engaging in such commercial activities (see Example 11.11). An increasing number of these professionals are defying tradition by putting their names in print and their faces on television. Consequently, a new market for public relations practitioners has opened.

EXAMPLE 11.7

Corporate Image Ad

The eagle has landed.

In Oklahoma and Mississippi. Georgia and Alabama. Where few bald eagle nests have produced young in the last 50 years. Using precious eggs and dedicated effort, the Sutton Avian Research Center is successfully raising eaglets from fuzzy to fierce. And releasing them into the habitats bald eagles used to call home. Phillips Petroleum supports this unique program to re-establish our endangered national symbol.

After all, if Man can land an Eagle on the moon, he can surely keep them landing on the earth.

PHILLIPS 66

For more information, contact the George Miksch Sutton Avian Research Center, Inc., P.O. Box 2007, Bartlesville, OK 74005, (918) 336-7778.

Reprinted with permission.

EXAMPLE 11.8

Nonprofit Image Ad

ADVERTISING UNSELLS.

In 1986, drug abuse officially became America's number-one concern.

In that same year, the Partnership for a Drug-Free America was organized by the American Association of Advertising Agencies (AAAA). Its mission: to decrease drug use in this country by changing attitudes.

Many of the country's top persuaders–members of the AAAA–were enlisted by the Partnership. Some 200 ads created for all major media have been donated by the agencies. The messages have been run by the media on a pro bono basis at an estimated weight of $310 million since the program began in April 1987. Massive consumer surveys have tracked the results.

Some highlights:

From 1987 to 1989, children who think "it's easy to get hooked" rose 5 percentage points. Those who are "scared of drugs" rose 4.

Most significant: Changes in attitudes and consumption were greatest in markets where the advertising appeared the most:

Among Adults	Low Media	High Media
Basic Attitudes	+5.2%	+9.7%
Fear of Drugs	−1.0%	+3.7%
Act Against Use	−1.7%	+4.5%

Two independent studies confirm declining usage. One, from the University of Michigan, found drug use among high school seniors to be down. Marijuana usage dropped from 21.0 percent in 1987 to 16.7 percent in 1989. Cocaine use fell from 4.3 percent to 2.8 percent in the same period.

The second was conducted by The National Institute of Drug Abuse (NIDA). It found that, between 1985 and 1988, trial of marijuana and cocaine among people 18 to 25 declined at a significant rate.

Releasing this data, NIDA's director, Dr. Charles R. Schuster, said, "...a significant decrease in trial and occasional use of illicit drugs is a result of major changes in social attitudes. In my opinion, the Partnership's messages have had a direct impact on these attitudes and usage declines."

At a special White House conference, Gordon S. Black, Ph.D., president of the firm that conducted the Partnership research, concluded, "If these were the results of a tracking study for one of your own advertising campaigns, I think your advertising director would be rather pleased, to say the least."

To get a booklet that summarizes the findings, please write to The Committee on the Value of Advertising, Department B, American Association of Advertising Agencies, 666 Third Avenue, New York, New York 10017.

These studies confirm the power of advertising. It can change attitudes. It can cause action.

Or, in this case, inaction.

AAAA

%
21.8 — Tried Marijuana 15.5
7.6 — Tried Cocaine 4.5
1985 1988
The Results We're Proudest Of.

Reprinted with permission.

Image/Identity Ad

THE WALL STREET JOURNAL   11/4/91

The Dial Corp

The name behind some of the best names you know

A tradition in most homes

Dial makes some of the best-known brands in the personal care market. Dial bar soap is the best-selling deodorant soap in the world. Liquid Dial is the first antibacterial liquid hand soap. Tone soap is one of the fastest-growing brands in the country. And we recently acquired Breck hair care products.

We also make outstanding household and laundry products. Like Brillo soap pads. Purex bleach and detergent. Borax and Borateem. Parsons' Ammonia. And many others.

In the kitchen, we serve up healthy foods that fit consumers' busy schedules. Four years ago, we developed shelf-stable microwave meals that stay fresh without being refrigerated. Today, Lunch Bucket remains the best-selling brand. And Armour Star canned meats are a familiar sight on tables everywhere.

Convention services and duty free shops are major contributors to the services group

Exhibitgroup, Inc., designs and builds exhibits for shows, museums, marketing centers and showrooms. Greyhound Exposition Services is a leading general contractor for conventions and trade shows west of the Mississippi, handling more than 750 major events every year.

The largest operator of shipboard duty free shops is Greyhound Leisure Services, selling fine products to travelers aboard 32 cruise ships and in select airports.

Travelers Express is number one in money orders

Travelers Express, with its Republic Money Orders division, is the nation's largest issuer of money orders, providing this important service through more than 55,000 retail stores and financial institutions. Approximately 800 million money orders are sold each year, and the company has recorded 15 straight years of sales increases.

Dobbs is a leader in airport services

As air travel grows, we're there to make the most of it. Dobbs International Services, for example, is the nation's second largest independent in-flight caterer, serving 60 airlines. And Dobbs Houses operates restaurants, lounges, newsstands and gift shop concessions at 28 airports.

Our continued financial growth and market success make us confident about our future. Call us at (602) 207-5600. Or write us at: Department PR, The Dial Corp, Dial Tower, Phoenix, AZ 85077. We'd love to tell you more.

The Dial Corp
Profit Through Leadership

Healthy growth continued at The Dial Corp in the third quarter. For the nineteenth consecutive quarter, we recorded an increase in income — a share from continuing operations — a rise from percent — to $.83 per share on income of $33,293,000, up from $.80 per share on income of $31,990,000 in the same quarter last year. For the nine months of 1991, this brings revenues to $2.72 billion, up from $2.65 billion a year ago.

Very importantly, on October 29, 1991, the board of directors gave preliminary approval to a restructuring plan that would spin off Dial's commercial lending and mortgage insurance business to our shareholders.

The purpose of the plan is to help Dial focus on its core business, consumer products and services, and enable each company to pursue separate growth opportunities to maximize shareholder returns.

The board also authorized management to consider strategic alternatives for disposition in 1992 of its Transportation Manufacturing and Service Parts business.

The goal is to give our financial and transportation manufacturing businesses the freedom to pursue their own, unique opportunities, which are quite different from those in consumer products and services. The result will be that each business will have a very clear identity, enabling it to develop growth opportunities and enhancing the likelihood that it will achieve appropriate market recognition for its performance.

The plan underscores our determination to deliver value to our shareholders and build on the strong position in consumer products and services achieved over the last decade.

**John W. Teets
Chairman, President and
Chief Executive Officer
The Dial Corp**

Reprinted courtesy of The Dial Corp.

EXAMPLE 11.10

Cooperative Ad

Our Next Program Contains Some Very Graphic Material.

Nigerian batik by Oyenike

Exquisite batik designs. Kinetic metal sculptures. Abstract wood carvings. Paintings, prints, reliefs offered as prayers to enrich the earth.

On the next episode of Smithsonian World, you'll take a fascinating look at modern Nigerian art through the eyes of the artists who create it. Designers, sculptors, painters and print makers who bring their ancient traditions to life in surprisingly contemporary ways. Drawing on a variety of cultural influences, African and Western, to fashion something rich in meaning and diverse in form.

So watch "Nigerian Art- Kindred Spirits," proudly brought to you by Southwestern Bell. It'll be broadcast on PBS May 2 at 8 p.m. Check your local listings.

Then get ready for a program that's very revealing.

SMITHSONIAN WORLD 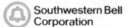 Southwestern Bell Corporation

Reprinted with permission of the Smithsonian Institution, Southwestern Bell Corporation and Terry Heffernan, photographer.

EXAMPLE 11.11

Advertising for Professionals

Hyatt Legal Services was a pioneer in legal advertising. Founder and senior partner Joel Hyatt presented the case for advertising before the Ohio Supreme Court, arguing that it was the constitutional right of the public to be informed. The company's 1991 campaign used three commercials, "Street Scene," "Law Office," and "Circuit Court." The storyboard shown here is for "Law Office."

HYATT LEGAL SERVICES

"Law Office"

And on top of that, Abraham Lincoln *advertised*.

and he took all comers, big and small.

His fees were so low, they alarmed his fellow lawyers.

His office was just across from the State House,

For the same reason Hyatt Legal Services does today:

To bring the law closer to people.

Lincoln always told you his fee up front. And we do that today.

Reprinted with permission.

Hyatt Legal Services. A good idea that just keeps getting better.

I'm Joel Hyatt, and you have my word on it.

In 1975, after the Federal Trade Commission began attacking advertising restrictions on lawyers, doctors and dentists, self-promotional advertisements began to appear—particularly in local newspapers and on local television. Several Supreme Court decisions supported creating a new market for the media among the professional groups. Although some PR practitioners are understandably pleased by the development, others consider handling some professional clients to be ethically questionable. The most recent ethical problem has arisen over testimonial ads for lawyers—especially televised testimonials. Although such ads are growing in popularity, many lawyers feel that they are in poor taste and may be misleading.[2]

▼ ADVERTISING AS CONTROLLED/ UNCONTROLLED COMMUNICATION

Controlled Advertising

One significant advantage of using paid advertising is that the advertiser nearly always has *total control*—over the message itself, over the context in which it will appear (size, shape, color) and over the medium in which it will run. And, of course, the advertiser knows approximately *when* an audience will receive the message. In addition, the advertiser has access to media research about the medium's audience, indicating *who* will receive the message and *how often* the audience will be exposed to it. Finally, media research will tell the advertiser the typical *impact* an ad schedule will have on the target audience's behavior.

Uncontrolled Advertising

Uncontrolled advertising consists of PSAs prepared for use on radio and television stations. The message is controlled, but the delivery time is not.

Only nonprofit organizations qualify for free public service time. But because such time is scarce, the United Fund and local symphony season ticket drives must compete for it just as fiercely as any business competes for dollars. National organi-

zations like the Heart Association and the American Red Cross send stations highly professional tapes, usually cut with a celebrity's voice. These are mailed far enough in advance to give station personnel time to find good slots in the daily programming for these announcements. In contrast, local organizations are more likely to put in a frantic call the day before a local blood drive asking the station to run some announcements starting immediately—with no tape and probably not even any copy. Or someone drops by with a dozen slides and two pages of copy and does not understand why this can't be aired. Remember, however, that any PSA is used only if the station has time available to give, and even this slot may be sold and the PSA bumped at the last minute.

Because most commercial radio and television stations are generous with their public service time and make every effort to cooperate with those who request it, many people imagine that the stations are required by the Federal Communications Commission to devote a certain percentage of each broadcast day to PSAs. But a station is not compelled to do so by law. Furthermore, an FCC action in 1984 erased a guideline for TV that recommended devoting 10 percent of airtime to nonentertainment programming. The corresponding guideline for radio was abolished in 1981.

Station policies on PSA time are so diverse that they defy any general description. The effective practitioner simply learns and then meets the demands of the stations.

▼ PREPARING ADVERTISING MESSAGES

A person writing advertising copy needs more than a list of details from marketing and sales describing what is supposed to be pushed. The copywriter must also know the purpose of the ad or commercial, its audience and the media it will appear in.

Copywriters must clearly define an ad's purpose. Is the purpose to *inform*? Is it to introduce a new product, attract a new market, suggest a new use for a familiar product, give a corporate identity to a conglomerate or familiarize an audience with a new trademark? Is the purpose of the ad to *persuade*? Should the ad or commercial try to get its audience to think or do something? The following ad from a laundry company appeared in a British newspaper; its purpose is quite clear: "Strong, fat women who wish to lose weight wanted for hard but well-paid work."

Sometimes an ad's purpose is "positioning." Advertisers developed this technique as a way of finding a foothold in the marketplace, and publicity strategists are now borrowing it. Here is the way it works: Have you ever asked yourself why Miller High Life is for sippers and Schaefer's is for guzzlers? Why Nyquil is the "nighttime" cold remedy, while Dristan and Contac work all day? The difference is not so much in the product but in positioning, which isolates a segment of the market in a highly competitive field by creating a unique image for a product that is fundamentally the same as its competitors. Thus, this technique artificially segments the audience.

After determining the audience and the appeal, the copywriter must find out which media are planned to carry the ad. Often adjustments must be made, since the copywriter may be thinking in terms of a medium that has not even been considered for the advertising. When the media have been chosen, the copywriter takes the facts learned, tested and validated through research; considers the audience to be reached; and with the *specific* media in mind, develops copy for the ads.

Broadcast Advertising Mechanics

Writing for broadcasting has its own set of rules, many of them related to the fact that broadcasting is less flexible than print. When a printed message won't fit, you can increase the space or use smaller type. But if a message won't fit the time slot in broadcasting, and you don't condense it, the message just can't be used.

Often PR practitioners willingly turn the job of writing copy over to an advertising agency that specializes in producing commercials. The only writing some PR people attempt is for public service announcements. They forget that poor preparation is as apparent in PSAs as it is in paid commercials.

PSAs   When you plan PSAs, you should become familiar with the preferences of the individual stations within your market area. Most television stations use videotape cassettes, 16-mm color film (sound or silent) and color slides (with sound on disks, reel-to-reel tape or cassette tape or with a script for an announcer to read). Most radio stations can use records or scripts, although professional-quality cassettes and reel-to-reel tapes are preferred. Cable systems prefer videotape cassettes and, like most broadcast stations, are willing to use more than one length of the same spot concurrently (such as 10-second, 30-second and 60-second versions). If you plan to mount a national campaign, you must make sure all actions and words are acceptable to the various regulatory agencies and to the in-house review committees of the national networks. This involves submitting any proposed PSA to various interested administrative bodies for review and approval.

The following six points about PSAs are important to remember:

1. If you send tapes or disks, send a typed copy of the message with them.

2. Indicate on the copy a cutoff date.

3. Mark the precise timing on the copy.

4. Identify where you can be contacted if any questions arise.

5. Send the material about four to six weeks ahead of time, to ensure that the station has ample time to consider and schedule it.

6. Make sure that both the video and the audio are of broadcast quality. Your own recordings or slides are not likely to qualify unless you are a professional.

Sometimes a local station will be generous enough to work with a nonprofit organization to help produce PSAs. If offered such an opportunity, accept with alacrity. A television station, for instance, may provide the studio, crew and director, with the PR practitioner handling script, talent, costumes, props, special effects or music, and any extra video components such as slides, art or film clips. The charge for these PSAs and for dubbings to enable other stations to use them is minimal.

In a small-market area, you can help get your PSA on the air by catering to the whims and idiosyncracies of each station. This can vary from matching your PSA's length to the number of seconds each station prefers for its PSAs to satisfying the PSA director's preference for having all PSA scripts typed on 4 × 5 cards so that they fit into his or her special file box. If your audience is much larger, however, settle for the format most stations can readily use.

If you are in an area of linguistic diversity, consider producing PSAs in languages other than English (most commonly, Spanish). Use standard broadcast Spanish, and avoid idioms and slang. Spanish-speaking peoples, even in the United States, are culturally diverse.

Experienced public relations practitioners usually have good working relationships with the people in charge of PSA time in their own areas; and in preparing national releases, they generally produce top-quality materials. Agencies like MediaLink will prepare PSAs and even add closed captioning if you wish.

Commercials Commercials are more common than PSAs in broadcasting. If you intend to prepare commercials, you should plan to invest a lot of time, trouble and money. It is advisable to hire a production company, unless you work with an agency experienced in producing commercials. Tasks include writing the copy, planning the audio (announcer and actors, voices, music and sound effects) and, for television, planning the video. You may have to audition acting talent and hire a producer, director, light crew, engineers and other special personnel. You may have to take the entire group on location. You may have to commission special music to be written or electronically generated.

▼ **In broadcast advertising, whether for PSAs or for commercials, knowledge of the medium's technical requirements is essential.**

Before you buy space, you must pretest your commercials to make sure they have the desired effect on a target audience. In addition, because of the innumerable legal problems that advertising can involve (particularly in this era of consumer consciousness), it is best to have your attorney check copy and art for a national or large regional campaign while it is still in the planning stages. In dealing with a regulatory agency or a network's ad clearance committee, you usually have to provide a copy of the finished product. Your ad still may be rejected. To help recover an investment, remember that some cable systems will run network rejects.

Print Advertising Mechanics

PR professionals can benefit from working directly with the advertising staff of a particular newspaper or magazine. Some media advertising representatives will help you design the ad and will get it typeset for you, but you will be charged for these professional services just as if you had gone to an outside agency or studio. The only advantage in-shop production gives you is the assurance of the ad's usability by that newspaper or broadcast station. You remain the person responsible for getting all the information needed for the copy or special art. You must also be available for consultation when needed—not when it is convenient for you.

If you personally are handling a national campaign, you may write the copy but go to an artist for layout and design, and you may get the type set at a typesetting house. Have the artist prepare camera-ready art and type, and take the ads to a printer to get slicks or glossies for offset reproductions. To make sure the sizes are correct, consult media sources like Standard Rate and Data Service, Inc.'s books for the various media. These will give you the mechanical specifications of the publications where you want to place the ads. Although not as rigid as broadcast criteria, these restrictions are important considerations.

In working with magazines, remember that most magazines have a specialized audience. You must tailor your ads accordingly: what works in *Cosmopolitan* misses by more than a mile in *Playboy.*

Advertising Costs and Evaluation

Television commercials are among the most expensive types of advertising. The cost of producing a one-minute commercial—including rehearsals, filming, reshooting, dubbing, scoring, animation and printing, is usually five times the cost of producing a minute of televised entertainment. A company may spend $1 million or more getting the commercial on the air. Commercials for movie theaters are even more costly than those for television, because they have to be more entertaining.

PR practitioners must become familiar with the scale of charges for broadcast time and print media space. They must learn to use local rate cards and to consult the appropriate volume in the Standard Rate and Data Service series. You can hire a media-buying agency, but you will get better results if you know as much about buying advertising time as the agency does and if you use this information to handle the actual placement of the ads.

You should also learn how to verify the audience data offered by the various media. U.S. magazines and newspapers with paid circulations have their readership claims substantiated by the Audit Bureau of Circulations, an outside agency. The resulting information is publicly available in various reference books that catalog media. Business publications are also audited, and these figures are published, too. However, some readership studies commissioned by newspapers and magazines are private and may not be communicated. Occasionally a publication's editorial department has readership studies done and does not even make the results available to the magazine's own advertising

staff. But audience information can be obtained from the advertising and promotion departments of most publications or from a research section within the promotion department. The promotion and advertising departments obviously have a vested interest, however, so it is best to get a clear statistical picture on competitors.

The figures on broadcast audiences are even more difficult to interpret. Radio stations have gone to a "magazine" format—that is, they appeal rather clearly to a particular audience—and the size of this audience is usually available from area ratings. Therefore, you can readily discover the station's general audience profile and listenership. Unless ratings for various programs are available, however, you can't tell to what program or at what time the audience is listening.

In television, the findings really get obscure. The basic problem is that television is a mass medium, and the mass is rather difficult to measure. National ratings exist for network shows, and local ratings for local shows. But often the ratings for the latter are not as reliable as even the stations would like them to be. If a considerable investment is involved in your advertising campaign, you may want to budget for a research study of your own.

One consideration in measuring effectiveness goes back to the planning stages: the purpose for the commercial. Some commercials are designed to win awards, and often they do. But the recognition for these awards generally benefits the agency more than it does the client—perhaps because award-winning commercials aren't necessarily the same as message-effective commercials. A study of the Clios, a now discontinued international commercial award competition, showed that the initial opportunity for product or service recognition (which generally appears within the first ten seconds in successful "selling" spots, because it aids viewer recall) was delayed in one out of every two Clio award winners. Furthermore, the duration of exposure to the brand name or logo (which is also positively identified with recall) was relatively brief in most Clio winners.[3] This gives you one more thing to consider when involved in the planning and creative process: you want results, but the producers may just want an award.

You also need to evaluate carefully the best way to deliver your message. In doing so, you must seek the proper media mix. When you buy a portion of that mix through advertising, you want every advertising dollar in each medium to help deliver the message effectively to your priority public. You have to plan how to allocate resources so as to remain within budgetary constraints, as well as putting aside some money for uncontrollable problems, which often have expensive solutions.

▼ UNCONTROLLABLE PROBLEMS

One of the biggest problems you will face in using advertising is that, if you get a good idea, it's likely to be imitated. Christian Brothers created a very successful ad campaign for its beverages using puns, only to see J&B, a competitor, launch a similar campaign. *Rolling Stone* magazine was also a victim of copycat when several magazines imitated or used takeoffs on its "perception-reality" campaign.

Another seemingly uncontrollable problem that advertising campaigns frequently encounter involves the undesirable placement of ads in a newspaper or magazine relative to the adjacent copy. The same thing can happen in broadcasting, although it's fairly standard to have standing "kill" orders for, say, an airline commercial when the evening news carries the story of an airline crash. Most media try to avoid placement errors because it makes advertisers unhappy and can result in demands for compensation.

Yet another difficulty has to do with campaigns that attack the competition. These may take the form of a product-to-product affront, like soft drink taste tests, or one politician lambasting another. Some companies don't consider it much of a problem if the competition mentions their name in an ad. They reason that consumers will forget which product was supposed to be better. Like P. T.

Barnum, they seem to respond, "Say anything you want to about me, just spell my name right." But anyone who has watched some of the battles among the fast-food hamburger chains might question the legitimacy of such a view.

Election campaigning in the United States and abroad (perhaps due to either direct or indirect U.S. influence) is increasingly negative. One perceived effect of this is lower voter turnout due to disgust with the whole affair—a rather dangerous trend in democracies. Some evidence suggests that negative advertising works for the attacker if a decision is forced within a time frame, such as elections create. But the decision to use negative advertising, either in an attack or in a counterattack, demands careful consideration because of its longer-term public relations costs, some of which may be intangible.

Myths are the source of two other problems advertising must face. The first is the notion that one ad campaign can be effective across national boundaries and cultures. Evidence from an experienced agency, Gray Advertising, Inc., indicates that global campaigns only work when three conditions exist: 1. The market developed the same way from country to country. 2. Consumer targets are similar. 3. Consumers have the same wants and needs around the world. If even one of the conditions does not exist, a global campaign will not work. For example, Gray says that Kellogg's Pop-Tarts failed in Great Britain because toasters aren't widely used there. The General Foods Corporation positioned Tang in France as a substitute for breakfast orange juice, but it subsequently found that orange juice was not popular among the French and that they drank almost none at breakfast.

The second myth is that a single advertising design or concept will work within a culture. Psychographics indicates the need for different appeals that might not be apparent from demographics. Whether the format is movie ads or paperback covers, it's important to adjust the advertising appeal to the audience. In many cases, different appeals must be designed to sell exactly the same product to different audiences.

▼ **Publicity media include in-house, industry and trade or association publications; employee handbooks; the organization's newsletters, handbooks, films and videos; speeches; and meetings.**

▼ TYPES OF PUBLICITY USED IN PR PRACTICE

A second major category of messages placed in various media by PR practitioners is publicity. What is publicity? Is it a column item in a local newspaper? A cover story in a national magazine? Thirty seconds on the 6 P.M. television news? A bit of chatter by a radio disk jockey? The mention of the company's name once or twice in a long story about the industry? A single photo in a newspaper or magazine? A 2-inch item in an association publication? An annual report? A house publication? A film? It is all of these and more.

Publicity is information about an organization that is carried as editorial (not advertising) content in a publication or news medium. Often it's news, but it can also be a sales or promotional message. Candidates for public office who make frequent speeches and expect these to be reported in the news are selling two things: themselves and their ideas. They hope you will buy them at the ballot box. Other publicity, of course, may be strictly informational. Most of a daily newspaper's business pages are filled with publicity releases and stories based on publicity releases. Here PR people function as reporters, and what they write about their organization or client is hard news.

Reporters who cover a certain area—for instance, public affairs—rarely get to talk with the top officials and executives in their field. Consequently, they must rely on public relations people who know what the news media want, need and

will use. The PR people must know their own organization thoroughly, have access to the top echelons (where they can get the information they need) and prepare it in a form that the news media can use (see Chapter 12). The news media also depend on PR people because they never have enough reporters on a staff to cover everything going on in a metropolitan area. Much of the information the news media use comes to them from public relations sources. These are facts they did not have to gather, stories they did not have to write and pictures they did not have to take. But public relations representatives who expect to remain effective must justify the trust of the news media by being accurate, truthful and reliable.

Although much of the publicity information that PR people provide to the news media is "packaged" as news tip sheets or news releases, many other publicity tools are used to reach nonmedia publics. These include publications, films and video productions, speeches, various employee media and other special media. Chapter 12 discusses tactical details of "how to do it."

Publications

Three broad categories of publications carry publicity directly to audiences: organizational, industry and trade or association.

Organizational Publications   Organizational magazines, sometimes called house publications, are distributed to employees and perhaps to stakeholders of a company. The distribution is usually vertical: copies go to everyone in the organization, from top to bottom. Occasionally in a very large organization a publication may go to just one type of employee and thus get horizontal distribution—for example, a publication for supervisors. Some organizations' publications are intended for external audiences (see Example 11.12). Others are for financial/stakeholder audiences (see Example 11.13); and still others are primarily internal (see Examples 11.14 and 11.15).

EXAMPLE 11.12

Organizational Publication for External Audiences: Oil

(Continued)

C O N T E N T S

oil progress

Caltex Petroleum Corporation.
Chairman and Chief Executive Officer: R.F. Johnson. President and Chief Operating Officer: P.J. Ward. Vice Chairman, S.S. Miller. Vice Chairman, C.A. Boyce. Vice Presidents: F.W. Blue, G.J. Cernarata, W.C. Dunning, J.M. McPhail, R.J. O'Connor, R.H. Paredes, L.A. Rayburn, M.W. Saunders, E.M. Schmidt.

Published by Corporate Affairs Department, R.A. Coccola, Editor.

© 1990 by the Caltex Petroleum Corporation, P.O. Box 619500, Dallas, Texas 75261-9500 U.S.A. All rights reserved under U.C.C. Berne, and Pan American Copyright Conventions.

Each Company affiliated with the Caltex Petroleum Corporation is a separate corporation that manages and controls its own affairs. The use of such terms as "Company," "Caltex," "organization," "our," "we," and "us" when referring to affiliates is only for convenience and is not intended as an accurate description of corporate relationships.

Credits: Front cover, inside front cover and pages 2-9 and 11-13, Joseph Brignolo for Caltex. Page 10, Lincoln Potter. Pages 14-24 and 31-33, K. Conley Associates, New York. Pages 25-30, Bahrain Ministry of Information, Nazem Choufeh and Mel Baglin.

OIL PROGRESS   Vol. 40   Spring 1990

BRIDGES

Soaring spans of structural steel require tough, nonstop protection against the weather and water that promote rust buildup. Right reason for using Caltex Texacoat to provide a fast-drying, waterproof, hard-as-nails film on exposed metal surfaces. Trusted by maintenance crews in over 60 countries spanning 3 continents because it is effective, economical, and easy to apply. For information concerning our complete line of metal-savers, call Caltex. If there's a better way to help you cut costs, raise productivity, and conserve energy, let us work with you to find it.

**Caltex helps you run
your business better.**

CALTEX

Reprinted with permission.

PHILLIPS PETROLEUM
COMPANY NORWAY

NORWEGIAN BRANCH

ANNUAL REPORT
AND ACCOUNTS 1989

Reprinted with permission.

Industry Publications   A company or even a nonprofit organization may be a member of an industry organization. Such groups often publish periodicals aimed at bettering the entire industry. Industry organizations' magazines often gain wide distribution. They are received not only by industry executives but also by business editors, financial analysts, economics specialists, government officials and anyone else who has a particular interest in the industry.

Trade or Association Publications   Also distributed horizontally are trade or association publications—magazines, newsletters, newspapers or annual reports published at the national headquarters of a group whose members share common goals or interests. Among them are labor union publications, religious magazines and newspapers, and fraternal and professional publications.

Other media include corporate, industry or association films, which are supervised (though rarely produced) by the organization's public relations staff.

Sponsored Magazines   Both profit-making and nonprofit organizations may publish sponsored magazines. They are a costly venture, however, and some profit-making organizations have quietly folded their efforts, while others accept outside advertising for support. One new magazine going to court personnel and attorneys in a large Southwestern city focuses on issues that often underlie court cases (domestic violence, delinquency and the like) and is being published for a nonprofit, human-services organization.

Among sponsored magazines published by profit-making companies, the one with the largest circulation is Philip Morris's, with 10 million copies nationwide. Although it does accept outside advertising, it charges less for its ads than do newsstand magazines. Some companies seek cosponsors because the venture is so expensive. These magazines differ from a company's own service magazines that also are costly. Examples of service magazines include various airlines' in-flight publications and American Express's *Departures,* which goes to its platinum card holders. Sponsored magazines are "custom-published" by major media companies that want to expand their business. However, companies may find it impossible to sustain them during an economic downturn, because they are so expensive to produce. An exception might be companies like Philip Morris, which see their magazines as a key to corporate survival; the cigarette manufacturer began its sponsored magazine to promote "smokers' rights."

Newsletters   Newsletters can be internal, external or both. Some external newsletters are income generators, because their audiences pay for them through subscriptions.

Internal newsletters offer an effective means of communicating with employees. A newsletter should not be a collection of trivia, but it should contain items of interest. Many newsletter items later become subjects of fuller treatment in the institution's magazine. One company newsletter editor describes her publication as a "circulating billboard." In other companies it is much more, containing short articles, bits of humor, important announcements and notices.

External newsletters are also a publicity vehicle. Some are used for addressing issues (see Example 11.16). Others are created for and subscribed to by members of the public. Subscription to a newsletter can come through membership in an organization or through direct subscription, like a regular commercial magazine. The paid newsletter business is a big one. More than 10,000 subscription newsletters exist, and most cover highly specialized subjects and are obviously intended for a particular target public. Generally, they enjoy a high readership.

Desktop publishing has made newsletters of all kinds more attractive as a means of communication and has enabled them to resemble publications more than "letters."

EXAMPLE 11.14

Association Newsletter Primarily for Internal Audiences

VITAL SIGNS

Volume 8 • Issue 3 • Spring 1990

American Heart Association
Texas Affiliate, Inc.

HeartGuide Changes Focus

THE AMERICAN HEART ASSOCIATION has changed the focus of the HeartGuide program. The modifications, which include the immediate discontinuation of the food product seal of approval, will be finalized and announced this summer.

According to Myron Weisfeldt, M.D., president of the AHA, the revamped HeartGuide will continue to focus on public nutrition education, but with added emphasis on legislative and regulatory actions to provide understandable food labeling, and on consumer research.

Weisfeldt said it's important for the public to know the AHA will not be changing the basic objectives of the program. "Its (HeartGuide's) primary goal is still to help Americans improve the way they select and prepare foods, and ultimately reduce their risk of heart disease."

Weisfeldt, chief of cardiology at the Johns Hopkins Medical Institution in Baltimore, said the decision to modify the program was due to new government initiatives announced on March 7 by Health and Human Services Secretary Louis Sullivan, M.D., and to the U.S. Food and Drug

Administration's recently announced opposition to third-party endorsements. "We have said many times that when the government develops a program that meets the public's needs, we will modify HeartGuide. The rapidly changing regulatory environment clearly indicates we need to modify HeartGuide now."

"Our efforts throughout the past three years have led to a significant victory for the American people," the AHA president said. "After 17 years, the government says it is going to move forward with a comprehensive nutritional food labeling plan and the regulation of health claims."

Weisfeldt said there is a definite role for voluntary health organizations to develop educational programs that fill the void between the FDA's proposed regulations and the educational needs of consumers.

"Everyone realizes labeling is not enough. The FDA's own proposed regulations say consumer education programs are vital to providing dietary advice," Weisfeldt said. "The FDA has

Continued on page 11

THE REVISED HEARTGUIDE PROGRAM WILL FOCUS ON:

• *public nutrition education*

• *legislative issues*

• *regulatory issues*

• *consumer research*

Inside

Volunteers Enter '90s at Annual Meeting

"A DECADE OF DREAMS" is the theme for this year's Annual Meeting of Membership for the American Heart Association, Texas Affiliate. The meeting will be held July 14 at the Hyatt Regency in Dallas. Delegates from Texas' 150 divisions are invited to attend.

This year's keynote speaker is James N. Patrick, a noted motivational speaker and consultant who will address "Trends in the '90s." As a futurist, Patrick will discuss changes to

expect in the 1990s while offering thought–provoking ideas on how AHA volunteers can prepare for these changes.

The purpose of the Annual Meeting is for volunteer delegates to:
• consider and review activities of the organization,
• recommend policies to guide the Affiliate Board of Directors,

Continued on page 3

Handbooks One major employee publication that PR departments produce is the employee handbook, which functions as both a reference piece and an effective orientation tool. It should provide a definitive statement of what is expected from employees and what the organization offers

them. The handbook should thoroughly explain policies, rules and regulations, and it should indicate how management helps to further the education and career development of the employee. The handbook should also detail how and under what circumstances the corporate name and logo can be

Former Chairman of the Board Testifies Against Sound-Alikes

In December, the U.S. Senate Judiciary Subcommittee on Antitrust Monopolies and Business Rights heard testimony on abuses in charitable and nonprofit solicitations.

AHA National Board Member and Treasurer Don Joseph of Austin testified on behalf of the organization.

In his testimony, Joseph, a former Texas Affiliate chairman of the board (1981-82), cited problems associated with "sound-alike" organizations.

Former Texas Affiliate Chairman of the Board Don Joseph (right) presents testimony with representatives from the American Cancer Society and American Lung Association on sound-alike organizations before a Senate Judiciary Subcommittee.

"These fly-by-night operations, through the use of computers and other devices, are able to reach large segments of our population. Many of the people solicited are those who have suffered from some disease or hardship or know someone close to them who has. Such contributors sincerely believe that they are making a real contribution to efforts to improve society. But too often those dollars are not returned to society."

Continued on page 11

Perspectives:

How can physician-driven programs, such as Heart Rx, help patients to reduce their risk for cardiovascular disease?

COUNCIL I   *Paula Winkler,* El Paso Division
◆ ...because the physician can influence treatment. Physicians are still the primary source of healthcare information for individuals. They have the greatest amount of knowledge about healthcare and are the most credible to recommend prevention and treatment activities.

COUNCIL II   *Greg Phillips, M.D.,* Fort Worth Division
◆ ...because the physician takes the first step. I find it more effective to offer information or advice, rather than waiting for the patient to ask for it—the patient seems to appreciate this initiation too. It's essential, however, for the physician to be enthusiastic about offering this education to the patient.

COUNCIL III   *Tom Fitzharris, M.D.,* Dallas Division
◆ The New England Journal of Medicine had an article that pointed out the importance of risk management. It suggested the decline of CVD disease is due to behavior modification and altering of lifestyle to change risk factors. The Heart Rx program is an excellent way for the physician and patient to affect behavioral changes, thus lowering risk factors and the incidence of cardiovascular disease.

COUNCIL IV   *J. James Rohack, M.D.,* Brazos County Division
◆ Most patients believe the physician is working in their best interest. Therefore, any educational materials given to the patient by the physician will not be viewed as entrepreneurial, but rather as valuable to their treatment. This form of education will have more impact than information the patient would pick up in a shopping mall.

COUNCIL V   *Tim Bricker, M.D.,* Houston Division
◆ One of the difficult aspects of prevention, from the viewpoint of those who try to encourage it, is to establish the milieu or theoretically ideal environment in the medical office. Ideally, a general practitioner would do well to have a full-time psychologist and health nutritionist in the practice, but this is neither realistic nor cost-effective. We can therefore offer a patient education program, like Heart Rx, as a substitute to help provide this milieu—to provide materials and resources which are beneficial to the patient, while cost effective for the physician.

COUNCIL VI   *Debbie James, R.N.,* San Antonio Division
◆ An effective patient education program is one that provides information which is easy to read, readily available and free to the consumer. With Heart Rx, these components are rolled into one package. When the physician gives the information to the patient, they say "hey, this must be important information because my physician keeps it in the office." They read it, and become informed.

5

---

used. Inclusion of a management organizational chart with the names of individuals whom employees need to know about or contact in various departments is essential. Workers at all levels should be made aware of the way to get questions answered and problems solved. Most corporations find it necessary to produce handbooks annually in order to keep the information current.

Some organizations also publish handbooks for external use. For example, a hospital may publish a handbook with physician references and first-aid information. This book is then distributed to

American Heart Association

Texas Affiliate, Inc.

P.O. Box 15186
Austin, Texas 78761

DOUG NEWSOM PH D
TEXAS CHRISTIAN UNIV
DEPT OF JOURNALISM
P O BOX 32930
FT WORTH TX 76129

FW-705
002502

NON PROFIT
ORGANIZATION
U.S. POSTAGE
PAID
PERMIT NO. 2401
AUSTIN, TEXAS

IMPROVED DIVISIONS

Vital Signs salutes the following divisions, who over the past year have made substantial improvements in communications, development, program and overall organization.

Panhandle Region: Hutchinson County Division–Development goals nearly doubled, increased income by 100 percent; JRFH returned after eight-year absence; Celebrity Waiter raised $11,000, received substantial media coverage; Food Festival, CRP.

South Plains Region: Lubbock Division–Best year in development; conducted balanced campaign; program and communications efforts remained outstanding.

North Texas Region: Young County Division–Conducted first Celebrity Waiter, raised $6500; JRFH success; schoolsite and volunteer commitment strong.

Concho Valley Region: Sutton County Division–Tripled Turkeywalk participation, raised $2500, key media relations; programs maintained.

Northeast Texas Region: Gregg County Division–Balanced campaign, exceeded best year; Heart At Work, schoolsite increased; active committees; nominating committee looked to future, established vice-chairman and chairman-elect positions.

Fort Worth Area Region: Arlington Division–Board recruited broader base of new volunteers, encouraged more community involvement in programs; $19,000 telepledge; first Turkeywalk and Cardiac Arrest.

Heart of Texas Region: Hill County Division–Board has instilled attitude that AHA belongs to the community; surpassed development goal by $9000; good media relations, leadership; board unafraid to take risks.

Golden Triangle Region: Mid and South Jefferson Division–Excellent leadership and board spirit; development income increased over 100 percent; program committee established, reached over 200 teachers with Getting to Know Your Heart; Food Festival success.

Capitol Area Region: North Caldwell Division–Excellent leadership, goal increases in all areas; conducted balanced campaign through Neighbor-to-Neighbor, Telepledge, Celebrity Waiter, JRFH; exceeded goal by $5000.

Coastal Bend Region: Victoria County Division–Increased community awareness, volunteer base; media sponsorships; Heart At Work increased; development goals doubled.

Golden Crescent Region: Grimes County–Completely new board revitalized division; returned JRFH to schools after two-year absence; active CPR instructor-trainers in schools, conducted school board visits for Getting to Know Your Heart; best year ever in development, Cardiac Arrest raised $11,000.

Permian Basin Region: Ector County Division–Media relations improved; best year in development through telepledge, Cardiac Arrest, Celebrity Waiter; maintained outstanding programs.

Rio Grande Valley Region: South Cameron Division–Excellent leadership and board commitment; income increased 50 percent; held first big ticket event, raised $15,000; Getting to Know Your Heart presented to all teachers; improved relations with daily newspaper, Heart Month insert.

East Texas Region: Nacogdoches County–Conducted more teacher inservices than ever before; exceeded fund-raising goals, best year ever; increased volunteer depth.

West Central Region: Brown County–Increases in Heart Rx, Heart At Work; excellent communications; reached goals.

Houston Metropolitan Region (A): Clear Lake Division–Improved communications, concentrated on cardiovascular education messages; excellent programs; Celebrity Waiter, telepledge success; board diversity.

Houston Metropolitan Region (B): Cy-Fair Division–Doubled JRFH participation; good communications; inserviced every teacher on Getting To Know Your Heart, over 1000 teachers inserviced.

Bay Area Region: South Brazoria Division–Rebuilt division; conducted successful business drive; excellent communications; effective schoolsite trainings.

Alamo Region: Webb County–Key communications program, volunteer representatives from all media outlets; best year in fund-raising through JRFH, Celebrity Waiter; "Lose It Laredo" healthy weight-loss program, Food Festival "Heart Cart Races."

Dallas Metropolitan Region: Plano Division–Best year in development; Heart At Work task force created; exceeded communications goals.

Reprinted with permission.

---

patients of all the physicians listed, and sometimes to all residents in an area likely to use the hospital's services.

Film/Video

As audiences become increasingly oriented toward graphics and audiovisual presentations, PR practitioners cannot afford to ignore films and videos as informational and publicity vehicles.

Sponsored Films   One type of film to consider is the long feature, or *sponsored film.* This is a film without stars put out by an organization or corporation and distributed free of charge. Such films can be produced for as little as $15,000 or as much as $500,000. Most fall in the $40,000-to-$50,000 range. Large companies may have their own film-producing units, but most hire independent film producers. The observations of magazine columnist Stuart Little on such films are informative:

One sees corporations presenting films on urban development, on consumer protection, on ecological problems, and the only time the sponsoring company allows itself recognition is in a few sunset frames toward the end of the picture when, for example, the wing of the plane tilts skyward and the name of the airline, for an instant, fills the screen like an unexpected rainbow.

The sponsored film can, of course, serve an explicitly commercial purpose. General Motors and Ford, for example, which are among the largest producers of sponsored films, have libraries of instructional, training and driving safety films that directly relate to commercial goals. The airlines freely distribute travel films that are clearly designed to foster wanderlust.[4]

The customary audiences for sponsored films are schools, community organizations, television stations and movie theaters that use exhibitors' shorts to flesh out their schedules when a 105-minute feature leaves 15 minutes to be filled in the theater's two-hour schedule.[5]

Feature Fillers   Another type of production to consider is the one- to five-minute film clip, usually done on 16-mm film with sound or on videocassette. These generally serve as fillers for feature programs, talk shows or local sporting events. To win acceptance, fillers must be newsworthy and timely, must show activity and must have only one mention or plug for the sponsor. They are generally presented in a news magazine format.

Corporate Videos for Internal Uses   Although some internal videos—such as video "newsletters" for employees—use the news magazine format, other formats are borrowed from television—such as MTV-style videos and game-show spoofs.[6] The videos are used to communicate the corporate culture, to inform employees about corporate resources available for dealing with such problems as substance abuse, to instruct and train employees in new techniques or new jobs and to give employees the organization's side of controversial public issues in which it may become involved.

▼ **As audiences become increasingly oriented toward graphics and audiovisual presentations, PR practitioners cannot afford to ignore films and videos as information and publicity vehicles.**

The reasons for using videos to reach internal audiences start with the fact that most employees now are products of total television immersion: they get most of their news from television, and they use VCRs for home entertainment. In addition, video offers drama. "It's the seeing is believing; the personalization of a message backed up by pictures," says Dan Droege, manager of internal communications at Phillips Petroleum Company in Bartlesville, Oklahoma.[7]

The average corporate video budget has increased by approximately 200 percent in four years, from $87,000 in 1987 to an estimated $171,000 in 1991. Although four out of ten U.S. companies produce fewer than ten programs each year, 17 percent produce between twenty-one and fifty videos; and 14 percent, fifty-one or more.[8]

Employee information (training) remains the primary use for corporate videos, but they are also being used in employee relations (benefits) and crisis communication (informing employees of the organization's side of a controversial issue so that they can pass that view along to external audiences).

Some corporate videos are directed toward a combination internal/external audience such as investors who "own" the company but don't work there. Some crisis communication videos are specifically designed to reassure such audiences. Other videos deal with investor relations and address "recommenders" of corporate investment such as brokers and analysts.

EXAMPLE 11.15

Corporate Magazine Primarily for Internal Audiences

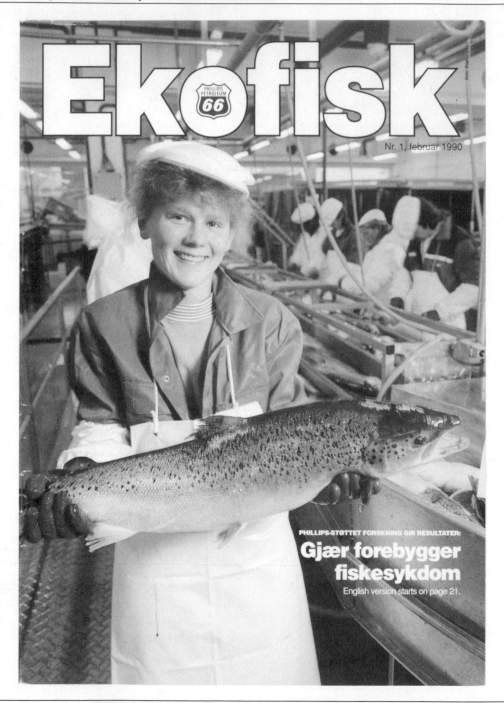

Ekofisk

Nr. 1, februar 1990

PHILLIPS-STØTTET FORSKNING GIR RESULTATER:

Gjær forebygger fiskesykdom

English version starts on page 21.

Returadresse: Ekofisk-magasinet, boks 220, 4056 Tananger

Dette bladet utgis av informasjonsavdelingen i Phillips Petroleum Company Norway på vegne av den norske Phillips-gruppen og Norpipe A.S.
Redaksjon: Torunn Mo, Liv Marit Baardsen, Sturle Hagen og Evy Aase Ravndal. Red. avsluttet 20. februar 1990.
Konsulent og utforming: Eirik Moe Grafisk Design. Trykk: Industritrykk.
Ettertrykk tillatt når kilden oppgis. Ettertrykk av foto er ikke tillatt.

Sist, men ikke minst:

Sponsormidler til Voss

Bak fra venstre: Tore Gjernes, Helga Øvsthus Fenne, Gisle Fenne (med lille Thomas) og Anne Elisabeth Elvebakk. Foran fra venstre: Bjørn Ståle Lærdal, Eirik S. Finne og Hans Ellingsen.

Fredag 9. februar signerte selskapet en sponsoravtale med Voss Skiskytterlag, og 170.000 kroner per år er summen som står i kontrakten. Avtalen er gjeldende i fire år, med mulighet for oppsigelse hvert år.

Phillips var en av sponsorene under junior-VM på Voss i fjor vinter, og i følge Sto Lærdal i informasjonsavdelingen var det her grunnlaget for den nye avtalen ble lagt.
-Erfaringene fra junior-VM var udelt positive, og det la et godt grunnlag for videre avtaler. Det blir lagt ned et imponerende frivillig arbeid for idretten på Voss, og tilbudet om å være med å sponse skiskytterlaget var for godt til å kunne si nei til, sier Sto Lærdal.
-Slik denne avtalen er lagt opp forplikter også Voss Skiskytterlag seg til visse gjenytelser. Selskapet får

hytter stilt til disposisjon, samt fiskerettigheter i lakse-elv. Voss er jo kjent både for sine skiheiser og sin gjestfrihet, og denne avtalen gir oss mulighet til å utvide velferdstilbudet, sier Lærdal. -For våre ansatte i Bergens-området er Voss et yndet utfartssted, samtidig som også flere og flere fra andre kanter av landet velger å legge ferien dit. I tillegg er også skiskyting en publikumssport, så rent PR-messig regner vi med å få stort utbytte av avtalen. Ved alle mesterskap arrangert av Voss Skiskytterlag vil vi få fribilletter til arrangementene, og første arrangement med Phillips som støttespiller er NM, som blir arrangert i perioden 1. til 4. mars.

Voss Skiskytterlag har omlag 150 medlemmer. Flere av verdens beste skiskyttere, som for eksempel Eirik Kvalfoss, Gisle Fenne og Anne Elisabeth Elvebakk, har alle fått sin trening i skiskyttermiljøet på Voss. Phillips har ikke satt krav til hvordan pengene skal brukes, men Eirik S. Finne, leder i Voss Skiskytterlag, sier at sponsormidlene fra Phillips primært skal brukes til arbeid i de yngste klassene, samt til innkjøp av geværer og annet utstyr.

-Vi føler at avtalen er gunstig både sett fra de ansattes side, for Voss Skiskytterlag og for selskapet. Samtidig som vi støtter skiskytterlaget, får vi noe tilbake som kan komme de ansatte til gode, avslutter Sto Lærdal.

Innsamling til Romania

I alt kroner 36.700 er samlet inn blant de Phillips-ansatte på Ekofisk til nødlidende i Romania. I administrasjonen på Hotellet får vi opplyst at det for en tid siden gikk ut beskjed til alle om at de kunne bli trukket et visst beløp i lønn som skulle gå til Røde Kors' Romania-aksjon. En honnør til dem som fulgte oppfordringen!

USA-besøk til Ekofisk

Tirsdag 6. februar var representanter fra ledelsen i Phillips Petroleum Company på Ekofisk. De fem, Jack Perryman (Projects and Design manager), John Mihm (vice president Corporate Engineering), Bob Ceconi (Drilling and Production manager), Vic Baldridge (Planning and Development manager) og Jim Woods (Corporate Procurement and Materials Control manager), reiste sammen med representanter fra ledelsen for Phillips i Norge. De hadde et hektisk program med omvisning på Ekofisk-senteret, 2/4 Alfa, Tor og 2/4 Bravo-K. Turen til Ekofisk var ledd i et større program som blant annet inneholdt informasjon og oppdatering på en rekke prosjekter og oppgaver i den norske divisjonen.

Reprinted with permission.

The Point Is...

No. 126, February 28, 1989

A SUMMARY OF PUBLIC ISSUES IMPORTANT TO THE DOW CHEMICAL COMPANY

Risk Perception Versus Fact

The following is an excerpt from the newly revised Dow brochure "Life is in the Balance" concerning questions of risk and benefit in today's world. The brochure was written by Elyse M. Rogers, a free-lance science/medical writer.

The idea that somehow life today is more dangerous, more difficult and more hazardous has gripped many of us despite the fact that we are healthier statistically, live longer and enjoy more leisure time than ever before.

We have learned how to measure, probe and publicize our environment, yet we often have difficulty putting it all into perspective. Just because we have the capacity to measure substances in concentrations as miniscule as one part per quadrillion doesn't mean that the world is more contaminated — it merely means that we have the ability to know what's there. As Shakespeare said sometime back around the beginning of the 17th century:

> *"But no perfection is so absolute*
> *That some impurity doth not pollute"*

We must ask ourselves: "Was the water purer, the food safer, the environment cleaner when we didn't know what was in it?" Or is it simply true, as one scientist has said, that we all enjoy the confidence that comes from innocence?

Learning to perceive risks correctly is important to the average citizen because there are so many factors that make proper perception difficult. Voluntary risks that we assume of our own volition, such as motorcycle racing or smoking, are usually far easier to tolerate than involuntary risks, over which we have no control, such as having a munitions factory built next door to our home.

Also, personal anxiety plays a part. One citizen may have more anxiety about one certain risk, and it may not matter to her personally that the risk is not really a substantial one. But, if that person is helping to make decisions on an issue of risk for the entire nation, then she must also learn to recognize the personal "dread" factor in risk decisions, as well as the tendency among most of us to fear most those risks that we don't understand.

> **"Security is mostly a superstition. It does not exist in nature, nor do the children of men as a whole experience it. Avoidance of danger is no safer in the long run than outright exposure. Life is either a daring adventure, or nothing."**
> **Helen Keller**
> *The Open Door* **1902**

RISK COMPARISONS

One way to rate risks and provide some comparisons of those risks is to portray them in "days of life expectancy lost." Dr. Richard Wilson, professor of physics at Harvard University, has devised a mathematical formula that measures risks in terms of the minutes and seconds of life lost. Taking the average person of 30 who has a life expectancy rate of about 74 years, Dr. Wilson says that "statistical" person cuts time from his life in the following ways:

Smoking one cigarette . . . . . . minus 12 minutes
Drinking a diet
   soft drink . . . . minus 9 seconds
                             (estimated)
Driving without
   a seat belt . . . . minus 6 seconds
                           (for every trip)
Being an
   unmarried male . . . . minus 1800 days
Being male rather
   than female . . . . minus 2700 days

➠

PUBLIC ISSUES ● 2020 DOW CENTER ● MIDLAND, MICHIGAN 48674

Risk comparisons are interesting, informative and sometimes even humorous; they also demonstrate that almost everything we do involves at least some risk.

RISK AND UNCERTAINTY

Life is at best uncertain. And with risks and risk assessment, uncertainties abound. Scientists tend to give us "probabilities" and "statistical analysis;" we average citizens tend to want facts and hard data.

To get risk assessment data, scientists look to history. Although it might seem that history cannot predict the future, it can be surprisingly accurate with proper statistical methods, which is why the "predicted" deaths from cancer or estimated number of traffic fatalities for the following year are often very close to the mark.

Still, we must be careful that we understand statistics and what they can and can't tell us. Greatly overrated risks and severely underated risks can be wrongly extrapolated from data and must be guarded against, particularly by those who wish to "use" statistical data either to alarm or to placate.

When risk assessments are made, the way the data are presented may influence our thinking. This is called the "framing effect." If we are told that 1 out of 100 will die from a disease, we may make a different personal evaluation of that risk than if we are told instead that 99 out of 100 people will be saved.

Even with good data, we have trouble accurately assessing risks. This can happen because the data are very complicated, as in biochemical research, because we find it hard to change preconceived ideas (i.e., that we are safer-than-average drivers so the statistics don't apply to us), because our worries about risk are tied up with other problems (i.e., that nuclear energy is associated with nuclear war), or for a host of other reasons.

Ultimately it will not be just one group that makes decisions about risk. The public, the politicians and the scientists all will be and should be involved; for good, thoughtful decisions on risk/benefit questions are of growing importance.

> **"Do we look with pride, or view with alarm?"**
> **Theodore Roosevelt**
> **former President of the United States**

PRIORITIZING RISKS

Using risk assessment techniques and learning to perceive risks correctly is an important goal for the future. For we must, as a national society and as members of a global community, decide where to put our time, energy and resources of both people and money. As Bob Hope once quipped, "We are a nation that wants to ban saccharin and legalize marijuana."

The point is... there are many threats to people today, and planning and deciding what risks we will tolerate and those we will not is vital.

Judicious risk-taking is part of the balance that makes life worth living. We can't deny our children that legacy of hope and challenge by deciding for them that life should be cushioned against all risk. They should have some choice in their own tomorrow — a choice to risk sorrow and learn from it and, above all, the right to risk failure for success and joy.

Copies of the 21-page brochure are available by writing to Corporate Communications, 2020 Willard H. Dow Center, Midland, MI 48674.

SOURCE: Reprinted with permission of the Dow Chemical Company.

Videos focusing on community or environmental issues may be produced originally for internal audiences, but then may be adapted for special external audiences. The flexibility of the medium, which allows minor adaptations to be made on basically the same video, makes it especially useful for targeting messages to special audiences.

Teletext and Videotex   Teletext is a one-way system of information transmission that is delivered via a regular TV broadcast signal; subscribers to the service are given a decoder (similar to a cable television converter) that allows them to read the text on the TV screen at any time. Videotex is a two-way system of information transmission that can be delivered via a cable TV system or telephone lines and can be received on a TV set or a personal computer monitor; subscribers to videotex services can request specific information from these sources.

Although teletext and videotex have struggled to find a market niche as an adjunct to newspapers, the technologies' usefulness to public relations is growing. Both are increasingly being used to deliver highly "perishable" information such as investment news and agricultural information.

Teletext and videotex systems can be used to reach farmers electronically by telephone line, satellite, FM sideband (extra space on an existing station's bandwidth) or television (in one of the blanking intervals in a station's signal).[9] Upscale and younger farmers use electronic sources to complement more traditional sources.[10] Much of the information they seek on new agriculture options, grain and livestock futures or meat trade comes from videotex and teletext, as does government information such as weather service and USDA reports and analyses.[11]

Speeches/Meetings

Speeches are also publicity. When the president of an organization speaks to the local Monday club, the result is publicity, whether or not the local media cover the speech. This is because a person is also a medium. The PR person usually gets the job of researching and writing speeches. To be well received, the remarks must be particularly tailored for that particular group. The speech writer must also remember the personal characteristics of the speaker delivering the speech: the speech has to sound like the speaker, not like the writer.

Speeches are often published as brochures and sent to special audiences. This extends their usefulness as publicity tools. Sometimes, a copy of a speech is sent with just a special card (not a business card) attached. In other cases, the speech consists of a reprint with additional information. Occasionally, the speech is packaged as a publication—for example, a brochure. More unusual is a package that shows the visuals of the presentation (see Example 11.17).

Meetings often generate publicity, too, whether they are for internal or external audiences. Increasingly, meetings are used for external audiences as a proactive device to share concerns about an issue or environmental situation, and these are often covered by media. Internally, meetings are used to enable management to interact with employees and to gain feedback. Small group meetings are seen as an effective management tool,[12] and they often generate publicity in internal publications.

Other Promotional Messages

Another category of public relations messages used to promote organizations and individuals appears neither as editorial content nor news in media. Examples of those promotional messages include exhibits and characters identified with the organization (Mickey Mouse appearing for Disney; the Cookie Monster from Sesame Street appearing for PBS). Other forms are books, multimedia presentations and closed-circuit television appearances. Many presentations, like the ones this book's publisher puts on, occur at trade shows or conventions. Some organizations invest in videotapes or slide tapes that can be used at display areas or meetings with little support from organization representatives. Your college's admissions office probably uses such a traveling exhibit to recruit students.

© King Features Syndicate, Inc. 1973. World rights reserved.
Lew Little Syndicate

11-21

Reprinted with special permission of North America Syndicate.

Closed-circuit television is used a great deal in investor relations. Top executives can give a report on the company and then be interviewed by investment analysts. Reuters Information Services, Inc., owners of the British news service, uses "Reuters TV 2000" to transmit corporate presentations directly to analysts, giving them a chance to phone in questions. Paine Webber, a stockbrokers group, broadcasts a radio program to its 250 offices around the world on its global network.

In addition to using high-tech communications such as satellite broadcasts and computer networks, companies can rely on the old standby: print. Examples of self-promotion books are Lee Iacocca's *Iacocca: An Autobiography*, Stanley Marcus's *Minding the Store*, John F. Kennedy's *Profiles in Courage* and Richard Nixon's *Six Crises*. A book gives prestige to the subject and can be worth the time invested in producing it. Organizations usually save this device for an anniversary or other special occasion. Some books miss being connected to an organization because they are written by a well-known author commissioned to prepare the manuscript. When a political figure, celebrity or executive's name is on the book as author, the chances are that a ghost writer was employed. Much of the writer's time is devoted to tracking down elusive information, validating information given as fact and searching for illustrations. Nevertheless, a sincere effort, well done, often proves to be an asset.

Organizations also take advantage of their history by opening museums. Museums are gradually replacing plant tours, which sometimes raise legal problems. (Kellogg and Gerbers have quit offering plant tours.) Coca-Cola opened a museum in Atlanta in 1990, but it's a latecomer to the museum business. Some companies put a mini-museum on tour or establish small displays in historical districts (such as at a country store among a group of restored homes).

If books don't usually come to mind when promotions are mentioned, certainly stamps don't. However, any PR person who has shepherded an idea through the bureaucratic maze and actually succeeded in getting a commemorative stamp issued can assure you that it does attract attention to the organization or cause. A postal service panel sifts through 4,000 suggestions each year to select its annual batch of commemoratives. Organizations and individuals proposing stamps often go to considerable lengths to influence the committee. The *Wall Street Journal* reported on Montgomery Ward's highly effective campaign to get a stamp issued for the one-hundredth anniversary of the mail-order industry.

The company sent expensive promotion kits to influential members of Congress, including New York's Rep. Thaddeus Dulski, chairman of the House Post Office Committee. Store managers

EXAMPLE 11.17

Speeches as Publicity

This is the full set of visuals accompanying a speech by Michael Cooper made to PRSA. A speech like this one can be put on slides or on vinyl sheets to use with an overhead projector. An increasingly common device is to put the speech on a portable computer and use an attachment that allows the speech to be projected on a screen as the speaker talks. Subsequently the speech can be printed out, copied and distributed as "publicity."

MEASURING AND MANAGING CORPORATE REPUTATION FOR STRATEGIC POSITIONING

Dr. Michael R. Cooper, President & CEO
Opinion Research Corporation

PUBLIC RELATIONS SOCIETY OF AMERICA
NATIONAL CONFERENCE
NEW YORK
NOVEMBER 4, 1990

OPINION RESEARCH CORPORATION

MEASURING AND MANAGING CORPORATE REPUTATION FOR STRATEGIC POSITIONING

- Value of a Strong Corporate Reputation
- Importance of Corporate Reputation Positioning
- Elements of a Corporate Reputation Positioning Assessment Program
- How Positioning Assessment Sets A Framework for Strategic Marketing
- ORC's Corporate Reputation Positioning Value Index
- Managing Reputation Positioning

Opinion Research Corporation

VALUE OF A STRONG CORPORATE REPUTATION

A strong Corporate Reputation . . .
- Helps generate revenue growth and command premium pricing
- Provides a platform for new products, line extensions and ventures
- Enhances company stock valuation
- Facilitates M & A prospecting
- Enhances company attraction and retention of high caliber employees
- Avoids boycotts of company products

Opinion Research Corporation

CORPORATE REPUTATION IS A CORPORATE ASSET

- It is often not measured for valuation

- It is often not deliberately managed

Opinion Research Corporation

CORPORATE IMAGE AND MARKET VALUATION 1990

P/E Ratio
Top Quartile

P/E Ratio
Bottom Quartiles

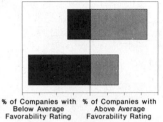

% of Companies with
Below Average
Favorability Rating

% of Companies with
Above Average
Favorability Rating

Opinion Research Corporation

CORPORATE REPUTATION POSITIONING

- Can be measured for strategy alignment

- Can be compared to strategic/peer companies

- Can be managed for strategic advantage

Opinion Research Corporation

CORPORATE REPUTATION POSITIONING ASSESSMENT PROGRAM

Opinion Research Corporation

CORPORATE REPUTATION POSITIONING ASSESSMENT PROGRAM

- Identify Issues

- Develop Measurement Tools

- Gather Information

- Interpret Results

- Translate Findings into Marketing Strategy

Opinion Research Corporation

OPINION RESEARCH CORPORATION CORPORATE REPUTATION POSITIONING ASSESSMENT PROGRAM

KEY PUBLICS
- Financial Community
- Customers/Buyers
- Employees
- Stockholders
- Business Executives
- Media
- Thoughtleaders

Opinion Research Corporation

OPINION RESEARCH CORPORATION CORPORATE REPUTATION
POSITIONING ASSESSMENT PROGRAM

KEY ATTRIBUTES
- Imaginative/forward-looking management
- Aggressive R & D programs
- Good midterm personal investment
- Responsive to customer needs
- Offers high-quality products/services
- Leader in corporate social responsibility
- Effective corporate communications
- High ethical business standards
- Responsive to environmental concerns

Opinion Research Corporation

(Continued)

EXAMPLE 11.17

Speeches as Publicity (*continued*)

OPINION RESEARCH CORPORATION CORPORATE REPUTATION POSITIONING ASSESSMENT PROGRAM

ADDITIONAL ATTRIBUTES

- Clear strategic direction
- Competes effectively at home and abroad
- Attribute strengths and weaknesses by geographic area
- Buyer values relating to product quality, price, and service quality

Opinion Research Corporation

REPUTATION POSITIONING MAP

CORPORATE REPUTATION POSITIONING ASSESSMENT PROGRAM ANSWERS KEY QUESTIONS AND SETS FRAMEWORK FOR STRATEGIC MARKETING

1st • Positioning Assessment
  - What is the company's corporate reputation? How is the company perceived by its key publics?
  - What are buyer values?

2nd • Familiarity and Favorability
  - Do they know us, ... our brands, ... our business?
  - Do they like us?

Opinion Research Corporation

CORPORATE REPUTATION POSITIONING ASSESSMENT PROGRAM ANSWERS KEY QUESTIONS AND SETS FRAMEWORK FOR STRATEGIC MARKETING

3rd • Repositioning
  - Build on buyer values and familiarity/ favorability strengths to design communication themes that match buyer values

4th • Strategic Marketing
  - Integrating buyer values, familiarity, favorability, and reputation positioning into strategic marketing plan

Opinion Research Corporation

MARKETING STRATEGY IMPLEMENTATION

Opinion Research Corporation

ORC CORPORATE REPUTATION POSITIONING VALUE INDEX

Opinion Research Corporation

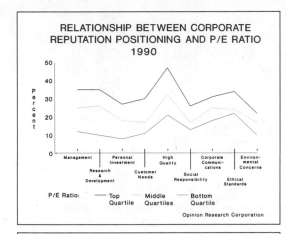

RELATIONSHIP BETWEEN CORPORATE
REPUTATION POSITIONING AND P/E RATIO
1990

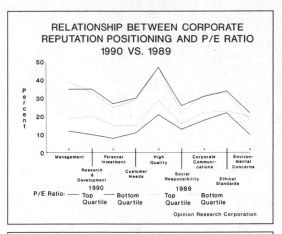

RELATIONSHIP BETWEEN CORPORATE
REPUTATION POSITIONING AND P/E RATIO
1990 VS. 1989

SPECIFIC REPUTATION POSITIONING ATTRIBUTES ARE CLOSELY LINKED TO P/E RATIO

Opinion Research Corporation

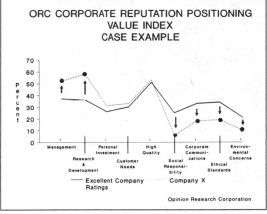

ORC CORPORATE REPUTATION POSITIONING
VALUE INDEX
CASE EXAMPLE

MANAGING REPUTATION POSITIONING

1st • Identify Key Strategic Objectives
2nd • Design Attribute Measures to
   Assess Strategy/Reputation
   Positioning Alignment
3rd • Perform Comparative Profiling:
   Company vs. Competitors/Peers
4th • Identify Strategy Gaps:
   Company vs. Competitors/Peers
5th • Prioritize Reputation Attributes for
   Management Focus and Alignment
   with Corporate Positioning Strategy

Opinion Research Corporation

Reprinted with permission of Opinion Research Coropration.

Reprinted with permission: Tribune Media Services.

were prodded to write their own legislators. And Walter Trohan, the *Chicago Tribune*'s veteran Washington correspondent, now retired, wrote a column pushing the stamp.

The proposal, which Montgomery Ward began pushing only last December, was rushed through the advisory panel, and the stamp was issued September 18; the time elapsed was several months less than it usually takes to get a commemorative issued.[13]

One reason companies, institutions and special-interest groups develop symbols and logos is for the visual promotion of their identity. Although "obvious," these devices are not obtrusive, and sometimes they are almost unconsciously accepted. Once such representations become identifiable, a public need only see the symbol to be reminded of its meaning.

Such a symbol does not have to be a logo; it might even be a picture. In one case, PR practitioners had pictures made of children using milk cartons with the tops cut off as modeling clay forms. The publishers of a national children's educational book accepted the photo as showing an example of the creative application of everyday household items. The photo of the cartons subsequently appeared in the book, with the name of the milk company clearly visible. Such pictures, with the product in the background or foreground, are often used. If you ever wondered why hotels always have speak-er's rostrums clearly labeled with the hotel's name and insignia, now you know.

An entire industry has developed around making sure that identifiable brand-name products are used in television shows and in movies. As a viewer, you may have noticed that you can read the label of a star's soft drink, or that a billboard is clearly visible in a street scene or that a particular make of car is used. These are not accidental choices of the prop department.

▼ PUBLICITY AS CONTROLLED/ UNCONTROLLED COMMUNICATION

Determining where to place publicity demands an objective look at what is likely to happen to it, from creation to delivery. This means considering how much control you can exert over the delivery of the message by the medium.

Controlled Media

Many specialized media, such as company, industry, trade and association publications, are under *their* editors' control. If you are the editor, it is a controlled publication; but if you are the PR director for a company submitting publicity to an industry or trade publication, your submissions are subject to editorial discrimination and revision. Thus, if you are not the editor, specialized media fall in the uncontrolled category. Another person decides whether and how to use your material. On the other hand, magazines, brochures, newsletters and videos you produce and distribute are controlled, because you decide when, where and how to deliver the message.

Uncontrolled Media

News releases may be exceptionally well written, but once they are in the hands of an editor anything can happen and you can't do much about it. An editor may run a release as you wrote it, give it to a reporter to rewrite, give it to a reporter to use as a take-off point for an independently researched story or junk it entirely. Trade publication editors discard 75 percent of the releases they receive, and radio news people discard 86 percent. Most discarded PR material, however, richly deserves such an end. The news media treat a professionally prepared release from a trustworthy source with respect, although it still may not be used if there is no space or time for it that day.

News tip sheets alert editors to possible news or feature stories. In addition, "calls for coverage" or queries may be used to elicit media coverage of PR events—a presidential press conference, the arrival of Santa to open a store's Christmas buying season, ribbon cuttings and groundbreakings. Whether these get any attention is up to the editors, who decide whether or not to assign reporters. Of course, even when reporters are assigned, they may not cover the event as the PR person would have wished. But if the event is well planned, the coverage will reflect it.

▼ PREPARING PUBLICITY MESSAGES

Some publicity messages go directly to audiences as controlled communications; others go to the news media, who constitute an intermediary audience.

▼ **The first problem in putting out an institutional publication involves finding out what is going on; the second involves restraining management's tendency to use the publication as a propaganda organ.**

Direct Publicity for Audiences

Public relations offices prepare material for audiences directly in both print and video formats. Most video production, though, is done outside the organization.

Publications   PR practitioners encounter two principal problems in putting out institutional publications—newsletters, magazines or newsletters—beyond the problem of justifying its existence to some dollars-and-cents-minded person in accounting.

The first involves finding out what is going on. Usually this is handled by setting up departmental "correspondents" who report monthly to the editor on significant events in their departments. To avoid a stream of unusable gossip, you should seek out the people in each department who have been there the longest and ask their supervisors if they can be correspondents. Then invite all your correspondents to a "news clinic," in which you explain the publication needs of an editor and how they can help. Devise a form that takes care of all the basic information you are looking for each month. Be sure the deadline is stated boldly and clearly. You must design this yourself, because you set the editorial policy for the publication and know what the content should be (see Example 11.18). Then figure out a way to reward your correspondents. Listing their names in the publication usually works best, because then others know whom they should approach with information.

The second problem involves the tendency of management to view the publication as a propaganda organ for telling readers what it would like

EXAMPLE 11.18 ▬▬▬▬▬▬▬▬▬▬▬▬▬▬▬▬▬

Employee Publication Form

SPECTRUM NEWS

Reporter's Name: _____

Reporter's Department: _____

News Event (please check appropriate category)

____ Promotion
____ Award
____ Sports
____ Announcement
____ Other (please explain): _____

_____

About the event:

What happened: _____

_____

When did it happen: _____

Where did it happen: _____

Who was there: _____

_____

Names _____

Department _____

Division _____

Use this space for additional comments.

Mail to publication office.

them to believe rather than what they would like to know. When the editor yields to this kind of pressure, the result is an ego treat for management, but an unread publication and a truly unjustifiable budget item. Eventually, when enough complaints are heard about the publication, executives conduct a readership survey, discover that the publication is not read and, instead of changing policy, fire the editor. An editor should not let this drama play itself out.

As editor, you should include what the employees want and need to know about the company. Brighten it with entertainment and humor. Reprint articles from professional publications (which will charge little or no fee to nonprofit organizations). When management insists that you include certain stories, be sure to do a readership survey testing the readability of various articles. When management finds that its choices lose the poll consistently, it usually backs off and lets the editor edit.

Often PR people inherit house publications almost as an afterthought ("By the way, you'll also be doing our publication"); however, there is no need to put writing and editing a publication in the same category with washing the coffeepot. Much of what happens depends on attitude and careful planning.

Some corporate publications accept advertising as a way to expand a small budget. Consider what types of ads you could accept and who would sell them (if your staff is small, it may take too much time).

Editing a house publication is an opportunity to be creative. The first thing to consider is the layout. If you have three people on your staff, make sure that one is skilled in art and layout. If you can hire someone with a background in art, layout and photography, count your blessings. Most house publications are plagued by amateurish efforts. If you can't afford a professional photographer, even part-time, try to find someone in the company who is an experienced photographer and has a darkroom at home. Offer to supply him or her with the necessary film, photographic paper and chemicals. Incidentally, the art for some institutional advertising is available without charge, including the color separations. Often the source wants only a credit line.

Desk-top publishing has brought new freedom and flexibility to editors of house publications. However, its value drops precipitously in the hands of individuals who cannot write or edit and who have no graphics background. You need to inquire regularly about new computer software packages that will help you do your job better and more easily. If you don't have budget money for a layout artist/photographer, a good graphics software package can be a lifesaver.

If you use a computer, you may rely on a copying facility for copies. But if you have more elaborate publications, you will go to a printer. In that case, you must specify for the printer the special effects (screens, duotones and such) you intend to use per issue, as well as the cost of color separations, cover stock and colors for the cover, interior paper stock (make sure the printer warehouses it for you; it is disconcerting to have to change stock in mid-year because the printer ran out), number of pages, deadlines and agreements about corrections, delays and delivery. Ingenuity, creativity and determination are essential qualities of a good house publication editor.

Annual reports are often done in house, especially by nonprofit organizations. Large publicly held companies may hire an individual practitioner to work with the public relations staff to produce the report, or they may use a public relations firm. The importance of the annual report to investors was reduced by legislation requiring companies to complete and issue 10K forms, so most annual reports now serve primarily as public relations tools.

Preparers need to remember to use a theme or storyline, interesting headings that lead into credible (and readable) copy and good-quality four-color art.

Some annual reports are distributed as videos, too.

Videos Producing instructional and motivational videotapes is a standard public relations assignment.

Many institutions consider television a better medium than print for certain purposes. In other situations, television is used in concert with print.

An industry instituting a new profit-sharing plan, for example, put the executive who could best explain it on closed-circuit TV. The show then ran each day during lunch, and PR followed up with handouts so that the more complex aspects of the program would be available for reference.

The success of closed-circuit TV is attributable partly to employee experience with the medium and partly to the medium itself, which is the next best thing to face-to-face contact. A Navy public information officer put the captain of a carrier on the ship's closed-circuit TV because, as he put it, "This place is like a city and someone is likely to not even know what the captain looks like if they don't see him on TV."

Land-based telephone lines and dish antennas have enabled U.S. businesses to create their own private TV networks. Only four such corporate networks existed in 1983, but now there are nearly a hundred. Merrill Lynch has used its network to introduce new products to special publics. Texas Instruments connected its executives in five U.S. cities and Paris with reporters to discuss integrating its LISP artificial intelligence processor into Apple personal computers. Penney's delivered antidrug programming to the community by showing "Plays for Living" over its network. Countless PR opportunities exist for using the private networks.

Publicity Through Mass Media

In contrast to both advertising and publicity prepared directly for audiences, publicity prepared for the mass media generally is totally uncontrolled, both as to the delivery and as to the message. Information about an institution, product or person that appears as news in newspapers or magazines or on radio or television is used at the discretion of news editors. Thus it may be used in any context or not at all.

Print Publicity   Information reaches the news media through many routes, but three are basic: news releases, coverage of an event and interviews. To be acceptable, a *news release* must be written in the style used by the particular medium, and it must be presented in a form suitable to the technology of the medium. Awareness of the technological demands of each medium is also important if you expect *coverage of an event*. A speech may be an event, and certainly a news conference is, but the *interview* is not. The public relations person may formally arrange for a reporter to interview someone in a position of authority. Or the reporter may interview the PR person as representative or spokesperson for the institution. This informal situation—it may be a phone call or a visit by news media representatives—can be an organization's most significant source of publicity. Generally it is the source used most often by the media, which often ignore events and throw away publicity releases.

More and more often, media interviews are handled by the chief executive officer (CEO) with the aid of the PR person. The PR person's job therefore extends to preparing the CEO to be an effective, efficient spokesperson. Some PR agencies, notably Burson-Marsteller, have become specialists in providing such training for their clients.

Most of the bad publicity an organization gets can be attributed to errors by management: poor planning, ineffective communication or bad policies. Not getting any publicity at all, however, is probably the fault of the publicist. Newspeople say they throw away 80 to 90 percent of the news releases they get, because they are not usable. "Not usable" may mean the stories are incomplete (full of holes), inaccurate, not timely or just don't fit the news need.

Back in 1973, *pr reporter* carried an item about faulty press kits as a warning to its readers. The information remains just as relevant today:

One of our volunteer reporters scooped up at random an armful of press kits at the recent National Boat Show in New York's Coliseum, scanned them with the professional eye of a seasoned public relations executive, then sent them along to us with some interesting—if discouraging—observations.

After checking his comments against material in the kits and adding a few findings of our own to the list, we came to the conclusion that some product publicists in the marine field are careless, some are lazy, and some simply don't know how to put together a proper news release. For example:

1. Three-quarters of the releases were undated.

2. At least half either lacked any followup press contact information (gave only name and address of manufacturer) or the information was incomplete (no telephone number, or PR firm name but no individual to ask for).

3. Some picture captions were stapled to photographs, while others were so flimsily attached they came apart when handled.

4. One company's release was single spaced flush left, contained quotes without attribution, and misspelled "Coliseum."

5. The lead in another company's nine-page release was exactly the same this year as last except that 1973 was substituted for 1972; the president's statement about the new product line also was precisely the same in both years; and the balance of the nine pages closely followed the 1972 pattern—word for word in some short paragraphs.

6. In one almost unbelievable case, a PR firm handling the publicity for three marine equipment companies (two are competitors, incidentally) not only single spaced all the releases but left practially no margins and then framed the stories with a heavy rule. Included in the kit were several unidentified photographs. Compounding the agony: Every release had a return card attached so the editor could report when and how he planned to use the story.

In all fairness to some 50 companies which had kits stacked in the boat show press room, it should be noted that we looked at only nine. But of those

▼ **Most publicity that the news media reject is inappropriate, inaccurate or poorly prepared.**

nine, only two came through with flying colors. One was Raytheon Co., whose marine subsidiary makes electronic devices for watercraft. The other was Evinrude Motors—which, as a matter of added interest, included a fascinating story, complete with pictures, of how one of its outboard engines propelled a boat 110 feet through the air for an upcoming James Bond movie.[14]

For a good media kit, see Example 11.19.

Many other horror stories like the ones uncovered by *pr reporter* could be told, but you need not become a victim in one yourself. To avoid bad publicity and nonpublicity, you need only observe the following rules:

1. Make sure that the information you offer is appropriate to the medium in content and style, and is timely.

2. Check all facts carefully for accuracy, and double-check for missing information.

3. To deal with any questions that may arise, give the name and phone number of the person newspeople should contact.

4. Include on photographs the name, address and phone number of the supplier, stamped or written in felt-tip pen on the back margin, so the ink won't soak through; attach captions with rubber cement (not glue, paper clips or Scotch tape); and most importantly, make certain the captions are there.

5. Never call to find out why a story or photo did not appear; and certainly don't ask, as you submit an item, when it will appear.

6. Do not send out a note with mailed releases asking for clippings. Newspapers do not run clipping bureaus.

EXAMPLE 11.19

Media Kit

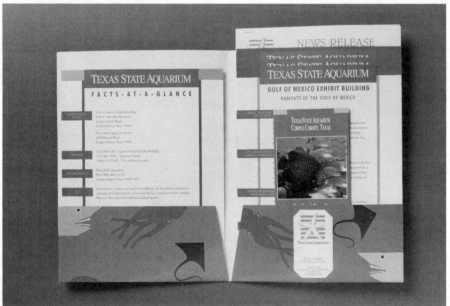

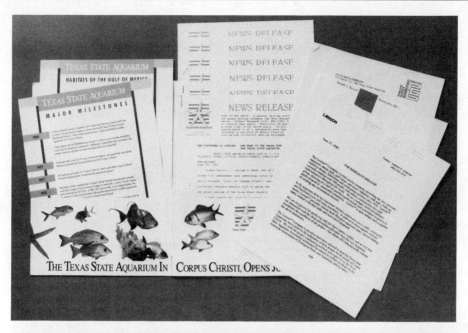

Reprinted with permission. Courtesy of the Texas State Aquarium, Corpus Christi, and the Parker & Wood Association, San Antonio.

Another mistake that publicity release writers commit involves failing to pay attention to the medium's audience. Trade publications often receive more general "mass media" releases that can't be used because they are not tailored to the publication. Some general media publications, although not technically trade publications, are by specialization much like trade or industry publications. One example is *TV Guide*, the largest-circulation magazine in the United States. (*Reader's Digest* is second.) Another is the magazine *Country America*, published by the Nashville Network with a primary focus on country music.

Some organizations would do well to pay attention to another type of specialized media—the so-called alternative media—especially if they need to reach activists and special interest groups. Examples of alternative newspapers include the *Boston Phoenix*, the *San Francisco Bay Guardian*, the *Chicago Reader*, Phoenix's *New Times* and the *L.A. Weekly*. These are often better read and have higher credibility (especially among activists) than traditional newspapers. Other relevant media are activist networks like PeaceNet, Public Data Access in New York City and the WELL in San Francisco; each such network is run by grassroots activists concerned with civil rights, feminism, peace, ecology or some other issue. The opportunities are endless for public relations practitioners to reach their audiences if they think "micro" rather than "macro" in terms of publicity, and if they target releases especially for the audience of the medium selected.

Broadcast Publicity   You need a sophisticated knowledge of the medium to be able to prepare broadcast-quality publicity. Television generally uses videotape cassettes with sound or satellite "feeds," but it can also use either sound or silent 16-mm color film. TV news directors prefer to use their own staff's material or something from another news source, but they will use publicity videos (film or tape) to show the project plans for a new sixty-story office building, the opening of an airport or the complexity of a space launch. Such VNRs (video news releases) usually cover hard news, not features, and may be transmitted by satellite.

Educational TV often uses PR-produced feature videotapes and films if they contain no commercialism, and on rare occasions so does commercial TV. Frequently television stations show a short feature film or videotape offered by a group. These are usually 90 seconds long, but some are three minutes long; most are entertaining, light and informative. Local stations use these most often on weekends, when news is slow and they have time they can fill with non-network shows.

Publicity never supplants spot news—news recorded at the time an event occurs (usually by journalists)—but it is the best way to tell an advance story. However, such a videotape or film is just as subject to editing as a written news release is, and it too may not be used at all. This is definitely an uncontrolled area—nearly as uncontrolled as the spot coverage of news that results when a television crew is alerted to an event.

Most stations use ½-inch VHS tape. A few employee-produced materials are still on ¾-inch Betamax. Stations may or may not have the equipment to transfer from one size to another.

Occasionally, the television medium may use color slides and an accompanying script (or audio cassette). Or the director might have a new script written. Sometimes an organization or profession is the subject of a television documentary. The PR practitioner can cooperate with those who are researching, writing and filming the documentary, but that is all that the PR person can do: help and hope for the best.

A form of television publicity that cannot be overlooked is the talk show. Daytime and evening talk shows continually present people promoting their latest book, movie, song or persona. Most local stations have a format that allows for local bookings. In such events, the PR person should be sure of three things: (1) that the show fits the PR objective; (2) the organization or sponsor gets credit; and (3) that the spokesperson is well coached or skilled in television appearances. Some interviews may be sent by a news distribution service like MediaLinks via satellite. However, most stations still tape the "send" for later use.

One of the myths that haunts public relations people is the notion that television exposure is critically important. This is not so. Television exposure is so fleeting and the audience so fragmented that, unless all networks use the information, the impact will be minimal. Most of the impact from local coverage comes from documentaries or news features.

Just as the possible benefits of being on television or in newspapers or magazines are exaggerated, so is the damage caused by negative stories. But some balanced stories that tell both sides of a story are seen within an organization as being "negative" because they say something against the organization. You can't avoid that, but you can be sure you tell the organization's story successfully.

▼ THE HYBRIDS: DIRECT MAIL AND 900 PHONE NUMBERS

Direct mail is a hybrid of publicity and advertising. In certain instances (such as newsletters from politicans), direct mail can be considered publicity. On the other hand, direct mail that seeks magazine subscriptions, for example, most certainly is advertising. Direct mail is a form of controlled communication: the message can say anything that does not violate a law, it can be any size or shape the postal service will accept, and it can be sent any time its sender chooses. Mailing lists are available for almost any audience you might wish to reach (if not, you can send it to "Occupant" at a particular address). However, just because the envelope arrives does not mean the message will be received.

The newest form of direct mail is electronic mail. Many associations now list, along with members' office and home addresses, their fax and electronic mail addresses. These systems are best for "perishable" messages that need instant delivery and a prompt response.

Traditional direct mail has a high mortality rate, which is why so much is invested in designing ap-

▼ **Direct mail is a hybrid channel used sometimes for publicity and sometimes for advertising.**

peals and in doing multiple mailings. The hope is that at least one effort will reach its intended audience.

The seven cardinal rules governing direct mail are as follows:

1. Know what the objective of the mailing is, and concentrate on it.

2. Use the correct mailing list. Remember that December through February is a significant job-change period; if you don't have time to check the accuracy of your list, mailings at this time should go to the title and not to the person.

3. Write copy that explains what the product or service does for the recipient.

4. Design the layout and format to fit the image of the product or service you are presenting.

5. Make it easy for the prospect to take the action you want taken.

6. Tell the story at least three times, and repeat the mailings two or three times.

7. Research all direct mail by testing the offer, package and list. Test to see if the offer is attractive to target audiences. Use alternative offers to make sure you have the best incentive. Test the package (presentation). Make sure respondents know what to do with the offer, and keep the directions simple and clear. Test the list with a sample mailing to ensure that it's accurate. Test the mailing even if it is as little as 1,000 pieces. Don't ever drop untested pieces in the mail.

Example 11.20 shows an attractive and professional-looking direct-mail piece.

EXAMPLE 11.20

An Attractive and Professional-Looking Direct-Mail Piece

THERE'S NOTHING FUNNY ABOUT ILLITERACY.

We knew that if you had a simple, joyful way to help the millions of Americans who are saddened by illiteracy, you would. And you're looking at him.

This is Ira Wordworthy, a tearful badger who doesn't know how to read. He's the main character in a wonderful children's story by Stephen Cosgrove. When you order this book, the proceeds will help fund important literacy projects across our country.

"Ira Wordworthy" is a heartwarming gift. And even if you don't have children, buying the book can be a very special way for you to help dry the tears of illiteracy in America. Show you care. Order yours today.

IRA WORDWORTHY. A stunning 32-page soft cover book and an incredible value at just $3.95. Order yours today. Send $3.95 to Coors Foundation for Family Literacy. P.O. Box 46666, Denver, Colorado 80201. U.S. check or money order only. Allow 4-6 weeks for delivery. Denver, Colorado residents please add 7.2% state and local sales tax. Other Colorado residents please add 3% state sales tax. ©1991 Coors Brewing Company, Golden, Colorado 80401 Brewer of Fine Quality Beers Since 1873.

Name _____

Address _____

City/State/Zip _____

Phone _____

Coors Foundation For Family Literacy.

Reprinted with permission of Coors Foundation for Family Literacy.

Three important considerations go into planning a direct mailing: recency, frequency and monetary matters. The *recency* of a direct mailing is significant in evaluating response; stories of delayed-action response are rare. *Frequent* mailings increase your chances of response by providing reminders. The *monetary* aspect—what you can afford to spend—influences the design and outcome of a direct mailing.

Usually direct-mail investments more than pay their way. The key to success is the mailing list you select. *Occupant* lists—lists organized by addresses—are easy to find and inexpensive but very impersonal, and often inaccurate. If you are mailing to a limited geographical area, you can make up your own list from the crisscross, or city, directory. *Specialized* lists are available according to age, income, educational status and almost any other kind of breakdown you want. Many organizations sell lists of their membership, and you can buy other lists from direct-mail list companies. Some base their lists on auto registrations, others on phone directories and others on complex sampling strata.

The U.S. Postal Service is compiling the first nationwide list of American addresses. The plan is to license the list to private database companies that service mailers. Although names won't be attached to the addresses, privacy has become an issue. Direct-mail services already have about 80 percent of U.S. households located, but about 6 percent of all third-class mail still goes undelivered.[15]

The price you pay for use of a list entitles you to use it only once. To protect its list, the mailing house actually sends out the material for you. It is important to remember that 23 percent of a general list, 22 percent of a business list and 35 percent of a business executive list go bad in a year. Planning a periodic check of your list is the best way to safeguard the integrity of your basic mailing file. The U.S. Postal Service will help. If your address list is on a diskette, you can send it in and the post office will standardize addresses, make sure cities match zip codes, validate the zip codes and add four extra digits to each code. Your post office also will report any addresses that can't be coded.

Remember that every piece of correspondence going out of the office is an image maker or breaker. Careful attention to spelling indicates that you care about the recipient. Typographical errors suggest that the message was not important enough to command the writer's attention, and the person receiving the letter might wonder why it should deserve his or hers. Accurate spelling and syntax also imply knowledge and authority. Perhaps the most compelling reason for making every piece of copy perfect is that your letterhead is your signature.

Every bit as personal as a note bearing your letterhead is a telephone call. The promotional tool 1-900-Telephone charges calls to the customer. The voice information system offers callers access to a prerecorded message or other public relations information, if they have a touchtone telephone. Callers can be charged anything from 50 cents to as much as $50 per call and billed at a flat rate or at a cost per minute.

The 900 numbers have been used for fundraising, for offering live or prerecorded messages, for promotions and for marketing games. In the 1980s, Johnson & Johnson set up a 900 line during the Tylenol tampering crisis so that callers could get immediate information.[16] More recently, AT&T set up a 900 line for the USO so that stateside callers could talk to troops involved in the 1991 Persian Gulf "Desert Storm" war (see Example 11.21).

▼ NEW CHANNELS

You have to be alert for new channels you can use to reach audiences, and two such channels may be in popular use soon. Both provide an experience for the audience. One is a computer program (for Commodore Computer) developed by Professor William Lynch of the School of Education and Human Development at George Washington University in Washington, D.C. His program, "The Virtual Historic House," uses digitized audio visual images to take the viewer/visitor on an electronic "tour." When the user chooses a room, its floor plan is displayed on a computer monitor, activating a media presentation of that location, including audio

EXAMPLE 11.21

900-number Ad

How does the USO bring a little bit of home to our troops 10,000 miles away?

AT&T 900 Service.

We're happy the USO can use our 900 service to help 350,000 Americans feel a little less lonely. And we hope the goodwill sent through AT&T *MultiQuest*® 900 Service will continue to keep spirits high in the Persian Gulf.

The USO chose to work with AT&T and Call Interactive℠* because we're as dedicated to quality as they are to support. They know we'll make sure America's voice will come through loud and clear.

1 900 820-2USO

By calling this number, you will be charged $3. The net proceeds go to the USO so they can provide personal gift packages, celebrity visits, off-duty centers and, most of all, a vital link to home. Call by December 25, 1990 and you can have your name added to a massive thank-you card sent to our troops in the Persian Gulf. That way we can all lend a hand to the brave Americans overseas.

AT&T
The right choice.

*Call Interactive is a joint venture between the
American Express Information Services Corporation and AT&T.

© 1990 AT&T

of the sort you might hear from a tour guide if you were visiting the location. Additional text and even period music are further options. The first presentation was arranged for Chester County (Pennsylvania), to present historical buildings and explain the relationship between architecture and history.[17]

Lynch's creation does not make use of cyberspace. This is a more experience-centered medium, and it is also much more complex to use—at least as it now exists. Cyberspace relies on computer-generated images, but the user must wear goggles and gloves (or hand attachments) that electronically create the illusion of a three-dimensional experience. The simulations vary from walking around inside a patient who has a tumor so a surgeon gets a good look at it and all the surrounding organs before making an incision or planning radiation therapy, to looking inside a storm system so a meteorologist can get a better view of the storm's potential. It could also be used to let a potential customer "fly" a plane—perhaps one not yet built—or to enable a user to explore an underwater site as a "dry" scuba diver. This technique, called "virtual reality," seems capable of creating countless artificial worlds for people to experience.[18]

▼ SUMMARY

Channels of communication are public or private paths for messages. Messages travel along these channels through media. Public channels are where you find mass media like newspapers, television and radio; and private channels are where you find the print and electronic media of organizations. These private channels may be directed to internal or external audiences, or sometimes to both. Media in private channels are controlled, but the public channels include both controlled and uncontrolled messages.

The two principal types of public relations communication used by organizations are advertising and publicity, both of which take many media forms. In planning public relations strategy, the practitioner chooses channels and media based on the purpose of the communication, the intended audience, the message to be delivered, the resources available, the time limits for delivery of the message and the credibility of the medium chosen to carry the message. A mix of different media is generally used.

Types of advertising used by public relations practitioners include house or self-directed ads in organizational publications, public service announcements (if the organization is nonprofit) and various types of institutional advertising such as issue, advocacy and image ads. Advertising also appears in other formats such as posters (which in their smallest form are flyers and in their largest are billboards), goods packaging, displays and specialty advertising that bears the organization's logo. Sometimes organizations get involved in cooperative advertising, where costs are split among two or more companies who share an advertisement.

Advertising for professional services has generated some ethical concerns, especially in relation to the services of physicians and lawyers.

Most advertising is controlled because specific time or space is purchased. But public service announcements are not, since they are free and are used at the discretion of print and broadcast media. Preparing advertising messages of any kind—whether PSAs or commercial messages—is generally a costly process, and evaluations of effectiveness are limited.

Among the uncontrollable problems associated with advertising are imitation of good advertising ideas, occasionally unfortunate ad placement and ill effects of negative advertising. Advertising also has two myths associated with it: that a single concept can be used globally, and that a single concept will work with all audiences even within one culture.

Messages that do not constitute advertising often do rate as publicity—some form of news or information about the organization. These messages publicize the organization to a number of different audiences. Sometimes the publicity is direct to audiences, and sometimes it is through the mass media, in which case public relations people act as sources and resources to the news media. Material that goes directly to audiences may take the form of publications by the organization or by industry, trade or other associations. Some organizations produce expensive sponsored magazines that advance a cause or idea but look similar to general consumer publications.

In addition to publishing magazines, organizations often produce newsletters for internal and/or external audiences. Some of the external newsletters are money-making subscription publications. Public relations departments also produce handbooks for organizations.

While publications are generally done in-house, an organization's film and video productions often are produced by outside specialists because of technical demands. Some sponsored films are shown as features in theaters and can be purchased or rented by special groups. Shorter videos are sometimes used as feature fillers by television and theaters. Organizations also use corporate videos internally to educate and train employees, to tell them about employee benefits and to give them organizational messages they want shared with external audiences—especially in a crisis.

Messages intended for special audiences are now being sent by other electronic means, especially videotex and teletext. These are used when the information is highly perishable. Audiences especially enjoy the interactive aspect of videotex. Both meetings and speeches are additional ways to generate publicity, either through reports in internal publications or through coverage by mass media.

Other media for promotional messages include exhibits and characters identified with the organization, multimedia presentations, closed-circuit television, books, stamps and even cartoons.

Publicity the organization sends directly to audiences is generally controlled, but that transmitted through the mass media is not. For print and broadcast media messages to be successful, they must be newsworthy, timely and presented in the appropriate format for the medium.

Two hybrids (combinations of advertising and publicity) are direct mail and 900 telephone numbers. The success of direct mail depends on research to keep target audiences identified.

The effectiveness of communication depends on the appropriate and inventive use of existing channels of communication and their media.

▼ NOTES

[1]Planned Communication Services (PCS), 12 E. 46th St., New York, NY 10017. Organizations like MediaLink Video Broadcasting Corporation will send PSAs by satellite, monitor them, send hard copies and ¾-inch cassettes, depending on what type of service the customer needs.

[2]Ellen Joan Pollock, "'I Love My Lawyer' Ads May Spread to More States," *Wall Street Journal* (Deccember 7, 1990), pp. B1, B4.

[3]Alice Gagnard, "Elements of Timing and Repetition in Award-Winning TV Commercials, *Journalism Quarterly*, 66(4) (Winter 1989), pp. 965–69.

[4]Stuart Little, "Sponsored Films Are Better Than Ever," *Saturday Review* (September 12, 1970), pp. 90–92.

[5]Robert Finchout, "A Funny Thing Happened at the Cinema Last Night . . . I Saw Your Film," *Public Relations Journal*, 30(10) (October 1974), pp. 6–7.

[6]Adam Shell, "Reaching Out to the TV Generation," *Public Relations Journal*, 46(11) (November 1990), pp. 28–32.

[7]Ibid., p. 29.

[8]Ibid., p. 29.

[9]Eric A. Abbott, "The Electronic Farmers' Marketplace: New Technologies and Agricultural Information," *Journal of Communication*, 39(3) (Summer 1989), pp. 124–36.

[10]Ibid., p. 124.

[11]Ibid., p. 129.

[12]Zoe McCathrin, "The Key to Employee Communication, Small Group Meetings," *Professional Communicator* (Spring 1990), pp. 6, 7, 10.

[13]Timothy D. Schellhardt, "Why Tom Sawyer and Not Whooda Tom Is on Your Stamps," *Wall Street Journal* (November 30, 1972), pp. 1, 8.

[14]*pr reporter* (February 12, 1973), p. 1. For a first person account of dealing with the flood of publicity, see Anne Groer, "Paper Madness in Washington," *Gannett Center Journal* (Spring 1990), pp. 69–82.

[15]Michael W. Miller, "Post Office's Planned Address List Raises Privacy Jitters," *Wall Street Journal* (December 13, 1990), pp. B1, B6.

[16]Adam Shell, "1-900-A-PR-TOOR," *Public Relations Journal* (August 1990), p. 9.

[17]"Being There," *Historic Preservation* (March/April 1991), p. 11.

[18]Doug Stewart, "Through the Looking Glass into an Artificial World—via Computer," *Smithsonian* (January 1991) pp. 36–45.

Selected readings, activities and assignments appropriate to this chapter can be found in the *Instructor's Guide*.

Tactics and Techniques: Details
That Make PR Strategies Work

By speaking out you can control to some extent . . . perhaps to the only extent . . . the way in which you are perceived, and if you are both candid and cooperative with the press, they will give you an even chance and the benefit of the doubt . . . and that . . . is all you should expect in today's world.

Antonio Navarro, senior vice-president, W. R. Grace & Co.

Corporations are wise to accept the premise that it is better to dine on 50 percent of a large, plump turkey than 100 percent of a sparrow.

Translated by *Washington Journalism Review*

We have to recognize that the magnitude of communication possible through the advent of technology will add to the din, making it even more difficult, not easier, for messages to get through undistorted. In essence, the method of communication will become so deceptively easy that it could mislead practitioners as to the effectiveness of their activities.

John Budd, Chair and CEO, the Omega Group

Public relations work is somewhat like a giant jigsaw puzzle: there are many pieces, and each must fit perfectly with the others to make the whole picture. In Chapter 10, you learned strategies to help you develop the picture. In Chapter 11, you surveyed the communications channels PR practitioners use as the framework for that picture. In this chapter, you get a look at the pieces. Have you ever worked a jigsaw puzzle by first separating what appeared to be ground from what looked like sky? Well, you can divide the major sections of the public relations puzzle—advertising and publicity—in the same way. However, in trying to sort out puzzle pieces by "sky" and "ground," you may sometimes have found pieces that included parts of both, and others that looked like one but were actually the other. That's also the case with advertising and publicity in public relations.

▼ ADVERTISING

Advertising has been defined as paid-for time or space, except in the case of public service announcements (PSAs) where the time and space are donated to a nonprofit organization. But in some situations advertising looks a lot like publicity. Usually when advertising takes on the appearance of publicity, there is no intention to deceive. Ads are supposed to be clearly labeled as such, but they can be labeled and still look very much like editorial copy. Sometimes when a newspaper publishes a special section on something like the opening of a hospital, the reader may not be aware that almost all of that section—even the news columns—consists of advertising.

The tendency of some public relations people to view public service announcements as publicity, because no money changes hands, is confusing to most students and mystifying to others. Clearly, though, print PSAs looks exactly like ads, and broadcast PSAs sound exactly like commercials. Moreover, they are handled through the advertising departments of print media and through public service directors at radio and television stations. Publicity, on the other hand, is handled by media news staffs and must compete for time or space with staff-generated material. Perhaps the most clearcut difference, however, is that PSAs, like other advertising, are controlled communications whose precise content is dictated by the originating organization. In contrast, publicity is subject to whatever truncation, dismemberment, supplementation or revision the news medium sees fit to impose.

Ads as News Lookalikes

Ads sometimes look like publicity. Although the copy is clearly marked as advertising, it resembles a news feature and may pass for one. These ads frequently appear in local publications and highlight products and services offered by local businesses (see Example 12.1). Stories like these are promotional pieces, however, and wouldn't pass muster as a news column if submitted to an editor.

Sometimes public relations people have difficulty with ads that closely resemble publicity releases, because unsophisticated managements don't know the difference between the two. Often whole sections of copy may be involved, all consisting of display advertising, in the weekly real estate section of the newspaper (see Example 12.2). In addition, newspapers sometimes run special sections—whole sections of the newspaper devoted to

▼ **Ad copy sometimes looks like news, but there's a big difference between news releases and copy in newspaper advertising sections.**

a special topic or event and built around the advertising that is sold.

The editorial copy in such a section is essentially written for those who have taken out ads. The amount of space purchased determines the length of the stories, as well as the amount of illustration material that accompanies them. The only "free" copy in the section is what you write about the event or the topic itself, such as a historical feature, a current "what's going on" news item, profiles of people from previous events and photos related to the topical content of the section. The copy in most special sections, other than the Sunday real estate sections, looks like news, but it is not straight news.

Special sections may appear in many different forms. One on health care, for example, may look like a regular newspaper section, as might a *single advertiser* supplement for a new store. Alternatively, a store may use a magazine format to be inserted within a newspaper or some special sections. A chamber of commerce annual report may look like Sunday tabloid inserts similar to the *New York Times Book Review* section (which is editorial matter, not advertising). Advertorials, magazine advertising supplements, often look like special features. Broadcast advertorials, though, look like editorials and deal with ideas or issues and not with products or services. Another area that invites confusion is broadcast news promos (the broadcast equivalent of house ads). These often sound like actual news soundbites and can mislead the viewer or listener.

To maintain credibility with the news media, you have to know the differences in their styles of copy but be able to write appropriately for all.

EXAMPLE 12.1

Feature-length Ads That Look Like News Items

WESTERN TARRANT COUNTY

BUSINESS PROFILES

Computer Place helps customers

Computer Place helps its customers in an unusual way by having a sidewalk sale every second Sunday from 1 to 5 p.m., where people can bring their computer items to sell.

There is no fee, said Jim

PROFILE
BUSINESS: Computer Place
LOCATION: 5214 Wedgmont Cir. N.
HOURS: Noon to 6 p.m., Tues-Thurs;
10 a.m. to 5 p.m, Fri-Sat
PHONE: 292-1584

Jim Thompson holds a computer sidewalk sale every month.

Thompson, and in the three years the store has been open, they have had about 30 sidewalk sales. This is the only computer sidewalk sale in Fort Worth, Thompson said, and the crowds are always good.

Thompson has been in the computer business about 10 years. He has worked at several other computer stores and also worked as a computer consultant before striking off on his own.

"We build and sell computers, and we do service on computers," he said.

They also tutor newcomers to the computer field, he said.

"We sell public domain software, which is reasonably priced," he added. Computer Place has 800 or 900 public domain software choices at $5 a disk, he said, including PC Write (word processing), PC Calc (spreadsheet), PC File (database) and educational software and games.

Thompson feels his store can offer personal service that larger stores cannot. "We try to take care of our customers," he said.

Computer Place does service calls in the mornings and on Monday.

PAID ADVERTISEMENT

Used with permission from Fort Worth Star-Telegram, Thursday, December 13, 1990.

EXAMPLE 12.2

Opening Page of Whole-section Display Advertising

SUNDAY'S NEW HOME GUIDE

CLASSIFIED ADVERTISING SECTION

Written and Produced by the Classified Advertising Department

Sunday, January 20, 1991 · Fort Worth Star-Telegram · Section G, Page 1

Fox & Jacobs Builders

Fox & Jacobs Builders is now offering spacious New Generation homes, priced from $109,000 to $135,000 in The Knoll at the master-planned community of Park Glen.

Meeting with tremendous success, the community offers fine values in a beautiful setting. Designed to be a town unto itself, it has schools, playgrounds, shopping centers and churches. Located in northeast Fort Worth, it offers convenient access to area employers.

The gas-heated homes are enhanced by designer wall coverings, ceramic tile entries, crown molding in living and dining rooms, six-panel interior doors, formal entry doors with beveled-glass insets, plush carpeting throughout, fully sodded and landscaped front yards and fenced back yards. Exteriors are further complemented by all-brick porches and Palladian windows.

Kitchens feature name-brand appliances, 42-inch cabinets, easy-care, no-wax flooring, hand-crafted cabinetry and convenience packages that include a pull-down cookbook rack.

Featured this week is the Elgin. Priced from $106,500, this 2,339-square-foot, two-story home spotlights two bedrooms, two and one-half baths, a spacious kitchen with adjacent morning room, family room with fireplace, upstairs game room and formal dining area.

In the kitchen is an abundance of cabinets and space along with a pantry and pass-through serving bar to the breakfast room.

The Elgin's master suite is on the first floor and features a window seat. Its bath has a garden tub and window seat; separate, glass-enclosed shower; and his-and-her lavatories.

Fox & Jacobs also offers plans in The Meadows of Park Glen. Created for first-time home buyers, the one- and two-story designs are priced from $81,950 to $102,950.

To visit Fox & Jacobs at Park Glen, take Loop 820 north to Beach Street. Go north on Beach Street two and one-half miles to Basswood and turn right. Proceed one-half mile to the models, which are open for viewing from 10 a.m. until 8 p.m. daily.

Custom Classics

Custom Classics is building fine homes in Hurst, Colleyville and Keller, bringing a new perspective of quality construction and tailor-made options to the custom home-buying market.

Homes are priced from the $150s to $500s, allowing Custom Classics to build to suit a variety of tastes or lifestyles, depending on what an individual home buyer is looking for.

Custom Classics builders and consultants work with each home buyer to help create a uniquely personalized home and include all of the innovative features and exquisite amenities desired.

Some of the features included in a Custom Classics home are: marble entryways, hand-crafted staircases, spacious, showcase kitchens with top name-brand appliances, built-in microwave ovens; ceramic tile; and sunny breakfast nooks.

Rich, crown molding providing elegance and style can be found in the family, living and dining rooms, as well as the master bedroom. Master bedrooms are built downstairs or upstairs and offer baths with a marble, jetted tub; marble shower and double, marble vanity.

A wet bar and built-in entertainment center are usually included in an upstairs game room. Plans also highlight a built-in security system, garage door opener and allowance for extended landscaping.

Since 1986, Custom Classics has grown steadily and expanded throughout several major Texas cities. The company began building in the Dallas/Fort Worth metroplex more than one year ago and has successfully introduced its creative designs.

A beautiful two-story model, 2728 Woodbridge Drive, in Woodbridge Estates of Hurst is nestled amid many available home sites, including several cul-de-sac lots. Woodbridge Estates is centrally located, close to shopping facilities, schools, hospitals and restaurants. Located at the corner of Highway 26 and Long Boone in north Hurst, it is easily accessible to downtown Fort Worth and D/FW Airport.

Custom Classics also builds homes priced from the $220s in Colleyville at neighborhoods such as Hidden Oaks, Summertree, Summerbrook and Lakes of Somerset and in Keller at Williamsburg. For more information, contact Larry Myers or Cary Clarke.

Decor Score

BY ROSE BENNETT GILBERT
Copley News Service

Q. We're looking for a new house. The children are all married and this is our chance to have exactly what we want — fewer rooms, but suited to our lifestyle.

The problem is, after 27 years of marriage, it turns out we have different ideas about what that lifestyle — or should be. My husband thinks the family room is the important factor in what we buy. I want a large, elegant living room so I can start entertaining, at last.

How do we compromise? — L.C.

A. First, relax. Your husband is no stranger to you; he's just following what one California designer says is a typical male pattern when it comes to buying a new house.

According to Larry Kilb of San Diego, a woman typically looks at two areas — the kitchen and master bath, while a man focuses on the family room.

"He wants something of size, something that's functional, something where he can come home and relax for some down time," Kilb points out. "He could care less about a show place living room."

With that in mind, I'd suggest shopping for a house that has a good-sized den he can dominate while you keep your living room company-ready. If that sounds selfish, Kilb has an answer: He cites a recent Wall Street Journal survey, which estimated that upper-management male executives typically work a minimum of 57 to 60 hours a week. That's a lot of time away from home for a home, so sexist or not, she who's there most deserves a stronger say. (I look forward to letters of response to that!)

Kilb, by the way, practices what he preaches: He recently designed a town house in Davidson Communities, San Diego, specifically for women. Among the special considerations he says women want.

— A kitchen that's light and airy.
— Lots and lots of cupboard space.
— Kitchen floor plans that open into adjoining rooms "so a woman doesn't feel abandoned."
— Low walls over the sink area that allow for visual contact between family members while hiding dirty dishes from view.

— Lighting that comes from two angles, so there are no uncomfortable shadows.

— Separate sides of the master bath so his-and-her things don't get mixed up (she gets more space, by the way).

— Vanity countertops that are 3 to 4 inches higher than in secondary baths "so we adults can stop stooping to brush our teeth."

Kilb's town house also offers another comfort that comes under the heading of luxury with a capital L: a two-way fireplace in the master suite, which warms both the bedroom and the bath.

Q. I want to put a wood floor in the kitchen of our house. Everything has a country theme, and I think the floor would be perfect. My husband says it's a bad idea, that the wood will never stand up. What do you think? — K.W.

A. Wood floors have come a long way, thanks to modern technology.

The key to lasting happiness underfoot lies in protective finishes. As long as you pay routine attention to maintenance, a wood floor protected

Please see Decor, Page 3

A two-way fireplace lends warmth and luxury to both the master bedroom and bath.

Westchester Homes

Westchester Homes features Plan 1774, ready for immediate occupancy, in the garden home community of Eagles Landing in Bedford.

Priced from $105,900, this completed home was designed for entertaining, as well as quality living in an easy-care setting, says sales consultant David Stockel.

This two-story design features three bedrooms, two baths and two spacious living and dining areas, as well as some extra amenities usually found in custom homes.

A gourmet kitchen is complete with work island, expansive pantry, lazy susan, built-in microwave and an abundance of counter space.

The master bath boasts a jetted tub, separate shower, double marble vanity and a skylight.

Other luxurious amenities and finishes include: a split-level entry; marble entryway; plush carpet; designer wall coverings; natural oak bannisters; six-panel interior doors; a fireplace; imaginative window treatments with stacked, triple and fan-shaped windows; cathedral ceilings; ceiling fans; plant ledges; polished-brass fixtures; complete security system; brick exterior; a room-finished, two-car garage; energy efficient package; and landscaping with a sodded lawn and fenced back yard.

More than one dozen garden home designs are found at Eagles Landing with prices from $93,900 to $125,900 and sizes ranging from 1,253 to 2,350 square feet of living space.

The gracious surroundings at Eagles Landing are enhanced by the neighborhood parties and pool with sundeck area. The community is a few blocks away from a 55-acre, wooded public park that has jogging trails, a lake, picnic areas and a recreation center.

Shopping malls, restaurants, health clubs and a post office are nearby. D/FW Airport is easy accessible, as are other parts of the metroplex.

At Eagles Landing in Bedford, Westchester Homes spotlights Plan 1774, an elegant garden home priced from $105,900.

The Eagles Landing information center/model home is open from 10 a.m. to 7 p.m. Tuesday through Saturday and from noon to 7 p.m. on Sunday and Monday.

To visit the community, take Highway 183 to Central Drive and exit north. Turn left on Harwood and go past Forest Ridge west to Falcon Trail. From Highway 121, exit west on Harwood, go past Forest Ridge to Falcon Trail and turn right. The sales office is at 1206 Falcon Trail.

J.B. Sandlin Homes

Building homes for 33 years, J.B. Sandlin's goal is to give home buyers fine quality.

The maximum in amenities and square footages is found in Sandlin custom homes. A locally owned company, J.B., Mike and Terry Sandlin take a personal interest in buyers and their individual needs.

Fine craftsmanship and materials are used throughout and after a home is sold, a comprehensive customer service department and the HOW warranty continue the quality. Each dwelling is built with a high-efficiency energy package earning it the E-OK rating.

A professional decorating staff blends colors and patterns of wallpaper to create unique living areas. All homes have custom-designed kitchens and baths, ceiling treatments, hand-crafted cabinetry and detailed brick work. Underneath the home, the slab is supported by extra foundation piers around the perimeter beams and under the fireplace.

Several subdivisions in different locations offer various lot and home sizes and amenities.

With more than 200 plans to choose from with spacious baths and bright, Hollywood-style bath with vanity counter. Wallpaper is bold red, blue and green plaid.

With a fine view of the Iron Horse Golf Course, this home is ready for immediate occupancy and is priced $179,000. It is located at 6214 Skylark Circle.

J.B. Sandlin is building fine custom homes in many metroplex communities.

kitchens and a design staff ready to assist buyers, J.B. Sandlin is building homes in Bedford Park Estates, priced from the $130s; Park Hill Estates and Woodbury Forest in Euless, priced from the $130s; Wintergreen North and Oak Ridge Estates with homes from the $120s to $140s; Fox Meadows, from the $140s, Hidden

Oaks and Highland Meadows IV, from the $200s in Colleyville; Countryside Estates in Grapevine, from the $130s; Trophy Club, $100s to $180s; Thornbridge in North Richland Hills, from the $200s; Quail Valley Estates in Keller, $150s; and Cranbrook Estates, from the $200s and Ross Downs in Colleyville, $170s.

Meadowlakes

Introducing a new approach to living, Meadowlakes style, is the Golf Villa by R.J. Frank and Co., a custom home built for today's active life style.

Whether one is an on-the-go executive or retiree with better things to do than yard work and home maintenance, this 2,117-square-foot home is exciting.

Inside is an open, ceramic tile entry with a semi-circular stairway to the right. An 11-foot-high window above the front door brightens the entryway. A marble fireplace in the living room fills the home with warmth and charm, while the wet bar makes for entertaining ease.

The traditional dining area features wallpaper in blue, green and rose. The guest/powder bath, decorated in bright blues and greens, has a white, pedestal sink and angled mirrors. Warm, taupe carpeting is found throughout the home.

Food preparation is a breeze in the custom, total-electric kitchen with ceramic tile flooring. Over- and under-the-counter lighting and milk-wash cabinets keep the atmosphere airy. The oversized range offers a built-in griddle and the self-cleaning oven and microwave have a stylish white-on-white finish.

The breakfast area has traditional wallpaper complementary to the dining room's and a tiffany lamp of clear and navy blue glass.

The master bedroom suite's sitting area provides windows overlooking the back patio. A wall of built-in storage leads to the master bath. An elegant jetted tub and marble shower enhance this room with soft pastels of gray, green, blue and rose along mirrored walls.

Above the entry is a game room with vaulted ceiling, stable windows, ceiling fan/light and closet for storage.

Two spacious bedrooms share a

veloper of Meadowlakes, has lots available on the new Iron Horse Golf Course, priced from the low-$60s. Most are golf-course frontage lots with excellent views. For more information, visit or contact the sales office at 6340 Skylark Circle.

The Meadowlakes community is located at Rufe Snow Drive and Loop 820 in North Richland Hills.

With 2,117 square feet, 6214 Skylark Circle is priced $179,000.

In Today's Section

History Maker Homes	Pulte Homes
Centennial Homes	Choice Homes

Used with permission.

▼ **Although print and broadcast PSAs are ads, they can generate publicity.**

Print and Broadcast PSAs

Public service announcements are examples of publicity-generating advertising copy that are similar to special sections and display advertising. In all of these forms, you do *not* work with the publication's editorial staff in placing them. With print PSAs, you will probably deal with newspaper or magazine designers and layout artists who position ads and editorial matter in the publication. You might also work with a newspaper's advertising director to get a drop-in ad placed in a regular advertiser's space, with that advertiser's permission. Or you might work with a regular (also large) advertiser to sponsor your space. Regular advertisers usually agree to do this only for nonprofit organizations or in conjunction with special civic events that are open to all, such as a Fourth of July fireworks celebration.

If your message is for the broadcast media, you will deal with public service directors who are usually partial to general interest subjects like health and safety or to specific social problems like substance abuse or child molestation. You can sponsor a PSA if you are a profit-making organization as long as you are delivering a nonprofit organization's message. An example would be AT&T's sponsorship of a PSA on illiteracy for the Assault on Illiteracy program, a nonprofit organization. AT&T's corporate advertising district manager explained why the company sponsored the ad: "We wanted a subject related to information and communications because that's the business we're in. We also wanted the public to know that while we are a gigantic corporation, we are committed to performing deeds in the public interest." The AT&T spot went to 400 TV stations, was aired 1,374 times on 296 stations and made an estimated 682,280,000 audience impressions.[1]

In a survey of 1,057 VHF and UHF TV stations about their PSA preferences, Planned Communication Services (PCS) received 665 responses. The survey found that stations have moved from film to tape and from wider to narrower tape standards, with 2-inch tape receiving the greatest acceptance. Stations will accept both 30- and 60-second spots, and tapes for children and the elderly got the best reception.[2]

When you are planning a PSA, you first need to consider its purpose. Then you must consider the budget, the amount of money you have to spend and the amount you can get from donations. You must also try to foresee problems you are likely to encounter in shooting, including actors, location, permissions, music and sound. Example 12.3 provides a quick reference for planning time.

For just the reasons stated by AT&T's ad director, a profit-making organization may sponsor a whole campaign or a portion of one.

Preparing Successful Ads

Your most important consideration in preparing any type of advertising copy is effectiveness—achieving your purpose. The purpose must be clear because it's difficult for even the best copy to create awareness, convey specific information, get action and affect attitude. You must decide where the public is in relation to the product or service (including a nonprofit organization's service) and go from there. The fact that memory is multidimensional means that you have to know exactly what you wish to achieve and how prepared a specific public is to receive your messages, in order to be able to measure your ad's effectiveness with some degree of reliability.[3]

Decisions about effectiveness include whether or not to use humor, to make comparisons or to use negative comments. Again, what you decide depends on what you are trying to accomplish and whom you are trying to reach. Humorous ads seem

EXAMPLE 12.3 ∎∎

PSA Preparation Schedule

Task	Time Required	Task	Time Required
Choosing a cause or topic	4 to 12 hours	Setting up shoot (crew) plus meeting with camera crew	2 to 4 hours
Script research	3 to 8 hours	Shoot day (on set)	8 to 14 hours
Finding a nonprofit sponsor	12 hours to 3 days or more, depending on your persuasiveness	Music selection	1 to 3 hours
		Casting narrator	1 to 4 hours
First-draft script	2 to 6 hours	Recording narrator at sound studio	1/2 to 1 hour
Script rewrites	1 to 3 hours		
Script approvals	3 to 8 hours, depending on the number of drafts	Choosing takes and editing	5 to 10 hours
		On-line edit to finished master with title	4 to 9 hours
Location scouting	5 hours to 2 days		
Casting	5 to 8 hours		
Prop shopping	3 to 5 hours		

SOURCE: Margie Goldsmith, "How to Get Results with PSAs," *Public Relations Journal* (January 1986), p. 34. Copyright January 1986. Reprinted by permission of *Public Relations Journal,* published by the Public Relations Society of America, New York, NY.

to get attention (see Example 12.4), but they convey less information and don't always ensure recall of the advertiser.[4] There's a risk, too, in comparative ads, especially as regards credibility. Credibility also can be at stake in negative advertising, but you can usually count on recall. And while most people say they don't like negative advertising, they do respond to political negative advertising that seems to offer insight into an issue or personal characteristic.[5]

One of the most memorable parts of any ad is the organization's logo, designed not only for high recognition, but also for a positive attraction or reaction. According to one study by Frank Thayer, "Successful corporate symbols will be those which effectively evoke the positive and powerful responses already present in the mind of the subject and those which were learned at a much earlier stage of their cultural education."[6] The latter point suggests that, as organizations become involved in global communication, these logos should be pretested abroad to ensure that they meet with cultural acceptance. Organizations often change their logos so that these "grow" with the organization and reflect a more modern look. (See Example 12.5.) Other organizations cling to an established logo for high recognition.

EXAMPLE 12.4

House Ad Using Humor

Everyone knows that children and dogs always attract attention. Furthermore, anyone who has ever owned an Irish Setter (as one of the authors does) appreciates the validity of this illustration. The illustration is memorable and is closely tied to the message and the source.

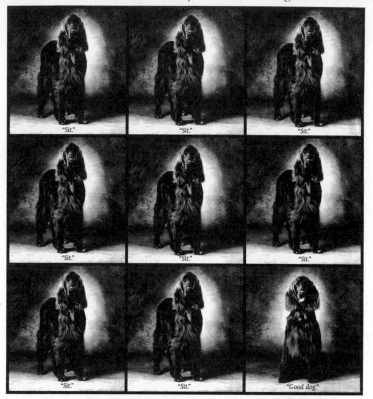

SOURCE: Reprinted with permission of Dow Jones & Co., Inc., publisher of *The Wall Street Journal*. Copyright 1991.

EXAMPLE 12.5

Logos

The Audit Bureau of Circulations has been monitoring the circulation of print media since 1914 and has changed its "look" or logo several times over the years to modernize. The newest logo, introduced in 1989, coincided with ABC's 75th anniversary.

Reprinted with permission.

▼ PUBLICITY AND PUBLICATIONS

Just as some advertising resembles publicity, some publicity and promotional pieces look like advertising. This is particularly true of brochures, which are just as likely to be sales pieces as to be news or information pieces.

Brochures are just one type of publication that organizations regularly produce themselves. Desktop publishing has increased the number of such in-house publications. Except for brochures, house publications generally follow a magazine format, although some are designed as megapapers—oversized papers folded for a magazine or newsletter look.

One of the most important magazines an organization produces is its annual report. Although only publicly held companies are required by law to produce annual reports, many nonprofits offer them to their stakeholders as well. But nonprofit organizations are less likely to produce quarterly reports. Publicly held companies must do so, and these often take the form of brochures of variable size and format. Sometimes speeches by top executives and reports by researchers are produced in brochure or magazine format and sent to stakeholders as publicity.

Publicists often get extra mileage out of their newspaper and magazine stories by reprinting them for their own mailings.

Producing Brochures and House Publications

Publishing is a highly technical part of public relations activity. It is full of traps for the unwary—and unfortunately, mistakes are very tangible and easily noticed. With the technology of desktop publishing, more materials like brochures and house publications are now computer-generated, but not all of these are prepared by the PR department. Thus, the public relations practitioner may have to publish some guidelines for the publications' physical appearance so that they look as though they belong to the same organization, no matter who produces them. Publications from an organization should appear to belong to a "family." If you don't control this, the organization's image will suffer fragmentation.

Brochures The first decision you have to make in producing a brochure is to determine its purpose and its *audience*. This will suggest not only the number of copies to print but also the distribution method to use. Distribution is critical to planning.

Brochures come in all shapes and sizes, but these are virtually predetermined if the piece has to be mailed. If it is going in the mail, you must decide whether to enclose it in an envelope at additional expense or to send it as a self-mailer—that is, a folded piece with a tab or staple closing and part of the surface reserved for mailing instructions. In either case, it is important first to check with the Postal Service, particularly if your piece requires a specially designed and irregular envelope, since there are regulations governing acceptable envelope size. There are also regulations about sealing and addressing self-mailers and about sending a bulk mailing. Finding out all this in advance is important because it affects brochure design, including the choice of paper stock.

After determining the physical properties of the brochure and its envelope (if there is to be one), use a folded piece of paper as a mockup. Visualizing helps. Make sure the size exactly matches that of the finished piece.

Next decide what is to be said and how. Figure out what can be said with illustrations. Brochures usually succeed or fail because of their graphics, so it is important to begin working early with an artist. The artist responsible for the design must know the concept and the purpose, as well as the distribution method and how it affects the design. Together you must reach some decisions about color (ordinarily a financial, rather than an aesthetic, decision) and about the method of reproduction, whether offset or letterpress (today most printing is offset). Ask for rough layouts, and ask the artist to offer a choice of several different ideas.

Once you have approved the design, you must decide on the exact paper stock, finish, weight and color; the precise color of ink; and the kind and size of type for each portion of the layout. Paper supplies, printers and typesetters usually have samples, which many artists also keep on hand. Choose the printer carefully, because even an attractive layout that is clumsily executed is unusable. The number of brochures printed affects their cost: the more printed, the less the cost for each.

The artist can go ahead with production after all details are settled, copy has been written and supplied and either illustrations have been supplied or artwork approved.

Copyfitting and layout may fall to the artist or to a layout person, but public relations people should also master these techniques. Since the advent of desktop publishing, it is generally accepted that the PR person can write the copy, design the format and produce a camera-ready piece. If you do not produce the piece on a computer, you will send out the copy, marked for type sizes, to be set by a typesetter. After the type has been set and proofread, the finished art readied and everything pasted up, it is time to begin work with the printer. Be sure to arrange with the printer to check proofs before the entire printing is run. Mistakes can happen. Instructions on the layout can be misunderstood or stated incorrectly. Proofing is your last chance. Take it.

When a large printing is complete and the folding is done, it may be worthwhile to have the stuffing and mailing handled by a mail service. Such firms offer different services, but nearly all will work with a mailing list and either charge for labeling or use your labels. Since most operations are computerized, it is best to provide a mailing service with a printout of the addresses on mailing labels.

After the mailing, be sure to keep enough brochures on hand to meet additional requests. Keep at least five as file copies. You may need them for reference.[7]

▼ **Steps in brochure production include determining the purpose, audience and physical properties of the brochure; deciding what is to be said and how; choosing materials and procedures to carry out the design; and carrying production through printing.**

Some brochures are costly pieces, like one for a construction company that took the form of a paper house when unfolded, or the Accord brochure whose headlights came on when it was opened, or a music company's brochure that played a tune. The limits are set not by creativity but by costs.

House Publications   When you are producing a house publication, all other decisions depend on the first: who the audience is. Since a house publication goes to employees or members only, it is likely to have quite a different design from a publication that receives broader distribution. What type of publication, then, is most likely to be accepted and read—a newsletter, a tabloid newspaper format or a magazine? This decision is usually influenced by the budget allotted, which sometimes makes such a question academic.

The next decision involves frequency of publication. Frequency usually depends on the public relations department, and monthly issues are about all most PR departments can cope with. Some produce quarterly publications.

The method of distribution is another consideration. If it is entirely internal, with distribution either in pick-up boxes or by supervisory personnel or in-house mail service, you need not be concerned about mailing regulations and labeling. However, many companies have found it advantageous to send the publication to the recipients' home. In this case, it is important to keep up with address changes, which the personnel department should have in the employee records, and it is critical to consult with the mailroom so that delivery can be worked into a reasonable schedule, with consideration given for their other duties.

Once these elements are decided, content deserves the most careful attention. Enlightened management knows that what the employees want to know about the company is more important than what the company wants to tell the employees. Built into the publication should be ways to convey information and allowances for two-way communication—perhaps through letters to the editor or a response column that answers questions of general concern. The tone of the publication—which includes writing style, layout, artwork, type choice and general design—greatly affects the attitude the employees adopt toward it.

To help determine content, and even type and frequency of publication, PR staffs have used questionnaires to find out what employees might like in the way of employee publications. The difficulty here is that some employees have no idea of what is possible. Choosing among unknowns is a bit of a problem. What seems to work better is to get a sample of house publications put out by others (not necessarily in the same type of company), and select a representative panel to meet on company time and discuss the type of employee publication that might be effective and that could be produced within budget, time and talent restrictions.

It is a good idea to retain the panel even after the publication appears, since panel judgments provide a check on whether the publication is being read, what part of it is best liked and what is missing.

Develop a dummy or mockup suggesting design and general type of content. Estimate how much copy and artwork will appear in each publication and approximately how many pages each will be; then determine how the publication will be printed. Larger organizations may have in-house printing plants; however, if you need to choose an outside printer, make sure to get bids from several. The printer will need to see the dummy, know about how many copies are needed and how often the publication will appear. Together with the printer you have to decide on paper stock for the cover and inside pages and also headline and body type. The printer will have a price list for artwork and special effects, to help in estimating the costs of each issue.

In selecting the printer, you may choose between offset and letterpress. Offset is usually chosen for cost, flexibility and convenience. The printer then has to know whether the publication will be coming to the shop camera-ready or whether the printer will be responsible for setting type and preparing the art (as in getting color separations).

Staff is a major concern in starting a house publication. Who will write and edit? Where can help and talent be found and put to work? Writers, photographers and artists are all important to the success of a house publication, and some reasonable assessment of potential must be made before a publication can be launched. Again, budget is a factor in deciding how much talent can be bought. In the case of an employee publication, however, ego appeals, esprit de corps and gentle persuasion often work in lieu of remuneration.

A system for gathering information and preparing it for publication on schedule must be developed. Deadlines must be set for all art and photos, as must specifications for the way material is to be submitted. Some successful operations use reporting sheets, which are handled by a person in each department. These are turned over to the editor and help in gathering news. Longer articles are generally determined by editorial/administrative decision and worked out on an assignment basis. Some editors plan a whole year's content; others plan one issue at a time, working only two or three months in advance on major stories.[8]

Some publications are prepared by institutions to be a customer or client service, offered at no charge. These bonus publications, from institutions like insurance companies, are designed to make the customers feel good about the organization. The publications act as subtle ads suggesting that the company cares about a customer. Often the publications do not call attention to their sponsorship. An example is a fitness magazine sent out by a hospital group.

Some organizations produce magazines that compete with consumer periodicals. Examples are *Smithsonian* (the Smithsonian Institution's magazine) and *Audubon* (an environmental club magazine that holds its own well against independent commercial environmental magazines such as *Buzzworm* or *Garbage*).[9]

Producing Annual Reports

Responsibility for the annual report should be shared by two key people, according to William Ruder and David Finn: a communications specialist responsible for deciding the *character* of the report; and a high-level management representative (generally the chief financial officer or the chief executive officer) responsible for the *content*.[10] The design and the language of the report are the province of the communications specialist, who should not have to yield to the style preferences of others whose expertise lies in different areas.

To give these two individuals the authority they need, all key management personnel should be informed about who has the responsibility for the report and should be involved in contributing to the point of view the report ultimately reflects. Through meetings, a consensus may be reached on theme and approach.

The communications expert should prepare the first draft, working with content supplied by the other key person, and this document should be circulated for comment and contributions. Its impact on all audiences should be weighed, but specifically its *effect* on priority publics should be determined. For example, many annual reports contain copy that touts diversity in the workforce and professes a commitment to teamwork but then show disdain for employees in the illustrations or have pictures that clearly reveal power resting in the hands of a few white males. In addition to being sensitive to such representations while the report is being planned, the communications expert should suggest to other members of management how the published report might be used with various publics, because this could have some bearing on the presentation adopted.

▼ **Annual reports should be the shared responsibility of a communications specialist, who decides the character of the report, and a management representative, who oversees the content.**

Annual reports used to be almost synonymous with complex and obscure prose, but some are now down-to-earth and occasionally even entertaining. The *Wall Street Journal* quotes Wisconsin Securities Company of Delaware as describing one of its ventures as "a flop," and the annual report contains enough additional candor for the *Journal* writer to comment, "Now that's telling it like it is."[11] New Hampshire's Wheelabrator-Frye, Inc., has aimed its annual report toward youngsters. The educational effort—to tell fourth through sixth graders about the free enterprise system—consisted of a twenty-page cartoon report telling what this manufacturer of environmental and energy systems did with its money that year. Not only did the company get publicity from the circulation of the report among youngsters (whose parents and teachers also were exposed), but the report's novel approach generated a lot of publicity. Several companies have bought enough pages in magazines like *Time* to present the entire annual report to an audience of millions.

"Millions" may represent overkill, but to make the most of the published report, it does need to be in the hands of all interested publics. Again, the communications expert should suggest to other departments the most effective use of the published piece.

Some annual report planning begins nearly a year in advance. It is common to begin at the end of the first quarter, and certainly work should commence no later than three to six months before the close of the fiscal year. The wise public relations person builds some padding into any schedule, and the annual report is the publication most likely to need it, since it is such a significant document. After all, it constitutes the organization's most comprehensive statement about itself.

The annual report is a process as much as it is a publication—a comprehensive review of the past year. Because approvals and participation are so important and because the report must be produced on a deadline, the schedule needs to be structured so as to prevent delays. You'll have to work with outside auditors, who are responsible for the financial content, and have the entire report reviewed by legal counsel. The chief financial officer generally has oversight of the annual report, as does the investor relations person, who usually reports to the CFO and who may or may not be in the public relations department (see Example 12.6)

Every annual report normally contains the same kind of information, but reports differ from company to company as to their order or their headings. Most contain the following elements: (1) a letter from the chairman; (2) the auditor's report; (3) financial statements; (4) a longer section narrating pertinent facts about the past year's operation; (5) photos and charts.

Shareholders also get quarterly reports, and some companies package these attractively as newsletters. Others use a brochure format or create packages that resemble thick statement stuffers. (Chapter 9 discusses SEC requirements for the annual report and the 10-K.)

Ever since the SEC began requiring that a company publish its 10-K in addition to its annual report, the annual report has ceased to serve primarily as a financial document and has instead become primarily a public relations piece.

Even though annual reports have taken on a different significance, many remain hard to read. To many CEOs, then, the idea of an executive summary, or shortened version of the report, seemed a good one. In 1987, the Financial Executives Institute devised the summary format, according to which financial information is relegated to the 10-K and to the annual meeting proxy statement. More companies might have used the new format, but 1987 was the year of "Black Monday" (October 19),

when stock prices tumbled precipitously in twenty-four hours. It clearly wasn't the year for abbreviated explanations to investors, but this format may gain acceptance in the future. In the years since 1987, businesses have come to use the executive summary format routinely, in addition to the annual report, although not all companies favor it.

Speeches as Publicity or Publications

For all the time and trouble that goes into preparing an executive's speech, you need to get more out of it than just one-time media coverage at the event. That's likely to be limited at best, even if the speaker is important. When George Bush became a candidate for president of the United States in 1988, his campaign managers asked CBS to send a television crew to cover his first campaign address following the announcement of his candidacy. CBS declined, but CNN showed up, and his campaign managers said they thought the cable network's coverage might actually have been preferable, since it was an all-news network and was therefore likely to give the story more time and to repeat it more frequently on succeeding newscasts.

A speech is one of many types of meetings that an organization may hold and use for publicity (by sending speech texts or meeting transcripts to the news media). These events are often videotaped as an additional way to generate publicity. Some videotapes (and some films) are made expressly for publicity.

Most organizations reprint major addresses in brochure format and mail them to their special publics with a printed notice or a business card attached. Remember also to send copies to publications like *Vital Speeches of the Day* and *Executive Speeches.* These periodicals review and analyze the speeches sent to them and print the best ones.

You need to circulate copies of the speech internally as well. Remember that your employees are PR's front line. What would their response be if someone told them about a major speech by your organization's president that they were unaware of? Employees need facts to help you. You might even

EXAMPLE 12.6 ▰

Production Timetable for Annual Reports

Conception, copy and design for a calendar year annual report should begin shortly after mid-year. A production schedule should be developed early, and a firm delivery date established. Working back from this date to set week-by-week goals can help avoid confusion and save time and money.

WEEK 1:

Start analysis of previous books; develop goals/themes: contact division/department heads for ideas/copy. Circulate timetable with delivery date.

WEEK 2:

Begin rough design exploration. Begin copy outline.

WEEKS 3–4:

Continue design and copy outline.

WEEK 5:

First design review and copy outline.

WEEK 6:

Start photography. Develop copy and comprehensive design.

WEEKS 7–8:

Continue developing copy and comprehensive design.

WEEK 9:

Begin production and type estimating.

WEEK 10:

Final review of comprehensive with photos. Copy review.

WEEK 11:

Start retouching. Develop charts, illustrations and typesetting, if possible.

WEEKS 12–13:

Typesetting and mechanicals.

WEEK 14:

To printer, check blueprints.

WEEKS 15–17:

Printing and binding.

WEEK 18:

Delivery.

SOURCE: Reprinted from Doremus, *Public Relations Checklist for 1989–90 Annual Reports.*

▼ **Speeches need to be used as publicity tools through followup dissemination as well as contemporaneous coverage.**

consider videotaping the speech for internal use over closed-circuit TV or over other internal audio-visual communication systems. You can also refer to the videotape the next time you write a speech for that person to ascertain what gestures the individual is comfortable with and what idioms she or he is likely to use. The question-and-answer session after a speech is especially helpful in these areas (see Example 12.7).[12]

Special Events

While a speech can be a special event, other events are really just occasions or celebrations, like an open house. Then there are big events like a celebrity visit; a convention; or a trade, commercial or consumer show.

Sometimes you may plan for a celebrity's visit, and the celebrity fails to come; but if you think creatively, you can have the event anyway. Stanford University did when then-President of the then–Soviet Union Mikhail Gorbachev was unable to make a planned appearance at the Hoover Institute. The institute had spent a frantic twenty-one days preparing in a short-notice situation. But in three weeks it had created media packets for the anticipated 1,500 reporters, assembled 4,000 presentation folders, written eight facts sheets, disseminated three news releases and prepared prints of 1,000 special photographs from the Institute's Soviet archives.

The official reason given for the cancellation was "time constraints," but no one is sure about this explanation, since Gorbachev spent two hours at Stanford University and spoke to 1,700 faculty, staff and students. The Hoover Institute's staff didn't let three weeks of planning go to waste, though. They exhibited Russian archival material, released the commemorative poster planned for the exhibit and opened their doors to the news media, with scholars available to respond to questions. While they hoped until the last minute that Gorbachev would make an appearance, they also took the initiative and had former Secretary of State George Schultz, a Hoover Institute Distinguished Fellow, present Gorbachev with a 1921 Russian pro-literary poster (a rare item from the collection), and that event was covered by television. Then the staff put out news releases on that presentation, which resulted in over 100 newspaper stories and more than 50 radio and television news items.[13] Thorough planning for special events is the key.[14]

Setting up for Events

There are nine steps or stages in planning for meetings or special events such as dedications, open houses and plant tours:

1. Start planning early. Depending on the size of your event, a year in advance is not too soon.

2. Make a blueprint and a timetable. Plan every detail, no matter how minor, and assign people responsibility for each. Have alternates selected as "backups." These can be one or two extras—people without specific assignments but involved in planning so they can step in if necessary. Once you have all details listed, "walk through" the event mentally as a participant. That way, you will find what you overlooked.

3. Form as many committees as you deem feasible. By involving management and employees in this event, you spread the workload and get the employees enthusiastic and knowledgeable.

4. Use company professionals wherever possible: artists, design personnel, copywriters, exhibit specialists and the like.

5. Provide special attractions to ensure attendance and to make the event memorable. Examples: prominent personalities, parades, concerts, dances, films, exhibits of historical materials, citations or awards, prizes and drawings, product demonstrations, tours of the plant in operation.

EXAMPLE 12.7 ▬▬▬▬▬▬▬▬▬▬▬▬▬

Meeting or Speech Checklist

This is perhaps the most common arrangement asked of PR people and one that is often carelessly handled. The following detailed list may be adapted to suit particular situations.

1. Set up a day in advance when possible; if not, set up at least two hours before program. Check the *podium* for proper height (short or tall speakers); test the podium light and microphone.

2. Find out what activity will be going on in the *room next to your speaker*; you don't want the speaker to have to yell to make him- or herself heard. When planning for a large group, it is important to see whether the hotel or restaurant expects another large group and, if so, what that group is. If your group consists of retired schoolteachers, they may not enjoy being housed in a hotel with a group of boisterous rodeo riders.

3. Check out the *sound system,* amplifiers and speakers. Find the cutoff for piped-in music.

4. Find access to the *lighting* controls.

5. Check access to *electrical outlets.* Have spare heavy-duty extension cords ready for broadcast media.

6. If visuals are to be used, check out the *projector* and check for extra equipment such as a spare projector and extra reels. Test the proper distance for projection. Make sure a table for the projector is set up at the proper distance. Run both projectors, one on blackout so it's ready if the other fails.

7. Have the proper number of *chairs and tables* on hand, and have them placed correctly. It may be desirable to cover the tables with cloths. Arrange the tables so they are as close to the speaker as possible without crowding. However, a smaller room with some crowding is preferable to the yawning cavern of a big hall if attendance is light. If you get enough warning about impending light attendance, most hotels can use screens to help "shrink" the room space.

8. Make arrangements for *water and glasses*; also, for coffee or other refreshments. Be sure there is a firm understanding about the *service*: when delivered, replenished and removed, and what quantity.

9. Locate a *telephone.* If one is in the room, be sure to arrange for an immediate answer if a ring should interrupt the speaker.

10. Make out *name tags* and have additional blank tags on hand. Remember that women guests may not have pockets for the pocket insert tags. Use pressure-sensitive tags, clips or pin-ons.

11. Set up a table for *guest registration* and name tags.

12. Maintain a *list of guests* invited, marked for those who confirmed their acceptance and for those who sent their regrets.

13. Have *place cards* or attendants to help guests to their seats.

14. Prepare a *program* of activities for the speaker and for guests, too, if possible.

15. Have *writing materials,* including cards, available in case the speaker wants to make last-minute notes.

16. Have *information kits* to give to guests.

17. Have an easy-to-read *clock* or stopwatch for timing.

▼ **Planning events successfully involves at least nine steps: (1) start early; (2) make a timetable; (3) form committees; (4) use professionals; (5) offer extra attractions to get people there; (6) have giveaways and souvenirs; (7) control the flow of traffic at the site; (8) publicize the event well in advance; (9) thank people who helped.**

---

6. Have giveaways and souvenirs (they need not be expensive) for everyone. There should be different souvenirs for different target audiences. Personalize all items and tie them to the event. (Advertising specialty companies have catalogs filled with suggestions.)

7. To ensure smooth flow of traffic, arrange for parking or, if the plant is some distance from the population center, provide bus transportation from points of departure. Train guides to conduct tours for visitors, and have knowledgeable employees positioned at strategic points to provide information and answer questions. Use signs and printed maps to direct visitors.

8. Publicize the event well in advance through all possible channels. Use all available controlled media to keep employees and other publics informed. Use the mass media for a broad appeal. If necessary, use advertising.

9. When the event is over, thank everyone who helped and participated. A successful dedication or open house requires the services of many—and hard work by quite a few—and their efforts should be gratefully acknowledged (see Example 12.8).

Handling Visual Presentations

Public relations practitioners frequently plan presentations that involve the use of visual materials—for example, a presentation to financial analysts, or one to employees explaining a new benefits package.

Visual Devices   You will be using various devices for visual presentations. Easel pads, overhead projectors and slides are described here.

Easel Pads   An easel holding a chart pad or other visual aid is the best tool for helping executives generate ideas and reach conclusions in the shortest time possible. It can stimulate group interest, help organize discussion, help explain or clarify and help summarize and review. Be sure to keep a supply of markers and masking tape on hand so you can tape torn-off pages onto a wall for a review. (Don't tape directly onto wallboard, though, or the paint will peel off.)

Overhead Projectors   Overhead projectors are simple to set up and use; but make certain you understand how to operate the projector. You may be using the projector in connection with a computer, in which case you can project directly from the computer screen to the overhead projector screen. Always be careful not to clutter your presentation with too much material. The information put on the overhead must be clear and easy for anyone in the room to read. It should be the type of material that would be difficult to capture in words only and should include graphs, charts and statistics.

Slides   Not everything can be made into a good slide. Poor color choice, intricate diagrams, cluttered charts and wrong-size type or lettering can leave your audience red-eyed and discouraged. Slides must have good color contrast, clear details that are kept to a minimum and type or letters of an appropriate size. You may want to provide handouts of the slide material for audiences to follow along with or take away.

A good four-step rule of thumb that almost always works can help you evaluate whether a given piece of material can be translated into a slide:

1. Measure the widest part of the material being considered for a slide.

2. Provide a reasonably wide border, and measure the border on both sides.

3. Add items 1 and 2 together.

4. Multiply the total by 6, giving you a total distance in inches (or feet, as the case may be) from your eyes or from the eyes of a person with 20/40 vision to the material. This is important.

If someone with 20/40 vision can read the material easily and see all the pertinent details, then the material could make a good slide. If the material can't be easily read, it must be modified until it does pass the test.

Artwork prepared for 3¼ × 4-inch slide projection should be prepared in a 3 (high) to 4 (wide) proportion, because the image should be masked down in photography and slide binding to 2¼ × 3 inches, which is a 3 to 4 proportion. Artwork for 35-mm double frame slides (2 × 2s) should be prepared in the proportion of 2 (high) to 3 (wide); and art for a 35-mm filmstrip should be prepared in a proportion of 3 (high) to 4 (wide). The use of these proportions is very important. If they are not used, effective space on the slide is lost.

Many slides can be computer-generated. Your own organization may have this capability. If not, you can buy the service. Such slides can be very simple, or they can be so elaborate that they give the impression of movement, resembling the animated art used in cartoons.

When you plan a slide show, you need to consider its eventual development into a videotape. This is especially important if you intend to present it often. A videotape presentation requires more slides and more consideration of visual "bridges" established by transition slides.

Dos and Don'ts of Visuals   Some general dos and don'ts for visuals deserve mention. The function of a visual is to illustrate a point, to clarify and to fix a fact or image in the minds of the audience. It should correlate with the spoken narrative, whether it is a recorded sound track or a live presentation. People retain more information when it is presented to them in a combination of sight and sound than they do when only one of these two senses is employed.

A good visual must have simplicity. It must be capable of being instantly absorbed by the mind.

▼ **Easel pads, overhead projectors and slides are three visual presentation methods that require technical familiarity.**

Variables that influence simplicity include color choice, design elements, typeface and lettering and how photos are used. Following are a few common pitfalls to avoid if you want to retain simplicity in visuals.

Backgrounds   Never use black type on a dark background. This is so elementary you might think that it is never done. Yet people who should know better, such as qualified commercial artists, make this mistake every day. The usual error involves black type on a blue background that never seems to photograph as light as they thought it would. Blue is never a good color for background use with black type. If the blue is light enough to contrast strongly with the type, it invariably washes out and results in a weak visual. Similarly, white letters should never be used against a pastel background.

Overloading   The use of a visual with too much detail is another common mistake. Don't use too many design elements or too many shapes—circles, triangles, rectangles, square blocks—in planning a visual. A design may be made so "arty" that the message is lost in a maze of shapes, curlicues and clashing colors. Better to be simple than sorry. For the same reason, don't use too many typefaces in a single visual, and don't overload a visual with too many words. It is better to break up a statement or thought into two or three slides, and let the audience take it in short bites. Similarly, bear in mind that script type is about 50 percent harder to read than simple, uncluttered Roman letters.

Color   At the other extreme, don't make the mistake of having too much white space in a visual either. Remember, white means clear film, 100 percent light transmission and an overpowering glare from a white screen. If you must show a white

Checklist for Facilities

Organization is essential to ensuring that significant details are not overlooked. One of the easiest ways is to make a checklist far enough in advance—so that you can add those "middle of the night" thoughts to it in plenty of time to plan for and implement them.

One Week Before	Day Before	Day of Event	Following Week
Complete media kits, including speeches, bios and photos, with event timing indicated for broadcast news.	Have kits available for news media on request.	Meet with news media representatives, distribute kits.	Followup letters to news media represented.
Advance release out.			
Find out what special facilities news media will need, and make arrangements for. Order all supplies and equipment for newsroom or media use area. Check lighting, sound levels, electric outlets and so on.	Set up media area. Check out all equipment and special facilities. Check all visual displays and logos.	Recheck news media area to be sure all supplies and equipment are ready for use.	
Draft final guest-acceptance list.			
Prepare guest information kits including program, brochures and the like.		Distribute guest information kits with badges.	
Prepare media, guest and host badges.	Set up physical facility and procedure for badge distribution.	Check badges and be sure badge issuance is recorded.	
Make arrangements definite. Be specific and agree on contingency plans. Plan cleaning of site and arrange for any special decorations. Remember logos, displays and so on.	Check eating area and order. Be sure time of service, place and cleanup are clear. Check site, grounds, all facilities.	Check food preparation, delivery, service.	

One Week Before	Day Before	Day of Event	Following Week
Complete speeches and get adequate number of copies for kits, requests and files.	Have kits available for news media who cannot cover.		
Assign hosts for VIPs.	Check with VIP host to confirm schedules.	Be sure all VIPs' needs are met.	
Arrange for any citations or presentation materials.	Check to be sure special presentation materials are on hand.	Be sure persons making presentation have materials.	
Detail any necessary safety precautions. Outline plan for emergency situation. Anticipate and be sure to communicate all emergency planning to all who might be involved.			Mail thank-yous.
Arrange for message board for media and guests. Have local airline schedules, taxi numbers, hotel and restaurant lists, with times and phone numbers available.			
Make final transportation and hotel arrangements for guests. If remote, plan transportation and hotel accommodations for news media also.			

form, photograph only the essential areas, and cover the rest with color-aid paper or a colored bourgess, with cutouts to allow the important areas to stand out on the screen. Your visual will be much more effective. Make sure that the slides maintain consistency of format, color and placement of material.

Conflicting Messages   Visuals should complement the audio portion of your presentation. They should not fight each other for supremacy. The word or words on the screen should be identical to the words to be spoken. Don't say one thing visually and something else orally. The mind simply cannot accept two conflicting statements simultaneously.

Putting a Show Together   The sequence of events in developing a slide show production is as follows: (1) set your objectives; (2) work out a budget; (3) prepare the conceptual plan (an artistic development of the idea); (4) write the script; (5) test concept and script on an audience; (6) shoot the visuals; (7) produce the visuals; (8) edit visuals and script; (9) complete for presentation (record script and synchronize, add music and so on). The show should capture the mood of the message as well as provide visual content.

Adding Sound   If you are a production expert, you can add sound effects and musical themes from suppliers such as audio archives (Films for the Humanities and Sciences, Box 2053, Princeton, NJ 08543-2053). They can provide anything from a convoy of diesel trucks to an orchestra tuning up. However, many large metropolitan areas also have professional sound studios and sound suppliers. Hire a professional if you aren't one. Example 12.9 provides estimated production timetables.

Handling Audio Presentations

A sound system can make or break a presentation. Here are four general rules to follow.

1. *Sound Reinforcement:* Never accept the word of a hotel that adequate sound reinforcement will be provided. Few hotels own acceptable professional equipment. The electronic rostrums, microphones and portable loudspeakers they provide vary widely in age, quality and condition. Frequently the parts are not physically or electronically compatible with one another.

Do not check the sound item off your list until a dry run—held in the meeting room—has established that every component in the system functions properly. Make certain that any assistant who must operate the equipment knows exactly how it works, knows the location of all switches and controls, knows the proper volume and tone-control settings and knows how to operate auxiliary equipment such as phonograph turntables, tape recorders or additional microphones. It is always exasperating to both audience and speaker to have to break the bond of communication between them in order to give mechanical instructions to an equipment operator.

Check out the loudspeaker systems. Adjust their volume level to a point slightly higher than you would normally set it—recognizing that the room, when filled with people, will be much more sound-absorptive than when it is empty.

2. *Rented or Company Equipment:* If you cannot rely on the hotel sound equipment, you can rent suitable gear from a nearby audio rental facility. Or you can bring it in and have your own firm set it up (subject to local union regulations and convention requirements). The last approach is probably the most reliable—and the most economical, too, if your annual investment in sales meetings exceeds $3,000.

3. *Simple Equipment:* When selecting the equipment you will use, remember the auto mechanic's maxim: you'll never have trouble with the accessories they *don't* include. A bewildering array of microphones, loudspeaker systems, amplifiers and

EXAMPLE 12.9 ■■■■■■■■■■■■■■■■■■■■■■■■■■■

Estimated Timetables*

Items Needed	Advance Time for You (working days)**	Advance Time for Media (weeks)	Media	Total Time (weeks)
35-mm film/videotape			Local or network TV	16–20
Approved storyboard	5–10			
Set bids, casting	10 (more for animation)			
Production planning	10			
Filming	7			
Sound track	3 in canned, otherwise 10–15			
Editing	10			
Master prints	3			
For film: 16-mm reductions and print	1–3	6		
For film: 4-color process plates	8–10 for color separations	6–8, if they make color separations; 4–6 if color separation provided	Magazines	8
Finished art	Negotiable	8–10 to print and get up; less if 24 sheets delivered; printer needs time, about 4–6 weeks	Outdoor ads	8–12
Finished art	Negotiable	8 if list bought, 4 if own list	Direct mail	12
Mats (plastic) and repro proofs	5 for shooting and processing	2	Newspapers	3–4
Slides and script or tape	10–40 depending on subject and length, whether advertising or publicity	6 6–8	Local TV, network or local radio	7 8–12
Slides/transparencies	2–3		Presentations, local TV	3–7

* Varies with proximity to suppliers.

**Add approval time and correction time—about 6 weeks.

accessory equipment are available for highly specialized uses and for startling effects. But keep your equipment basic and simple.

4. *Choosing Components:* The technical information you need to make a wise choice regarding components is not great, and most manufacturers furnish helpful literature that even a novice can readily understand.

It's a good idea, nevertheless, to choose components to suit your individual needs. Microphones, for instance, are available in a great many varieties and prices, but no other element is so vital to the sound system. However good the other components are, they cannot compensate for a poor microphone. Be sure it is suited to the use for which it is intended. Price is no index to suitability.

Numerous evils commonly associated with poor sound reinforcement are actually side effects of unsuccessful attempts to offset microphone deficiencies. Amplifier hum or background noise may be caused by a microphone with a low output, inadequately compensated for by turning up amplifier gain (volume). Ear-splitting treble emphasis often occurs because an amplifier's treble control was turned up to overcome a loss of articulation at the microphone. When amplifier gain is held so low that the audience must strain to hear, the microphone is often to blame. In this case, if the gain were turned up, ear-splitting feedback would result because of the microphone's inability to distinguish wanted from unwanted sound.

For a worst-case example, consider this true account of Murphy's Law. It comes from the experience of Chuck Werle, now of Werle & Brimm and Associates of Chicago, from a time when he was with the Leo Burnett Company. He and his colleague Richard Criswell were giving a presentation before the Florida Public Relations Association:

> My collaborator had told me by phone that he was bringing a reel of 16 commercials. Turns out he said *60*—not 16. That was the first thing. We asked for an overhead projector. It never showed up. I asked for a slide projector. It jammed. We asked for a video-cassette recorder. The first one came late, then didn't work. The second one did work . . . un-

til we stopped it to make a point and then it never started again. After all these horrendous problems, I went to pick up a rental car. It was in stall 1311 and it stalled two blocks from the airport. This all happened on Friday the 13th.[15]

Producing Institutional Videotapes and Films

Some annual reports are now published on videotape as well as in print. The videotapes are often used to introduce the firm to new audiences, such as security analysts who have not previously followed the firm, communities in which the firm has not previously operated, large groups of new employees hired for specific tasks or successful job candidates who have been hired for high-level positions. Companies and nonprofit institutions—including the U.S. government—make considerable use not only of videotape cassettes but also of 16-mm film. Beginning in the early 1970s, the trend was to make these films in 35 mm, and then reduce them to 16 mm. Technology has lowered the cost of this type of treatment, and the larger film gives higher quality and increases potential use, including possible distribution to movie houses. The life of a film is usually about seven years, with potential audiences in the millions. The technique of using clips from the film or taking clips from the outtakes for corporate advertising distributes the costs over a broader marketing range. Furthermore, the unit cost per public impression must be considered.

When considering whether to produce a film, the first decision to make is what your message is and for what audience it is intended. Then you must consider how much it will cost, and who is going to produce it—an in-house unit, an outside commercial studio or both? Most corporations have in-house film production units, but their size and capacity varies; and even large units occasionally farm out a large undertaking, at least in part. Although a number of commercial studios exist, only a few are known for award-winning films. Some commercial studios are just film producers; others are producers and distributors.

More than half the institutions with film titles in circulation use part in-house and part commercial studio for production. An in-house film unit generally handles such things as record shooting, in-plant filming and shepherding the script and budget approvals through the corporate structure. The commercial studio is used for filming that requires extensive staging, a remote location or special talent. Sometimes the film is shot entirely by the in-house unit but processed and edited externally.

Distribution must also be considered. Ordinarily, it is better to pay a distribution company to take care of the enormous amount of paperwork, the shipping and the film care. However, some companies large enough for in-house film units can handle distribution easily and at a lower cost. Bypassing the commercial distributor also means bypassing the contacts, and they may be important.

A film should have an objective—a specific, stated purpose. It cannot be expected to "tell the whole story." The more numerous the objectives, the weaker the film. The sponsor must determine why a film is needed and must have one made to accomplish that purpose. Another decision that needs to be made involves the impression or attitude the film should communicate.

Often this is suggested by the audience. Obvious audiences for business films include customers or prospective customers; industry groups or other business groups in related fields; management; stockholders and the professional investment public; employees; the community (through direct distribution to clubs, church groups, social agencies and professional associations); government on all levels (federal, state, local); educational institutions; television, either through purchased time or public service time; theaters; and international distribution through any of these channels.

Multiple uses of the film have a great deal to do with the planning. Is it going to be made with an eye toward the mass public? If so, you should consider a contract with a producer/distributor who can deliver the movie theaters for the 35-mm production, as well as offering the film in 16 mm for private audiences. Should it also be available in 8

▼ **Although producing institutional films and videotapes can be costly and time-consuming, they can be put to many uses.**

mm? What about distributing finished copies in videocassettes? All of these usage questions affect the design and length of the film.

Entirely different approaches are used for a publicity-slanted film and for a more personal corporate statement. To be acceptable for public use, the corporate message must be almost indiscernable, with the only blatant tie in the credit line: "sponsored by." Of course, if the film is mostly for corporate use, it can be much more inwardly focused.

But whether the film is produced commercially or internally, a great deal of research is involved. Often this falls to the sponsoring PR department, which works with a writer and a producer. The first step is to analyze the purpose of the film, along with how it will be used and with what audiences. Then you must get enough information so the writer can come up with a story outline or suggested script. The next step is a rough storyboard. At this point, it is important to consider getting approval clearances; testing the storyboard and script with the potential audience may also be desirable. You may wish to invest in a finished storyboard, since it is difficult for inexperienced people to visualize from a rough.

Once the script is approved and some consideration is given to the footage needed, the producer must determine what is available in stills, slides and footage. Even if none of it is ever used, this material might suggest ideas or approaches. If film on hand is used, clearances for using stock footage and the people appearing in it must be obtained.

Another question is whether to use *professional talent* in a film. If a producer is good at getting unstilted performances from nonprofessionals, then this solution is probably preferable to hiring talent. Casting takes time and adds to costs. However, casting is preferable to a distractingly and obviously amateur "performance."

Sound is a major consideration and often is the primary reason why corporations with film units go outside for the production of their footage. Technical knowledge is important, too, to make sure either that all music used is in the public domain or that permission has been granted. An expensive film can increase in price overnight if it has to be shelved to avoid a lawsuit or if a lawsuit is actually filed.

Editing is another expert's job. Costs vary according to the complexity of the film and the skill of the editor. After the initial editing effort, the producer usually holds a screening of the work print, which shows picture scenes arranged and spliced in approximate relationship. Some sequences may be missing, and it is a very rough product. PR people should be familiar enough with work prints to know what to expect, but it can be a rather unsettling experience for the untrained eye. Much reassurance may be necessary if top management sits in on this approval session. It is important, though, to get as much input as possible, because if changes are to be made, this is the time. Later changes probably will cost more money than they would be worth.

The sound usually involves narration, which requires a talent fee. Narration and the other sounds in films can be finalized only after approval of the work print. The next stage is the answer print, sometimes called the "first release print" because it combines picture, sound and optical into one print for the first time. Revisions now come with high price tags.

The master print of the film is never used and should be stored in climate-controlled conditions while the prints are distributed as prearranged.

Promotion of the film is an additional consideration. Usually it is handled by the distributor, but often the film's sponsor must also do the touting, and the sponsor may find—with some dismay—that this has not been anticipated in budgeting.

The biggest user of institutional films is the U.S. government. About 2,300 films are made each year by the various federal agencies and departments. Their purposes vary—training, public information

and promotion. Users of government films include schools, civic groups, theaters and television stations, as well as some individuals and other agencies. The costs of this taxpayer-supported movie making dwarfs those of any commercial film corporation. While a commercial movie studio in Hollywood may spend roughly $100 million or more per year on movie and TV productions, the government spends more than $500 million on movies, TV shows, filmstrips and similar productions.

Commercially made films are well received by schools and civic groups. About 30,000 requests come from such groups annually and 1,200 more come from commercial, public and cable TV stations. TV stations also use videotapes.

Videotapes are also expensive productions. A video news release can cost anywhere from $7,000 to well over $75,000. The variables are much the same as for film: length, shooting schedules, travel, editing, placement and so on. First, before you get into the area of video news releases (VNRs), you need to make sure you have a market. Talk to some news stations' personnel to see whether you have the right angle. Your topic should have either broad or local appeal. Then be sure you have both the professional help to accomplish it and the time to get it filmed, edited and distributed. The size of tape may be ½ inch or ¾ inch, and most large stations have equipment to dub to other sizes. You may decide to hire a media service that keeps a log of which stations use which size.

Cable systems tend to use more videotapes of nonnews from various sources. Some of the segments could almost be called "shows." These provide information, not entertainment, but the advertiser-made or -sponsored shows have high interest. A 30-minute show can cost as little as $30,000. In many cases the show is a setting for commercial messages; and by using particular products, it certainly suggests if it doesn't actually sell.

Instead of producing your own film, you may only want to see that your product is used prominently in someone else's. This is a highly competitive business. However, since you are paying, you can make demands. Mercedes-Benz, for instance, likes to see its cars used in films but never wants the villain at the wheel. When you see a product close enough to recognize it in a film, the company undoubtedly paid for it to be there. It is a subtle form of promotion/advertising.

The following checklist for critiquing films and videotapes was compiled by Howard Back, president of National Television News, Inc. (23480 Park Sorrento, Calabasas Park, CA 91302).

Before looking at the film, be sure you know its subject, purpose, and the nature of the audience it purports to reach. Only then can you judge whether it meets its goals, or is suitable.

As you look at the film, rate it on each of these ten points:

1. *Attention Span:* Is the film "gripping," or "interesting," or just plain able to hold the audience's attention throughout? This is critical: if the film is boring, *nothing else really matters!*

2. *Subject:* Does the film adequately cover the subject in a clear way, and fulfill its expressed purpose? Is the film too long? Or (seldom) not not long enough?

3. *Audience Suitability:* Does it clearly address the audience it's aimed at . . . or the group you plan to show it to?

4. *Visuals:* Are the pictures in focus? Properly exposed? Are the colors true? If there are graphics, do they help to clarify and explain, or are they just there for effects?

5. *Timeliness:* Are the visuals up to date? (Nothing turns off an audience faster than an old-fashioned haircut or clothing style, or any printed matter on screen that shows the age of the film.)

6. *Talent:* Are the participants or actors real, and natural? Do you believe them? Can you hear and clearly understand what they're saying?

7. *Sound:* Are the sound effects and/or music appropriate to the action? Is there proper balance among words, sound effects and music, so that the message gets across in the most effective way?

8. *Editing:* Does the story flow naturally? Is the editing pace good, so the story neither drags, nor moves too fast? Are you jolted by unusual angles, jumps in action, scenes that are too short or too long, or by bad sound?

9. *Script Content:* Someone once said (or wrote) that the best script for a film is one with the fewest possible words. A well-done informational film should rely heavily on visuals to tell the story. Words should fill in, adding information that cannot be seen. Most films have too many words. And words should be simple. Long words or cumbersome phrases are distracting.

10. *Believability:* Is the film "professional," in the sense that it moves along smoothly, in a logical fashion, and you're not distracted by the mechanics of the medium? In summary, did you find the film or tape honest and believable?[16]

Handling Celebrities

The presence of celebrities almost guarantees publicity, so luring them and making them glad they came is important. Arrangements for a celebrity's appearance may be made through an organization with which the celebrity is involved—for example, as the national chairperson of a charity. Or if the celebrity is a columnist or television star, contact may be made through his or her syndicate or network, using a local publication or network affiliate station as a starting point. Ultimately, though, you will probably deal with the celebrity's agent. It is important to remember that this person is a *business* agent.

Once you have the celebrity scheduled, you should request updated biographical information from his or her agent or public relations person and 8 × 10 glossies of at least two different poses. The biographical data will give you a start in preparing the advance publicity. It is helpful if you can also get a telephone interview to fill in details, since vita sheets are sometimes outdated or incomplete. Further, personal information and a personal contact offer insight into the celebrity's likes and

---

dislikes and give some indication of what type of promotion would be best. It is important to determine what that person likes to do and does best because this is where he or she will perform best for you.

In planning the celebrity's schedule, you will probably work with the agent or with a person charged with scheduling. Make sure your communications with this person are clear, concise and definite. Your dependence is mutual, so you should try hard to establish rapport. Get off to a good start in your first contact by providing the following information: (1) travel arrangements, including who will be meeting the celebrity (and whether an airport arrival interview is planned); (2) where the celebrity will be staying; (3) what provision has been made for transportation; (4) what financial arrangements have been made (get this ironed out early!); (5) what the schedule of appearances is; (6) what other group appearances have been scheduled and what special events the celebrity will participate in. Make multiple copies of the schedule so your staff and the celebrity's have contact information. Include phone numbers at various locations.

Give the celebrity as much background as possible, not only on relevant groups and people, but also on the city. Personalize by tying the information into the celebrity's own background, career or special interests. It will help prepare the celebrity for the questions that he or she will have to field and also make him or her feel comfortable and welcome rather than exploited.

Be sure all newsmaking events on the schedule are covered by your own staff reporter and photographer. In fact, don't go anywhere without your photographers. Some of the best picture possibilities can be missed if you depend on news media photographers working only on assignment. Moreover, the celebrity may want pictures, and these are easier to get from your staff than from the media. Someone in the office should keep a log of television appearances and clippings to present to the celebrity or to the accompanying PR person or agent.

Media information kits should be prepared and distributed in advance of the celebrity's appearance, but keep extra ones with you at all times. If reporters assigned to the story have not seen the kit, they may ask you numerous questions that are answered in the kit.

Arrangements should not only reflect the celebrity's star status, but also be personalized. One television actor found that the PR director at an affiliate station had keyed everything, even the fruit in his room, to the TV series in which he portrayed a teacher (the fruit was, of course, apples). For another celebrity, who was an art lover, pictures in the hotel suite were replaced with valuable paintings on loan from the local art museum.

The red-carpet treatment begins at the airport, where most major airlines maintain luxurious VIP rooms for interviews. It may be the best place to have an initial press conference and have the celebrity greeted by a city official. Make arrangements through the airline's local public relations department. Most airlines will also expedite baggage handling. The hotel's PR department is also eager to cooperate in seeing that the star's room is specially prepared with flowers or fruit. You should check the celebrity in before arrival and have the room key in hand, to make this a smoother operation.

For transportation, a chauffeured limousine is almost a must for important celebrities; if this is impossible, try to get a new car on loan, say a demonstration model from a promotion-conscious dealer. Get a driver who understands time schedules and knows the city. Be sure the celebrity knows how to contact the limousine service or driver in case of an emergency or a change in plans. One solution is to put up the driver in the same hotel as the celebrity so that immediate access is possible.

Assign someone who is understanding and sympathetic to be with the star throughout the schedulc. This person should be able to handle special requests like hairdressers at 6 A.M. or filet mignon at midnight. Be sure it is someone with patience, tact and diplomacy who also understands the significance of keeping on schedule. After an appearance is over, this person can probably suggest the best way to say thank you.

Take care of all departure details such as checkout, bills, airline flight confirmation, baggage check-in. Attention to the celebrity cannot be relaxed just because the itinerary is closed. The farewell remarks of a celebrity are usually recorded and remembered, too. One thought to keep in mind is that celebrities talk to other celebrities. A public relations director who was having difficulty getting a particular celebrity happened to mention it to another celebrity who had once been the organization's guest for the same event. To the PR person's surprise, the celebrity said, "Well, I'll just call and tell her she needs to be here. It's a good promotion vehicle, and you people know how to do things right."

Some celebrities you may be responsible for handling are relatively new at public relations appearances. For example, the book publishing business is so highly competitive that authors are frequently sent "on the road" to garner sales for their books. Some of these new celebrities may be more difficult to handle than more seasoned people because, while they are less likely to have high expectations of recognition, they are more likely to expect some "privacy" or time for themselves.

Some celebrities are extraordinarily generous with the demands of self-promotion. The *Wall Street Journal* tells of author Ken Follett's willingness to be the prize in a contest advertised in bookstores promoting his novel, *Pillars of the Earth*. Follett's novel is about the building of a medieval cathedral, and the contest prize was a free trip to England with the author and a guided tour by him of Westminster Abbey. Not only was Follett willing to be a tour guide, he also agreed to write for *Good Housekeeping* a romantic short story called "The Abiding Heart," set in the same cathedral he described in his novel. In exchange, Fol-

lett's publisher, a division of Penguin USA, got two full pages in the magazine to advertise the trip and tour contest.[17]

While some authors like Follett may be accommodating and may see promotions as opportunities, many others may resent the time spent doing such mundane things as going to television stations to give interviews, making guest appearances in bookstores or speaking to various clubs and organizations. You must build some personal time into their schedule, and you must handle them in such a way that you preserve their dispositions for the public appearances.

Preservation of talent may be necessary if the celebrity is a performer. Some performers are asked to make a number of appearances and play, sing or do whatever they do either too close to their performance schedule or in conditions that might jeopardize their being able to perform—soloists singing outside in cold night air, for example. You may be responsible for the schedules of some celebrities who are traveling without their own staffs, and you need to think of their needs in planning their appearances.

▼ PUBLICITY THROUGH THE MASS MEDIA

Good working relationships with media personnel are always important for smooth functioning, but they are particularly crucial when they can facilitate, impede or even destroy a public relations program. The secret of success in placing publicity is in developing a good working relationship by *knowing and anticipating the needs of the media*. Your PR efforts in handling publicity are usually a two-part operation: providing the information you want to convey to that medium's public; and responding to inquiries. Your contacts are valuable as a source for placing stories or story ideas and as a resource for keeping you advised of media changes in personnel or procedures.

Fortunately, some things never change, and among them are the standards by which publicity

▼ **A successful publicist must know the production schedules of the news media and provide the appropriately prepared message for each audience.**

---

is measured. Publicity is ranked by editors and TV news directors for news value. It should meet three criteria:

1. Is it important to this medium's readers? It must be of local significance to be considered.

2. Is it timely? It must be news, not something the beat reporter had three days ago.

3. Is it accurate, truthful and complete?

One PR person, who had heard a newspaper's assistant city editor chew out an unfortunate publicist for offering copy with "more holes than a sieve," was asked by the editor if the reaction had been too harsh. "Not at all," he replied. "Sloppy copy just makes it harder for the rest of us."

Strict news value is one yardstick of value. Another is human interest, a story or picture with humor, drama or poignancy. Humorous stories, especially, have an edge because so much of what editors must print is serious. A publicity piece that is genuinely funny or appealing is usually given good display.

In handling publicity you are concerned with offering news releases to mass and specialized media, both print and broadcast. Your primary task is to interest the media in story and picture ideas they might cover. In doing this job, you must prepare materials that tell about the institution, such as newsletters, brochures and pamphlets, television and radio spots, slide presentations and perhaps films. When necessary, you must arrange for the media to talk directly to management in interviews and conferences. Therefore, you must master the styles of all media and develop working relationships with professionals in all of these fields.

A PR person must know, for example, the exact copy deadlines for all local media and the approxi-

mate deadlines for state and national media. If you are involved in international PR, you must be prepared to work late (in some cases very late) to reach your contacts abroad during their working day, because of time differences.

Knowing the media's working schedules will save you a great deal of grief. No experienced PR person would call a city editor at 11:30 A.M. and offer lunch, if the editor is working on an evening paper. Why? Because the editor probably began work at six that morning, has already had lunch and is presently fighting a deadline to get the paper out. (Actually, buying the editor lunch or dinner is not the key. If you do take someone to lunch, it should be because you want to, not because you expect a favor or free professional service.) And it might be wise to call a sports, business or other section editor to check on the possibility of new deadlines. Such attention to details separates the professional from the inept amateur.

Knowing whom to contact at the various media with your news is also essential. You need to make sure your releases get to the reporter or editor who covers your organization. Since media people change jobs and assignments frequently, your current media contact may not be the same person you dealt with last week.

Technology and Public Relations

A PR person must keep current in the area of new technology for mass communications. Recent developments of particular significance to public relations include (1) the use of computers for storing, sending, receiving and printing information and art; (2) the growth of satellite transmission and cable video; (3) the growth of specialized PR services, including broadcast monitoring services to catch publicity (a parallel to the print media clipping services) and computerized graphics design services.

Typesetting and Printing Processes   Public relations practitioners began to feel the impact of new technology in the newsrooms early in 1973, and it has increased continuously since then. All news releases that came in used to be "processed" with all other newspaper copy, including stories generated by the staff. Often a good publicity release would be checked over by a reporter and then go to the copy desk for editing. It thus had a reasonably good chance to survive and get into the paper.

Now, however, with newspapers converted to photo-offset printing and using visual display terminals (VDTs) to put stories directly into their computers, publicity releases *must* be retyped (unless they are electronically transmitted). The chances of typewritten PR releases being used have decreased considerably, and the chances of releases being used "as is" are almost nonexistent. For releases to escape being discarded, both staff and agency public relations practitioners must originate electronically acceptable copy.

PR Wire and Video Services   Specialized wire and video services carry public relations news directly into the world's broadcast and newspaper newsrooms (see Example 12.10). This capability is especially important for newspaper technology, since the PR newswires provide copy that can be processed by a medium's wire capture program and stored on a hard disk. It can then be called up on a terminal for editing and subsequent direct transmission to the typesetting equipment. First begun in 1954, the publicity wire concept began to catch on as a result of the technological advances of the media. Its use was further stimulated by the simultaneous disclosure decision in the Texas Gulf Sulphur case (see Chapter 9).

The increasing importance of television has heightened the need for video releases. Satellite transmission has made the world's broadcast stations readily accessible to such releases. Many public relations media services provide a complete publicity package of video news releases and satellite transmission.

The privately owned publicity services offer simultaneous transmission of news releases and provide a rather efficient national network. Although they charge for their services, they are run much

▼ **Recent developments in mass communications technology include the use of computers for information storage and retrieval, the growth of satellite transmission and cable video, and the growth of specialized PR services.**

---

like news bureaus, and their editors may reject copy as they try to exercise some judgment about what to send. Most operate only during business hours, Monday through Friday, although special arrangements can be made for evening or weekend transmission. An exception is PR Newswire, which is staffed seven days a week, 24 hours a day.

These PR suppliers provide journalists (via computer) with news releases, facts sheets, graphics and other information that PR people pay to have sent. Such services charge clients an annual fee and then charge for each release. The price depends on the distribution ordered. A surcharge is usually added for larger-than-average releases (more than 400 words), and video rates are more expensive. In addition to publicity, clients may send advisories and invitations, such as notifications of news conferences.

One particular advantage of public relations wire services to practitioners is the resulting national and international coverage now available for clients of a practitioner working from a single base. Before these services appeared, many practitioners tried to make arrangements with agencies in other cities to help handle out-of-town releases. It was a Rube Goldberg operation at best, and it depended greatly on the PR contacts the practitioner had in other cities. Now it is strictly a business arrangement, easily structured and with more predictable results.

Another advantage to the practitioner is editorial acceptance of the PR sources. Because copy is carefully checked before it is moved (even though the practitioners supplying the material are "clients"), news media are assured of a double check on details, timeliness, and other elements that often

EXAMPLE 12.10

New Technology and PR News

TRY THIS APPROACH FOR BREAKING NEWS

Daniel Johnson

Pratt & Whitney had a very big story to tell. It expected to win a contract from Delta Airlines for production of the most fuel-efficient jet aircraft engine ever developed. If the deal came through (and it was by no means certain until the day it was announced) Pratt & Whitney would ring up the largest commercial engine sale in aviation history—$600 million.

This story was a natural for audiences all over the country affected by such news—air travelers, of course, but much more particularly the communities, subcontractors, and competitors involved with Delta, Pratt & Whitney and Boeing (which was building for Delta the fleet of 757s that would receive the engines). We were dealing with a technological breakthrough designed to save significant amounts of energy and enhance U.S. leadership in the aviation industries.

Our suggested approach for breaking the story was the first satellite video release. Pratt & Whitney agreed and we began phase I: determining what would be needed.

Our shopping list:

▼ A fully equipped TV news crew to cover the news conference, which probably would be held at Delta

headquarters in Atlanta but could be held in Hartford, Pratt & Whitney's home base;

▼ A satellite and time reserved for the transmission;

▼ A prepared-in-advance videotape showing and explaining the new engine and the new Boeing aircraft it would power;

▼ Arrangements to quickly edit the videotaped news conference to present the highlights in a five-minute segment;

▼ Arrangements for a local station, in Atlanta or Hartford, to handle the first stage of the transmission to the satellite;

▼ Advance notice to TV news directors at stations in some 35 major markets detailing what they could expect and exactly when they would be able to receive the feed from the satellite. (We decided on three feeds, spaced 15 minutes apart, to give the stations some flexibility in receiving the feed and to give our people a maximum amount of time to alert the news directors.)

Everything Fell into Place

Assembling the crew was no problem. DWJ has crews going on "shoots" all over the country and abroad for a variety of clients. We do our own editing and other production and supply the results.

---

make PR copy unacceptable. To preserve their own reputations, the PR news bureaus won't move inferior or inaccurate copy. Business Wire even reminds clients: "Write to wire style and member newspaper computerization [constraints]. Following AP/UPI style and keeping computer specifications in mind are marks of communications professionalism that improve your release's chances. Again we'll be glad to help whenever you need us." The company has built a reputation for reliability with the media it services.

Yet another advantage of public relations wire services is that they are already in the newsroom. Many metropolitan dailies have a PR news wire ticking away right beside the Associated Press, United Press International and Reuters wires. Copy is pulled from that source and considered for use on its merits. Broadcast releases are often a direct feed, after an advisory is wired. Often mailed releases (print and videocassettes) that reach reporters are never even opened. In addition, mail service may be delayed by lack of weekend deliv-

Similarly, production of the videotape B Roll, showing the Pratt & Whitney engine and the new Boeing 757, edited to 90 seconds, was done in our own studios. We also edited the news conference tape.

Hartford was picked for the news conference and we got WFSB-TV to handle the transmission to the satellite ground station in northern New Jersey, where it was combined with the pretaped B Roll.

We selected Western Union's Westar III satellite as the facility best suited to our needs, and reserved time early in the week of December 15 for what we expected would be transmission from Atlanta on December 18 at 4 P.M. Before the eventual transmission from Hartford shortly after 5 P.M. on the 18th, the reservation had to be changed twice, once to Friday when it appeared the conference would be delayed.

We were able to complete editing within an hour of the close of the news conference and get the transmission from WFSB-TV to Western Union and via Westar III to TV stations around the country by 5:30 P.M., one hour after editing began.

Our reports show we reached an adult audience of 9 million (Nielsen figures) on the 21 stations carrying the Delta-P&W story in such cities as New York, Washington, Los Angeles, Seattle, Miami, Atlanta and Chicago. This compares quite favorably with the estimated total viewers of ABC's "World News Tonight" each evening.

We define the satellite video release as breaking news recorded on videotape and released via satellite and local satellite-receive dishes to local TV news operations in widely separated markets.

The key phrase is "breaking news." Prebreak announcements or news reported well after the fact are not candidates for this approach.

The satellite video release solves the problem of getting your story covered—and, usually, with sufficient time devoted to your news event. The story is covered because your crew covers it. It arrives in the local TV newsroom in a form and length you select. Of course, local stations may cut your story, but certainly not down to network length.

The concept is less than a year old, but it has enormous potential for solving difficult communication problems.

SOURCE: Daniel Johnson, "Try This Approach for Breaking News," *Public Relations Journal* 37(9), pp. 28–29 (September 1981). Copyright September 1981. Reprinted by permission of *Public Relations Journal,* published by the Public Relations Society of America, New York, NY. Mr. Johnson is a managing partner of DWJ Associates, Inc., New York, and former executive producer of the WNEW-TV (New York) "10 O'Clock News."

ery or by holiday closing. For all of these reasons, a newswire service is a good investment when broad coverage is desired, timing is significant and the budget allows.

All of these wire services have flooded the news media with information. What is the likelihood that an item of local interest will get lost in the flood? It can happen, but here again current technology helps. Most newspapers have WireWatch, a software program that scans all AP wire copy for local names so that relevant stories aren't missed.

Computer technology helps outside the newsroom as well. Reporters use terminals to cover news outside the office. At a special event, they can use a computer billboard service to keep up with what's going on from their hotel room. They can even download a news conference release and work their stories from that information, if they wish. They can then send the stories directly to the newspaper's computer. PR practitioner Steve Lee, who has spent a good bit of time in London servicing a major client, says that he experienced increasing acceptance of computer releases that can be sent to media at the cost of a long distance telephone call. Direct radio and television feeds, of course, are not viewed as unusual by the broadcast media. Most take a direct feed, after an advisory is sent.

A side benefit of PR wire services is that most also supply basic news data banks for storing releases and published stories. These data banks give a news story a longer shelf life. Probably the most important databases for news stories are CompuServe, Nexis, X-Press Information Systems, Dialog, Vu/Text, Dialcom, News Net, Dow Jones News Retrieval Service and the Informaster Electronic Library of 630 databases.

Most of these services, as well as specialized clipping and monitoring services like Burrelle's, Luce and Video Monitoring Services of America, provide an accounting of media use. Some users complain that the services (particularly some of the video services) are not exhaustive, but inflated figures are probably more of a concern than underreporting. Many organizations supplement their data services by hiring at-home workers to monitor video releases for them. Following up on print releases yourself is more difficult, because you won't have the list of print media that the service uses. Distribution and clipping services do maintain up-to-date media lists, because that's the heart of their business, but you will be given a copy of only a general distribution list.

You'll probably develop your own limited media lists from using *SRDS, Writer's Market, Editor and Publisher* and the like. Lists of media abroad are now more readily available, with the new European Community (EC) market coming into being and with the new focus on Pacific Rim nations.

You'll also keep lists of where you placed your advertising, of course, and the monitoring services will trace your advertising as well as your releases if you want to purchase that additional service. The services will also perform an analysis of both. Television services that handle production for your public service announcements sometimes monitor the use of your PSAs, too. But even the best services won't catch everything. They may misreport or misinterpret events. Use information from these services as a monitoring device; use your own research to measure results.

Now software packages like Right Brain's News Track and Cambridge Communications' Media Map offer solutions to building and maintaining media lists and measuring results.

Media Electronic Systems   When a PR person gets a story of regional or national interest in a local paper, there is a good chance that the story will receive regular newswire service attention. The Associated Press wire service uses an "electronic carbon"—a computer-to-computer hookup that allows newspapers to send copies of their local stories instantly into local AP bureau computers. The increased flow of stories from member papers to the bureaus increases the use by other papers of PR-generated stories of regional or national significance.

Another AP computer advance offers greater control over laser photos, so that photoeditors can crop, enlarge, reduce, brighten, darken or otherwise improve the quality of overseas photos sent. By 1986 the technology had developed to the point where it was possible to send an image and get a color photograph of it without a negative.

Newspapers' electronic information delivery systems (EISs) are copy cannibals—devouring vast amounts of incoming material and immediately relaying facts, breaking news, sports scores, recent stock reports and such. EISs have enlarged the news hole. Cable is another cannibal, using programming 24 hours a day. Much of cable's programming gives PR practitioners special opportunities to reach some TV audiences without commercial costs. For example, sponsored films can be used on cable, health information from the American Heart Association or the Cancer Society can be shown and museums can preview new exhibitions.

In-House Electronic Systems PR agencies and departments are finding that computers make preparing graphics much easier. Computer graphics programs permit instant call-up of common illustrations such as bar charts and pie charts. A computer system coordinated by General Electric has programs stored in it for each type of chart or graph.[18] The artist works on a visual display terminal (VDT) with a lighted display board. The programs contain different designs and type sizes so that, to create a pie chart, for example, the artist simply types the percentages of the various pie slices to be drawn and the computer does the work. The pie can even be tilted for a three-dimensional effect. The system also allows slides to be produced for meetings and publications. The rule for using charts, especially if you are sending them with news releases, is to keep them simple (uncluttered) and clear (no artsy gimmicks that confuse or distort meaning).[19]

Computer graphics for three-dimensional color designs can be made either with an electronic pen or directly by a computer. Laser graphics require more technical skills but also provide movement and three-dimensional effects. Laser artwork can be entered into a computer graphics console and synchronized for incorporation into slide and film presentations. These graphics can represent the special effects of movement to a multi-image slide show.

Computer graphics also enhance the software that automobile manufacturers and some car dealers now distribute instead of brochures. In 1987, to attract consumer attention, Buick sent out 20,000 floppies to Apple personal computer owners, giving them answers to questions about the Buick line of General Motors cars. A brochure might not even get a glance.

Finally, PR in-house use of technology includes access to a variety of data banks, word processing to store and manipulate large amounts of data, computer generation of art, desktop publishing (from concept to camera-ready, with art and copy combined), and communication by teleconferences and electronic mail systems.

▼ **A PR person has to have the news sense, the judgment and the appropriate professional skills of news media people.**

Preparing to Work with the Media

Because you must constantly sell ideas in stories or pictures to the media, you have to do advance work in gathering ideas and information.

Preparing the Story You should have some basic training as a reporter; this is because, in order to write about news, you have to be able to recognize it when you see or hear it. In a large institution, where people may be too busy to be bothered with giving you "news tips," you must be able to search out the news yourself. One way to encourage news cooperation in a large organization is to tell people exactly what you need and how and when to get it to you. Of course, once you have the information, you are often expected to make banner headlines with it.

Sometimes a PR person's news sense becomes dulled by spending too much time reading company materials and too little time perusing outside news and newscasts—not to mention talking too much to company people instead of to newspeople. When this happens, he or she is likely to produce a three-page story in response to the boss's suggestion for a "great news story," when in fact the story deserves only three paragraphs. Although you should listen to the suggestion carefully (never discourage any news source), you should assess the story from a news editor's perspective, not from a company perspective. Is it really worth three pages or is it simply a column item or does it deserve no exposure at all? Maybe the idea is good but the medium is wrong. Maybe the idea is good for the company publication but lacks appeal outside the institution. A publicity person must keep his or her sense of news value finely honed.

In gathering information for a release, a publicity writer must act the way a reporter would with the same access. Start with secondary sources, finding out if the company files contain anything written about the subject—any research or sales reports, any memos. Then seek out the primary sources, interviewing people to learn everything they know and are willing to share.

A good publicist keeps a basic file of the following:

▼ Statistical information

▼ Governmental information—regulatory and other

▼ Basic reference books for the field of interest and for related fields

▼ All legislation on problems—pending or proposed

▼ Trade association data

▼ Trade union literature—each union, how it operates

▼ Record of the organization—a file copy of *all* your own publications

▼ File of ads run

▼ File of speeches of officials

▼ Clippings of all information about the company, with publication name and date for each

▼ List of individuals and organizations interested in the company, including civic groups appealing for contributions

▼ Biographies of top executives

▼ Pictures of stores, plants, products, other activities

▼ Lists of editors and publications

▼ People in all media; contact as potential sources of releases or information

▼ File on major competition and antagonists and their efforts

▼ Timetables of occasions for publicity; indicate news releases

Like a reporter, you should never begin work with some predetermined idea about the length of the story. Find out everything you can, since you must have complete information before you can properly condense it—and otherwise news people won't later be able to get answers from you regarding questions you never anticipated (which they will ask). In doing your research, you may find that you have accumulated information for not one but several stories. You may find that, with a different emphasis, the story could be used by the newspaper, the local chamber of commerce magazine, an industry publication and your company's own house periodical. If your story focuses on a person, there may be even more opportunities for publication, because (again with a different emphasis) the story may be used in professional, religious or other publications of organizations in which that person is active. Research represents your principal investment in time. Make it pay off for you.

You should be familiar enough with the medium to which you are submitting copy to be absolutely certain the writing style you used precisely matches the style of the medium (see Example 12.11). For instance, it is important to know whether a newspaper has an "up" or "down" style—that is, whether it uses capital letters frequently (up) or seldom (down). Find out and accommodate. Beware especially of writing the way people from whom you got your information talk, because they often use unintelligible jargon (business, professional, educational, governmental or whatever). Don't write what someone says, write what the person means. Of course, this is impossible if you don't understand it yourself, so never be afraid to say to a source, "I'm sorry, that is out of my area. You'll have to explain. I don't understand."

EXAMPLE 12.11

News Releases

Here are two examples of a story prepared for broadcast (left) and newspaper (right) news. Daily newspapers in the area *each* got different stories.

EMERGENCY: DIAL 911
1800 Main St., Suite 330
City Center, XX 12345
Leslie Brown, (123) 456-7891
7/15/89

FOR IMMEDIATE RELEASE

Calling for emergency police, fire or ambulance service in Center City gets a lot easier after August the first. Just dial nine-one-one.

You can even dial nine-one-one from pay phones without using a coin. All telephones in City Center and in the county are equipped for the nine-one-one emergency response.

Your emergency calls will be answered by nine-one-one dispatchers. The dispatchers' electronic screens will tell them where you are calling from. You tell them what the emergency is and where it is. They will relay the message to the police, fire or ambulance services. Residents and businesses with telephones voted to pay for the service a year ago.

EMERGENCY: DIAL 911
1800 Main Street, Suite 330
City Center, XX
Leslie Brown, (123) 456-7891
7/15/89

FOR IMMEDIATE RELEASE

When there's an emergency in Center County after August 1, the telephone number 9-1-1 will bring police, fire or ambulance services.

The number can be dialed from pay telephones without a coin.

Dispatchers will answer 9-1-1 calls and alert the required service. When the call comes in, the dispatcher's electronic screen will give the address of the caller's telephone. The caller is asked to describe the emergency and to give the exact location of the emergency.

Dispatchers will relay the information to the required services with a direct connection. The 9-1-1 service in other parts of the state has reduced emergency responses by as much as ten minutes, says 9-1-1 area coordinator Jayne Johnson.

Johnson says that Center County's response rate may be even better since the electorate chose the enhanced message system that allows dispatchers to tell where a call is originating.

Dispatchers will stay on the line until they get the needed information from the caller and, in some cases, may remain on the line to convey emergency information to the caller.

The enhanced system also makes it possible for the dispatchers to track false emergency calls. The County Commissioners have voted to charge $250 to callers who make a false emergency call. If the call comes from a pay phone, police will be sent to the location.

For calls to police, fire and ambulance that are not emergencies, callers should continue to use the seven-digit numbers listed in the blue pages of the telephone directory, Johnson said.

-30-

They probably don't know anything about communications either, so you're even. Most PR people emphasize the need to be creative and conceptual—to be able to see the "big picture." Although they agree with that idea, experienced PR people will tell you it is the details that matter.

News Releases Public relations people are news managers, whether they are dealing with news releases that they initiate and then distribute, mail or put on PR wires or whether they are issuing responses to media inquiries. Sometimes these inquiries result from leaks of information that the PR person was trying to "manage." At special events, PR-sponsored newsrooms facilitate both news releases and response releases because a PR newsroom manager is on duty who either has the information or knows where to get it promptly. The

EXAMPLE 12.12

News Story Deadlines for Various Media

Media	Type of News Story	Deadline*
Newspapers		
A.M. daily, local	General news	4 P.M. day before publication
	Breaking news	8 P.M. day before publication
	Breaking major stories	11 P.M. absolute last
	Features	Several weeks before anticipated publication
P.M. daily, local	General news	8 A.M.–4 P.M. day before publication
	Breaking story	7–9 A.M. day of publication
	New material or important development	10:30–11 A.M. day of publication
	Critically important, but late-breaking news	12:30–1 P.M. (will make only last edition, and then only maybe)
	Features	Several weeks before anticipated publication
Sunday local	General news	First section and front pages close Saturday, usually by noon or early afternoon
	Section news and features	Usually noon Wednesday deadline for preprinting on Thursday or Friday
Weekly	All material	Four days prior to publication's own deadline, generally day before issue.
News Wire Services	All material	Any time, but more amenable 9–4 weekdays; short-staffed weekends
PR Wire Services	All material	Some services available on week after business hours by arrangement

*Deadlines are general guidelines. Specific media may differ.

news manager also knows the needs and schedules of the news media.

Whatever the circumstances, you have to be sensitive to media schedules. Your news schedules have to be worked out to fit the media served in each case (see Example 12.12). *Deadline* means just that. It is the *last* minute for handling new information, not the *preferable* time for doing so. When you are initiating a piece of news, you should let editors know your plans in advance, if possible, so that they can put your story on their schedules.

Each story for newspaper and broadcast news should be prepared in a style and form appropriate to the particular medium. You must use the inverted pyramid or modified inverted pyramid format for news releases and accepted formats for features. In all cases, you must write the story as if you were a reporter. The broadcast version in Example 12.11 went to radio and television stations, with the longer newspaper version attached, so that the story could be rewritten during the broadcast day. The TV version was accompanied by color

Media	Type of News Story	Deadline
Television		
Network	Straight news	Call in to desk or feed to affiliate if locally available 4–6 hours prior to airtime
	Breaking story	1 hour prior to airtime
	News on videotape	Send day in advance
Local	Straight news	2 hours prior to airtime
	Breaking news	1 hour prior to airtime
	News on videotape	4 hours prior to airtime
Radio		
Network	General news	Send release one day in advance
	Breaking story	Call newsroom
	General news	Give release one day before
Local	Breaking news	Need 45 minutes before newscast
Magazines		
Weekly	News	No later than Saturday noon for following Tuesday
	Features	Several weeks before expected use
Monthly	All material	On 10th of month preceding month of publication
	Photos (especially color)	First of month preceding month of publication

slides. The newspaper story was accompanied by color slides and black-and-white glossy photographs, with captions attached. (Formats for news releases and news tips appear in the *Instructor's Guide.*)

Planning Publicity Photos and Illustrations

A publicity story generally has a better chance of being accepted by a news medium if you can offer an illustration to go with it. Many newspapers prefer to shoot their own photos, and the wire services almost always do. In such cases, you must work in advance of the day the newspaper intends to use the story to preserve its timeliness and still allow the editor to schedule a photographer at a time when you can set up the picture. You should have all the elements of the photo assembled—people, things or both—before the photographer arrives. But how the photographer arranges or uses the subjects is his or her business. Don't interfere.

If you have hired a photographer to take the picture for you, you may have to offer substantial

▼ Keeping a complete, updated file is essential in working with news media, as is anticipating news media needs and treatments.

guidance, depending on the photographer's background. If the photographer has news experience, you can probably trust the person's news judgment. But if he or she is a commercial photographer with no idea of newspaper requirements, you must make sure (1) to keep the number of subjects down to four or less; (2) to get high contrast and sharp detail; (3) to avoid clichés (people shaking hands or receiving a plaque); (4) to position your subjects close together; and (5) to keep the backgrounds neutral.

Make the most of the photographer you have hired and get the photos you need—not only for one particular story but for other possible versions of the story for different media. Once you have good photographs, you can use them in a number of ways.

In ordering photographic prints, be sure to get some for your own files. Keep your photographic files up to date, so you aren't caught offering an old photo to a news source. The news media often pull photos out of their own libraries to use, but they expect to get something new from someone seeking publicity—even if they initiate the request. Anticipate this with adequate photo files. In addition, do not give competing media the same picture, even if it is only a person's photograph.

Try to arrange with a photographer for your organization to buy the negatives or disks (floppy or compact). This is particularly important for high-cost assignments that involve color or aerial photography. Get a written contract. Otherwise, because of copyright law, the pictures belong to the photographer, and you have only bought specific rights. If the photographer will not sell the negatives or sign releases on "work for hire," you must anticipate all future uses of the photos you order for the file (publicity, ads, promotional materials) and identify those uses in the contract. If you own

the negatives, you may for convenience ask the photographer to store them for you at his or her studio so that additional prints can be made later.

The same is true for other artwork and film. If you plan to invest in elaborate schematics, maps, charts or graphs, make sure they become yours. Similarly, when you hire someone to shoot film or videotape to use in releases to television (although most TV stations and all networks prefer to shoot their own footage), it is all right to let the company that processes and duplicates the film or videotape keep the master, because they have the temperature-controlled environment to preserve it; but be sure you own that master. Although all you may have planned at the moment is a short segment for a news clip or news feature, you might need that footage later for a corporate film. Make sure everyone knows and understands who the owner is and how much reprints cost.

News photographers do not have time to develop and print film other than their own or to make extra prints for you; neither do the wire services. Both newspapers and wire services have photo sales departments to take care of reprint requests. Television stations have commercial operations that develop film. Be prepared to pay for whatever you ask for. If you ask for videotape to be prepared at a station or for illustrations to be handled by a newspaper's art department—whether it involves photo retouching or designing the cover for a special section—get your checkbook out. The news media are businesses. They cannot make money on gratuities.

When you hire a photographer or when one is assigned by a publication to cover some event, try to think of an original pose to replace unimaginative stock poses. Make sure all the people and the props the photographer will need are ready well before the time for the shot. Action shots are best because they help tell a story, but a character study of a person whose face shows deep emotion is also desirable.

You should have at least two specific shots (including camera angles) in mind before going to the event. Discuss these with the photographer before-

WE'RE HAVING OUR ANNUAL KIWANIS CLUB PANCAKE BREAKFAST, AND WE'D LIKE TO GET SOMETHING ON IT IN THE PAPER...

WHAT WOULD IT TAKE FOR YOU GUYS TO SEND A PHOTOGRAPHER OVER TO COVER IT?

YOU'D HAVE TO HOLD THE PANCAKE BREAKFAST AT A NUDIST COLONY.

Jefferson Communications, Inc. 1984
Distributed by Tribune Company Syndicate, Inc

MACNELLY 6/19

Reprinted by permission: Tribune Media Services.

hand. Consider publication needs in terms of horizontal or vertical shots, the number of people to be included in the pictures and whether you need color or black-and-white photos. You also need to consider the event from the standpoint of the photographer, including how close the pictures can be taken. In some cases, the photographer needs to be unobtrusive. For that reason, many PR directors insist that their staffs have first-hand knowledge of photography, to understand lens openings and lighting. When you have a picture in mind, look through the lens to be sure it is there. If it isn't, work toward what you want. The more professional the photographer, the less direction he or she needs. Allow for travel time and rest periods in shooting, and be prepared to pay half or all the agreed-upon fee if you must cancel at the last minute.

Video News Releases   Some organizations prepare their own video news releases, but most hire out this form of release. Many public relations services will handle video news releases for you, transmitting them worldwide by satellite. They also can monitor use of your video news release.

Initially, video news releases met with some resistance from news directors who felt they had less control over packaging news stories that came in this form from an outside source. However, it's so easy to edit videotape cassettes that few news directors balk any longer at accepting a video release. Still, they do have some preferences (see Example 12.13). Public relations services that produce and distribute video releases make it their business to know what the trends are, and they keep up with the preferences of network, cable and major station news directors.

Promotions

The notion that media attention follows good promotions is not new. Edward L. Bernays says that the idea is to make news—to create really newsworthy events. One news photo that has come to symbolize white resistance to the civil rights movement of the 1960s shows former Alabama Governor George Wallace standing at the door of the University of Alabama confronting the first two blacks who sought admission. That was a true media event, according to both Wallace and Macon L. Weaver, who was at that time the U.S. attorney responsible for enforcing the federal court's mandate:

> Few people knew, but those two black students were already *officially* registered before George Wallace stood in the schoolhouse door for the benefit of press and television. The students had been registered by the Alabama dean of admissions inside the library of a federal judge. . . . Everything was coordinated [among Wallace's office, the university and the federal government] . . . the route

EXAMPLE 12.13

Video News Release Preferences

A survey of news directors by Nielsen Media Research in 1987 sought to determine what sorts of video news releases were likely to find acceptance. The results are listed here.

TOPICS

What is the most useful subject for a video news release?

1. Health/medical
2. Business
3. Political and lifestyles/fashion
4. Sports

What general type of video news release do you prefer?

▼ VNR/timely news angle   46.8%

▼ Evergreen   25.5

▼ No preference   23.4

Do you incorporate video news releases, in whole or in part, into local interest stories?

▼ Yes   83.0%

▼ No   14.9

Does a suggested local angle increase the likelihood of using a video news release?

▼ Yes   83.0%

▼ No   17.0

Would you consider picking up and airing an "issue-oriented" video news release?

▼ Yes   74.5%

▼ No   23.4

PRODUCTION, PACKAGING AND CONTENT

How long should a video news release be?

▼ One minute   8.6%

▼ 90 seconds   52.1

▼ Two minutes   9.3

▼ No preference   9.3

What is the most useful format of a video news release?

▼ Produced and packaged as a news story   2.9%

▼ B-Roll only   15.0

▼ Combination   69.3

▼ Don't know   12.9

What would you advise a company if it were to produce a ninety-second VNR to optimize news usage and exposure of the company or its message?

▼ Mention product once   8.8%

▼ Make product name visible   41.2

▼ General message across without mentioning product or company directly   39.7

When video news releases are transmitted by satellite, do you prefer audio signals on:

▼ Separate channels   83.8%

▼ Same channel   10.3

▼ No preference   1.5

Should video news releases be clearly identified to stations as public relations releases?

▼ Agree completely   62.1%

▼ Agree somewhat   11.4

▼ Disagree completely   1.4

▼ Disagree somewhat   7.1

When a VNR is aired, the station should identify the source of the release.

▼ Disagree completely   9.3%
▼ Disagree somewhat   7.9
▼ Neither   10.7
▼ Agree somewhat   11.4
▼ Agree completely   48.6

This station will not use a produced release using a stand-up news reporter.

▼ Disagree completely   14.3%
▼ Disagree somewhat   5.0
▼ Neither   12.9
▼ Agree somewhat   9.3
▼ Agree completely   46.4
▼ Don't know   12.1

In your opinion, how many video news releases should be in a VNR series?

▼ No preference   5.0%
▼ Two-part series   5.0
▼ Three-part series   50.0
▼ Four-part series   10.0
▼ Five-part series   5.0

Are you interested in receiving video news releases with simple digital effects and/or animation when these effects help explain the story?

▼ Yes   83.0%
▼ No   12.8

When your station broadcasts a video news release, is it your station's practice to . . . ?

▼ Identify company   45.6%
▼ Identify if clearly relevant 26.5
▼ Not identify   17.6

How many video news releases do you use in full during a week—with no editing at all?

▼ None used in full   55.3%
▼ One   25.5
▼ Two   10.6
▼ Three   4.3

How many *edited* video news releases do you use in a week?

▼ One   34.0%
▼ Two   21.3
▼ Three   6.4
▼ Four   8.5
▼ Five   4.3
▼ None   23.4

DISTRIBUTION

If a video news release had a timely or hard news angle to it, would you prefer it be delivered by. . .

▼ Satellite with pre-notification   91.5%
▼ Regular mail delivery   6.4
▼ No preference   2.1

Do you prefer that video news releases, with a news angle, be delivered to your station by. . .

▼ Satellite with pre-notification   36.2%
▼ Regular mail delivery   40.4
▼ No preference   23.4

(Continued)

EXAMPLE 12.13

Video News Release Preferences (*continued*)

Approximately how many video news releases do you receive each week either by satellite or mailed cassette?

▼ None — 1.5%
▼ One — 2.9
▼ Two — 7.4
▼ Three — 10.3
▼ Four — 5.9
▼ Five — 16.2
▼ Six — 10.3
▼ Seven — 7.4
▼ Eight — 4.4
▼ Nine — 1.5
▼ Ten — 8.8
▼ Twelve — 2.9
▼ Thirteen — 1.5
▼ Fifteen — 7.4
▼ Eighteen — 1.5
▼ Twenty — 4.4
▼ Twenty-three — 1.5
▼ Twenty-five — 2.9
▼ Thirty-two — 1.5

In your opinion, is it helpful to transmit a video news release on both C-Band and Ku satellite?

▼ Yes — 54.4%
▼ No — 33.8

What is your general satellite preference for down-linking a video news release?

▼ C-Band — 42.9%
▼ Ku — 16.4
▼ No preference — 27.9

What is your specific satellite preference for down-linking a video news release or public service announcement?

▼ Westar (General) — 16.4%
▼ Westar 4 — 12.9
▼ Westar 5 — 1.4
▼ Telstar (General) — 5.0
▼ Telstar 301 — 8.6
▼ Telstar 302 — 1.4
▼ No preference — 28.6

When should video news releases be transmitted?

▼ A.M. in general — 10.1%
▼ 9 A.M. — 6.3
▼ 10 A.M. — 43.0
▼ 11 A.M. — 20.3

Second choice for VNR transmission time?

▼ P.M. in general — 12.5%
▼ 1 P.M. — 19.6
▼ 2 P.M. — 26.8
▼ 3 P.M. — 14.3
▼ Noon — 10.7

What format do you prefer for mailed video releases?

▼ ¾-inch tape — 89.4%
▼ Betacam — 6.4
▼ Other mention — 2.1

If you were to receive a multipart series video news release, would you prefer it be delivered by . . .

▼ Mail — 70.2%
▼ Satellite — 19.1
▼ No preference — 10.6

The respondents to this Nielsen Media Research opinion survey were news directors at stations nationwide. The sample for each question included 106 responses. News directors were not told that MediaLink sponsored the survey.

Survey of news directors by Nielsen Media Research for MediaLink. Used by permission.

for the students . . . the circle for the press. . . . His standing in the schoolhouse door was a charade. He got some publicity out of it. He got his wish.[20]

Wallace later said he stood at the schoolhouse door only because, without a symbolic protest, Klansmen and other extremists would have stormed the campus.

Pseudo-events have earned some "bad PR" for promotions. And, of course, promotions themselves often earn a bad name for PR. In promotions you see PR's closest ties to marketing—so close that some have called promotions "marketing PR." You are even likely to hear a component of marketing described as "advertising, selling and public relations."

Sometimes you have to sell an idea or concept in order to sell a product, as Bernays promoted the "American breakfast" of bacon and eggs to sell his client's product. Similarly, film competitors Kodak and Fuji engaged in big-time selling at the 1986 celebration of the restoration of the Statue of Liberty. Kodak promoted itself through its American Family Album, a permanent exhibit of portraits of American individuals and families. Rival Fuji promoted itself by entering a blimp adorned with its logo in the Great Blimp Race that ended at the Statue of Liberty. Why? People take pictures at big events, according to Ted Fox, spokesman for the Photo Marketing Association.[21]

Selling an image along with a product doesn't work, though, when the product isn't there to sell. At the America's Cup, the world's premier yachting event, RayBan sunglasses, a division of Bausch & Lomb, wanted to keep the French company Vuarnet from cutting into its market. Obviously people watching such an event wear sunglasses. So during the races at Newport, Rhode Island, RayBan sponsored a boat-ferry system, known as RayBan launches, and distributed a newsletter about the yacht races and other Newport activities. All of these activities were under the direction of the sports development division of Hill & Knowlton, now a part of Hill & Knowlton's marketing communication unit. But local stores had not stocked

▼ **Promotions are news makers, but you have to supply the information.**

anything but their normal supply of RayBan sunglasses, and thus RayBan couldn't deliver enough of the product its promotion had created a demand for.[22]

A coordinated effort works best and often involves advertising as well as publicity and promotion. For example, Denver city officials are aware of the bad image that its Stapleton Airport has among travelers, and they are trying to promote improvements to Stapleton and plans for a new airport about 10 miles away. The airport has run ads in national travel magazines, and George Doughty, Stapleton's director of aviation, has been interviewed by national news media. He is reported to have said, "Denver's Stapleton is the Rodney Dangerfield of airports. We don't get a lot of respect; we've got a bad reputation for delays and problems." Surely he also knows that promotion without problem correction is worse than no promotion at all.[23]

When you see an ad that focuses on an event or a problem, look for the publicity. And when you see the publicity, such as stories about champagne around New Year's or exotic recipes using particular fruits in newspapers and magazines, look for the advertising. Sometimes there is also direct contact with the product itself, such as food samples in grocery stores. It's all promotion.

Image Marketing   An image is the impression of a person, company or institution that is held by one or more publics (see Example 12.14). An image is not a picture; that is, it is not a detailed, accurate representation. Rather, it is a few details softened with the fuzziness of perception.

The difference a public relations effort makes is apparent in the story of an orthopedic surgeon who uses a miniature TV camera inserted in bone joints while he operates. He is not the only surgeon using the technique, but he has been the subject of a number of magazine articles and has appeared

EXAMPLE 12.14

A Symbol as Publicity

Dallas News staff photo by Rick Young

The Goodyear blimp — the ultimate in company trademarks.

Blimp gives PR big lift

By TOM BAYER

...year.
...name just about everybody — many today learn it as chil-...wed at the intriguing Goodyear ...hich happens to be mak...

A station wagon and sedan provide additional transportation for the crew. Moran, who said the crew spends about 50 to 60 per cent of its time away ...me, explained the principle on ...p operates and ...

FOR NIGHT FLYING and presenta-tion of the "Super Skytacular" display, as Goodyear calls it, the crew replaces the seats in th... with elec-tronic ...

which will lift heavy loads straight up and then move them away.

"OUR GOAL... NASA

SOURCE: Reprinted with permission of *Dallas Morning News*.

---

on many radio and television talk shows. Why? Because he pays a PR firm $1,500 a month to publicize his practice.[24]

Marketing reaches out to external publics, and institutions that historically have not had open communication systems are today more likely to make marketing a number one priority. Examples of typically closed communication systems are museums (often because of security and protection of benefactors), hospitals (usually because of privacy), banks (for privacy and security) and airlines.

Until the 1960s, neither museums nor hospitals bothered a great deal with either public relations or marketing. In the 1970s, however, museums sought to broaden their constituency and to expand their collections and buildings. Hospitals found it necessary to explain skyrocketing costs. They also were caught up in the litigious climate that positioned patients against their physicians in malpractice suits.

Banks and savings and loans have become financial supermarkets, offering a variety of services in a competitive marketplace fraught with the danger of closings caused by bad investments and overextended loans. Airlines have found that deregulation has created a highly competitive marketplace, contributing to the bankruptcy of some major airlines and the merger of others.

Publicity Spinoffs TV audiences frequently see newsmakers and celebrities on talk shows. The whole purpose of these appearances is to create spinoff publicity. In calling the press secretaries of nineteen leading Democratic Senate newsmakers in 1987, Terry Michael, news and information director of the Democratic National Committee, asked them to rank the three major interview shows: "This Week with David Brinkley" (ABC), "Meet the Press" (NBC) and "Face the Nation" (CBS). His question: "If you had the choice, which show would you want your boss on and why?" The press secretaries knew, of course, that the power of the shows was spinoff. One is reported to have told Michael: "There's no difference between the shows, and the listening audience is so small. It's the spinoff news that's important. And you can get that if you have something to say, no matter which show you're on." Roger Simon made the point by saying, "On December 7, 1986, ABC's 'World News Tonight' led off the news with clips of interviews from all three Sunday news shows."[25] In the 1990s talk shows became the medium of choice for politicians seeking to exploit a technique used by former President Ronald Reagan when he was a presidential candidate: to go directly to the people. By this period, talk shows had proliferated on both TV and radio and were commanding increasing audience numbers. The show appearances also create publicity in other media.

Often promotions generate publicity without much stimulation. One such situation was the publicity surrounding Burson-Marsteller's advertising campaign for Dannon yogurt. The Dannon commercials were filmed in Russia and featured a number of elderly citizens (such as an eighty-nine-year-old farmer and his mother), still hale and hearty, who were yogurt eaters. The commercials were filmed in Soviet Georgia where in pre-Glasnost days even some Russians were not allowed to go, so that in itself created some interest. Then the commercials began to win awards, which inspired more attention. The photo of the eighty-nine-year-old farmer was chosen for the cover of a book, *The Best Things on TV Commercials,* by Jonathan Price, and the story of the filming of the Dannon commercials appeared as "Diary of a Commercial: Soviet Georgians Eat Yogurt" in Judy Fireman's *TV Book: The Ultimate Television Book.*

In promoting film talent, publicity is the name of the game. Writer Marguerite Michaels explains the formula like this:

> The new system is based on four parts—the agent, the manager, the publicist and the would-be star. They generate their own law of supply and demand: the publicist creates the demand, the manager and agent supply the star.[26]

The promoter of Farrah Fawcett, Jay Bernstein, took as a client Suzanne Somers, who was in ABC-TV's situation comedy, "Three's Company." The publicist on the job was Stu Ehrlich, who said Suzanne "had a real Hollywood story. She was pregnant at 16, married at 17, divorced at 18. Carried the baby on her back to college classes. Waited tables, did modeling, lots of struggle. Published two volumes of poetry. Wonderful homemaker, wonderful mother." When an unfavorable story about the actress passing some bad checks threatened the image, Ehrlich turned it around by calling news media that hadn't broken the story and offering them an "exclusive" account of the other side of the story. The actress was broke and hungry at the time, he said, the rent had been due and her son was ill. As Somers's agent, Edgar Small, said, "It doesn't matter if the hype is vulgar or dumb. . . . It only matters if it works." P. T. Barnum would not have quarreled with that, but most PR people would.

▼ Celebrity spinoffs from promotion can be positive or negative.

Celebrity Spinoffs Promotion planners often look for a "big name" to attract media attention. It's not a novel idea, but sometimes it can result in negative publicity that has nothing to do with the product. For instance, the celebrity's private life may make the news in a way that hurts the promotion, such as when athletes are involved in drugs. Advertising has used celebrities frequently enough to have a long history of good and bad experiences. Although celebrities can increase recognition, they can't rescue a product, and they may actually harm it.

An example of the harm a celebrity can do comes from the recent experience of the Paddington Corporation. Paddington distributes the Italian liqueur Amaretto di Saronno. Desiring to give its product a more contemporary image, Paddington ran a series of ads that featured avant-garde celebrities. One of the celebrities chosen was Phoebe Légère, a well-known musical performer in New York's more trendy nightclubs. After the ads had run, Ms. Légère appeared in the film *Mondo New York,* performing a very steamy nightclub routine. Shortly after the film's appearance, she bared all in *Playboy,* alongside a copy of her liqueur ad. Paddington's reaction is unknown, but the company probably did not intend to promote the image that Ms. Legérè's subsequent actions portrayed.

When celebrities are used and media spinoffs occur, you may find media calling a well-recognized source, Celebrity Service International, a subscription service that tracks celebrities and their doings.[27] So, if you *do* use a celebrity and you are counting on spinoffs, check with CSI to see what they know about your "star," and be sure to give the service an itinerary of the celebrity's appearances for you.

Celebrities' names and pictures are often used in the pre-promotion of a special event. Be sure you have the celebrity's specific, written permission before using his or her name and picture in any advertising. Some who may agree to come to an event will not let their name or photograph be used in advertising because of previous advertising contracts for products or services. You must also make sure that any prior advertising association of the celebrity will not conflict with the image you want to create for your organization.

In using a celebrity for promotion, you may encounter the same problem that advertisers have when they use celebrities: people remember the celebrity, but not the message. You should also be aware that the celebrities are not as concerned about the promotion as you are, and they are not under the same control in a publicity event as they are in producing a commercial. Don't expect them to be. Things that you didn't plan for can and do happen.

Publicizing Special Events

A special event may be any newsmaking situation—from a corporate open house to a freeway ribbon cutting to the preview of an exhibition of rare paintings. The publicity for each event requires its own unique handling, but a few basic rules apply to virtually every case.

The Mechanics First, you must establish a timetable because so many events have to dovetail. The timetable should include the dates for the first announcement, which must be coordinated with any special invitations and advertising. Second, mailing lists must be prepared for both special activities and the news media. You must start early and set firm policies on handing out news media credentials. (You should not invite your PR colleagues to any media-day functions, unless they had an active part in the planning.) Third, the promotion campaign itself must be planned in detail, with a theme selected that will carry through all advertising, publicity, letterheads, invitations and posters.

A media kit should be prepared for the event, and it should be one of the most carefully thought out pieces of the entire promotion. Media kits are mailed in advance to people who may not attend the special event but who may write something about it. They are also handed out at the event itself.

Because the kits must serve a variety of media—specialized and mass, print and broadcasting—parts of the kits will differ. Publications will receive 8 × 10 glossy photographs with cutlines glued to the bottom or the back. Broadcast media will get cassettes or small tape reels with important information spoken by the central figures involved in the news event, so that these can be used by the broadcast media as "actualities" (recorded quotes). Accompanying the tapes will be brief stories written in broadcast style and format, with a suggested release date. Television media kits will also contain a list of specific activities that have visual appeal for television camera people to photograph, as well as videotape cassettes (VNRs), 16-mm film or slides.

Some special event publicists supply an electronic news kit containing an assortment of interviews, background footage and location shots. This allows stations to create their own story instead of being forced to use or edit the prepackaged version. The word *press* should never be used in a media kit. Press relates only to the *print* media; a PR person who thinks only in print terms is in the dark ages.

Some news distribution services will prepare media kits for you and will coordinate their delivery. But you must provide the information the service will need to prepare the kits, along with any special instructions that you want them to have. For example, the American Heart Association has found it especially effective to put the guidance heads (suggested headlines for news releases) on the front of envelopes going to the news media. If you want something special like this, you have to tell the distribution service.

Media Kit Contents   Media kits have to be tailored to each occasion; if mailed, they should also include a cover letter that briefly explains the event. The contents are as follows:

▼ **Media kit contents may vary, but basically they include the following: facts sheets, program of events, news story, list of participants with photos and bios, visual materials, special facts and special stories.**

1. A *basic facts sheet* that details the newsmaking event and explains its significance in strictly factual terms. Include important dates, times, participants and relationships (for example, how a company might be connected to a holding company). Be sure to include your name and address and the phone numbers where you can be reached for additional information.

2. A *historical facts sheet* that gives background information on the event and identifies the individual or organization involved. Use a simple date-event format.

3. A *program of events or schedule of activities,* including detailed time data. Provide a script, when possible, for the broadcast media.

4. A *straight news story,* never more than a page and a half of double-spaced typescript for print media and one or two short paragraphs for broadcast media. Give both print and broadcast versions to broadcast newspeople. The print news media need only the print version.

5. A *complete list of all participants,* with accompanying explanation of their connection with the event.

6. *Biographical background information on principals,* updated with emphasis on current information, unless something in their background is particularly relevant.

7. *Visual material,* consisting of 8 × 10 (or 5 × 7, if head shots of a person) black-and-white glossy prints for newspapers and magazines and 35-mm color slides (transparencies) for television and publications using color. Be sure all are of good quality, have significance (tell a story or show an important participant) and have attached identification. (If media kits are being mailed, you may want to send slick proofs, but certainly only to the print media.)

8. A *longer general news story* that ties in background information. It may be as long as three double-spaced pages for print media or one full page for broadcast media (about 60 seconds of copy).

9. Two or three *feature* stories of varying lengths for print media. There will be no broadcast versions, but the features should be included in broadcast news kits for background.

10. A *page of special isolated facts* that are interesting and will stand alone. These often are picked up for incorporation into copy written by newspeople or used as fillers.

11. Any *brochures* that are available about the event or organization or person, prepared either for the event or earlier (if the latter, be sure to update in pen).

12. A *list of useful additional information,* with the telephone numbers and addresses of local news organizations. Include a list of restaurants in the area that are known for their quick service and a list of food services that deliver. A map of the area should also be included. If media from outside the area are invited, provide a summary sheet that gives information about climate and likely weather conditions.

Don't forget electronic networks that can help. Put your material on a PR wire service. Have releases and photos (stills and slides) ready for the newswire people, and have actualities on cassettes for the radio networks (many state and regional ones extra), as well as films clips and videotapes for television.

Setting up a Newsroom   The next most important planning should go into arranging the media facilities during the event. Find out from the local media what they will need, and then plan for the out-of-town reporters.

Setting up and maintaining a newsroom or media facility for a convention, meeting or any special event requires planning and constant attention. You will need three to four weeks for phone installations, although in a crisis, you can get a portable phone bank installed at considerable extra cost. The facility you set up is for people responsible for getting the news and getting it out, so it must operate efficiently. When a newsroom is cramped, badly located or understaffed, it can result in poor coverage. The following elements are essential for a smooth-running operation.

First, have a sign-up sheet in the newsroom. Provide space for each representative's name, the medium that he or she represents and the local telephone number and address where the person can be reached.

Second, use a rack or display stand to keep media kits from falling apart and to let you know when supplies are running low. Have a separate place for the "newstips of the day," pick-up schedules, new facts sheets and new news releases. Daily news releases should list the day's events and cover results of the previous day's events in summary. All information must be easily available to media representatives. This means accessibility of news information, background material and releases, illustrations and people to be interviewed.

Third, select for the newsroom staff an experienced crew cognizant of the need to be helpful and friendly. The number of staffers depends on the size of the event and the expected news coverage, as indicated by past occasions. The importance of having one well-qualified person in charge cannot be overemphasized. That person is an "anchor" who should always be available during regular hours and should be replaced by another "anchor" at other times. (When you have international coverage of an event, you have to run a 24-hour newsroom.) This person should be able to handle emergencies and opportunities and should know how to deal with delicate press or personality relations. Leaving the goodwill of an organization up to an inexperienced person can be damaging. Give all staffers pagers, and have a supply of cordless telephones available for their use. You and other key people associated with the event should also wear pagers.

Fourth, separate the newsroom from the traffic of the convention or meeting.

Fifth, provide separate interview rooms for print and broadcast reporters. It is advisable to have an interview "set" for television coverage, another area for radio interviewing and a third location where newspaper and magazine reporters can talk with people. There should be plenty of wall plugs and extension cords for lights and other electronic equipment.

Sixth, plan for special equipment needs. Mini-cams and TV vans have made coverage easier for TV reporters, but some television equipment is still so bulky that large doors must be available nearby to allow this equipment to be brought into the newsroom area. Get information in advance about electrical outlets and other essentials that the TV crews require. At large news conferences, risers are usually necessary in order for each camera to have a clear shot.

Seventh, be aware that most print journalists now use laptop computers to send their stories directly to the home office. These devices function most efficiently over plug-in telephones and *single* telephone lines, so make sure that phone jacks are available. The telephone company has to be notified that an FCC-registered device is going to be used. During some special events, you may be dealing with two telephone companies. Be sure to check this situation in advance and clear it with both companies.

Eighth, make certain that the newsroom has the following supplies: (a) telephones for local and long-distance calls, plus metro lines so surrounding cities can be dialed free of toll charges, voice transmission equipment for broadcast newspeople, telephone directories, modems and direct lines that are always kept open; (b) typewriters, both electric and manual (power has been known to fail); (c) copy machines; (d) terminal keyboards and printers for electronic equipment; (e) Telex transmitters (electronic message senders) for wire sto-

ries; (f) bulletin boards and thumb tacks or boards with chalk or erasable markers and erasers; (g) individual desks or tables with comfortable chairs and good lighting; (h) coat hangers and space to hang coats; (i) wastebaskets; (j) paper, shorthand spiral notebooks, envelopes, pencils, correcting tape/fluid and erasers; (k) drinking water and paper cups for hot and cold liquids; (l) paper towels; (m) a supply of 35-mm color and black-and-white film, both 100 and 200 speeds, with twelve exposures; (n) an extra camera with a flash unit, batteries of all types, computer cables, jewelers' tools for quick repairs and basic tools such as hammers, pliers and regular and Phillips-head screwdrivers in assorted sizes. Ideally, you would have an electrician available. The building may have one. If so, make special pay arrangements for the help you might need, and then be prepared to pay by the hour for the actual work.

Ninth, darkroom facilities should be provided for wire services, which may or may not bring their own portable labs. This space needs electrical outlets, running water and blackout curtains. You don't want to have to commandeer a restroom. Building supply rooms with sinks sometimes can be temporarily converted if you clear it with the building manager and alert the cleaning crews. When you make these arrangements in advance with the building people, they generally cooperate, but they don't like surprises. If they seem possessive about the building, it is because they are held responsible for its condition. You may have to sign a contract and put up a deposit.

Tenth, providing food in the newsroom is practically a must. Food is worth the cost because reporters expect it, and it keeps them from wandering away from the meeting. How elaborate the food table is depends on the budget and generosity of the organization operating the newsroom. The basic requirements are coffee with donuts or rolls in the morning, sandwiches for lunch, and coffee and soft drinks throughout the day. Parties, however, should be held elsewhere. The distinction between working newspeople and partying newspeople is important to maintain. Never call a news conference unless it is a working session; never have a party for newspeople and expect them to work. However, it is customary at large conventions to have a cocktail hour for the reporters at the end of the working day and to provide free tickets for evening meals. If lunchtime includes a regular session of the program, a media table should be set up in the eating area.

Eleventh, be sure restroom facilities are nearby and that they are kept locked, but keep several keys in the newsroom. Check periodically on their cleanliness and on the availability of supplies. Arrange for building maintenance people to help, and be prepared to pay them. It is useless to know that you need towels if you can't get to a supply.

Twelfth, to protect the equipment, secure the newsroom for use only by authorized media representatives. It cannot be a social lounge for curiosity seekers, people looking for a cup of coffee (or other nourishment) and registrants to the meeting, who always seem to prefer the newsroom but get in the way. Visitors and unaccredited persons—regardless of who they may be—should be handled firmly and not admitted to the news area, where they are resented by the working newspeople.

Thirteenth, to ensure a good news operation, put yourself in the place of the reporter or editor. Evaluate what you would need to cover the meeting properly, and then plan from that point. If your event didn't get the proper coverage, it's probably because the PR people didn't put the time, money and staff into a sincere effort.

Other Special Event Considerations   The day before the event, call local media as a reminder; you can check on their technical needs again at this time too. If you have arranged for something like the Goodyear blimp as a symbol of publicity, you don't want to miss getting coverage. If you are presenting a boat show, football bowl game or state fair, having the Goodyear blimp attracts attention to the event, as well as to the blimp's sponsor.

Plan tie-ins to the special event. Motels and businesses around town are usually willing to display special messages on their marquees, especially if the event is an annual attraction or has some civic interest. Exhibits and displays can be developed and placed with institutions such as banks, utilities, schools and libraries. The chamber of commerce usually has a list of simultaneous conventions and meetings, and a special offer might be made to the sponsors to show your exhibit or display at these, if attracting crowds is one purpose of the special event.

Gimmicks   Some public relations people plan newsmaking gimmicks that will attract attention to their clients. For women recruits who failed to meet the Los Angeles Police Department's upper-body strength test, Nann Miller Enterprises arranged free workouts at Jack LaLanne Health Spas, Miller's client. At a groundbreaking for the SPCA (Society for the Prevention of Cruelty to Animals), two trained dogs manipulated the shovel. Planes are available to tow banners over large crowd assemblies, such as football games and music festivals. Helium balloons, painted with logos, can be rented to float over the event. Even squadrons of aircraft that puff smoke on computerized command (called sky typing) can be obtained, and there are always biplanes to do classic skywriting. (Pepsi bought two such planes for a $200,000-a-year skywriting campaign that senior vice-president Alan Potasch described as "the most singularly dollar-effective promotion we have.")[28]

Stunts of this type are clever and are accepted for their general interest. Any stunt that misleads, however, or creates a hazard—such as a human fly who walks up the side of a building, tying up traffic and rescue forces from the police and fire departments—is not generally regarded too highly by the news media.

Extending the Publicity Coverage   To get as much mileage as possible out of your publicity, you can send clippings and stories to special publications, such as trade magazines and newsletters, as well as to other media that serve special publics. If possible, it is always newsworthy to get a mayor, governor or state legislator to issue a proclamation to mark the event.

You can also produce your own magazines and books for a special event, such as a corporate anniversary or a merger. Banks and newspapers have been known to commission books from historians for their anniversaries, but most often the job falls to a public relations writer. Whenever possible, give the job to a historian. You will probably have many disagreements along the way, but the historian's reputation and desire not to compromise her or his scholarship will bring a credibility to the publication that cannot be purchased. Management may not appreciate the historian's "warts 'n all" approach, however; and management may also dislike the fees that will have to be paid.

Sometimes "extended coverage" of promotions and events is neither favorable nor desirable. Promotions that are tied to sales often turn negative, for several reasons. The promises stated or implied in sales promotions may result in some disenchanted consumers whose complaining can create negative media attention. Furthermore, business editors are likely to look for the bottom-line consequences of sales promotions, which are increasingly seen as unprofitable. (Some are not intended to be, especially when the product is new and the purpose is to introduce the product.)[29]

Sometimes news coverage can be negative in near disastrous ways. For example, after journalist Ward Bushee wrote an editorial criticizing the dangers of ceremonial jet flyovers, he was invited to fly with a National Guard pilot. Special permission for a civilian to go along had to be cleared through the public affairs office at the Pentagon, so this wasn't a casual invitation. Nevertheless, the plane that Bushee was in collided with another, and his pilot had to push the eject button to save both of their lives. Fortunately, the journalist was not critically injured, and the Iowa National Guard said the accident wouldn't affect its policy on public relations flights.[30] But the episode is something to consider.

▼ **Four groups of people are especially important to the publicist: newspeople, production people, other PR people and freelance writers.**

▼ ON THE JOB WITH MEDIA PEOPLE

Successful publicity is often closely tied to the relationships you form in getting and disseminating information. Four groups are especially important to the publicist: newspeople, production people, other PR people and freelance writers. You need to know whom to turn to first in all four categories. Next you need to know the level of their skills, either by examining their work (when possible) or by checking their reputations (second best, but the communications world network is a source). Remember, you too will be known by your trustworthiness and by the quality of your work.

Relations with Newspeople

PR people go to great lengths to meet the requirements of media people and sometimes they still get nothing to show for it. Such was the case when *Fortune* contacted K-Mart Corporation Chairman Bernard M. Fauber in Troy, Michigan, about being on its cover. Although the story had been in the works since the middle of July, it was in the middle of August, on a Friday at 11 A.M., when K-Mart was told that the picture would have to be in hand that weekend in order to make the cover. *Fortune* wanted a photo of Fauber on the roof of a K-Mart store. So after the call, Fauber's schedule was cleared, a store in Troy was selected and the PR staff began looking for a "cherry-picker"—a truck-mounted elevator, to lift Fauber to the roof. After the publicity director found a cherry-picker operator in the yellow pages, the weather turned bad and the *Fortune* photographer canceled. The shooting was reset for Saturday morning; it rained. Saturday afternoon was clear, but Fauber had to go to a wedding. *Fortune* ruled out Sunday. Monday morning the shot was finally taken, and couriers took the film to the Detroit airport to be flown to *Fortune*'s headquarters in New York. Unfortunately for K-Mart, Fauber got crowded off the cover by President Ronald Reagan, although the company's story was in that issue. The magazine has a practice of selecting three possible covers. The decision was made to go with Reagan. Fauber's graceful comment was, "If I had to lose out, I can't think of anyone I'd rather lose out to."[31]

A good PR practitioner knows newspeople's jobs almost as well as they do, and is courteous and considerate toward them. The PR professional also knows the importance of getting to know the newspeople, and therefore initiates contact. One of the best ways is to hand-carry news releases to all the local media. It is time-consuming, but by regularly hand-delivering releases, the PR person establishes a working relationship with the media that permits extra consideration when the institution he or she represents may be under attack. Take the release to the particular editor or reporter who should receive it. Make sure no questions are left unanswered. Visits should not be long. Speak to others briefly, and leave. Don't engage in extended conversation unless the newsperson invites it (say, by offering you a cup of coffee), and then be sure to take the time. Plan a delivery schedule that gives you the needed flexibility but still allows you to get the releases to other media with deadlines. You probably will find that you have to call ahead to get in. Most media now have security checks, so you can only get in to see someone if the person knows you are coming.

Include on your list of local media not just the daily metropolitan newspapers but also television and radio stations and suburban newspapers. Include ethnic and alternative media, too.[32] If it is necessary to translate the release into a different language, call on the faculty of commercial language schools and local college language departments or on one of the relatively new firms of language specialists handling business and industrial translations. (Be sure the translator knows current idiomatic use of the language.)[33]

An illustration of fractured media relations appeared in the *Business Wire Newsletter.* According to the newsletter, the San Francisco bureau chief for *Business Week* received in the mail a seven-page feature sent by a local public relations person to the magazine's New York office. New York had kicked the story back to the San Francisco bureau; and in checking, the bureau chief found that the "leapfrogging" of his office in favor of New York was a product of simple ignorance. The PR person did not know that *Business Week* had regional offices, including one in San Francisco. In sending releases to national publications, be sure to check whether they have local offices or representatives; if so, deal directly with them.

On the other hand, you do need to know what you are doing, what the headlines are and what these may mean. For example, the Dallas bureau chief of the *Wall Street Journal* says that, if your release is issued before the Dallas office opens at 8:30 A.M., you need to wire it to New York *WSJ* offices, too, so it will make the Dow Jones ticker.

When special events attract newspeople from outside the local area or members of the specialized media such as travel or outdoor publications, be sure to make personal contact while the opportunity is there. Contacts make smoother one of the more effective PR efforts—alerting news media to stories that might interest them. Usually this is a personal, individual effort, but some organizations have had success by publishing collections of news tips or story ideas for the state and national media.

If you are sending out many releases a week to the local media, you obviously cannot hand-deliver all of them, but it is important that you see all local newspeople on your mailing list at least once a month; there are no little or insignificant newspeople.

Most importantly, *be available*. PR people not only should not have unlisted telephone numbers, they should deliberately list their home phone number (as well as business phone) at the top of each release. A story may be processed after 5 P.M., and if you want it on the 10 P.M. news or in the morning paper, you should be available to answer questions. Often the caller is not an editor but someone from the copy desk who wants to check the spelling of a name in your story or to get some background to flesh out the story. You should immediately oblige them. The need comes with the request, not later, when it is convenient for you.

In working with news photographers, never tell them how to take their pictures, since they know what their editors expect. But remember that, as the PR practitioner, you know the event, the institution and the people, so you may be able to think of other pictures that might be newsworthy and *suggest*—the word cannot be too strongly emphasized—them to the photographer.

This additional advice comes from a corporate manual:

> When you think you have a story that rates a picture, call the city editor, the business editor or reporter and present your idea. If the editor thinks it has merit, you will usually find it gets coverage. If you're turned down, there's probably a good reason for it. Try again, but come up with a better idea next time. Unless the picture possibility comes up suddenly, give the paper several days' notice. You'll have a better chance of scoring.
>
> Don't try to get an iron-clad promise from a paper for photo coverage of an event days in advance. An important news break may occur which will prevent the photographer from taking your picture at the last moment. [If you are simultaneously visited by several competing photographers, be sure you do not suggest the same pictures to each.]
>
> Newspapers will accept and publish well-executed pictures by photographers other than their own staff members. There are a number of excellent freelance press photographers whose services can be acquired at reasonable cost.
>
> Ask other PR people for recommendations and look at their work. Tell the photographer what type of pictures you need, how they will be used and the format. Unless you negotiate, the photographer owns the negatives. Also be sure to let the photographer do the "directing" of the subjects.

In working with television journalists, think and talk in 30 second sound bites, and remember the visual aspect of the coverage.

Relations with Production People

PR people need to work effectively with two types of production people: those in the media and suppliers. In the media, much of the technical work is handled electronically. However, knowing the production staffs and understanding production processes make it easier for you to avoid problems with the material you supply and to unsnarl problems that do occur. You need to know what is and is not technically possible in the various media, and it helps to be familiar with the terminology.

Knowing the terminology and production processes can be critical when you are dealing with suppliers. Technical suppliers produce the typeset copy for your printed pieces, the printed pieces themselves, color separations for your artwork, slides, videotapes and sound. You have to know what you want, and you have to appreciate and be able to pay for quality (or accept less if you don't have the budget). More importantly, your directions will be followed by the producers. If you have scaled a picture wrong, failed to fit the copy correctly or, worse, misspelled a word, you will be charged for your mistake when it is corrected. Just as with other craftspeople, if the mistake is the suppliers', they will correct it at no charge. Mistakes always cause delays, and if the errors are yours, they are costly. A PR project can go over budget quickly if it encounters technical problems.

When production people contribute to a nonprofit effort, as typesetters and printers often do, you are likely to get a credit slip, like the ones you receive from broadcast stations after your PSAs have run. A gracious "thank you" certainly is in order.

Relations with Other PR People

On occasion you may work with PR people from other firms. It may be in a cooperative promotion; it may be because you've hired the firm to help with a special event; or it may be that you have a long-standing relationship with an advertising agency.

Fiascos have occurred when a practitioner who is supposedly directing the agency's efforts has suddenly felt threatened by them and has withdrawn his or her support and cooperation. To avoid such trauma, be sure to spell out in the beginning who has final approval over copy, and make sure deadlines and timetables are worked out to preserve your long-established relationships with the media. Then relax and manage. It is your job to supply the major source of information to the firm or agency, and to see that work is expedited, that deadlines are kept and that quality is maintained. It should be a rewarding experience from which all participants benefit.

Relations with Freelance Writers

Although it may be time-consuming, you should try to cooperate with freelancers who may be using your PR department as a source of information for a story they hope to sell or for a book they are writing. The freelancer may have a contact you lack; and the writer's status as a free agent lends greater credibility to the material.

Of course, freelancers can also waste your time, especially if they are really nonwriters on a fishing expedition. There are a couple of ways to check, without offending them. One is to ask them what and for whom they have written, and then look up the articles in the *Readers' Guide to Periodical Literature*. Another way is to ask them if they have sent a magazine or newspaper a query on the article idea and received a response; if they say they have, you can call the editor for confirmation. (To make it seem less of a "corroboration" check, you can suggest to the editor that you certainly are willing to cooperate but that perhaps you could help the writer better if you knew what direction the story was to take and whether art might be needed.) Most editors will tell you immediately if the writer is working on assignment or on speculation. You should not dismiss the writer working without assignment, however; on the contrary, you may be able to help an inexperienced writer.

Many magazines use staff for stories or assign writers. Working with a magazine's experienced people usually increases your own appreciation for what you are publicizing and is a pleasurable, albeit time-demanding, experience. One news bureau director and university magazine editor, contacted by a nationally syndicated Sunday supplement about a story on the university, found that three weeks' work with the magazine writers produced not only national coverage but a handsome reprint she could use as the primary portion of one of her magazines.

Sometimes a writer has malicious intent, but an experienced PR person can take the offensive to advantage. As one practitioner says, "I give them the straight stuff, and I try to keep them busy. Every time I say something, I try to think how it could be distorted, contorted, twisted beyond recognition, and if it still seems to shake out okay, I spit it out. One thing I do know, while they are talking to me they are not talking to the opposition or gathering facts against us." The key here is to anticipate how the truth might be used against you.

If a story seems unfair or distorted, employers are likely to blame the PR person, but the PR person cannot pass it on to the media without aggravating the situation. Most professional public relations people have never registered a complaint with any news medium in their entire careers. The standing rule with respect to the media is to call only if they have made a substantial error. If the story is libelous, let your institution's lawyer make the call. On the other hand, some PR practitioners think talking back gets attention, consideration and corrections.

Protecting Relationships: Contracts and Deadlines

One way to establish some understanding about what is to occur in PR-media relationships is to sign contracts and to keep to your written and unwritten obligations.

Contracts   Trouble with some media arrangements, such as exclusive cover stories or special TV appearances, can be avoided through contracts. Contracts have enormous value as preventives. The PR person also arranges contracts with suppliers of services. You should consider having contracts with an outside agency or studio, with a printer, with models and with any artists or photographers, even if they are your best friends or relatives. If your close friend, the photographer, has a contract, you can say, "The boss wants one of those color prints for his office," and your friend can say, "Well, it's not in the contract. How much do you think we ought to charge him for it?" A contract gives you the chance to suggest a fair price or say, "Forget it!" Bad feelings resulting from unexpected charges can be avoided if things are spelled out—in friendly but specific language.

Deadlines   Meeting deadlines is essential to a smooth operation. Allow enough flexibility in planning for mistakes—yours and others'. Once you have promised copy to the artist or typesetter or ads to the media, you *must* make that deadline. This is an unforgiving business, and either you function within the framework of allotted time segments or you don't function at all. Remember the significance of both contractual agreements and deadlines. The former may be invalid if the latter are not observed. Make sure that you get the ad or commercial to the proper person at the agreed time in a form usable to the medium.

Direct Contact: Client or Boss and Newsperson

Public relations people usually have to prepare top management for an interview situation with the media. It may be one-on-one in the office of the

▼ **PR people must prepare management and other corporate spokespeople for their contacts with news media and with the public.**

executive, or it may be a press conference on familiar or unfamiliar ground with many reporters. On occasion there may be a series of interviews on what is termed a "media tour," where the executive spokesperson is taken to different media that have accepted "bookings" (that is, made arrangements) for the executive to talk with editors, specialized reporters or representatives of special-interest publications. The tour may also include visits with news departments of broadcast stations and perhaps appearances on talk shows. On the latter, the executive may appear alone or as part of a panel or as the guest of an on-air personality. In any event, the success of the interview depends less on the interviewee's personality (although that is certainly important) than it does on his or her preparation for the interview situation.

Some problems occur when the executive being interviewed has not done the necessary homework and is not fully prepared for questions. The interviewee must not only be consistently ready with a brief, concise, clear and honest response, he or she must also be aware of the interviewer's style and personal background. One exasperated PR executive said it was a problem to get his company's spokesperson to remember even an interviewer's name, much less his or her background and style. As a consequence, this PR person insists on a role-playing exercise for the executive before any scheduled appearance. The executive is not pleased with the PR person's aggressive interviewing, but does prefer preparing in this manner to "reading all that dry stuff." Even if an executive is willing to prepare, however, it helps to have a run-through, with someone playing the devil's advocate and asking potential embarrassing questions. It is also important to have the executive listen carefully to the questions asked—a skill that can be learned in rehearsal.

In planning for an appearance, the executive and the PR director should develop some quotable material—ideally something carefully researched to appear fresh and newsworthy. Remember, the reporter is looking for a story, and it is wise to be able to offer one. If the reporter gets into a sensitive area, it is a mistake to mislead or skirt the truth, since most good reporters can spot such devices quickly and then they move in for the kill. Rarely should one try to go "off the record" (although this is possible in certain circumstances with print media). It is usually better to say something, rather than "No comment." It is also a good idea to ensure that the reporter has followup access to the executive in case he or she needs to clarify something (see Example 12.15).

The best way to get an accurate representation in the news media is to give a good performance. Does that mean a mistake-free performance? No, but it means correcting any mistakes immediately, says former ABC affiliate broadcaster Dan Ammerman, who now trains executives to appear on television. Ammerman points out both the importance of television as a medium and the significance of getting your message straight by relating the story of Gerald Ford's slip during his televised debate with Jimmy Carter in the 1976 presidential campaign.

Ammerman claims that Ford lost the presidency of the United States by failing to correct his mistake *immediately*. During the debate Ford declared that Eastern Europe was not under Soviet domination, and despite being given three chances to correct his mistake, he did not. Ammerman says Ford could have said, "I'm sorry, I didn't phrase that correctly, what I meant to say was" and then say what he meant. Had he done so, according to Ammerman, the slip would not have made headlines the next day. Furthermore, Ammerman quotes Ford's campaign strategists as determining that they had to convert 174,000 voters each day from the day their candidate was nominated to the day of the election. This would have assured Ford a slim victory. For two weeks following the crucial debate, however, no voters were converted. A Gallup poll taken after the election led George Gallup to state that "to the best of my ability to judge," President Ford lost to Jimmy Carter on that one misstatement in their debate. If the strategists had been able to acquire 174,000 voters per day for the fourteen days between the debate and the election, Ford would have beaten Carter.[34]

George Bush's PR people helped him limit the damage he inflicted on himself in a similar gaffe during a campaign speech on September 7, 1988, when he startled his audience by recalling Pearl Harbor: "September 7, 1941, forty-seven years ago today—I wonder how many people remember . . ." Aides quickly slipped their man a note of warning, and later in the same speech Bush was able to offer a correction that made the error appear to be merely a slip of the tongue: "Did I say *September* 7? Of course it was *December* 7 . . ." While media accounts of the speech still noted the mistake, they also duly reported that the then Vice President had made the correction himself soon afterward.

The role of the PR person in the interview is that of preparer, facilitator and clarifier. The public relations person who tries to inject him or herself into the process during the actual interview is asking for a hostile reaction. The role of clarifier includes interpreting facts and technical language, offering background information, reminding the interviewee of questions that might have been overlooked and perhaps extending the interview if necessary.

Phillips Petroleum printed "golden rules" for handling newspeople on 3 × 2 plastic cards and gave them to executives who took the company's media training class. The flip side of the card lists the company's public relations contacts with home and office numbers. Among the seven rules was the admonition to *"be brief and to the point*. Be pleasant even when the reporter is hostile. Answer the question, then shut up. Dead air isn't your problem. Correct misstatements." Another rule states, *"Never answer hypothetical questions*. These get you into trouble with speculation." And still another good piece of advice: *"Never use expert talk*. Sharks are sharks, not marine life."[35]

EXAMPLE 12.15

Conducting Press Interviews

The element of control that is present with written communications is far less so in an interview situation. As a consequence, the danger of looking bad in print is far greater when news is provided through this method. Certain ground rules, however, can make the interview more manageable and less burdensome to the person being interviewed. Following are guidelines for public relations people and executives to follow in conducting press interviews.

RULES FOR PR PEOPLE

1. Select the place for the interview, one preferably on the home ground of the person being interviewed.

2. Be sure to allow sufficient time for the interviewer to complete an assignment.

3. Know the topic of discussion, and have supporting material at hand.

4. School the person interviewed beforehand as to what questions to expect. Be prepared to handle touchy questions.

5. Know your reporter's habits, etc., and give the person being interviewed a verbal sketch. At the same time, make sure the reporter is completely aware of the person being interviewed—background, hobbies, and so on. These things can help establish rapport in preliminary conversation.

6. Set ground rules for the interview, and make sure both parties understand them.

7. Avoid off-the-record remarks. If it's off the record, keep it that way. Exceptions might occur if the reporter is known and trusted.

8. Help the reporter to wind up the story in one day.

9. Make sure the reporter gets the story sought. In agreeing to do the interview, you have said in essence that you will give the reporter the story.

10. Stay in the background, and do not try to answer questions. If the question is one that requires an answer contrary to company policy and the person being interviewed starts to answer, remind him or her it is not policy to disclose that information. Or if the interviewee wants to hedge on a question that is perfectly all right to answer, say it is OK to answer.

11. Offer to answer further questions later.

12. Do *not* ask the reporter when the story will run or how big it will be.

RULES FOR EXECUTIVES BEING INTERVIEWED

1. Know the topic you are to discuss.

2. Anticipate touchy questions.

3. Be completely honest.

4. Answer questions directly. If you cannot answer the question, say you cannot.

5. If you don't know an answer, say so and offer to get one. Follow up on this offer.

6. Keep the meeting as cordial as possible even in the face of bantering and pushing.

7. Avoid off-the-record remarks unless you know and trust the reporter. Explain that the information is not for public disclosure and politely decline an answer.

8. Be sure to answer questions that are matters of public record or not against company policy.

9. Use the personality that helped get you into a management position, and look professional.

10. Offer help later if the reporter needs it.

To these rules, Jim Blackmore and Alex Burton add, "Never say 'never' such as 'that never happened here before'"; and they advise tape-recording the interview yourself. They also advise correcting an inaccuracy or misrepresentation immediately.

You can hire a professional coach from a good firm like Audio-TV Features or the Executive Television Workshop to help prepare the executive to be interviewed. Some agencies like Burson-Marsteller and Hill & Knowlton also prepare their clients for these experiences and others, such as appearing as an expert witness or giving government testimony. People who are going to give depositions or appear on the witness stand can benefit a great deal from role-playing sessions in which they are questioned aggressively and challenged, because that's what's going to happen to them.

Some top executives haven't been seriously challenged face to face, much less insulted, in years. They may need some training in proper reactions and responses under verbal fire. They also may need to be reminded of the different types of audiences who will respond to their remarks. These audiences include news media, employees, other industry or association people, consumers and various others. They need to think through responses to see how each sensitive public is likely to react.

John Meek, president of Hartz/Meek International, a public relations and telecommunications firm in Washington, D.C., makes the following suggestions:

1. Go to the location prior to the presentation, if possible, and get an idea about the physical setting.

2. Go early to get a seat so you can hear and see before you appear or before your client or boss appears. Get a seat for the person who will be interviewed.

3. If prepared testimony is to be given and if it is longer than two pages, attach a summary statement to the front.

4. Bring extra copies of the testimony and of your news release about it for the media's table at the hearing.

5. Know how to address the person in charge.

6. Dress conservatively and in your best outfit.

7. Be courteous and respectful, but stand your ground.

8. Thank the person presiding for giving you an opportunity to speak when you begin and when you finish.

9. Have an adequate supply of business cards to give reporters.

10. Plan your schedule so you will have time to meet with reporters afterward.[36]

When the client or the boss comes into direct contact with the news media, both sides probably have some misperceptions of the other. But the greatest misperceptions probably are held by the client/boss. Most have had limited contact with newspeople, and some have had bad experiences. Your job is to see that all encounters are productive, if not altogether positive, experiences.

Again, two steps you can take will help you accomplish this. First, prepare your client or boss for the experience by going over the issues that are likely to come up, whether or not these are the main topics to be discussed. Be sure she or he understands how responses are likely to be interpreted and reported. Second, make sure you are there to see what happens and to follow up with information, interpretation, pictures or whatever else is needed.

News Conferences and Results   In general, don't call a news conference if you can avoid it, and never call one unless you are sure that what is to be said is newsworthy. But especially if there is a controversy, call a news conference in such a way that the organization doesn't appear to be hiding something. Call a news conference if you have a celebrity whose time is severely limited, and you believe many newspeople would want to meet her or him. If you can, separate print and broadcast media by holding two news conferences; however, you may not be able to. If you do separate news conferences, be sure that deadlines do not give one medium an unfair advantage. Some general rules to follow are these:

1. Choose a convenient (to the news media) location with adequate facilities. Try to choose a site that makes sense for the story—unless it's miles away from all central facilities.

2. Choose the right day and time, if you have a choice. Monday is good for coverage, and in some metropolitan locations Sunday is acceptable because news crews are working.

3. Plan to have the news conference covered for your own organization (videotape, audio—in addition and separate from the sound-on tape—and still photography). You need to be sure what was said, and you may be able to use some of the material later in your own followup story.

4. Take all of the background information on the person and the organization that you will need. Have someone assigned to get the names of reporters and the media they represent, with phone numbers for call-backs.

5. To news media who didn't make it, offer a story and pictures (print and still, sound bites and videotape release when possible). Give them the same background material you prepared for those who attended. You should have media kits for all news conferences.

6. Rehearse your spokesperson and be as aggressive in your drill as you can possibly be. Play devil's advocate.

7. Evaluate with your spokesperson the results right after the conference and again when the stories are in. Show him or her how the news media used what was said.

Media Tours: Print and Broadcast Although you can hire a PR news service or an agency to arrange a tour, you must be aware that, while your client or boss is providing information, he or she is also creating an image. A national business publication described an interviewee—an author on a book promotion tour—as looking like a "wrung-out politician." A newspaper columnist told how another interviewee asked him what day it was; this person, a film star riding the circuit to promote a new movie, did not know what city he was in either. The agenda is rigorous: one-night stands in major market cities talking with entertainment columnists, appearing on TV talk shows, opening new buildings and being the guest celebrity for special events in places like shopping malls. The name of the game is *exposure*. Winning national exposure is a bone-wearying job. It requires a lot of calls and a lot of small efforts to create some momentum toward major recognition.

Politicians use the personal appearance as a media event to help create exposure. Candidates develop a message (called The Speech by media who travel with them) and present it as often as a dozen times in one day to different audiences. The most skillful emphasize some particular portion of it for a particular audience. The result of this single-message presentation is that the news media stop reporting on the speech and begin to report instead on audience reaction to it or on trivia of the campaign. One gubernatorial candidate, capitalizing on the scarcity of things to report once his campaign was underway, had media kits constantly updated with "The Campaign to Date," his own version of the varying emphasis he gave his speech in different towns or to particular audiences. A political columnist who was a member of the opposing political party admiringly called the update "useful to us and damn smart politics." What is being sold in tours by personalities is the image of the individual.

The satellite media tour is easier on the individual involved because the person can stay in one location and reach stations all over the nation.

Here are some rules for on-the-road media tours to get the best results:

1. Become thoroughly familiar with the people you will meet on the schedule. Know their medium. Be familiar with their work.

2. Be sure all physical arrangements are firm, and confirm these by letter. Call your office or agency daily to get changes and messages.

3. Take plenty of money and letters of credit. You may have to charter a plane to keep on schedule.

4. Be sure your person keeps on schedule and fulfills all commitments. Take advantage of any "down" time to make phone calls to let people know you are in town. Watch the person's health and personal appearance. Anyone going through this ordeal needs help.

5. Keep up with props, supplies of media kits, luggage and so forth.

6. Make notes at stops of what followup is needed. If some of it can be done by the office, pass along instructions in your twice-daily calls to staff.

7. Keep clippings if you are in town long enough to get them. In any case, take notes of who attended all sessions.

8. Be responsive and sensitive to both sides. Keep your client or boss from getting depressed or burned out.

More Informal Contact   Trade shows are in the category of special events, as are most PR parties. The problems that can arise from these are due to the less controlled circumstances involved and the consequently increased opportunities for Murphy's Law—what can go wrong will go wrong—to operate. At trade shows, you must be alert to the presence of media people from specialized publications. Many feel that they deserve special attention, and they should get it. They shouldn't be ignored.

Parties come in all sizes, but Suzanne Hemming might hold a record for being in charge of the largest street party of all, the Fourth of July celebration in New York City that marked the unveiling of the restored Statue of Liberty. Hemming was hired by the City of New York, given 45 staff members and hundreds of volunteers to oversee 800 food and souvenir vendors and 2,500 performers. The three-day street festival started July 4, 1986, and featured continuous ethnic entertainment every twelve minutes on seven different stages. She had to coordinate the city's planning and assist with the four-day event being planned by the Statue of Liberty/Ellis Island Foundation, which began July 3 when the refurbished statue's torch was relit by President Ronald Reagan. Hemming had countless details to attend to personally. And she had to do a tremendous amount of troubleshooting, since many well-known celebrities were involved in the events.[37]

Although you might not get involved in something quite as large as a party with 5 million guests, it's fairly easy to get involved in a party for 500. It has the same sorts of problems, on a smaller scale. The challenge begins with trying to attract attendance. One type of PR writing you may not expect to practice is creating invitations. You may try a number of ploys: series invitations (teasers), singing telegrams and some just fun and attention-getting invitations.

Contact from the Media's Point of View   Why does Hugh Sidey tell young reporters to go directly to the source? When the contributing editor to *Time* and author of its weekly column, "The Presidency," wanted to get some answers on the Iran-Contra controversy, he called Ronald Reagan directly. (The other side of that is that Reagan knew him and would talk to him.) But reporters might avoid public affairs or public information people, even though such people know media news values. The reason that they do appears in some recent research.[38] As advocates for their agencies, public information officers (PIOs) are often compromised by conflicting roles. The findings of one particular study of government information people showed considerably less use of PR-generated materials (48 percent) than did other studies that included all PR sources. It also showed less use of business sources.

Apparently some PIOs send copy that they know won't be used. This stimulates distrust of the source by news media. However, Hodding Carter, a former newspaper reporter, editor and PIO, says journalists often return to sources they don't trust because they never know when the source might give them something important. As a result, reporters often get used as John McWenthy, the ABC national security correspondent, said he was used. McWenthy reported three days before the retaliatory raid on Libya that U.S. military action was not impossible but was unlikely. He says he was "passed half a loaf"—that is, a partial truth—which is an unethical act.[39]

Journalists are wary of all sources, and they are especially suspicious of advocates. But they don't reject PR-generated materials out of hand. The following checklist comes from the assistant editor of *Progressive Grocer* magazine, who probably has to suffer more bad copy than do most newspaper editors.[40]

As an editor at a trade magazine, my job is to open and read approximately 1,000 press releases a month, route them to the appropriate editor, and write the new products column. Please help me in my job (and enjoy more success in yours) by considering the following:

▼ **Update your mailing list.** Our address changed several years ago, yet we still get mail addressed to our old office. We can't use your news in a timely manner if we don't get it until it's been forwarded all over the city. Check your directory each year, or better yet, call to double-check the address. And the same goes for our staff members. Editors who left 10 years ago are still getting mail.

▼ **Proof your copy** before it goes out. Don't depend on the typist. We've received releases from *Fortune 500* companies—as well as from small businesses—with the company's name spelled wrong. How can we rely on such a release? If the name is wrong, what else might be?

▼ **Include the name and address of the client you're representing,** if you work for a public relations firm. Our new products column includes the address of the manufacturer.

If my deadline is tight and I can't easily call you, I won't use the item.

▼ **Date your release.** For your records and mine, I prefer that directly under "for immediate release" or your release date, you type the date it was mailed. That way you'll know when you sent it, and I'll know whether it's up-to-date. We're a monthly publication and work two months in advance; a winter promotion received in early January isn't relevant.

▼ **Alert your switchboard** where calls from editors go. The way they answer the phones and to whom they send our calls is important for our relations, too.

▼ **Please don't call to see if I've received your release.** If you've updated your list, I've received it. If I have any questions or need more information, I'll call you. And I don't know whether I'm using it or not—don't pressure me. But if you absolutely have to call, call *me*, not the publisher. He has seriously considered making a recording for you—and it's not a very polite one.

▼ **Send one and only one release**—not the same release to the entire masthead. That's a time-waster for both of us. I promise you, I will make sure it gets passed to the right editor. Generally, it's best to send the release to the managing editor, or call to see who edits the section the release would most likely go into.

▼ **Know the publication.** It's insulting to us when you ask what the magazine is about, or who reads it. Read some copies before you send the release to see whether the magazine uses the type of material you are planning to send. When I see a story targeted towards our industry (supermarkets, food), it's apt to catch my eye. And if you're confident our readers can benefit from your story, sell me through a cover letter.

▼ **Please don't ask the editor to send you a tearsheet.** We truly don't have the time. Take a subscription, go to the library, or just buy the magazine if you don't have a clipping service. Or, if you must, call the editorial department—not the publisher—to see if it was published in the latest issue.

▼ PR people and their bosses need to understand the news media's perspective.

▼ **Don't promise you'll advertise** if I give you editorial space. Most publications separate their editorial staffs from their advertising staffs and will take offense at such a suggestion.

▼ **Follow up after an article is written.** Send me a thank-you note sometimes. I'm only human, and it's nice to hear when you liked the write-up.

In addition to the relationships of PR people with media representatives, there is the relationship between the client or boss and the news media. This is a factor in the PR person's relationship, too. Most executives prefer a reactive rather than a proactive stance in dealing with news media. They feel this way because of a lack of trust, some of which may be justified. Many executives fear being misquoted, and they are likely to be,[41] which is why you need to tape-record their interviews and call for a correction when an error is serious. They also feel that the news representatives don't understand their business, and they question in general the objectivity of the news media.

But executives also feel that they don't know as much as they need to about the way the news media work, are not very accessible, don't communicate well and aren't open.[42] If that is the case, a lot of potential business exists for companies that teach executives to deal with the news media. They might like to know that the publisher and CEO of the *Los Angeles Times* says:

> The trend with major companies is greater candor, openness and cooperation with media. This new generation of corporate officers has more awareness of public relations and greater skill in working with the media. And, most important, there is a growing acceptance on their part that most companies receive the press they deserve—that there is a direct relationship between good public policy and a good public image.

Some newspapers do their PR best to be helpful.

▼ GOOFS AND GLITCHES

Today world markets are the only markets, and translating materials is therefore a commonplace task. Perhaps in the future PR offices will consider as standard equipment the hand-held computer that translates words and phrases into any of thirteen languages, with the help of the appropriate tape cassette. Actually, few agencies handle their own translations, with or without language computer assistance. The problem involves the nuances of a language.

For example, a PR and advertising agency director in Mexico City tells about the agency's U.S.-based affiliate, which insisted on sending them billboards ready to put up for a client, Parker Pen. The Mexico City agency had wanted to handle the art and translations. When a billboard of twenty-four sheets arrived, a secretary in the office opened one package of poster duplicates of the billboards, gasped and began laughing. The Spanish translation had not taken into consideration local usage—and it was advertising that its new product would help prevent unwanted pregnancies! The Mexico agency's experience is not unique. Otis Engineering Company displayed a poster at a Moscow trade show saying that its oil well completion equipment was effective in improving one's sex life. Ads for "rendezvous lounges" on an airline's flight in Brazil startled and offended patrons. "Rendezvous" in Portuguese translates as a place to have sex. In Southeast Asia, a promise by Pepsodent to brighten teeth was not impressive. Chewing betel nuts is common, as are the discolored teeth that the practice causes.

Countless such goofs have occurred. When Dr Pepper, the soft drink manufacturer, designed its logo for the Middle East, where its product was to be bottled for the first time, it could have used some expert help. In July 1978 the Dallas-based beverage company took a copy of its new logo for the Middle East production to the *Dallas Morning News*, where Aziz Shihab, chief editor of the newspaper and former editor of the *Jerusalem Times*, noticed a problem. Shihab explained that Arabic has no letter *p* and that Arabs consequently often

EXAMPLE 12.16 ■

Dr Bebber—Something Lost in Translation

SOURCE: Reprinted with permission of *Dallas Morning News*.

confuse the letters *p* and *b* when reading English. The Arabic symbol that is used for *p* in translated works is the Arabic letter *b* with three dots, instead of the usual one, under it. The company was thus alerted to the problem, and the *News* shared the story with its readers (see Example 12.16), showing both the incorrect (left) logo, which spells "Dr Bebber," and the corrected (right) version.

Most international news services will do translations, but costs can be high and finding type for a foreign language's unique symbols can be difficult. When Gerber's faced that difficulty with its labels, it went to King Typographic Service, a Manhattan-based advertising typographer. According to the *Wall Street Journal*, King offers "Happy New Year" in 600 languages "all the way from Abenaqui to Zulu with such exotic stops in between as Ewe, Guipzcoan, Gyengyen, Kanarese, Lur, Ma, Tamul, Tsimihety, Wa, Xhosa and Yahgan."[43]

Words, emblems and gestures all have cultural connotations. It pays to be aware of meanings, especially taboos. Paul Ekman, Wallace Friesen and John Bear have developed a technique for identifying cultural emblems and their significance to certain groups (see Example 12.17). U.S. industry and

even international associations must be alert to such problems now that they are catching up with practices already firmly established in Europe. A resort in the Bahamas, owned and operated by Americans, casually keeps brochures available in other languages.

The problem with PR mistakes is that the whole world is likely to know about them, often because the news media tell. The *Wall Street Journal* seems to take special delight in this. The July 10, 1987, "Washington Wire" carried a note about two releases sent in the *same* envelope. Both were from Congressman Doug Barnard, Jr. (D–Georgia). One attacked the House budget resolution for not cutting enough spending, but the other carried a headline, "Barnard's Favored Projects Pass in Energy/Water Appropriations Bill."[44]

Another goof the *Journal* caught was by *Time*'s Home Box Office. HBO sent a flier for cable companies to use in their March bills. Included was a photo of Sam Kinison, described as a "hot comic who's a real scream," but who is, perhaps, best known for NBC's censoring his act on "Saturday Night Live." In the photo Kinison is wearing a black T-shirt decorated with various forms of an obscene

EXAMPLE 12.17

The International Language of Gestures

On his first trip to Naples, a well-meaning American tourist thanks his waiter for a good meal well-served by making the "A-Okay" gesture with his thumb and forefinger. The waiter pales and heads for the manager. They seriously discuss calling the police and having the hapless tourist arrested for obscene and offensive public behavior.

What happened?

Most travelers wouldn't think of leaving home without a phrase book of some kind, enough of a guide to help them say and understand "Ja," "Nein," "Grazie" and "Où se trouvent les toilettes?" And yet, while most people are aware that gestures are the most common form of cross-cultural communication, they don't realize that the language of gestures can be just as different, just as regional and just as likely to cause misunderstanding as the spoken word.

Consider our puzzled tourist. The thumb-and-forefinger-in-a-circle gesture, a friendly one in America, has an insulting meaning in France and Belgium: "You're worth zero." In parts of Southern Italy it means "asshole," while in Greece and Turkey it is an insulting or vulgar sexual invitation.

There are, in fact, dozens of gestures that take on totally different meanings as you move from one country or region to another. Is "thumbs up" always a positive gesture? Absolutely not. Does nodding the head up and down always mean "Yes?" No!

To make matters even more confusing, many hand movements have no meaning at all, in any country. If you watch television with the sound turned off, or observe a conversation at a distance, you become aware of almost constant motion, especially with the hands and arms. People wave their arms, they shrug, they waggle their fingers, they point, they scratch their chests, they pick their noses.

These various activities can be divided into three major categories: manipulators, emblems and illustrators.

In a manipulator, one part of the body, usually the hands, rubs, picks, squeezes, cleans or otherwise grooms some other part. These movements have no specific meaning. Manipulators generally increase when people become uncomfortable or occasionally when they are totally relaxed.

An emblem is a physical act that can fully take the place of words. Nodding the head up and down in many cultures is a substitute for saying, "Yes." Raising the shoulders and turning the palms upward clearly means "I don't know," or "I'm not sure."

Gestures, called illustrators, in semantics are physical acts that help explain what is being said but have no meaning on their own. Waving the arms, raising or lowering the eyebrows, snapping the fingers and pounding the table may enhance or explain the words that accompany them, but they cannot stand alone. People sometimes use illustrators as a pantomime or charade, especially when they can't think of the right words, or when it's simply easier to illustrate, as in defining "zig-zag" or explaining how to tie a shoe.

Thus the same illustrator might accompany a positive statement one moment and a negative one the next. This is not the case with emblems, which have the same precise meaning on all occasions for all members of a group, class, culture or subculture.

Emblems are used consciously. The user knows what they mean, unless, of course, he uses them inadvertently. When Nelson Rockefeller raised his middle finger to a heckler, he knew exactly what the gesture meant, and he believed that the person he was communicating with knew as well. . . .

In looking for emblems, we found that it isn't productive simply to observe people communicating with each other, because emblems are used only occasionally. And asking people to describe or identify emblems that are important in their culture is even less productive. Even when we explain the concept clearly, most people find it difficult to recognize and analyze their own communication behavior this way.

Instead, we developed a research procedure that has enabled us to identify emblems in cultures as diverse as those of urban Japanese, white, middle-class

Americans, the preliterate South Fore people of Papua, natives of New Guinea, Iranians, Israelis and the inhabitants of London, Madrid, Paris, Frankfurt and Rome. The procedure involves three steps:

▼ Give a group of people from the same cultural background a series of phrases and ask if they have a gesture or facial expression for each phrase: "What time is it?" "That's good." "Yes." And so on. We find that normally, after 10 to 15 people have provided responses, we have catalogued the great majority of the emblems of their culture.

▼ Analyze the results. If most of the people cannot supply a "performance" for a verbal message, we discard it.

▼ Study the remaining performances further to eliminate inventions and illustrators. Many people are so eager to please that they will invent a gesture on the spot. Americans asked for a gesture for "sawing wood" could certainly oblige, even if they had never considered that request before, but the arm motion they would provide would not be an emblem.

To weed out these "false emblems," we show other people from the same culture videotapes of the performances by the first group. We ask which are inventions, which are pantomimes and which are symbolic gestures that they have seen before or used themselves. We also ask the people to give us their own meanings for each performance.

The gestures remaining after this second round of interpretations are likely to be the emblems of that particular culture. Using this procedure, we have found three types of emblems:

First, popular emblems have the same or similar meanings in several cultures. The side-to-side head motion meaning "No" is a good example.

Next, unique emblems have a specific meaning in one culture but none elsewhere. Surprisingly, there seem to be no uniquely American emblems, although other countries provide many examples. For instance, the French gesture of putting one's fist around the tip of the nose and twisting it to signify "He's drunk," is not used elsewhere. The German "good luck" emblem, making two fists with the thumbs inside and pounding an imaginary table, is unique to that culture.

Finally, multi-meaning emblems have one meaning in one culture and a totally different meaning in another. The thumb inserted between the index and third fingers is an invitation to have sex in Germany, Holland and Denmark, but in Portugal and Brazil it is a wish for good luck or protection.

The number of emblems in use varies considerably among cultures, from fewer than 60 in the United States to more than 250 in Israel. The difference is understandable, since Israel is composed of recent immigrants from many countries, most of which have their own large emblem vocabularies. In addition, since emblems are helpful in military operations where silence is essential, and all Israelis serve in the armed forces, military service provides both the opportunity and the need to learn new emblems.

The kinds of emblems used, as well as the number, varies considerably from culture to culture. Some are especially heavy on insults, for instance, while others have a large number of emblems for hunger or sex.

Finally, as Desmond Morris documented in his book *Gestures*, there are significant regional variations in modern cultures. The findings we describe in this article apply to people in the major urban areas of each country: London, not England as a whole; Paris, not France. Because of the pervasiveness of travel and television, however, an emblem is often known in the countryside even if it is not used there.

Source: Paul Ekman, Wallace V. Friesen and John Bear, "The International Language of Gestures," *Psychology Today* (May 1984).

verb that the *Journal* left to its readers' imaginations. (HBO's explanation was that the picture was taken from a slide, and the words just looked like stripes.)[45]

That was an accident, at least. The *Journal* also reported that Eastern Airlines was going to honor a passenger just before his two-thousandth trip. Media were called for the plaque presentation. The recipient's plane broke down just before he boarded, so his flight from Miami to New York was delayed for two hours and forty-two minutes. To prevent further delays for their honoree, Eastern towed away the broken plane and substituted one from a nearby gate. That plane was to leave for San Juan, so its crew and passengers were delayed two hours and fifty-one minutes, They were told *their* plane had mechanical difficulties.[46]

As you can see, goofs and glitches have a way of creating problems, some of them serious. Sometimes you only find out about them when you get an early morning phone call, "Have you seen the morning paper?" or "Do you have the morning news on (radio or TV)?"

▼ TALKING BACK AND CORRECTING

The PR edict for years was "suffer in silence" when the news media made a mistake in their coverage. There was reason for such a decision: "You can't fight with a pen people who buy ink by the barrel." There were also adages such as "Why spit in the wind?" and "I was taught not to kick jackasses."

Today, for most PR people, the idea of talking back is still limited to demanding and getting their side of the story presented. Some, however, launch a campaign.

Ronald Rhody of Bank of America offers several observations and postulates for responding to media, which he calls the Ben Franklin approach to the problem because they are based on this Franklin quote: "A little neglect may breed mischief: for want of a shoe the horse was lost; for want of a horse the rider was lost; for want of a rider the battle was lost; for want of a battle the kingdom was lost."[47] The following are Rhody's principal postulates of the Ben Franklin approach:

1. No contest was ever won from the sidelines. Be players, not spectators.

2. The public has a right to accurate and balanced information about your operations.

3. The public's right to know is as much your responsibility as it is the responsibility of government or the media.

4. Fear of controversy or criticism is a luxury no institution in today's society can afford. Silence never swayed any masses, and timidity never won any ball games.

5. Take the initiative in all circumstances, whether the news is good or bad.[48]

Rhody thus disputes the conventional wisdom that is employed when dealing with this constituency (namely, remember that the news media represent a public). The only caution he considers appropriate in taking on the news media is the same one you would exercise with any other public: making sure you have documentable facts on your side.

Will talking back make the problem you are responding to go away? Thomas Burke, vice-president of Superior Oil Company, doesn't think so. He says the following media circumstances "keep the fires hot": short deadlines; limitations on newspaper space and TV time; inexperienced reporters; news by nonattribution; absentee editing; the mentality of prize journalism; competitive juices. He also cites some suggestions gained from his own "media massacres." First, if you are controlling the release of significant and/or sensitive news, plan for things to go wrong. Second, if you get pasted, stay cool. Third, remember, it's your bosses who panic. Fourth, do not automatically assume that you should never take on the media, no matter what. Fifth, be ready for the risk. Sixth, make your tactics fit the crime and the media's response to your objections. Burke advises: "We're no longer just a conduit for information. We're watchdogs over inaccuracy and antagonism."[49]

Most PR people now endorse the notion that you can get substantial errors corrected—preferably editorially, and if not, by advertising. If redress seems necessary, file a lawsuit.

▼ SUMMARY

Advertising often looks like news, features, editorials or (on television) even programming. While some public relations people refer to public service announcements (print or broadcast) as "publicity," these are in fact advertising on time or space donated by the medium. Few members of the media public think of PSAs as anything but advertising, because they look like ads.

Whether or not space or time is paid for, the most important aspect of advertising is its effectiveness. You have to be clear about what you want an ad to do, and its purpose affects your style—whether you will use humor, make product comparisons or risk negative advertising.

One of the most memorable parts of an ad is the logo, which is also the organization's signature. These may change over time as design trends change, but the identification of the logo and its association with the organization are essential.

The mark of the organization should be in character with the organization, as should its publications and audiovisual productions. All of these generate publicity for the organization.

While many organizations do everything in-house, suppliers are often used for audiovisual components, and sometimes for media distribution and monitoring, since such technology is expensive.

Among the publicity and promotion tools generated in the office are brochures and magazines; some organizations also do their quarterly and annual reports in-house. Speeches are almost always written in-house, and although these are classified as "events," the speeches themselves may find broadened distribution by being packaged as printed pieces.

Speeches, scripted meetings and special events need to be carefully planned to ensure that they succeed with their primary audiences, as well as to guarantee their value in generating positive publicity. Events are often videotaped and circulated to reach larger audiences, and institutional videotapes and films may be made for their publicity, informational and instructional value.

While publicity is often directed toward special publics through controlled media, it may also be generated through the release of news to the mass media in both print and broadcast formats. Technology enables public relations departments to connect directly with mass media electronically, so it's important for materials prepared for the mass media to be in the proper style and format for immediate, direct use by the media. Organizations use both print and video news releases to distribute their stories through the mass media.

Often instead of using the material generated by the public relations department, the medium will cover promotions and special events. In these situations, the PR person needs to make sure that the participants have complete cooperation *and* that the news media get a positive story to tell about the organization. Celebrities are often involved in events and promotions, and their experiences are often reflected in media coverage. Making arrangements for celebrities and handling their experience with the media (as well as with the event or promotion) must be carefully planned to ensure a positive outcome.

A PR person needs to establish and maintain good relations not only with celebrities and media representatives but also with production people, other PR people and freelance writers who sometimes supply material to trade and mass media. Good relations with suppliers are critical to a smoothly functioning public relations operation. To protect these relationships, it's wise to keep deadlines and honor contracts.

Although the public relations person often has direct contact with media representatives, the officers of the organization may have occasion for such an experience, and they need to be prepared for it. Some of the preparation should be done in-house, but it may be necessary to obtain special media training to keep organization spokespeople out of trouble.

Even with the best preparation, some goofs and glitches will occur. In fact, there's more of a chance for this now with so much international exposure (some intentional and some unintentional) of an organization's materials. When mistakes are made, either by the organization or by the media, it's important to make corrections quickly, setting the record straight so the mistakes are not perpetuated.

▼ NOTES

[1] Jennifer Bingham Hull, "If the Doc's on TV, Maybe It's Because He Takes the PR Rx," *Wall Street Journal* (August 23, 1983), pp. 1, 16.

[2] "Getting PSAs Aired Requires Knowing Broadcasters' Needs; Survey Tells What Stations Want," *pr reporter* (May 13, 1985).

[3] Victor V. Cordell and George M. Zinkhan, "Dimensional Relationships of Memory: Implications for Print Advertisers," *Journalism Quarterly*, 66(4) (Winter 1989), pp. 954–59.

[4] Bob T. W. Wu, Kenneth E. Crocker and Martha Rogers, "Humor and Comparatives in Ads for High- and Low-Involvement Products," *Journalism Quarterly*, 66(3) (August 1989), pp. 653–61, 780.

[5] Karen S. Johnson-Cartee and Gary Copeland, "Southern Voters' Reaction to Negative Political Ads in 1986 Election," *Journalism Quarterly*, 66(4) (Winter 1989), pp. 888–93, 986.

[6] Frank Thayer, "Measuring Recognition and Attraction in Corporate, Advertising Trademarks," *Journalism Quarterly*, 65(2) (Summer 1985), pp. 439–42.

[7] For production details, such as copyfitting and scaling photographs to fit the designated space, see Doug Newsom and Bob Carrell, *Public Relations Writing: Form and Style*, 3rd ed. (Belmont, Calif.: Wadsworth, 1990).

[8] For a full discussion of this topic, see Newsom and Carrell, *Public Relations Writing*, pp. 320–55.

[9] David Mills, "Publications at No Charge Are Subtle Ads," *Wall Street Journal* (August 5, 1983), p. 19. See also Rodney Ho, "Environmental Magazines Defy Slump," *Wall Street Journal* (September 10, 1991), p. B1.

[10] William Ruder and David Finn, *How to Make Your Annual Report Pay for Itself*, second booklet in *Management Methods*, a series on public relations by members of Ruder and Finn, Inc.

[11] N. R. Kleinfield, "An Annual Report Is No Comic Novel, but It Can Be Fun," *Wall Street Journal* (April 15, 1977), pp. 1, 29.

[12] "Formal Guidelines for Reviewing Information Films or Videotapes," *pr reporter* (February 23, 1982), p. 4. For information on writing scripts and speeches, see Newsom and Carrell, *Public Relations Writing*, pp. 336–79.

[13] Michele Horaney, "The Russian President Is Coming . . . No He's Not!" *Public Relations Journal* (August 1990), p. 11.

[14] Details by Jim Haynes on planning an event appear in the *Instructor's Guide* to this text.

[15] "Murphy's Law at Meetings Comes True, Has This Ever Happened to You?" *pr reporter*, 27(10) (March 5, 1984), p. 2.

[16] "Formal Guidelines for Reviewing Information Films or Videotapes," *pr reporter* (February 23, 1982), p. 4.

[17] Meg Cox, "L:iterary World Is Debating How Much of a Huckster a Book Writer Should Be," *Wall Street Journal* (August 2, 1990), pp. B1, B4.

[18] See Hirotaka Takenchi and Allan H. Schmidt, "New Promise of Computer Graphics," *Harvard Business Review*, 58(1) (January/February 1980), pp. 122–31.

[19] For the ten pitfalls to avoid in supplying graphics, especially for newspaper use, see James W. Tankard, Jr., "Quantitative Graphics in Newspapers," *Journalism Quarterly*, 64(2&3) (Summer and Autumn 1987), pp. 406–15.

[20] Macon L. Weaver, quoted in Michael Leahy, "Thanks to TV . . . He'll Always Be Remembered for Standing in the Schoolhouse Door," *TV Guide* (April 4, 1987).

[21] Clare Ansberry, "Do People Really Buy Film Based on Entries in a Great Blimp Race?" *Wall Street Journal* (July 8, 1986), p. 33.

[22] Donna M. Lynn, "If the Shoe Fits: The Success of Sports Marketing Programs Seems to Depend on Matching the Right Sports to the Right Mix of Public Relations Objectives," *Public Relations Journal*, 43(2) (February 1987), pp. 16–20, 43.

[23] "Business Travel," *USA Today* (April 20, 1987), p. 6B.

[24]Jennifer Bingham Hull, "If the Doc's on TV, Maybe It's Because He Takes the PR Rx," *Wall Street Journal* (August 23, 1983), pp. 1, 16.

[25]Roger Simon, "TV's Sunday Interview Shows—They're Tougher Now, but Are They Better?" *TV Guide* (March 14, 1987), pp. 4–5.

[26]Marguerite Michaels, "How Hollywood Harvests the New Crop of Stars," *Parade* (July 23, 1978), pp. 4–5.

[27]For more information, see Joan Kron, "Is Madonna in L.A.? Is Sean Penn in N.Y.? Does Anyone Care?" *Wall Street Journal* (April 8, 1986), p. 1.

[28]Frederick Rise, "Last Few Skywriters Strut the Write Stuff Doing Ads on the Fly," *Wall Street Journal* (May 28, 1987), p. 1.

[29]Some negative financial aspects of promotions are detailed in two articles: John Philip Jones, "The Double Jeopardy of Sales Promotions," *Harvard Business Review* (September–October 1990), pp. 145–52; Magid M. Abraham and Leonard M. Lodish, "Getting the Most Out of Advertising and Promotion," *Harvard Business Review* (May–June 1990), pp. 50–60. The latter carries this observation: "Managers must cut back on unproductive promotions in favor of hard-to-imitate promotion events that directly contribute to incremental profitability. And they must use the new data to shape distinctive promotional efforts for specific local markets and key accounts." (p. 50)

[30]Associated Press, "Flyover Foe Gives Ride a Try and Nearly Dies," *Fort Worth Star-Telegram* (June 4, 1990), sec. 1, p. 3.

[31]Charles Stevens, "Cherry Picker Got Him to the Roof but Not onto Fortune's New Cover," *Wall Street Journal* (September 15, 1981), sec. 2, p. 1.

[32]Andrew Patner, "Papers Take Alternative Path to Success," *Wall Street Journal* (June 19, 1990), p. 31.

[33]Many U.S. publics do not recognize English as their language of choice, and the variety of languages in the United States alone can present a challenge. *PR News* reports that some 100 languages are spoken daily in the southern part of California alone. *PR News*, 66(46) (November 26, 1990), p. 3.

[34]Dan Ammerman, speech to the Texas Public Relations Association, Fort Worth, Texas, February 25, 1978.

[35]*pr reporter* (September 20, 1982), p. 3.

[36]John Martin Meek, "How to Prepare Your Client for Government Testimony," *Public Relations Journal* (November 1985), pp. 35–37.

[37]Meg Cox, "Planning a July 4 Party for Five Million? Ms. Hemming Is, and It's Not an Easy Task," *Wall Street Journal* (June 19, 1986), p. 29.

[38]Judy VanSlyke Turk, "Information Subsidies and Media Content: A Study of Public Relations Influence on the News," *Journalism Monograph*, 100 (December 1986), pp. 26–27.

[39]John Weisman, "Betrayal and Trust: The Tricky Art of Finding—and Keeping—Good TV News Sources," *TV Guide* (March 7, 1987), pp. 2–3.

[40]Marcia S. Clark, "Checklist: Getting Your News Releases Through," *Public Relations Journal* (November 1986), p. 57.

[41]Adrienne Lehrer, "Between Quotation Marks," *Journalism Quarterly*, 66(4) (Winter 1989), pp. 902–6.

[42]Judith A. Mapes, "Top Management and the Press—The Uneasy Relationship Revisited," *Corporate Issues Monitor*, 11(1) (1987), pp. 1, 3.

[43]"Company Sets Type in Almost Any Lingo," *Wall Street Journal* (January 3, 1973), p. 1.

[44]Rich Jaroslovsky, "Washington Wire," *Wall Street Journal* (July 10, 1987), p. 1.

[45]Cynthia Crossen, Andrea Rothman and John Bussey, "Shop Talk: If You Look Closely," *Wall Street Journal* (March 27, 1987), p. 19.

[46]Johnathan Dahn, "A Delayed Honor," *Wall Street Journal* (October 29, 1987), p. 29.

[47]Ronald E. Rhody, "The Conventional Wisdom Is Wrong," *Public Relations Journal* (February 1983), pp. 18–31.

[48]Ibid., p. 19.

[49]Thomas E. Burke, "Advice for PR Folks Facing Reporters: Expect Foul-ups, and Don't Be Afraid to Fight Back," *ASNE Bulletin* (September 1984), pp. 30–31.

Selected readings, activities and assignments appropriate to this chapter can be found in the *Instructor's Guide*.

CAMPAIGNS

Experience keeps a dear school, but fools will learn in no other, and scarce is that; for it is true, we may give advice, but we cannot give conduct.

Benjamin Franklin, *Sayings of Poor Richard*

Public Relations must move forward from the realm of constructing corporate and institutional images to promoting debate and education of the great issues of our time.

Frank Vogel, Director of Information and External Relations, World Bank

The interactions of organizations with their publics provide the setting for specific efforts such as public relations campaigns; such interactions also form the background against which all case studies must be examined. The study of campaigns and cases is more than a shared learning experience or the basis for developing a public relations repertoire; it is ongoing research into what gives an organization viability and credibility in a fluid socioeconomic and political environment. In this chapter we look at the planning, implementation and evaluation of campaigns. In Chapter 14, we look at case studies for analysis and discussion.

▼ TYPES OF CAMPAIGNS

Campaigns are coordinated, purposeful, extended efforts designed to achieve a specific goal or a set of interrelated goals that will move the organization toward a longer-range objective expressed as its mission statement (see Example 13.1).

Campaigns are designed and developed to address an issue, to solve a problem or to correct or improve a situation. They accomplish these purposes by changing a behavior; by modifying a law or opinion; or by retaining a desirable behavior, law or opinion that is challenged.

A campaign may be constructed around a *positioning statement*—an objective operating statement for the organization. For example, the American Heart Association decided in the 1980s "to be known as *the* source for information about cardio-vascular disease in the U.S." This statement described the organization's central mission: to reduce death from cardiovascular disease. Communication planning is then structured to help the organization achieve its mission, in light of how the organization has positioned itself.

The term *positioning* is often used in marketing to refer to a competitive strategy—a way to identify a niche in the market for a product or service. Public relations people tend to talk about positioning in terms of the entire organization and to build a communications effort around a statement that describes the organization's positioning of itself. When the positioning is to set a new course, it calls for a campaign.

Various types of PR campaigns exist. Six are described by Patrick Jackson, senior counsel and cofounder of Jackson, Jackson and Wagner, an international firm located in New Hampshire:

> There are a number of public relations campaigns, in fact about six. First we have the skills to put on a public *awareness* campaign, to make people aware of something. School is starting again so please don't run over first graders on their way. Simple awareness.
>
> Second, we have the skills to mount public information campaigns, to offer *information along with awareness*. Totally different than a simple awareness campaign.
>
> Third, we have the skills to do a *public education* campaign, using the word education in the pedagogical way, meaning that a person has encompassed the material sufficiently, and is emotionally and attitudinally comfortable enough with it that he or she can actually apply it to daily behavior. We have the skills to run those campaigns.
>
> But there are other kinds of campaigns that we must also prepare. Fourth, sometimes we must *reinforce the attitudes and behavior* of those who are in agreement with our position. All they may need is a reminder of shared values.
>
> And sometimes, fifth, we have to *change or attempt to change the attitudes* of those who do not agree with our position. This requires creation of cognitive dissonance and is much tougher.

▼ **Campaigns are designed and developed to address an issue, to solve a problem or to correct or improve a situation.**

Sixth, and finally, we have the skills today to carry out *behavior modification* campaigns. To convince people, for instance, that they ought to wear their seatbelts or that drunk driving is neither in their or society's best interest. These are light years different from awareness or information campaigns.

These six types of public relations activity—and this is my list, of course; you should make your own and it may have five or eight types—are the process of our field. But note that each type attempts to motivate different levels of behavior. That's the reason we mount the campaigns. It's a little hard for us to deny, therefore, that *behavior is the outcome we seek*—not the thinking or feeling or even social interaction that precedes behavior. They are the means to an end.[1] [Emphasis added.]

▼ **CHARACTERISTICS OF SUCCESSFUL CAMPAIGNS**

Regardless of how you categorize campaigns, experience suggests that successful ones share some basic principles and characteristics. Five principles of successful campaigns can be identified: (1) assessment of the needs, goals and capabilities of priority publics; (2) systematic campaign planning and production; (3) continuous monitoring and evaluation to see what is working and where extra effort needs to be made; (4) consideration of the complementary roles of mass media and interpersonal communication; (5) selection of the appropriate media for each priority public, with due consideration of that medium's ability to deliver the message.

Studies of successful campaigns indicate that five elements or characteristics are always present. First is the *educational* aspect of a campaign. A campaign should always enlighten its publics—

EXAMPLE 13.1

Campaign Model

MODEL OF THE SUCCESSFUL ORGANIZATION

Begins with, and invests much energy in, a

1. Definitive Mission Statement (Values)
   - ▼ the distilled essence of the organization's reason for being
   - ▼ implies its USP, positioning, goals, policies.

This is carried out by

2. Corporate Culture (Shared Values)
   - ▼ demonstrated by role models, heroes
   - ▼ reinforced by rituals, stories
   - ▼ the source of teamwork, morale, productivity.

This in turn lets the organization speak with One Clear Voice to penetrate the changing and competitive environment by building

3. Positive Public Relationships (Expressed Values)
   - ▼ more than marketing or communication
   - ▼ the source of loyalty, credibility, trust.

Over time this creates

4. Reputation (Understood Values)
   - ▼ generates latent readiness to like, accept, trust, believe
   - ▼ a serendipitous, self-powering force that lies at the core of all human interface
   - ▼ epitomized in the old Squibb motto, "The priceless ingredient of every product is the honor & integrity of its maker."

SOURCE: "Opportunity '85: Bring Rigor and Process Management to Building Public Relationships by Creating an Easily Applied and Simple to Explain Conceptional Framework." Reprinted with permission, *pr reporter*, 28(1) (January 7, 1985), and Bob Thompson.

---

telling them something they didn't know or giving them a different perspective or way to look at something they already knew, or thought they knew.

The second element is *engineering*—a factor critical to behavior change, which is the objective of almost all campaigns. Engineering involves ensuring that the means are there (and convenient) for publics to do what you want them to do. Thus, if you want them to throw trash in containers instead of on the ground, the containers must be conveniently located. (One city put slanted barrels on the median at left-turn signals so that drivers waiting for the green arrow could dump trash there instead of pitching it out the window.) Asking women in developing nations to have their chil-

dren inoculated against disease can only achieve the desired result if the doctors and the serums are readily available—probably taken to women and their children in the villages. You can't expect a woman who works from daylight to dusk, and often beyond, to take a day off to walk miles carrying an infant to get a shot and then to walk miles back carrying the same, now unhappy, child.

The third element of successful campaigns is *enforcement*. There must be something beyond incentive to underscore the significance of the campaign. Many automobile seatbelt campaigns went through the education and engineering phases but failed to elicit behavior change until laws approved fines for noncompliance. The same has been true for campaigns in favor of wearing motorcycle helmets, and in many developed nations for campaigns to inoculate children. Today children are not allowed to attend school until they can prove that they have had certain inoculations.

The fourth element in successful campaigns is *entitlement*, which is also a form of *reinforcement*. Entitlement means that publics are convinced of the value of the appeals of the campaign and in a sense "buy into" the message. This helps with reinforcement, because it extends the message statement by having others outside the campaign give it voice. Such reinforcement is needed not only because people forget, but because new members of a public are added daily, and the messages have to be available for them. Those who are complying also need the reinforcement, so they will continue to do what they have been doing. The "Smokey Bear" campaign in the United States to prevent forest fires is one of the most successful information campaigns ever; it's more than 40 years old and still going, as the need for it remains as great as ever.

The *evaluation* of a campaign is the fifth significant element. In ongoing campaigns like Smokey, there are annual evaluations, as well as three- and five-year checks. The same is true for public health organizations like the March of Dimes, which looks each year at its "walk" to see what the focus should be and has changed that focus from time to time as a result of these evaluations. The evaluation is a campaign's report card. It identifies what kind of desired behavior change occurred, when and in which publics.

▼ PLANNING A CAMPAIGN

As discussed in Chapter 10, the first task in planning a campaign is to look at the organization's mission statement in order to clarify the objectives and goals of the PR program (see Example 13.2). Within the limits of the organization's objectives and goals, you must set those for the PR program that your research suggests are needed. Define the objectives—what you want to accomplish—as precisely as possible and in long-range terms. Then attach

▼ **You must clearly delineate your publics before planning your strategy.**

measures to your short-range goals. A clear statement of goals means you will be able to evaluate the success of your campaign because you can measure how close you came to achieving them or by how much you surpassed what you expected.

Look critically at the goals you've set, and ask some probing questions. Are they compatible with the current PR program? Where are they headed, ultimately? Would any conflict with your institution's policy? Is there possible conflict with a major public? With any particular public? How significant is the conflict? Could it destroy a program? More pragmatically, how will you measure success along the way?

You must clearly delineate your publics before planning your strategy. The demographics and psychographics will give you insight into the tactics you should employ to make your strategy succeed. Demographics represent objective, statistical data like age, sex, education and income. Psychographics represent the value statements you can make about audiences, their lifestyles, their likes and their dislikes. Part of your strategy involves deciding the most effective way to reach each public. What do you want to have happen as a result of the communication? How far do you need to take a public to get that to happen? Since there are six steps in the persuasion process, a public is likely to be at *one* of the six levels. You have to reach them at that level and bring them along through the other levels to acting (see Chapter 7).

Setting Goals, Timetables and Budgets

Results can be identified on several levels. Suppose, for example, that you are in charge of public relations for the local public library system. Your first goal may be to get a bond issue for a new

EXAMPLE 13.2

Organization's Mission Statement

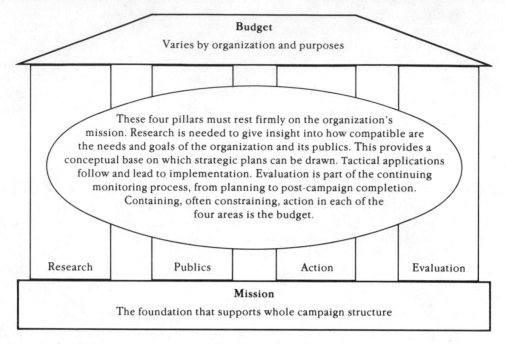

The organization's mission statement governs all action and functions as a foundation.

Initial *research* is a *situational analysis* of organizational strengths; weaknesses; objectives; product/service/idea being offered; publics—characteristics, segments, priority, behavior; opposition or competition; media—tools and tactics; previous experience with communication elements.

Organizational objectives include the objectives of the organization's total program and how the campaign is to help achieve them.

Publics are considered by priority, in terms of the expected behavior for each segment and also by area and by time elements.

Once the analysis is complete, organizational objectives studied in light of the analysis and publics studied, the size of the total communication campaign budget is reviewed.

---

library passed. But you also want to increase awareness of library services in specific areas and, perhaps, to stimulate demand for more bookmobiles to serve more distant areas. You may lose the bond issue, but if results are positive with the other two objectives, you will have accumulated ammunition that can be used at future budget hearings to help increase services and to provide more bookmobiles.

Estimates or timetables for achieving results need be no more elaborate than a marked calendar, but the deadlines must be realistic, given the

A *tentative budget mix* is developed with proportions assigned to communication elements such as publicity, advertising, promotion, marketing—such as product or service trials or sampling, merchandising—including possible changes in presentation or packaging, monitoring of each element during the campaign and evaluation measures.

The *public relations budget* fits with other organizational resources such as marketing, human relations and information systems.

Action communication goals are set for each public in general terms and specifically for segments of priority publics.

Message strategy, positioning and format are created to present the organization the way it wants to be seen in the campaign by all publics.

Tactics are developed to use specific media for a message distribution plan that includes all events and all publics.

Budget allocations are either special allocations for phases of the campaign or are designated by categories such as publicity, promotion, special events and such.

A *timetable* is detailed to specify implementation by particular *action* and the *person responsible* for seeing that it happens, and designated *reporting procedures* are outlined.

Evaluation is for control during the campaign and for a final assessment. There is continuous measurement of effects for all campaign aspects, adjustment as monitoring suggests by time, area and priority publics, segments and other publics. The final evaluation of the campaign effects is set against the accomplishment of measurable goals and how these goals help the organization meet overall organizational objectives.

SOURCE: Adapted from Michael L. Ray, *Advertising and Communication Management* (Englewood Cliffs, N.J.: Prentice-Hall, 1982), forepiece, and Russell H. Colley, *Defining Advertising Goals* (Association of National Advertisers, Inc., 1961), where Colley distinguishes between marketing *objectives* and the achievement of specific, measurable advertising *goals* toward that objective. This was the "management by objective" technique (a much older concept) as applied to advertising. Public relations people were even later in adapting the MBO to PR.

objectives involved. Allow for foul-up time, and try to finish work ahead of schedule. Avoid the need to explain continually why you are behind. Contingency planning means deciding in advance who will pick up the ball if someone drops it and what effect the substitution will have. Downtime from mistakes can be reduced considerably if you have a realistic timetable. Don't crowd yourself or your staff. Consider how to integrate the project into the overall schedule of PR activities so it won't conflict with regular duties such as writing the annual report or preparing for a stockholders' meeting. If necessary, allow for calling in extra clerical help when there is an overload.

You have to know at this point whether you are working from your department's regular allocated budget or from a special project budget. If it is a special project budget, you must know its size and be aware of whatever conditions or restrictions are placed upon it. Alternatively, the budget may be a mixture of your regular budget plus specific additional amounts for specific purposes. It might also be that some money must be raised before your budget is complete. Accurate knowledge of your budget will allow you to see what extra help you can contract for, how creative you can get, which media you can use and how often you can go to them.

Setting Creative Strategy: Choosing Theme and Media

The success or failure of a PR campaign depends largely on your creativity—in deciding on the theme, in choosing the media and in using the media. Go back and ask what you expect to achieve. How will you monitor progress toward that expectation, and how will you measure results? What does each public need to know? What is the best way to say it? What would be the most likely way to get that public's attention? This is where creativity—in use of words or symbols in an original approach to the medium—makes the difference.

Deciding on the theme may come about in a number of ways—from several persons brainstorming together, from one person's new idea or from adaptation of someone else's successful idea. It is important to entertain *all* ideas without passing judgment. Criticism kills creativity and may snuff out a good idea at birth. Stimulate people to share ideas—no matter how wild—by offering en-

couragement and enthusiasm. A good theme won't save a poorly executed campaign, but well-oiled campaign machinery won't save a bad idea either. You also need to pre-test ideas as well as completed materials, getting feedback from the publics.

Your choice of media depends both on the publics you want to reach and on the message you want to deliver. You should be able to make a preliminary decision as to which media are right once your goals are determined; however, the *creative choice* of media is something different. What is a unique way to reach a special public? What media have not been used before but could be? Someone, after all, was the first to use bumper stickers, skywriting and silk-screened T-shirts.

The *creative use* of media is also important. A media schedule that lists which media to use and when can be the key to a campaign's success—and also to its failure. Cereal companies that began advertising in the comics might have been laughed at by those who advertised in women's pages, but the comic-page advertisers knew who their real consumers were and how to reach them. A PR person has to be careful about the complementary use of advertising and publicity. Advertising is definite, scheduled communication that appears along with whatever planned activities it is designed to promote. Publicity is indefinite communication that cannot be guaranteed except in controlled media. If the planned activities are newsworthy enough, there may be mass media attention.

In both advertising and publicity, you are presenting a message—information. People either seek information or just process it. If involved enough in the subject to seek information, they are not likely to turn to mass media, says PR researcher James E. Grunig.[2] Grunig found that only people with extra time to spend are exposed to mass media. The more active people are, the less time they spend with mass media. To reach the involved, you need to use specialized publications because that is where people actively seeking information on the subject go. However, if you are aiming for low public involvement and perhaps just want exposure to an issue, then a mass medium is appropriate, especially one like television that forces audiences to process information. Remember, though, that the public you most want to reach might not be there, and your effort (if publicity) or expense (if advertising) may be wasted.

Your budget has a great deal to do with how much flexibility you have in choosing media, and with how many publics you can reach effectively.

Contingency Planning

One cheerful PR person says his smile is the result of always anticipating the worst that could happen, and then being pleasantly surprised when it doesn't. Unhappy possibilities always have to be kept in the back of your mind. What if a billboard company confuses dates, and your ads don't go up on time? Can you use newspaper advertising and radio or TV commercials to take up the slack? What if your publicity is pushed off the news by a disaster or other breaking story? What if your TV time is preempted? Flexibility and contingency plans are needed.

A PR director can get help in contingency planning from his or her staff. The staff will not only make creative suggestions and come up with good alternative proposals, but they will support the project, particularly when it is likely to consume a lot of their time. The director should evaluate accurately and honestly what each individual can best contribute to the project (and think about individuals' talents rather than just about the jobs each has done before). After the project is accepted by management, the director must write down everyone's duties and responsibilities to avoid misunderstandings over who does what when.

Remember to allow for contingencies in the timetable, too. You needn't allow for the ten minutes it takes a messenger to deliver copy to the typesetter, but you should allow for the eight to ten days required for color separations to be made. Build in some leeway, or one missed deadline will jeopardize the entire effort. Also, retain enough elasticity in the schedule so that you can take advantage of opportunities and make changes.

▼ **You must develop an internal strategy to get approval and cooperation within the organization for your campaign.**

You will undoubtedly experience having some critical element in a project barely make it—programs delivered from the printers with the ink barely dry, artwork delivered only an hour before it is needed for production. But if a PR director allows this to happen often, his or her staff will find the work environment too harrowing and unpleasant, and the PR practitioner will risk his or her mental and physical health as well as job and reputation.

Setting Internal Strategy: Selling the Program Within the Organization

After you have set your goals, you must plan the strategy you will use to achieve them. One of your first tasks in mapping your strategy is to sell your plan to management. You do this with a carefully reasoned and well-designed presentation, based at least in part on what has received approval in the past.

People doing a job tend to get so caught up in their enthusiasm that they forget that others, including top management, may not know what they are supposed to be doing or why. In addition, some CEOs demand to know more than others, and some are more quantitatively oriented than others. Cultural differences can complicate matters, too. One U.S. employee in a Japanese company was excited by some successful promotions, but in reporting these to his Japanese boss, he had his enthusiasm considerably dampened by questions like: "How much are you going to spend? What are you going to accomplish? How much more are you going to sell next month, next quarter, next year as a result?" He resisted, but finally was pushed into putting numbers on the board for the demanding manager.[3]

The greatest danger in presenting a plan rests in not anticipating questions and challenges. Listen to opposing points of view, but maintain control and do not allow "a good plan to get nibbled to death," as one PR director put it, before you have a chance to test its effectiveness. One PR director who has to work in a hostile climate makes a practice of duplicating her presentations and circulating them to management instead of calling a conference, because she says people will approve ideas on paper that they would never approve in an open meeting. If necessary, show your plan to several important people first, so you can anticipate the reception it will get, before you actually present it formally. The whole process is not unlike caucusing in politics before calling for a committee vote. Much verbal battle can be eliminated by careful listening in the planning stages.

▼ IMPLEMENTING THE CAMPAIGN

Implementing the project involves adapting and applying tactics to strategies while adhering to the timetable and budget, keeping people informed and solving problems positively.

Adapting and Applying Tactics to Strategies

The framework for your whole campaign must be suited to its institutional environment of either a closed or open communication system, as determined by top management. This is not synonymous with proaction and reaction. A campaign *is* proactive. But some campaigns are mounted by closed communication organizations.

You will choose messages and messengers for *each* public, drawn from what your research tells you are the best choices. You will select a master communications strategy—a functional strategy based on differentiation, segmentation or modification. This, with other factors such as what your image research tells you is the goal to be achieved will determine your campaign's emphasis—public-

ity, advertising and/or promotion. You will set persuasive strategies for your publics because you want to make sure that something happens.

You will use tactics to shape specific messages for delivery to each public in order to achieve the purpose you have determined. You have to keep on a schedule and within the budget in making these choices. If the publicity writer says it is impossible to get the information needed for a story in time for it to go in the media kit as scheduled, determine how long the delay may be, set an absolute deadline and make sure it is one you can live with. Most importantly, keep people informed of changes as well as of first plans. Most foulups occur because one person does not know the problems besetting another person whose work is related.

Keeping People Informed

There are many ways to solve internal communications problems. The head of one small PR firm, noting that his staffers headed for the coffeepot between 9:30 and 10:00 A.M., scheduled a coffee-break conference time with free doughnuts. In persuading his staff members to sit for a while and discuss their successes and problems, he helped them integrate their staff work. Staffers, hearing the problems of others, discovered how their own timetables were going to be affected.

The chief executive of a larger PR operation, after observing the most horrendous arguments among his staff over who was to blame for a delay, insisted that written communications be sent to everyone. Although he admits that sometimes snafus still occur, he says it is only because someone did not read a communique. Some companies use computer message systems so that memos are waiting when a terminal is turned on each morning.

A multibranch operation has another alternative to written communication in the form of a weekly loudspeaker telephone conference (telecon). Every week the advertising and PR staff of a Dallas company, for example, sit around a conference table with a phone loudspeaker operation hooked up to their counterparts in branch offices in other parts of the country. Each person summarizes what he or she is doing and outlines travel plans. As a result of the conference, plans are frequently changed. It may be brought out that someone from Dallas and someone from Chicago are both heading for, say, a plant in Montreal. The PR corporate director, then, can tell the Chicago person to take care of both assignments, thereby reducing costs in travel expenses and staff.

Solving Problems Positively

Still, even in the most carefully planned and well-managed effort, complications and confusion do occur. The important thing is to resolve each problem and get the job done successfully. Placing blame wastes time and energy and can damage working relationships. Good working relationships are imperative for smooth functioning any time, but particularly where personal relationships can facilitate, impede or even destroy the public relations program.

Whatever the PR projects, all internal publics should be kept informed. This is easy to overlook, especially when there is dynamic leadership. For instance, the director of a concert group that suddenly was given the opportunity to tour Europe was about to relay the story to the news media when someone suggested that the concert group's board of directors should be asked first to grant permission for the tour. Although approval seemed certain, and asking for it necessitated calling each of the twenty-three directors, the effort was worthwhile, because people in authority feel their status has been undermined when they learn of important actions first from the newspapers.

Pleasing everyone is impossible, but the PR practitioner who works according to policy—real policy, not "unwritten policy"—is usually safe. Unwritten policies may seem as compelling as written ones, but persistence and diplomacy can often change them—although this may be difficult if they represent the principal interests of the major stockholders. Written policy generally is much less flexible and should be followed carefully until changes

▼ **Campaigns must be evaluated by monitoring as they develop and by postmortem after they end.**

are adopted. Policies can be changed by the bold, but you must first devise a strong justification for the change and then determine how to sell it to the publics involved, anticipating how they will perceive it.

▼ EVALUATING THE CAMPAIGN

Two types of evaluations have to occur in a campaign: monitoring and postmortems.

Monitoring

You need an ongoing system for monitoring all major activities. Some measures can be unobtrusive, such as counting the number of color-coded tickets collected for an event, the number of gift certificates redeemed or the number of phone calls received. Other areas require the more careful monitoring of formal research (see Chapter 5). Monitoring is important in a campaign because you may need to change directions, reallocate resources or redefine priorities to achieve your objective. Monitoring makes it possible, for instance, for political candidates during a campaign to increase television exposure in an area where their name recognition or support is low or to arrange for an unscheduled appearance in the area.

Although results of such monitoring are less visible in other types of campaigns, the need to monitor remains. Think about it on a personal level. You wouldn't want to plan a party, send out invitations and not know if anyone was coming. You would be buying food or guaranteeing a certain turnout for a caterer. Before you did these things, you would certainly want to know how many people to expect.

Reprinted with special permission of North America Syndicate.

Postmortems

Every PR campaign deserves a thorough and honest autopsy. What worked, what didn't and why? What was accidentally a success? What could have been done better?

Formal research is needed here. You need to uncover some solid evidence that objectives were achieved or not achieved. You need to establish what missed the mark and by how much. Anecdotal evaluation is useful and often insightful, but it does not make a good budget defense.

To make a postmortem successful, you must keep all analyses on a professional level; no witch hunts should be permitted. If something did not work, there is usually more than one reason for its failure and more than one person responsible. Use constructive criticism to suggest, "If we had attempted to do this, would it have worked better than what we did try?" Egos, especially creative egos, are fragile things, yet no one minds looking in the mirror unless she or he sees someone in the background pointing an accusing finger.

As mentioned in Chapter 5, you need to evaluate several results. These include the impact on publics; the effect on the organization's goals and mission; the effect on the attitudes of publics toward the organization and on their perception of the organization; and the effects on the organization's financial status, ethical stance and social responsibility.

The most effective evaluations are continuing programs—for instance, annual surveys of what

audiences like or dislike, surveys of employee attitudes and measurements of consumer attitudes. Evaluations may also be done by reading letters and taking phone calls from happy and unhappy publics and by talking with various publics to ascertain their attitudes. These give you benchmarks against which to measure a campaign's effects. If you say after a campaign, "It's all over, we can forget it," instead of instituting an ongoing evaluation program, you will put yourself in the position of, as one astute advertising executive put it, "constantly reinventing the wheel."

Although this discussion has addressed campaigns mounted for a specific purpose and for a specific period of time, an organization should have an overall public relations program tied to its fundamental mission and goals. This should be a written program complete with rationale, policy support statements, listed priorities, identified publics and illustrations of the tools to be used. Most importantly, it should receive top management endorsement, just as budgets do.

In each campaign you need to look for the "self-interest" appeal to each target audience—the key to all effective communication. Search out the other communication strategies in message structure and media delivery that have proved successful (or unsuccessful) in informing and influencing the target audience.[4] Look beyond the strategies for their base in some theoretical concept so you can apply that to other campaigns. Then plan your program by integrating all of these elements into a flexible and feasible timetable, and secure management and staff support. Select media that will ensure successful and on-time implementation of the program. Finally, evaluate the results or effectiveness of the program through formal post-testing research and through less formal methods of responses from staff and publics. You are measuring for financial impact, ethical impact and social responsibility.

▼ CAMPAIGN OUTLINE

Before narrowing our focus to the issue of changing behavior, let's review the steps involved in the whole process of developing and executing a campaign. In summary:

1 ▼ Define the problem. Set goals for the *campaign* within an organizational framework.

1 ▼ Evaluate the impact of the problem on publics and on the organization, and define clearly the issues involved in the problem.

2 ▼ Develop an organizational strategy consonant with the mission.

2 ▼ Determine a communication strategy to reach the stated goals.

2 ▼ Plan actions, themes and appeals to publics. In developing a functional strategy, plan where the emphasis will be—ads, publicity and/or promotion.

3 ▼ Develop an organizational responsibilities plan, with budgets and timetables.

3 ▼ Decide which tactics fit the strategy best and how you will monitor each aspect.

3 ▼ Evaluate the results or effectiveness of the program.

▼ CHANGING BEHAVIOR

Public relations practitioners are often depicted as masters of manipulative techniques designed to get people to think or act in a certain way. And in fact most campaigns do strive to produce behavior

▼ Changing behavior is a central objective of many PR campaigns.

changes. This is the case even when campaigns start at the awareness level, since the purpose of a campaign to create awareness (of a problem, of a product or service or of a person) is to eventually get action. The same goes for "information campaigns" as well: what is desired is action, which may mean getting people to behave differently from how they usually behave.

The ethical question of the propriety of such campaigns is not always raised, especially when the campaign appears to reflect strong social values. But sources behind the campaign pay for it, and their values or "social agenda" may not match that of individuals who lack the means and (in some cases) the access to communicate through public and private media. Imbalances of means and access are part of the concern over development campaigns in some countries. These "public information campaigns" usually are handled by the government, which may not allow much input from those who are the objects of the campaign. All information campaigns, Charles T. Salmon says, represent weapons in conflicts of interest, and social intervention involves conflicts of values.[5]

A successful campaign—one that changes behavior—has three elements, according to the U.S. Forest Service: education, engineering and enforcement.[6] The educational part consists of telling people what you want them to do, which in the case of the Forest Service was to not destroy the forest (see Example 13.3). The second step, engineering, enables people to accomplish what you are asking. To this end, the Forest Service built "fire safe" camp sites and put up steel signs that were difficult to vandalize. The third step is enforcement, where the will of the people begins to get restricted. Laws were enacted to protect the national forests, and people who failed to obey the laws could be fined. In some cases, access to forests is restricted if the

EXAMPLE 13.3

A Campaign That Affected Behavior

Perhaps repetition is an answer. Smokey is well over 40 years old.

Smokey Bear, one of the best-known symbols in the history of advertising, is celebrating his 40th year as the national symbol of forest fire prevention—and one of the most successful programs of mass appeal. Smokey is credited with reducing forest fires by 50 percent since 1944, with resulting savings in human life, wildlife and timber.

The Smokey Bear program has been effective because it accomplishes the three objectives of any successful information campaign: It creates a cognitive structure (awareness), a motivational structure (desire) and behavioral structure (action). Awareness is measured by recognizability, and Smokey has certainly become a well-known character since he first appeared on a poster dressed in dungarees and campaign hat, pouring water on a campfire.

Surveys show that 98 out of 100 people know who he is, and that most know what he stands for. It is difficult, for instance, to visit or travel through a forested area without encountering some evidence of Smokey and his message: "Only You Can Prevent Forest Fires."

The Smokey Bear program (actually, the Cooperative Forest Fire Prevention Program) goes beyond the familiar posters. In addition to television spots, the campaign uses personal appearances by Smokey-costumed forest rangers, Tournament of Roses Parade floats and a giant Smokey Bear balloon. Smokey gets so much mail he has his own zip code (20252), and his commercial use is regulated by an Act of Congress.

Motivation would appear to be no problem: Who wouldn't want to prevent forest fires? Well, not quite everyone does—one fire of every four is started deliberately. But, if Smokey is even 75 percent successful in convincing us that we shouldn't burn the woods, that's a lot better than the seat-belt folks have done.

Sixty percent of all forest fires result from human carelessness. (Only 9 percent are started by lightning.) What we have, then, in an average year is about 76,000 careless acts that result in forest fires. No one knows how many near-misses occur, but this record isn't bad when one considers the millions of people who live in and visit forested areas.

Although there is room for improvement, Smokey's record in creating a desired behavior structure is the envy of the advertising world. And because Smokey's keepers know they have a good thing, it's very likely that your children and your grandchildren will be just as familiar as you are with Smokey's admonition—"Only You Can Prevent . . ."

Source: Larry Doolittle, "Only He Can Prevent Forest Fires," *Psychology Today* (May 1984), p. 14.

Forest Service determines that the danger of damage to the forest is too high.

But laws can be overturned, or people can be flagrant about violating them. What is it that makes people accept and obey? William Paisley says that, because the public in the United States accepts the notion of a "free marketplace of ideas," campaigns (even conflicting ones) are common. But to gain public support, a social issues campaign must get on the public agenda of issues, and the issue must be seen as having some public merit.[7]

Then, in addressing the merit of an issue, that fourth "E," entitlement, is added to the list of campaign elements.[8] Some public issues are seen as obligations and others as opportunities, but entitlement involves laws, public policy and public acceptance. Laws can be upheld or changed, and laws tend to change with society's social agenda, as drinking age laws illustrate. Public policy becomes a part of the entitlement consideration when more than one group or agency claims a social issue; and certainly environmental issues of all kinds have multiple sponsors who usually carve out their own part of the issue and try to make the identification with it distinctive. The final part of entitlement, as Paisley sees it, is public acceptance. In the United States, the issue requires association with first-party stakeholders—those whom the issue affects directly—to have credibility and thus win widespread public support.[9]

Who Is Entitled?

Whether the government should decide what's best for everyone or whether those who are governed should participate in the decision-making process is at the root of most social issues.

How fundamental this question can be is reflected in the campaign strategy for "selling" the nuclear freeze, worked out by science writer and environmental PR specialist Peter Sandman, who was media and outreach coordinator for the New Jersey Campaign for a Nuclear Weapons Freeze in 1982 (see Example 13.4).

Getting Grassroots Involvement

Changing behavior works best when the people who are being asked to change are encouraged to participate in formulating the behavioral goals. Top-down information campaigns in most countries are doomed to failure. On the other hand, if members of the public become partners in the planning, they share ego involvement in the push for successful outcome; and self-persuasion is a major ingredient.

A good example is the campaign by the Crime Prevention Coalition using McGruff the Crime Dog "Taking a Bite out of Crime." The program is implemented through local police departments, which handle the campaign materials—videos, brochures and other information on how to protect yourself from crime. These efforts are reinforced by a media campaign showing McGruff dressed in a fedora and trenchcoat. The dog is a favorite with children, who take messages home from school and also take part in the watch program. The neighborhood local watch programs are a major ingredient of the program. The focus on community partnerships means that the program takes on a slightly different character for each community.[10]

Community involvement has always been a part of the MADD (Mothers Against Drunk Driving) movement, which has community chapters and state offices. MADD's Minnesota state office put up a billboard that included the actual car in which a man and his three children were killed (see Example 13.5).

The billboard was a shocker, drawing national and international media attention. The victims in the crash were a 36-year-old University of Minnesota agricultural researcher from Nigeria and his three young children. All were killed instantly on September 28, 1989, when their Toyota was so crumpled when struck by a speeding pickup truck that the rear end of the car was pushed to within 6 inches of the dashboard. The accident scene was so hideous that rescue workers called to the scene had to undergo counseling later to overcome what they had witnessed. There were no skid marks from the pickup truck, which slammed into Ojobona Oju's car at 65 miles per hour. Its drunk driver had himself lost a leg to a drunk driver in 1981.

The idea for putting the crumpled car on the billboard came from a retired public relations director who felt it would send a strong message. Implementing the idea wasn't easy. The widow had returned to Nigeria, with her entire family in coffins in the plane's cargo hold. She had to be located to get a release. The car itself couldn't be released until after the driver, Brian Patterson, was tried and all criminal charged against him adjudicated. (He was sentenced to 63 months in prison and an additional 10 years of probation, during which time he must totally abstain from alcohol and nonprescription drugs.)[11]

EXAMPLE 13.4 ■■■■■■

Notes on "Selling" the Freeze

Most of the recommendations listed below are based on communication theory, poll data, or both. Some are just my political instincts. *All* are meant to supplement your own political instincts, not to replace them. If what I am suggesting feels wrong, do what feels right instead.

1. Aim at involvement, not knowledge. Well-informed futility and paralyzed concern are of little value to the freeze movement, short-term or long. Besides, people who become actively involved will find and absorb huge quantities of relevant information. Becoming well-informed, on the other hand, is no guarantee of involvement.

2. Don't bury people in information. Newcomers, especially, have a limited appetite for technical detail; that will come *after* they're involved. Respond to the questions people are asking, of course, but try not to feed their fear that they must become arms experts before taking a stand. Especially avoid prolonged "our experts versus their experts" battles: their experts have more Pentagon titles and classified numbers; the basic issues require far less expertise than people imagine; newcomers respond to technical debate with glazed eyes and paralyzed wills. (But information *is* crucial after involvement; see #18.)

3. For any given presentation or document and for the campaign as a whole, identify 3–5 points that you will keep stressing. For each point, focus on a handful of convincing arguments, statistics, and quotations—including ones from military and other "unexpected" sources. Hold in reserve prepared responses to the most likely hostile questions on each point, again relying heavily on "their" sources. Fight *hard* to stick to these basics. Move beyond them only if the audience as a whole (not just one questioner or a debate opponent) seems to want you to. The winners of political contests are usually the people who define the terms of the contest. Your goal is to sell the freeze, not to answer its opponents (but see #11). Fight on your own turf.

4. Accept the legitimacy of feelings. People get involved in arms-control issues, not because they are "interested," but because they *care*. This is true even of freeze opponents—they too are feeling people, worried about the survival of what they love. The feelings of potential supporters point the route to more active support; try to sense what feelings are on top (fear? anger? love?) and respond in a way that legitimates them. (But don't necessarily pander to them—see #19.) The feelings of hostile questioners also deserve respect; accepting and responding to the feeling is often more important than answering the question itself.

5. Remember that our audience is not ourselves. Whatever your politics, whatever your moral and religious values, whatever your reasons for working on the freeze, they are *yours*. Other people will become involved for their own reasons, not for your reasons—and your goal is to facilitate the involvement, not to debate the reasons. Bear in mind especially that the audience is not yet involved for *any* reasons; presuming more interest or commitment than is there risks nipping its growth in the bud. Newcomers need nurturing; they grow into seasoned activists in their own time and on their own path. This growth process is determined by a complex amalgam of their histories, feelings, actions, values, and knowledge, probably in that order. We can affect it but not control it.

6. Focus on top prospects. Activating supporters is easier than persuading neutrals, and persuading neutrals is easier than converting opponents. Especially early in the campaign, when you need help and contributions more than votes, concentrate your efforts where you expect to find supporters. As summer moves into fall shift more emphasis into mass persuasion of uncommitted voters. Never waste time on opponents unless there is a neutral audience to win over. But note that your top prospects may not be who you think they are (see #7).

7. Don't write off any group. The freeze movement so far has proved to be wide but shallow—supported by a large majority of virtually every demographic group, but supported with fervor by many fewer.

8. Be patriotic. Showing respect for key U.S. institutions and symbols (the flag, the presidency, elections) is essential. Showing disapproval of repression is extraordinarily helpful as well; so is a healthy (and visible) skepticism about good will from suspect countries or their leaders ("verifiability" wins more votes than "trust"). This reality neither requires nor excuses enemy-baiting, or denying such home-grown injustices as racism and sexism. It does, perhaps, suggest a muting of ideology in the interests of the widest possible freeze coalition.

9. Go easy on the rhetoric of ideology. Make the connections you want to make, but try to pick connections you think will be meaningful to your audience, not necessarily to yourself.

10. Reinforce audience values. People change more, and act more, when you support their values than when you challenge them. The golden rule of persuasion is thus to look for *existing* audience values to which you can hook your message, values that already incline your audience toward your message. If there are existing values that incline your audience the other way, the less you mention them the better—you want to remind people why they want to agree with you, not why they want to disagree.

11. Respond to key counterarguments. Although it generally pays to fight on our own turf (see #3), four issues are or will soon be so widely debated as to require an explicit response.

a. "The freeze would tie the hands of the experts at the Strategic Arms Reduction Talks." Respond with respect for START—argue that it is not enough, not that it is a fraud. In fact, claim credit for it; the president's arms-control policy changed in response to the freeze movement, and can change more if we maintain the effort.

b. "The enemy is ahead in the arms race, as shown by the following incomprehensible chart." According to poll data, the parity issue is *at the core* of freeze support and opposition; believing that an enemy is not ahead is virtually a prerequisite for supporting the freeze. (Most Americans would feel safest—mistakenly—if the U.S. were ahead, but they will settle for a standoff.) Parity here does not mean quantitative equality; it means essential fairness. So skip the incomprehensible charts for most audiences and rely instead on quotations from military experts to the effect that they would not trade places with their enemy counterparts. And explain that both sides have enough weapons to obliterate the other no matter who strikes first; this secure deterrent is the only parity that means anything. . . . Make your point without slinging arrows.

c. "We can't trust these people, as the record on chemical/bacteriological weapons, or whatever proves." The most effective answer here is not that we can trust another country—though it is helpful to point out that honoring a freeze treaty would be in that country's interests. Nor is it wise to put great stress on the parallel record of international untrustworthiness of the United States—though you may want to note that trust has never figured greatly in diplomacy. The key response is that we do not *need* to trust another country, nor they us. Carry a satellite photo of a Chinese or Iraqi license plate with you, and argue that the freeze is verifiable.

d. "The United States needs a strong military." The response that the U.S. does not need a strong military, that U.S. military strength threatens the world's peoples, lacks appeal to most audiences, even profreeze audiences. The response that the U.S. already has a strong military goes over better, especially when tied to nuclear parity. But the most effective answer by far is to argue that weapons too

(Continued)

EXAMPLE 13.4

Notes on "Selling" the Freeze (*continued*)

powerful to use confer no strength, that the arms race diminishes national security, that a Pentagon grown overdependent on nuclear arms is ill-prepared to fight. Stop short of asserting that the freeze makes the world safe for war.

As the campaign continues, other issues may grow important enough to require an answer—nuclear proliferation is a likely addition to the list, and subversion may become an issue if opponents decide to fight dirty. If you are quite sure your audience is already concerned about an issue (*any* issue), respond to it before you're asked. But don't spend too much time "answering" the opposition; we want to keep the opposition answering us instead.

12. Help people give themselves permission to support the freeze. No one wants a nuclear war, and almost everyone intuitively senses a freeze would help prevent one. But the cost of being wrong is frighteningly high. People worry that the freeze might be a communist plot, or a cowardly cop-out, or a con—or just a terrible mistake. They thus need to hear that experts and authorities also support the freeze; this gives them permission to support it too. (The bandwagon of support from other nonexperts is also important—see #14.) The ideal list of endorsers depends on your audience, of course. Military experts are essential; state and national political leaders confer establishment respectability, especially when the list is bipartisan; religious, moral, and cultural dignitaries help; national heroes can be invoked. Be sure to include *local* persons of stature. Though the freeze movement rose mainly from the grassroots, prestige endorsements are probably crucial to further growth—and it is wise to secure them early while the mood of consensus remains strong.

13. Make working for the freeze personally attractive to people. All of us are concerned about many more issues than we actually commit our time and money to. And that all-important first commitment, the evidence shows, comes because we are given a chance to do something personally fulfilling. Why do people start working for freeze groups?—to meet interesting people; to get out of the house; to feel more a part of the community; to improve old skills and develop new skills; to feel needed; to enjoy a social evening, a rock concert, a stimulating conversation. None of these is enough reason to *stay* involved; once involved people learn about the issue and build a better rationale for their involvement.

14. Help make people feel powerful. Paralysis, fatalism, apathy, and "psychic numbing" are inevitable responses to feeling powerless; acting, caring, and learning make no sense if they will do no good. . . . To unfreeze nonsupporters, stress efficacy and empowerment in three senses: (a) the effectiveness of the individual—that the things we are asking people to do are *useful* and *important*, not makework; (b) the effectiveness of the movement—that they are about to join an irresistible bandwagon, a mass upwelling of grassroots fervor, democracy in action (but guided by experts—see #12); and (c) the effectiveness of the freeze itself—that a nonbinding referendum can genuinely influence national policy and lead to a treaty that works. Supporters as well as newcomers need to hear these things; the single greatest reason why people abandon political movements is that they began to feel futile.

15. Stress the urgency of the freeze movement. People contribute their time and money where they feel their time and money will make a difference. This means they must feel effective (see #14); it *also* means they must feel needed. . . . This stress on urgency is especially important for committed audiences; newcomers need to hear more about confidence (see #19).

16. Make working for the freeze feel like a "controllable commitment. People normally join new causes tentatively, a step at a time. The first steps must be easy, like wearing a button or signing a petition. And they must be reinforced (see #18) before people are asked to do more. Aim at a graduated series of increasingly serious commitments, alternating with information about the issue and about the effectiveness of past commitments. Avoid "the four outs"; (a) Burnout results from asking for too much too fast. When last week's newcomer is this week's committee chair, s/he may well become next week's ex-member. (b) Cool-out comes from asking for too little, and giving too little reinforcement. People want to be told explicitly what to do next, and why, and what you think about what they did last. (c) Pull-out is what happens when people feel trapped, afraid that unless they quit now the movement will suck up all their energy. Feeling suffocated does not lead to good political work. (d) Keep-out is the feeling many newcomers get from ongoing political groups—the sense that there are invisible walls to be climbed; social, ideological, or informational entrance requirements to be met. Think of the four outs as the corners of a room; commitment grows best in the room's center.

17. Personalize the movement. Perhaps "movement" is the wrong word to begin with. People join groups; they decide to try working with Mary and George. And peace work is not a penance. It can and should be joyful. At every level, then, try to make the freeze movement human and fun. Include quotations and photographs of "ordinary citizens" in your literature. Encourage people to bring their children to meetings, and provide relevant child-care activities. Serve food. Introduce newcomers. Share good news. Consider fielding a freeze softball team.

18. Use information strategically. Instead of inundating newcomers with technical details (see #2), use information to reinforce that first commitment; this leads people to adopt a what-shall-we-do-next? attitude instead of I-gave-at-the-office. Three kinds of information are especially useful:

a. Ammunition is information about the issue itself. People need it to do a good job, of course—but they need it even more to justify their commitment to themselves and their skeptical friends. Though people become involved for personal reasons (see #13), they need sound arguments to *stay* involved.

b. Mobilizing information tells people what to do next and how to do it. (This article is an example of mobilizing information.) When passive supporters of political movements are asked why they don't do more, their two biggest answers are "I don't know what" and "I don't know how." Mobilizing information meets these needs.

c. Efficacy information stresses the value of what people have already done (see #14). It tells them that they're not wasting their time, that their work is appreciated, that their neighbors are working too.

19. Go easy on fear, guilt, and depression. These are all inward-turning, negative emotions. They may shock the totally ignorant into recognizing the issue, and they may actually galvanize hardened fanatics into further action—but most audiences respond better to uppers than to downers, better to solutions than to problems, better to progress than to catastrophe, better to confidence than to desperation. We must come to terms with nuclear terror slowly or we risk reverting to psychic numbness and paralyzed inaction. . . . In contrast to fear, guilt, and depression, *anger* provokes action rather than avoidance, because it looks outward instead of inward. But even anger is too negative to stand alone without turning sterile; it is best paired with *love* and *efficacy:* someone to fight against, someone to fight for, and the conviction the fight can be won.

20. Don't neglect the mass media. The most *effective* outreach is of course person-to-person. But we're talking about reaching millions of people, and we can't do it without the megaphone of the mass media. In any case, grassroots organizing and media reinforce each other. Active supporters get much of their ammunition and sense of efficacy from media coverage of "their"

(Continued)

EXAMPLE 13.4

Notes on "Selling" the Freeze (*continued*)

movement. Potential supporters are far more likely to become involved if they are hearing about the freeze from the media, not just from their neighborhood activist. And millions of politically inactive people will vote almost exclusively on the basis of what they learned from the media. Early in the campaign, then, use media to reinforce your grassroots organizing, to confer visibility and credibility on the freeze. Later, use media to reach those who have not been touched by organizing. Advertising, pamphlets, and the like give you the most control over what you say and to whom you say it. But unpaid media attention—news, talk shows, letters-to-the-editor—is cheaper and more credible. Whatever your budget, you can affort to talk to local reporters—and you cannot afford not to.

21. Trust yourself. If you'd asked them, most experts would have told you a year ago that a mass movement

for nuclear arms control wouldn't get to first base right now. These notes may be out of date by the time you read them; or inappropriate for your group, your style, your constituency, your situation; or flat-out wrong. Merge what looks helpful with what you're already doing.

This is a model for any movement to get public opinion mobilized and into action. It can be analyzed to watch pressure groups at work, and it can also be used as a predictor. The model blends communication theory with social movement action.

SOURCE: Used with permission. Dr. Sandman is now director of the Environmental Communication Research Program at Rutgers University.

The MADD billboard joins other dramatic and controversial signs of the times. One of the most controversial artists is Mark Heckman of Grand Rapids, Michigan. Many of Heckman's clients are private individuals who want to make a political statement. Sometimes his billboards are so provocative that they get a response from "the other side." When the Gannett outdoor sign company put up Heckman's billboard urging people to fight AIDS by wearing condoms, a Grand Rapids businessman threatened to cancel his own billboard. A Kalamazoo group later leased the same billboard for its message: "Abstinence! It beats AIDS."[12]

Billboards often play an important role in development communication campaigns, and they often rely on drama and symbols more than on words. That's important, given the communications problems of a high rate of illiteracy and/or a multiplicity of languages. Language problems make radio an important campaign medium, as well. Unfortu-

nately, many development campaigns have depended on mass media, top-down message construction, with no development of infrastructures to make carrying out the messages possible. The result has been some information or education about what the government wants people to do, but not much in the way of "engineering" to see that it's feasible. And very little interactivity and feedback, although that is improving as governments realize that even when governments are authoritarian, they need "entitlement" to gain compliance.

One type of campaign that has received widespread mass media attention is the campaign for population control. Although various countries' experience could be cited, the pattern is the same for many. Billboards and radio spots carry slogans and jingles. In some countries television is also used. A few countries have tried taking folk media, puppets and plays to outlying villages.

EXAMPLE 13.5

MADD Billboard

For this billboard, Mothers Against Drunk Driving used the actual wreck of a car in which a man and his three young children were killed by a speeding pickup truck whose driver was drunk. The car's engine block had to be removed so the sign would support it; but five months after the accident, and with the help of five different agencies, the car was mounted on a billboard on a heavily traveled freeway between Minneapolis and St. Paul. It immediately caught the attention of national and international media, including *Time* and *Newsweek* magazines.

SOURCE: Used with the permission of MADD, Minnesota State Office.

These campaigns encounter at least two basic problems. First, the message of having few children makes little sense in a rural community where many hands are needed and mortality rates are high. Second, too few family-oriented clinics or health programs are available for followup counseling and materials, and in any case the male typically makes most of the family-planning decisions. Women living in these societies could tell the planners why their messages won't work, but while many people talk to them, few people ask them anything and even fewer listen.

One difficulty in getting useful interaction or feedback from people in many countries relates to their social relationships. Recognizing this prob-lem, Hernando Gonzales has offered a revised interpretation of the interactive model that doesn't look at the flow of information up or down in situations where status and power are likely designators.[13] Instead, his model looks at the already established norms of interactivity, with a view toward building coalitions so that power can accrue to these groups, which can then act as representative voices.

One campaign that did seek help from its publics with message development was Family Health International's population control/health campaign in the Caribbean. The campaign, "Condoms . . . Because You Care," was developed by AIDSTECH[14] (see Example 13.6).

EXAMPLE 13.6

Public-generated Messages for a Caribbean Campaign

"CONDOMS . . . BECAUSE YOU CARE"

The Creation of a Condom Promotion Campaign in the Eastern Caribbean, December 1990

The campaign button and the poster carry messages generated by their publics and the entire promotion was built on field research.

The condom promotion campaign was initiated on 26 November, 1990. Preliminary evaluation data (see chart) demonstrate changes in condom sales (83%) before and after campaign implementation from randomly selected outlets.

In addition, qualitative research (focus groups) with shop owners and members of the target audience indicate very high message recognition for all aspects of the campaign. For example, in initial campaign design, focus group participants were unable to recognize the condom "symbol" without the word "condoms" beneath it. One year later, focus group participants demonstrated high awareness of the campaign: symbol recognition without the defining word was high. In addition, familiarity with the poster (tested without the text) was also high, and responses to the graphics and text separately were equally positive.

Shop owners indicated that both condom sales and discussion about condoms in shops had increased noticeably and that people responded very favorably to the display boxes. Many shops requested that the artwork also be produced on the back of the box so that they can turn the box around if they wish to have the dispensing slot facing the shop clerk rather than the customer. Additional boxes have already been printed with artwork on both sides.

Response to the campaign has been so positive that two additional steps have already been initiated to expand the program:

1. Installation of condom promotion materials and display boxes in all Ministry of Health clinics nation-wide as part of their condom distribution system.

2. Training of CBD outlet managers in condom sales and logistics strategies to further increase numbers of condoms purchased.

EXECUTIVE SUMMARY

A series of focus groups and interviews were conducted in Antigua and Dominica to pre-test several ideas for use in a condom promotion campaign that had been designed based on prior field research. The participants in the various aspects of the qualitative research provided input in the selection of the text for a condom promotion poster, as well as for the graphics and standardized condom symbol to be used as point-of-purchase materials in the community-based distribution outlets in the Eastern Caribbean. Interview participants, both men and women, responded most favorably to the poster text of **"It's not the end of anything. It's only the beginning. Condoms . . . Because You Care."** Focus group participants—young men, older men, and young women—strongly favored the "Cool Man and Woman" visual (close-ups of man and woman on front of display box) for the point-of-purchase materials and made concrete recommendations for changes in the current design to make it more appealing and target-audience specific. Of the range of choices, condom symbol #4 was chosen (among the 5 options) as representative of the preferred style; the color preference, however, tended much more strongly toward the bright blues, greens, and pinks. Recommendations, therefore, are made for the needed changes in the picture and the condom symbol.

"Condoms...Because You Care" A Lifestyle Approach to Condom Promotion in the Eastern Caribbean

Ostfield, Marc*; Fevrier, W**; Jagdeo, T***; Cole, L*; France, B*.
*AIDSTECH, Family Health International, RTP, NC, USA
**Dominica Planned Parenthood Assoc., Dominica, West Indies
***Caribbean Family Planning Affiliation, Antigua, West Indies

Goal: To reduce the spread of HIV in the Eastern Caribbean by changing social norms about condoms in order to increase condom sales and use.

Methodology: This campaign uses an innovative approach to position condoms in a "lifestyle" format — associating condoms with the "good life," the things that the "in" people use, rather than linking condoms with AIDS, family planning, or general health messages. The campaign seeks to make it more comfortable for people to discuss condoms by altering social norms and reducing the stigma associated with condom purchase and use.

Strategy: The campaign uses a range of promotional and point-of-purchase materials to convey the carefully designed "lifestyle" message in Community-Based Distribution (CBD) outlets (such as shops and bars) in the Eastern Caribbean nation of Dominica (pop. 82,000): (1) a poster developed in conjunction with the Caribbean Family Planning Affiliation, (2) a display/distribution box, durable enough for long-term use and easy to assemble, (3) a sticker with a condom symbol for CBD outlets to indicate "condoms available here," (4) a button with the "lifestyle" tag message for all CBD outlets.

Results: The promotional campaign was initiated 26 November, 1990. Data below demonstrate changes in condom sales before and after campaign implementation from randomly selected outlets. A dramatic increase (83.15%) occurred in average monthly condom sales across sites following campaign implementation in all CBD outlets.

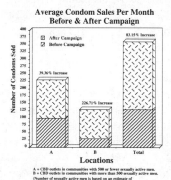

Average Condom Sales Per Month Before & After Campaign

Number of Condoms Sold / Locations

After Campaign / Before Campaign

A = CBD outlets in communities with 500 or fewer sexually active men.
B = CBD outlets in communities with more than 500 sexually active men.
(Number of sexually active men is based on an estimate of 25% of the total population).

Conclusion: Condom sales can be increased in Community-Based Distribution outlets, with a relatively small amount of promotional work using a "lifestyle" message in innovative ways to change social norms. The use of additional channels of communication such as radio or television, which were not utilized in this campaign, may significantly increase the impact of such a campaign on condom sales. Further evaluation will measure changes in non-CBD sales, reported usage, and campaign recognition.

Funding: Partial support for this project was provided by AIDSTECH/Family Health International with funds from the Regional Development Office/Caribbean of the United States Agency for International Development.

 DOMINICA PLANNED PARENTHOOD ASSOCIATION

 AIDSTECH

Reprinted with permission.

(Continued)

EXAMPLE 13.6 ▪

Public-generated Messages for a Caribbean Campaign (*continued*)

BACKGROUND

This project grew out of AIDSTECH's work in the Eastern Caribbean during the course of the past year. The staff at the Dominica Planned Parenthood Association and at the Health Education Office of the Ministry of Health, as well as in similar offices in other Eastern Caribbean nations, had requested assistance in effective ways to promote condoms that are currently being sold in their community-based distribution (CBD) outlets (bars and shops in villages throughout the country). Currently, all condoms sold in the CBD shops are sold directly from their white, A.I.D. boxes; as a result, they are not very visible in the shops and customers often do not know that they are even available. The shop owners are interested in promoting condom sales, both for health and financial reasons.

Simultaneously, AIDSTECH began negotiations with Dr. Tirbani Jagdeo, Chief Executive Officer of the Caribbean Family Planning Affiliation (CFPA) about the possibility of designing and distributing a regional condom promotion poster—one that is not specific to AIDS, STDs, or Family Planning. CFPA has taken a leading role in the design and distribution of positive, well-received posters to promote Family Planning messages throughout the Caribbean. AIDSTECH was impressed with CFPA's work and track record and approached them about the condom poster idea. CFPA was enthusiastic about the project and arranged to work with AIDSTECH creative staff in the poster design.

The idea for this project grew out of conversations between AIDSTECH staff and Family Planning Associations in a variety of OECS nations in the Fall of 1989. Dominica was selected as the pilot country for this campaign because of its strong interest in the program and its well-organized CBD system and meticulous record-keeping detailing numbers of condoms sold in all CBD outlets throughout the country. AIDSTECH began its field work on this project in early 1990, with initial field research (including interviews with Family Planning personnel, shopkeepers, and MOH staff in several countries) conducted January

through March of that year. Based on the data collected, a graphic artist was hired to begin production of possible designs for use in the CBD distribution program, as well as for the condom symbol to be used throughout the entire campaign (CBD program and CFPA poster). In April, 1990, AIDSTECH sent a team to Antigua and Dominica to work with CFPA on the poster design, conduct interviews to pre-test poster messages, and run focus groups to pre-test CBD promotion ideas. The joint team made up of AIDSTECH staff and consultants with CFPA staff worked closely for several days to identify possible themes and messages for a "lifestyle" condom promotion poster. These themes, and accompanying ideas for visual images, were then pre-tested in both Antigua and Dominica.

Materials were produced by AIDSTECH and CFPA in the subsequent months; campaign materials (posters, boxes, buttons, stickers) were delivered to Dominica in early October, 1990 for distribution throughout the Family Planning Association CBD network and the initiation of the campaign.

OBJECTIVES

The goals of the campaign are to increase condom sales throughout Dominica's CBD outlets by increasing condom awareness and condom visibility. Based on principles used in advertising in many regions of the world and some preliminary research conducted in Mexico by AIDSCOM/Porter Novelli, the "lifestyle" approach was selected to be tested in this campaign. By increasing condom visibility in a fun, socially acceptable and relevant way, this campaign can set the stage for further education and information about condoms throughout the society, reaching marginalized populations at high risk. In addition, a highly visible, acceptable campaign can increase overall societal comfort levels in dealing with issues of condoms, sexual health, and AIDS prevention. The campaign, from its inception, was designed to be a low-cost way to promote condoms and increase visibility and sales.

Rather than using the tools of traditional condom social marketing, such as re-packaging and re-marketing the condoms themselves, this campaign seeks to provide additional ways for NGO's and shop-owners to display and promote the condoms they are currently selling. Social marketing of condoms has been effective in some countries (e.g., Zaire), but it is a very expensive means of increasing sales. In addition, social marketing campaigns focus on specific brands and may not have as much impact on overall condom sales and use. This condom promotion campaign, however, is not brand-specific and can contribute to the overall acceptability of all types of condoms and, presumably, condom sales.

The objectives of the qualitative research that supported this campaign were to:

▼ Outline the design of a condom promotion poster and select visual elements for use in the poster photo.

▼ Identify the most appropriate textual message for use on a condom promotion poster designed jointly by CFPA and AIDSTECH.

▼ Select the most appropriate promotional design for use in the CBD program for point-of-purchase materials.

▼ Pre-test and select the preferred condom symbol for use throughout the campaign.

▼ Identify shop-owners' concerns and needs regarding condom display/distribution boxes.

METHODOLOGY

To accomplish these objectives, the AIDSTECH team conducted a series of interviews and focus groups with the target audiences in Antigua and Dominica. The qualitative research participants were segmented based on age and gender. The process was as follows:

Structured Interviews: The AIDSTECH team conducted a series of 23 interviews (14 men, 9 women) in St. John's, Antigua to pretest the three possible messages developed by the CFPA-AIDSTECH team and the potential visual images to accompany them. Participants for the interviews were recruited from 5 different shops in downtown St. John's.

In addition, AIDSTECH staff conducted a series of interviews with shopkeepers and bar owners in six villages in Dominica to pre-test the artwork and structure of the condom display box. These interview participants were those who worked in or owned CBD outlets in Dominica.

Focus Groups: AIDSTECH staff conducted a total of four (4) focus groups in Dominica. Two focus groups took place in Roseau with women, and two in Grand Bay with men. Participants were recruited by the staff of the Dominica Family Planning Association. The data from these interviews and focus groups were used to determine visuals and text for the condom promotion poster and the artwork for the condom display box and condom symbol.

FINDINGS AND RECOMMENDATIONS

Condom Promotion Poster: In keeping with the idea of developing a "lifestyle" campaign, the CFPA-AIDSTECH team developed three possible sets of text for the poster to accompany the visual image.

Text: The text ideas that were developed and pre-tested were:

1. **I was strong enough to talk about it. We talked. We listened. Now we use condoms. Not for her. Not for me. But for both of us.**

2. **People who care use condoms. How about you?**

3. **It's not the end of anything. It's only the beginning. Condoms . . . Because You Care.**

(Continued)

EXAMPLE 13.6

Public-generated Messages for a Caribbean Campaign (*continued*)

Reprinted with permission.

Each of these sets of text was designed to convey a social message, one that positioned condom use in the context of people's relationships with one another, in much the same way that traditional advertising of soft drinks or other consumer goods does.

Visuals: The text above was to be framed against a backdrop of a social situation to emphasize the "life-style" aspects of the campaign. The possible options all involved public places that would not require showing someone's home (such as a party). The visual images that were pre-tested were:

1. **Beach scene**
2. **Sporting event**
3. **Restaurant scene**

Of the visual images, the beach scene was preferred overwhelmingly. When interview participants were asked what place they thought of when they were having fun, the most prominent and enthusiastic responses involved the beach. In addition, the beach was cited as the place to meet friends and possible boyfriends/girlfriends. In focus group discussions in Dominica, when participants were asked to describe the activities of a "fun day at the beach," the most frequently mentioned activities were having a barbecue or going on a picnic. Participants said that the people they were most likely to go to the beach with were friends and siblings. In addition, they often meet other friends at the beach.

The restaurant was cited as a friendly environment, but was perceived to be too formal—not as much fun. It was also less likely to be a place to go with a group of friends for the focus group participants.

Some of the men in the focus groups also mentioned football matches as "fun" environments; the women, however, indicated that, while they were a fun place, it seemed to be more so for men. So, if a site was to be chosen that was considered to be equally enjoyable for men and women, the beach was the most appropriate selection.

Based on these responses from the interviews and focus groups, the beach scene was selected as the most appropriate visual image for the poster.

For the text, the three ideas were presented in both the interview and the focus groups. Ideas #1 and 3 were most well received by all participants. Idea #2 was perceived to be too "weak." Focus group participants in Dominica (especially women) felt that it did not make the point about using condoms in a strong enough fashion. Among the men, in both interviews and focus groups, #2 was consistently liked least of all the choices. Idea #2 generated little discussion in the focus groups and minimal responses in the interviews.

Among the other ideas, there was much discussion. Many interview participants liked #1 for its literal message. Respondents pointed out that it was very clear about telling people what to do. When asked who was speaking, however, all respondents said that it was a man. The women in the focus groups, while they liked that the man felt "strong enough to talk about it" did not like the fact that, as they saw it, the man seemed to be the primary deciding factor. In the interviews, idea #1 was usually most well-received by people who put the least time into thinking about the messages; thus, for those people who were interested in the campaign and took active part in the interviews, this idea received only a lukewarm response. For those interview participants who seemed to want to conclude the interview as quickly as possible, idea #1 was usually their first choice. The interview team felt that this was most likely because it was the most literal of the three options; choosing it was easy and gave the respondents a feeling of having completed the interview quickly and easily.

Those who actively discussed each message overwhelmingly preferred #3 ("It's not the end of anything. It's only the beginning. Condoms . . . Because You Care"). Interview participants frequently commented that this one had a bit of mystery about it.

(Continued)

EXAMPLE 13.6

Public-generated Messages for a Caribbean Campaign (*continued*)

Some asked the interview team what it meant; when the question was turned back to them to try and answer, they had a range of creative ideas. Those who came up with explanations for it always favored this text over the other options.

In the focus groups, this text generated by far the most discussion of the three options. Both women and men in their respective groups debated its possible meaning and, as one group rightly noted, **the fact that the phrase could generate so much discussion made it a very valuable tool for getting people to think about condoms**. In one focus group, a woman pointed out that it reminded her of a perfume advertisement, with a little bit of mystery attached. This notion was quickly echoed by the rest of the group. Both men and women felt that the slogan could refer to any of the following things (all of which were seen as positive kinds of condom promotion messages):

1. It's not the end of hope . . .

2. It's not the end of sex . . .

3. It's not the end of the day . . . (more chances to get to know other person)

4. It's not the end of romance . . .

5. It's not the end of the relationship . . .

6. It's not the end of fun . . .

In addition, women in particular felt that this message spoke to their concerns about relationships with men, not just sex. In other words, the message told them that having sex was simply the prelude to a relationship—and not an end in itself. For the women in the focus groups, this was a very significant and positive attribute of the message.

Overwhelmingly, all respondents liked the "Condoms . . . Because You Care" tag line. Even for those participants for whom #1 was preferable, many suggested concluding with this tag line as well. When asked why they liked this line, interview participants responded that it made them "feel good" and that it made them think very positive things about condoms. The caring referred to in the line, they felt, could refer to caring about your partner, caring about yourself, or even caring about people with AIDS. For virtually all respondents, these were seen as very important and powerful messages.

When this tag line was combined with the more "mysterious" feelings in the first part of #3, it was seen as a powerful combination that emphasized positive feelings and encouraged people to think about and talk about the issue of using condoms.

Given that this program seeks to increase awareness and use of condoms without promoting any kind of AIDS, STD, Family Planning, or health-specific message, it was felt that #3 best represented the ideas behind the condom promotion campaign: that it epitomized the "lifestyle" message by presenting somewhat ambiguous text that could lead people to think more about the poster and the issue in general.

Recommendations:

> **It's not the end of anything.**
> **It's only the beginning.**
> **Condoms . . . Because You Care.**

Against backdrop of beach scene. [Frye's Point in Antigua discussed as possible option for shooting photograph].

Condom Symbol: The campaign included a condom symbol for two reasons:

1. To help shopkeepers have a recognizable way of indicating "condoms available here."

2. To create a unifying theme for the campaign.

During the preliminary research phases of the campaign, AIDSTECH staff met with a range of people involved in AIDS prevention and condom promotion throughout the region to discuss the idea of a condom symbol. Early drawings were pre-tested in shops in Dominica and it was found that respondents could not identify an abstract condom symbol (e.g., a circle in a square, like a condom in its package) without some kind of identifying label. During a second round of pre-testing in the region in March, 1990, another set of possible symbols were pre-tested. Interview participants expressed a strong preference for the more literal of the condom symbols. During the final pre-testing in April in Antigua and Dominica, focus groups strongly favored the most literal-looking of the possibilities presented. In addition, the word "condoms" was added to the bottom of the symbol to clarify its meaning. When the selected symbol was pre-tested, with the additional textual label, its meaning was very clear for focus group participants. When asked what they would think about a shop that had this symbol and label on its door, the overwhelming response was that the shop sold condoms. The only other response given in the focus groups was that the shopkeepers were trying to promote condom use. The team conducting the research felt that this symbol was clearly understood by participants. The campaign would eventually like to remove the label—when the symbol has achieved a sufficient level of recognition.

For the symbols' colors, all qualitative research participants favored very bright colors, particularly blues, greens, and pinks. Symbols in all three of these colors were printed after shopkeepers requested a variety of colors to use in their shops.

The final condom symbol is integrated into both the CFPA-AIDSTECH condom promotion poster and the condom display box to enhance the unifying theme of the campaign.

Condom Display Box: The purpose of the condom display box is to increase condom visibility in the CBD outlets. Prior to campaign implementation, all shopkeepers stored and displayed condoms in the white cardboard USAID boxes. Photographs taken during preliminary fieldwork conducted in March, 1990 indicate how the white boxes were virtually invisible in the shops. After speaking with a variety of shopkeepers and bar owners, AIDSTECH developed three different box design structures.

Needs for the newly-designed box structure, as identified by AIDSTECH and the shopkeepers included:

▼ Durable, yet resistant to heat and moisture

▼ Easy to assemble and lightweight for shipping

▼ Easy dispensing of condom strips

▼ Condoms dispensed from front or side so that boxes can be stored on top

▼ Wide enough to support other boxes on top

▼ Opaque, to prevent light from harming condoms

▼ Easy to change artwork

▼ Dark enough so that dirt does not show

The box designs that were pre-tested were developed by AIDSTECH in conjunction with an artist and packaging specialists to ensure that these needs were met. Three box designs were taken to Dominica and pre-tested with 14 shopkeepers and bar owners in six villages throughout Dominica. The box design chosen was the only one that reflected all the needs listed above.

For the front panel of the display boxes, a series of artwork ideas were pre-tested, all with a variation on a lifestyle theme. The interviews with shopkeepers revealed several main themes:

▼ The artwork needed to be large enough to be visible from a distance.

▼ Artwork showing faces rather than animals, blue jeans pockets, etc., were strongly preferred.

(*Continued*)

EXAMPLE 13.6

Among focus group participants, artwork with faces was also strongly preferred. In addition, groups expressed a strong preference for artwork in which the faces were looking out (toward the consumer) rather than at one another.

The condom symbol, when integrated into the box artwork, was preferred when positioned between the man and woman, rather than above or to the side. Focus group participants, especially women, felt that this drew attention to the reason for the display.

The artwork for the box is produced separately from the box itself. In this way, campaign themes and styles can be changed without requiring box replacements each time.

Written by Lynda Cole, Associate Director of AIDSTECH, and used by permission.

▼ GOVERNMENT CAMPAIGNS

What about public relations campaigns for governments? Most governmental agencies and departments have a public relations function, whatever it is called. In the United States, it is called public affairs. In some countries it has no name but encompasses the activities performed by the ministry of propaganda. Just as the names differ, the missions often differ too. But leadership can change a mission. The leadership of Mikhail Gorbachev in Russia, for example, made the Ministry of Propaganda more PR conscious. At the 1987 Washington, D.C., Reagan-Gorbachev summit meeting, the Soviet ministry came close to beating the United States at its own game.

The USIA (United States Information Agency) is the U.S. government's public relations department, but it functions primarily outside of the United States. In the 1980s, it was run by Charles Z. Wick, a California businessman and Reagan fundraiser who is reported to have said he didn't know anything about foreign affairs or journalism.[15] He changed the agency dramatically, making it more responsive by holding people accountable. He spoke out readily and developed new programs, including controversial documentaries that made the agency more visible. Not everyone liked that, and more than a few didn't like Wick himself. But even those who didn't like him could not dispute his effectiveness

in dramatically increasing the overall budget, modernizing the Voice of America and developing Worldnet, the first international satellite television network. Washington is now linked to fifty U.S. embassies and other overseas stations with two-way audio and one-way video hookups that permit all types of programming, from presentations to news conferences.[16]

In the United States, the Federal News Service (FNS) broadcasts White House briefings (generally twice a day: morning and midday), as well as briefings from the State Department (once a day) and the Defense Department (twice a week). FNS also broadcasts statements by the President, cabinet officers and other U.S. officials. It also broadcasts Congressional hearings, National Press Club meetings and news conferences and various other meetings held in Washington when the topics discussed are of national interest. The FNS also presents points of view of other nations as expressed to U.S. embassies abroad or to the United Nations. On weekends, FNS transmits the President's radio address and other public affairs programs with guest interviews of national or international interest. FNS transmits by satellite, and the signal is received by FNS radio stations. These transmit to a printer or a computer. FNS also has a private wire system in Washington, D.C., which is available by subscription and is part of Dialcom, a hardware-independent on-line worldwide service whose transmissions can be received by personal computers, word processors and computer terminals anywhere.

Governments are interested in commercial development and especially in tourism. Many nations publish books and magazines and buy advertising space and time in the media. Although these agencies try to be responsive to media inquiries in times of crisis, they don't always succeed in overcoming government censorship, which compounds the problem. An exception is the U.S. Commonwealth protectorate of Puerto Rico, which cooperated with the media in the coverage of a tragic hotel fire and even followed up on the story. Because of Puerto Rico's sensitivity to public relations, Edward L. Bernays encouraged them to help interpret North America and Latin America to each other by establishing a North-South Center. (There is an East-West Center in Hawaii.)[17]

With all of the turmoil in the Philippines in the 1980s after Corazon Aquino took over following the expulsion of Ferdinand Marcos, the nation hired a U.S. firm to help its tourist bureau.[18] Antonio Mapa, regional coordinator for the Philippine Department of Tourism, said Japan and the United States were the major foci of the campaign. To run the campaign, the government hired Hill & Knowlton. In doing so, the Philippines joined more than 125 foreign governments in retaining U.S. firms.

The governments are interested primarily in tourism, trade, internal investments, industrial development and image building, says Amelia Lobsenz, whose firm represents a number of foreign countries.[19] Normally agencies are hired after the U.S. embassy in the country's capital has invited bids. Lobsenz says that in international PR practice the diverse needs of U.S. society have to be identified and interpreted to clients through research and analysis and that the agency has to get to know the country's leaders in order to obtain substantive facts. She also says that the agency has to be an authority on the country's culture and therefore must remain abreast of current events. It has to be especially careful in serving as the country's U.S. spokesperson, because everything it sends abroad can have tremendous repercussions.[20]

Many countries use their own PR firms instead of government agencies to do extra work in representing the country. One of these is Kyodo Public Relations, the largest independent PR firm in Japan, which counts as one of its clients the U.S. embassy in Tokyo. The Japanese public relations counsel Ohashi notes that in Japanese corporations only the best people in a company can qualify for the public relations specialists' jobs, because they deal with top management directly. They also have top titles, major authority and are candidates for the CEO position.[21] As the United States put plants in other countries and as other nations set up shop in the United States or buy U.S. facilities, culture shock sets in for both owners and employees, underscoring the need for first-rate corporate communications, both internally and externally.

▼ GLOBAL CAMPAIGNS: DOES ONE FIT ALL?

Historically the nations of the world have always engaged in a great deal of economic interaction, but something quite different happened after World War II. First, many national economies were shattered, and the United States invested heavily in the Marshall Plan to rebuild them. As the various nations began to recover their economic strength, they turned to the United States first as a marketplace for their goods and later as a place to invest their new wealth.

Along with the increase in international economic activity came the need for help in dealing with different governments, with the languages and customs of foreign and unfamiliar customers and with the effects of two new technologies—aviation and television. This need existed both in the United States and in the foreign countries. The United States was rapidly expanding its political and commercial involvement abroad and the foreign nations were discovering the United States as an eager customer. The borders between countries seemed to vanish, and business people talked of "jet lag." Later, the micronization of electronic technology and the advent of the computer made virtual face-to-face contact possible throughout the world.

From bankers putting together financial packages in Brussels or Paris, to loan participants coming from Caracas, Frankfurt, Tokyo and Madrid, to hospital administrators convening in Geneva, the world began to look more like a community, although a few neighbors would do battle from time to time over one issue or another. The vision that many people had held for the role of public relations in its 1950s growth period seemed on the verge of becoming reality. Expansion in the social sciences and in communication theory seemed to provide the needed support.

Companies that had waded into the international waters early found many requests for their services, so they began to formulate public relations campaigns to reach their new-found publics. Some of these campaigns were product-oriented; some were political; some were service-centered; and some were professionally focused.

Going global is even more necessary today, but it is still a very untidy and uncertain business. The PR firms that got in early (in the 1960s and 1970s) are still at the top of the heap: Burson-Marsteller, Hill & Knowlton and Ogilvy & Mather. They control a campaign, "a seamless campaign" as Burson-Marsteller calls it. One well-recognized network is the Pinnacle Group, headed by Amelia Lobsenz, chairman of Lobsenz-Stevens and 1985 president of the International Public Relations Association.[22]

Although PR firms and networks are available to do the job, some companies still handle their PR/advertising/marketing/sales campaigns at home and abroad. Their PR and marketing people may or may not work together. A survey of service industries showed their PR departments to be small compared to marketing. And in most instances these departments reported to marketing, which reported directly to the principal office. This suggests that PR, at least in service industries, is being used for publicity and promotion. Certainly PR is not in a hierarchical position in these industries that facilitates interaction with management.

One of the most intensive global campaigns is the World Health Organization's AIDS campaign. In addition to experiencing the problems of any campaign (language barriers, government regulations and media), the AIDS campaign suffers from a lack of infrastructure—a problem not limited to nonindustrialized nations. Add to that the cultural taboos of many societies regarding any discussion of sexual matters, as well as the objections of social conservatives in all cultures who fear that sex education encourages promiscuity, and you have a real campaign challenge.

WHO has responded by creating basic educational materials that it furnishes to health authorities in various countries to adapt to their own cultures. Many countries have turned the development of their plan (and the funds to implement it) over to public relations firms. While many nations have taken aggressive action, others have not, perhaps because they face too many other issues that demand immediate attention. But the problem is global and involves essentially the facts everywhere, so at some point the campaigns tailored for various countries and for the ethnic and cultural groups within those countries will offer a remarkable case study.

▼ SUMMARY

Campaigns are designed to accomplish specific organizational objectives. The three elements of the campaign discussed in detail are planning, implementation and evaluation.

Planning means setting goals, creating timetables and developing budgets. Setting the creative strategy involves choosing a theme and media to use in communicating with the designated publics. Internal strategy is critical to establishing organizational support for the campaign. Implementation has three major components: adapting and applying tactics to strategies; keeping people informed; and solving all problems positively. While the campaign is in progress, all elements must be monitored so that goals are achieved. Afterward, a post-mortem offers an objective look at what worked and what didn't—where goals fell short or exceeded expectations. This final evaluation helps with successive planning.

Campaigns are usually built around a desire to establish, change or modify behaviors. Some government campaigns (primarily information-based) have succeeded when education is supported by engineering (making it possible for people to do what you are asking them to do) and by enforcement (some sort of regulation or reward).

Most campaigns, even for a product that is being sold globally, do not work well across cultures. The cultural aspect is more important than national borders or languages, although laws can affect certain campaign tactics.

▼ NOTES

[1]Patrick Jackson, speech for Vern C. Schranz Distinguished Lectureship in Public Relations, Ball State University, Muncie, Indiana, 1984.

[2]*pr reporter* (May 29, 1978), p. 1.

[3]John E. Rehfeld, "What Working for a Japanese Company Taught Me," *Harvard Business Review*, 68(6) (November–December 1990), pp. 167–76 (p. 171).

[4]Ronald E. Rice and William J. Paisley, eds., *Public Communications Campaigns* (Beverly Hills, Calif.: Sage, 1981), p. 7.

[5]Charles T. Salmon, ed., *Information Campaigns: Balancing Social Values and Social Change* (Newbury Park, Calif.: Sage, 1989), p. 47.

[6]William Paisley, "Prologue," in Ronald E. Rice and Charles K. Atkin, eds., *Public Communication Campaigns* 2d ed. (Newbury Park, Calif.: Sage, 1989), p. 17.

[7]Ibid., p. 21.

[8]Ibid., p. 23.

[9]Ibid., p. 23.

[10]Campaigns Can Change Behavior if They Involve a 2-step Process: 3 Examples Show How National Efforts Using Partnerships & Grassroots Programs Are Making Headway," *pr reporter* (December 10, 1990), 33(10), p. 1.

[11]"Billboard Displays Powerful Message," *MADD in Action* (May–August 1990).

[12]John Pierson, "Political Statements Take Graphic Form" in "Form + Function" column, *Wall Street Journal* (September 24, 1990), p. B1.

[13]Hernando Gonzales, "Interactivity and Feedback in Third World Development Campaigns," *Critical Studies in Mass Communication*, 6 (1989), pp. 295–314.

[14]Lynda Cole, Associate Director of AIDSTECH, Research Triangle Park, North Carolina, furnished all of the material on the Caribbean campaign reproduced in this example.

[15]Andreas Rosbach, "Marketing and Public Relations in the International and Domestic Markets of North American Service Companies: Partners or Adversaries," unpublished masters thesis, Texas Christian University, August 1987.

[16]Marguerite Michaels, "The Surprising Success of Charles Wick," *Parade* (March 31, 1985), pp. 8, 9, 11.

[17]Alan Patureau, "Creation of a North-South Center Urged," *San Juan Star* (May 2, 1984), p. 32.

[18]Arne N. Masterton, "Public Relations Firm Hired to Promote Philippines," *Tour and Travel News* (October 12, 1987), p. 55.

[19]Amelia Lobsenz, "Representing a Foreign Government," *Public Relations Journal* (August 1984), pp. 21–22.

[20]Ibid., p. 22.

[21]"Ohashi: Public Relations in Japan," *Public Relations Journal* (August 1984), pp. 14–19.

[22]Alyse Lynn Booth, "Going Global," *Public Relations Journal*, 1986, pp. 22–27.

Selected readings, activities and assignments appropriate to this chapter can be found in the Instructor's Guide.

▼

CASE STUDIES

Learning teaches how to carry things in suspense,
without prejudice, til you resolve.

Francis Bacon, author, statesman and philosopher

That man is wise to some purpose who gains his
wisdom at the expense and from the experience
of another.

Plautus, Roman poet and playwright

Case studies (often referred to as *cases*) demonstrate how campaigns to achieve specific public relations objectives are planned, implemented and evaluated.

PR practitioners and educators use case studies in two ways. First, they may pose a PR problem and outline a possible solution according to specific guidelines, as suggested by an existing case. Second, they may dissect an historical case as a learning experience to determine what worked, what didn't and why. The historical case is generally referred to simply as a *case*. The existing situation in need of a PR solution is generally called a *problem*. Many PR courses in fact use the title "PR Cases and Problems."

A PR firm keeps a special library containing files of the cases it has handled. These are often written as historical case studies and are not merely the final evaluation of PR action. The firm's new employees often are assigned to research these cases in the firm's library, which also serves as a resource center for the entire staff.

▼ CASE ANALYSIS

An analysis of a historical case can be broken down into four parts. The first part should include a summary of the case—that is, an explanation of the nature of the problem or problems the campaign addressed and the problem background—and the research-based purposes of the PR actions that were taken to address the situation or problem, based on discovery research and remedial research.

The second part involves additional research into publics; an assessment of the impact of the problem, situation or proposed action; prioritizing of the publics; a discussion of the evolution of the problem, together with its probable causes; and an explanation of what was done to deal with the problem. In looking at the steps taken to solve the problem, you should pay special attention to research into the problem itself, how the publics were selected and what was learned about them. Study the techniques and tools used to reach these publics, and compare these with other possible techniques and tools. Study, too, the role of the public relations person in the solution, especially with regard to the interaction of PR with other departments. The solution should offer some evidence that it was a workable way to handle the problem. Evidence may be available from the continuation of the program, from letters of endorsement, from evaluation research or from other data such as responses to the program.

The third part of the analysis should consist of a detailed description of the institution involved in the problem—what it does, what it is. Samples of all materials used in the program should be included: news releases to all media, special coverage, scripts, posters, advertising, letters, special publications and so on. Copies of progress reports should be examined and included in the analysis. Such reports are generally available if the PR problem was handled by a PR firm, because the firm must report to management periodically. Internally handled problems are sometimes less well documented, because there is some informal reporting. The action taken and all communications efforts made should be explained in detail.

The fourth part of the analysis should be a consideration and evaluation of what worked particularly well and what could have been improved. Especially valuable are thoughtful recommendations about how such a program might be handled better if a similar situation confronts the same institution in the future.

▼ **Cases are analyzed by looking at their four components: research, publics, action (including communication) and evaluation.**

This type of dissection of a PR event is useful for students trying to develop approaches to PR problems; and the same careful, detailed study and documentation is also useful for practitioners after a campaign. Such a dissection is part of the postevaluation discussed in Chapter 4.

Elements included in both the existing and the historical cases are basically the same (see Example 14.1).

Availability of Cases

Cases serve as idea resources for PR practitioners in solving problems and for PR scholars in theory building. The Public Relations Society of America each year solicits documented cases in 45 categories for its Silver Anvil competition. The structure of those cases generally follows the outline in Example 14.1, although the designations are Research, Planning, Execution and Evaluation. (You may recall from Chapter 10 that two other sets of frequently used designations are Research, Action, Communication and Evaluation and Research, Objectives, Publics and Evaluation. The elements of each set are much the same, although the emphasis may differ.) Case entries from each PRSA competition are kept for two years and are available for review in the Information Center of PRSA's New York headquarters (33 Irving Place, New York, NY 10003) by appointment. The phone number is (212) 995-2230.

Self-generated case studies that have won awards are also available from the International Association of Business Communicators (IABC). IABC's Golden Quill Awards are published each year in booklet form, and each volume offers about 100 cases. These are available from IABC, One Hallidie Plaza, Suite 600, San Francisco, California 94102. IABC's phone number is (415) 362-8762.

EXAMPLE 14.1

Elements of PR Cases— Existing and Historical

Existing Case/Campaign Development	Historical Case
RESEARCH	
To help identify the problem and establish objectives.	To describe the nature of the problem and its background—the evolution and probable causes. To define the objectives involved in the solution. To consider other possible solutions and their consequences.
PUBLICS	
To designate publics and recognize which are target publics. To learn what they know and believe and how to reach them with available media.	To determine how priority publics were selected and how each was involved in the solution.
ACTION	
To plan ways of reaching publics in an effective, efficient manner within a flexible, feasible timetable. To develop a persuasive strategy. To get management and staff support.	To examine the tools and techniques used in terms of their effectiveness with the various publics. To look for evidence of management and publics' endorsement through continuation of the program or through other results that give evidence of a solution. To include samples of action taken—PR tools and techniques.
EVALUATION	
To evaluate the results or the effectiveness of the program as revealed by post-testing research or less formal methods such as responses from publics and staffs.	To recommend better ways to approach similar problems, should these occur in the same organization. To analyze lessons to be learned from the solution implemented.

In addition, the Harvard Business School publishes various case studies, some of which address public relations problems. These are available from Harvard Business School Publications, Boston, Massachusetts 02163. Unlike the PRSA cases, which are self-reporting for a competition, the Harvard cases are field studies performed by graduate students. Of course, the field studies are done with the cooperation and consent of the company being investigated. Harvard's Business School dean in 1908 began looking for ways to build theory in his newly established discipline and got the idea for case studies from Harvard Law School. The first cases were a bit of a "hard sell," since the researchers tended to unlock closets that hid corporate skeletons; but the case study approach now has a prestige factor attached to it.

A 1990s case from Harvard Business School Professor Stephen A. Greyser's corporate communications class analyzes the evolution of Mazda's public relations strategy over a 20-year period. The case documents how Mazda used public relations to build relations with consumers during the 1970s and to establish its reputation in the United States.

Considerably more difficult to find are cases that document problem solving when culture is an issue. However, resources in other disciplines such as anthropology and sociology (including social work) offer some help. If you explore that literature, you need to be familiar with the social science approach, which is as follows: problem definition, purpose, problem *solver*, process and, finally, solution (usually with some evaluation). But whereas in social work the researcher usually becomes the problem solver, in anthropology the researcher looks at indigenous problem solvers who may be village elders, or others of status. Why look at such cases for guidance in addressing public relations problems? Here's one example. The object was to get health information to Indian tribes living in remote parts of Mexico who deliberately maintain their distance from the mainstream of Mexican affairs for fear of "cultural contamination." In that sense, they are much like the Amish in the United States who preserve their own culture and traditions in "island communities." The Indian tribals depend on a shaman for guidance and care in their physical and mental health. The shaman is therefore the key to getting the health information to the tribe. A more direct approach to tribe members might be possible, since many of them speak and read Spanish and their communities are accessible, but the results would be ineffective at best. A worst-case situation would be a serious domestic disturbance resulting from the effort.

The only reasonable solution, then, seems to be to "sell the shaman" on the health programs. But that's not easy either, since the shaman stays in the community. However, a village elder does have some connection to the larger Mexican society because he travels to other communities bringing goods to sell and then buys provisions to take back. (In these tribes, it's always a "he." The women and young people are never allowed out of the community.) The contact has to be made, trust established, and the representative granted access to the tribe's shaman. Usually this process takes months or even years. But it is the only way to deliver health

▼ **Cases serve as idea resources for PR practitioners and theoreticians.**

information and get any kind of compliance or adoption.

As public relations efforts continue in the global community, observations from anthropologists and case studies from the fields of social work and agriculture (which is the source of the diffusion process and resulting theory) will have increasing significance and bear careful study by PR practitioners and scholars.

Learning from Experience and Borrowing Ideas

PR practitioners who work in the public affairs area may be more familiar than those from the marketing/promotions area with the situation of having a priority public of one. Often a case depends on the support of one person—a key staff member of an agency or a committee chair. Often in such cases the PR person will work with the organization's lobbyists. Ronald N. Levy offers the following suggestions, based on his experience, for helping your lobbyist win in such situations:

1. Get started early and use material from an executive's speech, because it already has been researched and cleared for release.

2. Use arguments people can relate to, ones that affect them.

3. Show what impact winning on your issue will have on the major concerns of the day.

4. Don't put all your arguments into one release (except for the trade publications). No one wants to know everything, at least immediately, and you need additional material to keep sending.

5. Present only your case, not the opposition's.

6. Don't engage in pejorative name calling. If you have to, refer to the other side as "less informed" or "well intentioned."

7. Keep in touch with the lobbyist to get feedback on which arguments seem to be working best.

8. Don't cover just the news media. Send information to important constituencies, too, so they will have information to reinforce their support.

9. Keep in mind that the key objective is to win, not to accumulate more clippings, interviews, editorials and photo layouts. Winning is the bottom line.[1]

Even with the best of help, though, things can go wrong, as the American Heart Association (AHA) found out in its public affairs campaign to put a seal of approval on foods that met AHA standards. After three years of planning and working with all regulatory agencies as well as industry, and just five days before the first labeled foods were to become available to consumers, the AHA got a letter from the Food and Drug Administration (FDA) threatening regulatory action to stop the program. At first the AHA said it wouldn't cancel the launch of the first phase of its program: labeling of margarines, spreads, crackers, oils and canned and frozen vegetables (altogether, fewer than 100 labeled foods). However, the AHA did eventually fold the campaign. James S. Benson, acting commissioner of the FDA at the time, cited possible consumer confusion over the meaning of the labeling as grounds for intervening. Critics of the FDA's decision to intervene, however, argued that political pressure from beef and dairy producers provided a more plausible explanation for the FDA's behavior. The Department of Agriculture already had told the AHA that it would not support the program; but that agency had no regulatory power to affect such a program as the AHA's labeling.[2]

Various supporters of the AHA plan felt that the campaign was stymied by three unavoidable problems. One was the power of some industries over the agencies that supposedly regulate them. A second was the fact that the AHA had previously attacked the tobacco industry, which now owns a number of food product companies, leading many observers to conclude (justly or unjustly) that these companies had objected to the program out of simple vindictiveness. A third problem was that the very existence of the campaign represented an affront (or embarrassment) to the federal government, which had done little in response to consumers' demands for information about what they were eating. The subsequent regulatory activity by the government mandating better labeling was viewed by some AHA supporters as confirming this last point.

Nonprofit organizations always have to be careful about their public affairs efforts. They are restricted in how much pressure they can exert on government, because direct lobbying may endanger their tax-exempt status. They have, therefore, focused on promotions designed to compete for funding dollars, to convince people to take advantage of their services (so they can prove they need money), and to increase or maintain their image-share of the marketplace. The most competitive have been health organizations and organizations that represent the arts. In fact, their promotions have been called marketing/public relations.

Nonprofit institutions that emphasize the selling aspect of marketing without paying enough attention to their publics can encounter hazards. Alan Andreasen, a professor of marketing at the University of Illinois in Champaign-Urbana, warns nonprofits to pay as much attention to their clients as they do to their products.[3] He points out that nonprofits are always in financial difficulties and really suffer when the economy is bad and the federal government makes substantial budget cuts in social services. Clients will remain loyal if they see themselves as part of the institution.

Loyalty of clients has become a national problem for MADD, which found itself the subject of a TV network investigative piece in March of 1991. The problem centered on the organization's distancing of itself from its founder, Candy Lightner, which caused some loss of identity. The organization has also been accused of spending too much of the money it takes in from donors on raising more money instead of on the cause. That accusation is not an unusual one to hear about fund-raising efforts. Some people who give to university appeals and then receive a package of expensive gifts in response wonder how much of their money goes to the real appeal. The national public broadcasting stations, which also use gifts in fundraising, have tried to get around this by offering a check-off option that enables the donor to relinquish the standard gift so that all of the money can go to programming. Many museums and other organizations will tell donors how much of their "membership" can be counted as an outright "donation." It appears that the Internal Revenue Service is as interested as consumers in how these donations are used.

Reports of the six-figure salary commanded by United Way's (now former) chief executive touched off a major flap in early 1992. Local groups affiliated with United Way scrambled to establish that they were abiding by the standard of spending no more than 12 percent of the contributions they received on administrative expenses; but published audits showed that in many cases they were over the limit.

Failure to listen to publics is still pervasive, and many cases document the unfortunate consequences of this. One such case came from General Electric, which is considered to have one of the best management training programs in industry. GE had an embarrassing and costly failure with a refrigerator. The product failed so badly that the company had to take a $450 million pretax charge in 1990, and beginning in early 1989 it replaced nearly 1.1 million faulty compressors.[4] The whole disaster had been attributed to poor corporate communications. Low-level, salaried GE employees who did the pre-production testing told their superiors that the compressor might be defective. The word never got up the six levels of oversight to senior executives.[5]

While no theory links corporate values and economics, Johnson & Johnson's former chairman Jim Burke thinks that his company's credo enabled it to take rapid and correct action during the Tylenol crisis. He commissioned a study of the financial performance of 20 U.S. companies that had written value statements for at least a generation. The study showed a net income for the 20 companies that increased by a factor of 23 at a time when the gross national product (GNP) increased by only 2½.[6]

Obviously, corporate values have to be accepted by the employees in order to be recognized by others, particularly consumers. As noted in Chapter 6,

employees are PR's front line, and most of the concerns of middle management deal with personnel. Thus, top management is often relieved of these chores. But unfortunately top management is where the attitude toward employees is set. Middle managers adopt the corporate culture and treat their employees, generally, as they are treated and as they perceive their boss to be directing them. Some companies, aware of this interpretation problem, have developed management guides, which are especially popular with companies coping with mergers or diversifications.

You can borrow ideas from the experiences of others on your own. When you see something that catches your attention, find a way to file it. You may need it sometime. You'll have to create your own system for retrieving your collectibles. Some practitioners use a publics typology, like the one in Chapter 6. Others use a media typology, as in Chapter 11. Others use a less formal method and simply maintain a collection they label "gimmicks," or "good strategy." The following pages present two "collectible" cases you can put in your file for future reference.

In the first case, Southwest Airlines' research that led to development of company policy before any policy was needed provides an example of proactive (versus reactive) policy.

The second case illustrates the celebration of historic occasions. Such celebrations are usually a lot of fun for public relations practitioners; and if the company is 100 years old, all the better. The planning by McCormick & Company was especially good because it recognized that employees develop an organizational identity in part from a shared history. Although all publics were involved in the McCormick centennial year, the employees were central.

Southwest Airlines—Putting Policy Before the Problem   Southwest Airlines, one of the first carriers to design a special appeal to people over 65 (first product created in 1971), began to realize that some of the customers it had pitched just might want to take their battery-operated wheelchairs along. Vice-president of special marketing

Camille Keith says she does a lot of her preliminary market research "hanging out" in the terminals—watching, talking to customers and listening. As she watched a group of seniors involved in Southwest's special promotion arrive at the departure gate, she thought, "What if one of them wants to take a wheelchair along? Can we do it? What are the physical properties of the chairs? How many of our customers use them?"

Keith had some research done first among the makers of motorized wheelchairs to determine the chairs' size and what their batteries were made of. And she talked with the airline's safety and mechanical experts to determine what restrictions might limit the plane's ability to carry such items—either in the cabin or below in storage. She found out that spillable, wet-cell batteries could not be carried in the cabin, and she also discovered that the height of the airplane cargo bin prohibited many chairs from being carried upright in the luggage hold.

She drafted a proposal for company policy on carrying the chairs, got it checked by the airline's technical people and, once it was approved, communicated the information to all of Southwest's senior travelers.[7]

Dealings with consumers should be handled considerately, creatively and candidly. Responses, rather than reactions, are more effective. Institutions can defuse hostility and modify negative positions by creating respect for another point of view, making sure that everyone knows all sides of an issue, and having the facts translated from scientific, technical or legal data into something consumers and news media can understand. Thinking ahead also helps in educating audiences.

McCormick & Company's Celebration and Sharing of 100 Years of Corporate History

McCormick & Company, Inc., founded in Baltimore in 1889 and based today in Hunt Valley, Maryland, is an international producer of seasonings, flavorings and specialty foods. Annual sales of the company are over $1 billion, and it has more than 7,500 employees.

Five years before its centennial year, the company had its archives organized and cataloged by the History Factory of Washington, D.C. Besides providing background resources for the centennial event, the archives exercise elicited a corporate commitment to continuing preservation of the company's history. Employees were asked for ideas about how to observe the anniversary, and other large consumer product companies were asked how they had celebrated major anniversaries.

These three types of research helped frame the program objectives, which were: "to reach every major McCormick public; reaffirm and celebrate the company's basic philosophy, values and culture; draw upon company history to promote employee loyalty, pride and teamwork; and demonstrate the company's commitment to and participation in worthy community activities."

The celebration began with a dinner and dance for 650 Baltimore-area current employees and retirees in December 1988. Guests were presented with cookbooks of the 100 best recipes of 100 years of McCormick, and each chapter covered a decade in the company's history (see Example 14.2). Another feature of the dinner and dance was a "Spices of the World" board game produced in cooperation with Baltimore gamemaker Avalon Hill. In the game, six players using miniature vials of real spices compete at delivering spice cargoes around the world. Each card has the picture of a spice and a description of its major features on one side, while the flipside has a recipe that uses the featured spice. The tokens carry the McCormick logo.

Both the 1988 and 1989 annual reports were spice-scented and used pictures from the archives. Shareholders at the annual meeting were served birthday cake. Throughout the year the centennial logo was used on printed materials and postage meters.

In June, Chairman and CEO Charles P. McCormick, Jr. presented Baltimore Mayor Kurt Schmoke a $2 million endowment gift for the city, to be used primarily for (but not restricted to) the city's literacy program.

On the anniversary date of the company's founding, September 27, the donations of the company to the community were announced, one of them resulting from Charity Day contributions. Each year the employees work an extra day (Charity Day) and their wages are matched by the company and given to United Way.

Four thousand employees celebrated at the 100th anniversary dinner party for Baltimore-based employees and their spouses, where the featured attraction was "Up With People"—a group of 150 youngsters from all over the world who perform internationally. Similar celebrations with employees and for customers were held at other McCormick locations. And at other locations, too, donations to the surrounding community were announced.

Following the celebrations, a survey of McCormick employees indicated that the centennial events had met the company's expectations.[8]

▼ CASES FOR STUDY

Cases abound that can provide learning experiences. In this section, we look at two that provide an opportunity to explore solutions others have used. In the case of the 20th anniversary of an incident like the students' deaths at Kent State University on May 4, 1970, you know that commemoration and remembrance of the event will go on and on, so there's plenty of time to plan. Yet this case is special because observation of the 20th anniversary offered an important opportunity for the university to reflect on its past, present and future. The second case comes from India, but the financial world is global, and many companies have had similar experiences.

Kent State University's Commemorative Event

The 20th anniversary of four campus deaths during a State National Guard action is something that Kent State University certainly anticipated. However, it was an important opportunity to take the initiative and focus public attention not just on the past but on the future of the university as well. This case was written by co-author Judy VanSlyke Turk with the cooperation of the university's public relations office.[9]

Escorts Limited (India)

This case from Escorts was presented at a public relations workshop in India in 1988 by its author, Murad Ali Baig. He had written the case earlier (September 25, 1986) for the Public Relations Society of India's annual meeting. The case is presented here with the author's permission.[10] Mr. Baig is now a public relations and management consultant. He offers the following key to some references that might be unfamiliar:

▼ Escorts: Escorts Limited, one of India's top ten engineering companies.

▼ Swraj Paul: The largest private steelmaker in UK and a non-resident Indian of British nationality.

▼ FICCI: Federation of Indian Chambers of Commerce and Industry.

▼ ASSOCHAM: Associated Chambers of Commerce.

▼ PHDCCI: Punjab, Haryana and Delhi Chambers of Commerce.

▼ A.P.J.: Anuin Chand Pyarelal companies, owned by Swraj Paul's brother in Calcutta.

▼ FERA laws: Indian government laws under the Foreign Exchange Regulation Act, which are very strictly monitored.

▼ RBI: Reserve Bank of India, the bankers' bank.

▼ LIC: Life Insurance Corporation. A huge government company formed out of all the private companies nationalised in the 1960s.

▼ Unit Trust: A big government-managed mutual fund company.

▼ Financial institutions: Industrial Development Bank of India (IDBI) controlled the nominees of L.I.C., Unit Trust, nationalised banks, etc., on the boards of private limited companies.

▼ NRI: Non-resident Indian; any person of Indian origin settled abroad with Indian or foreign passport.

EXAMPLE 14.2

Materials from the Centennial Celebration for McCormick & Company

Reprinted with permission.

Kent State University: Commemorating the 20th Anniversary of a National Tragedy

INTRODUCTION

Description of Kent State University

Kent State University is one of 13 public four-year colleges and universities in Ohio. The University's main campus is in Kent, the largest city in Portage County. Other cities nearby in northeastern Ohio are Cleveland and Youngstown, each approximately 45 minutes away, and Akron, about 15 minutes away. The University also has regional two-year campuses in Ashtabula, East Liverpool, Geauga County (Burton), Salem, Stark County (Canton), Trumbull County (Warren) and Tuscarawas County (New Philadelphia).

Kent State University is the oldest state university in the region, established by the State of Ohio in 1910.

The University's enrollment in the fall of 1990 was 24,434: 19,636 undergraduate students and 4,798 full- and part-time graduate students. With more than 3,200 full- and part-time faculty, staff and administrators, the University is the largest employer in Portage County.

The University's academic programs are grouped into several colleges and schools: the colleges of Arts and Sciences, Business Administration, Education, and Fine and Professional Arts; the schools of Nursing, Library Science, and Physical Education, Recreation and Dance; an Honors College; and a Graduate College. A College of Continuing Studies that coordinates the University's lifelong learning efforts also offers programs in conjunction with these other schools and colleges.

Purpose of the Case Study

This case study describes how one institution—Kent State University—planned and implemented a commemoration of the 20th anniversary of what many describe as an American tragedy: the shooting of Kent State University students by Ohio National Guards-

University materials used with permission.

men on May 4, 1970, that left four students dead and nine others wounded.

Kent State and May 4, 1970, have become for many Americans a symbol of the war in Vietnam. The tragic shootings were just part of that larger conflict, yet the impact on the University, past and present, and its surrounding community, was profound. The shootings created a public relations problem—one of public confidence and public opinion—that the twentieth anniversary commemoration had to address.

Like the war itself, the events of May 4, 1970, remain controversial. And in the intervening 20 years since the shootings, there hadn't been much success at bringing together the divergent opinions about what really happened and why, or in bringing about an emotional healing that might permit the University and its community to face its future rather than dwelling on this tragedy of its past.

The University and groups within the University community had commemorated the shootings each year on May 4. But May 4, 1990, would be a special commemoration, for on that day a permanent memorial to the slain and wounded students would be dedicated. Many at the University—administrators, faculty, students and alumni—as well as others in the community who had lived through the tragic events of 20 years ago hoped the dedication of the memorial might begin a healing process that would enable the University to face this moment in its past with grace and to look ahead to its future with dignity.

The task of planning and implementing the 20th anniversary commemoration and dedication of the memorial fell to a campus-wide May 4 Twentieth Anniversary Commission appointed by the University's president, Dr. Michael Schwartz. University News and Information Services, the public relations "arm" of Kent State University, was a planning "partner" with the Commission and implemented many of the tactics with public relations implications that were used in the campaign.

(Continued)

This case study is a success story, an example of a public relations program that worked. It provides an illustration of effective public relations, and of the way in which thorough research and planning can result in public relations tactics and messages that produce desired, positive results.

Research for the Case Study

The case study is based on interviews with individuals who had primary responsibility for planning and implementing Kent State University's commemoration of the 20th anniversary of the May 4 shootings. Those interviewed were Janet Thiede, director of University News and Information Service; Dr. Jerry M. Lewis, professor of sociology and co-chair of the May 4 Twentieth Anniversary Commission; and Prof. Myra R. West, assistant professor of physics and chair of Kent State University's Faculty Senate who served as the Commission's other co-chair.

The author of the case study, Dr. Judy VanSlyke Turk, also was an administrator and faculty member at Kent State University, and participated in or witnessed first-hand many of the 20th anniversary commemorative events.

Records kept by University News and Information also were examined, along with copies of correspondence, documents, publications and other materials generated by the Commission and the University prior to, during and immediately following May 4, 1990.

BACKGROUND: MAY 4, 1970

The Events of May 4, 1970

The spring of 1970 was a turbulent time on the campuses of many colleges and universities across the United States. The war in Vietnam was escalating, with the U.S. bombing raids over Cambodia and dead American servicemen in body bags as close to home as the living room television set. Student protests, most peaceful but a few violent, were as common on college campuses as all-nighters and mid-term exams.

Students at Kent State University, like other students all across the country, rallied to protest the presence of Reserve Officer Training Corps (ROTC) units on campus. They demonstrated against the presence on campus of recruiters from Dow Chemical and other corporations that had commercial ties to the unpopular war. They held teach-ins and sit-ins against the war and for peace.

But at Kent, student opposition to the war took a shocking and tragic turn on May 4, 1970, when Ohio National Guardsmen fired into a crowd of students at 12:24 P.M. In that 13-second volley of gunfire, four students were killed and another nine were injured. All were Kent undergraduates.

Many of the students in the crowd were bystanders, on their way to or from class or lunch in their dormitory cafeterias. Some had gathered at noon for another anti-war demonstration. None could have anticipated the tragic outcome.

National Guardsmen had been dispatched to campus several days earlier on orders from then-Ohio Governor James A. Rhodes at the request of Kent city officials, concerned for the safety of those on campus and in the surrounding community. The Guard's presence on campus was seen as a precaution in case demonstrating students turned on each other or on bystanders, in case the student demonstrators turned violent.

Some say that on May 4, 1970, the demonstrating students turned on the Guard. Others say it was the Guard that turned on the students. But there is no disputing the outcome: four students dead and nine others wounded in a 13-second volley of firing from Guard rifles.

Here's the chronology of significant events in the period surrounding the May 4, 1970, Kent State shootings:

PRIOR TO THE SHOOTINGS

▼ April 30, 1970: President Nixon announces the invasion of Cambodia, triggering massive protests on several of the country's college campuses.

▼ May 1: Rampaging anti-war protesters smash 47 windows and build a bonfire on Water Street in Kent's downtown.

▼ May 2: Ohio National Guardsmen are sent to Kent State University after the University's ROTC building is burned by protesters.

▼ May 3: Ohio Governor James A. Rhodes appears on campus and promises to use "every force possible" to maintain order. Rhodes vows to keep the Guard in Kent "until we get rid of them" (the protesters).

MAY 4, 1970

▼ 11 A.M.: Students begin collecting on the campus commons as their 9:55–10:45 A.M. classes end, in preparation for an announced noon demonstration.

▼ 11:15 A.M.: National Guard leaders ask the University's National Public Radio station to broadcast a warning that "all outdoor demonstrations and gatherings are banned by order of the governor. The National Guard has the power of arrest."

▼ 11:30 A.M.: National Guard commander arrives at the ROTC building on the edge of the commons that had been burned by students two days earlier, and concludes that the crowd gathered there is orderly and not a threat.

▼ 11:45 A.M.: Guard commander, astonished to see more than 600 students gathered on the commons, gives an order to Guardsmen to disperse the students.

▼ 11:48 A.M.: Two student demonstrators issue calls to action, and the crowd on the commons grows as students arrive from classes ending at 11:50 A.M.

▼ 11:49 A.M.: A University policeman reads the state's Riot Act over a bullhorn, but most of the crowd can't hear him because he's at the edge of the commons, too far away from where most students have gathered.

▼ 11:50 A.M.: The University policeman repeats his reading of the Riot Act from a National Guard jeep that circles the commons.

▼ 11:55 A.M.: The Guard commander gives the order to load and lock weapons, and to prepare to move out.

▼ 11:59 A.M.: The Guard commander gives the order: "Prepare to move out and disperse this mob." At this point, more than 2,500 people have gathered on the commons or on the nearby hill leading to the closest University building, Taylor Hall.

▼ 12 noon: An unidentified spokesman from the crowd runs up to the Guard commander and says, "General, you must not march against the students." The commander replies that the students need to learn what law and order are all about, and orders his men to shoot tear-gas cannisters into the crowd.

▼ 12:01 P.M.: The Guard captain in charge of one company of troops begins to march with his men toward Taylor Hall, firing tear gas.

▼ 12:02 P.M.: A demonstrator throws a handful of rocks at the Guard captain as he and his men advance toward Taylor Hall; the captain breaks his baton on the demonstrator.

▼ 12:03 P.M.: A second Guard company crosses the commons and begins to climb a wooded hill, approaching Taylor Hall from the other side.

▼ 12:04 P.M.: The first Guard company passes alongside Taylor Hall and approaches a pagoda-like structure on the hillside, where they are greeted with rocks and Guard tear gas cannisters thrown back at them by students.

(Continued)

▼ 12:06 P.M.: Both Guard companies face thousands of students who are fleeing the tear gas on the commons as well as other students on their way to or from classes.

▼ 12:07 P.M.: Guardsmen marching from the pagoda through a nearby football practice field are trapped by the crowd at a fence on one side of the practice field. Students begin to close in on the field from the Taylor Hall parking lot. They are throwing rocks, waving flags and cursing the Guardsmen.

▼ 12:18 P.M.: The Guard commander orders his troops to regroup back at the burned-out ROTC building, back across the commons.

▼ 12:19 P.M.: A Guard colonel radios for more tear gas.

▼ 12:22 P.M.: The commander of the Guard unit trapped by the practice field fence gives the order to march, and his unit leaves the fence, heading back toward the commons. The closest students are about 20 yards away; most students are more than 100 yards away.

▼ 12:24 P.M.: The Guard reaches the crest of the hill, about to descend onto the commons. Some turn around, facing back toward the practice field, and drop their rifles to a ready position. A single shot rings out. Immediately, there is a burst of shots lasting about 13 seconds. Silence follows, then two final shots are heard. Four students lie dead on the Taylor Hall parking lot. Nine other students lie wounded.

▼ 12:25 P.M.: The Guard ceases firing.

▼ 12:29 P.M.: Order is restored to the Guard. Guardsmen reform and retreat to the ROTC building, where they surrender their guns for registry and inspection.

AFTER THE SHOOTINGS

▼ 1970: Two and a half months after the shootings, key portions of a secret Justice Department memorandum are disclosed by the *Akron Beacon Journal*. The memorandum describes the shootings as unnecessary and urges Portage County (in which the University is located) to file criminal charges against the six Guardsmen implicated in the shootings. Later that year, U.S. Attorney General John Mitchell says that both students and Guardsmen apparently violated federal laws, and the President's Commission on Campus Unrest concludes the shootings were "unnecessary, unwarranted and inexcusable." Governor Rhodes orders a special state grand jury, but the grand jury declines to indict any Guardsmen. Instead, it indicts 25 people involved in the protests that weekend, including several of the wounded students. The U.S. Justice Department reviews the evidence to determine if a federal grand jury should be convened.

▼ 1971: Allegations of a conspiracy surface, but Attorney General Mitchell closes the case, dismissing the conspiracy allegations and claiming "there is no likelihood of successful prosecutions of individual Guardsmen." A petition bearing 10,000 student signatures, urging President Nixon to overrule Mitchell's decision is submitted to the White House. Ohio officials dismiss charges against 20 of the 25 individuals indicted by the state grand jury.

▼ 1972: The President and new U.S. Attorney General refuse to reverse the earlier decision to close the case. Parents of the slain students file suit in U.S. District Court, asking for a court order compelling the Justice Department to convene a federal grand jury.

▼ 1973: Parents of the slain students renew their demands for a federal grand jury, and students plan to resubmit their petition. The Justice Department says it has sufficient evidence to prosecute six

Guardsmen, and the Attorney General reopens the case. The *Akron Beacon Journal* confirms reports that a House Judiciary subcommittee is investigating the Justice Department's handling of the Kent State investigation. The Justice Department announces that it will officially conduct a new inquiry. Ohio Senator William Saxbe, nominated by President Nixon to be the new U.S. Attorney General, says he will terminate the new investigation if his nomination is approved. Parents and students petitioners demand that Saxbe disqualify himself because of conflict of interest. On the eve of Saxbe's confirmation hearings, the Justice Department announces that a federal grand jury will be empaneled.

▼ 1974: The federal grand jury indicts eight Guardsmen on charges that they deprived the students of their rights to due process. No Guard officer is indicted. The U.S. Supreme Court overturns a series of lower court decisions dismissing civil damage suits filed by the parents of the slain students and the nine surviving student victims, paving the way for a civil trial. The eight are indicted, but charges are dismissed after the judge rules that prosecutors failed to prove their case beyond a reasonable doubt. Governor Rhodes is re-elected.

▼ 1975: A three-month-long wrongful death and injury trial begins, five years after the shootings. The jury decides not to award damages to the parents of those killed or to the nine surviving wounded students.

▼ 1977: Students erect a makeshift "Tent City" on the practice football field that had figured prominently in the 1970 shootings, to protest plans by the University to construct a gymnasium annex over part of the site of the May 4 confrontation, but the University proceeds with construction. An appeals court overturns the decision in the wrongful death and injury trials brought by victim's parents and the surviving wounded students.

▼ 1978: A second wrongful death and injury trial begins.

▼ 1979: The victims and parents settle the trial out of court, and the State of Ohio awards a total of $674,000 to be split 13 ways. Defendants in the case sign a "statement of regret." While some see the statement as an apology, the defendants dispute that conclusion.

▼ 1982: A U.S. Appeals Court rules that government documents on the shootings, sealed seven years earlier, must be opened. Major litigation over the shootings officially ends when the U.S. Supreme Court declines to hear an appeal of the ruling that ordered the documents released.

▼ 1984: Kent State University President Michael Schwartz receives a petition bearing more than 80,000 signatures that calls for a memorial to be built to the May 4 shootings. Schwartz forms a committee to study the idea and to make recommendations on whether a memorial should be erected.

▼ 1985: The University's Board of Trustees announces that a memorial will be built on campus, and sets up a nationwide competition for a design for the memorial.

▼ 1986: The winning design in the competition is disqualified, and the runner-up design for the memorial is selected.

▼ 1988: The University's Board of Trustees announces that only $42,000 has been raised in donations to pay for the memorial, and that a scaled-down version of the winning design will be built at a total cost of $100,000. The announcements spawn a brief flurry of protest.

▼ 1989: Ground is broken for the memorial at the top of the hill overlooking the commons adjacent to Taylor Hall. Construction of the memorial begins, 19 years after the shootings.

Kent State University: Commemorating the 20th Anniversary of a National Tragedy (*continued*)

▼ 1990: The memorial is dedicated on May 4, 20 years after the shootings. Former U.S. Senator and presidential candidate George McGovern addresses the dedication ceremonies, and Ohio Governor Richard Celeste apologizes on behalf of the State of Ohio for the tragic events of May 4, 1970. The families of two of the slain students participate in the dedication ceremonies, as do most of the wounded students. But families of some victims and one of the surviving wounded students refuse to take part. Dr. Schwartz, University president, says the words inscribed on the memorial—"inquire . . . learn . . . reflect"—call upon those who view the memorial to "inquire, learn and reflect on the events that happened here and in our nation in order that the past is not our future."

PREVIOUS COMMEMORATIONS OF MAY 4

The Kent State University community has commemorated each anniversary of the May 4 shootings, beginning with the first anniversary in 1971. An annual candlelight walk and vigil is conducted by the Center for Peaceful Change, established at the University a year after the shootings to study the role of higher education in creating non-violent social change. The idea for the walk and vigil originally came from Dr. Jerry M. Lewis, a Kent State sociology professor and eyewitness to the events of May 4, 1970, and two Kent students.

Each year at 11 P.M. on May 3, students, faculty and others from the University and surrounding communities take part in a candlelight procession around the perimeter of the campus. The walk begins in the commons area, and ends at the parking lot adjacent to Taylor Hall, where the shootings took place. Following the walk, the vigil begins in the parking lot, with individuals positioned at the spots where the four dead students fell to the ground. The vigil continues until 12:24 P.M. on May 4, the time the Guardsmen opened fire.

At noon on May 4, an annual commemoration program begins on the commons. Originally sponsored by the University, the program is now a project of the May 4 Task Force and includes speakers, music and a look back at the events of May 4, 1970.

In addition to the permanent memorial that would be dedicated on the 20th anniversary of the shootings, other memorials to the shootings exist on the University's campus. A May 4 Resource Center was established in 1973 on the first floor of the University Library. Items in the Resource Center include books and selected materials from University Archives dealing with May 4, campus unrest in general and the involvement of U.S. military forces in Southeast Asia. The room also includes four stained-glass windows, a gift from a former art student at Kent who fabricated the windows to depict the shootings.

B'nai B'rith Hillel Jewish Services Center at the University donated a plaque bearing the names of the four slain students; three of the students killed were Jewish. The plaque was placed in 1971 in the parking lot where the students were killed, but was stolen two years later. Members of the University's faculty then raised money and purchased a granite and marble marker to replace the plaque. The marker was put in place during the 1975 commemoration.

A sculpture, entitled "The Kent Four," by former faculty artist Alastair Granville-Jackson was erected on campus near the School of Art in 1971. The sculpture is based on four rifle barrels, which the artist described as "symbols of destruction."

In 1978, sociology professor Lewis and Dr. Thomas R. Hensley, professor of political science, initiated a course, "May 4 and Its Aftermath," which has been taught on the average of every three years since then. The course is popular with Kent students, many of whom had not even been born in 1970 when the shootings occurred. The class is a laboratory of sorts, with students learning firsthand the "how tos" of researching a watershed event of historical and legal significance. Students simulate a re-enactment of the trial of the suit brought by victims' parents and the wounded students against the State of Ohio; view a collection of documentaries and film dramatizations related to the shootings, and hear from a variety of guest speakers, many of whom witnessed what happened on May 4, 1970.

CASE STUDY: COMMEMORATING THE 20TH ANNIVERSARY OF MAY 4

"Landmark" anniversaries—whether of birthdays, weddings, or events of national and international significance—seem to command special observance. That certainly was the case as the 20th anniversary of the Kent State shootings drew near, especially with the University having broken ground for a permanent memorial to the tragic events of May 4, 1970.

Dr. Schwartz, the University's president, and the University's Board of Trustees agreed that the memorial should be dedicated on May 4, 1990, to coincide with the 20th anniversary of the shootings. Schwartz and others wanted the University to mark the anniversary with a commemoration different from the annual events that had, since 1971, marked the May 4 anniversary.

Two days after she took office as chair of the University's Faculty Senate, Myra West, assistant professor of physics, got a call from President Schwartz. "'You know what happens this spring,'" West recalls the President telling her in their June 1989 telephone conversation. And indeed she did: most of the University community was already aware that this May 4 anniversary would be the object of particularly intense public and media interest, because media inquiries about the University's anniversary plans had already been received by Kent State's University News and Information Services department.

President Schwartz asked West and the Faculty Senate to help with the planning of the 20th anniversary commemoration. That led to the appointment of a May 4 Twentieth Anniversary Commission, composed of faculty, students and University staff, to plan, schedule and coordinate all events related to the commemoration, including dedication of the May 4 memorial.

West and sociology professor Lewis were elected co-chairs of the commission.

The Commission approached its task the way a public relations practitioner would approach solving a public relations problem. The problem, clearly, was how to commemorate the 20th anniversary of May 4 and dedicate the memorial with events appropriate to the occasion, in a manner that involved the entire campus community as well as families of the slain students and the surviving wounded students, and in an atmosphere of dignity and sensitivity. The Commission was aided in its task by the advice and staff support of the University's public relations staff. John R. Quattroche, vice-president for institutional advancement, and Janet Theide, then director of University News and Information Services, offered day-to-day assistance and implemented many of the Commission's recommendations. Jackie Parsons, a member of the Commission and director of the University's Conference Bureau and Scheduling Office, also provided day-to-day assistance and coordination of many of the scheduled events.

The Commission, working with this assistance, followed a four-stage problem-solving model commonly used by public relations practitioners: research, planning, implementation and evaluation.

Research

Commission members and University News and Information staff gathered a great deal of factual information to guide them in their planning. Included was information about the events of May 4, 1970, about the University then and in 1990, about the slain students

(Continued)

and the surviving wounded students, about the memorial to be dedicated in 1990, about how the University had planned and implemented other ceremonial events and commemorations.

Co-chair Lewis recalls that a model planning document developed by the campus committee appointed to study the desirability of a permanent May 4 memorial was particularly helpful to the Commission. Thiede noted that the Commission also benefitted from planning and evaluation documents from earlier campus events such as groundbreakings and the May 4 candlelight processions and vigils held annually since 1971.

The Commission held frequent open meetings in the eight months leading up to May 4, 1990, seeking input at these meetings from a variety of publics: faculty, administrators, students, and the May 4 Task Force. Co-chair West believes the Commission's openness to a wide spectrum of viewpoints and opinions contributed significantly to its success, even though at these open meetings, "emotions ran high, with some nasty verbal attacks that made me afraid we'd never agree on anything."

Goals

The Commission, working closely with President Schwartz, set these goals for the May 4 20th anniversary events it planned and implemented:

▼ To dedicate the May 4 memorial in a dignified ceremony that would have special meaning and significance for the parents and families of the slain students and for the surviving wounded students.

▼ To develop a program of commemorative activities that would enable all those who participated to learn about and reflect upon the events of May 4, 1970, and their significance in the present and into the future.

▼ To provide accurate information to all publics, particularly to the news media, about what happened

at the University 20 years ago and what had occurred in the interim.

▼ To begin to heal the emotional and psychological wounds the shootings had inflicted among campus publics, in the surrounding community and especially among the parents and families of the slain students and among the surviving wounded students.

"The University's primary concern was to make sure people knew the importance of what happened here in 1970 to the University and to the country," recalls Thiede. "We needed to communicate that the University understands the events of May 4, 1970, were an important part of our history we'll never forget, but that we're going to also move forward."

Commission co-chair Lewis says many Commission members wanted to make it clear that "the University was a victim of May 4, 1970—not just the students who were killed or wounded, but the faculty, staff and other students who were here at the time and the others who have come to the University since."

Planning and Implementation

The Commission's plan, which was approved by University President Schwartz, included a variety of special events and communication vehicles to accomplish its goals. Target publics to be reached were families of the four slain students; the nine surviving wounded students; faculty, students and staff of Kent State University; alumni, especially those who had been on campus in 1970; residents of the community in Kent and other nearby towns and cities; and the news media.

Implementation of the plan involved all segments of the University community: faculty, administrators, staff, students and alumni. In particular, the University's Facilities Planning, Physical Plant, Conference Bureau and Scheduling Office staffs assumed responsibility for many of the facilities and site arrangements and details, while University News and Information Services assumed responsibility for publicity, promotion and media relations activities

Activities generally fell into one of three categories: special events, publications and media relations.

Special Events The primary special event was dedication of the memorial at 11 A.M. on May 4. Speakers at the dedication included former U.S. Senator and presidential candidate McGovern; Florence Schroeder, mother of William Schroeder, one of the students killed; Dean Kahler, one of the wounded students and now a county commissioner in Athens County, Ohio; Ohio Governor Celeste; and three University administrators and faculty members.

More than a dozen other special events were part of the 20th anniversary commemoration held during what the Commission called "Remembrance Week." Here's a chronological listing of those special events:

▼ April 24: An exhibition of paintings, prints, poetry, plays, sculpture and other art that evolved around the events of May 4, 1970, opened in the Kent Student Center. The exhibit, displayed through May 7, also included copies of letters sent to the University in the aftermath of May 4, 1970.

▼ April 29: The first in a series of nine Faculty Forums, sponsored by the Commission and open to the general public, was held on campus. The theme for all forums was "Inquire, Learn and Reflect," the three words etched on the May 4 memorial.

▼ April 30: Three more Faculty Forums were held.

▼ May 1: Two more Faculty Forums were held. At noon, "Echoes of Hyde Park: Then, Now, Next" on a plaza outside the Kent Student Center provided a public forum for May remembrances reminiscent of London's famed Hyde Park speakers' corner.

▼ May 2: The last two Faculty Forums were held.

▼ May 3: A "Gathering of Poets," a series of poetry readings, ran through May 6. The May 4 Task Force sponsored two panel discussions. At 11 P.M., the traditional candlelight procession, sponsored by the Center for Peaceful Change, began, ending at the parking lot where the shootings took place. At midnight, the vigil at the parking lot began, lasting until 12:24 P.M. on May 4.

▼ May 4: The memorial was dedicated at 11 A.M. At noon, the traditional May commemoration program sponsored by the May 4 Task Force began, featuring as speakers William Kuntsler, attorney for the "Kent 25" and "Chicago 8." At 7 P.M., a documentary on 1990 Kent students compared with 20 years ago received its premiere showing, followed by a folk music concert.

▼ May 5: A national student conference, "The Jackson State and Kent Commemorative Conference," began under the sponsorship of the Kent Progressive Student Network. The conference continued through May 6.

Publications The University News and Information Office, working closely with the Commission, produced a Remembrance Week program brochure that included a complete schedule of events planned in connection with the 20th anniversary of May 4. More than 12,000 copies of the brochure were printed and distributed to faculty, students, University staff, alumni, community residents and the media. A program brochure for the dedication also was produced; each of the 2,000 copies also included a commemorative bookmark.

A brochure describing the memorial and its symbolism, as well as the events of May 4, 1970, also was produced. Copies of the brochure are made available to those who visit the memorial in a permanent information rack installed at the memorial site, with the supply constantly replenished. More than 16,000

(Continued)

copies of the memorial brochure were distributed within the first six months following dedication of the memorial.

An issue of *For the Record*, a University publication distributed to faculty and staff, was devoted to coverage of the May 4 20th anniversary events. This internal publication supplemented regular coverage given the commemoration in the University's bi-weekly employee newsletter, *Inside Kent State University*. A special edition of *Inside* also was distributed immediately prior to May 4 to an audience of 4,200.

The *Daily Kent Stater*, the University's student-produced newspaper, produced a special pull-out section that appeared in the newspaper's April 27, 1990, issue. The section included a variety of articles, photos and informational graphics that depicted the chronology of May 4, 1970, as well as remembrances of those whose lives were touched by the shootings and background information on the memorial. Circulation of the pull-out section was more than 16,000 copies.

Media Relations One of the most formidable tasks involved in implementing the 20th anniversary commemoration was providing information to the hundreds of news media representatives who covered Remembrance Week events. Some of the media sent reporters and photographers to campus prior to or during Remembrance Week. Others requested information by telephone and satellite feed.

University News and Information Service's staff began researching and preparing media materials in January 1990, five months before the memorial dedication and 20th anniversary. More than 20 news releases and fact sheets were written and distributed to a media list that included newspapers, magazines, radio and television stations and wire services across the country. Every release and fact sheet was checked for factual accuracy by Thiede and her staff as well as by the University's legal staff, the co-chairs of the Commission and faculty quoted in the releases.

A media kit that included all the releases and fact sheets as well as photos, maps, architects' drawings of the memorial and background information on the University and participants in the Remembrance Week activities was distributed to media who arrived on campus for the memorial's dedication.

In addition, file news releases and chronologies of past events as well as file photos were collected for use in responding to media inquiries.

A news conference was held prior to the memorial dedication, and a press room was set up in Taylor Hall adjacent to the memorial site for use on the day of the dedication. Press credentials were prepared and issued to working media representatives, and special arrangements were made to accommodate the truckloads of television equipment and personnel who arrived to provide live coverage. University News and Information Services staff tried to anticipate and provide for the needs of working media: everything from parking passes and maps to special telephone lines, access to a FAX machine and umbrellas. That last item might have been among the most valuable, for the memorial dedication was held in a steady rain.

Special audio feeds on Remembrance Week and the memorial dedication were prepared for the University's Radio News Line, a toll-free number used year-round to disseminate sound bites to radio news departments. Audio tapes of the dedication itself were available one hour after the ceremonies concluded; one reporter had to rely solely on the tapes because his tape recorder malfunctioned.

Checklists were developed and used for the news conference and for the dedication to make sure all media needs were anticipated and met as well as to ensure that nitty-gritty details connected with the dedication itself weren't overlooked.

Evaluation

One of the measures of the success of the Commission in reaching its goals was the successful anticipation and "trouble-shooting" of potential problems that might have marred Remembrance Week.

One anticipated problem that could have seriously interfered with a dignified dedication of the memorial was a noisy or acrimonious protest by students and former students who had objected to the memorial from the start as a less-than-fitting measure of the University's respect for the dead and wounded students. There *was* a protest on May 4, 1990, but it was small and subdued.

Another problem the Commission anticipated was that the 58,175 daffodils planted around the memorial—to symbolize the number of U.S. servicemen who lost their lives in Vietnam—would not be in bloom on May 4. Winters in northeastern Ohio can be long and harsh, and there was a chance that the bulbs planted earlier would not be in flower in time for the memorial's dedication. But Mother Nature cooperated, and the hillside surrounding the memorial was a mass of yellow for the dedication ceremonies.

There also was some concern that a tabloid newspaper like the National Enquirer or what some call "tabloid television" (like Geraldo Rivera) would sensationalize coverage of Remembrance Week and the May 4, 1970, shootings it commemorated. That fear, too, proved ungrounded.

Of particular concern to Thiede, director of University News and Information Services, was the possibility that she might go into labor and deliver her baby before or during the various events scheduled for Remembrance Week. Her baby wasn't due until the end of May or early June (and in fact was born June 5), but the hectic pace of preparing for the dedication and handling the crush of media attention could have sent her to the delivery room early.

One problem that *did* materialize was bad weather—rain, to be exact. But that, too, had been anticipated: a tent had been erected adjacent to the memorial site, and dedication ceremonies were to be staged under the tent regardless of the weather. Tarps and ground covers also were used to protect the site and participants, and umbrellas had been purchased to shield dignitaries and the media from showers.

Mulch had been laid down over areas that might turn muddy if rain fell. There was no way to protect the hundreds of spectators who gathered to witness the dedication, but they didn't seem to mind: the rain might have been a nuisance, but it set the appropriate solemn, somber tone.

The Commission's planning, complete down to the most minute detail, and this successful anticipation of problems combined to make Remembrance Week successful in meeting its goals.

The dedication did take place, and in an atmosphere of dignity that satisfied Commission members and the University's top administrators. Commission co-chair West recalled that University President Schwartz "hugged me when it was all over, and said, 'We did it.' I think he was very proud, I think the institution was very proud of how it turned out." The Commission was less pleased with the Faculty Forum and some other Remembrance Week events that co-chair Lewis said were poorly attended. "It (the Faculty Forum) was a wonderful program but there was almost no one there to hear it," he recalled. "I consider it our biggest failure that we didn't involve the younger faculty more, even though they weren't here in 1970, so they can carry on our remembrance and can take over when those of us who were here are gone."

An estimated 3,000 witnessed the dedication first-hand, and many others watched on television both in the United States and Europe, thanks to a live satellite feed from CNN and coverage by all three commercial television networks. Media coverage was significant: in the month of April alone, University News and Information Services responded to 370 media requests for May 4-related information, and a total of 640 media calls about the 20th anniversary were logged that winter and spring.

(Continued)

Journalists are not known to heap praise upon the public relations practitioners who provide them with the information so essential to their reporting jobs. But one reporter who covered the dedication took the time and trouble a week later to write to Thiede and the University News and Information Services staff: "In 18 years as a reporter . . . , I have had occasion to attend hundreds of events, ceremonies and other gatherings. Some were small, some large; some well-organized, others more haphazard. But never have I witnessed such a series of events as well-managed, as meaningful, or as thoughtful and tasteful as what you helped organize surrounding last week's 20th anniversary of the May 4 tragedy. Media access, courtesy by students and staff of the university, background assistance . . . were exemplary."

The media used the releases, fact sheets and sound bite feeds made available to them by University News and Information Services. The Radio News Line received a record-setting 71 calls on the Monday prior to May 4, as radio stations across the country taped its audio feed for broadcast. A feed on the dedication itself was taped by 31 stations. In addition, 91 news media organizations were represented at the news conference and/or dedication ceremony on May 4. This news coverage resulted in 964 May 4-related newspaper clippings.

Even more important as a measure of successful media relations than the volume of clippings, radio feeds and television coverage, however, was the accuracy of the coverage. "Most media were very professional, very good to work with," recalled Thiede. "Their reports were fair. They weren't necessarily glowing reports, but they were accurate and fair."

Perhaps the Commission's highest-priority goal was to bring about some healing of the emotional and psychological wounds that remained from the May 4 shootings 20 years earlier. The memorial dedication and various Remembrance Week activities did seem to have a healing effect.

Commission co-chair West said planning and participating in Remembrance Week was, for Commission members and many other faculty and students at the University, "our vehicle for healing. Many of us had not been able to express openly how we felt until now."

Co-chair Lewis agreed, and noted that for the families of some of the victims and for some of the wounded students, "this was a touching event. They seemed pleased with the dedication . . . they seemed to achieve some kind of closure with what happened 20 years ago."

Videotapes of the memorial's dedication ceremony were sent to families of all the students who had been killed 20 years earlier as well as to all of the wounded students. The mother of one of the slain students, in a handwritten note sent shortly after the dedication, praised University officials for their thoughtfulness and sensitivity. "You were so unfailingly sensitive and it was evident to me that you *did* care," she wrote. "Thanks, too, for the tape, which made me feel satisfied and more at peace with the memorial and the whole situation than I would have thought possible just a short time ago."

And it is a sense of peace that visitors to the memorial feel as they walk amid its four symbolic granite slabs and stop to read the simple granite marker that bears the names of the four slain students. The visitors come in a steady stream, filling the nearby parking lot many weekends with license plates from New York, Pennsylvania, Florida, as far away as California. They come to make their own peace with the events of May 4, 1970. They pause before the words carved on the memorial's surface, "inquire, learn, reflect." They, too, like so many of those who participated in the May 4 20th anniversary commemoration, are experiencing the healing that will enable them, like Kent State University, to remember the past but to also move ahead into the future.

Illustrations for this case appear in the *Instructor's Guide*.

Escorts Limited of India in Crisis

A crisis is an exciting time of danger and stimulus which forces organisations to truly think strategically, as so much depends on success or failure. This means that, instead of having to address oneself to a large number of relatively minor tactical PR issues, one faces a "state of war" in which all aspects of the corporate and political environment must be studied and all of one's friends and enemies must be identified in order to formulate a strategic or tactical plan. From such an analysis comes a course for aggressive action, because action is the key element in public relations. What you say mainly depends on what you do.

Public relations is all about action. News stories can only flow from noteworthy action. No newspaper or influencer will otherwise take it seriously. One of the finest exponents of public relations in action was Mahatma Gandhi, who jolted the Congress Party out of being a virtual debating society—one that only made war with words—and into being a mass movement with a commitment for positive action. *Satyagraha* was exactly what it meant: "action for truth," and action and truth are indeed the very foundations of public relations.

Truth, like beauty, is often in the eye of the beholder. It is the task of the public relations practitioner, therefore, to remove the blinkers from the eyes of those who do not see the truth, by building an irrefutable body of facts to make the truth unassailable. The true definition of opinion is the absence of facts. If there are facts, there is no need for opinion. The collection and proper presentation of significant facts provide the foundation for destroying ignorance and other obstructions to the path of progress.

Another important element in successful public relations is imagery: being able to reduce complex facts to a few simple ideas that can graphically illustrate the issues to be promoted. In this dimension also, there are few practitioners who can better Mahatma Gandhi, who made a small handful of common salt into a symbol of colonial tyranny and by the symbolic burning of imported cloth was able to focus on the problems of India's textile industry and handicrafts.

After many years of involvement with the marketing of tractors and my earlier exposure to market research and advertising, I joined Escorts and found myself thrust suddenly into the middle of the greatest corporate war ever to hit the Indian business scene. It was a long-drawn-out, 3-year campaign, vigorously contested between Swraj Paul, a well-known nonresident raider and two Indian companies, the Delhi Cloth Mills (DCM) and Escorts—although eventually it was left to Escorts to carry the brunt of the battle.

In early 1983, Swraj Paul started quietly purchasing shares, first in DCM and then in Escorts. This went totally unnoticed till the 11th of April when his raid on the two companies was discovered. The matter was taken up immediately with the government and with a large number of industrial associations such as FICCI, ASSOCHAM, PHDCCI, etc., and there was a considerable hue and cry in the press concerning the injustice being done by a nonresident who possessed almost unlimited borrowing power in a foreign country, trying to take over and destabilise well-run Indian companies.

My department at Escorts had a great deal of work to do: organising the press meetings and conferences and ensuring that the press was provided with background notes of available material, public statements, copies of journalistic opinion, etc. There was at that time no clear strategy, and all the issues were rather muddled. There was a lot of speculation and wild gossip but no building blocks for an effective counterattack.

Used with permission.

(Continued)

BUILDING A DEFENCE

It was clear that we had a very insufficient knowledge of our adversary and of his associations with the A.P.J. group in India, as well as with the Caparo Group in the U.K. So our Market Research Department embarked immediately on a massive hunt for material. The first part of this search was for material on parliamentary debates in the library of Parliament, which almost immediately struck gold. We found that there were over 700 pages of acrimonious documentation concerning a large number of misdeeds of the A.P.J. Group including black marketing, underinvoicing and cheating, which had led to their being blacklisted on nearly a dozen occasions.

Simultaneously, material started coming in from Calcutta and London concerning the A.P.J. and Caparo companies, and it was soon evident that both worked on a generally similar pattern. In both countries, they had, by acquisition, taken over a large number of companies and other properties, working on the principle of taking over limping companies with good saleable assets and stripping these assets. We were able to put together evidence that their companies generally produced very little except money, which they certainly did know how to produce. The trading activities also occurred mainly in areas that were highly restricted or where there was a great premium on the licences, etc.—i.e., where there was scope for considerable black market margins.

Within two weeks of the battle's commencing, we were able to prepare an abstract of some of the key facts and ensure that this was circulated in many key quarters. It had a devastating effect because, firstly, it enabled us to regain some initiative and confidence and, secondly, the supporters of Swraj Paul became embarrassed and cautious, not knowing what additional data we had, since this abstract could well be only the tip of the iceberg. The document was also an important "ultimate deterrent" because it created a fear in the enemy camp that there might be other bombshells.

There had been speculation that Swraj was using Prime Minister Indira Gandhi's alleged funds to mount this raid. We did not believe this to be the case, either then or afterwards. A small group close to the P.M., with strong links in the Ministry of Finance had, we believed, been behind a purely opportunistic takeover bid. The same group had encouraged domestic takeovers of Kamani Engineering, Standard Batteries, CEAT Tyres, etc., and had nearly taken over Premier Automobiles. We, therefore, were convinced that, despite the influence of Swraj's friends, it was them we were fighting and not the government.

Swraj Paul, in the meantime, entered the fray with an aggressive and savage broadside against Indian industrialists in general and the managements of Escorts and DCM in particular.

In all fairness it must be stated that Swraj Paul was an excellent natural PR practitioner himself. He had enormous vigour and presence. He made the public aware for the first time that India's industrialists owned small percentages in the shares of their own companies. He alleged that they had sold out their shares to the financial institutions and then used the proceeds to live like Maharajas. He then went on the label them abusively as corporate pirates. Swraj Paul not only had a great deal of dynamism and force in his public utterances, he also maintained a close personal follow-up with many key journalists, who were often surprised to receive phone calls commenting on their editorial remarks, etc. He also had a way with catch phrases that soon made him out to be the saviour of the shareholders, who were allegedly being taken for a ride by Indian managements. Swraj Paul was no mean adversary.

REACHING KEY AUDIENCES

Escorts had developed a very good general image in Delhi, where its main plants and activities are located; and Mr. H. P. Nanda, the chairman, was a man of enormous charm, style and image. The company, therefore, was well known to all publics, including journalists, in the capital. India's financial capital was, however, in Bombay, which not only controlled the financial press but also was the main centre for investors in the stock market. The stock exchanges of Bombay and Ahmedabad were estimated to control nearly 60% of India's share purchasing. It was, therefore, vitally important that Mr. H. P. Nanda, as well as the vice-chairman, Mr. Rajan Nanda, and other top corporate executives, be seen and personally known to this vital audience.

Having complete confidence in the charm and sincerity of Mr. H. P. Nanda, I arranged for a simple discussion group with about 20 of Bombay's key financial journalists, followed by a series of smaller meetings with selected individuals and groups. Although the discussions were often acrimonious and critical, they succeeded admirably because the journalists were now able to establish flesh and personality to mere names they had previously heard of. Soon the journalists took a growing personal liking and respect for the Escorts executives. Moreover, they were impressed by the transparent fact that Mr. Nanda had with his own sweat, blood and tears created Escorts in his lifetime from the tiny initial Rs.5,000/- that he had brought in at the time of partition to the Rs.300 crore [ten millions] industry that Escorts had become by 1983. Journalists were also able to get an insight into the personalities of some of the other key executives and to see that Escorts had a very satisfactory track record of professional management that did not deserve to be destabilised.

Journalists have an influence on all publics and they soon decide in their minds who are the "good guys" and who the "bad guys" on every issue. If any PR practitioner can establish a firm public image that his or her company is on the side of the angels, it becomes a factor very difficult to fight against.

DIRECT ACTION

In June 1983, when Parliament was in recess, Swraj Paul again returned to India and started on a round of speeches to large packed gatherings in Calcutta, Bombay and Delhi. I missed his first set of speeches in Calcutta but these were extensively reported in the Indian press. Knowing that his next destination was Bombay, I rushed there with all the newspaper cuttings I could get hold of and analysed his speeches in the light of facts that, by then, I knew. While sitting in the plane to Bombay, I prepared a short 3-page note of some questions Swraj Paul needed to answer and ensured that these were immediately typed out on plain paper, cyclostyled and distributed to a large number of influential people who were likely to hear Swraj Paul. Some of the questions were:

▼ Swraj Paul had criticised Indian companies whose 10-year performance record was available through audited balance sheets. Could Swraj Paul provide similar data on the Caparo or A.P.J. companies, to show that he was in any position to criticise or to allege that "Sleeping Indian managements need a wake-up"?

▼ Swraj Paul alleged that Indian industrialists lived like Maharajas, but could he deny that as chairman or director of various Caparo companies, he received emoluments ranging from £10,000 to £40,000 a year from many of these companies and their subsidiaries? Were these emoluments going to charity or did he also live in style?

▼ The Caparo companies were controlled by Caparo Investments Jersey (a tax haven in the Jersey Islands). None of the 605,630 shares were purchased for cash. The entire capital was listed as "for considerations other than cash." How did he explain this?

▼ Swraj Paul proclaimed that Indian companies do not consider the interest of their shareholders. If

(Continued)

so, how was it that many of the shares held by him in his companies were 10p deferred ordinary shares, which earn the same dividends as £1 shares owned by ordinary shareholders?

▼ How could 13 Caparo companies, mostly with a capital base of less than £25,000 each, invest an average of £700,000 each? Where were these funds coming from? Furthermore, if these investments would give a yield of 3½% of the market value of the shares, what was the objective, as it could not just be returns on direct investment?

▼ Several legal issues were spelt out, especially the sanctity of FERA laws and the basic necessity that all foreign investments in any Indian company must have prior permission from RBI, etc.

I personally arranged for these notes to be widely distributed and, as an afterthought, sent one to Mr. Swraj Paul at his suite in the Taj Mahal Hotel, Bombay. This note, I believe, infuriated Swraj because it was a major spanner in his works. From that moment onwards, he carefully avoided all these and other listed issues and spoke instead in broad generalities and became more and more abusive and less and less factual.

INFLUENCING THE INFLUENCERS

One of the important influencers was the body of India's economists. I, along with several journalists, was invited to several seminars to debate the whole NRI issue. At these seminars, organized by the Delhi School of Economics, South Delhi Campus, etc., I was able to establish a few fundamental points, which were well received by this community of economists:

1. As a result of India's socialist policies, Indian industrialists had been forced to pay taxes (i.e., wealth tax and income tax) that, in combination, exceeded their incomes. For this reason industrialists had been forced, however reluctantly, to sell their shares to pay taxes—not with the objective of gaining wealth so that they could live like Maharajas, as claimed by Swraj.

2. Financial institutions, especially LIC and Unit Trust were the biggest shareholders in every good Indian company. As there was a shortage of good scripts, financial institutions had gradually increased their purchases of shares in well-run Indian companies. As their participation on the boards of these companies had been generally constructive, there had been no desire to refuse them these shares, even if it were legally possible to do so.

3. The financial institutions had actually got extremely good returns. LIC, for instance, had purchased all its Escorts shares before 1965, and as a result of bonus shares had bought its entire block of 30% of Escorts equity (its maximum permissible limit) at an average cost of Rs.2/25 per share; these were now worth over Rs.60/- on the market—i.e., they had got a return on their investment of nearly 30 times, without counting the value of dividends they had received during that period. In fact the annual dividend of 1982 was 80% of their total investment of Rs.1.02 crores. It could not, therefore, be argued that the Indian industrialists were using (i.e., misusing) government money, as alleged by Swraj.

4. The fundamental injustice lay in the fact that the takeover bid represented an unequal battle pitting the almost unlimited borrowing power of a foreign investor, operating under the terms of foreign banking laws, against the declining personal wealth of the Indian industrialists, who were by Indian law debarred from borrowing money from banks to buy shares in their own companies. It was literally a case of bows and arrows against machineguns.

SUPPORT OF SHAREHOLDERS

The next part of the unfolding drama was to promote the confidence of the shareholders. The hundreds of shareholders who came to the packed AGM in June 1983 were delighted to read a story in the *Statesman* about a Swraj Paul scandal, which caused great jubilation. The strong support of Delhi shareholders for Escorts management was quite clear to several journalists who attended meetings in which dozens of shareholders spoke at great (often embarrassing) length in favour of the company and its management.

Again Bombay was the crucial area. In Bombay a new association, the Investors Association, had been started and had invited Swraj Paul to be its first speaker. I immediately approached this group and requested them to make Mr. H. P. Nanda their second speaker. There was some protest from our colleague industrialists who advised against our association with this group, whom they alleged were in Swraj's pay. I, however, managed to convince my management that the promoters were all respected in the investing community, and that it would be a forum where we could reach a large number of people who were still undecided. We had a very good story to tell, so why not tell it at a good available forum?

I attended Swraj's speech, in which he had a packed house of over 700 in the audience. However, when Mr. Nanda spoke at the same forum in September, the crowd was even bigger, and we had to provide microphones and TV monitors for those who had to sit outside. Although there were initially some hostile questions, the meeting was a great success, and a large number of speakers eventually came forward to praise Mr. Nanda for his courage in standing up to the pressure he was facing. The mood of the house was not missed by the journalists covering the meeting.

For the day after this meeting of the Investors Association, we had organised another big informal meeting to which we had invited a large number of Escorts shareholders. We gave an audio-visual presentation of the company, which few of them had actually seen. Many shareholders who had never seen or heard Mr. H. P. Nanda were impressed by his charm, sincerity and good humour, despite the enormous pressures that they knew he was under. What also came as a surprise to them was the forceful and impressive presentation by Mr. Rajan Nanda, about whom they had heard very little. It was now clear to many journalists and other special invitees that Escorts shareholders considered their investment in the company to be one of their best investment decisions. They were quite satisfied with the company and its management and were deeply hostile to any move that would destabilise the working of the company.

LEGAL BATTLES

September 1983, however, turned out to be a traumatic month for Escorts. The company was soon embroiled in a long string of legal battles that had to be explained to the press and to the public. The investments of Swraj Paul in Escorts and DCM had been rejected by the companies because they grossly violated the published policy of the RBI.

In the case of Swraj Paul, there were many legal problems. Firstly, he started with a secret investment of about Rs.1 crore which was, in actual fact, borrowed rupee funds from his Indian companies and therefore could not possibly have qualified as an NRI investment. Secondly, his large second block of investments, to the tune of Rs.9 crores, came from a single company, and therefore could not be the individual investments of 13 Caparo companies as claimed. Thirdly, although the brokers of Swraj Paul had claimed to purchase 975,000 shares—i.e., 75,000 shares each by the 13 Caparo companies—the actual shares put up for registration accounted for only 462,000 shares (3% of the company's equity). Fourthly, despite repeated queries to the brokers and the bankers, there had been complete silence as to whether RBI had accorded sanction to these alleged purchases.

The two Indian companies had, therefore, consistently maintained the position that, in the absence of clarification on these and other fundamental matters, the registration of the shares would be a gross violation of the FERA laws by the Indian companies, making them liable to severe penalties of up to 5 times the value of the illegal investments. This view was supported by a considerable correspondence that we

(*Continued*)

knew existed between RBI, Caparo and their bankers. Therefore, without clear clarifications on these many legal issues, the companies could not have risked registering the shares even if they had desired to do so.

On the 17th of September, 1983, we received a severe blow in the form of a press release from the RBI that sought to legitimise the Caparo investments, followed by an RBI notification two days later that was clearly slanted to benefit only one investor—Caparo industries.

Rajiv Gandhi had made a statement in Parliament, in late May, that NRI investments should not exceed 5%. Pranab Mukherjee, the Finance Minister, then translated this into revised rules the following week, specifying that no individual NRI firm, company or society could hold shares in excess of 1% of a company's equity, subject to a maximum ceiling of 5% for all NRI investments.

We had discovered from the companies search in London that all of the 13 Caparo companies were subsidiaries of one holding company, Caparo Investments Jersey Limited. Thus, it had been our lawyer's view that each foreign corporation was, in the eyes of law, a foreign national and not an NRI investor. Furthermore, even if Swraj Paul was the single owner of the holding company, he could not seek to evade the 1% or 5% ceiling by infiltrating his investments through a multiplicity of subsidiaries. The RBI's new notice clarified that overseas bodies were eligible to invest up to 1% each, irrespective of whether the ultimate ownership was in the hands of nonresident individuals, etc., provided that NRI holdings accounted for at least 60% of its equity. Even more alarming was the fact that this notification was to be applied with retroactive effect.

The legal opinion, later supported by the judgement of the Bombay High Court, found many gaps and lacunae in this directive, and a hectic stream of letters followed, seeking clarification. Many of these doubts and ambiguities were shared by journalists, who vigorously objected to the obvious inequity of this notification and to the pressure tactics being applied to force the companies to regularise what clearly seemed to be illegal and irregular.

CASE TO HIGH COURT

The stalemate therefore continued until late December, when we received the rather alarming intelligence that the government was seriously considering an ordinance to compel the companies to register the shares. At this point, Escorts decided to move the Bombay High Court with a writ petition to settle the legal issues through courts of law, as it seemed that India's executive was not going to act impartially.

The Bombay High Court listed the case of hearing on 15 February. Four days before this, on the 11th, the Life Insurance Corporation, the company's largest shareholder, served notice to the company to summarily dismiss nine directors from the Board and to replace them with their own nominees. The company was privately told that, if the company did not withdraw the Bombay High Court case, the government would, through the reconstituted Board of Directors, force the company to do so in any case.

It was a time of great depression within the company, as the company was feeling increasingly isolated, and the pressures were even affecting a large number of colleague industrialists, who were unwilling to lend their support for fear of attracting executive wrath or vindictiveness. Some even told Mr. Nanda that he was being selfish and jeopardising the interests of the entire industry by his obstinacy. Mr. Nanda, however, stated to several colleagues that, as he had personally built up this company in his own lifetime, he was not going to just gift it away on a platter. He stated that he did not need the company for his own gain because his own fairly modest needs could easily be met through his other savings. What was at issue was his self-respect, and if he caved in to pressure, he would never be able to hold up his head in the corporate world.

Despite all the pressures, all of us in the small group around Mr. Nanda somehow could not believe that, in a country like India, justice would not prevail in the end. Even though most of our professional colleagues considered us quite mad, there was an unwavering feeling that justice must prevail in the end.

The hearing in the Bombay High Court took a full month and represented a mini trial in itself. Justice S. K. Desai's incisive questions and sharp remarks made excellent journalistic copy. After each day's proceedings, the journalists covering the trial would gravitate to the press room, where journalists who had a legal background and were accredited to the courts were soon outnumbered by the financial journalists, many of whom had difficulty in converting legalese into journalese. During these sessions, I was able to contribute quite a lot by being able to explain the significance of the legal issues being discussed each day.

I had to be extremely careful to ensure that my interpretations of the proceedings were absolutely fair; otherwise, I would not have been able to maintain the confidence of many new journalistic friends whom I met in that hot and humid room. My sharp little team of assistants also had to be quick in producing photostat copies of relevant documents and papers, so the press could be kept continuously informed as developments took place. In this process, we were able to make our services useful, carefully highlighting the vital points that we felt needed to be emphasised and ensuring that the press could provide good coverage of the unfolding drama.

The Bombay High Court started the case in the middle of June 1984, and arguments carried on for nearly 2 months thereafter, during which period we spent many sweaty hours in the Court and in the press room afterwards.

OFFENSIVE BY LIC

In the meantime, LIC was pressing ahead by demanding the removal of nine directors, and an Extraordinary General Meeting [EGM] on the 9th of June was demanded by LIC. It was held at the spacious Siri Fort Auditorium, as we expected a large turnout of the shareholders. The proceedings of this EGM came as a surprise to us and as a shock to the government, because the assembly of shareholders savagely attacked the government for their unprecedented action and even attacked Escorts management for agreeing to vacate the Chairmanship in favour of a government nominee for the purpose of moving a motion in which the Chairman had an interest. Field Marshal Sam Manekshaw, one of the directors facing ouster, made an absolutely brilliant speech that was widely reported and clearly highlighted the iniquity of this mess that LIC had been forced into.

The shareholders, to everyone's surprise, came up with a large number of legal and other points of procedure that forced the government to postpone the balloting it had demanded. On a large number of technical and legal issues, these minority shareholders forced LIC to go through eight successive meetings until LIC was with great difficulty able to force its will on the 28th of June. The vigorous and frequently brilliant efforts of these many unknown ordinary shareholders were an eye-opener to all, and the sheer drama of the proceedings began to attract a large number of journalists, very much to the embarrassment of the government.

In the final analysis, however, 41 shareholders and their proxies, representing 0.2% of the shareholders but commanding 54.5% of the shares, overwhelmed the votes and proxies of 7,600 shareholders who, although they represented 46% of the shareholders, commanded only 29% of the shares. The LIC victory, far from being the walk-over they had expected, thus proved to be a juicy press story and a great embarrassment to the government.

(Continued)

CHANGING GEAR

On the 9th of November 1984, the Bombay High Court delivered its historic judgement vindicating all the points that the company had fought for. In the meantime, a tragic event had taken place with the assassination of the Prime Minister, Mrs. Indira Gandhi. Mr. Rajiv Gandhi then took over as Prime Minister. Although he soon cleansed the government of many powerful influence brokers who supported Swraj, the government had embarked upon a course from which it could not suddenly retract. Thus legal proceedings continued, as LIC felt that it could not accept the verdict of the Bombay High Court and had to pursue the matter by appealing to the Supreme Court.

The company's public relations posture now had to change completely, because the company was no longer in an endangered defensive position from which it had to fight aggressively for survival. With the changed situation, a path towards a compromise was being sought, and this required a very low profile to keep such matters away from the hungry eyes and ears of the press, as premature disclosure or speculation could throw off the delicately balanced negotiations.

The matter came up for hearing in the Supreme Court, which eventually gave its judgement on the 19th of December, 1985. Although the judgement gave Swraj Paul and his brokers a severe rap on their knuckles, it also upheld the executive power of the government to act without restraint through its voting strength on the board of any company. Although it was a somewhat confusing judgement, it basically laid the foundations for an out-of-court settlement, which was completed a few months later. Swraj Paul received back from Escorts all the money he had invested, with an interest of 15% as well. Swraj Paul did not receive payment for a small part of his investments in some shares that had not been put up for registration, as they were tied up in a legal wrangle among himself, his principal broker and another broker in Calcutta. That, however, was of no concern to Escorts.

KEY PR FACTORS

Throughout these many ups and downs, I travelled constantly and kept the journalists and others continuously informed of the unfolding developments. Even when developments were going against our interest, I would make sure that the information was given fully and fairly because only by this means was I able to gain the full confidence of our journalist friends.

On many occasions, when there was bad news, I would deliberately seek out and give a scoop to a journalist who could otherwise be expected to be a savage critic; by being able to provide this small favour, I was quite often able to moderate the damage and even to persuade them to highlight a sensitive point that was important for our cause. Although I was criticised and reprimanded for this on a few occasions, I felt there was no harm in disclosing facts that would eventually have come out in any case. What was important was to ensure that we retained initiative over what was being written.

I also found that big papers were very conservative in handling any controversial story, so I would often begin such a story in one of the hungrier second-line papers. A fuller story could then be developed very easily, which the big papers would usually be happy to run. There was also the factor of "critical mass." As in a nuclear device, a multiplier effect can be created by running a series of news stories.

Journalists are highly individualistic, and they seldom write the way we might wish. However, the key ingredient to gaining some measure of success in dealings with them is to get their confidence that you are not merely offering slanted information as a biased voice of the company but are giving a fair and balanced analysis of the evolving events. Journalists are a very sensitive, even touchy group, and they have to be handled with great care. They are allergic to any approach from advertising agencies or even their own advertising departments. They are also highly cynical about the claims of any organisation. Their confidence takes a long time to earn and can be lost with one careless word.

The key journalists are the concerned correspondents who actually write the stories. Editors, chiefs of bureau, etc., should only be involved if there is a really big story; otherwise, they should only be kept in friendly contact. Another important personage is the news editor who usually clips the copy and gives the headline. He can be a useful friend.

Many organisations in public relations have been criticised for what is sometimes described as "suit-length public relations," referring to the practice among some textile companies of distributing suit lengths or other textiles to journalists attending their press conferences. Throughout this epic battle, Escorts gave few presents and had no lavish cocktail parties. In fact, very little entertainment was offered beyond businesslike lunches or drinks with discussions. There were no presents distributed except for the standard corporate presents given every year at Diwali, which usually consisted of a relatively low-cost item such as a China jar containing nuts. Never were any items presented that were of a value sufficient to obtain the services of any pen for hire, as alleged by Chotu Karadia in his *Swraj Paul Affair* (a rather scurrilous book promoted by Swraj Paul). I believe that gifts, presents, etc., should not be anything more than mere tokens of personal regard. The real essence of our effort was again rapid dissemination of information and interpretation along with a lot of personal follow-up contact on the basis of carefully established confidence and credibility.

In times of crisis, the PR practitioner often faces strong opposition from corporate lawyers, who are generally opposed to any utterances that they feel might irritate the feelings of judges and the courts. I, therefore, frequently faced the annoyance of these cautious, learned gentlemen. However, I believe that, if a corporate war is left entirely to law-

yers, PR initiatives will get sandpapered to death, and the company will sacrifice other important arenas of the corporate war and make itself totally dependent on just one line of defence.

I understand that the low level of PR activity evidenced by the Shaw Wallace Group, which is presently facing a takeover bid, is entirely due to the influence of their lawyers on their management. The result is that very few people are at all clear concerning the issues that are at stake, and there is no clear image about the company and its track record—or indeed about who are the "good guys" and the "bad guys" in this whole issue. Shaw Wallace has not been able to generate the positive groundswell of public sympathy that we were able to achieve; and without this popular feeling they are likely to suffer from a great drop of corporate morale, which may have damaging repercussions.

A vital factor in our success was the unfailing support that my little team received from our management—especially from our Chairman, Mr. H. P. Nanda, who has a wonderful instinct for public relations himself. Mr. Nanda's courage, unfailing humour, humility and optimism, even in moments of deep depression, was a great inspiration to all of us who worked with him. His enthusiasm and tact while handling many critical high-level contacts, as well as his guidance, were an example for us all.

There were, however, times when we had to take courageous initiatives, because a particular moment would not permit any delay. Hostile actions by government or corporate enemies, I believe, must be reacted to immediately. A new development only has the life-span of a few days in public interest. Consequently, if there is no immediate response to a false allegation, the allegation sticks. You are assumed to be guilty thenceforth, and a later declaimer is stale. A quick but mature

(Continued)

response firstly signals a determination to challenge any iniquity, and secondly enables the public to see your side of the story. Delays while waiting for corporate approvals or legal opinions often result in organisations' losing the value of a golden moment. Timing is vital in PR.

These initiatives did sometimes attract corporate irritation and wrath, but I firmly believed that, as long as I worked with commitment and sincerity, I could face the occasional prospect of a firing without worrying about being fired. Quick responses and reaction were vital, and this can only be possi-

ble when the PR person is confident about overall corporate support. In a situation of crisis, PR cannot operate in a passive mode, and I have always been a firm believer in the power of friendly aggression.

I consider that I have been greatly privileged to have had the opportunity to be drawn into a corporate battle of this national—even international—magnitude, because a person very rarely has the experience of being fully stretched in intellect, effort, imagination and courage. Such a thing can only happen in a time of real crisis.

▼ SUMMARY

Cases and case studies provide public relations practitioners with vicarious learning experiences, as well as suggesting ideas they might adapt and use in current circumstances.

Looking at what tactics worked under diverse circumstances provides useful information. The case analysis involves looking at research, publics, action and evaluation. Case studies abound in organizational files and in the literature of public relations, related social sciences and business.

The mini-cases presented here as useful learning experiences involve Southwest Airlines, where policy was enacted before it became essential, and

McCormick & Company, which shared its 100-year-old history with all of its publics but focused on employees.

Two cases were included for detailed study: Kent State University's 20th anniversary event commemorating the killing of four students on its campus in 1970, and Escorts Limited of India's three-year battle to defeat an attempted hostile takeover. The details in these cases demonstrate the command of public relations tools and tactics necessary to be a successful and useful member of the management team.

▼ NOTES

[1] Adapted from Ronald N. Levy, "How to Help Your Lobbyists Win," *Public Relations Journal* (August 1982), p. 31.

[2] Joanne Lipman, "AHA's Seal of Approval Dealt a Blow," *Wall Street Journal* (January 25, 1990), pp. B1, B4. See also Marian Burros's New York Times News Service story of Wednesday, February 7, 1990. It appears in the *Fort Worth Star-Telegram* of that date on page 1, section 6, under the headline, "Do Ya Gotta Have Heart?"

[3] Alan R. Andreasen, "Nonprofits: Check Your Attention to Customers," *Harvard Business Review* (May–June, 1982), pp. 105–110.

[4] Thomas F. O'Boyle, "GE Refrigerator Woes Illustrate the Hazards in Changing a Product," *Wall Street Journal* (May 7, 1990), pp. 1, A6.

[5] Ibid. See also Janet Gwyon, "Culture Class: G.E.'s Management School Aims to Foster Unified Corporate Goals," *Wall Street Journal* (August 10, 1987), p. 25. GE's guide, *New Manager Starter Kit*, is given to new employees during a mandatory one-week course at GE's Crotonville Management Development Institute. A *Wall Street Journal* writer calls GE's 31-year-old institute one of the nation's most intense and systematic.

[6] Rosabeth Kanter, "Values and Economics," *Harvard Business Review* (May–June 1990), p. 4. This same piece says, "Values should be inclusive—general enough to embrace diverse parts of the organization and diverse people. One company's attempt to spread a new management philosophy relevant to its traditional operations wing failed in a publicly humiliating way because the young marketing group—mostly young MBAs—rebelled."

[7] Camille Keith, vice-president of special marketing, Southwest Airlines.

[8] "Using a Corporate Celebration to Foster Goodwill for the Sponsor," *PR News* Case Study No. 2220.

[9] Judy VanSlyke Turk was, at the time this was written, Director of the School of Journalism and Mass Communication at Kent State University.

[10] Murad Ali Baig, formerly of Escorts, Ltd., Delhi, India, now a consultant.

Selected readings, activities and assignments appropriate to this chapter can be found in the *Instructor's Guide.*

▼

CRISES

When the crisis occurs the research must be at hand . . . its facts understood . . . the communicators ready to go into action.

The modern PR person must know how to research any subject, do it quickly, and summarize it well and briefly.

Frank W. Wylie, Fellow, PRSA, and past president, PRSA

It is no use putting whipped cream on the manure pile because the sun comes out in the morning and you have the same old manure pile.

L. L. L. Golden, PR counselor and author

Managers are like other people. They do not like to be told unpalatable facts. Too often they want only to be confirmed in their fixed opinions. But if the professional in public relations fails to perform his "no" function, others will be found to do it.

L. L. L. Golden, public relations counselor and commentator

Crises come in many forms, but public relations people for the most part deal with *public* crises. These can be described, categorized and usually (in general form at least) predicted.[1] Crises are like plays; there are only so many basic plots. Everything else is a variation.

Causes of crises are either physically violent or nonviolent. The physically violent ones come to mind immediately—earthquakes, fires, storms, plane crashes and terrorist acts, to name but a few. Then there are the physically nonviolent crises, such as Black Monday, October 19, 1987, the day of the stock market crash.

Each of these broad categories, *violent* and *nonviolent*, has subsets with more specific descriptors. Some violent crises are created by *acts of nature*, such as lightning that sparks a forest fire or a hurricane or typhoon that sweeps a coast. Some nonviolent crises, too are created by acts of nature—crises such as viral epidemics, insect plagues and droughts. These may take lives, but they are not cataclysmic or overwhelmingly violent. That factor alone calls for a different type of crisis management.

Some crises result from *intentional* acts committed by a person or group. Violent intentional crises are acts of terrorism that result in loss of life or freedom, such as hostage-taking. This category also includes product-tampering, when it results in loss of life or destruction of property. Nonviolent intentional crises include bomb and product-tampering threats, hostile takeovers, inside trading, malicious rumor and other malfeasance.

The third subcategory of crises includes *unintentional* events that are neither acts of nature nor deliberate acts of individuals or groups. This category includes violent unintentional accidents, such as explosions, fires and chemical leaks. On the nonviolent side are process or product problems, which often have delayed consequences such as stock market crashes, business failures or hostile takeovers. Example 15.1 provides an outline and summary of the various kinds of crises.

Whatever organization you are working in or with, you can predict and thus anticipate most possible crises. This means that you can plan for crises.

In responding to the notion that crises could be planned for, one corporate PR director said, "Research and planning sound great, but that's academic. I'm too busy fighting alligators to drain the swamp." Often such a response is a form of denial or simply an excuse—one that public relations counselors often hear, especially when they are called on a weekend and asked to put out a bonfire that had been smoldering for months. When the fire is either contained or extinguished, the alligator comment often follows. The problem for the PR person is that the CEO, whom the counselor is also dealing with, is asking how the fire got so big so fast. The key to good crisis management is anticipation.

▼ IMAGINING THE WORST

Always anticipate the worst thing that could happen to your organization. It might well occur, but probably not as damagingly as you can imagine—if you are creative. Then, when a crisis does happen, you will be prepared. If you are in the brokerage business, imagine the collapse of the Tokyo market. It might happen some night while you are asleep. Your working day, then, will consist of confronting the loss of investor confidence in the U.S. market, which is closely tied to Tokyo due to heavy Japanese investing. If you are in chemical manufacturing, imagine an explosion that contaminates a city of several million and results in thousands of

▼ **Crises are either violent or nonviolent. In each category, a crisis can be an act of nature, an intentional event or an unintentional accident.**

___

deaths. The airline industry? Imagine a 747 crashing into the U.N. building in New York at high noon on a Monday. Education? Imagine your entire endowment has been mishandled and it emerges that the crime involves the president, the head of the board of trustees and and the institution's development officer. A city manager in a major metropolitan area can imagine a tornado that rips through or a nearby volcano that erupts with no warning. A museum curator can think about an act of vandalism that destroys all of the masterpieces and other valuable holdings. Many municipal governments plan for physical disasters with simulations, and some companies now use simulations to test their crisis plans. Remember fire drills? They do help.

One thing that also helps is top management's acceptance of the two-way symmetrical model of public relations (see Chapter 2). When that model is used, resolving conflicts that a crisis might cause is likely to be easier, because the organization and its publics have been talking to each other all along.[2]

An organization confronted with a crisis is concerned with its own behavior and with the behavior of its members and of all its other publics. Some publics tend to be neglected in the planning process—unintended (often global) audiences of communication about the crisis. Such publics, known as "nimbus" publics,[3] often receive information about the crisis because of the global nature of technology. Every crisis plan needs to take into account the potential global impact of crises, even when these are viewed as being essentially domestic. Organizations experience a crisis, not as an isolated event or series of events, but as one or more occurrences that develop in the total environment of public opinion in which the organization

EXAMPLE 15.1

Crisis Typology

	Violent Cataclysmic—Immediate Loss of Life or Property	Nonviolent Sudden Upheaval but Damages, If Any, Are Delayed
Act of Nature	Earthquakes, forest fires	Droughts, epidemics
Intentional	Acts of terrorism, including product tampering, when these result in loss of life or destruction of property	Bomb and product-tampering threats, hostile takeovers, insider trading, malicious rumors and other malfeasance
Unintentional	Explosions, fires, leaks, other accidents	Process or product problems with delayed consequences, stock market crashes, business failures

operates. That total environment encompasses various nimbus publics that the organization may not have recognized as being affected by the crisis and by the organization's response to it.

Sometimes a crisis creates the nimbus public, as in the case of Muslim reaction to U.S. bookstores' selling Salman Rushdie's *The Satanic Verses* after Iran's Ayatollah Khomeini condemned it. Other nimbus groups may be identified for the first time as a result of a crisis. An example is the anti-American activism in Mexico when the United States invaded Panama in 1990.[4] Handling such nimbus publics means considering the environment of public opinion in the planning process (see Example 15.2.)

A crisis gets your attention and demands the immediate attention of top management. It may or may not come with preliminary hints or warnings. But whether the crisis involves violent or nonviolent dangers created by natural events, deliberate acts or accidents, it can be anticipated with good imaginative powers exercised through brainstorming. Various departments within the organization should participate.[5]

You need to hold brainstorming sessions with various departments because someone may be aware of a possibility that you couldn't imagine without having that person's special job-related knowledge. Look at all aspects of the organization. H. J. Heinz's vice-president of coordination for that organization's crisis management program said:

> We try to say, "What would we do if the president of the company were kidnapped, if a plant burned down, if somebody alleged tampering with the products?" The company then develops responses and stages simulated emergencies to make itself less vulnerable.[6]

The company got a chance to test its training with a false alarm at its Brisbane, Australia, plant in 1986. Plant officials thought that some products had actually been tampered with the day after a simulation. The Australian plant notified corporate headquarters, contacted local authorities and began an investigation, which revealed that it was a false alarm. Some organizations that resist crisis planning and simulations point to events like the Heinz experience and say that it is a good reason not to have drills. Drills simply start rumors. Heinz, though, maintains that simulations improve reaction time and confidence.

The "imagining" process, Ian I. Mitroff of the University of Southern California's Center for Crisis Management suggests, is designed for top executives to put themselves in the role of an intelligent

EXAMPLE 15.2

Public Opinion Node in Crisis Management

The minimum objective of crisis management with respect to public opinion is to maintain the positive public opinion the organization enjoyed before the crisis and to limit negative public opinion, collectively or from any single public, to pre-crisis levels. The public opinion node itself contains all opinions (positive or negative) held by all members of a specific public.

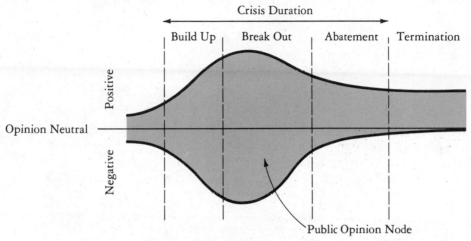

SOURCE: David Sturges, Bob Carrell, Doug Newsom and Marcus Barrera, "Crisis Communication Management: The Public Opinion Node and Its Relationship to Environmental Nimbus," *SAM Advanced Management Journal*, 56(3) (Summer 1991), pp. 22–27. Reprinted with permission.

adversary and ask, "What is the most creative way I could wreck this company? . . . Then they have to ask, 'What is the most intelligent way we could respond?'"[7]

In looking at "wreckable" areas, Dow Chemical's corporate communications director in Sarnia, Ontario, suggests these potential targets: (1) *products or services* in terms of safety, effects on the environment and use of scarce materials; (2) *processes* such as manufacturing, transportation and finance; (3) *locales* of operation, including sending and receiving facilities; (4) *people problems*—offices and executives, their corporate and private lives and personnel policies, especially employment and separation policies and benefits.[8] You should add health to the people-problems category, since AIDS

or some other epidemic in the workplace may cause panic.

While you are imagining the worst, consider the impact that each event you can identify will have on each public individually. When you do this, you can anticipate possible chain reactions—that is, for example, what an explosion that contaminates your product will do to your stock and how you are perceived by important publics (see Examples 15.3 and 15.4). The way you handle a crisis while it is occurring can lessen or increase its impact significantly. Planning can help you develop strategies out of the intensity of a crisis. It also helps you clarify or modify a management response, depending on whether management operates in a closed or in an open climate.

EXAMPLE 15.3 ▐

An Organization's Operational Environments in a Crisis

The direct environment includes the publics central to the organization, as well as other publics most directly affected by the crisis. The indirect environment encompasses other readily identified publics that usually are involved in the organization's ongoing relationships with constituencies. The cloud around an organization's environment is its nimbus, consisting of groups that are not normally identified as being among the organization's publics but that become such publics as a result of the crisis.

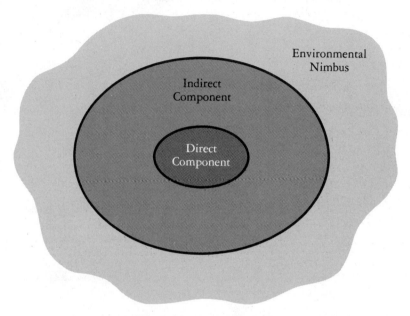

SOURCE: David Sturges, Bob Carrell, Doug Newsom and Marcus Barrera, "Crisis Communication Management: The Public Opinion Node and Its Relationship to Environmental Nimbus," *SAM Advanced Management Journal*, 56(3) (Summer 1991), pp. 22–27. Reprinted with permission.

Planning

An organization's communication climate has a great impact on how management handles crises.[9] Of all the wrong decisions an organization can make in a crisis, deciding to shut off the flow of accurate information is probably the worst. Closed and open communication systems have been described earlier; but in terms of crisis management, the open system is much the easier one in which to operate. Rumors are less likely to start when information is openly available and a residue of trust exists inside and outside the organization. You must always consider an organization's communication climate when you undertake crisis planning.

In planning for a crisis, you must always recognize that information is going to be in great demand. Unfortunately, you won't be able to get much information about the crisis itself ahead of time. You can make a crisis easier to handle, though, if you organize the information you *can* obtain in advance. You should collect information on products/

EXAMPLE 15.4

Stages of Public Opinion in a Crisis

Latent issues should be detected by environmental monitoring, but when a crisis occurs, groups tend to form in relation to the event and to responses to it by the organization and by other publics. The result may be public debate of issues, as occurred after the United States and its allies went to war in the Persian Gulf in 1991. As time lapses after an event, public opinion forms. It does so more dramatically if the crisis, like the Persian Gulf conflict, involves daily changes and additional events. The result of opinion formation is a form of social action—peace protests in the case of the Persian Gulf war. Then there is usually counteraction, followed by the eventual restoring of group norms.

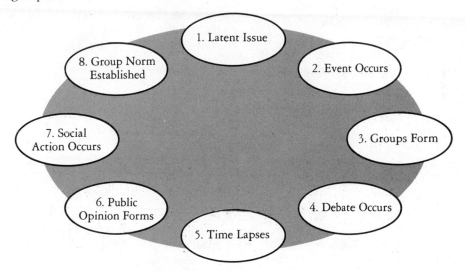

SOURCE: David Sturges, Bob Carrell, Doug Newsom and Marcus Barrera, "Crisis Communication Management: The Public Opinion Node and Its Relationship to Environmental Nimbus," *SAM Advanced Management Journal*, 56(3) (Summer 1991), pp. 22–27. Reprinted with permission.

services, processes, locales, people and the policies that govern the organization. Keep all of this information readily available to those most likely to need it, and keep it in a form that is most likely to be usable in a crisis. Information is useless if the people who need it don't know it is available or don't understand how to use it.

Materials What kind of information should be gathered, and in what form should it be kept?[10] You need details and descriptions of products or services, product contents and product development processes or service processes, as well as a list of general operating procedures. You should also have current safety and instruction manuals, and copies of all recent inspection reports. In case of an explosion or a fire, you will have to describe contents and processes, with full awareness of potential danger areas—that is, the explosive nature of stored grains or the use of inflammable chemicals in a cleaning operation. You need a full description of all locations, including what is kept in surrounding areas and specifics such as acreage, street names, and the location of nearby homes, businesses or nonprofit organizations.

For every operation, you need a list of personnel and the times specific personnel are likely to be occupying an area. If the organization has clients or customers who are likely to be on the premises, you need that information, too. In 24-hour-operations—for example, mines, manufacturing plants, some retail stores, medical facilities and resident educational or care-giving institutions that operate with shift changes—you must set up a system with your personnel or human resources department so that you have at your fingertips an up-to-the-minute record of which employees are working where at what particular time. This information must be kept *remote* from the location. For example, at the time of a disaster, one mining company had to call all families and ask which family members were missing to determine who was trapped in a mine. This occurred because an explosion close to the opening of the mine blew up the shack in which miners had signed on for the shift. You should also keep a list of personnel benefits that employees receive in the event of death or injury on the job.

Keep separation policies on hand in the event that an employee or employees are responsible for the crisis. You should have policies and processes governing access to facilities, since many crises are caused by disgruntled employees or former employees. You also need access to as much information as your personnel office has on all employees and officers in the event of a crisis that involves them. You may not use all of the available information, for reasons of privacy, but the undisclosed facts available to you may help you to put a situation into perspective.

Part of being prepared is routine and consists of maintaining current corporate facts sheets containing all necessary basic information in the files at all times. Such information should include the following:

1. Addresses of the home office and all branches or subsidiaries (if any) and all telephone numbers, including the numbers of security people and night numbers that override the main control and put you through to the person on duty.

2. Descriptions of all facilities, in detail, giving layouts and square footage and the number of people in each area (very important facts in case of fire or cave-ins).

3. Biographical information on all employees, and long, in-depth pieces on key executives. Often called "current biographical summaries," these are useful for speeches and introductions, but here they might become standing obituaries, material ready to use with only the addition of cause of death.

4. Photos of all facilities and all principals (recent photographs; not the architects' rendering of the ten-year-old building or the CEO's favorite photo from several years past).

5. Statistics on the facilities and the institution: number of people employed now; cost of buildings and equipment; annual net (or gross); descriptions of products or services, or both if that is the nature of the institution; major contracts with unions and suppliers; details of lawsuits pending or charges against the institution; information on regulatory or accrediting agencies with some sort of oversight covering the institution, its products and its services (for instance, the Food and Drug Administration over products in that area or hospital accreditation over health-care institutions).

6. A history of the institution, including major milestones, prepared like a facts sheet.

Simply keeping all these materials up to date is a major undertaking, but it is vitally important. Most institutions handle them piecemeal, updating employee biographies annually, and photos less frequently, and gathering new and relevant facts once the base is established. A periodic review of these materials is essential. Make a checklist and use it, marking the date of the most recent check next to it.

The crisis plan itself should be a guideline rather than a heavily detailed process, for two reasons: ease of recall and flexibility. Both features aid in the creative handling of a specific crisis.

Communication   Some crisis plans are thorough and comprehensive, but they are never communicated. Then, when a crisis occurs, employees either don't have a copy of the plan or don't know how to follow its instructions. A good plan should include an easy-to-use facts sheet and background information.[11]

You should hold regularly scheduled meetings with all managers and supervisors likely to have to deal with a crisis, to review crisis response procedures. "Regularly" really depends on an organization's structure. In an organization with high turnover, quarterly review meetings may be appropriate. An organization with more stable employment and a system for giving information to new hires may prefer annual reviews. Reviews not only renew familiarity with procedures, they also allow planners to review the procedures themselves to ensure that they are relevant. Reviews spaced more than year apart court trouble.

One reason to discuss crisis planning in advance is to get management involved in handling various publics before a crisis occurs. You may be able to alter some management tendencies to procrastinate through hypothetical examples of the effects of such behavior and through role playing. In organizations such as hospitals and banks, employees should be crisis-trained for the possibility that they may either have to negotiate with a hostage-taker or survive as hostages themselves.

As dismaying as it might sound, from 50 to 70 percent of the largest profit-making organizations in the United States haven't made any disaster plans. The percentage is probably even higher for nonprofit organizations, primarily because they are less likely to have personnel trained to handle this area and are not likely to have a public relations firm on retainer to plan for them and to help them through a crisis.[12]

Communicating During a Crisis

Three key elements that promote successful communication during a crisis are (1) the existence of a *communication plan* as a part of the overall crisis plan; (2) the ability to assemble a *crisis team* when a crisis occurs; (3) the use of a *single spokesperson* during the crisis.

In developing a communication plan, remember that employees are going to talk to neighbors and to casual acquaintances whether authorized to do so or not. Consequently, your communication plan must include strong internal as well as external communication. Determine the best system to use: memos, closed-circuit TV, computer terminals, telephone. Identify people likely to be the principal participants in a communication plan, and develop a system for checking message statements before these are disseminated through the media.

The message statements will be generated by the crisis management team that you assemble from staff. This team will be instructed by outside PR counsel (when you decide to retain outside help) and by the organization's legal counsel. Isolate the crisis management team from normal day-to-day business affairs during the crisis. If day-to-day business is interrupted, the company appears to be consumed by the crisis and unable to manage the situation.

Designate members of the crisis team as fact finders—people who will dig out facts, organize facts, resolve conflicting data and control and direct the flow of information to the team members and the spokesperson. Designate a person to evaluate the effects of the crisis on all publics and to monitor how the messages from the organization are influencing various publics and the factions within these publics.

You must include legal counsel in all planning because typically, when a crisis occurs, legal advice and PR advice to top management often conflict. Legal counsel tends to advise "no comment," while PR counsel urges "openness." The reasons for both are justified by what occurs. Since the opposition seizes upon every word, lawyers understandably believe that it is better to say very little. Openness clearly creates more difficulty for lawyers who are trying to defend an organization. Accept that fact. But at the same time, the openness of an organization in a crisis also affects public opinion favorably. Keep in mind that, whether the situation involves a jury trial or a Supreme Court hearing, the proceedings do occur within the climate of public opinion.

According to Robert L. Dilenschneider, former president of Hill & Knowlton, an organization in crisis needs to go public in the first three to six hours after the news breaks or "you're dead." Another PR executive, Richard Truitt, CEO for Doremus & Company, comments that, when reporters get stonewalled, "They know they're really onto something."[13] A seasoned counselor says, "Your choice is a simple one. Either you write the story or they will. It's better if you do."

As a result of one disastrous situation in which workers in Texas Eastern's pipeline field refused to talk to reporters, Houston media consultant Jim Young prepared a laminated card for all field supervisors to carry in their wallets. The card lists information they can divulge in an emergency, and lists the basic facts that reporters are likely to want to know. The card also cautions: "Confirm there is a problem, state its nature but do not speculate about its cause." The list of "dos and don'ts" on the card begins with: "Do be calm."

Another Houston media consultant, Dan Ammerman, who was one of the first in the field, says,

> Corporate people are taking a proactive stance now. They realize it's folly to hope nothing will happen. He who tells his story first has the greater

chance of surviving the recovery period. Exxon and the Valdez incident are good recent examples. For two whole days no one from the company was there, and they took a beating.[14]

As an example of a positive reaction to crisis from an oil company, Ammerman cites the 1988 Shell refinery fire in Louisiana, where the company set up a newsroom and brought in phones and coffee for the reporters. "Any time you help the media do their job, they'll do it without emotion, and that's what you want," Ammerman says.

After developing a plan for responding to a crisis and making people in the organization familiar with it, the next most important part of dealing with a crisis is designating *the* (as in single) most credible spokesperson. Some authorities say that choosing the spokesperson is the most important part of dealing with a crisis, because that person sets the tone for handling the crisis. It may or may not be the CEO. Frequently the CEO is involved in making critical decisions to resolve the crisis if that responsibility has not been delegated to someone else. In any case, the person designated should be someone who is perceived by the organization's publics as knowledgeable and who is kept up to date on all developments. The spokesperson must know all aspects of the crisis, must understand their implications and must have sole responsibility and authority for speaking in the name of the organization. The appropriate spokesperson may be different in different crises. When a university was dealing with a football scandal, the designated spokesperson was the coach. The same school when faced with an academic crisis used the academic vice-president. Each had been previously trained to deal with the news media.

The spokesperson is usually a member of the crisis team and functions as your key contact for all media. If for some reason (probably time pressures), you decide to use a different inside spokesperson for employees than for the news media, you must be sure that the two present *exactly* the same information. The only difference should be the inside slant that the spokesperson for employees

Reprinted with special permission of King Features Syndicate.

gives. Using an inside slant does not mean presenting biased information; it means taking into consideration the special concerns of employees. You might also choose an inside person because that person has greater credibility with inside audiences. But the external spokesperson must be someone respected and highly credible to inside audiences as well, or you will damage the credibility of the inside person in the process. The spokesperson should not be an outsider, even if that "outsider" is a quasi-insider, such as a staff member from the public relations firm of record. Jim Lindheim, senior vice-president of Burson-Marsteller, an agency that enjoys a fine reputation for crisis management, explains that the firm's role is not to play the wizard who waves a magic wand and makes all the trouble go away. Instead, its role is to work in partnership with the organization, fully realizing that the final decision is always the client's.[15]

Employees' Critical Role   You must truly believe your employees are the front line in public relations to use them effectively in a crisis. They are the organization's most credible representatives to the people outside the organization with whom they come in contact; and when you think about it, those people constitute all the rest of your publics—from media to customers, from clients to suppliers. People will develop perceptions from the way employees respond to their questions and

from their behavior. Unfortunately, most organizations in crises neglect their employees. This not only mistreats personnel, but also harms the organization.

Employees get depressed during a crisis. They worry first about themselves and then about the organization (see Example 15.5). They become overly dependent on internal networks fed by rumors and on the news media. Employees should *never* first learn something about their organization from the news media unless it is something that has just occurred, like a fire. "Employees may hold the key to the organization's ability to survive and then recover from life-threatening crises," according to two researchers who have looked at the stress that crises cause employees.[16]

Management's Behavior   In planning for crises, you need to be able to anticipate the communication climate by predicting how management is likely to act and react as the drama of a crisis unfolds. Relying on case studies and Hazel Henderson's pattern for typical management responses to problems, Bob Carrell has developed some guidelines for anticipating management reactions in the three stages of crisis mangement: prior to the crisis during normal day-to-day operations; at the moment some event triggers the crisis, and during the crisis situation that follows the event (see Example 15.6).[17]

EXAMPLE 15.5

Employee Crisis Communication Model

Employees personalize their organization's crisis, and if their needs are not attended to through appropriate communications, their responses to external publics and their interactions with each other can impede the organization's recovery from a crisis.

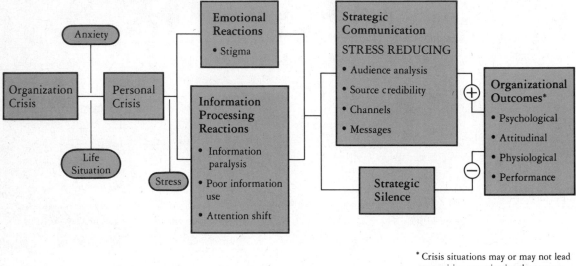

* Crisis situations may or may not lead to positive organizational outcomes. The use of strategic communication can minimize or neutralize negative outcomes, or create a climate for positive outcomes.

SOURCE: Reprinted with permission from J. David Pincus and Lalit Acharya, "Employee Communcation Strategies for Organizational Crises," in *Employee Responsibilities and Rights Journal*, 1(3) (1988), p. 190.

Carrell acknowledges that the crisis management effort can be hampered by the following elements:

1. The extent of a crisis may not be known immediately.

2. Persons or audiences affected by a crisis may be difficult to identify.

3. The cause of a crisis may be difficult to identify, and its cause(s) may never be fully known.

4. A crisis is always traumatic to audiences affected directly by it.

5. Accurate and appropriate information about a crisis is an expectation—sometimes rising to unreasonable levels—of audiences, especially by those directly affected.

6. Information decisions are made under conditions of high stress.

7. Because the situation is a crisis, the credibility of the organization is suspect among audiences directly and indirectly affected by it.

8. A crisis incites emotional behavior by everyone related to it.

EXAMPLE 15.6

Toward a Matrix of Crisis Communication Management

CRISIS-TRIGGERING EVENT

	Assessment of Environment	ON-GOING Development of Crisis Management/Communication Plan	ON-GOING Pro-Action	SITUATIONAL Activate Crisis Communication Plan	SITUATIONAL Arrest Triggering Event	SITUATIONAL Recovery	SITUATIONAL Evaluation
RESPONSIBLE MANAGEMENT BEHAVIOR LEVEL 4 (++)*	• Prudent evaluation of all categories of potential crises • Evaluates risks • Considers, prepares strategies and plans to prevent, minimize impact of crisis • Management is optimistic, confident, open-minded and aggressive	• Identify management team • Assign specific duties • Designate one person only to convey information to internal and external audiences • Train spokesperson, other members of crisis team • Plan viewed as positive way of meeting private and public responsibilities • Plan reviewed and revised regularly	• Implements, within capacity to do so, policies and strategies to prevent or minimize impact of crisis • Lobbies for government/public support for changes in laws and regulations • Aggressive, pro-active communication program to prepare audiences for crisis • Believes in principle of inoculation	• Spokesperson takes charge of communication function • Timely, consistent, candid information to internal and external audiences • Conveys information vital to public safety • Allays fears • Stifles rumors by supplying appropriate, factual information	• Inspires wholesome exchange of information with internal and external audiences • Seeks support as necessary • Makes adjustments in policies and strategies to arrest crisis	• Makes changes in policies and strategies to enhance recovery • Makes slight (if any) changes in organizational structure or personnel • Chances of recovery and turnaround are good	• Evaluates causes of recent crisis, responses to it, and outcomes • Reviews, revises crisis management/communication plan for future use in light of recent experience
RESPONSIBLE MANAGEMENT BEHAVIOR LEVEL 3 (+)*	• Evaluates some potential crisis categories, ignores others • Planning is spotty, myopic • Control systems questionable • Wants to prevent/minimize potential crisis but not fully committed to doing everything they can • Management often complacent	• Communication function regarded as defensive necessity • Communicates only as much and as often as required by internal and external pressure • Does some training but not much follow-up to keep plan current	• Selective implementation of policies/strategies designed to prevent/minimize impact of crisis, but could do more • Sporadic participant in lobbying programs • Little, if any, commitment to communication program to educate, prepare audiences for crisis	• Posturing messages with little substance • Face-saving approach • Rumors and propaganda often go unchallenged or uncorrected • Group think creeps in • Grudgingly admits crisis but often denies culpability • Offers plausible excuses	• Exchanges only limited information with internal and external audiences • Fears ridicule • Makes policy and strategy changes only sufficient to arrest crisis, no more • Audiences view organization with skepticism	• May make changes in policies and strategies, but usually these are very few • May make some changes in personnel but organizational changes are rare • Chances of recovery and turnaround are fair	• May change crisis management/communication plan, but changes often not taken very seriously
RESPONSIBLE MANAGEMENT BEHAVIOR LEVEL 2 (–)*	• Lip service to planning and preparation for crises • Management more concerned with sustaining power/status • Lacks sense of public responsibility	• Group think is common • Plan fully protectionist • Short-term solutions to long-term problems • Plan rarely reviewed and updated • Little or no training	• Does only what is demanded by law	• Often denies crisis exists • Rarely admits culpability • Places blame on others • Feelings of invulnerability are common	• Bunker mentality • Digs in and is often recalcitrant, inflexible • Communication channels are plugged up	• Reluctant to make changes in policies and strategies when changes made, usually are to conform to new public policies • In-fighting increases • Loss of confidence in leadership • Low morale • Loss of public confidence	• Existing plan remains unchanged • Rarely changes made in top management or in policies or strategies
RESPONSIBLE MANAGEMENT BEHAVIOR LEVEL 1 (– –)*	• Unable or refuses to recognize potential crises • Can't or won't develop a crisis plan	• Crisis management/communication plan does not exist	• Grudgingly does what is demanded by law	• Self-postulating as victim of circumstances, incompetent personnel	• Ostrich syndrome • Admits nothing • Does nothing more than is absolutely necessary • Relies on short memory of audiences	• Searches for persons to be offered publicly as sacrificial lambs • Changes in policies and strategies are only those mandated by law • Chances for recovery are very poor	• Organization may collapse • Replacement of top and some middle management is probable • Restructuring is common

* (++) = Open; (+) = Mostly Open; (–) = Mostly Closed; (– –) = Closed

SOURCE: Reprinted with permission of Bob Carrell.

> ▼ **Because crises always result in people going public with suppositions that can be treated as reality, you have to be prepared to correct misinformation with information.**

However, Carrell notes that the tendency of management toward an open or closed communication style and the corporate culture that such a style creates have a great deal to do with the way the organization responds both internally and externally.

Crisis Constants   Five communication elements that remain constant in any crisis help explain how people not directly experiencing the crisis will evaluate it. First, people learn about crises primarily from personal networks, if the situation is geographically close or if there is some relationship between the crisis and the network. An example would be an explosion in a nearby plant where employee networks carry the news to other employees faster than the mass media carry it. Second, people tend to interpret the seriousness of a crisis in terms of personal risk, or risk to people important to them. This perception may be based more on subjective than objective factors, so public and official perceptions of risk sometimes differ considerably. Third, government sources are relied on as the most authoritative. Fourth, the amount of mass media coverage indicates the significance of the crisis to a global public. Fifth, the availability of information in an open-communication environment reduces rumor and increases the accuracy of others' assessments of the situation.

Any crisis involves many more entities than just the organization that is experiencing the damage and is most responsible for the remedy. Developing an image that suggests the organization is successfully handling the situation depends on two factors: the reality of the organization's being able to cope with the problem; and how well the organization communicates its successful handling of the problem to those who didn't experience the crisis.

An organization's inability to cope with a crisis or the perception that it is bungling its efforts to cope can dramatically damage its credibility.

▼ COMMUNICATION AS A CRITICAL FACTOR

Two very costly and probably unavoidable crises occurred in 1989 and another in 1991 that should have made every industry realize its own vulnerability to disasters. The first was set off by an announcement from the National Resources Defense Council that apples treated with the chemical Alar could cause children to die of cancer. Reaction was immediate. Apples were pulled from school lunch menus throughout the nation, and they stayed in grocers' produce bins. Health authorities finally convinced the nation that the health risks of Alar treatment were well within the very conservative range set by the Environmental Protection Agency. From this crisis, the apple industry learned that public interest groups concentrate on hazards and that publicity often helps them attract and retain members. Apple growers already knew that they could face serious legal damages if they put a dangerous product on the market. While financial losses due to the Alar scare were considerable, the apple industry also had to be concerned about its credibility.

Also in 1989, the U.S. government banned the importing of Chilean grapes after *two* grapes were found to contain traces of cyanide. Attention was called to the situation by a terrorist threat. The financial losses to produce sellers were huge, and again the threat turned out to be highly exaggerated. While the government was probably justified in temporarily halting grape imports, the industry was put at the mercy of a terrorist.

That situation was reminiscent of the famous Tylenol crisis. In fact, in 1991, another pharmaceutical company (this time Burroughs-Wellcome of London) suffered a Sudafed product tampering crisis like the one Johnson & Johnson and its laboratory had with Tylenol in 1982, when several people in

Chicago died from taking Tylenol capsules that had been filled with cyanide. The two Sudafed deaths in Washington state during February of 1991 were only the fifth such poisonings with a consumer health product since 1982. Like Johnson & Johnson, Burroughs-Wellcome ordered a massive recall of the product. The deaths forced the entire industry to take another look at capsule pills. While industry officials want to protect consumers, they also hope consumers will be somewhat more vigilant.

The difficulty facing the companies in these crises was (and is) that consumers want their selections to be risk-free, and that, says *Science* editor Daniel E. Koshland, Jr., is "not only impossible, but intolerably expensive."[18] How does an organization communicate what it is doing to reduce risk, and how can it respond to crises like these?

Crises are evaluated in terms of the damage done or the risk of future damage. Evaluations not based on experience are based entirely on communication, and even people involved in a crisis rely heavily on communication in interpreting the crisis. Since many people depend on the mass media for information, those attempting to handle the crisis must try to get the most accurate information to the news media. This must be done not only to quiet rumors that exaggerate the situation and later damage credibility, but also to instill confidence in the organization's ability to manage the crisis.

Avoiding a Crisis with Good Communication

In Chapter 5, you learned to be on the lookout for problem areas. Knowing that you are likely to face a challenge means that you can open lines of communication with the potential opposition, with a group that supports or agrees with your position or with both.

Let's briefly examine two cases—one in which good crisis planning and communication averted a crisis for the company, and another in which taking the initiative put the organization in a good public light even though a crisis occurred.

Within hours after the August 2, 1990, Iraqi invasion of Kuwait, the crisis management team at AT&T was planning how to get AT&T employees working there out of the country. A month later, AT&T spokesman Herb Linnen shared some details of the successful escape. Linnen said that the AT&T security director was awakened at 3 A.M. by AT&T employees in Kuwait City on the morning of the invasion. The security director and his staff at the crisis center went into action within an hour.[19]

The AT&T crisis center is not located at corporate headquarters. It is situated at an undisclosed location in northern New Jersey. There, the converted conference room is full of communications equipment and stocked with maps, computers and telephones. Eighteen people staffed the crisis center around the clock, even after most of the Kuwait employees were out.

A telephone line from Kuwait City to the crisis center was left open as a "psychological lifeline," according to Linnen. "They [the employees] wanted assurance that AT&T's top management was looking out for their interests," Linnen said.

The crisis center directed the AT&T employees to form a caravan of cars and drive across the desert into friendly territory. Within a week of the invasion, more than 20 AT&T employees formed the first car caravan to make the 20-hour trip through the desert to Saudi Arabia. They made it safely through, despite confrontations with Iraqi tanks and soldiers.[20]

The Persian Gulf war that erupted on January 16, 1991, after Iraq ignored the United Nations' resolutions calling on it to evacuate Kuwait, was a public relations opportunity missed by one company embroiled in a continuing crisis, according to public relations executive Roger Ailes.[21]

Ailes said that Exxon, which was in 1990 still receiving much criticism for its handling of the Alaskan oil spill that occurred on March 24, 1989, should have used this as the opportunity to launch a public relations initiative. When other oil companies began raising prices in August immediately after the invasion of Kuwait, Exxon—according to

Ailes—should have launched a campaign pledging not to raise gasoline prices and urging other oil companies to do the same. According to Ailes, such an action would have done a lot to help Exxon recover from the bad public opinion it incurred by mishandling the Alaskan crisis.[22] Instead, Atlantic Richfield, which had many employees and a considerable investment in the area under crisis, took up the challenge from President Bush to hold prices. ARCO froze prices, as Bush asked all oil companies to do.

All of the oil companies should have anticipated the crisis and avoided the negative public opinion that resulted from their escalation of oil and gasoline prices at the onset of the Persian Gulf crisis. All were aware that no effective U.S. energy policy was in place, and all had weathered two previous international crises: one when the 1973 Arab oil embargo sent prices up and caused long lines of motorists to form at service stations; the second when the Iranian revolution of the late 1970s created another oil import shortfall.

Oil company executives complained as the Persian Gulf crisis developed that no one appreciated their side of the story—why the United States had returned to dependency on foreign oil, and why the oil companies had discontinued their domestic exploration and drilling. Complaining is not nearly as effective as anticipating and explaining.

When an organization fails to spot a crisis in the making, it's usually due to four shortcomings, according to Bank of America NT and SA senior vice-president and director of corporate communications Ronald Rhody: "ignorance, arrogance, bad judgment, negligence." Ignorance follows from the failure to get adequate information about the opponent and about potential allies of the opponent. Arrogance leads to making incorrect assumptions (primarily, underestimations) about the opposition. It frequently involves trying to be "above" a fight that's already on your doorstep. Bad judgment means making dumb mistakes. Often these are caused by failing to get objective information or by not planning. Mistakes also can be the result of negligence, such as failing to make sure everyone

hears your story and hears it first from you. This is especially necessary with respect to likely constituents, such as employees, suppliers and customers or clients whom you could expect to be "on your side." Rhody says: "Employees, and the families and friends of employees, in the aggregate, can be perhaps the most important of the communication weapons available."[23]

Public relations employees are particularly important because people expect them to know everything, and they themselves expect to know everything. In some cases this may not be possible, but at least make sure that the employees know enough not to get you in trouble. It's best to brief them completely, so they can put breaking news of the crisis in context. If you can't take them into your confidence, this may indicate the presence of a problem you need to explore. They will be subjected to a great deal of criticism anyway. One way to cut down on the likelihood of PR's being blamed for the crisis (or at least for whatever the news media do with the news of the crisis) is to adopt a procedure that Control Data uses.

Control Data has an exposure report that tells executives which issues the organization is dealing with make it vulnerable. Its developers say publication of the periodic exposure report has had at least five major benefits:

1. Senior management saw that the PR executives were managing crises.

2. Compiling the report caused the PR staffers to redefine their jobs.

3. It enabled the PR staff to respond quicker to fast-breaking situations.

4. The report's visibility changed the behavior of line managers, who began to think more about the PR aspects of events and to confide more in PR staff, alerting them sooner to iffy situations.

5. It reduced the recriminations that were leveled against the PR staff.

The developers of the report strategy are J. Arthur Boschee, CEO for the Alpha Center for Public/Private Initiatives (a national nonprofit organization), and Scott D. Meyer, chairman and CEO of Mona, Meyer & McGrath (a Minneapolis-based public relations firm).[24]

Responding in a Crisis

Every crisis produces an initial management consultation that occurs face-to-face, by telephone conference call or through a satellite teleconference. It is important to keep comprehensive notes of this meeting. After the meeting, you should write a response release, clearing it first with top management and the organization's attorney to be sure that it contains no mention of responsibility or damages and no assumption of either. You need a recorded actuality simultaneously with the spokesperson's statement. Depending on the status of crisis, you may need to call a news conference. If so, you must prepare a list of points you want to make, and, of course, you must be prepared for the reporters' questions (see Chapter 12—Tactics, News Conferences).

As news develops, you will issue bulletins to keep all publics informed. Some of these may be put on an electronic system, such as teletext or videotext; others will be written news briefs or taped actualities. All will quote the spokesperson.

If the situation attracts calls from media, employees or other publics (and most do), you must set up a telephone bank, train the responders and keep them supplied with updates of information and a list of people to call when they can't answer a question. If the situation involves consumers or large numbers of employees, not all of whom are located nearby, you may get an 800 number. When a large number of external publics, other than media, are involved, you may want to use a 900 number. Although this means that the caller must pay for the information, some callers will be glad to do so.

The telephone bank responders will direct some calls to the 800 or 900 lines. Media calls will be directed to yet another group of responders, preferably PR staff. Crises generate thousands of media calls a day, and a response system has to be developed, together with a method of recording who called when and with what questions.

▼ **Organizations that have an open communication policy are usually better off in a crisis because they have built up trust and goodwill with all of their publics over a long period of time.**

Constraints of the crisis situation will keep you from communicating as freely as you would like, but all responders must understand that responses should never be misleading or deceptive in any way.

Ineffective communication in a crisis can turn a difficult but manageable situation into a full-blown disaster, as Exxon discovered in 1989. When the supertanker *Exxon Valdez* ran aground on Bligh Reef in Prince William Sound off Alaska, many people in the oil industry said among themselves, "Thank goodness it happened to Exxon." It wasn't that they wished the company ill, and certainly no one was pleased about the accident, which promised to draw renewed scrutiny to past oil spills and the question of whether the industry's current safety measures were adequate. What the industry people had in mind was that Exxon had enough staff and crisis "know how" to handle the spill swiftly and professionally.

Such assumptions turned out to be unsound, however, because much of the infrastructure in Alaska and at Exxon for dealing with a crisis had been allowed to deteriorate over time since the original crisis planning was conducted. In addition, much of the research and development program had fallen behind.[25] Even so, Exxon could have fared better from a communications perspective if the company had firmly followed up the initial on-site response. The reaction of Exxon's chairman of the board Lawrence G. Rawl was to remain silent for two days and to stay in New York.

Exxon president William Stevens later conceded that some of what he and other company executives considered one-sided reporting of the accident was partly the organization's fault. Two news conferences a day were being held at Prince

William Sound, but as Stevens notes, "we should have provided electronic linkage to the lower 48, with two-way question and answer capability. That way, both our people in Alaska as well as our executives and the reporters could have pursued the story more directly and simultaneously." Stevens said that the coverage from the reporters on-site was well-balanced and fair.[26]

Nevertheless, some question remains about how much more damaging than necessary the effects of the crisis were because of the following problems: (1) the unavailability of top management, which made them appear to be "stonewalling"; (2) management's focus on the employee error of the tanker captain Joseph Hazelwood and the pilot on duty, which looked like "scapegoating"; (3) the fact that the employee substance abuse rehabilitation policy, while admirable in other respects, lacked a monitoring element, enabling people with a history of problems to return in many cases to their jobs without having overcome their addictions; (4) the statements that the cleanup was over at the onset of cold weather in September, despite contemporaneous television coverage of still-suffering wildlife and ruined fishing businesses, which gave the cleanup effort the appearance of a half-hearted and ineffectual "whitewashing." (In fact, only a tenth of the spilled oil was cleaned up through the efforts of everyone—Exxon, Alyeska, the Coast Guard and volunteers.)

With the *Exxon Valdez* disaster came public recognition that, assurances to the contrary, no organization has the capacity to clean up a spill of this size—11 million gallons or 240,000 barrels of crude oil, which at the time ranked it 30th among the largest spills in world history and first among U.S. disasters.[27] Subsequently, it was surpassed by the Persian Gulf spill engineered by Saddam Hussein in January of 1991. Yet, the *Exxon Valdez* disaster remains a landmark because it involved U.S. oil going to U.S. refineries for U.S. consumption—oil that was being carried in a U.S. tanker with a U.S. crew under the oversight of the U.S. Coast Guard and working in cooperation with a U.S. pipeline (Alyeska)—and because the wreck occurred in U.S.

waters that were among the nation's most environmentally sensitive.[28] It was also a U.S. media blitz of the first order.

Dealing with the Media in a Crisis   PR practitioners encounter a number of difficulties when working with mass media to communicate the reality of a crisis. One is the inclination of reporters to be more interested in the rare and unusual, especially in communicating risk. For example, a volcanic eruption, which is sudden and dramatic, may get more attention than dangerous water pollution, awareness of which often develops slowly and undramatically. In the latter instance, it may be difficult even to get access to communication channels.

Communication channels are usually disrupted by crises. The disruption may be mechanical (especially if the crisis is a natural disaster), or it may result from demands that the crisis makes on personnel who ordinarily would be taking care of the communication functions. In either case, extra efforts have to be made by the organization to get information to mass media.

Media representatives usually seek authoritative information about a crisis, primarily from government sources. When a crisis occurs, though, people in positions of authority are generally absorbed in helping solve the crisis. Therefore, they seldom see the value of setting aside time to communicate information about the crisis. In addition, those involved in solving the crisis may be a mix of government and nongovernment personnel, such as in a natural disaster or terrorist act, when law enforcement, fire and safety groups work with others from the government. These may also interact with nonprofit relief groups like the Red Cross. All must work with the organization at the center of the crisis, which may be a privately owned business.

Although each group involved may have its own traditional methods of dealing with the news media as a single organization, they are not as effective in responding to media inquiries as a loosely organized unit brought together by the crisis. Lines of authority are blurred, and some of the personnel may be out of their usual geographic boundaries. Beyond that, even the best-prepared organizations—and there aren't many of those—can seldom cope with the demands of the news media for information once the media have been attracted to the crisis. The more experienced an organization is with handling crises, the better the response will be (see Example 15.7).

Another problem is the tendency to close down the normal communication channels discussed earlier in this chapter. Often the crisis is such a threat to an organization that either the organization itself or others with control over it, like the government, severely limit information about the crisis.

Even in the best of circumstances, a crisis generates contradictory information. So much occurs at the same time, and so many people have different pieces of information, that it is difficult to present a clear picture. The situation is even more complicated if the crisis is the result of an adversarial action such as a hostile takeover. In an adversarial situation, the crisis is complicated by counterrhetoric that also helps to shape the reality for all publics. In such situations, the most credible source often wins the battle for public opinion.

Sometimes a crisis situation turns around for a while but then resurfaces because of an accident, investigative reporting or legal action. Some crises continue for years, so you need to plan for short- and long-term crisis management. The key is to maintain credibility.[29]

Credibility is always at stake. Burson-Marsteller's Jim Lindheim says that, when you look at a badly handled crisis communication situation, "It normally comes down to one or more of three elements: lack of openness or honesty in the beginning; not preparing for a worst-case scenario; and failing to communicate honest human emotion and concern by the company."[30]

A model of mass media behavior in a crisis has been developed by Joseph Scanlon and Suzanne Alldred of the Emergency Communications Research Unit, Carleton University, Ottawa, Canada. Drawing on their research and experience, reporters respond to hearing of a crisis by trying to get

▼ **Be aware of media needs and how they are likely to "play" certain parts of your crisis so that you can be prepared.**

---

information by "whatever ingenious or technical means are available, and use their background files to fill in the gaps."[31] In making the point that editors assign people so that the breaking story receives continuous coverage, to ensure that information is released as soon as it is gathered, Scanlon and Alldred note that the coverage consists of periods of high drama followed by lulls. Reporters often share information and attempt to fit it into a deadline-driven framework. Trends for coverage, the researchers say, are set by the prestige media, but while the national and international media cover the story only at its height, the local news media stay with it all the way through to resolution of the situation. The role of the public relations person is important (1) in conducting the delicate negotiations that have to go on between source and media about what to use and what not to use; (2) in providing enough opportunities, such as news conferences, for information to be given to the media; and (3) in educating as well as informing, so that reporters don't fall back on stereotyping to explain the incident itself or the people involved in it.[32]

Planning for communication in a disaster is imperative because the news media are prepared to cover it. For example, all California businesses, especially those in geologic fault zones, should be prepared for the possibility of an earthquake disaster. The news media are.[33] The *Wall Street Journal* says CBS may have the most elaborate battle plan for covering a major California earthquake. However, both the Associated Press and United Press International also have plans that include specific assignments. The *Journal* said it didn't have an elaborate plan, but its Los Angeles bureau did buy a battery-powered radio and television set recently and plans to buy shortwave equipment.

EXAMPLE 15.7

Crisis PR: Press Headquarters in Emergencies

Your operation must contain two specific areas that serve as a central clearing point for reporters and company PR personnel in a serious emergency. These areas should be equipped with several telephones and with some place for the people to sit and write.

If the emergency is centered in the area of one of the headquarters, the alternate location should be used. Additionally, company employees should be informed of this fact so they are able to direct reporters to the area from which news will be forthcoming.

At least two secretaries should be made available to the staff member handling public relations if the emergency takes place during working hours, since there will be times when this individual will, by necessity, be away from news headquarters.

If no news headquarters needs to be established, all calls from news media should be directed to one or two designated lines. While the PR person is out assessing the situation, names and phone numbers of callers are taken.

HANDLING PR IN THE EMERGENCY

1. Need for the establishment of the news headquarters will be determined by the PR person. News headquarters will keep all visitors to the site under control and out of the way of any emergency work being done. Also, having a news service indicates the company's desire to be cooperative. The size of the emergency will determine whether there is a need for a headquarters.

2. The person handling public relations will maintain contact with reporters, make sure they stay in approved locations while on plant property and provide as quickly as possible all information determined to be in the company's best interests.

3. The person handling public relations will check with a designated representative of management on the text of announcements and help formulate answers to questions.

4. The person handling public relations will be responsible for guiding reporters into the disaster area if company management will permit such a visit.

5. The fundamental responsibility for which facts are to be given to the press and ultimately to the public must remain with top management. It is the responsibility of the person handling public relations to operate with the approval of top management.

6. Maintain close contact with members of media. More often than not they will be able to tell you things you don't already know. This is a great way to stem the flow of false information.

7. Keep a log of all facts given out, with times they were released. This avoids duplication and conflicting reports should new developments change facts.

8. Do not release the names of victims until you know for a fact that the families involved have been notified. Tell the reporters that the name of the victim will be made available as soon as the next of kin has been told of the mishap.

9. When it is necessary to admit a fact already known to the press, be sure confirmation is limited only to definite information that will not change. If fire fighters carry a victim from the plant in a body bag and the reporter sees it, say only that one body has been recovered. DO NOT SAY that you "don't know how many are dead." Never speculate as to the cause of accidents, amount of damage, responsibility, possible down-time, delays in shipments, layoffs, and so on.

In other words, say no more than to confirm what is already known, and yet give the reporters the impression the company will give all the assistance it possibly can. As facts that won't be harmful become known, clear them and give to news media people.

QUESTIONS TO LOOK FOR IN EMERGENCIES

WHAT REPORTERS CAN GET FROM OTHER SOURCES IF FORCED TO

1. Number of deaths.

2. Number of injuries.

3. Damage. (Fire chief will give estimate in dollars— give yours in *general* terms of what was destroyed as soon as known.)

4. What burned and/or collapsed.

5. Time.

6. Location within plant (paint locker, press room, etc.).

7. Names of dead and injured, following notification of relatives.

8. Their addresses, ages and how long with company, as well as occupation.

9. How many people employed; what activities.

FACTS DESIRED BUT NOT NECESSARILY DESIRABLE TO GIVE

1. Speculate on nothing.

2. Any delivery delays or such. (Accentuate positive as soon as course is sure.)

3. How caused. (Let city officials release this— chances are story will die before report is completed.)

4. Specific damage estimates as well as what destroyed. (This information would be extremely valuable to competitors.)

DEALING WITH THE MEDIA DURING EMERGENCIES

In meetings with the press at the scene of emergencies, several things should be remembered. Basic is the fact that the public is represented by the press, and this medium has a recognized right to information that may vitally concern the community, employees, their friends and families and the victims. It is also common knowledge that the best way to prevent the spread of false rumors and misinformation is through issuance of factual information. At the same time, the company must guard its own interests and insist on relaying factual information only in an orderly, controlled manner.

REMEMBER:

1. Speed in reply to a query is all-important. All reporters have deadlines to meet.

2. Keep cool. If reporters get snappy, chances are it's because they are under considerably more pressure at the moment than you. Try to cooperate to the extent possible.

3. If you don't know the answer, attempt to get it for the reporters.

4. Eliminate obstacles wherever possible. Most reporters will agree that the more obstacles they find in their way, the harder they will work to ferret out the real story—from any source possible. They will almost always use something they have uncovered, and you have no control over what they might uncover.

5. Never ask to see a reporter's story. Time is usually a factor. If you feel the reporter may be misinformed, check back with him or her on the point to make sure.

6. There's seldom a reason why you should not be quoted by name. As a member of the management team and one charged with public relations, you are speaking for the company.

7. Never argue with a reporter about the value of a story.

8. Any information that goes to one source in the emergency is fair game to all. Don't play favorites. They listen to and read each other's copy anyway.

(Continued)

EXAMPLE 15.7 ▰▰▰▰▰▰▰▰▰▰▰▰▰▰▰▰▰▰▰▰▰▰▰▰▰▰▰▰▰

Crisis PR: Press Headquarters in Emergencies (*continued*)

9. Never flatly refuse information. Always give a good reason why it isn't available. Be sure facts are, indeed, factual.

10. Always know to whom you are talking. Get the reporter's name and phone number in case you need to contact him or her later.

11. Never give an answer that you feel might not stand up. It can embarrass you later.

12. Never falsify, color, or slant your answers. A reporter is trained to see a curve ball coming a mile away and has fielded them before. If a reporter thinks you are pitching one, he or she will remember it a long time and tell colleagues and other members of the news media over coffee. This will also set him or her off quicker than getting no information at all.

13. Be especially alert about photographs. You have no control of photos taken off company property, but you have every right to control photos taken within the plant. Consider the possibility of pool photos and film/video where it is impractical to have several photographers on the scene at once. Remember, photos can be as harmful as words.

14. Be sure no time lag comes into play between the time you get information that can be put out and the time it is actually given to news media people.

15. Have safety, labor and employee records available for your reference if possible.

16. Be quick to point up long safety records and any acts of heroism by employees.

17. If damage must be estimated for the press immediately, confine statements to general descriptions of what was destroyed.

18. Always accentuate the positive. If your public relations is good, so are your chances for an even break.

Problems with Instantaneous, Global Coverage of Crises An opportunity to see how industrious the news media can be in covering a disaster came on October 17, 1989, when the San Francisco Bay area was shaken by an earthquake that measured 7.1 on the Richter scale. While it only lasted 15 seconds, the quake took 67 lives and resulted in some dramatic destruction, including the collapse of more than a mile of Interstate 880 in Oakland. Forty-two of the 67 victims died there when the upper deck of the interstate collapsed onto the lower deck. A section of the upper roadway on the San Francisco-Oakland Bay Bridge also collapsed. In San Francisco's Marina district three-story buildings collapsed onto the first level, and a gas-fed fire raged there for days. Instant on-air coverage came from television sports reporters who were at the Giants' Candlestick Park to cover the World Series.

The experience of watching crises on television as they occur is part of the difficulty of dealing with the media in such times. Many major conventions scheduled in the San Francisco Bay area were canceled, despite the fact that the metropolitan area was certainly not dysfunctional. No reassurances from local officials could convince visitors that it was safe or that they could still get around the area, because they had seen so much destruction on television.

In addition to problems of perception versus reality that instantaneous coverage creates, "crisis while it happens" coverage raises credibility problems because, in any breaking news situation, information is sketchy and conflicting. When the information is released without benefit of editing (which involves checking), it places a heavy burden of responsibility on the news staff providing the coverage.

When the crisis involves confidentiality, the difficulty of getting accurate information to the public through the news media is increased. The role of the public relations spokesperson becomes more crucial, and the spokesperson is often subjected to intense media criticism. The military spokespeople who handled briefings during the Persian Gulf crisis were subjected to intense grilling. The U.S. government has, since the invasion of Grenada on Octrober 25, 1983, maintained tight control over in-the-field coverage of military conflicts. The U.S. media, accustomed to the freedom that accompanied the earlier system of self-censorship of the editing process, have not responded favorably to the new controls. But despite government censorship and controls, the instantaneous coverage that is transmitted globally has circumvented the traditional editing process, and editing now is left to reporters who often don't have the luxury of time to check and confirm their information.

Instant coverage has always been a source of difficulty in terrorist attacks, which, because of mounting problems in the Middle East, have been elevated there to the level of constant risk from the lower level of isolated incidents. Some observers have criticized the news media's role in this situation. While researchers have failed to document the most frequent accusation—that news media coverage legitimates terrorist activities—evidence suggests that the news media do fail to explain the underlying objectives behind many terrorist activities.[34]

There is some evidence that the news media, like witnesses, are less likely than government sources to use sensationalist, judgmental or inflammatory words in describing acts of terrorism, although they do often use inflammatory characterizations of the perpetrators of terrorism.[35] Presumably the political nature of government sources influences them to characterize terrorism as political violence. When an organization (whether a nonprofit group or a company), is the victim of terrorism, especially in the case of hostage taking, witnesses should be made available to the news media, when possible, because they have credibility and are less likely than government sources to use inflammatory words. It is also important to try to control the tendency of news media (and often of government officials) to use the victims of terrorism as symbols.[36] For example, if the hostage is depicted as representing the United States or American citizens, the hostage's value to a terrorist who is acting out a protest against the United States or its policies increases. The same could be said for employees of financial institutions, taken hostage to protest economic disparities.

There is a very fine line between keeping a hostage from becoming a valuable symbol and projecting an uncaring attitude about the person's fate. The role of the public relations spokesperson in working with the news media in this situation is critical. The media's contribution in a crisis as interpreters and educators could be enhanced in many instances if they were dealing with adequately prepared and trained public relations spokespeople who could supply accurate background information.

Talking Back in a Crisis   Organizations used to take their lumps in the news media silently when negative publicity occurred, especially if they had tried to be open and cooperative and the policy had backfired.

Hostility levels between business and the news media go up and down, and the PR person usually tries to ride the tide without drowning. Organization officers often admit that they rely on their PR person to handle all contact with the news media because their rage wouldn't permit civility. Of course, when PR people get along well with news media representatives—as they must—their internal loyalty sometimes becomes suspect. Nevertheless, the advice PR people gave for years to irate CEOs who wanted to talk back (or worse) to the news media was "let me handle them." And they handled them with kid gloves.[37]

However, the public relations stance is different now and more companies are talking back. For example, Dow Chemical became involved in the summer of 1983 in combating such "jokes" as "How do you spell dioxin? Some people spell it D-O-W." These were the words of David Stringham, deputy director of the waste management division in the Chicago regional office of the Environmental Protection Agency.[38]

Dow was named in a class action suit by Vietnam veterans over Agent Orange, a defoliant that the suit claims was contaminated with dioxin. In 1981 an EPA report blaming Dow for contaminating Michigan rivers with dioxin came into the hands of the chemical company, which sent lobbyists to defend its position. Although in 1964 Dow had called the attention of other producers to the potential trouble the presence of dioxin in herbicides could cause, almost twenty years later Dow fought the EPA at every turn on the issue because the company contended that most of the product research was Dow's, not EPA's, and that Dow should be the one to evaluate it. Dow also noted that, if one product were disallowed by the government, others might follow. Then in March 1983, when the EPA came under attack for staff irregularities, the company was accused of influencing the wording of an internal EPA report that involved Dow.

Hooker Chemical, now a part of Occidental Petroleum, took its problems with Love Canal to the public with a public television program responding to media coverage of the Love Canal problem. It distributed numerous printed materials, among them Hooker *Factline* covering such topics as "How would you like to be sued for hundreds of millions of dollars for something you didn't do?" The controversy stemmed from accusations that Hooker had not exercised sufficient caution in burying dangerous chemicals in a landfill that was bought by the Niagara Falls School Board in 1953. Subsequent development of the property, which Hooker had contested, caused penetration of canisters in which the chemicals had been buried and resulted in seepage.[39]

One of the first companies to speak out boldly and loudly was Mobil Corporation, which during the 1970s engaged the news media in a verbal fight. To Mobil, taking the offensive seemed critical to corporate survival during what executives knew was going to be a serious oil shortage. The company decided it didn't have to take anything and everything the news media decided to print or broadcast about who was responsible for what, and it structured an aggressive PR program that has since beem imitated by others.

The director of Mobil's public affairs campaign was then-vice-president Herbert Schmertz, now in private PR practice. Mobil began buying advertising space in key metropolitan newspapers for editorial columns, usually carrying a cartoon of editorial comment also. When media reports were wrong (from Mobil's point of view), the company purchased editorial space to name the offenders, present Mobil's position and offer facts, without getting into vituperative repartee. In addition, Mobil's chairman of the board and chief executive officer met with editorial boards of major print media—newspapers and magazines—to respond to questions and debate issues that were having an impact on the industry and on their company.

Getting into the ring with the news media requires the PR counselor to be a heavyweight in the realm of ideas and to know how to handle the company's position politically, economically and socially. Further, crafting aggressive programs that take the offensive requires thorough knowledge of the industry as well as of all factors that affect the climate of public opinion. In some cases, as in Mobil's, it also means defending yourself within the profession. Some PR people were highly critical of Mobil's aggressive posture and accused it of defensiveness instead of social responsibility.

Writing about Mobil in the *Public Relations Journal*, communications consultant Richard Detwiler commented that the result of the "high-decibel advocacy seems to be more low-yield persuasion." Detwiler quoted Herbert Maneloveg, a communications authority, as having said the public has quietly rebelled against such methods of communication. Detwiler also quoted the negative comments of two business publications. The *Wall Street Journal* had referred to "surprisingly widespread public hatred of the company [Mobil]" and *Forbes* had noted, "Mobil's monkeyshines would be funny if not so serious."[40]

The repercussions of Mobil's stance were felt in the defeat of Mobil's bid for an unfriendly takeover of Marathon, a smaller oil company, in 1982. Richard Chency, public relations counsel for Marathon, has discussed the positive role for public relations in the company trying to resist being taken over during such battles. He notes that Marathon was popular with its employees and the local townspeople (Findlay, Ohio). But, Cheney says, some of his clients have such poor public relations that when he asks company managers what their employees think about an impending takeover, they say they would ask them but the employees are out on strike.

Marathon's situation was a good public relations base from which to build, and the *Wall Street Journal* noted that the public relations campaign Marathon launched strongly influenced the judicial decision when the takeover battle wound up in court. A Mobil lawyer was quoted as saying that policy arguments helped convince the appeals court hearing the case that a combination of Mobil and Marathon would somehow be "morally wrong." Marathon had called on all its forces, employees and townspeople, to condemn Mobil's "perceived 'to-hell-with-them-all'" attitude, an action the *Wall Street Journal* called a highly effective guerrilla campaign.[41] This "guerrilla warfare in the jungle of public opinion," calls for aggressive media strategies, says public relations practitioner Jim Callahan. He says, "The media can be used as independent, third-party endorsers through which public relations can promote corporate positions and information."[42]

Mobil's PR campaign in the 1970s and other corporate "talking-back" actions have often been spurred by unfavorable investigative reporting from programs like CBS's "60 Minutes" with Mike Wallace—reporting that often amounts to trial by television.

Two communications scholars looked at three issues involved in such negative media coverage: (1) media criticism of organizations; (2) new (since 1970) response techniques by criticized firms; and (3) related issues of responsibility and performance, especially of media. The study concluded that the original sources of the information, the news media, suffered loss of credibility when they attacked firms.[43] While cautioning that studies of long-term effects of media credibility need to be made, the researchers' work offers some support to the belief that it's in the best interests of those attacked to enter the fray.

The quarrel between Mobil and the *Wall Street Journal* in the 1980s (stemming from the *Journal's* criticism of Mobil's aggressive editorial ads during the 1970s) was noted as an exception to the idea that talking or fighting back is usually desirable. Observers suggested that the hostility between the nation's leading business publication and the nation's third largest industrial corporation could have negative consequences for all news media and for business, generally.[44] Mobil had imposed a news and advertising boycott on the *Journal*, withdrawing advertising that amounted to more than $500,000 a year. The *Journal* in turn refused to print anything about Mobil. Other media covered the conflict as news. Mobil's boycott was really the culmination of a long-standing conflict with the *Journal*. In speaking—perhaps preaching—to the members of the Society of Professional Journalists, Mobil's President William Tavoulareas's theme was "It's time the media had a voluntary code of conduct." Of course, the organization he was addressing did, and he was aware of that, but he said it lacked enforcement.[45]

The *Wall Street Journal* was also attacked by another oil company, Pennzoil, which was fighting Texaco over the purchase of Getty Oil. The battle, which resulted in the largest court judgment in U.S. history ($11.1 billion against Texaco), is recorded in detail in the newspaper reports of the period and was very much fought in the press.[46] Texaco printed a brochure quoting favorable commentary on the case from the *Journal* and nine other newspapers to present its side of the story. It also used its 1986 third-quarter report, its 1987 annual meeting and its 1987 first-quarter report to tell its story.

Pennzoil used newspapers other than the *Journal* to present its position. A quarter-page ad sponsored by Pennzoil on responsible journalism was refused by the *Journal*.[47] Talking back in crises can be done, but it does have drawbacks.

Understanding Various Media Roles   Some of the most serious issues that occur in reporting global crises arise from a conflict in opinion about the function, role and responsibility of the mass media. In some countries, news media are privately owned and function with few government restraints. In other countries, news media are under considerable government regulation and supervision. There are differences in government oversight among the media, with broadcast media being the most highly regulated, even in the United States. Media roles are interpreted differently, too, with some countries seeing them as representative spokespersons for the country. Even more controversial is the view of media "responsibility," which varies individually among journalists as well as collectively among media organizations and is closely tied to values.

The way news media representatives interpret the function, role and responsibility of the news media affects how they report a crisis, how they interact with news sources in a crisis and how their media offices present information from reporters to their audiences. Regardless of where these media are situated, technology has made their reports potentially accessible to audiences all over the world. Accounts of crises are evaluated for the timeliness and usefulness of the information they contain. That information is the result of cooperation between the news media and the spokespersons for the organization in crisis.

When the organization sees news media coverage as a threat and withholds information or makes it difficult for news media to obtain information, reports of the crisis are much more distorted and the organization's perceived ability to cope with the crisis is much reduced. Fear that disclosure will damage an organization's image virtually ensures that the crisis will be reported in greater depth, over a longer period of time and with added sensationalism, since media will turn to outside sources that often deliver speculation and rumor rather than facts.

▼ DEALING WITH RUMORS

If an emergency is long-term and serious, as in natural disasters, rumor headquarters must be set up and staffed. In the absence of fact, there will be fabrication. Because rumors feed on anxiety, emotional topics such as threats to physical or emotional well-being are always an integral part. And the people most distressed by the "news" are the ones most likely to pass it on (see Example 15.8). The following advice on handling rumor comes from communications specialist Walter St. John.[48] First, try to avoid situations like these, which encourage rumors to grow:

1. Authentic and official information and news are lacking.

2. Authentic information is incomplete.

3. Situations are loaded with anxiety and fear.

4. Doubts exist because of the existence of erroneous information.

5. People's ego needs are not being met (satisfaction from possessing the "inside dope").

6. Prolonged decision-making delays occur on important matters.

7. Personnel feel they can't control conditions or their fate.

8. Serious organizational problems exist.

9. Organizational conflict and personal antagonisms are excessive.

The following strategies should be used to combat rumors:

1. Analyze the scope and seriousness of the nature and impact of the rumor before planning and engaging in any active correction.

2. Analyze the specific causes, motives, sources and disseminators of the rumors.

EXAMPLE 15.8

How a Rumor Grows

He Said, She Said

As rumors are passed on through a network of people, they undergo typical changes:

THE ORIGINAL STORY
"Two boys and two girls were fishing when their boat capsized. Only the girls knew how to swim; they grabbed the boys and guided them safely back to shore. The boys' parents were very grateful."

EXAGGERATION
The details become vivid and sharper, often for the sake of drama:
"Some teen-agers were having a party at night out on a boat when it capsized. One of the boys had a broken leg. Two of the girls were on the swim team and two other girls were lifeguards. They saved everyone else."

SIMPLIFICATION
As the story becomes rumor, it gets shorter and more concise as it is passed on; some details drop out altogether:
"Some boys and girls were in a boat that capsized. The girls knew how to swim and rescued the boys."

INTERPRETATION
The rumor is reinterpreted in terms of the world view of the teller, emphasizing stereotypes:
"The other night some teen-agers were drunk out on a boat, and it capsized. Two of the boys were on the swim team and two other boys were lifeguards. They saved the girls."

Source: Dr. Jack Levin/Northeastern University

SOURCE: Copyright © 1991 by The New York Times Company. Reprinted by permission from the *New York Times* (June 4, 1991), p. B1. Art by Keith Bendis.

3. Confer with persons affected by or being damaged by rumors —— level with them and assure them of your concern and of your sincere attempts to combat the rumors effectively.

4. Immediately (and massively, if it appears advisable) supply complete and authentic information regarding the matter.

5. Feed the grapevine yourself with counterrumors placed by trusted colleagues and confidants.

6. Call the key status and informal leaders, opinion molders and other influential people together to discuss and clarify the situation and to solicit their support and assistance.

7. Avoid referring to the rumor in disseminating the truth. You don't want to reinforce the rumor itself, *unless* it already is in wide circulation. In that case you *must* go public so that those passing on the rumor will be discredited.

8. Conduct meetings with the staff and others at the grassroots level to dispel the rumors, if necessary.

Once rumors begin to travel, they spread with considerable speed, and it is extremely difficult to stop them. The best way to combat rumors is preventively—restricting the need for them in the first place by keeping people promptly and accurately informed and by maintaining good two-way communication. But when rumors start, you need to act immediately to control them.

Two situations illustrate the importance of getting rumors under control. In 1987, a rumor broke that Corona beer was tainted with urine. Barton Brands, Ltd., of Chicago, Corona's largest importer, acknowledged the rumor's existence and proceeded to refute it. A story countering the false rumor, a chart listing Corona beer sales second among the top ten imported beers, and a picture of a lone beer bottle with the caption, "Corona: Squelching Rumors," appeared in the same edition of *USA Today*.[49] The beer is sold in clear bottles, something that might have contributed to the rumor. But, the "credibility factor" that fueled the crisis was the rumor that either ABC's "20/20" or CBS's "60 Minutes" would air a piece charging that

urine was found in Corona. Both denied that they would air such a story. In fighting back, Barton took the following action:

1. Barton filed suit against Luce & Son, Inc., a Reno, Nevada, distributor of Heineken (the top seller among imported brands) for $3 million. Barton claimed to be able to trace some of the rumors to Luce; and without admitting responsibility for the rumor, Luce agreed to an out-of-court settlement whereby it wrote a letter saying Corona was free of contaminants.

2. Barton asked for letters of retraction from twelve other Western beer distributors that it claimed had spread the rumor.

3. Barton notified 1,500 distributors in its 25-state territory that they would be sued if they were tied to the rumor.

4. The company sent to newspapers, TV stations and radio stations statements by J. E. Siebel Son's Company, a Chicago beer-testing company, that pronounced Corona contaminant-free.

"It was our intention to muzzle this by being aggressive in getting our message to retailers. It kept spreading, so we decided to take a grave risk by going public with it," said Barton's executive vice president and general manager, Michael Mazzoni. Sales had suffered as rumors of the contamination spread to Western markets. A full year later, the rumor was still alive but not affecting sales.

Squelching a rumor proved impossible for Procter & Gamble Company. The corporate trademark of a man-in-the-moon face with a cluster of thirteen stars inspired a story that the company was part of a Satanic cult (see Example 15.9). The rumor first surfaced in the 1970s, but it peaked in July 1982, when Procter & Gamble received 15,000 complaint calls on its toll-free lines. The rumor was refuted in 1982 by leading TV evangelists and columnist Abigail Van Buren; in 1984 her sister, columnist Ann Landers, also refuted the rumor. Most disturbing to the $13 billion per year company, however, were fliers that revived the rumors in 1984, urging "good Christians" to stop buying Procter and Gamble products.

EXAMPLE 15.9

The Logo and the Rumors

Yielding to the rumor mill, Procter & Gamble retired its logo from products.

SOURCE: Reprinted with permission of Procter & Gamble.

At that time, the Cincinnati-based company launched a direct-mail campaign. According to Public Relations Director Robert Norrish, the company would have sued if it had been able to determine whom to sue. Norrish said, "It's goofy. It's a ridiculous rumor. It's libelous. The whole thing is just absolutely without foundation. . . . It dignifies the rumor by denying that there's any truth to it."

Some people who had passed along the rumor retracted it, but others still felt there was "something to it." Attempts to pinpoint who was spreading the rumors failed, P&G's rumor tracker (and former FBI agent) James D. Jesse eventually gave up trying to find the originators, although he had even hired outside investigators to help, when he could "get them to stop laughing."

It was not a joke to P&G. The company finally removed the logo from its products, retaining it only on its corporate materials.[50]

▼ RECOVERY AND EVALUATION

For help in recovering from a crisis, Bob Carrell, professor emeritus of advertising at the University of Oklahoma, suggests looking again at the first phase in his matrix of crisis communication management—a phase before the crisis event occurs. He makes these recommendations for getting a crisis under control:

1. Determine the cause(s) of the crisis. It is important to undercut rumors and speculation that may have been rampant.

2. Decide which strategies and policies can be developed that will prevent similar or related crises. Direct experience with a crisis, although painful, teaches more than even the best scenario ever could. A crisis is the most severe test of existing strategies and policies.

3. Ask whether the crisis plan itself worked and whether changes should be made in it.

4. Evaluate the performance of all personnel in the crisis situation. Any failures in the crisis plan may have been caused by faulty provisions in the plan or by poor execution.

▼ CASES THAT ILLUSTRATE THE TYPOLOGY OF CRISES

In looking back at the typology of crises presented at the beginning of this chapter, the California earthquake of 1989 certainly is an example of the *act of nature, violent crisis*. On the opposite side of the chart, in the category of *act of nature, nonviolent crisis*, is AIDS, a tragic affliction that appears to be spreading, even though media coverage of the issue was eclipsed by the Persian Gulf war and other sudden crises. Concerned about public and media preoccupation with the Persian Gulf situation, some AIDS demonstrators got media attention January 23 and 24, 1991, by getting into the McNeil-Lehrer PBS newsroom in Washington, D.C., and the NBC newsroom in New York, drawing attention away from the anchors. AIDS remains an epidemic and a focus for crises.

The origins of the AIDS virus remain obscure. The virus has been found in humans and in monkeys. But it is unclear in which species it first occured, and how it crossed over from one species to the other is also unclear. Because AIDS is inevitably fatal, the epidemic is viewed as being more serious than previous epidemics: poliomyelitis, pertussis (whooping cough), cholera and the fevers— scarlet, yellow and typhoid. Dr. Jonathan Mann, director of the World Health Organization, said at the Fourth International Conference on AIDS in 1988 that as many as several hundred million people around the world may be at risk in almost every country in the world and that no country is immune. At the 1992 conference in Amsterdam, some more startling news of AIDS-like illness without HIV had been found.

For a health risk that wasn't even identified until 1981, AIDS quickly became a global problem. It was discovered only after it had claimed so many victims that researchers began to seek the source. The search turned up traces of human immunodeficiency virus (HIV) antibodies in laboratory blood serum samples from as long ago as 1959. The virus damages the body's immune system, leaving it vulnerable to infections and cancer. Everyone who gets HIV, the AIDS virus, eventually dies, although some remain healthy longer than others. The disease is transmitted through blood or bodily fluids, and initially (in the United States at least) two communities were at greatest risk of contracting it: intravenous drug users and homosexuals. However, anyone engaging without protection in any sexual activity with an infected individual is also at risk.[51]

Some victims have contracted AIDS by receiving contaminated blood during a blood transfusion. Until 1985 tests of donated blood for contaminants were unavailable. Other victims are infants born to mothers who are HIV-carriers. Because of negative social attitudes toward the two groups most popularly associated with AIDS and because of generalized fear of the disease, victims are often socially ostracized.

Employers and the government have had to mount education programs to prevent chaos in the workplace when an employee with AIDS is identified. One family whose hemophiliac sons had received contaminated blood were literally run out of town in Florida. Laws had to be passed to make it unlawful to keep children with AIDS out of school or employees with AIDS out of the workplace.

Unlike past epidemics, the progress of the disease does not involve simple exposure followed by a brief incubation time before physical evidence appears. A blood test can be used to detect the disease, but the margin of error is 3 percent. Some people who have been exposed do not want to take the test, perhaps because of the error rate, or perhaps because they prefer to deny the possibility.

In 1988, the Fourth International Conference on AIDS revealed that the AIDS virus can remain latent for four years without detection, that there is no cure on the horizon, and that no effective vaccine is anticipated. The only hope for control of the disease rests either in therapy that results in a cure (which seems distant now) or in education that warns of the risk. It is hoped that appropriate educational programs will persuade people to change high-risk behavior and to share information across cultures and national boundaries.

In the category of ***violent, intentional crises***, the bombing of Pan Am flight 103 captured public attention in December of 1988, and many feel that it contributed to Pan Am's filing for bankruptcy in 1990. The explosion of the 747 jetliner over Lockerbie, Scotland, killed all 259 people on board and 11 people on the ground. The flight from Frankfurt, Germany was en route to New York, via London. Public sympathy was generated worldwide because many of the passengers were students from Syracuse University returning from a semester abroad. The explosion was eventually determined to have been caused by Czechoslovakian-made Semtex plastic explosives, which had been hidden in a portable radio-cassette player. The worldwide investigation focused on the Popular Front for the Liberation of Palestine—General Command (PFLP-GC), which intelligence sources said had been hired by the Iranian government to plant the bomb in retaliation for the shooting down of an Iran Air jet carrying 290 civilians by the *USS Vincennes* in the Persian Gulf during July of 1988. Also implicated in the Lockerbie tragedy were the nations of Syria and Lybia; in 1992, Libya was subjected to UN sanctions for its refusal to extradite suspects in the bombing.

Pan Am security was criticized, as was the security at Frankfurt airport. All information about the possible cause remained highly sensitive because U.S. government relations with the new Iranian leadership had shown some signs of improvement until the disaster.

Stepped-up security did little to allay the fears of travelers, who stayed away from identification with the United States and were not reassured by statements of explosion experts that the plastic devices could not have been easily detected by standard scanning devices. Actually those statements made things somewhat worse, because an appropriate method of detection did exist, but it was termed "uneconomical." Furthermore, terrorist experts said that the international trend was away from hijacking and toward sabotage, especially with difficult-to-detect devices.[52]

When reports first appeared of a lethal gas cloud leaking from Union Carbide's Bhopal, India, plant on December 3, 1984, people had no inkling of the extent of devastation involved. The gas leak eventually resulted in the deaths of as many as 2,300 people and in the painful injury of thousands more. The event, initially labeled an "accident," focused attention on the safety of chemical plants all over the world (see Example 15.10).

Although Union Carbide attributes the disaster in Bhopal to employee sabotage—a violent, intentional act—many people blame a failure of the plant's safety system, which had not been inspected for 31 months before the accident. A 1984 safety report had warned of problems at the plant.[53] One of the publics affected most critically was a "nim-

bus" public: the squatters who had built homes just outside the plant.

The chemical that caused the damage was methyl isocyanate gas, used in pesticides. The event received intensive media coverage during the first week of the tragedy for a number of reasons: (1) the sheer numbers of human beings dead, dying and permanently injured; (2) the involvement of a U.S. company, although Union Carbide USA owned only 50.9 percent and the facility was entirely managed by the Indian subsidiary company and run by Indian nationals; (3) the existence of a "twin" plant in the United States in Institute, West Virginia.

The only U.S. reporter to file a first-hand report on the day of the event was the *Washington Post's* William Claiborne. Details were sketchy for a number of reasons. No one was sure why it had happened, and Union Carbide officials in the United States didn't know anything because they had been unable to talk with the Indian managers who were on duty when the leak occurred. There was some question about why it took authorities two hours to decide to alert townspeople, especially the squatters. Bhopal's population when the accident occurred was more than 900,000.

News coverage in the United States was analyzed by the Media Institute. The institute commented on the similarities of the coverage among the three major television networks. On the evening of December 3, each network led with the story, and two had interviews with Ken Silver of the Environmental Action Foundation. Silver suggested that Union Carbide had located the plant in India to escape stricter U.S. pollution control standards. The second night, when news of the thousands of deaths put the story in the lead again for all three networks, there were interviews with people in Institute, West Virginia, where Union Carbide USA operated a similar plant. These interviews were a part of "could it happen here" stories. ABC and CBS led with the story again on December 5, with footage of funerals and interviews with U.S. experts. ABC

EXAMPLE 15.10

Telling Union Carbide's Side of the Story

WHAT REALLY HAPPENED AT BHOPAL?

Since the tragedy in December 1984, Union Carbide Corporation's primary concern has been with providing relief and assistance to the victims and determining how the incident happened. Generally, initial details and subsequent news reports and books have contained a great deal of erroneous information. New information uncovered during an ongoing investigation has led UCC to the conclusion that the tragedy was caused by employee sabotage and that there was a cover-up afterwards by certain operators on duty that night.

The scientists and engineers who investigated the incident at Bhopal have proven that a substantial amount of water—enough to fill an oil tank in an average home—was necessary to cause the chemical reaction that occurred.

New information uncovered during Union Carbide Corporation's ongoing investigation has established that water was deliberately introduced into a methyl isocyanate storage tank from a source only a few steps away.

Investigators believe the pressure gauge was removed after a valve was closed and that the hose was deliberately attached to the pressure gauge opening. Then, valves were opened to permit water to flow into the tank.

Since the plant's manuals emphasize that water should be kept away from MIC, Union Carbide believes the incident was caused by employee sabotage and that there was a cover-up afterwards by certain operators on duty that night.

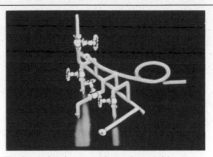

The investigation team has rejected this because:

Witnesses reported that washing water was flowing out through the filter system's bleeder valves onto the ground. This, in turn, meant that there was not enough pressure to force the water back up into the pipeline."

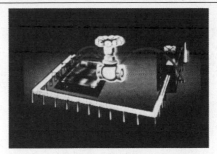

In addition, along the route there were four closed valves that would have stopped the water from reaching the storage area.

Here is what investigators have learned:

A few hours after the incident, a hose with water running out of it was found lying near the storage tank.

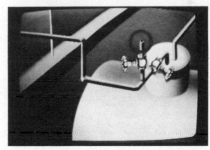

In addition, several witnesses discovered that a pressure gauge had been removed, leaving an unplugged opening into the tank.

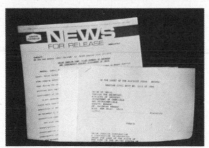

Additional evidence supports the employee sabotage finding, including: a shift instrument log indicating pressure gauges were present a few days before the incident, a sketch reflecting that water had entered the tank through a connection to the pressure gauge, logs that were altered or missing, and statements from other witnesses about the incident.

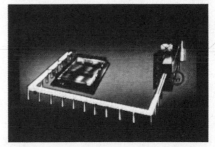

Previously, some people thought that routine washing of a filter system far from the MIC storage area caused water to back up through 400 feet of pipe and enter the storage tank.

(Continued)

EXAMPLE 15.10

Telling Union Carbide's Side of the Story (*continued*)

And finally, at the Indian Government's direction, a hole was drilled into the pipeline's lowest point. Had water gone into the pipe, it would have remained because there was no way for it to evaporate or escape during or after the incident.

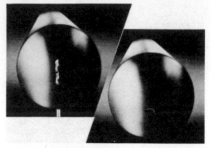

The drilling revealed that the inside was bone dry.

The evidence is overwhelming that the tragedy at Bhopal was an act of employee sabotage.

SOURCE: Reprinted with permission of Union Carbide Corporation.

also had footage of the student protest at Union Carbide's Indian headquarters in New Delhi.

The Media Institute observed that the coverage of this disaster showed both the strengths of television coverage—on-the-site scenes—and the weaknesses—superficiality in examining complex issues and thus creating "could it happen here" stories when it had to tell the story without pictures. On-the-scene accounts of death and suffering were not as prominent in the print media. The institute said the best followup coverage on the medical and scientific implications of the disaster was provided by the *New York Times*. The print stories, according to the institute, were first-hand accounts, on-the-scene reports, responses of Union Carbide officials, actions at the West Virginia plant, background stories on methyl isocyanate (including previous accidents associated with it), speculation about the legal and financial impact of the accident on Union Carbide USA, action of the U.S. government to prevent a similar occurrence in the United States, and discussion of the relative merits of such plants in Third World nations. The *Wall Street Journal* praised Warren M. Anderson, Union Carbide's chairman, for flying to India with a team of techni-

cal experts. Although he was put under house arrest along with the Indian plant manager and the chairman of Union Carbide India, he was released on bail and taken immediately to the airport. He never got to talk to the people in Bhopal. The Indian officials were kept in jail for ten days, leaving Union Carbide of India leaderless.

Even though Union Carbide USA was getting all of its information from the news media and couldn't get through on one of Bhopal's two trunk lines, the company decided to be open in all its communications. When the Media Institute interviewed editors in the print and broadcast media and industry executives about the coverage, both groups rated Union Carbide as above average in its responsiveness in providing information to the media. Not everyone agrees.

Everyone does, however, agree that it was the worst industrial disaster in the history of the world. The gas that escaped from Union Carbide India's pesticide plant in the province of Madhya Pradesh caused, by government count, 1,600 deaths at the time and 700 more from aftereffects. (Other reports estimate as many as 100,000 injured.) Many Bhopal residents still have illnesses related to the exposure. Many children were left orphans. Efforts by Union Carbide USA and Indian volunteers to help the victims have been thwarted by activists and by government action or inaction. Union Carbide USA offered to build a hospital and orphanage and was turned down. It had already gotten approval for a housing unit, but that was withdrawn. And a rehabilitation center outside Bhopal run by Arizona State University was closed after it was disclosed that Union Carbide had given the university $2 million for the center. Union Carbide also offered to convert the plant into a facility that made batteries, but the plant was closed. Then Union Carbide offered to turn the plant and its grounds, plus a nearby guest house and the research facility, over to the government to be used for medical facilities, a training center and a park. That too was refused.

The Indian government sued Union Carbide for $3 billion. Although there have been many efforts at settlement, none has been successful. The case was first tried in U.S. courts and then moved to Indian courts. Part of the problem may have been caused by U.S. lawyers who rushed to India to help people file suits against the company. Expectations of huge settlements climbed. India's state and national governments have rejected any Union Carbide aid because they thought it might damage their suit. However, about $5 million that was ordered to be paid to the American Red Cross by Union Carbide for Bhopal relief efforts was accepted. Only a portion of this amount was used by the Indian Red Cross. The Indian government's own relief programs have not been put in place. When the Red Cross offered to take over the government's entire child-care system at its own expense, it too was turned down.

The length of the crisis and the repeated frustration of the company's efforts to assist the victims, who were consequently left to suffer without help, caused a deterioration in the initially exemplary openness of management's handling of the crisis. The victims' continued suffering also turned more of India's people against the company. As one educator said, "We had considered Union Carbide a good neighbor until Bhopal."

Union Carbide's management also had to contend with more than one crisis. While the Bhopal situation was still very much in flux, the West Virginia plant had a minor crisis. But that was nothing compared to the attempted hostile takeover that developed when the Bhopal incident caused Union Carbide's stock to fall dramatically. To prevent a takeover, the company restructured, which caused another management crisis.

Union Carbide's public affairs officer at that time, Ronald S. Wishart, said the company is still paying the price for a decision made in March 1985 when

> the short-term need to satisfy the media's uncontrollable lust for culprits overcame our great reluctance to suggest any criticism of the affiliate company in India. We made the decision consciously because that's what the facts at hand suggested. But we know now, after two more years of intense study, that the tragedy was the result of an act of sabotage by a disgruntled employee, and that act overrode all other considerations.

Evidence shows that the employee connected a water hose to the tank and added several hundred gallons of water. Wishart, who is now retired, says that the employee probably didn't anticipate the consequences. What he probably intended to do was to spoil a batch of the product and discredit a supervisor.

Wishart saw himself as "chief of staff" to then-chairman Anderson and saw his role as being

> to identify what our objectives needed to be, to prioritize them in each moment of time, in each situation we faced, to assemble the appropriate resources from the legal, financial, technical, commercial, industry, governmental and consulting communities, and to coordinate those resources to achieve the desired results. What we said, and how we said it, had to recognize the games being played, and the stakes involved in each game . . . [B]ut I'm afraid that our balancing act among objectives sometimes prevented us from scoring the points—short-term—that we would have liked to."[54]

More recently Union Carbide USA was given permission to build the hospital it had offered to build earlier. But any good press this might have generated was largely negated in early 1992 by the Indian government's demand that former chairman Anderson be extradited to India to stand trial for murder.

While some observers have criticized multinational corporations like Union Carbide for building plants with "advanced technologies" in Third World countries,[55] India has its own advanced technological plants, and their operators make the same arguments heard the world over about the pros and cons of adequately warning their publics. One Indian plant manager at a crisis seminar got into an argument with another who said that the populace near the plant he managed would only be frightened if they knew the real dangers. The other manager said that for several years he and his employees had been communicating the dangers of their plant to the nearby residents, members of traditional tribal societies, and that the tribal residents felt comfortable with the plant. Elaborate displays and demonstrations had been developed to show them the dangers, and to help them identify early warning signs of trouble. In addition, an alarm system had been developed, and from time to time it was tested to see whether the residents knew how to respond.[56]

Compared to the violence of Pan Am 103 and Bhopal, crises in the **nonviolent intentional** category look tame, but the savings and loan industry's failure was a personal crisis for thousands who lost their life savings, and for many S&L employees who lost their jobs.

Symbolic of the crisis was the fall of the empire of California S&L owner Charles Keating. The 1990s began with a federal investigation focused on five U.S. senators accused of intervening on behalf of Keating and helping him keep his foundering empire intact. Keating had given more than $1 million in campaign contributions to the five senators, and one or more of the senators had subsequently met with federal banking authorities on Keating's be-

half. The U.S. Justice Department investigated, as did the Senate ethics committee, and the whole matter made many members of Congress uncomfortable, since intervening on behalf of a generous constituent is seen by many politicans as part of the normal course of legislative business.

This ethical aspect of the case caused serious credibility problems for the whole financial and banking industry, and the U.S. public was both hostile and cynical about "bailing out" the S&Ls with tax dollars. While many sympathized with those who innocently lost money, the perception was that even after the bailout most of the victims would remain uncompensated, while most of those responsible would go unpunished.[57]

Credibility was also a problem in July 1987 in another **nonviolent intentional crisis** that captured public attention: false mileage on Chrysler odometers and the sale of cars damaged at the factory but repaired and sold as "new." Initially, Chrysler defended its practice of testing new cars by giving 2 percent of all new cars to senior plant management to drive to and from work with the odometers disconnected. The corporate rationale was that, until the product had been tested, it wasn't ready for sale. Because the odometers were disconnected, the buyer still got the full mileage on the warranty.

Chrysler also repaired cars that had been damaged at the factory and sold them as new cars without buyers' being informed of the repair. The explanation here was that, when the car was sold, it met company standards for a new car.

Chrysler was charged with consumer fraud, mail fraud and wire fraud. At a news conference announcing the indictments, Chrysler defended its policy and said the U.S. district attorney was attacking a legitimate quality control system with a law intended to prevent used car dealers from rolling back odometers. Initially dealers reported no negative feedback, but the news media were full of negative cartoons, editorials and commentaries about Chrysler. When Lee Iacocca was asked by one U.S. senator if he should be worried about his new Chrysler that had been "product tested," Iacocca told the Chrysler executive committee that the company was going to apologize, offer compensation and reassure customers about Chrysler quality. But while the advertising was being prepared, the information about the charges began significantly affecting public opinion. Incoming mail was strongly critical of Iacocca for the first time, and a survey showed that 69 percent of people in the United States knew of the indictments and that 55 percent thought Chrysler had a problem.

Within a week, Iacocca was on television and radio making a public apology, explaining the odometer practices and saying that Chrysler had made a mistake in repairing the damaged vehicles and selling them as new. He offered a new car or truck to any buyer who determined that his or her vehicle had been damaged. He also said that owners with vehicles whose odometers had been disconnected could either get an extended warranty covering seven years or 70,000 miles (up from the five years, 50,000 miles available when the car was bought), or increased coverage for all the major systems not usually covered in the warranty such as the total brake and suspension systems, electrical and steering systems and the air conditioning. They also were entitled to a free inspection, during which any product deficiency would be corrected at no charge.

As Iacocca put it to the public, "Did we screw up? You bet we did." After his admission and the offer to compensate, another survey showed 53 percent of the people in the United States were aware of the apology, with 67 percent feeling that the damage had been undone and the problem solved.

Criminal charges were dropped against two executives, and Chrysler pleaded no contest to the remaining charges. A restitution fund of $16.3 million was established so that car owners who felt they had been injured could each get $500. Of the 42 damaged cars identified, 33 were replaced.[58]

In another, not so widely known **nonviolent unintentional crisis**, the public relations director (rather than the CEO, as in the case of Chrysler) acted as the chief spokesperson. Recognition Equipment Inc. is a publicly held company that makes electronic computer equipment in Irving, Texas. Crisis came in 1988 when the company's CEO and vice-president were indicted on charges of fraud, theft and conspiracy. The two officials resigned after they were indicted. But even though they were exonerated in November of 1989, the company's new leadership had to struggle to recover its 20 percent growth pattern and restore the company's reputation.

The charges that resulted in the indictment stemmed from Recognition Equipment's effort to supply the post office with electronic mail processing equipment and from its relationship with an Ohio public relations firm. In the eye of the storm thoughout the crisis was Jenny Haynes, who served as vice-president of corporate communication and was principal spokesperson except when she was unavailable as result of being called to testify before a grand jury in Washington, D.C.

At the onset of the crisis, she outlined a plan to preserve business and nurture employees. She presented a customer communications plan to ensure that current and prospective customers got answers about the problems facing the company. She wrote guidelines for dealing with customers for area sales managers and gave them a letter to distribute to employees who might be confused or upset by the situation. She wanted her company's sales representatives to be properly equipped to deal with customers, and she wanted them to understand the situation so they could feel comfortable explaining it.

Throughout the crisis, REI employees remained a primary public, beginning on October 6, 1988, when Haynes told all field employees of the impending indictments in a memo. Her memo covered the subject of the investigations and identified possible outcomes. She wanted to be sure employees could respond to customers and media when necessary. Employees were grouped into five areas: Dallas-based employees, domestic sales force, other domestic employees, international sales force and other international employees. Certain managers were designated to talk to employees during the crisis—to keep them briefed and updated. After the indicted CEO resigned, all employees received a personal letter from the interim CEO expressing gratitude for their loyalty.

The investment community was a major concern, and Haynes had a list of major contacts that she called before they called her. She kept the CEO and later the interim CEO supplied with a list of questions that influential stockholders and members of the investment community had asked her about the situation when she met with them. She wanted to document their concerns and get answers for them from the CEO. When the interim CEO took over, a letter explaining the situation went out to stockholders and to the investment community. The annual report was condensed and revised so that the major concerns of the stockholders and the financial community about the situation could be addressed. Since the situation was fluid and uncertain much of the time, Haynes canceled financial conferences if accurate predictions about Recognition Equipment's future couldn't be made.

In dealing with the news media, Haynes had a special problem. One local paper, the *Dallas Times Herald* (now out of business), had a well-placed source in the Justice Department, which meant that the newspaper often obtained information on impending events before the company did. On one occasion, the *Herald*'s story did considerable damage. Although Recognition Equipment had been banned from doing business with the post office, the company had reason to believe that the post office was about to lift the ban, and a multimillion dollar contract might have resulted. When the *Herald* reporter called Haynes for confirmation on the prospective lifting of the ban, she didn't deny the possibility. But after the story ran the next day, the post office denied that it was planning to lift the ban. After that story appeared, the possibility of getting the contract vanished.

Otherwise, Haynes felt that the company's media relations were good. Fortunately, she had been given some lead time in preparing for the crisis before the indictments were announced, and she offered reporters her home phone number so that she would always be available to offer Recognition Equipment's side of the issue. Her candor and availability helped promote friendly media relations.

Taking advantage of some warning time, developing a plan and carrying it through with one spokesperson helped Recognition Equipment avoid losing credibility during the crisis.[59]

Violent unintentional crises are numerous because accidents often result in loss of life and/or property, and serious events keep appearing in the news long after the incident. Even if the legal issues are resolved, there are always "anniversary of" reminders in the news media. Such an event was the Chernobyl nuclear disaster, which occurred on April 27, 1986, in the Ukraine and returned to the news in 1990 as the Supreme Soviet of the Soviet Union voted additional financial aid for parts of Byelorussia that had been affected by the accident. The region had announced contingency plans to evacuate more than 100,000 people from two provinces where high cesium-137 levels had been discovered years after the accident. Increases in the birth rates of deformed farm animals had been reported, studies of plant and animal life had revealed other deformities and there were additional reports of human cancer—especially of the thyroid gland and lips.[60]

The world learned of this first global nuclear crisis on Monday, April 28, 1986. First knowledge of the Chernobyl disaster really came the day before, however, when Swedish automatic monitoring stations began recording high radiation levels. By 10 P.M. Sunday, readings at a Swedish monitoring station on the Finnish border had started to record hourly increases. But these recorders were not read until the next day. By 8 A.M. Monday, Sweden's Forsmark plant on that country's east coast was showing unusually high levels of radiation. Within thirty minutes, the Swedes issued an alarm and began to evacuate about 1,000 nonessential employees from their plant. They were afraid that their plant had a leak somewhere.

Within four hours of the evacuation, Sweden's Nuclear Power Inspection Board was informed that an alarm had been declared at the Forsmark plant. In another four hours, news media were receiving information from the Swedish news agency Tidningarnas Telegrambyra. Two hours later, an Associated Press reporter was being told by a Swedish regional government official that the radioactivity was *not* coming from Forsmark, but from east of Sweden and Finland. He added, "If you know what I mean."

Within ten minutes of that statement to the AP, all news media organizations in Sweden were being briefed by Swedish Energy Minister Birgitta Dahl, who had called a news conference to say that the radiation was not from the Swedish plant, as authorities had first feared, but from somewhere else. The source was being investigated, she said, adding, "We are going to request complete information if there is proof pointing toward a certain country." It was 6 P.M. Monday in Sweden.

By now 26 hours had passed from the first detection of increased levels of radiation by the Swedish automatic monitoring stations. No word had come from any source but Sweden. At 9 P.M. Monday, three hours after the Swedish news conference, the then Soviet Union made its first public announcement. Tass News Agency in Moscow announced that "an accident has occurred at the Chernobyl atomic power plant, and one of the atomic reactors was damaged." Radio Moscow, the official broadcast source for the USSR, called the accident a "disaster":

> A government commission has been set up to investigate what caused the accident at the Chernobyl nuclear power station in the Ukraine where a reactor was damaged, and efforts are being applied to eliminate the consequences of the accident and to help the victims. The disaster was the first one at a Soviet nuclear power plant in more than thirty years. The use of nuclear energy for peaceful purposes is a vital necessity for humanity because of the gradual exhaustion of conventional fuels. Drastic measures are being carried out to guarantee the power reactor's reliability and safety.

Radio Moscow's broadcast was aired at 4 P.M. on Tuesday in the Ukraine, and it was heard early Wednesday morning in Europe. Victims of the Chernobyl disaster continue to be claimed in the 1990s, largely because people in the vicinity (including those who went in to help) were not told of the risks.

Before condemning the Soviets for their delay in reporting the nuclear accident, you should recall how U.S. authorities handled the United States' worst nuclear crisis, in 1979 at Three Mile Island. During the week-long crisis, the public received a baffling mixture of contradictory statements from Metropolitan Edison Company (the plant's owner), from the Nuclear Regulatory Commission and from companies that had built portions of the nuclear system. No lives were lost at Three Mile Island and nothing harmful escaped. That was not the case, however, when the British had a crisis in 1961 with a radiation leak. Are you saying to yourself, "I didn't know about that"? No wonder. The British didn't tell anyone about the leak or the toll it took in human and animal life, and details about it did not become public until after the Chernobyl disaster.

The Soviet authorities did improve as the crisis continued following the accident. Ultimately, the Chernobyl accident resulted in the total destruction of a power reactor and the spread of radiation to a considerable portion of the globe. In the first few months, 31 people died and 300 others were hospitalized with acute radiation sickness. Another 18,000 were hospitalized with lesser symptoms, and 100,000 more are under long-term medical observation.

The Chernobyl accident had global effects. Brazil delayed opening a recently constructed nuclear power plant, and almost all nuclear plants scheduled to come on-line in the United States ran into trouble, either with state regulators or with local communities.[61]

In the nonviolent unintentional crisis category is the crisis caused by publication in 1988 of Salman Rushdie's novel *The Satanic Verses,* which won the British Whitbread prize for fiction. In the novel, a fictional scribe, also called Salman, gets into trouble for blasphemy when he changes the words of God as dictated to him by a fictitious prophet called Mahound (read *Mohammed*). In the novel, the scribe escapes the punishment, death. Rushdie, however, was forced into hiding after receiving a death sentence in absentia from Iran's Ayatollah Khomeini, one that remained in force through the first quarter of 1992. This is not the first time the Indian-born British author has gotten into trouble with the members of the Moslem faith into which he was born. His parents moved to Pakistan during the 1947 partitioning of India. Rushdie's 1983 novel, *Shame* is banned in Pakistan, as is *The Satanic Verses*.

In 1990, Rushdie announced that he was turning down a lucrative contract to have *The Satanic Verses* published in paperback, as a conciliatory gesture to his critics. But he said he would never withdraw the hardback. His gesture was rebuffed in Iran, and he continues to live in hiding.

In 1991, the person who translated *The Satanic Verses* into Japanese was murdered in Japan, in an incident linked to his part in the book's publication. In 1992, Rushdie embarked on a high-security publicity tour to promote the paperback edition of the novel, which he had decided to go ahead with when he realized that the "death sentence" against him was not likely to be lifted.

Rushdie integrates his diverse cultural background into his novels, which are full of imagery and symbolism, and therein lies the difficulty. The images as symbols are interpreted differently by different cultures; and while Rushdie certainly could have predicted that the book might spark controversy, he probably did not expect to have to live in hiding as the result of publishing it.

The book was not distributed in the U.S. until 1989, after it already had created a stir in the Moslem community. At first bookstores throughout the United States displayed it prominently and it was selling well. But then threats and isolated firebomb attacks on bookstores occurred. Some bookstores, primarily chains that are not U.S.-owned, took the book out of their stores. Others took the book off the shelves, but made it available on request. Some courageous ones kept it on display and continued to sell it openly. Such a decision had to be supported by employees because any bomb threat affected them personally. One employee at a Taylor's

bookstore, when asked how he felt about having the book displayed with the other "new books" said, "I live under the U.S. government, which has a First Amendment, and I am under the protection of the city police. I'm sorry the Moslems are offended, but they don't have to read it. I sell a lot of things that probably would offend me if I read them, but I don't."

Culture is an important consideration in decisions about how to handle such crises. The book clerk's expression is perhaps typical of the United States, where church and state are separate and secular satires on religious themes are generally tolerated. In many countries of the world, though, including Iran, the laws are religious as well as civil. In places where religious offenses are crimes against the state, it's easy to see why a book like *The Satanic Verses* would be banned.[62]

A less sensational illustration of the nonviolent unintentional category of crisis is what happened to a publicly held company in the herbal product industry, Nature's Sunshine Products of Spanish Fork, Utah. For some time, the company was successful, but it wasn't attracting investors. The financial industry was a little leery of recommending it because of the unconventional appeal of the products and because these products were sold only through private distributors.

With a budget of $113,156, the company set about building an investor-relations program that eventually won it an IABC Gold Quill award. Nature became one of the smallest companies to make a presentation to the New York Society of Securities Analysts. And, as in most investor-relations programs, top management got a lot of attention. Then the crisis hit. Within a few weeks of the presentation, the chief executive officer and the chief financial officer left the company. They were the firm's principal contacts with the investment community, other than its consultants, Carl Thompson Associates of Salt Lake City.

The consultants developed a crisis plan to keep the organization stable, to establish a liaison between the board and the financial community and to rebuild credibility. A new CEO with good credentials was recruited and met with a good reception.

The company's monthly customer magazine was sent to the investment community, and PR consultants placed publicity about the company in major business publications such as *Business Week, Barron's, Forbes* and *Investor's Daily.*

The company did more than recover from the crisis. Its stock rose from $6 a share, before the first promotional efforts in January of 1989, to $14½ at the end of the year with the new CEO in place. Two other objectives were accomplished as well: the price/earnings ratio improved, and the number of institutional owners increased. Restoration of credibility went beyond the improved attitude of the investment community to demonstrated improvement in the company's financial situation.[63]

▼ SUMMARY

Public relations people deal with crises, usually played out in the mass media, that affect many publics but in particular have a tremendous impact on the employees of the organization. In some cases, the crisis may affect nimbus publics—publics who were not designated recipients of messages, activities or products/services of the organization.

Since communication technology is so highly developed, word of a crisis generally spreads to the world community.

While crises tend to be like snowflakes—no two exactly alike—some common characteristics permit development of a typology of crises. Within that typology an organization can discover its own areas of vulnerability to particular types of crises.

Two broad categories of crises in the typology are violent (meaning immediate, usually cataclysmic and involving loss of life or property) and nonviolent. Within each of these two categories are subcategories for acts of nature, intentional acts and unintentional events.

Whatever the crisis, there can and should be some advanced preparation. Some of this involves "imagining the worst" and deciding how to cope with it. Other preparation is physical: developing materials and strategies, plus communicating the plans to those who will carry them out. This is an ongoing process, since organizations change and employees come and go.

When a crisis occurs, there are three key elements for coping: (1) having a plan that can be activated even though it must be modified to fit the peculiarities of each event; (2) assembling a crisis team that can work independently of day-to-day management responsibilities; (3) using a single spokesperson from the crisis team to convey information about the crisis.

One of the most crucial publics to an organization during a crisis are the employees, because they have to keep the organization going and they tend to get depressed by crises. Furthermore, employees are seen by outsiders as highly credible sources of information about the crisis, so they need to be kept informed. The way they respond is usually a function of management's communication behavior, which typically fluctuates along a continuum between open and closed communication. In a crisis, the open communication management style works best, for three reasons: (1) rumor is arrested in the face of real information; (2) feedback can be obtained from employees and other publics who are exposed to what others are saying about the crisis (as opposed to management, which may be isolated and insulated); (3) credibility is higher because the information is shared instead of concealed.

Some crises can be avoided by effective communication, and all can be better managed. Outsiders often use how an organization responds in a crisis as a measure of the quality of its management. One of the biggest problems in responding is dealing with media—both mass and specialized. The task is time-consuming, and facts are sometimes difficult to come by. Furthermore, not all facts can be shared immediately. At the same time, media technology is such that the crisis is likely to be covered live by reporters who send messages directly to their audiences, without the benefit of the careful editing or fact checking that delayed media preparation permits. The effect is that the organization has to provide the news media with reliable sources who can explain in clear, simple language what is happening and what it means, without speculating.

Often in a crisis, media channels are difficult to reach or are disrupted. When possible, the organization must help media get their messages through. One perennial difficulty involves conflicting information drawn from equally authoritative sources. When possible, a unified message should be framed, and this may have to be done across organizational lines, as when a private company works with a government emergency relief team.

In any event, logs need to be kept of who told whom what from which medium when and under what circumstances. When possible, prospective spokespersons for an organization should undergo crisis communication training, so they will be better prepared to handle requests for information. When misinformation about a crisis does get out, the errors need to be addressed, not in an accusing way, but with insistence that corrections are made.

Reporters, regardless of where they are from, tend to look for something to symbolize the crisis, but spokespersons need to know how the news media function in different countries so they understand how information about the crisis is likely to be used.

Even under the best of circumstances, rumors may get started; in fact, a rumor may actually be the crisis. It's important to look at the rumor objectively and try to understand its scope and its potential to harm the organization. Looking behind rumors for their causes or motives may offer some insight into ways to handle the crisis. If a particular person or public is damaged by a rumor, you should work with each and show concern. Rumors can only be counteracted with massive amounts of concrete, authentic information. Sometimes such information is more successful when transmitted through the "grapevine" than through traditional media. When rumors are rampant, the visible support of key opinion leaders is critical. Yet spokespersons and others in the organization should avoid repeating the rumor as they disseminate the truth.

Once a crisis has passed, you must evaluate the plan, the people, the procedures and all other aspects of the effort to determine what worked, what didn't and what could have been done better. Often crises have a long life, such as when media publicize the anniversary of the original problem. There may also be legal action or other entanglements that return crises to the news periodically, delay resolution and continue to affect public perception of the organization. Knowing when and how a crisis is likely to reappear is part of managing and coping with it.

▼ NOTES

[1]Doug Newsom, "A Crisis Typology," paper presented at the Latin American and Caribbean Communication Conference, Florida, February 5, 1988.

[2]James E. Grunig and Larissa S. Grunig, "Toward a Theory of the Public Relations Behavior of Organizations: Review of a Program of Research," in Grunig and Grunig, eds., *Public Relations Research Annual,* vol. 1 (Hillsdale, N.J.: Lawrence Erlbaum Associates, 1989), pp. 27–61 (p. 60).

[3]David L. Sturges, Bob J. Carrell, Douglas A. Newsom and Marcus Barrera, "Crisis Communication: Knowing How Is Good, Knowing Why Is Essential," paper for Third Conference on Corporate Communication, Global Communications: Applying Resources Strategically, May 23–24, 1990, Fairleigh-Dickinson University, Madison, N.J.

[4]Ibid.

[5]Newsom, "A Crisis Typology."

[6]Nancy Jeffery, "Preparing for the Worst: Firms Set up Plans to Help Deal with Corporate Crises," *Wall Street Journal* (December 7, 1987), p. 23.

[7]Ibid.

[8]Donald R. Stephensen, "Are You Making the Most of Your Crises?" *Public Relations Journal* (June 1984), pp. 16–18.

[9]Joanne Lipman, "In Times of Trouble, Candor Is Often the First Casualty," *Wall Street Journal* (December 15, 1986), 30.

[10]One of the most comprehensive crisis planning books is *The Emergency Public Relations Manual,* 3d ed. (1987), by Alan B. Bernstein, president of PASE, Inc., printed by PASE, POB 1299, Highland Park, N.J. 08904. Another is *Crisis Communications Planning Guide* by Skutski & Associates, Inc., 100 First Avenue, Suite 800, Pittsburgh, PA 15222. The Texas Public Relations Association's 1988 *Crisis Communications Management Plan* is in the *Instructor's Guide* to this text.

[11]Doug Newsom and Bob Carrell, *Public Relations Writing: Form and Style,* 3d ed. (Belmont, Calif.: Wadsworth, 1991), 293–317.

[12]Jeffery, "Preparing for the Worst," p. 23.

[13]Susan Antilla, "Lawyers, PR Execs Compete in Wall Street Race," *USA Today* (December 22, 1986), p. 1.

[14]Gary Taylor, "When Worlds Collide," *Houston Metropolitan* (November 1989), pp. 26–27.

[15]James Wilson, "Managing Communication in Crisis: An Expert's View," *IABC Communication World* (December 1985), pp. 13–16.

[16]J. David Pincus and Lalit Acharya, "Employee Communication During Crises: The Effects of Stress on Information Processing," paper presented at the Association for Education in Journalism and Mass Communication, San Antonio, Texas, August 1987. Published as "Employee Communication Strategies for Organizational Crises," in *Employee Responsibilities and Rights Journal,* 1(3) (1988), pp. 181–99.

[17]Bob Carrell, "Predicting Ethical and Responsible Communication Behavior of Organizations in Crisis Situations," paper presented to International Association of Mass Communication Research, New Delhi, India, August 27, 1986.

[18]Daniel E. Koshland, Jr., "Scare of the Week," *Science,* 244(4900), p. 9 (editorial, April 7, 1989). For the Sudafed story see Michael Waldholz, "Sudafed Recall Shows Difficulty of Halting Tampering," *Wall Street Journal* (March 5, 1991), pp. B1, B4.

[19]Associated Press, "AT&T Crisis Team Helped Employees Flee Kuwait," *Daily Oklahoman* (September 4, 1990), p. 15.

[20]Ibid.

[21]James Cox, "The Oil War's Public Relations Battle," *USA Today* (August 22, 1990), p. 2B.

[22]Ibid.

[23]Ronald E. Rhody, "Hostile Take-overs: The Communications Edge," presentation at the *Fortune* Magazine Seminar, Palm Springs, California, March 17, 1987.

[24]J. Arthur Boschee, "Control Data's Crisis Control Team," *Management Review* (July 1987), pp. 14, 15.

[25]Staff of *Management Review,* "The Alaskan Oil Spill: Lessons in Crisis Management," *Management Review* (April 1990), pp. 12–21.

[26]Ibid.

[27]Ibid.

[28]Ibid.

[29]Newsom and Carrell, *Public Relations Writing,* pp. 193–197, 293–314.

[30]James Wilson, "Managing Communication in Crisis: Expert's View," p. 15.

[31]Alan B. Bernstein, "Handling the Press Under Stress," *Enterprise* (October 1984), p. 2607.

[32]Ibid.

[33]Scot J. Paltrow, "News Crews, Expecting the Worst, Prepare to Cover a Major Earthquake in California," *Wall Street Journal* (June 24, 1983), sec. 2, p. 1.

[34]Tony Atwater, "Network Evening News Coverage of the TWA Hostage Crisis," Terrorism and the News Media Research Project, funded by the Gannett Foundation, sponsored by the Association for Education in Journalism and Mass Communication, Robert G. Picard and Lowndes (Rick) Stephens, directors.

[35]Robert G. Picard and Paul D. Adams, "Characterization of Acts and Perpetrators of Political Violence in Three Elite U.S. Daily Newspapers," Terrorism and the News Media Research Project, funded by the Gannett Foundation, sponsored by the Association for Education in Journalism and Mass Communication, Robert G. Picard and Lowndes (Rick) Stephens, directors.

[36]Jack Lule, "The Myth of My Widow: A Dramatic Analysis of News Portrayals of a Terrorist Victim," Terrorism and the News Media Research Project, funded by the Gannett Foundation, sponsored by the Association for Education in Journalism and Mass Communication, Robert G. Picard and Lowndes (Rick) Stephens, directors.

[37]Public affairs/PR people often differ from CEOs on issues. Some research indicates that the major factor is age, since people tend to become more conservative as they grow older, and the longer a person is in corporate public affairs, the more likely he or she is to reflect the interests of the CEO. These two factors are discussed, along with other research on the topic, in Fred J. Evans, "Business: Attacked from Without and Undermined from Within?" *IPRA (International Public Relations Review)* (November 1983), pp. 27–32.

[38]Paul Blustein, "Poisoned Image, Dow Chemical Fights Effect of Public Outcry over Dioxin Pollution," *Wall Street Journal* (June 28, 1983), pp. 1, 20.

[39]Eric Zuesse, "Love Canal, the Truth Seeps Out," *Reason* (February 1981).

[40]Richard M. Detwiler, "The Myths of Persuasion," *Public Relations Journal* (April 1982), pp. 52–54.

[41]Richard E. Cheney, "PR to the Rescue in Takeover Battles," *Public Relations Quarterly*, 28(1) (Spring 1983), pp. 23–26.

[42]*pr reporter*, 195, "purview" (March 19, 1986), p. 1.

[43]David E. Clavier and Frank B. Kalupa, "Corporate Rebuttals to 'Trial by Television,'" *Public Relations Review*, 9(1) (Spring 1983), pp. 24–36.

[44]*Business and Economic Newsletter*, 3(25) (December 1984).

[45]William P. Tavoulareas, speech to Society of Professional Journalists, Sigma Delta Chi, Milwaukee, Wisconsin, November 12, 1982.

[46]Thomas Petzinger, Jr., *Oil and Honor, The Texaco-Pennzoil Wars: Inside the $11 Billion Battle for Getty Oil* (New York: G. P. Putnam's Sons, 1987).

[47]*Fort Worth Star-Telegram* (November 23, 1987), sec. 1, p. 8.

[48]Walter D. St. John, *A Guide to Effective Communication* (Keene, N.H.: Department of Education, Keene State College).

[49]James Cox, "Corona Importer Puts a Cap on Rumor," *USA Today* (July 30, 1987), p. 6B.

[50]Rumor About Trademark Bedevils Firm," *Fort Worth Star-Telegram* (October 24, 1984); and see Jolie B. Solomon, "Procter & Gamble Fights New Rumors of Link to Satanism," *Wall Street Journal* (November 8, 1984), p. 1.

[51]Compiled from "AIDS," *Medical and Health Annual 1988* (Chicago, Ill.: Encyclopaedia Britannica), pp. 254–59.

[52]Compiled from newspaper accounts and reports in the 1989 and 1990 *Encyclopaedia Britannica Book of the Year*.

[53]Otto Lerbinger, *Managing Corporate Crises* (Boston: Barrington Press, 1986), p. 16.

[54]Compiled from newspaper reports; speech by Ronald Wishart to the Public Relations Institute at the University of Northern Iowa, Cedar Falls, April 10, 1987; transcript of May 3, 1987, "60 Minutes"; Union Carbide employee brochure, "Setting the Record Straight on Employee Sabotage and Efforts to Provide Relief"; and *Chemical Risks: Fears, Facts and the Media* (Media Institute, 1985).

[55]Otto Lerbinger, *Managing Corporate Crises*, pp. 17, 18.

[56]Seminar conducted by Doug Newsom and Bob Carrell in New Delhi, 1988.

[57]Compiled from news reports and accounts in *Encyclopaedia Britannica 1990 Book of the Year*.

[58]*Corporate Directions, Corporate Secretary's Guide*, 53 (June 26, 1990).

[59]Drawn from research paper on "Crisis Management" by Sonja Ridgway, Texas Christian University.

[60]*Encyclopaedia Britannica 1990 Book of the Year*.

[61]Compiled from various news reports of the time.

[62]Compiled from various news reports and *Encyclopaedia Britannica 1990 Book of the Year*.

[63]"Investor Relations Program Gains Credibility for Small Company by Using Perception Management Techniques; Increases Marketability of Stock and Products Despite Unexpected Crisis," *pr reporter*, 33(24) (June 11, 1990), pp. 1–3.

Selected readings, activities and assignments appropriate to this chapter can be found in the *Instructor's Guide*.

▼

GLOSSARY*

A

ABC   Audit Bureau of Circulations, an organization giving accurate circulation data on U.S. print media.

A-B rolling   (1) Preparation of film for printing. All odd-numbered shots are put on one reel (A-roll), with black leader replacing the even shots. The even-numbered shots, with black leader replacing the odd shots, make up the B-roll. Both rolls are then printed together onto one film, thus eliminating splices. (2) Electronic A-B rolling means that on one film chain an SOF (sound on film) film is projected, while on the second film chain a silent film is projected. The films can be intermixed (A-B rolled) through the television switcher.

academy leader   A specifically marked film with numbers one second apart, used for cueing film in the projector.

accidental/convenience sampling   A type of nonprobability sampling that involves the selection of happenstance, as opposed to planned, samples. Standing near the information booth at a shopping mall and asking questions of shoppers who happen to walk by is an example of using an accidental or convenience sample.

account   A contract agreement with a client.

acetate   A transparent plastic sheet used in layouts, called "cell" for cellulose acetate; it also serves as a

base for photographic film and is used for magnetic tape too important to risk stretching. Acetate does not stretch and breaks cleanly.

across the board   A show aired at the same time daily at least five days a week. Also called a strip show.

adjacencies   Broadcast term referring to programs or a time period; usually means commercials placed next to specific programming.

advance   News story about an event to occur in the future.

advertorial   (1) In broadcasts, an organization's use of commercial time to state a point of view on an issue. (2) In print, a simulated editorial text with advertising content, usually run in consumer publications—product- or service-oriented copy.

aerial shot   A photo taken from helicopter or plane. (In movie film production and printing, the term refers to a particular effect.)

affidavit   A sworn statement, proof that commercials were aired at specific time periods.

affiliate   A radio or TV station that is part of a network but is not owned and operated by the network.

AFM   American Federation of Musicians, a union.

AFTRA   A union whose membership consists of anyone who performs live on videotape. Filmed TV shows require membership in SAG—Screen Actors Guild.

agate   Typographic term for 5½-point type, the standard unit of measurement for advertising lineage; fourteen agate lines to the inch.

*For a comprehensive book (668 pages) of communications terms, see *NTC's Mass Media Dictionary*, by R. Terry Ellmore, 1991 (Lincolnwood, IL: National Textbook Company).

air brush   An artist's brush that operates with compressed air; it is used to retouch photos or create special effects in illustrations.

air check   Tape made of a radio or TV program or a commercial when it is aired.

air time   Time when a radio or TV program starts.

alignment   (1) Straightness or crookedness of letters in a line of type. Also refers to the positioning of the elements in an ad for a desirable effect. (2) "Setup" of the head on an audio- or videotape machine.

alphanumeric   A set of characters used in computer programming that includes letters, digits and other special punctuation marks.

AM   May mean either a morning newspaper or standard radio broadcasting (amplitude modulation of 535 to 1605 kHz, soon to change to 1705).

angle   Particular emphasis of a media presentation; sometimes called a slant.

animation   Process of filming a number of slightly different cartoon drawings to create the illusion of movement.

annual report   Financial statement by management, used as a communication to all stockholders, security analysts and other interested publics; required by Securities and Exchange Commission for publicly held companies.

answer print   In 35-mm film, the first print off a negative (or in 16-mm, off a reversal) after the work print is completed; used to check quality.

AOR   Designation for a type of radio station format, album-oriented rock music.

AP   Associated Press, a cooperative or membership news-gathering service, dating from 1848, serving both print and broadcast media with stories and pictures. AP is international in scope and has its own correspondents, in addition to receiving material from member media.

Arbitron   Ratings company and sales research organization for broadcasting (also known as ARB).

arc   To move the camera in an arcing motion about a subject.

art   General term for all illustrations in any medium.

art-type   Adhesive-backed paste-on type used for special effects.

ASCAP   American Society of Composers, Authors and Publishers—a licensing clearing house that sets fees and controls artistic performance activity. *See* BMI.

ascender   The element of a lowercase letter extending above the body of the letter, as in b, d and h. *See* descender.

aspect ratio   TV picture measurement—three units high and four wide. Also used for film measurement, varying with the format.

assemble mode   Adding shots on videotape in a consecutive order.

attitude   A predisposition to behave in a certain way. People exhibit their attitudes by what they do or say; knowing someone's attitudes often helps predict how that individual will act.

audience   Group or groups receptive to a particular medium.

audio   Sound.

audio mixer   (1) Control room technician who mixes sound from different sources. (2) Equipment for mixing sound.

audit   In communications, a review analyzing perceptions of key publics (usually with an emphasis on internal publics), evaluating disparities between the two and formulating recommendations for improving the flow of communications.

author's alterations (AA)   Typesetter's term for changes made on proofs by the author after type has been set. *See* printer's errors.

availabilities   Unsold time slots for commercials.

B

back light   (1) Diffused illumination from behind the subject and opposite the camera. (2) In three-point lighting, a light opposite the camera to separate subject from the background.

back of the book   In magazines, the materials appearing after the main editorial section.

backroom or backshop   The mechanical section of a newspaper plant.

backtiming   (1) In broadcasting, a method of determining the time at which various program segments must begin to bring a program out on time. (2) In a PR campaign, scheduling to determine completion dates for various component parts to climax.

backup (1) In newspaper assignments, a second reporter or photographer used as a backup in case the first does not or cannot complete the job. (2) In printing, when one side of a sheet has been printed and the reverse side is being printed.

backup lead-in A silent lead-in to a sound film or videotape recording when the original recording preceding the sound is uncut; lead-in sound may be blooped or faded out by audio mixer.

bad break In typesetting, an incorrect word division at the end of a line of type.

bank (1) Composing-room table for galleys. (2) A strip of lights.

banner Also called a streamer; a long line of type.

banner head Headlines set in large type and usually stretching across a page.

barter Paying for advertising through goods, rather than money, or airing programs with commercials or time availabilities without paying directly for the program.

BASIC Beginners All-purpose Symbolic Instruction Code—a common time-sharing and business computer language for terminal-oriented programming.

beat A reporter's regular area of coverage, such as "city hall beat."

beeper (1) Recorded telephone conversation or interview. (2) Device frequently attached to the telephone that "beeps" every 14 seconds as required by FCC to indicate that a recording is being made.

beep-tape Magnetic tape reproducing a continuous beep.

belief A conviction firmly implanted in the bedrock of one's value system.

Ben Day Process carrying its originator's name that makes possible a variety of shadings in line plates through photoengraving rather than the more expensive halftone.

bicycling Transporting film or audio or video recording from one station to another instead of making a duplicate.

bit Binary digit—either a "0" (zero) or "1" (one).

black leader Also called opaque leader. (1) Black film used in editing. (2) Film used in 16-mm "A" and "B" or checkerboard editing. The black film, without images, makes putting sequences together easier.

blanking out Breaking or separating forms and placing spacing material where lines or illustrations have been lifted, in order to print in different colors. Also called breaking for color.

bleed Running a picture off the edge of a page. Allow at least ⅛ inch additional on all bleed sides of an illustration to be sure it "bleeds" after trimming.

block programming Scheduling the same types of shows back to back; the opposite of magazine format, which is varied.

bloop To erase sound track—by degaussing (wiping out) if magnetic, or by opaquing (blocking out) if optical.

blow up To photographically enlarge the visual size of an any item.

blurb A short promotional description of a story or article.

BMI Broadcast Music, Inc.—a copyright-holding organization from which permission for using musical selections may be received without asking individual copyright holders. Permission from BMI (or ASCAP) is obtained through a license fee. The copyright covers anything broadcast that exceeds four bars. Noncommercial stations get special consideration.

board The audio control board, which sends programming to the transmitter for broadcast or to the tape machine for recording.

body type Type used for text matter, as distinguished from display (headlines or headings) type.

boldface type (BF) Blacker, heavier type than the regular typeface, so it stands out from surrounding copy.

booklet A compilation of six-plus pages, printed with a paper cover and bound.

boomerang effect When a person affected by public opinion reacts oppositely from the expected way.

border The frame around a piece of typed matter.

box or boxed Type enclosed within printed borders.

break (1) Story available for publication. (2) Stopping point—may designate a commercial break.

breaking for color *See* blanking out.

break up To kill or break up a type form so it cannot be used to print from again.

bridge (1) A phrase or sentence connecting two stories. (2) In broadcasting, transitional program music.

bright Light, humorous news story.

broadside Message printed on one side of a single sheet no smaller than 18 × 25 inches, designed for quick reading and prompt response.

brochure A printed piece of (usually) six or more pages. More elaborate than a booklet, but without a backbone; differs from a pamphlet by its use of illustrations and color.

brownlines Lithographer's proofs.

BTA Best time available—commercial aired at the best time available for the station.

bulletin (1) Important news brief. (1) Wire-service message to kill or release a story.

burnish/burnishing Spreading dots in a halftone to deepen certain areas; also rubbing down to make pasteups stick.

business publications Periodicals published by and/or directed toward business.

bust shot Photographic framing of a person from the upper torso to the top of the head.

busy Too cluttered, as in a print illustration, still photograph or TV scene.

butted slug Type matter that is too wide to set in one line on a composing machine; it is set on two slugs and butted together to make one continuous line.

B&W Black-and-white (monochrome) photograph (as opposed to color photo).

byline Reporter's name preceding a newspaper, magazine or broadcast story.

byte A set of adjacent bits considered as a unit.

C

cable television *See* CATV.

CAD/CAM Computer-aided design and computer-aided manufacturing—systems of special hardware and software used in architectural or mechanical design that produce working blueprints or drawings from which the structure or product can be manufactured.

cameo lighting Foreground figures are lighted with highly directional light, with the background remaining dark.

camera chain TV camera and associated equipment, including power supply and sync generator.

camera copy Copy ready for reproduction. Also called repros.

camera negative Original negative film shot by a film camera.

camera-ready Material for a publication or printed piece pasted up in final form, ready to make a plate for printing.

campaign An organized effort to affect the opinion of a group or groups on a particular issue.

caps Capital letters.

caption or cutline Editorial material or legend accompanying an illustration.

card image Computer language for the image of a punched card as represented by some other medium, such as a tape or disk.

casting off Estimating the space required for copy set in a given type size.

cathode ray tube (CRT) An electronic vacuum tube with screen, on which information, news stories, etc., can be displayed.

CATV Community antenna television, also called cable TV—a system in which home receivers get amplified signals from a coaxial cable connected to a master antenna. CATV companies charge a monthly fee for this service.

CCTV Closed-circuit TV—programs telecast not to the public but only to a wired network of specific TV receivers.

cell or photocell Optical reader.

census Counting or asking questions of all elements or members of a population, rather than taking a sample of that population.

center spread Two facing center pages of a publication, printed on a single, continuous sheet.

central tendency The "average" direction or "middle ground" of data, usually expressed as the mean, median or mode.

chain *See* film chain, double chain.

channel (1) In broadcasting, a radio spectrum frequency assigned to a radio or TV station or stations. (2) In computer science, a path for electrical communication or transfer of information; an imaginary line parallel to the edge of tape along which lines are punched.

character Any single unit of type—letter, number, punctuation mark.

character generation Projection on the face of a CRT of typographic images, usually in high-speed computerized photocomposition system. The series of letters and numbers appears directly on the television screen or is keyed into a background picture.

chase Metal frame around a type form.

cheesecake Photographs that depend for their appeal upon display of sexual images.

chroma key Electronic process for matting (imposing) one picture into another. Called "shooting the blue," because it generally uses the blue camera signal of color TV cameras, but it may use any color.

circular Flyer, mailing piece, free distribution item, usually one sheet and inexpensive.

circulation (1) In broadcasting, refers to the number of regular listeners or viewers or area regularly tuned to a station. (2) In print, subscribers plus street or newsstand sales.

class publications Periodicals designed for well-defined audiences, with a focus limited to certain subjects.

CLC "Capital and lowercase" letters, used to designate a typesetting format.

client An institution, person or business hiring PR services.

clip (1) Newspaper clipping. (2) In broadcasting, a short piece of film or tape used as a program insert. (3) To cut off high and low audio frequencies of a program. (4) To compress the white and/or black picture information, or to prevent the video signal from interfering with the sync signals.

clip art Graphic designs and illustrations sold with permission to use, so designers of advertising or publications don't have to create their own artwork. Some is sold as books of camera-ready line art, other types come suitable for electronic scanning or already in electronic form for computerized desktop publishing.

clipping returns Clippings, mentioning a specific subject, from newspapers, magazines, trade journals, specialized publications and internal publications. Commercial services supply clippings from numerous publications for a monthly charge and a per-clipping charge or for a flat rate per clipping.

clipsheet Stories and illustrations printed on one page and sent to publications. Offers a number of releases in one mailing; works best with small publications that cannot afford syndicated matter.

close-up (CU) An object or any part of it seen at close range and framed tightly. The close up can be extreme (XCU or ECU) or rather loose (MCU) (medium close-up).

cluster samples Clusters or groups of elements in a population, such as particular cities or geographic regions, from which smaller samples are drawn. The population is first divided into clusters reflecting various traits; then a sample is drawn from each cluster.

coated paper Paper with an enameled coating to give it a smooth, hard finish suitable for best halftone reproduction.

cohort study Multiple samples drawn from the same population are studied longitudinally over time and then compared or contrasted.

coincidental interview Method of public opinion surveying in which a phone interview is conducted to gain information.

cold comp Type composition by various "cold methods"—from typewriter to high-speed computerized photocomposition systems.

cold light Fluorescent.

cold reading Broadcasting copy read by an announcer without prior rehearsal.

colophon (1) Credit line at the end of a book for the designer and printer; tells what typefaces and paper stock were used. (2) Publisher's logo. *See* logo.

color (1) "Mood" piece to go with a straight news story. (2) Lively writing. (3) Exaggerate, falsify. (4) Colored ink or art.

column rule A vertical line separating columns of type.

combination plate A halftone and line plate combined in one engraving.

commercial protection Specific time between competing commercials granted by a station.

community The immediate area affected by company policy and production.

community relations A function of public relations that involves dealing and communicating with the citizens and groups within an organization's geographic operating area.

compact disk (CD)   Digitally encoded storage medium for sound or text, decoded by scanning with a laser beam (CD-I is an interactive disk).

composition   (1) Typesetting and makeup. (2) Arrangement of words into a stylistic format.

compositive or composite   (1) In broadcasting, a sound track with the desired mix of sounds. (2) In photography, mixing elements from different negatives to create false image.

computer network   Two or more interconnected computers.

computer program   A set of instructions that, converted to machine format, causes a computer to carry out specified operations to solve a problem.

condensed   Type that is narrower than regular face.

conservation   Support of an existing opinion held by a public to keep it from changing.

console   Part of a computer through which the operator or repair person communicates with the machine and vice versa. Normally it has an entry device such as a typewriter keyboard.

content analysis   A research method that involves objective description or analysis of the language content of news releases, newspaper stories, speeches, videotapes and films, magazines or other publications.

continuity   Radio and television copy.

continuity strip   An ad in comic strip format.

control group   Group composed of members chosen for particular characteristics or opinions. Used as a comparison to a *test group*.

control track   The area of a videotape that is used for recording synchronization information (sync spikes), which is essential for videotape editing.

control unit   In a digital computer, the parts that effect retrieval of instructions in correct sequence. The unit interprets each instruction and then applies proper signals to the arithmetic unit.

conversion   Influencing opinion away from one side of an issue toward another.

co-op advertising   Sharing costs of advertising between two advertisers. In broadcasting, it nearly always refers to a national/local share.

coppering   Revising old news to give it a feeling of currency.

copy   (1) Any broadcast writing, including commercials. (2) Any written material intended for publication, including advertising.

copy desk   The news desk at a newspaper, magazine, radio or TV station where copy is edited and headlines are written.

copy fitting   Determining how much copy is needed to fill a certain amount of space in a design or publication, or figuring how much space is needed to accommodate a given amount of text.

copyreader   A newsroom employee who reads and corrects (edits) copy and writes headlines.

core   (1) The "memory" of computer. (2) A small hub on which film is wound for storage or shipping.

correspondent   Out-of-town reporter.

cost per thousand (CPM)   The cost to an advertiser to reach 1,000 listeners or viewers with a given message; figured by dividing time cost by size of audience (in thousands).

cover   (1) To a reporter, getting all available facts about an event. (2) Outer pages of a magazine—specifically, the outside front (first cover), inside front (second cover), inside back (third cover) and outside back (fourth cover).

cover shot   Shot of the scene used as a reserve if you miss the action with the first shot.

cover stock   Sturdy paper for magazine covers, pamphlets, booklets, tent cards, posters and other printed matter where weight and durability are important.

CPI   (1) In typesetting, characters per inch. (2) In computer science, the density of the magnetic tape or drum.

CPM   Cost per thousand (*M* means "thousand")—the ratio of the cost of a given TV segment to the audience reached (in thousands).

CPS   Characters per second—relates to paper tapes or typewriter speeds.

CPU   Central processing unit—the main frame of a computer, with circuits that control operations.

crawl graphics   Usually credit copy that moves slowly up the TV or cinema screen, often mounted on a drum (or crawl). More exactly, an up-and-down movement of credits is called a roll, and a horizontal movement a crawl. Both the roll and the crawl can be produced by the character generator.

credits   List of people who participated in a TV or film production.

cropping   Changing the shape or size of an illustration to make it fit a designated space or to cut out distracting or undesirable elements.

cross-fade   (1) In audio, a transition method in which the preceding sound is faded out and the following sound is faded in simultaneously. The sounds overlap temporarily. (2) In video, a transition method whereby the preceding picture is faded to black and the following picture is faded in from black.

CRT   *See* cathode ray tube.

crystallization   Creating an awareness of previously vague or subconscious attitudes held by a public.

CTC or CTK   Copy to come.

CTG   Copy to go.

CTR   Computer tape reader—attached when needed to a phototypesetting device.

CU   *See* close-up; usually head and just below shoulders of a person in TV, film or still photograph.

cue   (1) In TV, film or radio, a signal to initiate action. (2) A mark in a TV script for technical and production staffs. (3) White or black dots on film indicating the end. (4) To find the proper place of a transcription.

cumulative audience ("cume")   The audience reached by a broadcast station in two or more time periods or by more than one station in a specific time period (such as a week).

custom-built network   A network temporarily linking stations for a special broadcast.

cut   (1) To delete part of some copy or to end a program suddenly. (2) A track or groove in a transcription. (3) In engraving, a metal plate bearing an illustration, either lined or screened, to be used in letterpress printing (with a raised printing surface made from a matrix). (4) Instantaneous transition from one film or video source to another. *See* engraving.

cutaway shot   A shot of an object or event peripherally connected with the overall event and neutral as to screen direction (usually a straight-on shot). Used to intercut between two shots in which the screen direction is reversed. Also used to cut between two takes with the same shot, avoiding a jump cut.

cutline   The caption or legend accompanying an illustration.

D

daisy wheel   A type head used in letter-quality printers that contains a font of type on a circular wheel.

data   Information, often in numerical form and often obtained through systematic observation and surveys, that helps describe, explain or predict relationships, attitudes, opinions or behavior. *Data* is plural; the singular term is *datum*.

database/data bank   A collection of data used by an organization, capable of being processed and retrieved.

dateline   The line preceding a story, giving date and place of origin; usually only the location is printed.

deadline   The time a completed assignment is due and *must* be delivered.

dealer imprint   The name and address of the dealer printed on a leaflet, pamphlet, poster or similar matter, usually in space set aside for this purpose.

deck   (1) Part of a headline. (2) A recording machine only (audio or video).

deck head   A headline having two or more groups of type.

deckled edge   A ragged edge on a sheet of paper.

delphi technique   A research method that elicits an interactive exchange of ideas and information among a panel of experts to arrive at a consensus. Several rounds of questionnaires usually are involved, each incorporating and reporting responses from earlier rounds of questioning.

demographics   Certain characteristics in the audience for any medium—sex, age, family, education, economics.

department   Regular section on a particular subject in a newspaper or magazine.

depth of field   The measure in which all objects, located at different distances from the camera, appear in focus. Depth of field depends on the focal length of the lens, the f-stop, and the distance between object and camera.

descender Bottom part of a lowercase letter that extends below the body of the letter, as in p, q and y. *See* ascender.

dirty copy Written material with considerable errors or corrections.

disk Record or transcription.

display type Type or hand lettering for headlines; usually larger than 14 points.

dissolve In TV or film, a gradual transition from shot to shot whereby the two images temporarily overlap. Also called lap-dissolve, or lap.

documentary An informational film presentation with a specific message.

dolly To move the camera toward (dolly in) or away from (dolly out or back) the object.

donut A commercial in which live copy runs between the opening and close of a produced commercial, usually a singing jingle.

dope News information or background material.

dot-matrix printer A printer that forms type characters by arranging dots of ink in a grid, or matrix, pattern.

double chain A film story using two film chains simultaneously. *See* film chain.

double-page spread Two facing pages; may be editorial material or advertising, with or without illustrations.

double projection Shooting and recording sound and pictures separately for later simultaneous productions. Gives higher quality reproduction.

double-spot Two TV commercials run back to back.

double system sound In film and TV, picture and sound portions are recorded separately and later may be combined on one film through printing (married printing).

double truck Center spread, or two full facing pages.

downlink To receive audio and video signals or digitized computer information from a communication satellite, which acts as transmitter.

download To feed a news release from the organization's computer directly into the medium's computer for typesetting, etc.

dress (1) The appearance of a magazine. (2) In broadcasting, a final "dress" rehearsal, or what people will wear on camera. (3) Set dressing, properties.

drive out In typesetting, to space words widely to fill the line.

drop folio In books and publications, page number at bottom of page.

drop-in ads Small advertising messages added to or "dropped in" regular advertisements of a different character; e.g., a 1-column-inch community-fund-drive ad in a department store's regular half-page ad.

dry A "slow" or "dry" news day when not much is going on.

dry brush drawing A drawing usually on coarse board made with thick ink or paint.

dry run A rehearsal, usually for TV, before actual taping or airing, if live.

dub Duplication of an electronic recording or an insertion into a transcription. Dubs can be made from tape to tape or from record to tape. The dub is always one generation down (away) from the recording used for the dubbing and is therefore of lower quality.

dubbing Transcribing a sound track from one recording medium to another, such as from film sound to audio tape.

dummy The suggested layout for a publication, showing positions of all elements. A hand dummy is rough and general. A pasteup dummy is proofs carefully pasted in position.

duotones Two-color art. Two halftone plates are made from a one-color illustration and etched to produce a two-tone effect.

dupe Duplicate proof.

E

ears Boxes or type appearing at the upper left- and right-hand corners of publications alongside the flag (newspaper nameplate).

easel shots or "limbos" Still pictures or models videotaped by a TV camera.

edge key A keyed (electronically cut-in) title whose letters have distinctive edges, such as dark outlines or a drop shadow.

edit To modify, correct, rearrange or otherwise change data in the computer.

editing   Emphasizing important matter or deleting the less significant. (1) In live TV, selecting from preview monitors the pictures that will be aired, the selection and assembly of shots. (2) In print media, the collection, preparation, layout and design of materials for publication.

edition   All identical copies, printed in one run of the press.

editorialize   To inject opinion into a news story.

editorial matter   The entertainment or educational part of a broadcast program or publication, exclusive of commercial messages.

EDP   Electronic data processing.

electronic editing   Inserting or assembling a program on videotape without physically cutting the tape.

electronic film transfer   Kinescoping a program from videotape to film by filming the images that appear on a very sharp television monitor.

electronic newspaper   A videotex or teletext system in which the individual becomes his or her own gatekeeper, selecting a tailored mix of news and other information.

electros or electrotype   Printing plates made by electrolysis from original composition or plates. Made from wax or lead molds, they are much cheaper than original and duplicate photoengravings; used when long runs or several copies of plates or forms are required. If the expense of shipping is an additional cost factor, mats or flongs should be used instead of electros.

em   The square of any given type body, but usually refers to the pica em, which is 12 points square. A common method of measuring type composition is to multiply the number of ems in a line by the number of lines.

embossing   Making an impression by pressing a piece of paper between two metal dies so that it stands above the surface of the sheet.

en   Half an em, a unit of measure in typesetting. Equal to the width of a capital "N" in the particular size of typeface being used.

enameled stock   *See* coated paper.

end rate   The lowest rate for commercial time offered by a station.

engraving ("cut")   Zinc or copper plate that has been etched, generally with acid, to get a raised surface that, when inked, will print on paper. Engravings are reproductions of either line illustrations or halftones (screened); also called photoengravings, because they are made by being brought into contact with film negatives of illustrations. In commercial usage, *engravings* refers almost solely to letterpress printing, although in the past it referred to the intaglio processes.

essential area   The section of the television picture, centered within the scanning area, that is seen by the home viewer, regardless of masking of the set or slight misalignment of the receiver. Sometimes called critical area.

establishing shot   An orientation shot, usually a long shot with a wide angle giving a relationship of place and action; sometimes called a *cover* shot.

ET   Electrical transcription—like a record but produced only for broadcast stations.

etching proofs   Sharp, clean proofs from which zinc etchings can be made.

ETV   Educational TV.

evaluation   Measuring the relative success of a program or activity in terms of the goals and objectives set for it. Evaluation is a form of research, and may use various research methodologies to answer two basic questions, "Did we do what we set out to do? How well did we do it?"

exclusive   A correspondent's report or story limited to a single station, network or periodical.

experiential reporting   The sense of participation through computer-generated reality. One method is an interactive program with audio and video being used for armchair "tours." Another, not yet ready for the market, is cyberspace—a system of virtual-reality experiencing that requires wearing electronic "glasses" and hand-held devices or "gloves."

extended or expanded   Extra-wide typeface.

external publication   Publication issued by an organization to people outside its own employee or membership groups, such as to customers, the local community and the financial world.

extra condensed   Compressed, very thin type.

F

face   The printing surface of type. Also used to identify one style of type from another, such as plain face, heavy face.

facts sheet　Page of significant information prepared by PR people to help news media in covering a special event.

fade　(1) In audio, the physical or mechanical decrease of volume, either voice or music, to smooth a transition between sounds. (2) In video, the gradual appearance of a picture from black (fade-in) or disappearance to black (fade-out).

family　Complete series of one typeface, with all variations (bold, italic, small caps, etc.).

fax　Slang for "facsimile." Exact reproduction of printed matter (words and photos) by radio transmission; also used to refer to TV facilities.

FCC　Federal Communications Commission, the government regulatory body for broadcasting.

feature　(1) To play up or emphasize. (2) A story, not necessarily news; usually more of human interest.

feed　Electronic signal, generally supplied by a source such as a network from which a station can record. Also, what one station sends to another station or stations.

field study　Observation or experimental study in a natural setting.

file　To send a story by wire, Telex, etc. In computer language, information on a related record, treated as a unit.

fill　(1) In broadcasting, additional program material kept ready in case a program runs short. (2) To fill out for timing or space.

fill copy　Pad copy. Relatively minor material used to "fill out" a broadcast or page.

filler　A short, minor story to fill space where needed in making up the pages of a publication. Copy set in type for use in emergencies.

fill light　An additional direction light, usually opposite the key light, to illuminate shadow areas.

film chain　A motion picture film projector, slide projector and TV camera, all housed in single unit called a "multiplexor," used to convert film pictures and sound or still pictures mounted on slides into electronic signals.

film clip　A short piece of film.

film counter　A device used to measure film length while editing.

film lineup　A list of films in broadcast order.

film rundown　A list of cues for a film story.

financial relations　A function of public relations that involves dealing and communicating with the shareholders of an organization and the investment community.

fixed position　A spot delivered at a guaranteed time.

fixed service　Short-range TV transmission on the 2,500-megacycle band; generally used for closed-circuit TV.

flack　Slang for a press agent or publicist, primarily those in the entertainment fields; apparently coined by writer Pete Martin in the April 1, 1950, issue of *Saturday Evening Post*. Martin defined the term in a May 5, 1956, issue of the *Post* with these words, "And since 'flack' is Hollywood slang for publicity man . . ." This word has a few meanings from obsolete provincial English usage: As a verb: to palpitate, to hang loosely, to beat by flapping. Also as a noun: a stroke or touch, a blow, a gadding woman. The word flak came into use during World War II and is an acronym for the German Flieger Abwehr Kanone, an aircraft defense cannon, literally translated to mean "the gun that drives off raiders." The Old English word and the military word may or may not have anything to do with the inspiration of its application to PR.

flag　(1) The front page title or nameplate of a newspaper. (2) A device to block light in film lighting.

flagship station　The major network-owned station or the major station in a community-owned group of stations.

flighting　Broadcast advertising technique for interspersing periods of concentrated advertising with periods of inactivity; usually six-week patterns help a small advertiser get impact.

flong　*See* electros, matrix.

floppy disk　A flexible disk on which computer-generated copy or graphics can be stored.

flyer　*See* circular.

FM　Frequency modulation—radio broadcasting (88 to 108 megacycles) with several advantages over standard (AM) broadcasting such as elimination of static, no fading and generally more consistent quality reception.

focus group　A test panel of people, usually 20 or fewer at a time, selected and interviewed as representative of a particular public likely to have views and opinions on an issue or product.

fold Where the front page of a newspaper is folded in half.

folder A printed piece of four pages or a four-page, heavy-paper container for other printed materials.

folio Page number.

follow copy Instruction to the typesetter to set type exactly like the copy in every detail.

followup A story presenting new developments of one previously printed; also known as a second-day story.

font An assortment of typeface in one size and style.

form Pages of type and illustrations locked in a rectangular iron frame called a *chase*.

format (1) The size, shape and appearance of a magazine or other publication. (2) The skeletal structure or outline of a program, or even of the kind of programming a station does.

foundry proofs (1) Etching proofs. (2) Heavy borders of black foundry rules.

four-color process Reproduction of full-colored illustrations by the combination of plates for yellow, blue, red and black ink. All colored illustrations are separated photographically into these four basic colors. Four-color process is available to the letterpress, offset and gravure processes.

frame (1) A single picture on a storyboard. (2) A single picture in film footage. (3) $\frac{1}{30}$ second TV; $\frac{1}{24}$ second in film. (4) A command to a camera operator to compose the picture.

freelancer An unaffiliated writer or artist, available for hire on a per-story basis or on retainer.

freeze frame Arrested motion, which is perceived as a still shot.

frequency discount A lower rate available to volume advertisers.

fringe time Broadcast time generally considered to be 5:30–7:00 P.M. and 10:30 P.M.–1:00 A.M., the early and late fringes bracketing prime time.

front of the book The main editorial section of a magazine.

front timing The process of figuring out clock times by adding given running times to the clock time at which a program starts.

f-stop The calibration on a lens indicating the ratio of aperture diameter or diaphragm opening to focal length of the lens (apertures control the amount of light transmitted through the lens). The larger the f-stop number, the smaller the aperture or diaphragm opening; the smaller the f-stop number, the larger the aperture or diaphragm opening.

fully scripted A TV script that indicates all words to be spoken and all major video information.

fund raising Working with donor publics to solicit funds, usually through benefits, for charitable groups.

futures research Research designed to anticipate and predict future events. Organizations often engage in futures research to help anticipate and prepare for changes in their political, social and economic environments.

G

gain Amplification of sound.

galley A shallow metal tray for holding type after lines have been set.

galley proofs Proofs reproduced from the type as it stands in galley trays before being placed in page form or (with cold type) as photocopied from the master print or repro.

gel or cell A sheet of transparent colored plastic used to change the color of a still photo, key light or graphic, or clear material used in film animation. (Inserted in front of key lights, on top of art.)

ghost writer A writer whose work appears under the byline of another.

glossy print A smooth shiny-surfaced photograph; the most suitable form for black and white reproduction in print media. Also called glossy.

government relations A function of public relations that involves dealing and communicating with legislatures and government agencies on behalf of an organization.

grain (1) Direction in which paper fibers lie, and the way paper folds best. Folded against the grain, paper is likely to crack or fold irregularly. (2) Unwanted silver globs in a photograph.

graphics (1) All visual displays in broadcasting. (2) Art, display lettering and design in print media.

gravure A form of intaglio printing. *See* intaglio printing.

greeking Pasting dummy, "pretend" text set in the desired typeface and size onto a layout. The type on the layout gives the appearance of what the finished publication will look like, even though the words or characters may be nonsensical.

gross rating points The combined quarter-hour ratings for a time period when each scheduled commercial for a single, specific advertiser was aired.

guideline Slugline—title given to a news story as a guide for editors and printers.

gutter The space between the left- and right-hand pages of a printed publication.

H

halftone A screened reproduction (composed of a series of light and heavy dots) of a photograph, painting or drawing.

hand composition Type set by hand.

handout Publicity release.

hard disk A piece of computer hardware capable of storing as much computer-generated copy or graphics as could be stored on 20 or more floppy disks.

hardware Physical equipment of the computer.

head The name, headline or title of a story.

headnote Short text accompanying the head and carrying information on the story, the author or both.

headroom The space left between the top of the head and the upper screen edge in a television display.

highlight halftone A halftone in which whites are intensified by dropping out dots, usually by hand tooling.

hold News not to be published without release or clearance.

hold for release (HFR) News not to be printed until a specified time or under specified circumstances.

holdover audience Listeners or viewers inherited from a preceding program.

Home Box Office (HBO) A company that supplies pay TV programs to cable systems.

Home Information System (H.I.S.) A computer-based electronic information system that links the home to a variety of databases; the individual consumer controls the information mix delivered.

hometown stories Stories for local newspapers of individuals particpating in an event or activity, usually written so the name and perhaps address can be filled into a general story.

horsing Reading a proof without the original copy.

house ad An ad either for the publication in which it appears or for another medium held by the same owner.

house magazine House organ or company magazine—internal publications for employees or external publications for company-related persons (customers, stockholders and dealers) or for the public.

HTK Head to come—information telling the typesetter that the headline is not with the copy but will be provided later.

human interest Feature material appealing to the emotions—drama, humor, pathos.

HUTs Households using television—number with sets in use at one time.

I

ID Identification. In broadcasting, includes call letters and location in a 10-second announcement that identifies the station, usually in a promotional way.

impose To arrange pages in a chase so they will be in sequence when the printed pages are folded.

independent station A broadcast station not affiliated with a network.

indicia Mailing information data required by the Postal Service.

industry relations A function of public relations that involves dealing and communicating with firms within the industry of which the organization is a part.

initial letter First letter in a block of copy, usually two or three copy lines deep; used for emphasis; frequently in another color.

inline Letter with a white line cut in it.

input Information entered into a computer by typing, scanning, drawing, talking, singing or transfer from another computer.

insert (1) New material inserted in the body of a story already written. (2) Printed matter prepared for enclosure with letters. (3) In film, a matted portion of a picture or an additional shot added to a scene.

institutional ads, commercials and programs
All productions planned for long-term effects rather than immediate response.

intaglio printing   A process in which the design is scratched or etched below the general level of the metal and filled with ink, so the transfer in printing will show only the design. Rotogravure is intaglio printing.

integrated commercial   A "cast"-delivered commercial incorporated into a show, or a multiple-brand announcement for a number of products by the same manufacturer.

intercut   TV film technique of cutting back and forth between two or more lines of action.

internal communications   Communications within a company or organization to personnel or membership.

internal publication   A publication directed to personnel or membership of a company or organization.

interval measures   In social science, constructed measures based on experiences with distributions, rather than a true zero.

interviewee   A person being interviewed.

interviewer   (1) A person who seeks information by asking questions either formally or informally. (2) One who asks respondents the questions specified on a questionnaire in an opinion or market survey.

interviewer bias   A form of survey error that occurs when the interviewer asks questions slanted to get a response to support a particular point of view.

investigative reporting   Searching below the surface for facts generally concealed.

island   An ad surrounded by editorial material.

issues management   A function of public relations that involves systematic identification and action regarding public policy matters of concern to an organization.

italic   Type in which letters and characters slant.

item   A news story, usually short.

J

jingle   A musical signature or logo used for broadcast identification and as a vehicle for a message.

job press   A press taking a small sheet size, normally under 25 × 38 inches.

jump   (1) To continue a story from one page of a publication to another. (2) In film, to break continuity in time or space. *See* jump cut.

jump cut   Cutting between shots that are identical in subject yet slightly different in screen location. As a result, the subject seems to jump from one screen location to another for no apparent reason.

jump head   The title or headline over the continued portion of a story on another page.

jump lines   Short text matter explaining the destination of continued text.

jump the gutter   To continue a title or illustration from a left- to a right-hand page over the center of the publication.

justify   To arrange type and spacing in a line so the type completely fills the line and makes it the same length as adjoining lines.

K

keying   An electronic effect in which an image (usually lettering) is cut into a background image.

key light   The principal source of illumination.

kicker   (1) A short line over the source of directional illumination. (2) A headline. (3) A type of television light.

kill   (1) To strike out or discard part or all of a story. (2) In films or TV, to stop production.

kinescope   Film of a TV program film taken directly from a receiving tube. Also called a transfer.

L

lapel   Small microphone worn as a lapel button.

laser printer   A printer that uses a laser beam of light to create the printed image at a level of quality often equal to that of mechanical printing and far superior to the output of a dot-matrix or daisy wheel printer.

lavaliere mike ("lav")   A small microphone suspended around neck, worn on tie, collar, etc.

layout   Dummy.

LC   Lowercase (uncapitalized) letters.

lead ("led")   Spacing metal, usually lead alloy, placed horizontally between lines of type to give more space between lines. Leads can be 1, 2, or 3 points thick. Ten-point type lines separated by 2-point leads are said to be "10 point leaded 2 points." *See* slug.

lead ("leed") (1) The introductory sentence or paragraph of a news story. (2) A tip that may develop into a story. (3) The news story of greatest interest, usually placed at the beginning of a newscast or in the upper right hand corner of a newspaper, although some papers favor the upper left-hand position.

leaders (1) In print, dots used to direct the eye from one part of the copy to another. (2) In broadcasting, a timed visual used at the beginning of sequences for cues. *See* academy leader, black leader.

lead-in line A section of film, videotape or copy, such as the first sentence used by a newscaster, to cue the technical staff or news anchorperson.

leaflet A printed piece of about four pages, usually from a single sheet, folded.

leg Part of any network; usually a principal branch off the main trunk.

legend Cutline. *See* caption.

leg man A reporter who calls in information to a rewrite person.

letterpress A printing process in which raised type and plates are inked and then applied to paper through direct pressure.

letterspacing Putting narrow spaces between letters.

level (1) In audio, volume. (2) In video, number of volts.

lighting ratio The relative intensities of key, back and fill light.

light level Measured in foot-candles or in lumens.

light pen A penlike tube containing a photocell, which, when directed at a cathode ray tube display, reacts to light from the display. The response goes to the computer, and text in the data store can be deleted or inserted.

limbo Any set area used for shooting small commercial displays, card easels and the like, having a plain, light background. The floor and the background appear to go on forever.

lineprinter A drum, chain or cathode ray tube printer that usually is capable of printing a complete line of characters in one cycle of operation. The whole line is composed in the computer.

linotype A typesetting machine that casts lines instead of single characters.

lithographic printing Chemically transferring an inked image from a smooth surface to paper, as in offset lithography, offset printing, photo-offset.

lithography Printing from a flat surface.

live Performed at broadcast time.

live copy Copy read by station announcer, in contrast to electronic transcriptions or tapes.

live tag A message added to a recorded commercial by the announcer, usually to localize the spot.

localize To stress the local angle.

log A second-by-second daily account of what was broadcast.

logo Logotype or ligature: (1) A combination of two or more letters on the same body—e.g., *fl*. (2) A company trade name or product identification. (3) In broadcasting, a musical or sound signature used for identification.

long shot An object seen from far away or framed very loosely. The extreme long shot shows the object from a great distance.

loop (1) In audio, a technical way to keep up special sound effects or a background noise like rain by constant transmission from one spot of tape. (2) In video, loops used with videotape may replace kinescope pictures and sound recordings for national dissemination of TV programs. Loop feeds allow the affiliated local station's programs and news reports to be picked up by the network. Film loops permit continuous repetition of the picture.

LS Long shot, as with a TV or film camera.

M

machine format A broadcast format in which elements are not prefixed by time or relative position, but are varied. Opposite of segmented.

magazine format *See* block programming.

mainframe A large, fast computer usually programmed with several software packages and programming languages. Individual terminals may be linked to a mainframe for access to software and for manipulation or storage of data.

make good When an ad or commercial is not run because of media error or when it is run with a misprint or malfunction, the offender must publish or broadcast it free at a later date.

make ready To prepare a form on the press for printing.

makeup (1) Getting type and engravings in printing form correctly. (2) Placing information and pictures on a publication's page. (3) Planning a group of pages. (4) In film, putting several films on one big reel.

manifest In content analysis, the visible, surface content.

markup Proof with changes indicated.

mass publications Periodicals with wide appeal and large, general circulation.

master The original of a film or videotape.

master positive Positive film made from an edited camera negative and composite sound track with optical effects.

masthead Name of publication and staff that appears in each issue of magazine or paper, usually on the editorial page in a box also giving information about the paper such as company officers, subscription rates and address.

material In investor relations, a term applied to any event that is likely to affect the value of stock.

matrix or mats A papier-mâché impression of a printing plate that may be used as a mold for a lead casting to reproduce the copy or art. Used for some ads and publicity primarily because of the economy of mailing, and used by small publications without engraving facilities.

matte (1) Imposition of a scene or title over another scene, excluding background. Not a blend or a super. (2) Name for a box placed in front of a lens to shade and hold filters and effects. (3) Dull finish needed for still photos used by TV so lights will not be reflected.

mean The mathematical "average" calculated by dividing the sum of values or scores by the total number of scores; one measure of central tendency.

median The exact midpoint of an array of values of scores; one measure of central tendency. Half of the values or scores are above the median, and the other half are below.

media relations A function of public relations that involves dealing with the communications media in seeking publicity for, or responding to media interest in, an organization.

Mediastat A broadcast rating service.

medium shot *See* MS.

memory Same as storage.

MICR Magnetic ink character recognition—automatic reading by a machine of graphic characters printed in magnetic ink.

microwave relay Use of UHF radio relay stations to transmit television signals from one point to another in a line of sight, usually about 25 miles.

midcourse evaluation Evaluative research undertaken while a program or project is ongoing to determine if any adjustments should be made in the original plan to account for changing public, media or environmental conditions.

milline A unit of space and circulation used in advertising to measure the cost of reaching an audience. The milline rate is the cost per million for a one-column line of agate type.

minicam A highly portable TV camera and videotape unit that can easily be carried and operated by one person.

minority relations A function of public relations that involves dealing and communicating with individuals and groups of racial or ethnic minorities.

mixer (1) Audio control console. (2) Person working this console.

mixing (1) In audio, combining two or more sounds in specific proportions (volume variations), as determined by the event (show) context. (2) In video, combining various shots via the switcher.

mockup A scale model used for study, testing or instruction.

mode The most common or frequently found value or score in a data set; one measure of central tendency.

model release A document signed by a model allowing use of photographs or art in which he or she appears.

monitor (1) To review a station's programming and commercials. (2) A TV set that handles video signals.

montage In TV and film, a rapid succession of images to give idea association. *Also see* composite.

MOR Type of radio station programming that is "middle of the road."

more Written at the bottom of a page of copy to indicate that a story is not complete, that there is more to come.

morgue A newspaper library for clippings, photos and reference material.

MOS "Mitout sound"—film recorded without sound.

mouse A hand-held computer input device especially useful for applying features of graphics or desktop publishing software. When moved, it propels a pointer or cursor around the computer screen to select commands, functions or text.

movieola A device used to view film during editing.

MS Medium shot, as with a TV or film camera.

mult box A portable electronic box (usually resembling a large travel case) that allows dozens of tape recorders to be plugged in at once to record off the public address (PA) system so the speakers' remarks will be captured and transmitted to all simultaneously. *See* multiplexer.

Multigraphing A trademarked process for making numerous copies of typewritten or hand-drawn material. More closely resembles hand typing than does mimeographing.

multiplexer (1) A system of movable mirrors or prisms that takes images from several projection sources and directs them into one stationary television film camera. (2) An instrument for mixing signals.

must Written on copy or art to designate that it must appear.

N

NABET National Association of Broadcast Employees and Technicians—union for studio and master control engineers; may include floor personnel.

nameplate The name of the publication appearing on page one of a newspaper. *See* flag.

national rate A rate offered to advertisers in more than one market.

NET National Educational Television.

network Any link, by any technology, of two or more stations so they can each separately broadcast the same program.

network option time Broadcast hours when a network preempts on its affiliates and the stations it owns.

new lead Replacement for a lead already prepared, usually offering new developments or information. *See* lead.

newsprint A rough, relatively inexpensive paper, usually made from wood pulp, used for many newspapers and for other inexpensive printed material.

news release A news story written in print or broadcast style for use by a news medium.

news tip A news story idea not in story format given to a news medium for that medium's staff to write if the story idea is deemed to have merit.

news wheel A news show in which content is repeated with some updating.

Nexis Database.

Nielsen The A. C. Nielsen Company—the biggest name in broadcast ratings. Reputations and shows literally live or die on their Nielsen ratings.

nominal measures Used in ordering data, these variables have attributes that are mutually exclusive or exhaustive.

nonparametic In statistics, a method or test that is not based on distributions.

nonprobability sample A sample selected in such a way that it's not possible to estimate the chance that any particular member of the population will be included in the sample. Using nonprobability samples results in the risk of over- or under-representing certain segments of the population.

NPR National Public Radio.

O

obituary News biography of a dead person.

OCR Optical character recognition—electronically reading printed or handwritten documents.

offset Lithographic process.

ombudsman-woman Someone who researches complaints and problems brought by individuals or groups against an organization.

online In direct communication with the computer CPU.

on the nose (1) On time. (2) Correct.

open-end   A recorded commercial with time at the close for a "tag."

open spacing   Widely leaded spacing.

opinion   An expression of an attitude, belief or feeling, usually in writing or orally, held at a particular moment.

optical center   A point equidistant from the left and right sides of a sheet of paper and five-eighths of the way up from the bottom.

optical reader   An electronic reader of copy.

opticals   In film, any variations to the picture achieved after or during filming, such as mattes or dissolves. May be done during filming or by control board when multiple cameras are used.

optical scanner   A visual scanner that scans printed or written data and generates their digital representation.

ordinal measures   Used in ordering data, these variables have attributes that can be rank-ordered.

orphan   In publishing, an indented opening line of a paragraph that appears as the bottom line on a page or column of type. To be avoided.

outline   The gist of a written article or program.

output   The information that comes out of a computer or other device, such as a printer, linked to a computer. Output may be in hard copy form on paper, or it may be digitized information stored on a floppy or hard disk.

outtakes   Filmed or taped scenes or sequences not used in the final production.

overdubbing   Recording separate channels on a multichannel tape separately; then adding and synchronizing so the original sound track is supplemented. This allows a few voices to become a chorus and a few instruments, an orchestra.

overline   Kicker.

overrun   Established printing trade practice that permits delivery of and charge for up to 10 percent more than the quantity of printed matter ordered.

overset   More type set than there is space to use.

P

pace   The overall speed of a show or performance.

pad   Fill.

page proof   A proof showing type and engravings as they will appear in the printed piece unless subsequently altered.

pamphlet   A printed piece of more than four pages with a soft cover. Differs from a brochure in its size, simplicity and lack of illustrations.

pan   Horizontal turning of the camera.

panel   (1) An area of type sometimes boxed but always different in size, weight or design from the text and partially or entirely surrounded by text. (2) In broadcasting and communication research, a group brought together to discuss one subject or related subjects.

paper tape   A strip of paper on which data may be recorded, usually in the form of punched holes. Punched paper tape can be sensed by a reading head used to transfer the data. Each charge is represented by a pattern of holes, called a row or frame.

parametric tests   Tests of significance based on distributions that make different assumptions about the population from which the sample was taken.

participation spot   Shared time in a program for spot commercials or announcements.

pasteup   *See* dummy.

patch   A temporary equipment connection. Patch panels or patch boards are assemblies of jacks into which various circuits are permanently tied and into which patch cords may be inserted. They are essential at "on site" special events.

PBS   Public Broadcasting System.

perforator   A keyboard unit used to produce punched paper tape.

personal   A brief news item about one or more persons.

photo composition   A photographic method of setting type to produce proofs on paper.

photoprint   Reproduction of art or a printed or written piece by one of many different photographic copying processes.

Photostat   A trademarked device for making photographic copies of art or text.

pica   Standard printing measure of 12 points. There are six picas to the inch.

pied type   Type that is all mixed up.

PIQ Program Idea Quotient—annual study by Home Testing Institute to get reactions to new program ideas. Ratings are on a 6-point scale from "favorite" to "wouldn't watch."

pix Pictures.

place Any type of printing surface, engraving or electrotype.

play up To emphasize, give prominence.

plug A free and favorable mention.

PM Afternoon paper.

point Printers' standard unit of measure equal to 0.01384 inch. Roughly 72 points equals one inch. Sizes of type and amounts of leading are specified in points.

poll Survey of the attitudes and beliefs of a selected group of people.

position Where elements in any publication appear; usually indicates relative significance.

postdubbing Adding a sound track to an already recorded (and usually fully edited) picture portion.

poster type Large, garish letters.

pot Potentiometer—a volume-control device on audio consoles.

power structure The socially, politically and economically advantaged.

PR Public relations.

precinct principle Organization of a campaign through delegation of local responsibilities to chosen leaders in each community. These may be opinion leaders and not necessarily political leaders.

preempt In broadcasting, to replace a regular program with a commercial or a news event of greater importance.

preemptible spot Commercial time sold at a lower rate by a station, which has the option of taking it back if it has a buyer at full rate, unless the first purchaser pays to keep it at full rate.

presentational TV performance format where camera is addressed as audience.

presidential patch Portable sound system with outlets for amplifiers to be connected; unity gain amplifier with numerous mike-level outputs used in pool remotes to cut down on the number of mikes needed.

press agentry A function of public relations that involves creating news events of a transient, often flighty sort.

pretesting Testing a research plan, any of its elements or any elements in a campaign before launching the entire program.

printer's errors (PE) Typographical errors made by typesetter.

privilege Constitutional privilege granted the press to print with immunity news that might otherwise be libelous—e.g., remarks made in open court.

probability sample A sample selected in such a way that the chance that any particular member of the population will be selected for the sample is known. Using a probability sample enables the researcher to calculate the chances that the sample accurately represents the population from which it was selected.

process plates and progressive proofs Each of the color plates in a set printed singly, so they may be laid over each other for effect. In progressive prints, in addition to the single prints of each color, the colors are shown in proper color combination and rotation to suggest the final printed result.

program A set of instructions that make the computer perform the desired operations.

promo Broadcast promotional statement, film, videotape/recording, slide or combination.

promotion A function of public relations that involves special activities or events designed to create and stimulate interest in a person, product, organization or cause.

proof A trial impression of type and engraved matter taken on paper to allow the writer and publisher to make corrections.

propaganda A function of public relations that involves efforts to influence the opinions of a public in order to propagate a doctrine.

propaganda devices Specific devices—spoken, written, pictorial or even musical—used to influence human action or reaction.

PR wires Commercial wire services received by print and electronic media.

psychographics The attitudes and images held by media audiences.

public, publics Any group of people tied together by some common bond of interest or concern. *See* audience.

public affairs   A function of public relations that involves working with governments and groups that help determine public policies and legislation.

publicity   A function of public relations that involves disseminating purposefully planned and executed messages through selected media, without payment to the media, to further the particular interest of an organization or person.

public relations   The various activities and communications that organizations undertake to monitor, evaluate, influence and adjust to the attitudes, opinions and behaviors of groups or individuals who constitute their publics.

public television   Noncommercial broadcasting. Stations are financed by federal grants, private donations and public subscriptions.

puffery   Unsubstantiated and exaggerated claims that appear in either advertising or publicity.

pulp   Magazines printed on rough, wood-pulp paper, in contrast to "slicks"—magazines printed on coated or calendared stock.

punch   To give vigor to the writing or editing process.

Q

quads   (1) Blank pieces of metal used to fill large spaces in a line of type. (2) A type of videotape recorder.

query   A letter addressed to an editor that summarizes an article idea and asks if the piece might be considered for publication.

questionnaire   The body of questions asked of subjects in a research effort.

quoins ("coins")   Triangular wedges of steel used in locking up a type form.

quote   A quotation or estimate of costs.

R

RADAR   Radio's All Dimension Audience Research—a survey conducted by Statistical Research Inc., for NBC, CBS, ABC and Mutual networks.

radio-TV wire   (1) Broadcast wire. (2) The news service's wire copy written in broadcast style.

RAM   Random access memory—a storage device in which the time needed to find data is not affected significantly by where the data are physically located.

random sample   A sample in which each person or element of a population has an equal chance of being selected. A table of random numbers, sometimes generated by a computer, often is used to select sample members randomly from a population.

raster   The scanned area of the CRT tube; line scans traced across the face of a CRT tube by a flying spot.

rating service   A company that surveys broadcast audience for total homes or individuals tuning in or gives percentages of total listening for specific stations and specific shows.

ratio   Measures based on a true zero point (such as age, as opposed to temperature, which is an internal measure).

raw stock   Unexposed film. Called camera stock when it is unexposed film for use in a motion picture camera; called print stock when it is unexposed film for making duplicate copies of still photographs.

reach   The number of people or households a station, commercial or program is heard by in a given time period. Used with frequency to measure a station's audience for evaluation of worth, generally for advertising pricing.

real time   Online processing, with data received and processed quickly enough to produce output; interactive.

rear screen projection   Projection of positive transparencies onto a translucent screen.

rebate   An extra discount on ads earned by using more time or space than the contract specifies.

recap   A recapitulation of news.

reduce   To decrease the size of anything visual when reproducing it.

register   (1) The correct position for a form to print in so that the pages when printed back-to-back will be in their proper places. (2) In color printing, the precise position for superimposition of each color in order for the colors to blend properly.

rejection slip   A letter or printed form from a publication's editor accompanying a manuscript returned to its author.

release print   In TV, a film print made from a negative and given to stations to use.

relief printing Letterpress. Letters on the block or plate are raised above the general level so that, when an inked roller is passed over the surface, the ink can touch only the raised portions.

remote A videotape recording and broadcast live originating outside the regular studios.

reprint A second or new impression of a printed work, either text or art.

repro *See* camera copy.

respondents Those to whom questions are directed in a survey.

retail rate The local rate (or lower) for advertising.

retouch To improve photographs before reproduction as artwork.

reversal print A copy made on reversal print stock.

reverse To print text or art in white on a dark background, or, in making a cut from a picture, to turn over or "flop" the negative so that everything goes in an opposite direction.

review A critique or commentary on any aspect of human events—politics, society or the arts.

rewrite person A newspaper staff member who rewrites stories and takes phoned-in reports but does not leave the office to cover news.

rim On newspapers, the outer edge of a copy desk where copy readers work under the direction of a "slot" person or copy chief.

roots of attitudes Our institutions, observations, responses of others to us, socialization, education and media.

ROP Run of paper. Means that an ad may be placed on any page of the publication.

ROS Run of station or run of schedule. Costs less; usually preemptible.

rotary press A press that prints from curved stereotypes bolted to a cylinder.

rotogravure Printing by means of a sensitized copper cylinder on which is etched the image to be reproduced.

rough A preliminary visualization of art.

rough cut The first editing of a film, without effects.

roundup A comprehensive story written with information gathered from several sources.

routing Cutting out part of plate or engraving to keep it from printing.

rule A thin strip of type-high metal that prints as a slender line.

run in To combine one or more sentences to avoid making an additional paragraph.

running foot Identification information printed in the bottom margin of a magazine.

running head Identification information printed in the top margin of a magazine.

running story or breaking story A fast-breaking story usually written in sections.

S

saddle stitching Binding pages by stitching with wire through the fold.

SAG Screen Actors Guild.

sample The portion of the total population queried in a survey, intended to be representative of the total population.

sample error The degree to which a sample lacks representativeness; this can be measured and is reduced by having large samples or more homogeneous ones.

sandwich or donut In broadcasting, a commercial with live copy between musical open and close.

sans serif Typeface without serifs.

scaling Measuring and marking illustrations for engraving to ensure that the illustration will appear in the appropriate, designated size and in proper proportion.

scanner Optical scanner.

scanning Movement of an electron beam from left to right and from top to bottom on a screen.

scanning area The picture area scanned by a television camera's pickup tube; more generally, the picture area actually reproduced by the camera and relayed to the studio monitors.

segue An audio transition method whereby the preceding sound goes out and the following sound comes in immediately after.

set close To thin spaces and omit leads.

set open To open spaces with leads as slugs.

sets in use Rating service term for the percentage of total homes in the coverage area in which at least one radio is on at any given time; the radio equivalent of HUT (Households Using Television).

set solid   To set without extra space between horizontal type lines.

setwise   Differentiates the width of a type from its body size.

shared ID   When an organization or institution appears on the TV station's channel identification.

share of audience or share   The percentage of the total audience tuned into each station at any given time.

shelter books   Magazines that focus on housing or related subjects.

short rate   A charge back to an advertiser for not fulfilling a contract.

show   Program.

side stitching   A method of stitching thick booklets by pressing wire staples from the front side of the booklet and clinching them in back, making it impossible to open the pages flat.

silhouette or outline halftone   A halftone with all of the background removed.

silk screen   A stencil process using fine cloths painted so that the surface is impenetrable except where color is supposed to come through.

silver print or Van Dyck   The proof of negative for an offset plate taken on sensitized paper and used as a final proof before the plates are made.

simulcast   Simultaneous transmission over radio and television.

sizing   Scaling.

skip frame   A process in which only alternate frames are printed, to speed up action on film.

slant   Angle. (1) The particular emphasis of a media presentation. (2) To emphasize an aspect of a policy story.

slanting   (1) Emphasizing a particular point or points of interest in the news. (2) Disguised editorializing.

slick   A publication, usually a magazine, published on coated, smooth paper.

slicks   Glossy prints used instead of mattes in sending releases or art to offset publications.

slidefilm   Filmstrip. A continuous strip of film with frames in a fixed sequence, but not designed to simu-late motion. A recorded soundtrack usually is synchronized with the succession of the film frames.

slides   Individual film frames, usually positive but sometimes negative transparencies, projected either in the room where an oral presentation is being given or from a TV control room.

slip sheet   Paper placed between sheets of printed paper to prevent smudging.

slot   In newspaper rooms, the inside of a copy desk where the copy chief or copy editor sits.

slow motion   A scene in which the objects appear to move more slowly than normal. In film, slow motion is achieved through high-speed photography (exposing many frames that differ only minutely from one another) and normal (24 frames per second, for example) playback. In television, slow motion is achieved by multiple scanning of each television frame.

slug   Lead thicker than 4 points, used between lines of type.

slug lines   The notation placed at the upper left of a story to identify the story during typesetting and makeup of a publication.

slushpile   A collection of unsolicited manuscripts received by magazines.

SOF   Sound on film.

soft news   Feature news or news that does not depend upon timeliness.

software   The programs and routines associated with the operation of a computer, as opposed to "hardware."

SOT   Sound on videotape.

sources of motivation   Socially based or personal need and avoidance or elimination of stress often caused by the power of others.

splice   The spot where two shots are actually joined, or the act of joining two shots. Generally used only when the material (such as film or audiotape) is physically cut and glued (spliced) together again.

split run   The regional division of a national magazine before printing to accommodate advertisers desiring to reach a specific regional market and often with regional editorial emphasis.

split screen   A divided screen that shows two or more pictures; often used in TV titles and commercials.

sponsor   (1) The underwriter of broadcast programming whose messages are presented with the program. Most advertisers buy spot time and are not sponsors. (2) The underwriter of an event or activity who gets publicity for participation.

spot announcement or spot   A broadcast commercial that usually lasts less than one minute.

spread   (1) A long story, generally illustrated. (2) An ad group of related photographs. (3) Copy that covers two facing pages in a publication, generally without gutter separation and usually printed from a single plate.

SPSS   Social science statistical package used in research.

stakeholder   One who has an investment (time, money, etc.) in an organization.

stand-by   The signal given in a broadcast studio before the on-air signal is given.

standing head   A regularly used title.

standing matter   Type kept set from one printing to another, such as staff names on a newspaper.

station break   Break to a station for a contracted local spot. May include on-the-hour legal identification required of broadcasters by the FCC.

stereotype   A plate cast by pouring molten metal into a matrix or flong. Inexpensive form of duplicating plates generally used by newspapers.

stet   A proofreader's designation indicating that the copy should stand as originally written, that the change marked was an error.

stop-motion   A slow-motion effect in which one frame jumps to the next, showing the object in a different position.

storyboard   (1) Art work that shows the sequence of a TV commercial. (2) In film work, drawings and text showing major visual changes in a proposed show; this grew out of animated film, pioneered by Walt Disney.

straight matter   Plain typesetting set in conventional paragraph form, as opposed to some kind of display.

straight news   Hard news; a plain recital of news facts written in standard style and form.

stratified sample   The population is divided into strata (groups or subpopulations with common traits), and the sample chosen contains the same proportion of desired traits as the population strata from which it is drawn.

stuffer   Printed piece intended for insertion into bills and receipts, pay envelopes, packages delivered to customers or any other medium of delivery.

style book   A manual setting standards for handling copy and detailing rules for spelling, capitalization, abbreviations, word usage and such.

subhead   A small head inserted in the body of a news story to break up long blocks of type.

summary lead   The beginning paragraphs in a news story, usually including the H and five W's (who, what, when, where, why and how).

super   In film or TV, superimposition of a scene or characters over another scene; also called a take-out or add videotape.

supercard   A studio card with white lettering on a dark background, used for superimposing or keying a title over a background scene. For chromakeying, the white letters are on a chromakey blue background.

surprint   In printing, superimposing type or lettering on an illustration so the type remains solid, unbroken by a screen.

survey   An analysis of a market or of opinions held by a specified group.

suspended interest   A news story with the climax at the close.

sync   Synchronization—keeping one operation in step with another (1) between sound and picture or (2) between a scanning beam and a blinking pulse.

synchronization rights   Rights granted by a mechanical rights agency to use music licensed by them.

system cue   Network identification.

T

tabloid   A newspaper format—usually five columns wide, with each page slightly more than half the size of a standard newspaper page. A tabloid format often involves the use of just a picture and headlines on page one.

tag   (1) The final section of a broadcast story, usually stand-up (personally given rather than taped) following a film or VTR. (2) An announcement at the end of a recorded commercial or music at the end of live copy.

tailpiece   A small drawing at the end of a story.

take   (1) In print, a portion of copy in a running story. (2) In broadcasting, a complete scene. (3) To cut.

talent   Any major personality or models for ads or publicity photos. In TV or radio, anyone in front of the camera or on the air.

tally light   The red light on a video camera that indicates which camera is on air or being recorded.

teaser   (1) In print, an ad or statement that piques interest or stimulates curiosity without giving away facts; used to build anticipation. (2) A technique in which the beginning of a film has scenes and sounds related to the theme of the program rather than a title.

telecommunications   Long-distance transmission of signals by any means.

teleconference   Use of various telecommunication devices (computers, telephones, television and video systems) to permit three or more people at multiple locations to communicate with each other in a "live" and often interactive format.

tele line   The equipment room where film and slide projectors are located.

teleprocessing   Information handling in which a data processing system uses communication facilities.

teletext   A one-way electronic information system; noninteractive. *See* H.I.S.

Teletypesetter (TTS)   Trademark applied to a machine that transmits to a linotype and causes news to be set into type automatically.

terminal   Any point in a communication system or network where data can enter or leave.

test group   People selected and used to measure reactions to or use of a product or idea.

testing   Sampling the opinions, attitudes or beliefs of a scientifically selected group on any particular set of questions.

text   Written material, generally used in referring to editorial rather than commercial matter; excludes titles, heads, notes, references and such.

TF   Till forbid—advertising to run until advertiser terminates or contract expires.

thirty (30)   In newspaper code, "that's all." A reporter writing a story places this at the last of the written material to signify the end.

tie-back   Previously printed information included in a story to give background or a frame of reference and to refresh the reader's memory.

tie-in   (1) Joint or combined activities of two or more organizations on a single promotional project. (2) A promotional activity designed to coincide with an already scheduled event.

tight   In broadcast and print media, having little time or space left for additional material.

time base corrector   An electronic accessory to a videotape recorder that helps make playbacks or transfers electronically stable. Helps maintain picture quality even in dubbing.

time classifications   Broadcast time rated by audience level and priced accordingly, as Class AA, Class A, Class BB, Class B, etc.

timesharing   Use of computer hardware by several persons simultaneously.

tint block   A solid color area on a printed piece, usually screened.

tip   Information offered that could lead to a story.

tipping in   Hand insertion or attachment of extra pages in a publication, usually of a different stock than other items.

title slide   A graphic giving the name of a TV show.

total audience plan   A spot package designed to reach all of a station's audiences.

track   The physical location on magnetic tape where the signal is recorded for a specific source—the channel 1, 2, etc. of audio; the video signal; the control signal; etc.

trade publications   Periodicals carrying information of interest to a particular trade or industry.

traffic   The department in ad agencies that handles production schedules; in broadcasting, traffic handles everything that goes on the air.

trim   (1) In newspapers, to shorten copy. (2) In printing, the final process that cuts all pages to the same size.

turnover   In advertising, the ratio of *net unduplicated* cumulative audience over several time periods to average audience per time period.

TWX   "TWIX," a teletype machine.

typeface   A particular type design; may carry the name of the designer or a descriptive name.

type family   The name given to two or more type series that are variations of the same basic design.

type page   The printed area on a page bordered by margins.

type series   The collective name for all sizes of one design of typeface.

typo   Typographical error.

U

UC and LC   Upper- and lower-case—capitals and small letters.

UHF   Ultra high frequency TV channels broadcasting at frequencies higher than channel 13.

under and over   In broadcasting scripts, using sound dominated by (under) or dominating (over) another sound.

underrun   Printing practice that permits an allowance of 10 percent less than the total printing order as completion of an order when excessive spoilage in printing or in binding causes a slight shortage. *See* overrun.

upcut   In TV or film, to unintentionally overlap a sound picture with another sound.

update   To alter a story to include the most recent developments.

UPI   United Press International began as an international wire service to which any media could subscribe for news copy and photos, unlike AP, which is a membership corporation. UPI was bought in 1992 by MBC, a London-based company.

uplink   The transmission of audio, video, or digitized computer information to a communications satellite, which relays the information to other receivers.

upper case   Capital letters.

V

Van Dyck   *See* silver print.

varitype   A typewriter with alternate type fonts.

VDT   Visual or video display terminal—an electronic device used in typesetting and word processing, with a television-type screen to display data.

vertical saturation   Scheduling commercials heavily one or two days before a major event.

VHF   Very high frequency TV channels broadcasting at channels 2 through 13.

video   All television visual projection.

videoconference   A teleconference in which full video is transmitted, as well as voice and sometimes even graphics. The video signal can be from one point of origin to many receiving points, or two-way, simultaneously connecting two or more points, each of which can both originate and receive video.

videotex   An interactive electronic data transmission system; establishes a two-way link from an individual's television set or home computer to a database. *See* H.I.S.

vidicon   A special camera tube often used in closed-circuit operations and TV film cameras.

vignette   A story or sketch, often a "slice of life" drama.

vignetted halftones   A halftone with edges that soften gradually until they completely fade out.

visual scanner   Optical scanner.

VO   Voice over—broadcasting or film script designation for a narrator's voice to be used at a certain time in the production.

VTR   (1) In TV, videotape recording. Cheaper and more flexible than film, but less permanent. (2) In radio, voice transmitter and receiver—a small device attached to the phone, enabling a reporter to call in a story and preserve broadcast quality.

W

wash drawing   A watercolor or diluted India ink brush drawing requiring halftone reproduction.

watermark   An identification mark left in the texture of quality paper stock; revealed when the paper is held up to light.

when room   Designation on copy or art that means it is usable at any time.

wide open   A publication or news script with ample room for additional material.

widow   (1) A short line (one word or two) at the end of a paragraph of type. To be avoided, especially in the first line of a page or column and in captions. (2) In publishing, any less-than-full-measure line ending a paragraph that appears as the top line of a page or column. To be avoided.

wild track   Related footage with a soundtrack not intended to be in sync with the picture.

wipe   A transitional television technique in which one scene gradually replaces another.

woodcuts   Wooden printing blocks with the impression carved by hand. Now an art form; was the forerunner of zinc engravings.

woodshedding   In broadcasting, reading and rehearsing a news script.

word processor   A computer software program used to create, edit and manipulate documents. Word-processing software is used primarily for text, but also can be used for creating charts and graphs.

working drawings   Final drawings, usually black and white, prepared for use by an engraver; show how final art will appear.

work print   The film print used in first editing. Usually one "light print," not printed for full-quality reproduction.

workstation   A group of linked computer equipment used in accomplishing word-processing or design tasks. A workstation often consists of a computer terminal with keyboard and monitor linked to a printer and sometimes to a scanner.

wow   Pitch distortion or variation caused by changes in the speed of film or tape; also sound distortions in records.

wrap-up   Summary or closing.

wrong font   A letter from one font of type mixed with others of a different font.

X

XCU, ECU   In TV or film, an extreme close-up. For a person, this might show eyes and nose only.

Y

yak   Narration.

Z

Z-axis   The imaginary line that extends in the direction the lens points from the camera to the horizon. Z-axis motion is movement toward or away from the camera. (Not a standardized term in the industry.)

zinc etching   A line engraving etched in zinc.

INDEX

Globalization, 62, 72, 239. *See also* International PR.
Global society, 28, 59, 80, 101
Goebbels, Joseph, 33, 179
Gorbachev, Mikhail, 60, 61, 181, 183, 256, 502
Government, 13, 18
  ethical responsibilities of PR to, 235
  information campaigns by, 502–3
  relations, 4, 6, 75
  use of PR, 77. *See also* Gillett Amendment.
Gray, Daniel H., 24
Greyser, Stephen A., 19, 21
Griswold, Denny, 51, 82
Grunig, James E., 20, 21, 97–98, 172, 480
  information-processing model of, 97, 221, 222, 223
    interpreting behavior of publics using, 97–98
  models of PR practice by, 20, 105

H

Harris, Louis, 56, 183, 184, 230
Haynes, Jim, 12
Health care, 18, 71, 144
Heider, Fritz, 219
Henderson, Hazel, 22, 547
Hendrix, Jerry A., 140, 142
Hennessy, Bernard, 179
Hill & Knowlton, 14, 22, 49, 61, 91, 256–57, 447, 546
Historiography, 111, 112
History of public relations, 19, 32–69
  development as academic discipline, 32, 50, 57, 64, 65, 83–84
  five stages in, 19, 36
    era of communicating and initiating, 19, 38–42
    era of planning and preventing, 19, 49–59
    era of professionalism, 19, 59–64
    era of reacting and responding, 19, 43–49
    preliminary period, 36–38
Homeostasis, 213
House ads, 348
House publications, 368, 370–71, 372, 389–92, 413–15
Hovland, Carl, 210, 218, 220, 224
Human rights and PR ethics, 235, 239
Hunter, Barbara, 63
Hypothesis testing, 118–19, 209, 210

I

Ideology as new name for PR, 71
Image:
  advertising, 357, 358, 359, 360
  crises and, 550
  definition of, 169
  determining, 170–71
  external, 173–74
  internal, 169–173
  Levinson's theory of, 170–71
  marketing of, 447–49
  reality and, 178, 212
Image makers, 58, 169
Independent PR practitioner, 13, 14–15
  counselor, 71
  specialists, 75
Industry, 17–18
Industry relations, 4, 75
Infomercial, 273, 292–93, 314
Information, opinion vs., 186
Information processing, 219, 221
  cycle of, 218
  Grunig's model of, 221, 222, 223
Information seekers, 97, 122, 172
  processors vs., 97
Information withholding, 258
In-house publicity departments and bureaus, 41, 44
Inside America, 93
Insider, definition of, 279–80, 290–91
Insider trading, 57, 267, 309. *See also* Disclosure.
  definition of, 291
  guidelines for avoiding problems with, 291–92
Institutional advancement, 16
Insull, Samuel, 45
Internal publics:
  corporate image and, 172–73, 189
  media for, 347
Internal research, 132
Internal Revenue Service (IRS), 237
International Association of Business Communicators (IABC), 12, 81, 576
  accreditation process of, 261
  case studies, 507
  code of ethics, 235, 238
International PR, 17, 72, 238–39
  association (IPRA), 10, 51
  bribery in, 238
  ethics and, 236, 238–39
  foreign government, agent for, 238–39, 299

  human rights and, 235
  language of gestures and, 468–69
  legal requirements of, 276, 299
  message fidelity and, 221
  news media and, 256
  public affairs, 75
Interviews, 106, 111
  as publicity, 392, 396–97
    with the press, 459–62
    on talk shows, 449
  as research technique:
    broadcast measurement and, 131
    content analysis and, 115
    in-depth, 111, 112
Intuition in PR, 71, 109
Investigative journalism, 54. *See also* Muckraking.
Investor relations, 17, 75, 76, 82
  annual reports and, 287–90
  disclosures, guidelines for, 280–83
  ethical responsibilities of PR and, 234, 255
  social responsibility and, 254
Involuntary subeconomy, 55
IPRA, 63
Issue advertising, 353, 355
  fairness doctrine and, 243
  Mobil Oil, 57, 243, 296, 298
Issue forecasting, 95–96, 159
  techniques of, 96
Issues:
  checklist, 156–58
  evaluation, 154–63
  forecasting, 95–96
  life cycle stages of, 155–56
  management of, 4, 96, 154–63. *See also* Problem solving.
  monitoring vs., 99
  as opportunities, 154

J

Jackson, Pat, 9
Jefferson, Thomas, 32, 48
Johnson, Lyndon B., 55, 217
Journalistic research, 106
Journalists. *See also* Freelance writers; Media relations.
  code of ethics, 259
  PR practitioners and, tensions between, 45, 61, 250–51

K

Kalb, Bernard, 59
Kennedy, Eugene, 26

Special events, 418–20, 422–23
  publicizing, 450–54
  spinoffs from, 449–50
Speeches:
  checklist for, 419
  as publicity, 382, 385–87
  writing, 18
Spokesperson during crisis, 547–48
Sponsorships, 57, 241, 247. *See also* PSAs.
  IRS taxation of, 297
SRDS, 151
SRI International, 146, 148, 183
Staff member, 13–14
Standard of living, 55
Standard Oil, 42, 50, 63
Statistics, descriptive and inferential, 115, 116, 119
Stephens, Tom, 79
Stereotypes, 218, 343
Steward, Jane, 51
Stimulation-response (S-R) strategy, 207
Stress, PR practitioner and, 28
Subliminal advertising, 24–41
Survey of PR practitioners, 27–28
Surveys. *See* Public opinion surveys.

T

Talk shows, 396–97, 449
Tarbell, Ida, 42
Target audiences, 140–41
Target marketing databases, 151
Taxes on PR services, 314
Technology and public relations, 432–36
Technology assessment, 96
Telephone surveys, 120, 131
Teletext, 382

Television:
  audiences of. *See* Broadcast research; Audiences.
  credibility of, 211, 212
  public opinion and, 51
  sponsoring public programs on, 57
10-K form, 285, 287, 416, 433
Texas Gulf Sulphur case, 57, 279, 285, 291
Texture of a message, 214
Trademark, 241–42, 304
Transactional model, 19
Trend analysis, 16–17, 91
Trends, in business world, 71, 72, 85
Trends in PR, 75–85
  professionalism. *See* Professionalism.
  shift towards strategies vs. tactics, 73
  women. *See* Women in PR.
Triner, Alma, 63
Two-way asymmetric model of PR, 105
Two-way symmetric model of PR, 105
Tylenol:
  crisis about, 511, 550–51
  slogan case, 296

U

Uncontrolled advertising, 363
Uncontrolled media, 346, 347, 387
Uncontrolled publicity, 392
Union Carbide, Bhopal, case, 567–72
Unions. *See* Labor unions.
United Auto Workers (UAW), GM strike by, 50
University relations, 16, 75
U.S. Information Agency (U.S. Information Service), 59, 502

V

Vail, Theodore, N., 41, 47
VALS2 typology, 146, 148–50, 151, 183

Velvet Ghetto, 71
Video news releases, 443, 444–46
Videos, 391–92. *See also* Film/video.
Video services, 433–36
Videotex, 382
Visuals, 420–24

W

Wall Street Journal, 22, 23, 76, 91, 121, 184, 187, 241, 246, 248, 267, 291, 383, 431, 467, 555
  quarrel with Mobil, 560–61
War Advertising Council, 50
Wartime public relations, 35, 46, 50, 61
  American Revolution, 37, 64
  Civil War, 39
  Persian Gulf War, 61
  World War I, 39, 49
  World War II, 39, 49–50
Watkins, Frederick, 178
Wheaton, Ann Williams, 51
Whistleblower, definition of, 259
Wilson, Woodrow, 45, 46, 48
Wire services:
  government, 502
  news, 436
  PR, 433–36
Women in public relations, 51, 58, 63, 71, 81, 85
  PR prestige and, 82, 85
Wylie, Frank, 12

Y

Young, Davis, 229

Z

Zimbardo, Phillip, 208